The New Media and Technocultures Reader

The study of new media has developed within a wide range of academic disciplines and theoretical paradigms and has generated a great deal of excitement, hype and confusion. *The New Media and Technocultures Reader* gathers texts which map the cultural implications of new media, encapsulating and challenging key debates, theoretical positions and approaches to research.

    The New Media and Technocultures Reader offers students further reading on and exploration of key issues and topics raised in the textbook *New Media: A Critical Introduction*. The *Reader* draws on various disciplinary stances (including visual culture; media and cultural history; media theory; media production; philosophy and the history of the sciences; political economy and sociology), offering readers a rich and interdisciplinary resource. Critical and accessible editorial commentary guides the reader between the extracts and through the debates.

Contributors: Espen Aarseth, Jean Baudrillard, Michael Bull, Gabrielle Consentino, Michal Daliot-Bul, Shanly Dixon, Peter Galison, Félix Guattari, Donna Haraway, Larissa Hjorth, Erkki Huhtamo, Mizuko Ito, Mark Katz, Sarah Kember, Helen W. Kennedy, Dorothy Kidd, Norman Klein, Elaine Lally, Manuel De Landa, Bruno Latour, Pierre Lévy, Martin Lister, Geert Lovink, Marshall McLuhan, Lev Manovich, Laura U. Marks, Carolyn Marvin, Karl Marx, Ted Nelson, Mark Poster, Don Slater, David Sudnow, T.L. Taylor, Tiziana Terranova, David Tomas, Sandra Weber, Norbert Wiener, Raymond Williams, J. Macgregor Wise and Benjamin Woolley.

Seth Giddings is Senior Lecturer in Digital Media and Critical Theory in the Department of Screen Media and Journalism at the University of the West of England, where he teaches media and cultural studies, and particularly the theory and practice of new media. He is a member of the Digital Cultures Research Centre, and his research interests cross game studies, media ethnography, microethology, and everyday technoculture.

Martin Lister is Emeritus Professor of Visual Culture in the Department of Screen Media and Journalism at the University of the West of England. His research interests are in visual culture, photography, media history, new media studies and the role of technology in culture. He is editor of the Routledge journal *Photographies*.

The New Media and Technocultures Reader

Edited by

Seth Giddings with Martin Lister

Routledge
Taylor & Francis Group

LONDON AND NEW YORK

First published 2011
by Routledge
2 Park Square, Milton Park, Abingdon, Oxon, OX14 4RN

Simultaneously published in the USA and Canada
by Routledge
711 Third Avenue, New York, NY 10017 (8th Floor)

Routledge is an imprint of the Taylor & Francis Group, an informa business

Typeset in Perpetua and Bell Gothic by
Florence Production Ltd, Stoodleigh, Devon

British Library Cataloguing in Publication Data
A catalogue record for this book is available from the British Library

Library of Congress Cataloging in Publication Data
The new media and technocultures reader/edited by Seth Giddings
with Martin Lister.
        p. cm.
    Includes bibliographical references and index.
  1. Technology – Social aspects.   2. Technology and civilization.
  3. Digital media – Social aspects.   4. Communication and culture.
  I. Giddings, Seth.   II. Lister, Martin, 1947–.
  T14.5.N624 2011
  302.23 – dc22   2010031812

ISBN13: 978-0-415-46913-5 (hbk)
ISBN13: 978-0-415-46914-2 (pbk)

Contents

Acknowledgements

A number of thinkers have referred to the medium of the book in technological terms as a 'machine to think with'. Like all machines, it is made of parts, and constructed through a variety of processes and systems, by diverse actors and fabricators. Beneath this volume's sleek cover lies a heterogeneous circuit of permissions, extractions, condensations and annotations. It has been assembled through email, word processing software, pen and paper, photocopies, downloads, scans, conversation, the intriguing economics of academic publishing, library catalogue systems, Internet search engines and commercial book sites, negotiation, intellectual generosity and patience.

Though two names are on the cover, many people have made up its parts. So, many thanks to Martin Lister for encouraging, shaping, re-shaping, endless reading, and his critical rigour in the processes of development, organisation and synthesis. To the Routledge Media and Cultural Studies machine's many parts, in particular Charlotte Wood, Natalie Foster, Anna Callander and Monica Kendall for their good-natured patience and professionalism, but also to the others involved in permissions tracking, typesetting, indexing and design. Annie Lovejoy's beautiful cover image couples this machine to that of *New Media: A Critical Introduction* editions, and is augmented by Asha Pearse's elegant typography and layout.

Friends and colleagues who offered invaluable advice and suggestions in areas of new media and technocultural studies beyond my own expertise include Patrick Crogan, Iain Grant, Helen W. Kennedy and Hillegonda Rietveld. This volume is one product of a much longer process of intellectual and creative enquiry into new media and technoculture at the University of the West of England in Bristol, initially in the School of Cultural Studies, now the Department of Culture, Media and Drama. This process has been driven by my co-authors of *New Media: A Critical Introduction*, fellow members of the Play Research Group and the Digital Cultures Research Centre, and to many in the field of game studies: in addition to those already mentioned, Jon Dovey and Rune Klevjer.

Thanks of course to all the thinkers and authors assembled here by the remote processes of permission-seeking, editing and annotating. I hope they all feel that this volume does justice to their invaluable research, thought and writing. I will invoke – briefly – the unitary, autonomous and non-machinic author, but only to assure readers that the responsibility for any errors and omissions rests with me alone.

With thanks and love to Penny, Jo and Alex.
SG

Permissions

The following have been reproduced with kind permission. Whilst every effort has been made to trace copyright holders and obtain permission, this has not been possible in all cases. Any omissions brought to our attention will be remedied in future editions.

PART ONE: Genealogies of technoculture

1 *The Human Use of Human Beings: Cybernetics and Society* © 1989 by Norbert Wiener. By permission of Free Association Books.

2 Peter Galison (1994) 'The Ontology of the Enemy: Norbert Wiener and the Cybernetic Vision', *Critical Inquiry* 21(1), 228–66. By permission of the University of Chicago Press.

3 *When Old Technologies Were New* © 1988 by Carolyn Marvin. By permission of Oxford University Press, Inc.

4 *Computer Lib / Dream Machines* © 1987 by Ted Nelson. Published by Tempus Books. Reproduced by permission of the author.

5 Revised and updated version of the original essay, *From Kaleidoscomaniac to Cybernerd: Notes toward an Archaeology of the Media* © 1997 Erkki Huhtamo. *Leonardo* 30(3), 221–4. By permission of the author.

6 *War in the Age of Intelligent Machines* © 1991 by Manuel De Landa. By permission of Zone Books.

PART TWO: Models of technology, media and culture

7 Karl Marx, 'The labour process and alienation in machinery and science', from *Marx's Grundrisse*, David McLellan ed., Copyright © 1973, Paladin Press.

8 *Understanding Media: The Extensions of Man*, Copyright © 2001 by Marshall McLuhan, Routledge. Reproduced by permission of Taylor & Francis Books UK.

9 *Television: Technology and Cultural Form*, Copyright © 1974 by Raymond Williams, Routledge. Reproduced by permission of Taylor & Francis Books UK.

PART THREE: Bodies and agents

PART FOUR: Texts, forms, codes

23 Lev Manovich, *The Language of New Media*, excerpt from pages 218–49, © 2001 Massachusetts Institute of Technology. By permission of The MIT Press.

24 Laura U. Marks, 'Invisible Media', from *New Media: Theories and Practices of Digitextuality*, ed. Anna Everett and John T. Caldwell, Copyright © 2003, Routledge. Reproduced by permission of Taylor & Francis Books UK.

25 Geert Lovink, *Zero Comments: Blogging and Critical Internet Culture*, Copyright © 2010, Routledge. Reproduced by permission of Taylor & Francis Books UK.

26 Gabrielle Consentino (2006) '"Hacking" the iPod: A Look Inside Apple's Portable Music Player', from *Cybersounds: Essays on Virtual Music Culture*, ed. Michael D. Ayers, New York: Peter Lang, pp. 185–207.

27 *Capturing Sound: How Technology Has Changed Music*, revised and updated second edition, by Mark Katz © 2004, 2010 by the Regents of the University of California. Published by the University of California Press.

28 Norman Klein, 'Hybrid Cinema: *The Mask*, Masques and Tex Avery'. Previously published in *Reading the Rabbit: Explorations in Warner Bros. Animation*, ed. Kevin S. Sandler, Copyright © 1998 by Rutgers, the State University. Reprinted by permission of Rutgers University Press.

29 Martin Lister, 'Photography in the Age of Electronic Imaging', from *Photography: A Critical Introduction* (3rd edition), ed. Liz Wells, Copyright © 2004, Routledge. Reproduced by permission of Taylor & Francis Books UK.

30 David Sudnow, *Pilgrim in the Microworld*, Copyright © 1983 by David Sudnow. By permission of Grand Central Publishing.

PART FIVE: Network culture

31 Don Slater (1998) 'Trading Sexpics on IRC: Embodiment and Authenticity on the Internet', *Body & Society* 4(4), Sage, 91–117. Reproduced with permission of Sage.

32 Tiziana Terranova (2004) 'Free Labour', from *Network Culture: Politics for the Information Age*, London: Pluto, pp. 73–97. Reproduced with permission.

33 T.L. Taylor, *Play Between Worlds: Exploring Online Game Culture*, excerpt from pp. 36–62, © 2006 Massachusetts Institute of Technology, by permission of The MIT Press.

34 Donna Haraway, *Modest_Witness@Second_Millenium.FemaleMan©_Meets_Oncomouse*, Copyright © 1997, Routledge. Reproduced by permission of Taylor & Francis Books UK.

35 Geert Lovink, *Zero Comments: Blogging and Critical Internet Culture*, Copyright © 2010, Routledge. Reproduced by permission of Taylor & Francis Books UK.

36 Dorothy Kidd, 'Indymedia.org: A New Communications Commons', from *Cyberactivism: Online Activism in Theory and Practice*, ed. Martha McCaughey and Michael D. Ayers, Copyright © 2003, Routledge. Reproduced by permission of Taylor & Francis Books UK.

PART SIX: Everyday media technocultures

SETH GIDDINGS

INTRODUCTION
How to use this book

THIS BOOK IS DESIGNED TO complement and support another book: *New Media: A Critical Introduction* by Martin Lister, Jon Dovey, Seth Giddings, Iain Grant and Kieran Kelly. *New Media: A Critical Introduction* has been around for some time: it was first published in 2003, and a second, revised and updated, edition has now been issued. Readers do not have to buy or borrow both; the first has managed quite well on its own for some years, and this more recent collection, we hope, can stand for itself as an introduction to the field of new media and technocultural studies. However, the essays and extracts reproduced here have either significantly influenced our approaches and thought in the writing of *New Media: A Critical Introduction* or suggest ways of extending and developing these ideas and approaches. Not every topic or debate, new media form or technocultural practice covered by *New Media: A Critical Introduction* is addressed directly here, but where relevant we have cross-referenced the key ideas from this book to that one (these links are to the second edition of the book).

Each essay or extract here has a short introduction to orient the reader, outlining the main argument and approach, offering context or explanation of unfamiliar concepts where necessary, and making links to other extracts within this book (indicated by a surname in bold text, e.g. **Kennedy**), to relevant sections of *New Media: A Critical Introduction* and, where applicable, to key texts available online.

What are new media, and why technoculture?

Many of the key theorists and bodies of thought assembled here imply or assert in different ways that it is impossible to separate human culture from technology, that human society was made possible by the techniques, tools or machines of language, shelter, cooking, transport, art and manufacture. Moreover, for some, not only is all human culture always already technoculture but the distinction between technology and biology, nature and culture is by no means as clear as commonly understood. For Marshall **McLuhan** the electric lightbulb is a medium, for Donna **Haraway** nature, culture, science and technology are inseparable, epitomised by the science fictional *and* factual figure of the cyborg, whereas for Gilles Deleuze and Félix **Guattari** even molecules are machines. This is a challenge for a book on technology and culture: if culture has *always* been technoculture, and everything, including the natural world, is implicated in technoculture and new media, then which bodies of thought and critical approaches, which pieces of writing, should be selected – from, potentially, everything ever said or written?

To meet this challenge we have happily plundered other disciplines and cultural practices that address technology, culture, society and media, from film studies to philosophy, sociology to cybercultural studies, science and technology studies to media activism. But we have tried to maintain a loose focus in our own baggy discipline of media and cultural studies, tying in these broader questions and ideas about technology and culture with more familiar notions and categories from media and cultural studies.

New media are the product of the digital transformation of communication, information, entertainment media, including television, the press, cinema, telephones, photography and so on. However, these new media rarely exist as a straightforward remediation or digitisation of earlier media. For example, as both Larissa **Hjorth** and Michal **Daliot-Bul** point out, the contemporary mobile phone is already much more than a portable version of old fixed-line telephones. Videogames have their ancestry in both board games and pinball, but they are quite different objects and experiences. So, many of the extracts here are concerned with the *differences* and *newness* of new media, as convergences or as hybrids, as software and hardware, as networked and word-building. As in the writing of *New Media: A Critical Introduction*, we came up against the issue of the 'newness' of new media, in particular the temptation to play with only the latest gadgets and apps. We have followed a similar strategy and rationale to that of *New Media: A Critical Introduction*, i.e. to both insist on the importance of an understanding of media and technological history and change, whilst paying attention to broader contemporary developments that are reshaping media experience and everyday life. The critical negotiation of historical or genealogical trajectories on the one hand and the distinct or ruptural are pursued throughout the material gathered in this book.

Our starting point for 'technoculture' in this book similarly begins with the established media and cultural studies understanding of culture as a 'whole way of life'. Many of the extracts share media and cultural studies' emphasis on the quotidian and on the power relations and hierarchies that cut through or construct everyday life. The thinking behind our choice of material, then, was to offer resources for, first, the understanding and exploration of the ecologies and experiences of contemporary popular communications and entertainment media, media production and activism in a time of rapid transformation. And second, to explore conceptual refusals to see 'media' and 'technology' as discrete and bounded objects, their operations and effects somehow separate from everyday life until they 'impact' upon it.

We will zoom in on these everyday media technologies, practices and behaviours, but this will not be to classify or taxonomise them: we have no fixed working definitions of media or technology and are not interested in establishing their edges, in deciding what is and what isn't a medium or a technology. Rather we would like throughout to maintain a sense that any particular object, text, body, practice or machine is always connected to one next to, above or below it, is always part of larger assemblages and is itself always composed of smaller parts. From the start this approach necessitates a challenge to the humanist assumptions of media and cultural studies (and the humanities and social sciences in general). Many of the extracts collected here refuse to concern themselves only with human bodies, agency and practices. Like **Latour** we want to acknowledge, and study, the 'missing masses' of non-humans that co-constitute human culture.

All this said, to maintain some focus and coherence we have had to leave out topics that a more encyclopaedic approach might have included: we don't properly address issues of cultural or technological policy, of technoscience, biopolitics or biotechnology (though these issues are alluded to).

Many of the extracts ask their readers to think differently about contemporary digital media cultures, whether through a historical questioning of the perceived newness of new media or of alternative historical possibilities, or through a critical or creative rethinking of accepted forms, institutions, economics, relationships and aesthetics. So, this collection aims both to contribute to the fields of study addressing new media, technology and culture, whilst also challenging them.

Most of the extracts have been chosen not only for their pertinence for a particular object of study, but also for their richness, an excess that allows them to be read in different ways for different purposes. This will allow readers, we hope, to make connections across the extracts, to explore ideas, to follow arguments and to construct their own. In reviewing the selection we found many links across extracts, seams of ideas, approaches and concepts running through the book. In some extracts these seams were clear and glistening, ready to be mined, in others they were more deeply buried. These, for us, include: the history of, and concepts arising from, the science of cybernetics; the challenge of autonomous technologies and questions of technological agency; playful engagement with technologies and systems; questions of the reality of artifice and simulation; embodied engagements; and the strangeness or marvellousness of everyday technocultures. We hope this book's readers will find their own too.

Parts

These rich and polyvalent texts cannot be adequately categorised, and most could probably be placed under another of our headings without too much trouble. However, we decided to allow the reader some orientation and each part contains extracts the most salient point or approach of which addresses that part. For example, Larissa **Hjorth**'s essay on mobile media argues for a genealogical approach and cites Erkki **Huhtamo**. Yet **Huhtamo**'s essay is centrally concerned with media genealogy (or archaeology) and **Hjorth**'s is centrally concerned with understanding the contemporary everyday nature of new media, thus they have been placed in Parts One and Six respectively.

The part headings themselves could be completely different and the extracts organised differently. All we can do is hope that the reader finds some critical and analytical logic in our organisation.

PART ONE

Genealogies of technoculture

I N T H I S F I R S T P A R T W E A R E reminded of two things. Firstly, that our new media and the technologies on which they rely have histories and, secondly, that the very invention and emergence of these new media technologies raise new questions about the history of media and technology.

This book cannot offer a set of sources that do justice to the history of technoculture. This would have to include archaeological work on the first human uses of tools, the global development of techniques, technoscience and systems in China, early Islam, military technologies from Ancient Greece to the Great War, domestic technologies from weaving to microwaves ... to name but a few. Instead we offer a modest collection that aims to do two things.

Firstly, it offers historical insights into some key contexts in the development of contemporary digital media and technoculture. Whereas, as we have noted, all culture is, and has always been, technoculture, the relationships between culture, technologies and human experience change over time, and there are historical periods where this change is so intense and far-reaching that we can usefully talk of distinct 'revolutions' and subsequently new technocultural paradigms. The Industrial Revolution, particularly from the middle of the nineteenth century in Western Europe, addressed here by Norbert **Wiener** (and, in Part Two, by Karl **Marx**) is a powerful example. The next key moment in which emergent technologies and techniques intensified to such a degree that the identification of a distinct technological era seems reasonable and useful is the research on computing and simulation systems undertaken during and immediately after the Second World War. This is **Wiener**'s concern too. Indeed **Wiener** is a central player in this emerging computer research, as detailed by **Galison**.

Secondly, each extract can be read as a way of writing histories and genealogies of technoculture. Our concern in this part is not only to identify significant historical moments, but also, as importantly, to suggest to the reader ways in which these histories are written and interpreted. New technologies and systems do not spring into the world fully formed. They are always particular assemblages of existing and emerging technologies and techniques. Conventional histories of particular technologies often assume a clear, linear progression, whereas a genealogical or archaeological approach to media history, as propounded by Erkki **Huhtamo** and Carolyn **Marvin**, would look for non-linear connections, historical dead-ends and returns. New media often appear to bear a significant resemblance to much earlier or forgotten media technologies (as **Marvin** argues in relation to the spectacular displays of electric light in nineteenth-century cities) or appear as hybrids of technologies previously seen as occupying quite distinct historical paths (such as the connections **Huhtamo** draws between kaleidoscopes and virtual reality). We end this part with a short and seriously playful piece by Manuel **De Landa** that recasts the entire history of technology from an imagined future.

For further discussion of new media genealogy, see *New Media: A Critical Introduction*: 58–62 and 145–9.

Any selection necessitates exclusion. We have chosen not to include an extract on the history of the Internet, though of course this particular technological genealogy is fundamental to contemporary new media. A number of extracts in this book offer their own histories of the digital networks via their own particular concerns and genealogies (**Nelson**, **Lovink**, **Taylor** and **Terranova**, for example). There are a number of clear and accessible histories of the techniques, protocols and, to a lesser extent, the culture attendant on the development from the decentralised military communication network (ARPANET) to academic computer networks to the software innovations that led to the World Wide Web and later to Web 2.0, so we point our readers to them:

http://www.isoc.org/internet/history/brief.shtml
http://www.computerhistory.org/internet_history/
http://w2.eff.org/Net_culture/internet_sterling.history.txt

Chapter 1

NORBERT WIENER

THE FIRST AND THE SECOND INDUSTRIAL REVOLUTION

W IENER'S BOOK *The Human Use of Human Beings: Cybernetics and Society* was originally published in 1950, shortly after the end of the Second World War. Wiener was a key figure in the foundation of a new scientific paradigm that he called cybernetics. Cybernetics stressed the role of both human beings and new computers developed during the War as processors of information. The cybernetic project was to forge a theory of communication and control, applying to systems that might include humans, animals and machines.

Here, Wiener reflects upon two industrial revolutions in which, 'the machine [. . .] impinged upon human culture with an effect of the greatest moment'. The first occurred in the early nineteenth century and centred upon the steam engine, and the second, one whose early stages Wiener lived through and participated in, centred upon the early forms of the electronic mainframe digital computer. While Wiener sees the second revolution as qualitatively different from the first, in its far-reaching significance for work, production and communication, he also sees many connections and he repeatedly demonstrates how the invention of new technologies is 'conditioned by existing means'. In an essay that is alert to the complexities of technological change he shows how disparate machines and technologies converge and conjoin at an increasing rate, over some 300 years, to produce new technological possibilities and powers that are far beyond those that any single one possessed. From his standpoint in the 1950s, Wiener looks backwards to an industrial age (in which he sees his own present being prepared) and forwards to a time (our own) where he sees the second technological revolution as a 'two-edged sword'; one which may be used for the benefit of humanity or, he fears, may destroy it.

Terms and technologies that are key to cybernetics are outlined in this extract, including feedback, regulation, amplification and machine to machine communication. Peter **Galison** (below) goes into more detail of Wiener's life, cybernetics and the implications of his thought and work, as does David **Tomas** in Part Three. Their political implications are addressed by Donna **Haraway**.

Principia Cybernetica Web is an encyclopaedic site on cybernetic concepts and researchers: http://pespmc1.vub.ac.be/CYBSWHAT.html

[. . .] In this chapter, I shall discuss that field in which the communicative characters of man and of the machine impinge upon one another, and I shall try to ascertain what the direction of the development of the machine will be, and what we may expect of its impact on human society.

Once before in history the machine had impinged upon human culture with an effect of the greatest moment. This previous impact is known as the Industrial Revolution, and it concerned the machine purely as an alternative to human muscle. In order to study the present crisis, which we shall term The Second Industrial Revolution, it is perhaps wise to discuss the history of the earlier crisis as something of a model.

The first industrial revolution had its roots in the intellectual ferment of the eighteenth century, which found the scientific techniques of Newton and Huygens already well developed, but with applications which had yet scarcely transcended astronomy. It had, however, become manifest to all intelligent scientists that the new techniques were going to have a profound effect on the other sciences. The first fields to show the impact of the Newtonian era were those of navigation and of clockmaking.

[. . .]

Accordingly, the advance guard of the craftsmen of the industrial revolution consisted on the one hand of clockmakers, who used the new mathematics of Newton in the design of their pendulums and their balance wheels; and on the other hand, of optical-instrument makers, with their sextants and their telescopes. The two trades had very much in common. They both demanded the construction of accurate circles and accurate straight lines, and the graduation of these in degrees or in inches. Their tools were the lathe and the dividing engine. These machine tools for delicate work are the ancestors of our present machine-tool industry.

It is an interesting reflection that every tool has a genealogy, and that it is descended from the tools by which it has itself been constructed. The clockmakers' lathes of the eighteenth century have led through a clear historical chain of intermediate tools to the great turret lathes of the present day. The series of intervening steps might conceivably have been foreshortened somewhat, but it has necessarily had a certain minimum length. It is clearly impossible in constructing a great turret lathe to depend on the unaided human hand for the pouring of the metal, for the placing of the castings on the instruments to machine them, and above all for the power needed in the task of machining them. These must be done through machines that have themselves been manufactured by other machines, and it is only through many stages of this that one reaches back to the original hand- or foot-lathes of the eighteenth century.

[. . .]

We must thus consider navigation and the instruments necessary for it as the locus of an industrial revolution before the main industrial revolution. The main industrial revolution begins with the steam engine. [. . .]

The first place where steam power came into practical use was in replacing one of the most brutal forms of human or animal labor: pumping of water out of mines. At best, this had been done by draft animals, by crude machines turned by horses. At worst, as in the silver mines of New Spain, it was done by the labor of human slaves. It is a work that is never finished and which can never be interrupted without the possibility of closing down the mine forever. The use of the steam engine to replace this servitude must certainly be regarded as a great humanitarian step forward.

[. . .]

The next place where the industrial revolution made itself felt, perhaps a little later than in the field of the heavy labor of mine workers, and simultaneously with the revolution in transportation, was in the textiles industry. This was already a sick industry. Even before the power spindle and the power looms, the condition of the spinners and the weavers left much to be desired. The bulk of production which they could perform fell far short of the demands of the day. It might thus appear to have been scarcely possible to conceive that the transition to the machine could have worsened their condition; but worsen it, it most certainly did.

The beginnings of textile-machine development go back of the steam engine. The stocking frame has existed in a form worked by hand ever since the time of Queen Elizabeth. Machine spinning first became necessary in order to furnish warps for hand looms. The complete mechanization of the textile industry, covering weaving as well as spinning, did not occur until the beginning of the nineteenth century. The first textile machines were for hand operation, although the use of horsepower and water power followed very quickly. Part of the impetus behind the development of the Watt engine, as contrasted with the Newcomen engine, was the desire to furnish power in the rotary form needed for textile purposes.

The textile mills furnished the model for almost the whole course of the mechanization of industry. On the social side, they began the transfer of the workers from the home to the factory and from the country to the city. There was an exploitation of the labor of children and women to an extent, and of a brutality scarcely conceivable at the present time—that is, if we forget the South African diamond mines and ignore the new industrialization of China and India and the general terms of plantation labor in almost every country. A great deal of this was due to the fact that new techniques had produced new responsibilities, at a time at which no code had yet arisen to take care of these responsibilities. There was, however, a phase which was of greater technical than moral significance. By this, I mean that a great many of the disastrous consequences and phases of the earlier part of the industrial revolution were not so much due to any moral obtuseness or iniquity on the part of those concerned, as to certain technical features which were inherent in the early means of industrialization, and which the later history of technical development has thrust more or less into the background. These technical determinants of the direction which the early industrial revolution took lay in the very nature of early steam power and its transmission. The steam engine used fuel very uneconomically by modern standards, although this is not as important as it might seem, considering the fact that early engines had none of the more modern type with which to compete. However, among themselves they were much more economical to run on a large scale than on a small one. In contrast with the prime mover, the textile machine, whether it be loom or spindle, is a comparatively light machine, and uses little power. It was therefore economically necessary to assemble these machines in large factories, where many looms and spindles could be run from one steam engine.

At that time the only available means of transmission of power were mechanical. The first among these was the line of shafting, supplemented by the belt and the pulley. Even as late as the time of my own childhood, the typical picture of a factory was that of a great shed with long lines of shafts suspended from the rafters, and pulleys connected by belts to the individual machines. This sort of factory still exists; although in very many cases it has given way to the modern arrangement where the machines are driven individually by electric motors.

[. . .]

The electrical motor is a mode of distributing power which is very convenient to construct in small sizes, so that each machine may have its own motor. The transmission losses in the wiring of a factory are relatively low, and the efficiency of the motor itself is relatively high. The connection of the motor with its wiring is not necessarily rigid, nor does it consist of many parts. There are still motives of traffic and convenience which may induce us to continue the custom of mounting the different machines of an industrial process in a single factory; but the need of connecting all the machines to a single source of power is no longer a serious reason for geographical proximity. In other words, we are now in a position to return to cottage industry, in places where it would otherwise be suitable.

I do not wish to insist that the difficulties of mechanical transmission were the only cause of the shed factories and of the demoralization they produced. Indeed, the factory system started before the machine system, as a means of introducing discipline into the highly undisciplined home industry of the individual workers, and of keeping up standards of production. It is true, however, that these non-mechanical factories were very soon superseded by mechanical ones, and that probably the worst social effects of urban crowding and of rural depopulation took place in the machine factory. Furthermore, if the fractional horsepower motor had been available from the start and could have increased the unit of production of a cottage worker, it is highly probable that a large part of the organization and discipline needed for successful large-scale production could have been superimposed on such home industries as spinning and weaving.

If it should be so desired, a single piece of machinery may now contain several motors, each introducing power at the proper place. This relieves the designer of much of the need for the ingenuity in mechanical design which he would otherwise have been compelled to use. In an electrical design, the mere problem of the connection of the parts seldom involves much difficulty that does not lend itself to easy mathematical formulation and solution. The inventor of linkages has been superseded by the computor of circuits. This is an example of the way in which the art of invention is conditioned by the existing means.

In the third quarter of the last century, when the electric motor was first used in industry, it was at first supposed to be nothing more than an alternative device for carrying out existing industrial techniques. It was probably not foreseen that its final effect would be to give rise to a new concept of the factory.

That other great electrical invention, the vacuum tube, has had a similar history. Before the invention of the vacuum tube, it took many separate mechanisms to regulate systems of great power. Indeed, most of the regulatory means themselves employed considerable power. There were exceptions to this, but only in specific fields, such as the steering of ships.

As late as 1915, I crossed the ocean on one of the old ships of the American Line. It belonged to the transitional period when ships still carried sails, as well as a pointed bow to carry a bowsprit. In a well-deck not far aft of the main superstructure, there was a formidable engine, consisting of four or five six-foot wheels with hand-spokes. These wheels were supposed to control the ship in the event that its automatic steering engine broke down. In a storm, it would have taken ten men or more, exerting their full strength, to keep that great ship on its course.

This was not the usual method of control of the ship, but an emergency replacement, or as sailors call it, a "jury steering wheel." For normal control, the ship carried a steering engine which translated the relatively small forces of the quartermaster at the wheel into the movement of the massive rudder. Thus even on a purely mechanical basis, some progress had been made toward the solution of the problem of amplification of forces or torques. Nevertheless, at that time, this solution of the amplification problem did not range over extreme differences between the levels of input and of output, nor was it embodied in a convenient universal type of apparatus.

The most flexible universal apparatus for amplifying small energy-levels into high energy-levels is the vacuum tube, or electron valve. The history of this is interesting, though it is too complex for us to discuss here. It is however amusing to reflect that the invention of the electron valve originated in Edison's greatest scientific discovery and perhaps the only one which he did not capitalize into an invention.

He observed that when an electrode was placed inside an electric lamp, and was taken as electrically positive with respect to the filament, then a current would flow, if the filament were heated, but not otherwise. Through a series of inventions by other people, this led to a more effective way than any known before of controlling a large current by a small voltage.

This is the basis of the modern radio industry, but it is also an industrial tool which is spreading widely into new fields. It is thus no longer necessary to control a process at high energy-levels by a mechanism in which the important details of control are carried out at these levels. It is quite possible to form a certain pattern of behavior response at levels much lower even than those found in usual radio sets, and then to employ a series of amplifying tubes to control by this apparatus a machine as heavy as a steel-rolling mill. The work of discriminating and of forming the pattern of behavior for this is done under conditions in which the power losses are insignificant, and yet the final employment of this discriminatory process is at arbitrarily high levels of power.

It will be seen that this is an invention which alters the fundamental conditions of industry, quite as vitally as the transmission and subdivision of power through the use of the small electric motor. The study of the pattern of behavior is transferred to a special part of the instrument in which power-economy is of very little importance. We have thus deprived of much of their importance the dodges and devices previously used to insure that a mechanical linkage should consist of the fewest possible elements, as well as the devices used to minimize friction and lost motion. The design of machines involving such parts has been transferred from the domain of the skilled shopworker to that of the research-laboratory man; and in this he has all the available tools of circuit theory to replace a mechanical ingenuity of the old sort. Invention in the old sense has been supplanted by the intelligent employment of certain laws of nature. The step from the laws of nature to their employment has been reduced by a hundred times.

I have previously said that when an invention is made, a considerable period generally elapses before its full implications are understood. It was long before people became aware of the full impact of the airplane on international relations and on the conditions of human life. The effect of atomic energy on mankind and the future is yet to be assessed, although many observers insist that it is merely a new weapon like all older weapons.

The case of the vacuum tube was similar. In the beginning, it was regarded merely as an extra tool to supplement the already existing techniques of telephonic communication. The electrical engineers first mistook its real importance to such an extent that for years vacuum tubes were relegated simply to a particular part of the communication network. [. . .]

The vacuum tube was first used to replace previously existing components of long-distance telephone circuits and wireless telegraphy. It was not long, however, before it became clear that the radio-telephone had achieved the stature of the radio-telegraph, and that broadcasting was possible. Let not the fact that this great triumph of invention has largely been given over to the soap-opera and the hillbilly singer, blind one to the excellent work that was done in developing it, and to the great civilizing possibilities which have been perverted into a national medicine-show.

Though the vacuum tube received its debut in the communications industry, the boundaries and extent of this industry were not fully understood for a long period. There were sporadic uses of the vacuum tube and of its sister invention, the photoelectric cell, for scanning the products of industry; as, for example, for regulating the thickness of a web coming out of a paper machine, or for inspecting the color of a can of pineapples. These uses did not as yet form a reasoned new technique, nor were they associated in the engineering mind with the vacuum tube's other function, communication.

All this changed in the war. One of the few things gained from the great conflict was the rapid development of invention, under the stimulus of necessity and the unlimited employment of money; and above all, the new blood called in to industrial research. At the beginning of the war, our greatest need was to keep England from being knocked out by an overwhelming air attack. Accordingly, the anti-aircraft cannon was one of the first objects of our scientific war effort, especially when combined with the airplane-detecting device of radar or ultra-high-frequency Hertzian waves. The technique of radar used the same modalities as the existing technique of radio besides inventing new ones of its own. It was thus natural to consider radar as a branch of communication theory.

Besides finding airplanes by radar it was necessary to shoot them down. This involves the problem of fire control. The speed of the airplane has made it necessary to compute the elements of the trajectory of the anti-aircraft missile by machine, and to give the predicting machine itself communication functions which had previously been assigned to human beings. Thus the problem of anti-aircraft fire control made a new generation of engineers familiar with the notion of a communication addressed to a machine rather than to a person. [. . .]

During the period immediately preceding World War II other uses were found for the vacuum tube coupled directly to the machine rather than to the human agent. Among these were more general applications to computing machines. The concept of the large-scale computing machine as developed by Vannevar Bush among others was originally a purely mechanical one. The integration was done by rolling disks engaging one another in a frictional manner; and the interchange of outputs and inputs between these disks was the task of a classical train of shafts and gears.

The mother idea of these first computing machines is much older than the work of Vannevar Bush. In certain respects it goes back to the work of [Charles] Babbage early in the last century. Babbage had a surprisingly modern idea for a computing machine, but his mechanical means fell far behind his ambitions. The first difficulty he met, and with which he could not cope, was that a long train of gears requires considerable power to run it, so that its output of power and torque very soon becomes too small to actuate the remaining parts of the apparatus. Bush saw this difficulty and overcame it in a very ingenious way. Besides the electrical amplifiers depending on vacuum tubes and on similar devices, there are certain mechanical torque-amplifiers which are familiar, for example, to everyone acquainted with ships and the unloading of cargo. The stevedore raises the cargo-slings by taking a purchase on his load around the drum of a donkey-engine or cargo-hoist. In this way, the tension which he exerts mechanically is increased by a factor which grows extremely rapidly with the angle of contact between his rope and the rotating drum. Thus one man is able to control the lifting of a load of many tons.

This device is fundamentally a force- or torque-amplifier. By an ingenious bit of design, Bush inserted such mechanical amplifiers between the stages of his computing machine, and thus was able to do effectively the sort of thing which had only been a dream for Babbage. [. . .]

A computing machine so designed would have to work at extremely high speed, which to my mind put mechanical processes out of the question and threw us back on electronic processes. In such a machine, moreover, all data would have to be written, read, and erased with a speed compatible with that of the other operations of the machine; and in addition to including an arithmetical mechanism, it would need a logical mechanism as well and would have to be able to handle problems of programming on a purely logical and automatic basis. The notion of programming in the factory had already become familiar through the work of Taylor and the Gilbreths on time study, and was ready to be transferred to the machine. This offered considerable difficulty of detail, but no great difficulty of principle. I was thus convinced as far back as 1940 that the automatic factory was on the horizon, and I so informed Vannevar Bush. The consequent development of automatization, both before and after the publication of the first edition of this book, has convinced me that I was right in my judgment and that this development would be one of the great factors in conditioning the social and technical life of the age to come, the keynote of the second industrial revolution.

In one of its earlier phases the Bush Differential Analyzer performed all the principal amplification functions. It used electricity only to give power to the motors running the machine as a whole. This state of computing-mechanisms was intermediate and transitory. It very soon became clear that amplifiers of an electric nature, connected by wires rather than by shafts, were both less expensive and more flexible than mechanical amplifiers and connections. Accordingly, the later forms of Bush's machine made use of vacuum-tube devices. This has been continued in all their successors; whether they were what are now called analogy machines, which work primarily by the measurement of physical quantities, or digital machines, which work primarily by counting and arithmetic operations.

The development of these computing machines has been very rapid since the war. For a large range of computational work, they have shown themselves much faster and more accurate than the human computer. Their speed has long since reached such a level that any intermediate human intervention in their work is out of the question. Thus they offer the same need to replace human capacities by machine capacities as those which we found in the anti-aircraft computer. The parts of the machine must speak to one another through an appropriate language, without speaking to any person or listening to any person, except in the terminal and initial stages of the process. Here again we have an element which has contributed to the general acceptance of the extension to machines of the idea of communication.

In this conversation between the parts of a machine, it is often necessary to take cognizance of what the machine has already said. Here there enters the principle of feedback, which we have already discussed, and which is older than its exemplification in the ship's steering engine, and is at least as old, in fact, as the governor which regulates the speed of Watt's steam engine. This governor keeps the engine from running wild when its load is removed. If it starts to run wild, the balls of the governor fly upward from centrifugal action, and in their upward flight they move a lever which partly cuts off the admission of steam. Thus the tendency to speed up produces a partly compensatory tendency to slow down. This method of regulation received a thorough mathematical analysis at the hands of Clerk Maxwell in 1868.

Here feedback is used to regulate the velocity of a machine. In the ship's steering engine it regulates the position of the rudder. The man at the wheel operates a light transmission system, employing chains or hydraulic transmission, which moves a member in the room containing the steering engine. There is some sort of apparatus which notes the distance between this member and the tiller; and this distance controls the admission of steam to the ports of a steam steering engine, or some similar electrical admission in the case of an electrical steering engine. Whatever the particular connections may be, this change of admission is always in such a direction as to bring into coincidence the tiller and the member actuated from the wheel. Thus one man at the wheel can do with ease what a whole crew could do only with difficulty at the old manpower wheel.

We have so far given examples of where the feedback process takes primarily a mechanical form. However, a series of operations of the same structure can be carried out through electrical and even vacuum-tube means. These means promise to be the future standard method of designing control apparatus.

There has long been a tendency to render factories and machines automatic. Except for some special purpose, one would no longer think of producing screws by the use of the ordinary lathe, in which a mechanic must watch the progress of his cutter and regulate it by hand. The production of screws in quantity without serious human intervention is now the normal task of the ordinary screw machine. Although this does not make any special use of the process of feedback nor of the vacuum tube, it accomplishes a somewhat similar end. What the feedback and the vacuum tube have made possible is not the sporadic design of individual automatic mechanisms, but a general policy for the construction of automatic mechanisms of the most varied type. In this they have been reinforced by our new theoretical treatment of communication, which takes full cognizance of the possibilities of communication between machine and machine. It is this conjunction of circumstances which now renders possible the new automatic age.

The existing state of industrial techniques includes the whole of the results of the first industrial revolution, together with many inventions which we now see to be precursors of the second industrial revolution. What the precise boundary between these two revolutions may be, it is still too early to say. In its potential significance, the vacuum tube certainly belongs to an industrial revolution different from that of the age of power; and yet it is only at present that the true significance of the invention of the vacuum tube has been sufficiently realized to allow us to attribute the present age to a new and second industrial revolution.

Up to now we have been talking about the existing state of affairs. We have not covered more than a small part of the aspects of the previous industrial revolution. We have not mentioned the airplane, nor the bulldozer, together with the other mechanical tools of construction, nor the automobile, nor even one-tenth of those factors which have converted modern life to something totally unlike the life of any other period. It is fair to say, however, that except for a considerable number of isolated examples, the industrial revolution up to the present has displaced man and the beast as a source of power, without making any great impression on other human functions. The best that a pick-and-shovel worker can do to make a living at the present time is to act as a sort of gleaner after the bulldozer. In all important respects, the man who has nothing but his physical power to sell has nothing to sell which it is worth anyone's money to buy.

Let us now go on to a picture of a more completely automatic age. Let us consider what for example the automobile factory of the future will be like; and in particular the assembly line, which is the part of the automobile factory that employs the most labor. In the first place, the sequence of operations will be controlled by something like a modern high-speed computing machine. In this book and elsewhere, I have often said that the high-speed computing machine is primarily a logical machine, which confronts different propositions with one another and draws some of their consequences. It is possible to translate the whole of mathematics into the performance of a sequence of purely logical tasks. If this representation of mathematics is embodied in the machine, the machine will be a computing machine in the ordinary sense. However, such a computing machine, besides accomplishing ordinary mathematical tasks, will be able to undertake the logical task of channeling a series of orders concerning mathematical operations. Therefore, as present high-speed computing machines in fact do, it will contain at least one large assembly which is purely logical.

The instructions to such a machine, and here too I am speaking of present practice, are given by what we have called a taping. The orders given the machine may be fed into it by a taping which is completely predetermined. It is also possible that the actual contingencies met in the performance of the machine may be handed over as a basis of further regulation to a new control tape constructed by the machine itself, or to a modification of the old one. I have already explained how I think such processes are related to learning.

It may be thought that the present great expense of computing machines bars them from use in industrial processes; and furthermore that the delicacy of the work needed in their construction and the variability of their functions precludes the use of the methods of mass production in constructing them. Neither of these charges is correct. In the first place, the enormous computing machines now used for the highest level of mathematical work cost something of the order of hundreds of thousands of dollars. Even this price would not be forbidding for the control machine of a really large factory, but it is not the relevant price.

The present computing machines are developing so rapidly that practically every one constructed is a new model. In other words, a large part of these apparently exorbitant prices goes into new work of design, and into new parts, which are produced by a very high quality of labor under the most expensive circumstances. If one of these computing machines were therefore established in price and model, and put to use in quantities of tens or twenties, it is very doubtful whether its price would be higher than tens of thousands of dollars. A similar machine of smaller capacity, not suited for the most difficult computational problems, but nevertheless quite adequate for factory control, would probably cost no more than a few thousand dollars in any sort of moderate-scale production.

Now let us consider the problem of the mass production of computing machines. If the only opportunity for mass production were the mass production of completed machines, it is quite clear that for a considerable period the best we could hope for would be a moderate-scale production. However, in each machine the parts are largely repetitive in very considerable numbers. This is true, whether we consider the memory apparatus, the logical apparatus, or the arithmetical subassembly. Thus production of a few dozen machines only, represents a potential mass production of the parts, and is accompanied by the same economic advantages.

It may still seem that the delicacy of the machines must mean that each job demands a special new model. This is also false. Given even a rough similarity in the type of mathematical and logical operations demanded of the mathematical and logical units of the machine, the over-all performance is regulated by the taping, or at any rate by the *original* taping. The taping of such a machine is a highly skilled task for a professional man of a very specialized type; but it is largely or entirely a once-for-all job, and need only be partly repeated when the machine is modified for a new industrial setup. Thus the cost of such a skilled technician will be distributed over a tremendous output, and will not really be a significant factor in the use of the machine.

The computing machine represents the center of the automatic factory, but it will never be the whole factory. On the one hand, it receives its detailed instructions from elements of the nature of sense organs, such as photoelectric cells, condensers for the reading of the thickness of a web of paper, thermometers, hydrogen-ion-concentration meters, and the general run of apparatus now built by instrument companies for the manual control of industrial processes. These instruments are already built to report electrically at remote stations. All they need to enable them to introduce their information into an automatic high-speed computer is a reading apparatus which will translate position or scale into a pattern of consecutive digits. Such apparatus already exists, and offers no great difficulty, either of principle or of constructional detail. The sense-organ problem is not new, and it is already effectively solved.

Besides these sense organs, the control system must contain effectors, or components which act on the outer world. Some of these are of a type already familiar, such as valve-turning motors, electric clutches, and the like. Some of them will have to be invented, to duplicate more nearly the functions of the human hand as supplemented by the human eye. It is altogether possible in the machining of automobile frames to leave on certain metal lugs, machined into smooth surfaces as points of reference. The tool, whether it be a drill or riveter or whatever else we want, may be led to the approximate neighborhood of these surfaces by a photoelectric mechanism, actuated for example by spots of paint. The final positioning may bring the tool up against the reference surfaces, so as to establish a firm contact, but not a destructively firm one. This is only one way of doing the job. Any competent engineer can think of a dozen more.

Of course, we assume that the instruments which act as sense organs record not only the original state of the work, but also the result of all the previous processes. Thus the machine may carry out feedback operations, either those of the simple type now so thoroughly understood, or those involving more complicated processes of discrimination, regulated by the central control as a logical or mathematical system. In other words, the all-over system will correspond to the complete animal with sense organs, effectors, and proprioceptors, and not, as in the ultra-rapid computing machine, to an isolated brain, dependent for its experiences and for its effectiveness on our intervention.

The speed with which these new devices are likely to come into industrial use will vary greatly with the different industries. Automatic machines, which may not be precisely like those described here, but which perform roughly the same functions, have already come into extensive use in continuous-process industries like canneries, steel-rolling mills, and especially wire and tin-plate factories. They are also familiar in paper factories, which likewise produce a continuous output. Another place where they are indispensable is in that sort of factory which is too dangerous for any considerable number of workers to risk their lives in its control, and in which an emergency is likely to be so serious and costly that its possibilities should have been considered in advance, rather than left to the excited judgment of somebody on the spot. If a policy can be thought out in advance, it can be committed to a taping which will regulate the conduct to be followed in accordance with the readings of the instrument. In other words, such factories should be under a regime rather like that of the interlocking signals and switches of the railroad signal-tower. This regime is already followed in oil-cracking factories, in many other chemical works, and in the handling of the sort of dangerous materials found in the exploitation of atomic energy.

We have already mentioned the assembly line as a place for applying the same sorts of technique. In the assembly line, as in the chemical factory, or the continuous-process paper mill, it is necessary to exert a certain statistical control on the quality of the product. This control depends on a sampling process. These sampling processes have now been developed by Wald and others into a technique called *sequential analysis*, in which the sampling is no longer taken in a lump, but is a continuous process going along with the production. That which can be done then by a technique so standardized that it can be put in the hands of a statistical computer who does not understand the logic behind it, may also be executed by a computing machine. In other words, except again at the highest levels, the machine takes care of the routine statistical controls, as well as of the production process.

In general, factories have an accounting procedure which is independent of production, but insofar as the data which occur in cost-accounting come from the machine or assembly line, they may be fed directly into a computing machine. Other data may be fed in from time to time by human operators, but the bulk of the clerical work can be handled mechanically, leaving only the extraordinary details such as outside correspondence for human beings. But even a large part of the outside correspondence may be received from the correspondents on punched cards, or transferred to punched cards by extremely low-grade labor. From this stage on, everything may go by machine. This mechanization also may apply to a not inappreciable part of the library and filing facilities of an industrial plant.

In other words, the machine plays no favorites between manual labor and white-collar labor. Thus the possible fields into which the new industrial revolution is likely to penetrate are very extensive, and include all labor performing judgments of a low level, in much the same way as the displaced labor of the earlier industrial revolution included every aspect of human power. There will, of course, be trades into which the new industrial revolution will not penetrate either because the new control machines are not economical in industries on so small a scale as not to be able to carry the considerable capital costs involved, or because their work is so varied that a new taping will be necessary for almost every job. I cannot see automatic machinery of the judgment-replacing type coming into use in the corner grocery, or in the corner garage, although I can very well see it employed by the wholesale grocer and the automobile manufacturer. The farm laborer too, although he is beginning to be pressed by automatic machinery, is protected from the full pressure of it because of the ground he has to cover, the variability of the crops he must till, and the special conditions of weather and the like that he must meet. Even here, the large-scale or plantation farmer is becoming increasingly dependent on cotton-picking and weed-burning machinery, as the wheat farmer has long been dependent on the McCormick reaper. Where such machines may be used, some use of machinery of judgment is not inconceivable.

The introduction of the new devices and the dates at which they are to be expected are, of course, largely economic matters, on which I am not an expert. Short of any violent political changes or another great war, I should give a rough estimate that it will take the new tools ten to twenty years to come into their own. A war would change all this overnight. If we should engage in a war with a major power like Russia, which would make serious demands on the infantry, and consequently on our manpower, we may be hard put to keep up our industrial production. Under these circumstances, the matter of replacing human production by other modes may well be a life-or-death matter to the nation. We are already as far along in the process of developing a unified system of automatic control machines as we were in the development of radar in 1939. Just as the emergency of the Battle of Britain made it necessary to attack the radar problem in a massive manner, and to hurry up the natural development of the field by what may have been decades, so too, the needs of labor replacement are likely to act on us in a similar way in the case of another war. Personnel such as skilled radio amateurs, mathematicians, and physicists, who were so rapidly turned into competent electrical engineers for the purposes of radar design, is still available for the similar task of automatic-machine design. There is a new and skilled generation coming up, which they have trained.

Under these circumstances, the period of about two years which it took for radar to get onto the battlefield with a high degree of effectiveness is scarcely likely to be exceeded by the period of evolution of the automatic factory. At the end of such a war, the "know-how" needed to construct such factories will be common. There will even be a considerable backlog of equipment manufactured for the government, which is likely to be on sale or available to the industrialists. Thus a new war will almost inevitably see the automatic age in full swing within less than five years.

I have spoken of the actuality and the imminence of this new possibility. What can we expect of its economic and social consequences? In the first place, we can expect an abrupt and final cessation of the demand for the type of factory labor performing purely repetitive tasks. In the long run, the deadly uninteresting nature of the repetitive task may make this a good thing and the source of leisure necessary for man's full cultural development. It may also produce cultural results as trivial and wasteful as the greater part of those so far obtained from the radio and the movies.

Be that as it may, the intermediate period of the introduction of the new means, especially if it comes in the fulminating manner to be expected from a new war, will lead to an immediate transitional period of disastrous confusion. We have a good deal of experience as to how the industrialists regard a new industrial potential. Their whole propaganda is to the effect that it must not be considered as the business of the government but must be left open to whatever entrepreneurs wish to invest money in it. We also know that they have very few inhibitions when it comes to taking all the profit out of an industry that there is to be taken, and then letting the public pick up the pieces. This is the history of the lumber and mining industries, and is part of what we have called in another chapter the traditional American philosophy of progress.

Under these circumstances, industry will be flooded with the new tools to the extent that they appear to yield immediate profits, irrespective of what long-time damage they can do. We shall see a process parallel to the way in which the use of atomic energy for bombs has been allowed to compromise the very necessary potentialities of the long-time use of atomic power to replace our oil and coal supplies, which are within centuries, if not decades, of utter exhaustion. Note well that atomic bombs do not compete with power companies.

Let us remember that the automatic machine, whatever we think of any feelings it may have or may not have, is the precise economic equivalent of slave labor. Any labor which competes with slave labor must accept the economic conditions of slave labor. It is perfectly clear that this will produce an unemployment situation, in comparison with which the present recession and even the depression of the thirties will seem a pleasant joke. This depression will ruin many industries—possibly even the industries which have taken advantage of the new potentialities. However, there is nothing in the industrial tradition which forbids an industrialist to make a sure and quick profit, and to get out before the crash touches him personally.

Thus the new industrial revolution is a two-edged sword. It may be used for the benefit of humanity, but only if humanity survives long enough to enter a period in which such a benefit is possible. It may also be used to destroy humanity, and if it is not used intelligently it can go very far in that direction. There are, however, hopeful signs on the horizon. Since the publication of the first edition of this book, I have participated in two big meetings with representatives of business management, and I have been delighted to see that awareness on the part of a great many of those present of the social dangers of our new technology and the social obligations of those responsible for management to see that the new modalities are used for the benefit of man, for increasing his leisure and enriching his spiritual life, rather than merely for profits and the worship of the machine as a new brazen calf. There are many dangers still ahead, but the roots of good will are there, and I do not feel as thoroughly pessimistic as I did at the time of the publication of the first edition of this book.

Chapter 2

PETER GALISON

THE ONTOLOGY OF THE ENEMY
Norbert Wiener and the cybernetic vision

T HE WEALTH OF HISTORICAL detail in this account of Norbert **Wiener**'s work
on a predictor system for ground-based anti-aircraft (AA) weapons in the Second World
War provides a fascinating context for understanding the genealogy of cybernetics and digital
culture. Peter Galison explains that the significance of Wiener's AA predictor goes beyond its
immediate pressing (and ultimately unsuccessful) wartime application and instead forms the
basis for Wiener's 'cybernetic understanding of the universe itself'. Galison's explanation is
wide-ranging so in this introduction we will pull out just a few of the concepts and technological
forms that he describes, selecting those that can be productively connected with other extracts
in this book.

Firstly, Wiener's understanding of the 'enemy' in his prototype military technology is highly
significant. The enemy was not the dehumanised 'other' of wartime propaganda and ideology,
nor the anonymous and invisible targets of bombing raids, but rather a rational and mechanised
opponent. Wiener was hoping to design a device that could predict an enemy bomber's trajectory
a few seconds in the future based on past behaviour. That is, to predict the enemy plane's
position at the point when an anti-aircraft shell could hit it, based on its trajectory in the
seconds preceding the firing of the shell. In the pragmatic pursuit of this predictive system, it
made little sense to Wiener to consider the enemy pilot and bomber as separate entities. The
target was both: the combination of the cognitive and motor skills of one and the mechanical
capabilities and responses of the other. Moreover, it was not just the Enemy that could be
thus conceptualised: in considering the overall AA predictor system, Allied anti-aircraft
operators and weaponry were also elided, as in both these systems both the human and
technological elements functioned as servomechanisms. And, as Galison puts it, 'it was a short
step from this elision of the human and the nonhuman in the ally to a blurring of the human-
machine boundary in general'.

There are parallels here with the discussions of non-human agency elsewhere in this book
(e.g. **Latour** and **Wise** in Part Three), from the ostensibly trivial habit of pilots to blame
technical problems in their planes on 'gremlins', to key concepts in cybernetics, such as the
'black box'. In cybernetics it is often unnecessary to dwell on the material make-up or construction
of a particular organism or system – these are judged according to their output, behaviour or
effects. The internal workings of the 'black box' are invisible, inconsequential, just as the

precise ratio and nature of human to non-human components and activities in an enemy plane were irrelevant to the prediction of its trajectory.

Donna **Haraway**'s work draws on ideas from cybernetics and her Cyborg Manifesto (see extract in Part Two) is mentioned here. David **Tomas**'s essay in this book discusses the influence of **Wiener** and cybernetics for understanding the human and the human body in technoculture. The concept of cybernetics underpins Espen **Aarseth**'s cybertext, and Helen W. **Kennedy** describes online videogame play in cybernetic terms.

Galison mentions Wiener's working relationship with Vannevar Bush, another important figure in 1940s information technology. Bush's article outlining an idea for the memex, a personalised information system in the form of a desk, is often referred to as an important precursor to personal computing and hypermedia. The essay can be found here: http://www. theatlantic.com/magazine/archive/1969/12/as-we-may-think/3881/

1. The enemy

"I . . . hope you can find some corner of activity in which I may be of use during the emergency," the mathematician and physicist Norbert Wiener wrote the czar of American war research, Vannevar Bush, on 20 September 1940. Britain was under unrelenting aerial attack, and a Nazi invasion seemed imminent. Wiener scrambled across the disciplinary map to throw his weight behind a technological defense. He suggested procedures to improve Bush's computational device, the so-called differential analyzer, in ways that would facilitate faster design of war materiel from airplane wings to ballistic shells. More concretely, he reiterated a previous proposal that the Allies loft air-bursting containers of liquified ethylene, propane, or acetylene gases to engulf a wide volume of the sky in a prolonged detonation.[1] That repelling the onslaught of bombers had pushed all scientific questions aside is hardly surprising. For the German Air Force had dubbed 13 August 1940 "The Day of the Eagle," and with it the Battle of Britain had begun with an assault of almost 1500 aircraft flown against British air stations and aircraft factories. During the following two weeks over a thousand Londoners had died under the rain of bombs, and September was worse. On 7 September alone, 448 civilians perished; on 15 September the Germans pitched 230 bombers and 700 fighters against London, Southampton, Bristol, Cardiff, Liverpool, and Manchester.[2]

Over the next few years, Wiener's attention focused increasingly on the problem of destroying enemy airplanes. His early efforts at computation and antiaircraft fire coalesced in a remarkably ambitious calculating device that he called the "antiaircraft (AA) predictor," designed to characterize an enemy pilot's zigzagging flight, anticipate his future position, and launch an antiaircraft shell to down his plane. But Wiener's electronic manipulation did not stop with halting Nazi air attacks. In the course of characterizing the enemy pilot's actions and designing a machine to forecast his future moves, Wiener's ambitions rose beyond the pilot, even beyond the World War. Step by step, Wiener came to see the predictor as a prototype not only of the mind of an inaccessible Axis opponent but of the Allied antiaircraft gunner as well, and then even more widely to include the vast array of human proprioceptive and electrophysiological feedback systems. The model then expanded to become a new science known after the war as "cybernetics," a science that would embrace intentionality, learning, and much else within the human mind. Finally, the AA predictor, along with its associated engineering notions of feedback systems and black boxes, became, for Wiener, the model for a cybernetic understanding of the universe itself. This paper is an exploration of that expansion. In it, I will be backtracking from the widest ontological claims of cybernetics into a collocation of vacuum tubes, resistors, and condensers designed to replicate the intentions of a hidden enemy pilot.

Enemies were not all alike. In the killing frenzy of World War II, one version of the Enemy Other (not Wiener's) was barely human; to the Americans, British, and Australians, the Japanese soldiers were often thought of as lice, ants, or vermin to be eradicated. As General Sir Thomas Blamey told a unit in Port Moresby in 1942: "Beneath the thin veneer of a few generations of civilization [the Japanese soldier] is a subhuman beast, who has brought warfare back to the primeval, who fights by the jungle rule of tooth and claw, who must be beaten by the jungle rule of tooth and claw. . . . Kill him or he will kill you." A year later, Blamey insisted on the Buna battlefield that "fighting Japs is not like fighting normal human beings. . . . The Jap is a little barbarian. . . . We are not dealing with humans as we know them. We are dealing with something primitive. Our troops have the right view of the Japs. They regard them as vermin."[3] These monstrous, racialized images of hate certainly presented one version of the World War II enemy, but it was by no means the only one.

Another and distinct Allied vision held the enemy to be not the racialized version of a dreaded opponent but rather the more anonymous target of air raids. This enemy's humanity was compromised not by being subhuman, vicious, abnormal, or primitive but by occupying physical and moral distance. Viewed from afar, from the icy heights of thirty thousand feet, a city in Germany looked small, and individual people appeared to be invisible, partially shorn of their likeness to the bomber. After opening a spate of airmen's letters, one British censor from the Air Ministry reported on 21 June 1942: "[The letters] illustrate the effect of airmen's remoteness from their attacks on human beings. Expressions of satisfaction that the Germans are having to undergo the punishment they have hitherto meted out to others are found in almost all letters, but there is an absence of vindictiveness or fanaticism in the phrases used."[4]

But there is yet another picture of the enemy that emerged during World War II, less well known but in many ways more powerful and enduring than either the racialized or the anonymous enemy. More active than the targeted, invisible inhabitants of a distant city and more rational than the horde-like race enemy, this third version emerged as a cold-blooded, machinelike opponent. This was the enemy, not of bayonet struggles in the trenches, nor of architectural targets fixed through the prisms of a Norden gunsight. Rather, it was a mechanized Enemy Other, generated in the laboratory-based science wars of MIT and a myriad of universities around the United States and Britain, not to speak of the tens of laboratories in the countries of the Axis.

On the Allied side, three closely related sciences engaged this calculating Enemy Other: operations research, game theory, and cybernetics. Each had its own prototypical war problem. Operations research focused, for example, on maximizing efficiency in locating and destroying German U-boats in the North Atlantic and along the coast of the Americas.[5] Game theory, though it had mathematical roots in the interwar years, exploded into view with John von Neumann and Oscar Morgenstern's masterwork of 1944, *Theory of Games and Economic Behavior*;[6] strategists picked up the technique as a way of analyzing what two opposing forces ought to do when each expected the other to act in a maximally rational way but were ignorant both of the opponent's specific intentions and of the enemy's choice of where to bluff. Wiener, the spokesman and advocate of cybernetics, in a distinction of great importance to him, divided the devils facing us in two sorts. One was the "Manichean devil" "who is determined on victory and will use any trick of craftiness or dissimulation to obtain this victory." Wiener's rational Manichean devil could, for example, change strategy to outwit us. By contrast, the other, the "Augustinian devil" (and Wiener counted the forces of nature as such), was characterized by the "evil" of chance and disorder but could not change the rules.[7] Exemplary of the Manichean enemy, von Neumann's game theory postulated a logical but cunning opponent; it was designed precisely to analyze an antagonist who played against us and would bluff to win.

Building on Wiener's own usage of the term *Manichean* to designate the continuing struggle against an active oppositional intelligence, I will call this triad of wartime enterprises—operations research, cybernetics, and game theory—the Manichean sciences.[8] I choose the third war science, cybernetics, as an entry point to these machine-human systems.[9] Working with the Greek word for steersman, Wiener coined the term *cybernetics* in the summer of 1947 to designate what he hoped would be a new science of control mechanisms in which the exchange of information would play a central role.[10] If antisubmarine warfare was the formative problem for operations research, antiaircraft fire control was the key to cybernetics.[11] Faced with the problem of hitting fast maneuverable bombers with ground-based artillery, Wiener brought to bear his own established interest in feedback mechanisms, communication technology, and nonlinear processes.

I will argue that the system of weaponry and people that Wiener had in mind was predicated on a picture of a particular kind of enemy. On the mechanized battlefield, the enemy was neither invisible nor irrational; this was an enemy at home in the world of strategy, tactics, and maneuver, all the while thoroughly inaccessible to us, separated by a gulf of distance, speed, and metal. It was a vision in which the enemy pilot was so merged with machinery that (his) human-nonhuman status was blurred. In fighting this cybernetic enemy, Wiener and his team began to conceive of the Allied antiaircraft operators as resembling the foe, and it was a short step from this elision of the human and the nonhuman in the ally to a blurring of the human-machine boundary in general. The servo-mechanical enemy became, in the cybernetic vision of the 1940s, the prototype for human physiology and, ultimately, for all of human nature. Then, in a final move of totalization, Wiener vaulted cybernetics to a philosophy of nature, in which nature itself became an unknowable but passive opponent—the Augustinian devil.

Cybernetics no longer appears as a futuristic bandwagon or as a rising worldview that will leave mere mechanism in the dustbin of history, but it has much to tell us about the nature of the sciences in the mid-twentieth century and, as I will speculate, about postmodern theory in the late twentieth century.

2. The calculating enemy

Beginning on 10 July, German bombing attacks on British convoys grew significantly in number, ushering in the Battle of Britain. From 10 to 20 July the *Kanalkampf*, as the Germans dubbed it, was prosecuted with the goal of depleting the British supply of fighters, to be followed by an all-out assault on the fighter bases in Britain itself. It was this spate of Nazi bombing that precipitated Wiener's primary war work. By 23 July, Wiener had received notice that the armed forces had in hand his suggestion about the use of incendiary bombs and his reiterated desire to participate in the war effort.[12] But the main line of Wiener's military work centered on a general theoretical and practical inquiry into the possibility of radically improving antiaircraft technology. At root, Wiener's idea was to use electrical networks to determine, several seconds in advance, where an attacking plane would be and to use that knowledge to direct artillery fire. In an early simulated run of the AA predictor (November 1940), Wiener wanted to see how his machine would fare in four cases: a straight-line bomber trajectory, another having twice the slope of the first, a third with a parabolic slope, and a fourth with a curve following the integrated area of a semicircle. Since the circuit itself did not exist in wire and tubes, Wiener concocted a virtual mechanical equivalent and "tested" all four cases in simulated form on Vannevar Bush's differential analyzer.[13]

The scale of Wiener's work was not large. It was, in fact, infinitesimal compared with the scope of work getting underway at the Radiation Laboratory or at Los Alamos. Wiener's little group had, as its first 1941 budget (submitted in 1940), a paltry request for $2325, with $1200 devoted to circuit building, three man-months for differential analyzer studies at $450, and the remainder going to labor overhead.[14] Scale, however, can be measured in other ways. As the AA predictor came to fruition, Wiener came to see it as the articulated prototype for a new understanding of the human-machine relation, one that made soldier, calculator, and firepower into a single integrated system. His two thousand-odd dollars would be conceptually stretched to blanket the earth.

Preliminary circuit diagrams indicated that the AA predictor would be vulnerable to two kinds of sudden movements: irregularities introduced as the operator of the crosshair telescope cranked his gun to follow the plane and irregularities injected as the pilot zigzagged to escape. Both would have to be filtered to gain a smoother curve that the predicting circuit could handle. In the design of the filters, as in many aspects of the project, the underlying mathematical or calculational methods Wiener wanted to use for the AA predictor carried over from earlier studies of servomechanisms, that is, of feedback devices such as thermostats or self-guided torpedoes. Indeed, the only real difference between the two types of feedback problems was that in the AA predictor there was a longer time lag between action and effect: the shell took several seconds to reach its target. One striking indicator of the congruence of technological practice is that Wiener specifically asked for an enforcement of the same patent clause for the AA predictor as was used in the earlier servomechanism program.[15]

As Wiener and Bigelow gave form to the hardware in the summer of 1941, they desperately needed realistic information on the character of input data:

> We realized that the "randomness" or irregularity of an airplane's path is introduced by the pilot; that in attempting to force his dynamic craft to execute a useful maneuver, such as straight-line flight or 180 degree turn, the pilot *behaves like a servo-mechanism*, attempting to overcome the intrinsic lag due to the dynamics of his plane as a physical system, in response to a stimulus which increases in intensity with the degree to which he has failed to accomplish his task. A further factor of importance was that the pilot's kinaesthetic reaction to the motion of the plane is quite different from that which his other senses would normally lead him to expect, so that for precision flying, he must disassociate his kinaesthetic from his visual sense.[16]

Here was a problem simultaneously physical and physiological: the pilot, flying amidst the explosion of flak, the turbulence of air, and the sweep of searchlights, trying to guide an airplane to a target. As Wiener saw it, humans acting under stress tend to perform repetitively and therefore predictably.

To recreate this tense concatenation of human and machine, Wiener, Bigelow, and Paul Mooney, an accomplished technician, began a series of experiments before the end of 1941 to simulate the data input of an enemy plane that would enter the AA predictor. Bigelow, who was an active pilot, took special responsibility for creating a mechanical apparatus "designed to have the 'feel' of an actual [airplane] control."[17] On a laboratory wall, a light-spot projector shot an intense white spot that followed a smooth but irregular back-and-forth motion, careening its way from wall to wall every fifteen seconds. At the same time, an operator—simulating the pilot—was given a deliberately sluggish control stick that guided the position and motion of a second colored light spot. The "pilot's" task was to guide the colored spot onto the "target," mimicking (as one contemporary witness put it) "a plane which is dodging, but flying a mission, i.e. the pilot is holding a general course, but with large swings away from the course."[18] Quite deliberately, the experimenters made the task exceedingly difficult by racing the target across the wall at high speed and by inserting a mechanical lag into the control stick. This, they hoped, would create precisely the disassociation between kinaesthetic sense and visual information that the pilot had to face in the theater of war and would therefore lead to the same sort of feedback difficulties. Meanwhile, the position of the operator's light signal went down on tape alongside the position of the guiding light spot. The fluctuating difference between the "intended" position and the actual position of the operator's light dot provided "a way to duplicate . . . the properties of the type of irregular motion of an airplane in flight."[19] These data would program the AA predictor.[20]

In particular, the pseudo pilots' "nervous reactions" exhibited two crucial features. First, there was no particular correlation among the recorded fluctuations of different operators; second, there was a high degree of autocorrelation between an operator's earlier and subsequent performances. More specifically, Wiener chose the following definition of prediction. Imagine a number of flight paths (ten, for example) that all coincide for a given segment of their trajectory but may differ after a given time, t. Now pick a point in space where we expect a plane to be at, say, $t + 2$ seconds. For any such predicted point we can calculate the square of the difference between the predicted point and the actual position of the first plane at $t + 2$ seconds, and we can do the same for the other nine planes. The point for which the sum of squared errors is minimized is what Wiener calls the best prediction.[21] It turned out that prediction worked rather badly for one operator based on another operator's data, but any given operator was enormously self-consistent. "This suggests the use of such apparatus in the diagnosis of individual differences in reflex behavior, and of pathological conditions affecting the reflex arc. Many other extensions of these ideas will suggest themselves to the physiologist, the neuropathologist, and the expert in aptitude tests."[22] More to the point, it suggested that a more refined AA predictor would use a pilot's own characteristic flight patterns to calculate his particular future moves and to kill him.[23]

The core lesson that Wiener drew from his antiaircraft work was that the conceptualization of the pilot *and* gunner as servomechanisms within a single system was essential and irreducible. As Wiener put it a decade or so after the war, we might succeed in eliminating this or that human feature in a weapons system, but the enemy's human behavior would not go away:

> It does not seem even remotely possible to eliminate the human element as far as it shows itself in enemy behavior. Therefore, in order to obtain as complete a mathematical treatment as possible of the over-all control problem, it is necessary to assimilate the different parts of the system to a single basis, either human or mechanical. Since our understanding of the mechanical elements of gun pointing appeared to us to be far ahead of our psychological understanding, we chose to try to find a mechanical analogue of the gun pointer and the airplane pilot.[24]

Servo-mechanical theory would become the measure of man.

As the key discipline, servo-mechanical theory had a great deal to offer, and not just to laboratories devoted to enemy fire control. At MIT's huge and rapidly growing Radiation Laboratory, Wiener thought it obvious that suppressing noise and conveying information should be the central electronic mission. Here his views collided with those of an extraordinary collection of "fundamental" physicists—the likes of Lee DuBridge, M. G. White, N. F. Ramsey, I. I. Rabi, Julian Schwinger, Edward Purcell, and many others. On the evening of 21 March 1942, Wiener in frustration submitted his resignation from the laboratory, cut his relations with it, and handed in his identification badge. To E. L. Bowles, director of the Rad Lab, Wiener complained the next day:

> New members of the staff of your Laboratory are recruited from the theoretical physicists or mathematicians of the country, or indeed anywhere except from among the ranks

of communication engineers in the strictest and narrowest sense of the term. . . . It [noise suppression, operational notation, and circuit theory] is not something which a quantum physicist has any reason to know the slightest thing about, and to turn such an individual loose in your laboratory without special training, no matter what a big shot he may be in his own subject, is like ordering a corn-doctor to amputate a leg. Better three weeks delay while the big shot is learning his new trade than three months of puerilities and blunders.[25]

What the "big shots" lacked, Wiener contended, was a deep understanding of, for example, Brownian motion and generalized harmonic analysis. These were areas that Wiener had contributed to in fundamental ways; having found himself shunted off to trivial problem solving, he was furious. Without the requisite communications knowledge, Wiener prophesied, "the military efforts of the Laboratory will be about at a good boy-scout level."[26]

Pressure and frustration began to overcome Wiener. He was working frantically, often with the powerful stimulation of Benzedrine.[27] The day after his incensed letter of 22 March 1942 to Bowles, J. C. Boyce, professor of physics at MIT and technical aide to the National Defense Research Committee (NDRC), reported to Warren Weaver on Wiener's condition:

> He seems in an unusually bad nervous state the last few days, and I have been trying to get him to take a few days' rest. He had an unfortunate clash with the cleared patent attorney whom M.I.T. had asked to study some of his ideas on circuit theory, and at the same time he felt that the Radiation Laboratory was unappreciative of certain suggestions he had made to them on filter design. As a result of his state, Bigelow seems somewhat distracted, but I hope before very long this part of the zoo will be quiet again.[28]

Weaver replied the next day, after seeing Wiener pacing furiously up and down a room, "perspiring profusely," and apologizing for being unable to transform an integral into a more easily calculable, rapidly converging series that the great statistician Jerzy Neyman could use. "Upon inquiry," Weaver concluded, "it turned out that [Wiener] had not been doing any of the things we particularly wanted him to do and that his busyness consisted of 'holding myself in readiness in case other jobs turned up.'"[29]

If Wiener wasn't computing a faster-converging integral as quickly as Weaver wanted, he was already beginning to explore how the feedback mechanisms of his servo-mechanical theory might reshape rather distant fields. To J. B. S. Haldane, on 22 June 1942, Wiener put it this way:

> Behaviorism as we all know is an established method of biological and psychological study but I have nowhere seen an adequate attempt to analyze the intrinsic possibilities of types of behavior. This has become necessary to me in connection with the design of apparatus to accomplish specific purposes in the way of the repetition and modification of time patterns.[30]

Unmentioned was the content of these behaviorist studies. For security reasons Wiener would not reveal that the time-pattern behaviors were the pilot's evasive maneuvers and the test procedures Wiener employed to reproduce these patterns from the responses of test-subjects in the safety of the laboratory.[31]

The examination of an apparatus "from this point of view" is, Wiener told Haldane, a fundamental component of communication engineering, where the *function* of an instrument between four terminals is specified before anyone takes up the actual constitution of the apparatus in the box. He reported that this "black-box" vision of the nervous system had already generated information on a priori types of behavior, and it was clear that up to that point "no behaviorist ha[d] ever really understood the possibilities of behavior."[32] Whether his remarks were a spontaneous expression of excitement over the new results or a cryptic declaration of a priority claim, Wiener clearly saw the AA predictor, even before it was ready to shoot down a plane, as the prototype of a new behaviorist understanding of the nervous system itself. By the time Wiener wrote Haldane, he was in the final stages of preparing the machine for its great unveiling.

For a brief and shining moment, it seemed that the AA predictor would, in fact, foretell the future like a crystal ball and down enemy planes with ruthless efficiency. On 1 July 1942, G. R. Stibitz, Wiener's NDRC section chairman, visited Wiener's laboratory and registered his astonishment in his working diary:

> Most of the day is spent with Wiener, Bigelow, and Mooney. It simply must be agreed that, taking into account the character of the input data, their statistical predictor accomplishes miracles. Whether this is a useful miracle or a useless miracle, W[arren] W[eaver] is not yet convinced. The fact that predictions can at present be made only for a maximum of 2 seconds is a very serious limitation. . . . For a 1-second lead the behavior of their instrument is positively uncanny.[33] WW threatens to bring along a hack saw on the next visit and cut through the legs of the table to see if they do not have some hidden wires somewhere. ["D"]

These numbers were more impressive than they might at first seem, since the Wiener-Bigelow scheme compressed time by a factor of four to five, making a two-second prediction the equivalent of ten seconds in the real world. Since an antiaircraft shell took about twenty seconds to reach a bomber at altitude, the predictor seemed well on its way to success.

Even in the midst of a war project that did not yet approach field capability, Wiener clearly had already begun to reflect on the broader ramifications of this species of machine. On the same day he saw the predictor demonstrated, 1 July 1942, Stibitz recorded Wiener's wider ambition for the device:

> W[iener] points out that their equipment is probably one of the closest mechanical approaches ever made to physiological behavior. Parenthetically, the Wiener predictor is based on good behavioristic ideas, since it tries to predict the future actions of an organism not by studying the structure of the organism but by studying the past behavior of the organism. ["D"][34]

To get at the future behavior of the bomber-organism, Wiener and Bigelow made a tour that summer (1942) of the various installations charged with precisely measuring the flight of a plane. At Princeton and Tufts, they consulted on errors in tracking procedures; at Langley Field, experts offered them data on the regularities and irregularities of airplane motion; at the Aberdeen Proving Ground, at the Frankford Arsenal in Philadelphia, and at the Foxboro Instrument Company, additional information came pouring their way. But it was at the Anti-Aircraft Board at Camp Davis, North Carolina, that the two prognosticators received their most precious documents: tracking data on two test flights—the so-called flights 303 and 304—at one-second intervals.[35] These two trajectories through the sky were crucial because they gave, for the first time, realistic data that could be used as input to, and a test on the output of, the prognosticating machine.

Over the next five months, Wiener worked to reproduce these data—to little avail. By December 1942, it was all too clear that, however clever the general statistical analysis had been, it was barely able to compete with two simpler, geometrical prediction machines designed by Hendrik Bode. The first simply extrapolated the future from the derivative of the plane's trajectory, calculated at a fixed initial point. The second Bode method continuously recomputed its prediction on the basis of a trajectory derivative computed ten seconds back from the plane's current position. In December 1942 and January 1943, Wiener compiled the following chart for Weaver:[36]

Track	(1) Bode	(2) 10 Sec. Bode	(3) Statistical
303	6 hits	22 hits	23 hits
304	35 hits	55 hits	49 hits

Bode, from Bell Laboratories, had developed a geometrical fire-control predictor that had the virtue of being based on already-existing technology and the vice of not taking into account the random fluctuations and irregular trajectories of the bombers.

Quite clearly, Wiener's own method (statistical) was barely better than the ten-second Bode method for track 303 and inferior to the ten-second Bode for track 304. In light of this manifest inadequacy, Wiener judged the only hope for the method to lie in a vastly increased statistical base involving the calculation of tens, if not hundreds, of tracks. Since this would tie up the computing facilities of the country, and because the likelihood of improvement struck him as "too distant to be significant in the present war," Wiener hesitated to recommend further research until after the end of the war.[37] What went wrong? Wiener speculated:

> To what extent the negative result of this investigation is due to bad tracking, to what extent to the restriction of the useable past [flight path] to 10 seconds, and to what extent to the fact that the enemy plane has a very considerable chance to change its flight pattern, whether voluntary or involuntary, in the twenty seconds of projectile flight, is not yet fully clear.[38]

It may have been "not yet fully clear," but Wiener was "convinced" that it was the enemy's capacity to maneuver rather than anything else that would save him from inevitable destruction at the mechanical hands of the predictor. Failure came hard, for Wiener was frustrated by the predictor's weakness: "I still wish that I had been able to produce something to kill a few of the enemy instead merely of showing how not to try to kill them."[39]

3. From AA predictor to human nature

What Wiener was willing to do, even in the worst days of war, was to turn to psychological and philosophical implications of the predictor. In their 1943 article "Behavior, Purpose and Teleology," Wiener and Bigelow collaborated with the cardiologist Arturo Rosenblueth, then visiting Harvard Medical School, to present a new, behaviorist description of the very concept of purpose. Aside from the pure satisfaction of classification, the authors were pleased to single out the class of predictive behavior because "it suggests the possibility of systematizing increasingly more complex tests of the behavior of organisms."[40] Of particular importance, they contended that their classification rehabilitated "purpose" and "teleology" by bringing them under the aegis of a "uniform behavioristic analysis" that was equally applicable to living organisms and machines.

Where Darwin had assiduously tracked the similarities between human and animal in order to blur the boundary between them, Wiener's efforts were devoted to effacing the distinction between human and machine. Darwin's dog suffered remorse; Wiener's AA predictor had foresight. Indeed, over the course of the war, Wiener reported in 1945, men had grown ever more accustomed to attributing animation to servo-mechanical systems:

> The semi-humorous superstition of the gremlin among the aviators was probably due, as much as anything else, to the habit of dealing with a machine with a large number of built-in feedbacks which might be interpreted as friendly or hostile. For example the wings of an airplane are deliberately built in such a manner as to stabilize the plane, and this stabilization, which is of the nature of a feedback . . . may easily be felt as a personality to be antagonized when the plane is forced into unusual maneuvers.[41]

Our consciousness of will in another person, Wiener argued, is just that sense of encountering a self-maintaining mechanism aiding or opposing our actions. By providing such a self-stabilizing resistance, the airplane acts as if it had purpose, in short, as if it were inhabited by a gremlin.

Within the rubric of "purposeful behavior," then, Wiener and his collaborators Bigelow and Rosenblueth allowed for those acts that do not involve feedback while the process is underway (such as a frog that shoots its tongue out towards a fly) and those (such as a self-guided missile or torpedo) that gather information and use that information to correct themselves en route. But beyond any particular features of humans or machines lay Wiener's deep-seated commitment to a behaviorist vision of both. His was not a claim that no criteria differentiated humans and machines. Quite obviously there was no machine that could (as yet) write a Sanskrit-Mandarin dictionary; and, similarly, no living organism rolled on wheels. But it was the behaviorist impulse to focus on broad classes of actions, and to do so on the basis of the input and output he knew so well from communication technology, that led Wiener to his blurring of the man-machine boundary. *Black boxes*, as Wiener used the term, meant a unit designed to perform a function before one knew how it functioned; *white boxes* designated that one also specified the inner mechanism. In this language, the more sophisticated feedback mechanism of the AA predictor opened a new universe of black boxes to the engineer—and to the philosopher.[42]

[. . .]

Within a few weeks, Wiener's ambition left behind even the human mind. Collaborating with Howard Aiken, one of the pioneers in computer technology, and with von Neumann, the supremely versatile mathematician then at work on the computer, Wiener sent out a restricted letter on 4 December 1944 to a collection of seemingly unrelated experts:

> A group of people interested in communication engineering, the engineering of computing machines, the engineering of control devices, the mathematics of time series in statistics, and the communication and control aspects of the nervous system, has come to a tentative conclusion that the relations between these fields of research have developed to a degree of intimacy that makes a get-together meeting . . . highly desirable.[43]

Because many of the relevant developments were directly tied to the war effort, Wiener asserted, the assembly would necessarily be non-public. It was a new vision of the world that was to emerge from this secret confluence of war sciences, one that would embrace matters of "engineering, physical, and even economic and social interest."[44] Wiener, Aiken, and von Neumann named the group the "Teleological Society."[45]

The first meeting of the Teleological Society took place on 6–7 January 1945, and Wiener was delighted with its outcome. Rafael Lorente de Nó and Warren McCulloch, both physiologists specializing in the functional organization of the central nervous system, presented their work on the organization of the brain. "In the end," Wiener gushed to Rosenblueth, "we were all convinced that the subject embracing both the engineering and neurology aspects is essentially one."[46]

[. . .]

4. The philosophy of nature and the delivery of cannon fire

If humans do not differ from machines from the "scientific standpoint," it is because the scientific standpoint of the 1940s was one of men-machines at war. The man-airplane-radar-predictor-artillery system is a closed one in which it appeared possible to replace men by machines and machines by men. To an antiaircraft operator, the enemy really does act like an autocorrelated servomechanism. What is astonishing is the globalization of this technological *aperçu* into a new age for humanity and a general philosophy of human action. In 1947, as Wiener reflected on the events of the war, he divided the thoughts of the ages into three epochs. A first era was characterized by the clockmakers, surveyors, and planetary astronomers. Their science was one of prediction by laws and their economy that of the merchant. Boats sailed across seas based on the clocks and astronomical calculation of longitude; this was, as Wiener put it, the "engineering of the mercantilist" (*C*, p. 38). As the seventeenth and eighteenth centuries drew to a close, Wiener asserted, a new day dawned in which clocks gave way to the steam engine as the symbol and real center of technological work. Huygens and Newton ceded their place to Rumford, Carnot, and Joule, and it was the manufacturer not the trader who embodied the new culture. Finally, for Wiener, the present age, ushered in by the vast array of electromechanical devices of the war, was the age of information and control. If these developments reached back to Kelvin and Gauss, they found their real form (and interpreters) only in the laboratories and factories of radar and its associated systems. This age, our age, was that of the servomechanism.

As Wiener argued, each age engendered its own simulacrum of humanity—clockmakers of the eighteenth century made their pirouetting mechanical figures, steam engineers of the nineteenth glorified their engines as versions of the body. Our age? We make computers to calculate differential equations, open doors with photocells, and, not surprisingly, "the present automaton . . . points guns to the place at which a radar beam picks up an airplane" (*C*, p. 40). In a sweeping totalization Wiener had, within two years of the end of the war, elevated his AA predictor to the symbol for a new age of man. Whether or not we accept Wiener's techno-periodization of the history of humanity, there seems little doubt that he and many of his contemporaries saw themselves as standing at a historical and philosophical watershed in which the Manichean sciences would undergird the cybernetic age.

[. . .]

Nineteen forty-seven closed with Wiener still at MIT, despite his moral discomfort with the technical possibilities of cybernetics. In handing over the technology to what he called "the world of Belsen and Hiroshima," he could only hope to "confine our personal efforts [in cybernetics] to those fields, such as physiology and psychology, most remote from war and exploitation" (*C*, p. 28). Paradoxically, during the war Wiener had extended the cybernetic vision beyond its narrow applications because of the weakness of the AA predictor; now that he associated cybernetics with the power of cataclysmic weapons, he tried to push cybernetics away from the military arena because of its deadly efficacy. Either way, for Wiener and many colleagues, the association of cybernetics with its wartime origin was forcefully and deeply inscribed in the cultural meaning of the new science and its machines.

The Josiah Macy, Jr. Foundation opened the cybernetic age for the social sciences. On 8 and 9 March 1946, the foundation gathered psychologists and anthropologists to meet with mathematicians and physicists on the general subject of circular causal systems. Gregory Bateson, already persuaded of the importance of the new ideas, led the contingent of non-physical scientists and helped organize the second such meeting, "Teleological Mechanisms in Society," on 20 September 1946, and a third, "Feedback Mechanisms and Circular Causal Systems in Biology and the Social Sciences." Those invited included Paul Lazarsfeld, Margaret Mead, and F. S. C. Northrop, among many others. Backed strongly by Bateson and enthusiastically led by Wiener, von Neumann, McCulloch, and de Nó, the group's intense discussions brought systems, information theory, and feedback mechanisms onto the center stage of sociology, psychology, and anthropology.[47] Northrop later acknowledged the impact of servo-mechanical theory as "of revolutionary significance for natural science, moral as well as natural philosophy, and for one's theory of the normative factor in law, politics, religion, and the social sciences."[48] To Bateson, the new vocabulary of communication theory and cybernetics presented a turning point in his work; his biographer David Lipset called it a "theoretical conversion" in which his older terms, such as *schismogenesis*, were reworked into the language of the purposeful machine: "regenerative feedback."[49]

[. . .]

The impact of the Manichean sciences not only on computation and automata theory but also on the social sciences should not be underestimated. For Mead, Northrop, and Bateson, the impact of Wiener's models of feedback and homeostasis became essential components of their analyses. Even *Time* saluted Wiener in 1950 as one of the leaders of the new "computermen" who were blurring the boundaries between the wet sciences of the brain, psychological properties, and the machine (caricatured in fig. 5). Given such adulation, it is perhaps not too surprising to find many social scientists identifying themselves with the new sciences emerging from the war. The social scientists' fascination with systems in the 1940s and 1950s may have roots in older turn-of-the-century networks of telephony and power. Recent fascination with information-based feedback systems, however, tracks its roots more proximately—to the radar and tracking systems of World War II.

[. . .]

In "The Biological Enterprise: Sex, Mind, and Profit from Human Engineering to Sociobiology" (1979), [Donna Haraway] used the term *cybernetics* to characterize post-World War II biological sciences in terms, and with a periodization, that Wiener would have recognized. Before the war (according to Haraway) biological discourse had been organized around the organism viewed through the categories of medicine and the clinic. These included intelligence testing, human relations, physiology, and racial hygiene. After the war, the new sciences of information- and control-dominated systems reshaped biology, including sociobiology. This new, more cybernetic biology emphasized communication and feedback. For Haraway, E. O. Wilson's work typified the latter set of developments with his stress on information transfer among insects, including efficiency, noise, and capacity.[50] In her view, cybernetics, although often used to sanction the status quo, is ultimately far more open to a new and more liberating vision of the biological sciences than the psychobiological and organic functionalist theories that preceded it. The cybernetic biological view (sociobiology) is, in Haraway's view, *less* open to racism or sexism because in cybernetics the organic body is depicted as an engineering entity, always modifiable, and never defined essentially.[51]

Haraway opened "A Cyborg Manifesto" (1985) with a partial, ambivalent continuation of these Wienerian themes: "A cyborg is a cybernetic organism, a hybrid of machine and organism, a creature of social reality as well as a creature of fiction."[52] I say the continuation is partial and ambivalent because the cultural meaning she struggled to ascribe to the communication and information technologies is utterly different from the cultural meanings that emerged from cybernetics.[53] Haraway alluded to the "cyborg orgy" that she saw "coded by C[3]I, command-control-communication-intelligence, an $84 billion item in 1984's US defence budget." Just this cyborg root in military feedback systems is, she allowed, the "main trouble" with cyborgs: "But illegitimate offspring are often exceedingly unfaithful to their origins. Their fathers, after all, are inessential."[54] Can the cybernetic vision be so easily detached from its military historical origins and present location? After all, the very notion of a cyborg issued from an Air Force contractor's extension of Wiener's ideas.[55] I would argue that the associations of cybernetics (and the cyborg) with weapons, oppositional tactics, and the black-box conception of human nature do not so simply melt away.

For the classic cyberneticists (exemplified by Wiener, Rosenblueth, McCulloch, and their colleagues), the blurred boundary between human and machine opened an infinity of possibilities; Haraway, like Wiener, stressed the possibility that machines could be open-ended, non-dedicated in their function, and able to reproduce, learn, and interconnect with the human. But Wiener, unlike Haraway, saw power and control as absolutely central to the very definition of cybernetics, for better or worse. Indeed, by the end of his life, as if to push this theme to its theological *Endstation,* Wiener had come to see the human-machine relation as a model, if not an incarnation of the bond between God and "man." The paradoxes of religion ("Can God create a rock too great for him to move?") reemerged as questions about the cyberneticist and his offspring ("Can a human create an entity that can beat him at chess?"). On the last lines of the last page of his last book, Wiener put it this way: "Since I have insisted upon discussing creative activity under one heading, and in not parceling it out into separate pieces belonging to God, to man, and to the machine, I do not consider that I have taken more than an author's normal liberty in calling this book GOD AND GOLEM, Inc."[56] We who make cyborgs are, in the end, like gods.

Haraway, by contrast, took the variability, the unfixed nature, of the cyborg as grounds for the *partiality*, not the *omnipotence*, of what is human. As she put it, we are ourselves already in so many respects cyborgs—through our reproductive technologies, our psychopharmacologies, our prostheses (mechanical and computational)—that we can no longer put any stock in essentialist definitions of the classic dichotomies of mind and body, animal and human, organism and machine, public and private, nature and culture, men and women, primitive and civilized.[57] I understand her project to resonate with the more critical branch of postmodern theory: a refusal to espouse a nostalgia for a "natural" or "feminine" world that preexisted technology and a concomitant move to use (rather than simply shun) the built world of technology and science. Postmodernism holds cybernetics in an uneasy embrace. As a postmodernist challenge to a fixed human, racial, or gendered nature, the cyborg presents an alternative, a way out. But the successes of cybernetics in blurring the human and nonhuman have been most striking in the agonistic field, if not the battlefield itself; the choice between fighting Augustinian and Manichean enemies, as Wiener pointed out, is merely one of tactics. In choosing the cyborg to lead the flight from modernism, one risks reducing the picture of human capacities to one of tactical moves and countermoves in a metaphorical extension of automatic airwar.

Whether we accept or reject the ontology of the Manichean sciences, in discussing the technologies of cybernetics we find ourselves in the grip of a powerful set of cultural meanings. By this, I do not mean that feedback systems were born (so to speak) with a full complement of symbolic associations. As with any set of artifacts, it is possible to trace back fragments of servomechanisms, game theory, and operational reasoning long before 1940. One can cite, as

Wiener often did, fragments by James Clerk Maxwell, Leibniz, and many others who attended to issues of self-regulation, interconnection, and communication. Wiener, for example, knew perfectly well that the nineteenth century had a well-developed theory of the steam-engine governor, and by the 1920s electrical analogues in the form of voltage regulators were legion.

As Otto Mayr has so exhaustively demonstrated, pre-twentieth century feedback devices were culturally located quite differently from systems discussed here. Known in the golden age of Islam, feedback mechanisms—especially liquid-level regulators—flourished in antiquity. Then, from the Middle Ages through the baroque period, the technology vanished almost completely in Europe. Clocks, not self-regulating machines, held pride of place. Timekeeping machines served as a cultural symbol of authority; these were the mechanisms that appeared everywhere, celebrated from literature and poetry to philosophy and political theory. According to Mayr, "the authoritarian conception of order was directly and patently shaped by society's experience with the mechanical clock."[58] When the feedback device came back into European favor in the seventeenth and especially in the eighteenth century, it did so not on the Continent but in the British Isles, a manifestation, in Mayr's view, of the "liberal attitude" that at one and the same time shaped the "socio-intellectual" and the "technological" sides of culture. Regulating devices, especially as popularized by Watt's incorporation of the governor into the steam engine in the 1780s, were celebrated alongside political rhetoric of "dynamic equilibrium," "self-regulation," "'checks and balances,'" and "'supply and demand'" (A, p. xviii).

[. . .]

What we have seen in Wiener's cybernetics is the establishment of a field of meanings grounded not through zeitgeist but explicitly in the experiences of war. For however far telephone relaying technology or A. N. Kolmogoroff's statistics had come before the war, it was the mass development and deployment of guided missiles, torpedoes, and antiaircraft fire that centralized the technology to scientists and engineers. To the thousands of servicemen who used and faced this new generation of weapons, the "human" character of self-regulating machines seemed all too human. After all, trying to shoot down a Junkers JU 88 heading for London or a V-1 buzz bomb doing the same thing was not all that different. A skipper trying to dodge a self-guided torpedo could be excused for referring to the device as "trying" to kill him, as could the pilot ascribing airfoil self-adjustment to the work of "gremlins." And in the specific case of Wiener, Bigelow, Weaver, and their colleagues, it is perhaps understandable that the pilot of an enemy plane could be said to "behave like a servo-mechanism." While prewar behaviorists might have cautioned against the ascription of internal states, war made it impossible; reading the hidden enemy meant reading his actions. In the mechanized battlefield, in those life-and-death confrontations with an enshrouded enemy, the identity of intention and self-correction was sustainable, reasonable, even "obvious."

Face to face with another person, with no way to avoid the full depth and ambivalence of human interaction, feedback may seem to be a ludicrously simplistic representation of intentionality. But to Stibitz and Weaver, as they stood in Wiener's MIT laboratory that July day in 1942, the system of simulated pilot and AA predictor was positively "uncanny" in its capacity to predict a pilot's next move. World War II elevated the stakes of understanding the enemy's intention to survival itself; it stripped human behavior to moves of pursuit, escape, and deception; and it introduced a new class of self-regulating weapons. It is in this specific context that the identity of intention and self-correction was forged.

[. . .]

In general, the cultural meaning of concepts or practices, I would argue, is indissolubly tied to their genealogy. To understand the specific cultural meaning of the cybernetic devices is necessarily to track them back to the wartime vision of the pilot-as-servomechanism. In the air-ground battle, it was a short step for Wiener and Bigelow to take the pilot-as-servomechanism directly over into the AA gunner-as-servomechanism and thence to the operation of the heart and proprioceptive senses. From the body, it was us more generally—we humans—whose intentions could be seen as none other than self-correcting black-boxed entities and finally nature itself that came to be seen as a correlated and characteristic set of input and output signals.

If this cybernetic conception seems to differ from more familiar conceptions of the Other, it should. The cybernetic Enemy Other has little to do with the racialized Other so horrifyingly invoked by Blamey, and examined, for example, by Edward Said in *Orientalism*.[59] There is no sense in which Wiener sees the German bomber pilot as a racially lesser being. Nor is the German pilot an Other in being simply invisible. Finally, I take it to go without need of much elaboration that the servo-mechanical pilot is not Emmanuel Levinas's Other, where the recognition of the ineradicable humanity outside of oneself is the fundamental move in the establishment of an ethical philosophy.[60] No, Wiener's conception of the Enemy Other is more like his depiction of the game players in von Neumann's theory: "perfectly intelligent, perfectly ruthless operators" (*C*, p. 159). This is a theoretical representation in which information, statistics, and strategies are applied to moves and countermoves in a world of opposing but fundamentally *like* forces.

Surprisingly, the cybernetic Other is not negatively contrasted with us, nor are we the model upon which the Other is empathetically formed; our understanding of the cybernetic Enemy Other becomes the basis on which we understand ourselves. Wiener's image of the human and natural world is, in the end, a globalized, even metaphysical, extension of the epochal struggle between the implacable enemy from the sky and the Allies' calculating AA predictor that did battle from the ground. It is an image of human relations thoroughly grounded in the design and manufacture of wartime servomechanisms and extended, in the ultimate generalization, to a universe of black-box monads.

[. . .]

Notes

I would like to thank Arnold Davidson, Steve Heims, Gerald Holton, P. Masani, Howard Stein, George Stocking, Sheldon White, and especially Caroline A. Jones for many helpful discussions. Masani generously allowed me to see copies of Wiener's wartime papers and reports. Originals of these and other technical reports and general project files are housed at the National Archives, Library of Congress, Washington, D.C. References to the Norbert Wiener Papers are to collection MC-22 in the Institute Archives and Special Collections of the Massachusetts Institute of Technology, Cambridge, Massachusetts. I would like to thank Elizabeth Andrews of the MIT Archives and Marjorie Ciarlante of the National Archives for facilitating access to archival materials. I would also like to thank my able research assistants, Richard Beyler, Pamela Butler, and Jamie Cohen-Cole, for their help and Jean Titilah and Ann Hobart for manuscript preparation. This work was supported in part by a grant from the Andrew W. Mellon Foundation.

1 Norbert Wiener, letter to Vannevar Bush, 20 Sep. 1940, box 2, folder 58, Norbert Wiener Papers, collection MC-22, Institute Archives and Special Collections, Massachusetts Institute of Technology Archives, Cambridge, Mass. (hereafter abbreviated NWP).

2 Martin Gilbert, *The Second World War: A Complete History* (New York, 1989), pp. 117–25.

3 Quoted in John W. Dower, *War without Mercy: Race and Power in the Pacific War* (New York, 1986), pp. 53 and 71.

4 Quoted in Max Hastings, *Bomber Command* (New York, 1979), p. 146. Other recent literature on the moral, political, and military aspects of bombing civilians includes Michael Sherry, *The Rise of American Air Power: The Creation of Armageddon* (New Haven, Conn., 1987), which argues that the slide towards civilian bombing led inexorably to the use of atomic weapons against civilian targets, and Conrad C. Crane, *Bombs, Cities, and Civilians: American Airpower Strategy in World War II* (Lawrence, Kan., 1993), especially pp. 53–59, which

tracks aviators' attitudes in the field as differing according to their specific tasks: piloting, navigating, or bombing. Distancing, however, had to be maintained, often under immense stress. One pilot (who was killed in November 1944) wrote shortly before his death: "The whole idea was to blow up just as much Germany tomorrow as possible. From way up high, it wouldn't mean a thing to me. I wouldn't know if any women or little kids got in the way." Such remarks were followed in the very next sentence by doubts: "I'd thought about it before, but that night it was close. The more I thought of it, the uglier it seemed" (Bert Stiles, *Serenade to the Big Bird* [1947; New York, 1952], p. 21).

5   On the origins of operations analysis, see M. Fortun and S. S. Schweber, "Scientists and the Legacy of World War II: The Case of Operations Research (OR)," *Social Studies of Science* 23 (Nov. 1993): 595–642; and Robin E. Rider, "Early Development of Operations Research: British and American Contexts," paper presented at the Joint Meeting of the British Society for History of Science and the History of Science Society, Manchester, 11–14 July 1988, "Operations Research and Game Theory: Early Connections," in *Toward a History of Game Theory*, ed. E. R. Weintraub (Durham, N. C., 1992), pp. 225–39, and "Capsule History of Operations Research," in *Encyclopaedia of the History and Philosophy of Mathematical Sciences*, ed. Ivor Grattan-Guinness (forthcoming).

6   See John von Neumann and Oscar Morgenstern, *Theory of Games and Economic Behavior* (Princeton, N. J., 1944).

7   Wiener, *The Human Use of Human Beings* (New York, 1954), pp. 34–35; hereafter abbreviated *HU*. Elsewhere in the book Wiener writes that irrationality in human behavior (Freud) is of a piece with the chance element in the physical world (Willard Gibbs) and with the statistical system of reasoning itself (Henri Lebesgue): "This random element, this organic incompleteness, is one which without too violent a figure of speech we may consider evil; the negative evil which St. Augustine characterizes as incompleteness, rather than the positive malicious evil of the Manicheans" (*HU*, p. 11). Wiener emphasizes over and again that the evil opposition of nature is not active: "I have already pointed out that the devil whom the scientist is fighting is the devil of confusion, not of willful malice. The view that nature reveals an entropic tendency is Augustinian, not Manichean" (*HU*, p. 190).

8   It is part of my argument that the division between active and passive antagonists is not sustained in the cybernetic view of the world. In particular, within Wiener's vision of the world there is great continuity between the anti-entropic self-regulating strategy for controlling (or destroying) an enemy and controlling the built and found world around us. Indeed, Wiener himself contends that the Augustinian position easily breaks down into Manicheanism. *See HU*, p. 191.

9   On earlier human-machine links, see, for example, Anson Rabinbach, *The Human Motor: Energy, Fatigue, and the Origins of Modernity* (New York, 1990).

10 See Wiener, *Cybernetics; or Control and Communication in the Animal and the Machine* (1948; Cambridge, Mass., 1961), pp. 11–12; hereafter abbreviated *C*.

11 On Wiener, see the rich and provocative book by Steve J. Heims, *John von Neumann and Narbert Wiener: From Mathematics to the Technologies of Life and Death* (Cambridge, Mass., 1980). An extraordinary source for original writings by Wiener is the four-volume set of his collected works; there one finds the best technical summary and analysis of Wiener's antiaircraft predictor. See P. Masani and R. S. Phillips, "Antiaircraft Fire-Control and the Emergence of Cybernetics," in *Norbert Wiener: Collected Works with Commentaries*, ed. Masani, 4 vols. (Cambridge, Mass., 1985), 4: 141–79. I have also found very valuable the mathematically sophisticated treatment of Wiener's work on the AA predictor in Masani, *Norbert Wiener, 1894–1964* (Basel, 1990), esp. pp. 184–93.

    Three authors writing recently on the links between cybernetics and the biological and psychological domains include Lily E. Kay, "Who Wrote the Book of Life? Information and the Transformation of Molecular Biology, 1944–55," in *Experimentalsysteme in den Biologische-Medizinischen Wissenschaften: Objekt, Differenze, Konjunkturen*, ed. Michael Hagner and Hans-Jörg Rheinberger (Berlin, 1994); E. F. Keller, "The Body of New Machine: Situating the Organism between Telegraphs and Computers," *Representing Life: Changing Metaphors of Twentieth-Century Biology* (forthcoming); and Paul Edwards, *The Closed World: Computers and the Politics of Discourse in Cold War America* (forthcoming).

12 See C. Thomas-Stahle, letter to Wiener, 23 July 1940, box 1, folder 57, NWP.

13 See S. H. Caldwell, "Proposal to Section D-2, National Defense Research Committee," 22 Nov. 1940, introduction to Wiener, "Principles Governing the Construction of Prediction and Compensating Apparatus," Record Group 227, Office of Science and Research Development (hereafter abbreviated OSRD), Division 7, General Project Files, 1940–46, General Mathematical Theory of Prediction and Application, Massachusetts Institute of Technology (hereafter abbreviated MIT), Wiener, NDCrc-83, National Archives, Library of Congress, Washington, D. C. (hereafter abbreviated NA-LC).

14   See Caldwell, "Proposal to Section D-2, National Research Committee."

15   See ibid. A standard text on servomechanisms that Wiener approved of (and cited frequently) was Le Roy A. MacColl, *Fundamental Theory of Servomechanisms* (New York, 1945). MacColl clearly identified servomechanisms with slaved systems that used feedback; see pp. 1–9.

16   Wiener, "Summary Report for Demonstration," p. 6 (emphasis added).

17   George R. Stibitz, "Report on Visit to Prof. Norbert Wiener," 28 Oct. 1941, Record Group 227, OSRD, Division 7, Records of Chiefs and Members of Sections, 1940–46, George R. Stibitz, Section 7.1, Land-Based Fire Control Problems, "Predictions I," MIT, NDCrc-83, NA-LC.

18   Stibitz, Section 2 of Division D, Diary of Chairman, 1 July 1942, Boston, Project no. 6, Record Group 227, OSRD, Division 7, General Project Files, 1940–46, General Mathematical Theory of Prediction and Application, MIT, Wiener, NDCrc-83, NA-LC; hereafter abbreviated "D."

19   Wiener, *I Am a Mathematician: The Later Life of a Prodigy* (Cambridge, Mass., 1956), p. 251.

20   See Wiener, "Summary Report for Demonstration."

21   This method of prediction (least squares) was mathematically felicitous but controversial. Stibitz, for example, argued that a pilot heading into a burst of AA fire would turn right or left, but the Wiener Predictor would lay the next burst dead ahead, and he argued, "is almost certain to miss." Duncan Stewart (for whom Stibitz worked at OSRD) was not at all confident that the enemy would behave in a consistent way. Would he see the burst? Would he fly on to complete a bomb run? "Present predictors, I fear, are useful largely because the psychological effect on the enemy serves to keep them far enough away to . . . reduce the damage" (Stibitz, "Report on Visit to Prof. Norbert Wiener").

22   Wiener, "Summary Report for Demonstration," p. 7.

23   Because Wiener's AA predictor based its algorithm for prediction on statistical input from the pilot's past performance, the device was a kind of learning machine. As such, it came to stand in for Wiener as the prototype of other game-playing and potentially war-fighting machines. See, for example, Wiener, *Cybernetics*, pp. xi–xii. The central idea in Wiener's statistical approach is the quantification and characterization of noise. His analysis begins with the determination of the autocorrelation coefficients and an associated spectrum. Given a sequence of numbers, $a(n)$, where $a(n)$ is the value of a at time $t = n$, the autocorrelation coefficients $\phi(m)$ for lag m are defined as the mean value, taken over all time, of the product of one of these numbers with its mth neighbor. The spectrum is then defined as the Fourier series where the $\phi(m)$ are the autocorrelation coefficients of the original series. Wiener characterizes what it means for stability to exist for these time series and therefore establishes conditions under which predictions can be made in his crucial work, "The Extrapolation, Interpolation and Smoothing of Stationary Time Series with Engineering Applications," DIC Contract 6037, MIT, 1 Feb. 1942, declassified, box 11, folder 561A, NWP.

24   Wiener, *I Am a Mathematician*, pp. 251–52.

25   Wiener, letter to E. L. Bowles, 22 Mar. 1942, box 2, folder 62, NWP.

26   Ibid.

27   See Wiener, *I Am a Mathematician*, p. 249.

28   J. C. Boyce, letter to Warren Weaver, 23 Mar. 1942, Record Group 227, OSRD, Division 7, General Project Files, 1940–46, General Mathematical Theory of Prediction and Application, MIT, Wiener, NDCrc-83, NA-LC.

29   Weaver, letter to Boyce, 24 Mar. 1942, Record Group 227, OSRD, Division 7, General Project Files, 1940–46, General Mathematical Theory of Prediction and Application, MIT, Wiener, NDCrc-83, NA-LC.

30   Wiener, letter to J. B. S. Haldane, 22 June 1942, box 2, folder 62, NWP.

31   As he made clear to a conference organizer shortly afterwards, even alluding to the connection between statistics and prediction could be disastrous. When a joint meeting was planned in 1942 between the American Mathematical Society and the Institute of Mathematical Statistics, several papers were slated to discuss statistical prediction; Wiener shot off an urgent note to one of the organizers, J. R. Kline, contending that even titles might be "a tip-off" to the enemy on subjects "vital and secret in more ways, and vastly more important ways, than I have been able to tell you" (Wiener to J. R. Kline, 20 Aug. 1942, box 2, folder 63, NWP).

32   Wiener, letter to Haldane.

33   Stibitz invokes the term *uncanny* at just the moment—1 July 1942—when Wiener's machine began predicting as if it were animated (whence Weaver's half-joking call for a saw). One is reminded here of Stanley Cavell's reflection that Freud, in his essay on the uncanny, may be protesting too much when he claims (no less than four times) that the animate/inanimate conflation does *not* lie behind the uncanny.

For Cavell, the uncanny reflects precisely the philosophical anxiety exacerbated by the ambiguity created when it is unclear whether a mind or merely an inanimate object is at hand. The sentiment of uncanniness resulting from such an ambiguity is therefore tied to the philosophical problem of other minds. According to Cavell, this philosophical difficulty (surrounding the existence of other minds) is part of, not subordinate to, the psychology of uncanniness. See Stanley Cavell, "The Uncanniness of the Ordinary," *In Quest of the Ordinary: Lines of Skepticism and Belief* (Chicago, 1988), pp. 153–78. 1 would add this: each generation has its own conception of what constitutes a mind. Wiener's notion circulates around feedback, control, and the capacity to predict. Since characterizations of mind change, a philosophical-historical account of the uncanny would necessarily pass through many epochs.

34   *Behaviorism* as used by Wiener, Stibitz, Boring, and others encompassed a field and spirit of inquiry far wider than a behaviorism defined as a lineal descent from J. B. Watson to B. F. Skinner. For more on the scope of behaviorism, see Robert S. Woodworth, *Contemporary Schools of Psychology* (New York, 1931), pp. 43–92; Edna Heidbreder, *Seven Psychologies* (1933; New York, 1961), pp. 234–86; and Woodworth and Mary R. Sheehan, *Contemporary Schools of Psychology*, 3rd ed. (New York, 1964), pp. 111–213.

35   See Wiener, "Statistical Method Of Prediction in Fire Control," Final Report on Section D-2, Project no. 6, submitted to Weaver, Section D-2 NDRC, 1 Dec. 1942, Record Group 227, OSRD, Contractors' Reports, Division 7, NDCrc-83, OSRD Report No. 1863, MIT, NA-LC.

36   See Wiener, letter to Weaver, 15 Jan. 1943, Record Group 227, OSRD, Contractors' Reports, Division 7, NDCrc-83, enclosure with OSRD Report No. 1863, MIT, NA-LOC. See also Wiener, "Final Report," 1 Dec. 1942, NA-LC.

37   Wiener, letter to Weaver, 15 Jan. 1943.

38   Wiener, "Statistical Method of Prediction in Fire Control," p. 7.

39   Wiener, letter to Weaver, 28 Jan. 1943, box 2, folder 64, NWP.

40   Arturo Rosenblueth, Julian Bigelow, and Wiener, "Behavior, Purpose and Teleology," *Philosophy of Science* 10 (Jan. 1943): 22; rpt. *Norbert Wiener*, 4:184.

41   Wiener, "Operationalism—Old and New" (1945), box 11, folder 570, NWP, pp. 14–15. In particular, the wings of an airplane rise from the fuselage upward towards the wingtips (this rise is known as the dihedral). When the plane banks (while maintaining direction), the plane side-slips towards the lower wing. Since the lower wing is now positioned more nearly parallel to the ground, the lower wing encounters the relative wind strongly while the upper wing, now tilted more nearly perpendicular to the ground, encounters the relative wind more weakly. This raises the lower wing, righting the airplane. See, for example, the popular 1944 flight instruction book by Wolfgang Langewiesche, *Stick and Rudder: An Explanation of the Art of Flying* (1944; New York, 1972), especially the subsection "What the Airplane Wants to Do," pp. 125–27, which addresses the dihedral.

42   See Rosenblueth, Wiener, and Bigelow, "Behavior, Purpose, and Teleology," pp. 23–24. The term *black box*, commonly used at the MIT Radiation Laboratory during the war, became popular through the use of common black-speckled boxes to encase radar electrical equipment such as amplifiers, receivers, filters, and so on. Wiener himself referred during the war to "boxes" with unspecified interiors, as in his 1942 letter to Haldane, cited above. After the war, Wiener elaborated on the notion of a black box, contrasting it with a "white box" in the sense invoked here. See, for example, *C*, pp. xi and 180 and Wiener, "Über Informationstheorie," *Die Naturwissenschaften* 48 (Apr. 1961): 174–76. On the black box as part of "radar philosophy" at the Rad Lab, see Galison, *Image and Logic: The Material Culture of Modem Physics* (forthcoming).

43   Howard Aiken, von Neumann, and Wiener, letter to E. H. Vestine, 4 Dec. 1944, box 2, folder 66, NWP.

44   Ibid. See also Wiener, letter to von Neumann, 17 Oct. 1944, box 2, folder 66, NWP.

45   Wiener, Aiken, and von Neumann identified the common center of their interests to revolve around intention: "Teleology is the study of purpose of conduct, and it seems that a large part of our interests are devoted on the one hand to the study of how purpose is realized in human and animal conduct and on the other hand how purpose can be imitated by mechanical and electrical means." Their intention was to found a society, a journal, a patent and support mechanism, a means of popularization, and, finally, a protective net to guard against "dangerous and sensational publicity" (Aiken, von Neumann, and Wiener, letter to H. H. Goldstine, 28 Dec. 1944, box 2, folder 66, NWP).

46   Wiener, letter to Rosenblueth, 24 Jan. 1945, box 2, folder 67, NWP.

47   On the Macy meetings, see Gregory Bateson, memo to [invitees], 19 June 1946, box 2, folder 71, NWP; McCulloch, memo to the members of the "Macy Conference on Feedback Mechanisms, 17–19

Oct. 1946," n. d., box 2, folder 71, NWP; "Conference on Feedback Mechanisms and Circular Causal Systems in Biology and the Social Sciences," n. d., box 2, folder 71, NWP. Heims has a good discussion of the tenor of these meetings in *John von Neumann and Norbert Wiener*, pp. 201–7 and a wide-ranging study of the impact of cybernetics on the social sciences in *Constructing a Social Science for Postwar America: The Cybernetics Group, 1946–1953* (Cambridge, Mass., 1993).

48   F. S. C. Northrop, "Ideological Man in His Relation to Scientifically Known Natural Man," in *Ideological Differences and World Order: Studies in the Philosophy and Science of the World's Cultures*, ed. Northrop (New Haven, Conn., 1949), p. 414.

49   David Lipset, *Gregory Bateson: The Legacy of a Scientist* (Englewood Cliffs, N. J., 1980), p. 182. See also Heims, "Gregory Bateson and the Mathematicians: From Interdisciplinary Interaction to Societal Functions," *Journal of the History of the Behavioral Sciences* 13 (Apr. 1977): 141–59.

50   See Donna J. Haraway, "The Biological Enterprise: Sex, Mind, and Profit from Human Engineering to Sociobiology," *Simians, Cyborgs, and Women: The Reinvention of Nature* (New York, 1991), pp. 44–45.

51   See ibid., p. 67.

52   Haraway, "A Cyborg Manifesto: Science, Technology, and Socialist-Feminism in the Late Twentieth Century," *Simians, Cyborgs, and Women*, p. 149.

53   On "cultural meaning," see Peter Galison, "The Cultural Meaning of *Aufbau*," in *Scientific Philosophy: Origins and Developments*, ed. Friedrich Stadler (Dordrecht, 1993), pp. 75–93.

54   Haraway, "A Cyborg Manifesto," pp. 150–51.

55   The term *cyborg* itself was, as Matthew Price has shown, first used by Air Force contractors, in 1960, in the context of speculative research on biochemical means for extending the capability of astronauts. One line of inquiry was the search for drugs that would alter osmotic pressures within the body to allow unprotected "walks" in space. See Matthew Price, "'Man Must First Conceive'—A Critical Philology of the Cyborg," unpublished manuscript. This links rather closely on the one hand with Wiener (whom the Air Force contractors cite) and on the other with the bionic implants required by the space pilot in the science fiction representations of cyborgs cited by Haraway in "A Cyborg Manifesto," p. 179.

56   Wiener, *God and Golem, Inc.: A Comment on Certain Points where Cybernetics Impinges on Religion* (Cambridge, Mass., 1964), p. 95.

57   See Haraway, "A Cyborg Manifesto," p. 163.

58   Otto Mayr, *Authority, Liberty and Automatic Machinery in Early Modern Europe* (Baltimore, 1986), p. 197; hereafter abbreviated *A*. See also Mayr, *The Origins of Feedback Control* (Cambridge, Mass., 1970).

59   See Edward W. Said, *Orientalism* (New York, 1978).

60   See *The Levinas Reader*, ed. Séan Hand (New York, 1989).

Peter Galison is the Mallinckrodt Professor of Physics and History of Science at Harvard University. His work focuses on the history, philosophy, and cultural location of twentieth-century physics. His books include *How Experiments End* (1987), *Image and Logic: The Material Culture of Modern Physics* (forthcoming), *Big Science: The Growth of Large-Scale Research,* edited with Bruce Hevly (1992), and *The Disunity of Science: Boundaries, Contexts, and Power,* edited with David Stump (forthcoming).

Chapter 3

CAROLYN MARVIN

DAZZLING THE MULTITUDE
Original media spectacles

M EDIA SPECTACLE IS GENERALLY considered a twentieth-century phenomenon, evident from the early years of cinema, and coming into its own with the boom of advertising and consumerism after the Second World War. In this extract from a substantially longer chapter, Carolyn Marvin uncovers the nineteenth-century fascination with the then new technology of electric light and the spectacular ways in which this fascination was displayed. Before it wired and illuminated private homes, she points out, electric lighting was a public spectacle, transforming city spaces and monuments.

Marvin presents detailed historical research into the often bizarre (to contemporary eyes) electric spectacles, some of which – such as plans to project messages onto clouds – read like ideas from a steampunk novel, the past rethought according to alternative lines of technological development. Indeed the dreams and predictions of nineteenth-century scientists, engineers and entrepreneurs are inseparable from the actual technologies of the day, and throughout this chapter there is a sense of historical-technological possibilities opening up and closing down. Thus, visual spectacle by the late twentieth century is primarily the *other* brightly illuminating vacuum technology – domestic television, and television broadcasting captures a mass audience but not the collective audiences Marvin describes. She concludes with a warning against predictions of technological futures that simply extrapolate from current dominant forms: the nineteenth-century assumed that twentieth-century media would be dominated by electric light spectacle but on an even grander scale. This medium was, instead, largely superseded and forgotten. The history of media technology then is not a linear, evolutionary process, of gradual improvement and great leaps of invention, but rather 'a succession of distinct social visions, each with its own integrity and concerns'.

In this extract Marvin cites Marshall **McLuhan** and there are obvious connections here (McLuhan's provocative insistence that the light bulb is a medium) as well as deeper conceptual resonances. Norman **Klein**, in Part Four, traces a baroque genealogy for contemporary cinematic spectacle. See also **Huhtamo**'s 'media archaeology'.

. . . imagine the stars, undiminished in number, without losing any of their astronomical significance and divine immutability, marshalled in geometrical patterns, say, in a Latin cross, with the words *In hoc signo vinces* in a scroll around them. The beauty of the illumination would be perhaps increased, and its import, practical, religious, cosmic, would surely be a little plainer but where would be the sublimity of the spectacle?

—Santayana, *The Sense of Beauty*

Anthropologists and literary theorists are fond of emphasizing the particularistic and dramatic dimensions of lived communication. The particularistic dimension of communication is constituted in whatever of its aspects have the most individually intimate meaning for us. The dramatic dimension is the shared emotional character of a communicated message, displayed and sometimes exaggerated for consumption by a public. Its dramatic appeal and excitement depend partly on the knowledge that others are also watching with interest. Such dimensions have little in common with abstractions about information and efficiency that characterize contemporary discussion about new communications technologies, but may be closer to the real standards by which we judge media and the social worlds they invade, survey, and create. Media, of course, are devices that mediate experience by re-presenting messages originally in a different mode. In the late nineteenth century, experts convinced of the power of new technologies to repackage human experience and to multiply it for many presentations labored to enhance the largest, most dramatically public of messages, and the smallest, most intimately personal ones, by applying new media technologies to a range of modes from private conversation to public spectacle, that special large-scale display event intended for performance before spectators.

In the late nineteenth century, intimate communication at a distance was achieved, or at least approximated, by the fledgling telephone. The telephone of this era was not a democratic medium. Spectacles, by contrast, were easily accessible and enthusiastically relished by their nineteenth-century audiences. Their drama was frequently embellished by illuminated effects that inspired popular fantasies about message systems of the future, perhaps with giant beams of electric light projecting words and images on the clouds. Mass distribution of electric messages in this fashion was indeed one pole of the range of imaginative possibilities dreamt by our ancestors for twentieth-century communication. Equally absorbing was the fantasy of effortless point-to-point communication without wires, where no physical obstacle divided the sympathy of minds desiring mutual communion.

It is something of a historical irony that while late-nineteenth-century fantasies of perfect intimate communication are reasonably familiar, spectacles in which electric light played a widely admired communicative role have largely escaped our attention. Perhaps the reason lies partly in the fact that the electric light spectacle, emerging from inherited modalities— candles, bonfires, and oil lamps—was thought to point triumphantly in a future direction that, in the end, it did not. We think of the glittering spectacles with which modern audiences are familiar as something newer, invented by ourselves and perfected in cinema and television. On the contrary, elaborate visual spectacles were public occasions long before the introduction of electricity, and their transformation at its hands was very gradual. Besides enhancing the effective impact of familiar gatherings, electric lights provided occasions for novel ones, such as the outdoor electric light spectacle and the ball game after dark. A number of familiar spectacles were in time done in by the success of electric lighting, mostly by focusing attention on the newer and more private spectacles they made possible. Several popular applications of the electric light, the fastest-developing of all commercial electric technologies, demonstrated its potential for mass communication. Sometimes it was simply a large-scale ornament for traditional spectacles. Other times it was a novel spectacle of its own, or an iconic representation of texts or figures projected on a cloud or a wall for all to see.

Both the actually occurring large-audience spectacle of the late nineteenth century and the ardently felt desire for intimate contact at a distance reflected a yearning to realize what then seemed fantastic ambitions for the possibility of human connection, a yearning that has fallen out unremarked during the long trek to a present in which we take both achievements for granted. Historically speaking, it is a deceptive present, since our achievements are not precisely those the late nineteenth century had in mind. That we no longer remember the excitement of electric light spectacles testifies both to the fact that mass communication was implemented more directly in other forms and to the tendency of every age to read history backward from the present. We often see it as the process by which our ancestors looked for and gradually discovered us, rather than as a succession of distinct social visions, each with its own integrity and concerns. Assuming that the story could only have concluded with ourselves, we have banished from collective memory the variety of options a previous age saw spread before it in the pursuit of its fondest dreams. Of course, our amnesia simply complements theirs. In just the same way that we often see our own past as a less-developed version of ourselves, the late nineteenth century projected its past as a simpler version of itself, and its future as a fancier one.

[. . .]

In the twentieth century, the telephone and television are both pervasive media of effortless communication at a distance. Of these two, the telephone is our favorite intimate medium, wires notwithstanding. Television, at least as we know it now, is not communication on demand with a cherished other, but, on the contrary, a ringside seat at the grand but impersonal spectacles of the world stage. In modern television, the element of the spectacle recalls the electric light show, the most dramatic tradition of electrical experimentation in the late nineteenth century, itself an enhanced version of earlier public spectacles. It included both the lavish exposition whose express purpose was to celebrate electrical achievement and the public occasion convened for other purposes, but extended and made more exciting by the decorative drama of electric light. It is to these spectacles that we now turn.

Enhanced spectacles

It is instructive to recall Marshall McLuhan's argument of some years back that every medium "shapes and controls the scale and form of human association and action" surrounding it by virtue of its special physical configuration and capacities. According to McLuhan, each medium also conveys a semiotic eloquence about the culture of which it is part, which is expressively louder than any particular message content. McLuhan's notion of an information medium was unconventionally broad. In one of his best-known and most provocative examples, he insisted that even the electric light is an information medium. As it happens, this would have been a perfectly sensible claim in both Britain and the United States in the late nineteenth century, although understood somewhat differently than McLuhan intended. Whatever the salience of the electric light to current perceptions of the media environment, it was thoroughly familiar in this role to late-nineteenth-century observers.

Its legacy survives in gay electronic signs that light up urban streets each evening, in lighted scoreboards in gymnasiums and on playing fields, in traffic signals, and everywhere else that lights convey intelligible meaning to audiences. But this was not all. In the perceived novelty of its high-drama public role, the electric light also expressed the sense of unlimited potential that was a staple of nineteenth-century discourse about the future of electricity. For if electricity was the star of the nineteenth-century show, its most publicly visible and exciting agent was certainly the electric light. It was present in exhibitions, fairs, city streets, department stores, and recreation areas. It was physically and symbolically associated with whatever was already monumental and spectacular. It appeared in grand displays, processions, buildings, and performances. It borrowed from every established mode of dramatic cultural self-promotion.

Lighting for special occasions was indeed the most visible and aesthetically indulged side of the new electric revolution. Spectacles were the fun that experts unashamedly allowed themselves in public, fun that was also dramatic testimony to their civic contributions as electricians and scientists. Spectacles were an opportunity for popular audiences to display enthusiasm for electrical science and entrepreneurship, and for public officials and electrical experts to make common cause. What was new was the need for expert personnel to mount these spectacles, and the promise of profit they held out to private entrepreneurs. Less often acknowledged, although no less present, was the sense of theater deliberately cultivated by these professionally inspired and directed occasions, and the ideology of power they projected.

One story may illustrate. For Peace Jubilee festivities to celebrate the conclusion of the Spanish-American War, the city council of Chicago appropriated two thousand dollars to erect a grand municipal arch at La Salle and Washington Streets. It was discovered that aldermen were forbidden to earmark city funds for this purpose. In response, the Edison Electric Company, Western Electric Company, and General Electric Company joined forces to erect an arch of "striking and brilliant effect" modeled on the triumphal arches of the Roman Caesars and received by the city with great fanfare. Such favors were not soon forgotten. What electrical innovators and entrepreneurs could do for those in need of memorable displays of prestige made them useful friends to those in power.

The appreciation of electric light spectacles required no textual training, and electric lights were a professional achievement for which electricians were happy to be praised in the most extravagant terms. Technical discussions in the usual journals conferred scientific and technical legitimacy on entertaining and ideologically powerful social drama. Unlike discussions of other domains of electrical expertise, these were rarely accompanied by stories that rationalized the position of experts vis-à-vis others who misunderstood them or coveted their position. The very existence of these spectacles proclaimed cooperation between officials and experts and legitimacy for electrical endeavors.

The community ideology for which electric light spectacles were a vehicle was already well established by earlier modalities. Compared to the village bonfire that predated the Middle Ages, however, the float-wick oil lamp of the eighteenth-century garden fête, and even the carbon arc lamp, electric filament lamps seemed more colorful, elaborate, and versatile than other lights. Contemporaries claimed that their decorative illumination was more dramatic. The most immediate message conveyed by electric lights was that the occasion of their appearance was as colorful and as worthy of notice as they were. The association of experts with this new form of an old message confirmed their importance in every way. The purpose of *these* illuminated messages was not to intimidate heathen hordes, but to remind attentive audiences of the existence and justification of vested power, and to impress on them its size and majesty. This was communicated in the quality of wonder excited by displays of electric light, in their lavish scale, and in their clear and direct association with municipal and even national authority.

[. . .]

The symbolic possibilities of electric light attracted the interest of a variety of social groups that were eager to experiment. When the citizens of France presented Bartholdi's Statue of Liberty to the American people, "only the electric light [was] thought of" to illumine it. *Electrical World* declared that all serious propositions made by electricians would receive serious consideration from the government, and detailed a number of proposals that had already been made. One electrician suggested vertical beams of light projected upward from the torch, visible as "a pillar of fire by night." Another wished to have lights placed "like jewels around the diadem," and another suggested placing them at the foot of the loggia to light the entire statue, "and thus the illumined face of Liberty will shine out upon the dark waste of waters and the incoming Atlantic voyagers." The final plans called for five electric lamps of 30,000 candlepower thrown heavenward to illuminate the clouds at a hoped-for visibility of one hundred miles in every direction, four lights of 6,000 candlepower at the foot of the statue to illuminate it, and incandescent lamps on the diadem to give a jeweled effect. In every proposal the lighted statue was much more than a useful coast beacon; it was an icon of cultural grandeur.

[. . .]

But if on some occasions electric light projected public order and embodied it metaphorically, on others it strained some essential definition of the situation. In the south of England in 1896, a Jewish synagogue that had installed electric lights was criticized for violating the Sabbath. Electric lights aroused suspicion at the traditional celebration of St. Damasus in the Vatican in 1885. Amid two hundred chandeliers with two thousand tapers burning in the temple housing the saint's remains, a stream of electric light shone down from the cupola on the pontifical tiara and keys above the canopy over the body of the saint. This rich decoration was denounced as profane and accused of resembling an especially lively scene from *Excelsior*, a play being performed at the nearby Costanzi Theatre. Distrustful ecclesiastical authorities prohibited the use of electric, calcium, and magnesium lights for sacred celebration, but by 1892 the Vatican had been fitted with electricity by order of Pope Leo XIII. In 1894 the Church of St. Francis Xavier in New York City celebrated Christmas with three thousand electric lamps scattered throughout the church. Lights decorated the altars, the aisles, the statuary, and the pulpit. Additional effects included a lighted vase of porcelain lilies atop a lighted alabaster column.

But the most enduring contribution of the electric light spectacle to modern mass communication was to the syntax of popular mass entertainment spectacles and the reorganization of their traditional audiences. In the first instance, the electric light contributed to the vocabulary of effects that defined the public spectacle. In the second, the growing popularity of domestic illumination, partly stimulated by the demonstration effect of the spectacle, helped transfer certain features of those spectacles indoors to private audiences. The effect of electric light on the form and content of the new kinds of gatherings it illuminated makes the modern television special, for example, quite as much the fruit of the electric light as of wireless telegraphy or the kinetoscope, and the electric light as much a direct ancestor of broadcasting content as the telephone is of network programming distribution. The same imaginative impulse that mounts the striking visual effect and larger-than-life excitement of a television spectacle today seized on the electric light for much the same purpose in the late nineteenth century.

[. . .]

The vocabulary of electric light effects

The introduction of the electric light was everywhere dramatic. Often only nature itself, grandest of all spectacles, could provide a standard for comparison. When a small Illinois town installed electric lights, outlying farmers observing the glow were convinced that the town was on fire, and raced in their wagons to help. The electric light not only enhanced spectacles, it *was* a spectacle, captured in favorite descriptive metaphors of flowers, spider webs, lakes, and rainbows. A correspondent's account of the brand-new system of tower lighting in Detroit described each tower as a graceful structure

> as open to the wind and light as a spider's web. Five Brush lamps at the summit of each lofty tower shine down at night from the outer darkness, looking like so many crowns of living light shining above the city. . . . The five-pointed crowns of brilliant light, mile after mile along the avenue, far above the houses, and on a level with the

weathercocks of the churches, give one the odd impression that Detroit has a celestial lighting apparatus of its own.

Besides the comparison to nature, two other ways of rendering the emotional impact of electric lights were popular. One compared electric light spectacles to supernatural phenomena, fairylands, ghostly pointing fingers, and otherworldly, dreamlike settings. Another invoked the world of classical culture, clean, spare, and geometrically pure. All comparisons made it clear that the electric lights they described did not belong to the prosaic order of things. They belonged to a natural and supernatural world that seemed nearly, but not quite, beyond man's creative power, and to a legendary world of cultural giantism.

These worlds were often mixed. An electrical journal reporting on the First Greater America Colonial Exposition at Omaha in 1899 described its forty-five thousand lights as outlining "a veritable fairy city." A tropical garden by day was said to bloom again by night in "cunning clusters" created from more than three thousand electric lamps molded as roses, lilies, tulips, and other flowers, and nestled in real foliage: "a novel and brilliant work of art." Whirling globes of fire, festoons of colored light, broad shafts of a searchlight "now flashing here and there about the grounds, lighting up a pathway to the heavens above" were other details. To the observer reporting it for the electrical press, the complete effect was a benign "fairy scene, fleeting and unreal as the shadows of a dream." Above the white city after dark "will hang a misty cloud of light, playing on the heavens and shaming into shadow the twinkling stars. Viewed from a distance it might be mistaken for the light from a terrible conflagration but that it shines so clear and has no pall or pillar of dark smoke to mar its radiance."

Despite the standard vocabulary of most descriptive efforts, the best effects were always those that had "never before been created" and were guaranteed to "astonish the visitors" that observed them, phrases that were bestowed on the plans of William J. Hammer, "the electrical expert," for the Ohio Centennial Exhibition of 1888. The *Cincinnati Times-Star* published those plans with relish:

> Flashing lights will gleam behind the dashing waters of the cascade, there will be a fountain suspended by a single wire, the walks will be bordered with changing lights; sprays of electrical bulbs will gleam up from great vases of flowers—there will be lights, lights everywhere blinking and gleaming, and flashing, now brightness here and darkness there; then a total eclipse for a second, then a flood of light. A gorgeous electrical rainbow will appear and disappear over the miniature Niagara.

[. . .]

Texts of light: advertising and politics on the clouds

We have noted that the impulse to dazzle audiences with electric light effects was not limited to entertainments in which the very presence of electric lights was the message of the spectacle, but was also expressed in inscriptions and simple figural representations constructed from lights. Antecedents for texts of light go back at least to 1814, to the construction in St. James's Park, London, of an illuminated sign in the design of a star and the words "the Peace of Europe," assembled from more than thirteen hundred spout-wick oil lamps. These were attached to iron frames and were intended (prematurely, as it turned out) to celebrate the end of the Napoleonic Wars. Electric filament lamps made such achievements simpler, and inspired more ambitious ones.

At the wedding of Lydia Miller and David Rosenbaum in Baltimore, a variety of electrical effects decorated the reception. The bridal couple received their guests beneath an arch festooned with red, white, and blue electric lights, and lamps outlining the figure of a heart, the initials of bride and groom, and the year, 1892. When the guests reassembled in the supper room, a sudden outburst of bells and music was accompanied by a blaze of light. "At the completion of the first course the words 'Good luck' appeared over the heads of the newly-married couple and an electric hairpin, a gift to the bride, became incandescent and surrounded her head with a halo of light. Wine bottles were suddenly transformed into glowing candelabra."

In 1899 a wedding spectacle in Atlanta featured illuminated textual decorations, and transformed one message into another before the audience's very eyes as lights flashed on and off. The groom, an electrical contractor, had set the wedding scene with two hundred incandescent lights draped from one side of the sanctuary to the other. Directly above the altar hung a wedding bell fashioned of foliage and one hundred colored lights. An arc light suspended from the interior of the bell represented the clapper. Further details were reported:

> To the right of the bell a letter N, the initial letter of the name of the bride (Miss Daisy Nimmo), formed of white incandescents, set in pink flowers, was supported on invisible wires. A letter L [for F. H. Lansdale, the groom] was on the left. . . . As the bride with her brother entered the church by one aisle and the groom with his best man entered by the other the letters N and L flashed into view and sparkled with great splendor. A murmur of admiration arose from the auditorium at the superb effect.

Advertising and political spectacles that thrived on large audiences lent themselves to illuminated messages constructed on the large physical scale suited to group display. A common advertising device was the "sky sign" that spelled out a promotional slogan or the name of a firm, or projected an image against the blank wall of a building. At the instigation of Long Island Railroad president Augustus Corbin, anxious to increase his road's volume of passenger traffic, an especially ambitious sign was erected in 1892 on the side of the nine-story Flatiron Building at the convergence of Broadway and Fifth Avenue with Twenty-third Street in New York City. Fully lit, it consisted of fifteen hundred white, red, blue, and green incandescent lights arranged in seven sentences of letters three to six feet high. From dusk until eleven o'clock every evening, each of these sentences lit up in succession and in a different color, and brought "to the attention of a sweltering public the fact that Coney Island . . . is swept by ocean breezes," reported *Western Electrician*. So long as the changes were "being rung," it observed,

> The public is attracted and stands watching the sign, but as soon as the whole seven sentences are lighted and allowed to remain so, the people move on their way and the crowd disperse. This illuminated sign is not only a commercial success, but when all the lamps are lighted is really a magnificent sight. Its splendor is visible from away up town.

[. . .]

Spectacles of the future

Upon such experiments and spectacles, grand future schemes of communication by electric light were erected with imaginative flourish. The most fanciful were proposals to inscribe the night skies with powerful beams visible to all the inhabitants of the surrounding countryside.

Appearing in many variations, this proposal was a plausible extrapolation from existing technological achievements. It extended the familiar principle of the magic lantern and newer applications of electric light technology, including recent attempts to improve the reliability and safety of shipping.

The fact that vessels sailing the coast could often determine the locations of towns from reflections of their night lights off overhanging clouds inspired experiments in projecting brilliant Morse code flashes overhead from naval vessels. In one experiment these flashes were decipherable at a distance of sixty miles. In another, an astonished crowd filled the streets in the vicinity of the Siemens-Halske telegraph factory in Berlin, where a searchlight strong enough to illuminate handwriting at the distance of a mile was aimed at the sky. By means of a large mirror, signals placed in front of the light "were repeated, of course on a gigantic scale, on the clouds."

Other experiments attempted to implement optical telegraphy with luminous hot air balloons. An early French effort was made in 1881 by aeronauts who enclosed a spiral of platinum in a glass vial and kept it red-hot with current from two small batteries. In 1887 the citizens of Edinburgh observed "an unusual light" in motion in the mist above Castlehill, which excited their "wonder and curiosity." This was a signaling experiment with half a dozen incandescent lamps, each mounted in a wire cage and inserted into a large balloon. Military authorities in Belgium attached six lamps to the bottom of a balloon and connected them by wire to batteries on the ground in 1888. The next year in Antwerp, lights flashing in Morse sequence from a balloon three hundred feet above the ground were visible for several miles. French aeronauts using a lamp and reflector exchanged light signals with telegraph operators stationed high on the third platform of the Eiffel Tower in 1890.

But it was the prospect of illuminated messages on the slate of the heavens that most fascinated experts and laymen. "Imagine the effect," speculated the *Electrical Review*, "if a million people saw in gigantic characters across the clouds such words as 'BEWARE OF PROTECTION' and 'FREE TRADE LEADS TO H—L!'" The writing, it added, could be made to appear in letters of a fiery color. According to one electrical expert, "You could have dissolving figures on the clouds, giants fighting each other in the sky, for instance, or put up election figures that can be read *twenty miles away*."

[. . .]

Objections to the vulgarity of marketing messages on the sky were frequent. *Answers* called the possibility of sky signs "The Newest Horror" in 1892:

> You will be able to advertise your wares in letters one hundred feet long on the skies, so that they will be visible over a dozen counties. As if this truly awful prospect were not enough, we are told that these sky-signs can be made luminous, so that they will blaze away all night! A poet, in one of his rhapsodies, said that he would like to snatch a burning pine from its Norway mountains and write with it the name of "Agnes" in letters of fire on the skies.
>
> But he would probably not have cared to adorn the firmament with a blazing description of somebody's patent trouser-stretcher, or a glowing picture, as large as Bedford Square, of a lady viewing the latest thing in corsets.

An English newspaper decried "celestial advertising" as the means by which "the clouds are to be turned into hideous and gigantic hoardings. This awful invention deprives us of the last open space in the world on which the weary eye might rest in peace without being agonized by the glaring monstrosities wherewith the modern tradesman seeks to commend his wares."

If the sky was a logical surface upon which to reflect messages for the millions, so was the moon. *Science Siftings* reported in 1895 that an American named Hawkins planned to send a flashlight message from London to New York via the moon, using a gigantic heliograph reflector to catch the sun's rays and cast them on the moon's surface. Hawkins had conceived the intellectual principles of satellite relay using the only earth satellite available in 1895. The value of his plan, he announced, lay in covering long distances,

> but electricity would be required for local distribution from the receiving stations. If a flash of sufficient strength could be thrown upon the moon to be visible to the naked eye, every man, woman and child in all the world within its range could read its messages, as the code is simple and can be quickly committed to memory.

Discussions such as this often took for granted a technologically driven transformation in the scale of the audience for new modes of communication. Both fantasies of communication with intelligent aliens at interplanetary distances and fantasies of global communication titillated the collective capacity for imagining the social limits of new media. They likewise instructed collective imagination to explore the possibility of dramatic shifts in the social order in an age of communications transformed. Since laying a cable to outer space seemed unlikely, signaling schemes to strike up a wireless conversation with extraterrestrial beings received wide publicity. One suggestion was offered by Amos Dolbear, who proposed that a powerful searchlight

> such as was exhibited at the Columbian fair, having the power of millions of candles, can be directed in a dense beam and can be made intermittent; signals can thus be sent the same as from the tops of mountains. Once out of the air there would be no loss from absorption and the beam would speed on, reaching Mars in about four minutes when it is nearest us.

He added in his regular *Cosmopolitan* column, "The Progress of Science," in 1893 that communication with Mars would be possible "if it should chance to be peopled with intelligences as well equipped with lights and telescopes as we are."

[. . .]

Each of these otherwise highly various images of mass audiences viewing electric light messages in the night sky assumed that such audiences naturally belonged outdoors, and that familiar night-time social gatherings illuminated for dramatic effect as well as utility would be expanded on a grand scale in the future. As things have turned out, contemporary mass audiences congregate mostly indoors and not together. But other elements of early illuminated gatherings do point directly to one of our most familiar modern public spectacles, broadcast entertainment. Television's inheritance from the electric light is both technological and social. The original electronic effect, the so-called Edison effect, though poorly understood at the time of its discovery, was created in an electric lamp. The development of electronic tubes and transistors out of this puzzle in a light bulb eventually helped make many face-to-face public gatherings superfluous as families and individuals retreated indoors to well-lighted living rooms to watch on television the descendants of the public spectacles that had once entertained communities in the town square. The television special is a still identifiable heir of this genre, using brightly colored lights in striking patterns and images to create visual excitement and drama.

Because communication at a distance was mostly implemented in other forms, our cultural memories no longer recall predictions in nineteenth-century voices that twentieth-century media might include messages splashed across the sky by searchlight or projected on walls by banks of electric lights. The nineteenth-century conviction that important twentieth-century mass media would look like nothing so much as nineteenth-century electric lights writ large betrays the tendency of every age to read the future as a fancier version of the present. For late-nineteenth-century observers, the electric light was a far more likely mass medium than any point-to-point invention such as the telephone or even wireless, which the nineteenth century regarded as a vastly imperfect point-to-point medium. Most people made the acquaintance of electric light through its decoration of outdoor spectacles that candles and bonfires had once illuminated, and in new spectacles such as the sports event after dark, the night-time public amusement park, and the electrical exposition. Electric spectacles were the first dramatic ritual event created for the public by electrical professionals. These outdoor events were complemented by dramatically lighted indoor occasions for smaller gatherings, at first as a mark of conspicuous consumption, in time as a matter of routine.

Transformative patterns of this kind are common in technological innovation. Apparatus intended to streamline, simplify, or otherwise enhance the conduct of familiar social routines may so reorganize them that they become new events. The lines of their evolution remain, however. Ordinarily, we think of wireless telegraphy, cinema, and telephony as the direct ancestors of mass broadcasting, but this genealogy overlooks the role of electric light in the social construction of twentieth-century mass media. The communicative capacity of electric light survives today in illuminated signs, but its most important contribution to modern mass communication was to a vocabulary of popular forms in mass entertainment spectacles and to the reorganization of traditional audiences. In that sense, the glittering television special is as much the fruit of electric light as of any other invention.

Chapter 4

TED NELSON

SELECTED MATERIAL FROM
COMPUTER LIB/DREAM MACHINES

W E HAVE INCLUDED PAGES from this idiosyncratic and fascinating book for a number of reasons. The first is that it is in itself a historical document, a snapshot of an emerging computer culture. Or, more accurately, it is a double exposure, first published in 1974, then updated and republished in 1987. It documents the new smaller and faster computer technologies, their design, politics and cultural significance, all written by a man who was at the centre of these developments.

Ted Nelson documents the development of key aspects of computer technology and its transformation into popular computer media, including: the significance of the new (at the time) monitor displays, graphics and animation; the significance of computer games in the development of intuitive interfaces; to the possibilities of hyperlinked text and media (the foundation of the Web's media). This latter is an area of development in which Nelson's contribution was seminal – he coined the term hypertext in the early 1960s: his plans for the hypermedia Xanadu system are included in this extract and they make an interesting comparison with the subsequent development of the World Wide Web.

If Nelson is agitating for the popularisation of computers, it is not merely in the commonsense notion of the popular as 'widely enjoyed', but also, and more importantly, in the *political* sense of a popular uprising, say, a bottom-up and emancipatory movement, for 'computer lib' as one of the book's titles has it. In this his work is a link between the hacker culture of computer students in the US universities of Stanford and MIT in the 1950s and 1960s, and the 'homebrew' computer clubs that followed, and aspects of this tradition are evident in the open source and blogging cultures of the Internet today.

The form of the book itself, its cut and paste aesthetic, evokes the computer culture Nelson espouses. It is of the moment, concerned more with making an accessible, vivid and intelligent point, and connections to other thoughts, than with developing a scholarly argument. It offers technical advice and makes ambitious predictions. It is playfully serious, including jokes and cartoons, satire and, occasionally, vitriol against the unimaginative and the bureaucratic. http://ted.hyperland.com/

FROM INTERACTIVITY TO GRAPHICS

*We have been discussing interactive computers and terminals. The most important form of interaction, though, uses screens (referred to in this book as **display screens**) and interactive graphics.*

Almost everyone knows now what an interactive computer screen is, and interactive computer graphics. However, in 1974 this had to be explained.

THE WONDER OF INTERACTIVE DISPLAY SYSTEMS

(For much more on interactive display systems, see "Computer Graphics," p. DM 80)

If you have not seen interactive computer display, you have not lived.

Except for a few people who can imagine it—and I'm trying to help you with that as hard as I can—most people just don't get it till they see it. They can't imagine what it's like to *manipulate a picture.* To have a *diagram respond to you.* To change one part of a picture, and *watch the rest adapt.* These are some of the things that can happen in interactive computer display—all depending, of course, on the program.

For some reason there are a lot of people who pooh-pooh computer display: They say it's "not necessary," or "not worth it," or that "you can get just as good results other ways."

Personally, I wouldn't think of trying to justify computer display on "practical" grounds. So what if it offers you faster access to information and pictures and maps and diagrams, the ability to simulate extremely complex things by modifying pictures, the ability to go through complex transactions with the system in very little time, the ability to create things in the world almost instantaneously (say, by creating fabric patterns which are then automatically woven, or design 3D objects which are then automatically milled by machines), and never mind that it enables the user, say, to control entire oil refineries by the flick of a light pen.

As far as I'm concerned, these matters aren't very important compared to changing the world: making education an excitement rather than a prison; giving scholars total access to writings and notes, in new complex form; allowing people to play imaginatively, and raising human minds to the potentials they should have reached long ago; and helping people think at the deepest level about very heavy and complex alternatives—which confront us more ominously today than ever.

WOMEN, CHILDREN AND
MEN AT WORK

The computer display screen is the new frontier of our lives.

That such systems should (and will) be *fun* goes without saying. That they will also be a place to *work* may be less obvious from the tone of this publication, so I want to stress it from here.

Once you pass through the paradigm, to realize that computer screen systems will be the center of every kind of work, then the silly terminology that's been with us—terms like "microcomputer" and "word processing" and "CAD/CAM"—become seen for how inane they really are.

DESKTOP ANYTHING

At desktop computer screens—be you professional, student or some other type—you can now write books and typeset them, design buildings, compose music, do experiments in chemistry and physics, and much more. Whatever can be done through paper, blackboard, loudspeaker or machine tool can be done, or nearly done, on some computer screen.

*A popular term right now is "desktop publishing." But "desktop engineering" (presently called something else; see p. DM 83), desktop whatever, desktop **anything**, is here or on the way.*

The question is not whether it's "as good as" or "not as good as" what was previously done. The question is how to make it great.

(Another question is, why does the screen have to take up desktop space? But that's a separate issue.)

> The computer display screen will be mankind's new home.

> IF COMPUTERS ARE THE WAVE OF THE FUTURE, DISPLAYS ARE THE SURFBOARDS.

Another Viewpoint

(from handout, 1974 Natl. Joint Comp. Conf.)
John B. Macdonald
Research Leader
Computer Applications: Graphics
Western Electric Company
Engineering Research Center

PROBLEMS, PERILS, AND PROMISES OF COMPUTER GRAPHICS

I would begin with some definitions which may be obvious but bear repeating.

1. Engineering is the application of science for ($) profit,

2. Computer graphics does not make possible anything that was previously impossible: it can only improve the throughput of an existing process,

3. A successful application of computer graphics is when over a period of five years the cost savings from improved process throughput exceed the costs of hardware, software, maintenance and integration into an existing process flow.

Saving Energy With Computer Display

A timely criticism of computer display is that it needs electricity. But (as mentioned elsewhere) it saves paper, and importantly, it bodes to save energy as well.

IF WE SWITCH TO COMPUTER SCREENS FROM PAPER, PEOPLE WON'T HAVE TO TRAVEL AS MUCH. Instead of commuting to offices in the center of town, people can set up their offices in the suburbs, and share the documentary structure of the work situation *through the screens.*

This view has been propounded, indeed, by Peter Goldmark, former director of research for CBS Labs, the man who brought you the LP record.

Making pictures with the GE halftone system (see pp. DM 100).

THE CAVE OF PLATO.

(see DM 95)

TWO SPECIAL CHARACTERS ON THE SCREEN from its CHANGEABLE character memory (which can be loaded with Russian, Armenian, Katakana, Cherokee, or whatever, *even little pictures*, at the start of the lesson), or

A COMMAND TO THE MICROFICHE PROJECTOR, or

A COMMAND TO THE AUDIO PLAYER, or

A COMMAND TO WHATEVER'S IN THE GENERAL JACK.

Note that all lines and characters for the plasma screen can be turned *on* (orange on black) or *off* (black on orange).

WHERE ARE THEY NOW?
The PLATO terminal, tied to the original system, is a bit of a dinosaur. There are PLATO installations here and there, but it wasn't the big hit its developers foresaw. See "Plato's Retreat," p. DM 95.

This honey is the GT-40 from DEC ($12,000, including computer—the thing with teeth, below). It's a subroutining display (see p. DM 88).

Man is playing Moonlander game: controlling screen action with light-pen. Computer simulates real moon lander.

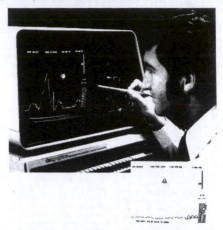

The thing about display screens—especially the high-performance, subroutining kind—is that the screen can become a place from which to control events in the outside world.

Example: I believe a town in New York state has its electrical system hooked up to an IDIIOM subroutining display (made by Information Displays, Inc., and coupled to a Varian 620 minicomputer). Instead of having a wall with a big painted map having switches set into it, like many such control centers, the switches are linked directly to the minicomputer, and a program in the minicomputer connects these circuits to the pictures on the screen. Thus to throw a switch in the real world, the operator *points with his lightpen at the picture of the switch,* and the minicomputer throws the switch.

There are oil refineries that work the same way. The operator can control flows among pipes and tanks by pointing at their *pictures,* or at symbols connected with them, and bingo, it happens Out There.

In another case, a person designing something at a screen can look across the room and see a machine *producing* what he just finished designing a few minutes ago. I wish I could say more about that particular setup.

There are now thousands of brands of graphical computer; at least half are based on the IBM PC or its clones (see pp. 48-49). Incredibly opulent graphic machines are now available.

Note that "Moonlander" was one of the first computer games, developed by Dave Ahl at DEC. Dave went on to found Creative Computing, which lasted a little over ten years, and helped whip up enthusiasm for personal computers. "Moonlander" came out in an arcade version.

GENETIC WORKSTATIONS used to be just barns and beds. Today, though, the operator can actually have the workstation create a DNA chain with an arbitrary sequence. From the screen. Scary?

There are workstations now set up for almost every occupation, every profession, every realm of endeavor, and every price. You can easily pay a hundred thousand dollars for a hot workstation, and get an excellent personal computer as well (see p. DM 113).

Display terminals aren't so common now, because the display is typically built right into the computer. A desktop machine with screen is often called a workstation now.

☞ These experiences are powerful and gripping, far more intense than anything else suburbia has to offer. Suicides have been reported over these games. Allegations of devil-worship have been heard. But there's nothing magical about the games themselves, really; these are just the only outlets for **companionate fantasy** available today.

There have been various one-person interactive games based on the fantasy role-playing games, but next to the **real** fantasy role-playing games they are as nothing. The real power of the fantasy role games is in the companionship, the crises together and the imagining together. Replacing the dungeonmaster with a machine throws it away.

COMPUTERIZED ADVENTURE GAMES

Actually, one mechanized variant of adventure gaming, with a certain limited appeal, has been very successful.

The text adventure game, beginning with what is now called Original Adventure at MIT (now available from Software Arts, as part of an album called Les Crane's Golden Oldies), began by telling you, textually, that you were in a strange land beside a stream. You then had to experiment with typed commands, such as go north and south, knock on doors, pick things up, eat, fight, and so on. Some people, especially programmer types, seem to find this exhaustive exploration an exciting challenge (sometimes nothing happens until you knock on something a THIRD time); others find it a bureaucratic bore.

There are many such adventure games on the market, some with illustrations. ZORK is the most popular. I think the market is limited to very specific personality types, but I don't know that anyone has formally researched this aspect.

Student programmer Alan McNeil, an art major, ponders something or other. It may be the program for the Nova space-game he and Pete Rowell are building.

Alan also made a film showing what may have been the motions of the continents, shooting straight off the PLATO screen.

Some PLATO purists point out that this is not exactly what PLATO was originally intended for. So?

WHERE ARE THEY NOW?

Alan created the bit arcade video game "Berzerk." He programs in FORTH, and (last I heard) lives in the country.

TOMORROW'S SYSTEMS

Those who have happened recently into the computer world may see today's screens and think, How puny! Computer screens show too little to be of real use.

That is true today, friend, **today**.

For instance, the standard screen of the IBM PC and its clones is 80 characters wide, 25 lines high. The standard screen of its yuppie-craftsy rival, the Macintosh, is 800 dots wide. Each of these is only about half a sheet of paper, and you can turn pages by hand much faster than flipping documents on their screens.

"Too limited," you may say.

But here a little historical perspective is called for. Just ten years ago personal computers had **no** screens, and then we were able to buy screens 24 characters wide, and **that** was a revolution. And then eighty characters wide, which is the present size.

But the next step up is ready. The hotter screens, those of the "professional workstations" (computers costing, say, $10,000 and up), go to 132 characters wide, and that can probably double in the next five or six years. (And Mac screens are now available with a million dots; and **that** number will be multiplied soon.

How much can eventually be put on the screen of a CRT we still don't know. But it's not advisable to bet on an upper limit (see p. DM 85).

How fast the screen can **change** is another matter; it has to do with the speed of memories and processors, also getting faster.

Tom DeFanti (see p. DM 96) has given us an excellent watchword for all this, inspired by Wizzywig (see p. DM 28). His motto is WIGGYPOOF, the way he acronymizes his motto: "What You Get Is What You Pay For." And that's the real issue.

Every year or so, more powerful computers and screens come into the Professional market, and the formerly "professional" screens come into the Personal market. Pricewise. So we can plan on getting this year's best as hand-me-downs a few years from now.

NO UPPER LIMIT

We are safest betting that there is no upper limit on how good screens and computers will get. When will the screens rival 70mm Dolby? 1995? 2005? Stick around.

Then there's the question of sheer processing power, raw crunch.

A class of machines they now call "Crayolas"—miniature Craylike computers (see p. 90)—will soon heave toward the personal price range. As may

Super TV As A Possible Standard

The high-resolution TV systems now in their experimental phases may offer the perfect resolution (pun intended) between text, sound, animation and playstation (see p. DM 23) monitor. The hi-res TV can in principle be broken into windows, and could combine text, computer graphics and video feed into a simple composite, especially with something like the DVI chips managing the video (see p. DM 99). This could be an ideal setting for many of the possibilities hoped for in this book.

See "Technically Better TV," p. DM 59.

such parallel machines as the Transputer (see p. 99), or even the extraordinary Connection Machine of Danny Hillis, with the power of thousands of regular computers all at once.

WINDOWS

But there will also be stylistic changes. Software for dividing the screen into "windows" will come soon: Microsoft Windows and Quarterdeck Desq for the PC, and competing windowing software for the professional workstations—vying presently are Xwindows, Sun windows, PostScript windows. (But see also "Qframes," p. DM 49.)

FLIGHT-SIMULATOR-CLASS MACHINES

However, I think that what is really coming for the personal market is another kind of interactive screen. The "flight simulator," of a class with the Evans and Sutherland and IRIS machines (see pp. DM 110, DM 112-113, DM 24, DM 113), but at breakthrough prices.

Given the ever-falling prices of current chips, a thousand-dollar IRIS-type machine might be with us in 1992, perhaps even sooner. And *that* will make a whole new world. For we must redesign education at once toward the time that every pupil can have one, attached to a common feeder network. (One avenue toward that cheap flight-simulator-class machine may be RCA's DVI chip; see p. DM 97). ☞

Quadrapong,

a swell video game now in bars, probably controls the four-player ping pong on the screen with a minicomputer or microprocessor.

Especially exciting is the social possibility of horizontal screens for other fun interpersonal stuff. As well as collaborative work. (But boy, let's hope the radiation shielding is good.)

There are various Interactive Graphics Standards being worked out by professional committees, standards with names like PHIGS and GKS, but such standards are usually decided by the marketplace. (There are de facto graphics standards in the personal computer market: on the PC it's write-to-screen on the color graphics adapter, and on the Macintosh it's called PICT format.)

ChAoS!

The Local Area Network Situation

So you want several connected computers that are able to share files and printers; that brings us to the problem of

LOCAL AREA NETS

As soon as you have two computers, you find you have to keep swapping disks all the time. Or putting serial cables between them and writing messy programs to transfer stuff.

As with most problems, there are many different ways to do it. And as with computers, the best advice is GO WITH THE STANDARD. Except there isn't any.

It's chaos out there.

Datapoint's ARCNET, first and best of the lot, blew the chance to be standard because Datapoint would not explain what it actually **was**. (I remember trying to find out at the NCC booth when it came out in the late 70s. The salesman acted as if he wasn't telling, but it was fairly obvious that he actually didn't know.) Xerox' Ethernet is expensive and has a lot of problems. General Motors, Intel and AT&T each offer their own, and IBM has announced at least three.)

However, in typically ibmish fashion, IBM has basically settled on something called the "token ring" network, thought by many to be technically the worst imaginable.

"One ring to rule them all,
one ring to bind them
In the land of Mordor
where the shadows lie."

—J.R.R. Tolkien, Lord of the Rings

Flat-panel displays, which can in principle be made much larger than CRTs, may yet be perfected.

A monitor, or operating system, is a master program that always runs a computer, even when other programs appear to be in control. (Compare the monitor to a stage manager who controls the curtain, while the audience sees only the comedian onstage. See p. 99.)

Our conventional monitor programs have assumed that a user is in charge of the computer and makes things happen by selecting programs to run. Thus the programs start when the user demands, and no outside events need to be synchronized.

Tomorrow's screen machines, however, will be playing in a new fashion: they will combine visuals and animations created inside the user's computer with visuals and animations arriving from various forms of storage or other feed. All these need to be synchronized to make one overall, coordinated presentation. Not only that, but data structures and new dimensions and details of data will have to be added and removed during smooth new animated performances for the user. (The media designer will synchronize these with a symphony-style notation.)

The same for sound. Sound and music created inside the user's computer will have to be synchronized with sound coming from something outside the computer.

I take this to be a new and necessary kind of software environment for tomorrow's educational and office systems. Just to give it a name, I call it the Playstation monitor. We need it now.

If you want an overall conjecture on the personal computer system of the future, here goes:

A flight-simulator-class graphical computer with 3D zooming and maneuvering display and real-time 3D image synthesis (see p. DM 111)—the IRIS will do (see pp. DM 24, DM 113); running a Playstation monitor for various real-time feeds with on-board sound and video and data structure swapping; symphonically coordinated by media designers; controlled by a user through controls such as the Walking Net™ and ZigZag™ systems, which are almost instantly learnable (see pp. DM 51, DM 47); and fed from a xanalogical network (see p. DM 144) permitting the linkage of all data structures.

Promotional robots. These are two-legged, or on wheels, and wander around the floor at conventions, typically making lascivious remarks to women.

As usual, some are fooled. But the fun is finding the person who's really controlling it. Wander through the crowd looking for someone who is watching the robot intensely with his hand in his pocket, her hand in a handbag, or the like, and possibly moving his or her lips slightly. Now that you've spotted the perpetrator the game is between you and him or her, as he or she acts casual and pretends not to be running the thing.

As yet there are no strip-tease automata (disrobots).

Medical instruction robots, such as those made by Ixxion. These are currently life-size dolls, or parts of them, that respond as the patient would—computer-based interactive systems with realistic humanoid input and output.

Note that in the future we may expect the continuation of these developments to lead to sexual-surrogate robots.

The home robot. This is a cheap version of the promotional robot, fairly useless. You can make it wander around by remote control, or at random; some come with a repertoire of prerecorded sassy remarks. My favorite was an advertised home robot named GARCAN: it was in fact a garbage can that had been put on wheels and remote control.

Toy robots. Well, there have been remote-controlled cars and stuff for decades. But of late there are some pretty amusing variants. Fuzzy-animal robots called "Petsters" can be programmed to explore randomly, act angry, or do various other things. "We installed one at the office and didn't see the cat for days," says a software developer I know.

Story robots. The latest wrinkle is the robot that tells a story. (Remember when *parents* told stories? Now you, too, can recapture the nostalgia of that bygone day, metempsychosed into a fuzzy doll with lips that move, for $79.95. Story cassettes are extra.)

The champ is Teddy Ruxpin™, a story-telling bear. Not only does his mouth move with his recorded tale, but his expressiveness is enhanced by the fact that his jaw and snout are separately controlled, making unpredictable double motions that don't look half bad. (And his eyes wink.) He also has a sidekick who talks back on the tapes, and may be bought separately

and plugged into Teddy for an animated duologue.

Fast on the heels of the successful Ruxpin comes The Talking Mother Goose™, a goose doll with similarly double-articulated beak, and a slightly English accent. There is also a story robot that **looks** like a robot, and has a changeable LCD face.

Pizza robots. Nolan Bushnell, inventor of "Pong" and founder of Atari, went on to invent the Pizza Robot. At Chuck E. Cheese's Pizza Parlors, various characters would wave their arms and do lip-sync to speeches, songs and jokes—all controlled, incidentally, by a multitrack tape recorder.

The characters were awful and the showmanship was poor—each supposedly sing-along song was terminated by the time you could find the key—but the concept lasted long enough to generate imitators.

The best part I heard, though, was what happened when a singing-robot pizzeria went out of business in Seattle. "A bunch of artists bought the robots," a friend tells me, "and did some very strange things with them." He did not elaborate.

BIBLIOGRAPHY

ARMS AND EYES FOR YOUR COMPUTER! (But just try programming them.)

Robotics Age magazine, and its ads, are largely concerned with moving output devices (arms, wheels, micro-manipulators and so on); languages to control them, interfaces, visual analyzers, etc.

"The best way to predict the future is to invent it."
—Alan Kay

One of the great unfinished dreams of the computer field, along with the Dynabook and the Architecture machine:

XANADU*
(pronounced "Zanna-Doo")
Literary System, Storage Engine, Hypertext and Hypermedia Server, Virtual Document Coordinator, Write-Once Network Storage Manager, Electronic Publishing Method, Open Hypermedium, Non-Hierarchical Filing System, Linked All-Media Repository Archive, Paperless Publishing Medium, and Readdressing Software. The Magic Place of Literary Memory™.

Xanadu, friend, is *my* dream.

The name comes from the poem (next page); Coleridge's little story of the artistic trance (and the Person from Porlock) makes it an appropriate name for the Pleasure Dome of the creative writer. The Citizen Kane connotations, and any other connotations you may find in the poem, are side benefits.

I have been working on Xanadu, under this and other names, for fourteen years now.

Make that twenty-seven years.

Originally it was going to be a super system for handling text by computer (see pp. DM 16 and DM 29). But it grew: as I realized, level by level, how deep the problem was. ☞

---

* "Xanadu," the Eternal-Flaming-X and FEBE are trade and service marks for computer, hypertext and software products and services offered by Project Xanadu, 8480 Fredericksburg #138, San Antonio, TX 78229, and licensed to XOC, Inc., a California Corporation.

For further information, see our videotape "A Technical Overview of the Xanadu Storage System" (VHS Extended Play, $50) or Ted Nelson's book *Literary Machines* ($20); add $5 for purchase order, $5 for overseas airmail.

Donations are accepted from those who would like to be on our mailing list. We also offer a universal network name or "Xandle" for $100 (subject to such complex and arbitrary rules and possible cancellation that the payment should be considered a donation).

By special arrangement with Microsoft Press, *Computer Lib* is accessible on the prototype Xanadu System.

KUBLA KHAN : OR, A VISION IN A DREAM.

A FRAGMENT.

In the summer of the year 1797, the Author, then in ill health, had retired to a lonely farm house between Porlock and Linton, on the Exmoor confines of Somerset and Devonshire. In consequence of a slight indisposition, an anodyne had been prescribed, from the effect of which he fell asleep in his chair at the moment that he was reading the following sentence, or words of the same substance, in "Purchas's Pilgrimage:" "Here the Khan Kubla commanded a palace to be built, and a stately garden thereunto: and thus ten miles of fertile ground were inclosed with a wall. The Author continued for about three hours in a profound sleep, at least of the external senses, during which time he has the most vivid confidence, that he could not have composed less than from two to three hundred lines; if that indeed can be called composition in which all the images rose up before him as things, with a parallel production of the correspondent expressions, without any sensation or consciousness of effort. On awaking he appeared to himself have a distinct recollection of the whole, and taking his pen, ink, and paper, instantly and eagerly wrote down the lines that are here preserved. At this moment he was unfortunately called out by a person on business from Porlock, and detained by him above an hour, and on his return to the room, found, to his no small surprise and mortification, that though he still retained some vague and dim recollection of the general purport of the vision, yet, with the exception of some eight or ten scattered lines and images, all the rest had passed away like the images on the surface of a stream into which a stone had been cast, but alas! without the after restoration of the latter :

> Then all the charm
> Is broken—all that phantom-world so fair,
> Vanishes and a thousand circlets spread,
> And each mis-shape the other. Stay awhile,
> Poor youth ! who scarcely dar'st lift up thine eyes—
> The stream will soon renew its smoothness, soon
> The visions will return ! And lo ! he stays,
> And soon the fragments dim of lovely forms
> Come trembling back, unite, and now once more
> The pool becomes a mirror.

As a contrast to this vision, I have annexed a fragment of a very different character, describing with equal fidelity the dream of pain and disease.—1816.

KUBLA KHAN.

Is Xanadu did Kubla Khan
A stately pleasure-dome decree :
Where Alph, the sacred river, ran
Through caverns measureless to man
  Down to a sunless sea.
So twice five miles of fertile ground
With walls and towers were girdled round :
And there were gardens bright with sinuous rills
Where blossomed many an incense-bearing tree :
And here were forests ancient as the hills,
Enfolding sunny spots of greenery.
But oh ! that deep romantic chasm which slanted
Down the green hill athwart a cedarn cover !
A savage place ! as holy and enchanted
As e'er beneath a waning moon was haunted
By woman wailing for her demon-lover !
And from this chasm, with ceaseless turmoil seething,
As if this earth in fast thick pants were breathing,
A mighty fountain momently was forced :
Amid whose swift half-intermitted burst
Huge fragments vaulted like rebounding hail,
Or chaffy grain beneath the thresher's flail :
And 'mid these dancing rocks at once and ever
It flung up momently the sacred river.
Five miles meandering with a mazy motion
Through wood and dale the sacred river ran,
Then reached the caverns measureless to man,
And sank in tumult to a lifeless ocean :
And 'mid this tumult Kubla heard from far
Ancestral voices prophesying war !
  The shadow of the dome of pleasure
  Floated mid way on the waves ;
  Where was heard the mingled measure
  From the fountain and the caves.
It was a miracle of rare device,
A sunny pleasure-dome with caves of ice !
  A damsel with a dulcimer
  In a vision once I saw :
  It was an Abyssinian maid,
  And on her dulcimer she played,
  Singing of Mount Abora.
  Could I revive within me
  Her symphony and song,
  To such a deep delight 'twould win me
That with music loud and long,
I would build that dome in air,
That sunny dome ! those caves of ice !
And all who heard should see them there,
And all should cry, Beware ! Beware !
His flashing eyes, his floating hair !
Weave a circle round him thrice,
And close your eyes with holy dread,
For he on honey-dew hath fed,
And drunk the milk of Paradise.

THE XANADU™ PROJECT

THE XANADU™ PROJECT is very well known; many have worked on it over the years. This visibility is both an advantage and a hindrance.

Many people know our goals and ideals, but only a few understand our real technical direction.

A new form of storage.

In ordinary computer storage, you have to keep copying files in order to reorganize them—a tedious and dangerous process, which (when done wrong) easily wipes out your work. For every hour spent usefully, perhaps half an hour must be spent copying, rearranging and backing up files. Most do not have the patience or resignation to do this, and many desert their computers as the work deteriorates into a rubble of confused and mislaid diskfiles.

Used on your personal computer, the Xanadu system is simply a storage manager. It will enable you to organize and reorganize what is already there without complication. The same materials may be organized in many different ways, and put to many different uses without significantly expanding the storage needed. It's

A SINGLE PROGRAM, RUNNING THROUGHOUT A NETWORK

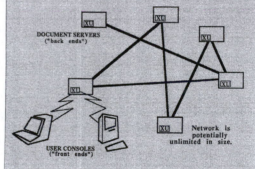

DOCUMENT SERVERS ("back ends")

USER CONSOLES ("front ends")

Network is potentially unlimited in size.

From *Literary Machines* 87.1.

People think that if the Xanadu system is going to store and supply so much *stuff*, it has to be an enormous *program*.

Not so. The same smallish program running in every computer of a network, makes the overall system. So we are much closer than generally realized.

all a unified structure, and no form of organization disturbs any previous one.

Offices need this just as much as individuals. With the advent of office computers, the blizzard of paperwork has melted into a slush of datafiles. (When an employee leaves, others dare not touch his or her data files for months, until some brave soul decides that things lost in them are no longer needed.)

The Xanadu system not only saves space—by not copying—but it shows the interconnections and commonalities among all documents. We believe this may lighten office work by as much as 75%.

We foresee new forms of education and new forms of writing, which show and make clear the interconnectedness of everything.

This reflects a fundamental philosophy. For those to whom the world is hierarchical, cut and dried, there is no reason to want to keep reorganizing ideas, writings, indexes, directories. But for anyone who must constantly work with ideas, writings, indexes and directories, the problem is their ever-swirling change.

Basically, then, the Xanadu system is just one thing: a new form of interconnection for computer files—CORRESPONDING TO THE TRUE INTERCONNECTION OF IDEAS—which can be refined and elaborated into a shared network. But if you truly understand this form of interconnection, you will understand its revolutionary potential. (K. Eric Drexler of MIT calls the Xanadu program one of the most important developments of our time.)

It is this concept of "true interconnection" that is central; the underlying technicalities, while themselves embodying very new principles of software, are merely the tricks we have found for making this happen.

Thus this supposedly wild dream, what the Whole Earth Review called "a retrieval system as big as the earth," is actually within reach.

It is in reality a single computer program which exists in prototype and needs debugging and reworking.

CUMULATIVE ORDER AND COLLAGING:

The ability to build new pieces from old without crippling multiplication of files helps things to become more and more ordered —unlike ordinary personal computer use, which tends to become more and more disordered.

The same facility, extended to a network, permits new forms of pluralistic publishing.

IMPROVED ORGANIZATION FOR SINGLE USER OR OFFICE

DOCUMENTS
are series of
POINTERS
into the changing
web of data

LINKS
are connections
between documents
which the user may follow.

Expanding Tissue of Text, Data and Graphics

From Literary Machines 87.1.

PUBLIC REPOSITORY SYSTEM WITH PLURALISTIC RE-USE,
publication by users

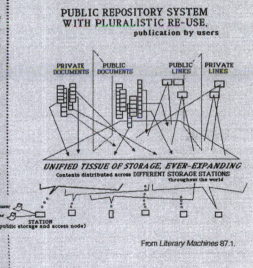

PRIVATE DOCUMENTS   PUBLIC DOCUMENTS   PUBLIC LINKS   PRIVATE LINKS

UNIFIED TISSUE OF STORAGE, EVER-EXPANDING
Contents distributed across DIFFERENT STORAGE STATIONS
throughout the world

user
user
STATION
(public storage and access node)

From *Literary Machines* 87.1.

☛ And the concept of what it was to be kept changing, as I saw more and more clearly that it had to be on a minicomputer for the home. (You can have one in your office too, if you want, but that's not what it's about.)

Now the idea is this:

To give you a screen in your home from which you can see into the world's hypertext libraries.

(The fact that the world doesn't *have* any hypertext libraries—yet—is a minor point.)

To give you a screen system that will offer high-performance computer graphics and text services at a price anyone can afford. To allow you to send and receive written messages at the Engelbart level (see p. DM 16). To allow you to explore diagrams (see pp. DM 47 and DM 134). To eliminate the absurd distinction between "teacher" and "pupil."

To make you a part of a new electronic literature and art, where you can get all your questions answered and nobody will put you down.

Originally Xanadu was programmed around the Parallel Textface (see p. DM 41). But as the requirements of the Parallel Textface were better and better understood, Xanadu became a more general underlying system for all forms of interactive graphic environments. Thus in its final form, now being debugged, it will support not only the Parallel Textface (see p. DM 41), the Walking Net (see p. DM 47), Stretchtext (see p. DM 134), Zoom Maps (see p. DM 134) and so on, but indeed any data structure that needs to combine complex linkages with fast access and rapid changes. Because the data structure is recursively extensible, it will permit hypertext (see p. DM 29) of any depth and complexity, and the collateral linkage (see p. DM 50) of any objects of contemplation.

THE REDESIGN, UP AT LAST

The reason that the Xanadu system has taken so long (and been prematurely announced from time to time) is that it's a **hard problem.**

When Computer Lib *was first written, there was already a good design using methods unkown in the literature. It was to be written in assembler on the PDP-11.*

However, a new invention by William F. Barus promised a whole new beginning: linkage not just between beginnings of chunks, but between **spans of bytes.** *Meaning that links could survive editorial changes very cleanly.*

Brought in by Computer Lib, *a new team (now under Roger Gregory) put an experimental version of the system on the end of a phone-line for public access in January of 1987.*

We welcome collaborating developers. Those interested in experimenting with the present system with an eye toward application and front-end projects should contact Project Xanadu.

THE XANADU NETWORK

First of all, bear in mind that Xanadu is a unified system for complex data management and display. This basically means that the *same* system (without the displays) can serve as a feeder machine for the data network itself.

So far, so good. That means that we can have a *mini*computer network handling the entire structure: sending out library materials to users on call, and storing any materials they want saved. This saves all kinds of hassles with big computer and big-computer-style programming.

But who will pay for it? To build the kind of capacity we're talking about—all those disks, all those minicomputers in a network—won't it take immense amounts of capital? Now, people ask me, will any American company ever back such a Utopian scheme?

Aha.

One method of financing has proven itself in the postwar suburban era, this time of drive-ins and hamburger stands.

Franchising.

What I propose, then, is the Mom-and-Pop Xanadu Shop. Or, more properly, the Xanadu *stand*. "Mom and Pop" are the owners of the individual stand. But the customers can be families, too.

From far away the children see the tall golden X's. "Oh, Daddy, can't we stop? I want to play Spacewar," says little Johnny. Big Sis adds, "You know, I have to check something for my paper on Roman politics." And Mom says, "Say, that would be a good place for lunch."

So they turn in past the sign that says "OVER 2 BILLION SCREEN HOURS," and pull into the lot. They park the car, and Dad shows the clerk his Xanadu credit card, and the kids run to

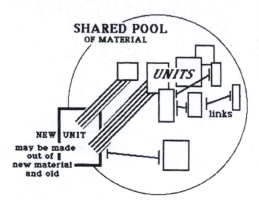

XANALOGICAL STORAGE

SHARED POOL
OF MATERIAL

UNITS

links

NEW UNIT

may be made out of new material and old

From Literary Machines 87.1.

The Xanadu system is built around a new concept of storage: that new units—we call them "documents"—may be freely built out of material in old units, and linked together arbitrarily.

2020 Vision And The **Near Sight**

In the year 2020, we imagine a network with at least a hundred million simultaneous users, adding a hundred million documents an hour to the system.

The immediate use, however, is as a clarification box: to make the interconnections of files, documents, correspondence, lists and figures clear at last in computer storage—and keep them that way.

screens. Dad and Mom wait for a big horizontal CRT, though, because there are some memories they'd like to share together...

Sis's paper, of course, goes to her teacher through *his* Xanadu console.

THE PLAN, IS IT AS CRAZY AS IT SEEMS?

Deep inside, the public wants it, but people who think of computers in cliches can't comprehend it. This means "the public" must somehow create it.

One way to go is to start a new corporation, register it with the SEC and try to raise a lot of money by selling stock publicly. Unfortunately there are all kinds of obstacles for that.

Through the miracle of franchising, now, a lot of the difficulties of conventional backing can be bypassed. The franchisee has to put up the money for the computers, the scopes, the adorable purple enamel building, the johns and so on; as a Xanadu franchisee he gets the whole turnkey system and certain responsibilites in the OVERALL XANADU NETWORK—of which he is a member. He is assigned permanent storage of certain classes of materials, on call from elsewhere in the net. (Naturally, everything is stored in more than one place.)

The Xanadu subscriber, of course, gets what he* requests at the screen as quickly as possible—or on priority if he wants to pay for it—and may store his own files, including linkages among other materials and marginal notations to other things that can be called. (See collateral structures, p. DM 50; these can automatically bring forth anything they're linked to. (See "Nelson's Canons," p. DM 149)) A user's historical record will be stored to whatever degree he desires, but not (if he chooses) in ways that can be identified with him.

Home users need only dial a local phone number—their nearest Xanadu stand—to connect with the entire Xanadu network. (The cost of using something stored on the network has nothing to do with where it is stored.)

(Special high-capacity lines need not be installed between storage stations, as

*Please read "he or she" and "him or her." This book was written back when the masculine included the feminine, or so we were taught in earlier days.

appropriate digital transmission services are becoming available commercially.)

Various security techniques prevent others from reading a subscriber's files, even if they sign on falsely; the Dartmouth technique of scrambling on non-stored keywords is a good one.

The Xanadu stand also has private rooms with multiple screens, which can be rented for parties, business meetings, design sessions, briefings, legal consultations, lectures, seances, musicales, and so on.

The choice locations for the Xanadu stands are somewhat different from hamburger spots. But that's probably not anything to go into here.

Within the Xanadu network, then, people may read, write, send messages, study and play.

Note: THIS IS NOT IN ANY WAY AN OFFER TO SELL FRANCHISES. Such an offer will only be made at such time as the experimental Xanadu program appears to be functioning and networking ☞

THE FIRST COMPUTER TALKIN' SINGING COMMERCIAL, continued from p. 15

So continuing under our guidance inertial, Let's have the XANADU SINGING COMMERCIAL.
[strings] It's got everything to give.
It'll get you where you live.
[chimes] Realms of mind that you may roam:
Grasp them all within your home.
[brass flourish] The greatest things you've ever seen
Dance your wishes on the screen.
[bass bautant] All the things that man has known
Comin' on the telephone—
[TUBULAR BELLS!] Poems, books and pictures too
COMIN' ON THE XANADU—
[kettledrums] XAN-A-DU, OO—
THE—WORLD—OF—YOUUUU!

The Golden X's welcome the mind-hungry traveller.

View from the snack balcony of a large Xanadu installation, overlooking the internal greenery. Hexagonal architecture permits physical expansion without interruption of services. (The mollusks have been telling us something about expansion.)

Local Xanadu Stand—First Floor.

correctly, and only to sophisticated individuals aware and fully warned of its unusual business risks and unproven technology, who can afford to lose all or part of their investments, and who are prepared personally to work long and difficult hours on the maintenance and supervision of a complex and unusual facility.

XANADU: BRASS TAX

WHAT IT IS: the heart of the Xanadu system, now being debugged, consists of a highly integrated program for use on minicomputers ("software"—see p. 52). It is an operating system with two programs: a highly generalized data management system for handling extremely complex data in huge files, and a generalized display system, married to the other, for handling branching animation and retrieval and canned display programs. These ordain retrievals by the data system. The Parallel Textface (see p. DM 41) and the Walking Net (see p. DM 47) are two such canned programs.

(See below, "Front And Back End.")

"Front and Back End"

The Xanadu system has become basically a storage management program for networks. This is the back end. Xanadu storage _remains standard across all applications_. Indeed, we would like it to become an archival standard for all data structures, permitting anybody's programs to use the shared data freely.

Anything you want to <u>do</u> with material stored in the Xanadu system is done by a program in your computer or workstation. This is your front end.

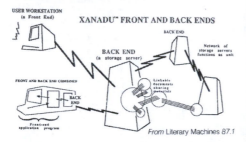

XANADU™ FRONT AND BACK ENDS

From Literary Machines 87.1

Many different front-end programs are possible for different possible uses of Xanadu storage. We invite software developers of every persuasion to write programs for any legitimate purpose to make use of these new storage forms and search mechanisms.

A TECHNICAL DESCRIPTION OF THE XANADU SYSTEM

© 1987 Project Xanadu

The Xanadu system—more properly, the Xanadu network storage engine—is a file-server program for linked compound documents. It is designed to run on a network and manage the update and delivery of document fragments on demand (not just full documents) from anywhere on the network. It operates in write-once mode and thus is especially suited to optical disk storage.

All documents are virtual, not stored in finished form (since there can be many "finished forms"), and assembled on demand as their pieces are requested. Material may be shared between documents with complete information available on its origin and other documents in which the same material is used.

Users requesting parts of these virtual documents need not be aware (but may find out) what documents their fragments originally came from. A request for a long piece of text from the user's workstation may bring back a shower of fragments from the separate documents of origin on different storage machines, which are assembled by the user's front-end program.

Links (separate from text and other data) are used for all demarcation, permitting data to remain uncluttered by special codes. Thus one use of material does not corrupt it for other uses. (For instance, paragraph marks and text attributes are stored as links, so the same text may be marked up many different ways.) Link types are open-ended. Searches of the link data are a specific class of user interaction. Any link to material shared between documents is available to all instances of that shared material.

With respect to any document or fragment, a user may request all other documents linked _from_ it, all other documents linking _to_ it, and all other documents presently containing portions of it.

The back-end program presently runs on a Sun Workstation under UNIX. It is written in C and presently (May '87) compiles to about 137K of 68000 native code on the Sun. This does not include buffer space, of which the more the merrier (1 megabyte and up recommended).

Front-end programs should include our protocol manager, a module which handles sending and receiving in the FEBE™ Front End-Back End protocol. It presently compiles to about 30K on the Sun.

The user operates from a workstation program set up to take advantage of the back end's special facilities. All operations which are not part of the file service are delegated to these workstation programs; these are "front-end functions." Such front-end functions include making bookmarks, keeping track of personal actions at the workstation, etc. Certain audit trailing of each document's modification is maintained automatically. Users may be easily informed about update of a document by various versioning features.

This design has been built with on-line network publishing as a goal. It will be possible to publish documents, links, or associated material on-line with royalties to their owners. These will be fragmentary royalties, automatically paid by the requesting user. Whenever a fragment is sent, a small financial increment will be credited for each byte shipped to the originating owner of that byte.

A WRITE-ONCE UNIVERSAL LINEAR ADDRESS SPACE
THE TUMBLER LINE

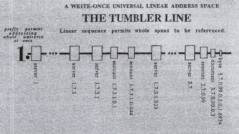

From Literary Machines 87.1

Four tumbler lines may be arrayed into a tumbler square, useful for visualizing both links and search requests. A link has a home in which it resides (the original copy of the link is in its native home); it has a from-set, the spans of bytes from which it links; a to-set, the spans of bytes to which it links; and a type (called for symmetry a three-set), which is some span of the tumbler line which has been assigned an arbitrary "type" meaning. A link request is that part of a FEBE command specifying the spans covering the home-sets, from-sets, to-sets and three-sets to be searched. (This might be a request for a list of links, or for the material actually connected to them.) This too may be mapped to the tumbler square.

TUMBLER ADDRESS
MASTER DIAGRAM

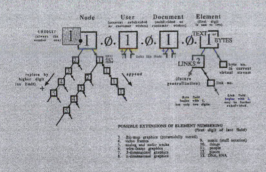

From Literary Machines 87.1.

The Xanadu network address is called a tumbler, which specifies the network node, user, document and element within that document. (A "user" may be a company or a department.) These fields may be subdivided in various ways. All tumblers may be mapped to a sequence called the tumbler line.

LINK AND REQUEST-SET BOTH MAP TO THE TUMBLER SQUARE

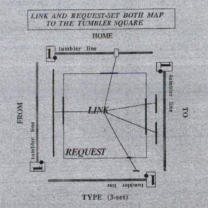

From Literary Machines 87.1

We might think of the system as a database of links connecting addresses in virtual documents. But what makes the problem (and this view) difficult is that all documents remain modifiable even while the links remain correctly attached to their shifting parts.

We expect to extend these linking facilities to all types of data structure; 2D and 3D graphical structures are of particular importance.

These matters are explicated more comfortably and fully in Literary Machines.

☛ Xanadu is self-networking, two on the phone make a network, and more can join.

Important features of the data system are huge addressability (in the trillions of elements) and Virtual Blocklessness.

COMPATIBILITY: because of its highly compacted and unconventional structure, it is *not* compatible with other operating systems (including time-sharing). Anyway, to put it on a larger machine is like having your Mazda driven around in a truck.

LANGUAGES: Xanadu programs will not be made available in any higher languages, mainly because of their proprietary character. The purpose of Xanadu is to furnish the user with uncomputerish good-guy systems for specific purposes, not a chance to do his own programming.

STANDARDIZATION. Taking a lesson from the integrated work of various people whose work has been described in this book, we see that if you want a thing done *right*, you have to do it yourself. (Great Ideas of Western Man: one of a series.)

Several levels of standardization are important with Xanadu. One, all Xanadu systems must be able to work with all Xanadu files (except for possible variations in screen performance and size of local memory). Now, there are those who would *not* be concerned for this sort of universality, and who might even try to make sure systems were *in*compatible, so that you had to buy accessories and conversion kits up and down the line. That is one of the things that must be avoided: "partial" compatibility, subject to expensive options and conditions, a well-known technique in the field.

Second, all Xanadu systems should be able to work with outside systems either through or off the net, *if* they conform to the unusual data rules required by the unusual design of the system. This assures that Xanadu systems will be compatible with any other popular networks. It also assures others who want to offer Xanadu-class services to system owners (through, e.g., conventional time-sharing) that if they adhere to the rules (see "Canons," p. DM 149) they can play the game on a certified basis.

By stabilizing the "Xanadu" trademark, I hope to prevent such shenanigans. Thus every accredited Xanadu system will offer full compatibility with the data structure, and either full performance or substitutes as necessitated by the hardware. The "Xanadu" trademark can in principle be made available to manufacturers abiding by all design features of the system.

AHEM. There is a lot to talk about, but a lot of time can be wasted talking. It is suggested that thoughtful computer firms, interested in some form of participation, study this book carefully—at least enough so no one's time need be wasted.

We're no longer setting dates, but it's going to happen.

Whether the Xanadu system will be available first as a service, or as a complete package for single-user personal computers, depends on whether we get backing in the near term.

So, fans, that about wraps it up. I'll be interested in hearing from people who *want* this system; many hardheaded business people have told me nobody will. Prove 'em wrong, America!

Of course, if hyper-media aren't the greatest thing since the printing press, this whole project falls flat on its face. But it is hard for me to conceive that they will not be.

I would like to thank (in chronological order) Elliot Klugman, Nat ("Kubla") Kuhn, Glenn Babecki, Cal Daniels and John V.E. Ridgway for the considerable time and involvement they gave to the Xanadu program design sessions; thanks also to various others who sat in from time to time.

The official credit line for the present system is: Theodor H. Nelson, William F. Burus, Mark S. Miller, Roger Gregory, Stuart Greene, Eric Hill, Roland King, John V.E. Ridgway and Calvin Daniels.

BIBLIOGRAPHY

Theodor Holm Nelson, *Literary Machines*, edition 87.1, published by the author.

K. Eric Drexler, *Engines of Creation*, Anchor/Doubleday, 1986.

Howard Rheingold, *Tools for Thought*, Simon & Schuster, 1985.

"Nelson's the Name, and What He Proposes Could Outdo Engelbart." *Electronics*, 24 Nov '69, 97.

Is Xanadu worth waiting for? That depends, doesn't it, on the value of the handbush differential bird utility ratio.

▼ ▼ ▼ ▼ ▼ ▼ ▼

Q. How many Xanadu people does it take to change a light bulb?
A. None, that's a front-end function.

Clearing up the problem of computer files, dissolving file boundaries and allowing their free connection and interpenetration, will lead the way to both the office and library of the future. And keeping track of things in open-ended and evolving categories—just the opposite of the "computerish" stereotype—is the most important thing that personal software needs.

Tell the world we're not just ducklings that followed an ice-cream truck.
—Michael Butler, Project Xanadu

What Nelson Is Really Saying

Told so that anybody can understand it without a Ph.D. and maybe some with.

From "Barnum-Tronics" (citation below)

1) Knowledge, understanding and freedom can all be advanced by the promotion and deployment of computer display consoles (with the right programs behind them).

2) Computer presentational media, coming soon, will not be technically determined but rather will be new realms for human artistry. This point of view radically affects how we design man-machine systems of any kind, especially those for information retrieval, teaching, and general writing and reading. Some practitioners see such systems as narrowly technical, with the computer hoisting up little pieces of writing on some "scientific" basis and showing them to you one grunt at a time. A Metrecal banquet. I disagree. The systems should be opulent.

3) The problem in presentational systems of any kind is to make things look good, feel right, and come across clearly. The things that matter are the feel of the system, the user's state of mind, his possible confusion, boredom or enthusiasm, the problems of communicating *concepts*, and the very nature of concepts and their interconnection. There will never be a "science" of presentation, except as it relates to these things.

4) Not the nature of machines, but the nature of ideas, is what matters. It is incredibly hard to develop, organize and transmit ideas, and it always will be. But at least in the future we won't be booby-trapped by the nature of paper. We can design magic paper.

It is time to start using computers to hold information for the mind much as books have held this information in the past. Now information for the mind is very different from "information for the computer" as we have thought of it, hacked up and compressed into blocks. Instead we can stretch the computer.

I am proposing a curious kind of subversion. "Let us design," I say; and when people see the systems, everybody will want one. All I want to do is put Renaissance humanism in a multidimensional responsive console. And I am trying to work out the forms of writing of the future. Hypertexts.

Hypertexts: new forms of writing, appearing on computer screens, that will branch or perform at the reader's command. A hypertext is a non-sequential piece of writing; only the computer display makes it practical. Somewhere between a book, a TV show and a penny arcade, the hypertext can be a vast tapestry of information all in plain English (spiced with a few magic tricks on the screen), which the reader may attack and play for the things he wants, branching and jumping on the screen, using simple controls as if he were driving a car. There can be specialized subparts for specialized interests, instant availability of relevancies in all directions, footnotes that are books themselves. Hypertexts will be so much better than ordinary writing that the printed word will wither away. *Real writing by people*, make no mistake, not data banks, robot summaries or other clank. A person is writing to other people, just as before, but on magical paper he can cut up and tie in knots and fly around on.

(From T. Nelson, "Barnum-Tronics," Swarthmore College Alumni Bulletin, December 1970, p. 12.)

I want a world where we can read the world's literature ____ _____ _____ ____ _____ _____ ___ ___ physical books. A world without routine paperwork, because all copying operations take place automatically and formalized transactions occur through formalized ceremonies at consoles. A world where we can learn, study, create, and share our creations without having privately to schlepp and physically safeguard them. There is a familiar, all-embracing motto, the jingle we all know from the day school lets out, which I take quite seriously: "No more pencils; no more books; no more teachers' dirty looks." The Fantic Age.

From T. Nelson, "Computopia and Cybercrud," in Roger Levien (ed.), *Computers in Instruction*, Rand Corporation, 1971.

Chapter 5

ERKKI HUHTAMO

FROM KALEIDOSCOMANIAC TO CYBERNERD
Towards an archaeology of the media

THIS IS A SUCCINCT BUT influential article. In it, Erkki Huhtamo offers a model and approach for studying the development of media technoculture. Rejecting the widely evident impulse to chart the history of technical innovation in a straightforward chronological account of inventions, he proposes instead what he calls an archaeological method.

On the one hand his media archaeology simply recognises broader trends in historical research in recent decades, trends that insist on the social and cultural contexts of historical events and developments. In this sense, his approach is similar to that of Carolyn **Marvin** (whom he quotes here). For example, he argues that the 'invention' of television as the broadcast medium we know today was not a historical inevitability. There were in the nineteenth century, for example, other predictions of how 'far-seeing' media might facilitate one-to-one communication over great distances. Today's dominant model (albeit a model that is currently challenged by Internet distribution of moving images) was shaped as much by political, economic and cultural factors as by the innate possibilities of the various technologies that constitute, or could have constituted, television.

On the other hand, and more radically, Huhtamo presents a model of media technological history that is non-chronological and even 'cyclical'. He notes the remarkable similarity of contemporaneous accounts of audience responses to diverse and unconnected media technological spectacles across the nineteenth and twentieth centuries, from kaleidoscopes to stereoscopes in the early to mid-nineteenth century to virtual reality and theme parks in the early 1990s (see also **Klein**). For Huhtamo this triggers a sense of *déjà vu*, as newspaper cartoons and reports of these new experiences across the centuries share a fascination with the rapt immersion of hapless viewers in these all-encompassing machines and their images.

The emphasis here is on the ephemera that attends these new media experiences: cartoons, promotional literature, newspaper reports, not the actual technologies nor the responses of audiences at the time. This is partly due to the difficulties of recovering these events, events which could not of course be recorded on video or audiotape. However, it is also due to Huhtamo's insistence on the discursive construction of new technologies. Ideological factors not only shape the adoption and uses of particular devices at particular historical moments, they also generate what he calls 'dream machines'. These speculative devices (sometimes in SF literature, sometimes the product of over-optimistic marketing) may never be realised, but,

Huhtamo argues, through their ideological circulation, they 'imprint' the development of new technologies and systems. The reader may find it interesting to compare this last assertion, that 'the reality of media history lies primarily in the discourses that guide and mold its development, rather than in the "things" and "artifacts" that [...] form the core around which everything (r)evolves' with the debates and arguments set out in Part Two of this book: debates about the nature of causality and determination in technoculture. Or, the reader might find it amusing to accept Huhtamo's suggestion that we apply his archaeological approach to the more recent phenomenon of virtual reality. This article was written at the height of excited speculation (and anxious misgivings) about VR, but younger readers may have only the faintest sense of that excitement. How might, say, the players of massively multiplayer online games or denizens of virtual worlds such as Second Life be understood in relation to the cybernerd of the VR dream machine, or the kaleidoscomaniac?

In his classic exposé of the "archaeology of the cinema," C.W. Ceram puts the prehistory of motion pictures straight. He states that

> knowledge of automatons, or of clockwork toys, played no part in the story of cinematography, nor is there any link between it and the production of animated 'scenes.' We can therefore omit plays, the baroque automatons, and the marionette theatre. Even the 'deviltries' of Porta, produced with the camera obscura, the phantasmagorias of Robertson, the 'dissolving views' of Child, are not to the point. All these discoveries did not lead to the first genuine moving picture sequence.[1]

In another paragraph, Ceram elaborates on his position: "What matters in history is not whether certain chance discoveries take place, but whether they take effect".[2]

Curiously, the profuse illustrations collected by Olive Cook for the English language edition (1965) openly contradict these statements. Plenty of "chance discoveries" have been included, supported by meticulously prepared captions. No doubt, for many readers this polyphonic array of curious traces of the past remains the truly exciting aspect of the book, not Ceram's pedantic attempts to trace one by one the steps that led to the emergence of cinema at the end of the nineteenth century.[3] The writer's primary focus is on the narrowly causal relationships that supposedly guided the development of moving-image technology. Tracing the fates of the personalities who made this happen comes next; other factors matter little. The reasoning is matter-of-fact and positivistic. Ceram never ventures upon speculations rising above the materiality of his sources.

The illustrations in Ceram's book, as well as the historical collections on display at such wonderful places as the Frankfurt Film Museum, can, however, be persuaded to tell very different stories, full of intriguing possibilities. As French historian Marc Bloch taught, our conception of the past depends on the kind of questions we ask.[4] Any source—be it a detail of a picture or a part of a machine—can be useful if we approach it from a relevant perspective. There is no trace of the past that does not have its story to tell. Another historian with a comparable attitude towards historical sources was, of course, Walter Benjamin, who (according to Susan Buck-Morss) "took seriously the debris of mass culture as the source of philosophical truth".[5] For Benjamin (particularly in his unfinished "Passagen-Werk") the various remains of nineteenth-century culture—buildings, technologies and commodities, but also illustrations and literary texts—served as inscriptions that could lead us to understand the ways in which a culture perceived itself and conceptualized the "deeper" ideological layers of its construction. As Tom Gunning puts it, "[i]f Benjamin's method is fully understood, technology can reveal the dream world of society as much as its pragmatic rationalization".[6]

Continuing the Benjaminian tradition, German cultural historian Wolfgang Schievelbusch has shown us how a broad concept of history can be used to shed light not only on the topic in question—the railway, artificial lighting, stimulants—but on the ways in which artifacts are embedded in the complex discursive fabrics and patterns reigning in a culture. From a predominantly chronological and positivistic ordering of things centered on the artifact, the emphasis is shifting into treating history as a multi-layered construct, a dynamic system of relationships. Such a shift can also be detected in the field of media studies. Tom Gunning, Siegfried Zielinski, Carolyn Marvin, Avital Ronell, Susan J. Douglas, Lynn Spiegel, Cecelia Tichi, William Boddy and others have recently researched the histories of media technologies such as telephone, film, radio and television by (re)placing them in their cultural and discursive contexts.[7]

This new media history clearly distances itself from the, "objectivist fallacy" of the positivist tradition, admitting that history is basically just another discourse, a voice in the great chorus of voices in a society. Historians have begun to acknowledge that they cannot be free of the web of ideological discourses constantly surrounding and affecting them.[8] In this sense, history belongs to the present as much as it belongs to the past. It cannot claim an objective status; it can only become conscious of its ambiguous role as a mediator and a "meaning processor" operating between the present and the past (and, arguably, the future). Instead of purporting to belong to the realm of infallible truth (with religion and the Constitution), historical writing is emerging as a conversational discipline, a way of negotiating with the past.[9]

In line with this development, I would like make a few preliminary remarks about an approach I call "media archaeology".[10] While I share with many interests with new historicist tendencies, emphasizing a synthetic, multi-perspective and cross disciplinary approach and historical discourse analysis, I see the aims of media archaeology in a more specific focus. I would like to propose it as a way of studying recurring cyclical phenomena that (re)appear and disappear and reappear over and over again in media history, somehow seeming to transcend specific historical contexts. In a way, the aim of this media archaeology is to explain the sense of déjà vu that Tom Gunning has registered when looking back from present reactions to the ways in which people have experienced technology in earlier periods.[11]

Fantasmagorie, *La Ciotat, and Captain EO*

In the Frankfurt Film Museum, in a display case with different samples of nineteenth-century kaleidoscopes, there is an engraving titled *La Kaleidoscomanie ou les Amateurs de bijoux Anglais* ("Kaleidoscomania, or the Lovers of English Jewels"), presumably dating from the first part of the nineteenth century. We see several people (and, indeed, a monkey!) immersed in their kaleidoscopes.[12] There are two "kaleidoscomaniacs" so mesmerized by the visions they see inside the "picture tube" that they do not even notice that other men are courting their companions behind their backs. When stereography became a fad in the 1850s, the same motif soon began to appear in stereographic photographs depicting humorously the less salutary effects of the new fashion.[13] The effect is the same, the only difference being that for the "stereoscomaniac" the immersion is "total": the eyepiece of the stereoscope covers both of the viewer's eyes, as if drawing him or her into a three-dimensional field of vision.[14]

Recalling the convictions of C.W. Ceram outlined above, we could wonder if these occurrences are just "chance discoveries" with no causal relationship and thus no historical interest. And is it only chance that leads us to the discovery that the current revival of immersive peepshow-like experience in the form of the virtual-reality craze has again brought forth the figure of the kaleidoscomaniac—this time in the disguise of the "cybernerd," whose passion for the other world makes him or her a fool in this one? The figure has already made its appearance in the cinema and in satirical cartoons, as well as on Music Television—just recall the animated figures Beavis and Butt-Head in their head-mounted displays performing the song "I Got You Babe" with (real-life) popular singer Cher.

Here is another example: according to C.W. Ceram, there is no historical connection between Étienne Gaspard Robertson's *Fantasmagorie* shows, begun in Paris at the very end of the eighteenth century, and the Lumière brothers' *Cinématographe* presentations a century later. Even the use of the *lanterna magica* principle for projecting the images on a screen does not, for Ceram, provide sufficient grounds to warrant positing a relationship.[15] However, if we compare contemporary illustrations of *Fantasmagorie* audiences' panicky reactions to ghosts attacking them from the screen with reports of early cinema audiences fleeing in terror when the train in the Lumière film *L'Arrivée d'un train à La Ciotat* (1895) seemed to rush straight onto them, we probably cannot avoid a sense of déjà vu.[16] For someone who has visited Disneyland, for example, an association that might come to mind is the stereoscopic movie spectacle *Captain EO*, featuring Michael Jackson. The "onslaughting" aspect of this film has been enhanced by laserbeams (in addition to the customary 3-D effects), which are released as if from the screen world to the audience space.[17] Even though the audience may not have reacted very vividly on the spot, the publicity, the media and the contemporary oral traditions retelling the theme park experience make sure they did.[18]

Again, we may ask if there is any sense in looking for connecting links between these occurrences, which are wide apart in time and space. I would like to claim that these parallels are not totally random coincidences produced indigenously by conglomerations of specific circumstances. Instead, all these cases "contain" certain commonplace elements or cultural motives that have been encountered in earlier cultural processes. I would like to propose that such motives could usefully be treated as *topoi,* or "topics," applying to the field of media studies the ideas that Ernst Robert Curtius used in his massive study *Europäische Literatur und lateinisches Mittelalter* (European Literature and the Latin Middle Ages) (1948) to explain the internal life of literary traditions.[19]

The idea of *topoi* goes back to the rhetorical traditions of classical antiquity. According to Quintilianus, they were "storehouses of trains of thought" (*argumentorum sedes*), systematically organized formulas serving a practical purpose—namely, the composition of orations. As the classical rhetoric gradually lost its original meaning and purpose, the formulas penetrated into literary genres. According to Curtius, "[t]hey become clichés, which can be used in any form of literature, they spread to all spheres of life with which literature deals and to which it gives form".[20] Topics can be considered formulas, ranging from stylistic to allegorical, that make up the "building blocks" of cultural traditions; they are activated and deactivated in turn; new *topoi* are created along the way and old ones (at least seemingly) vanish. In a sense, topics provide "pre-fabricated" molds for experience. Even though they may emerge as if "unconsciously," they are, however, always cultural, and thus ideological, constructs. This is my main objection to Curtius, who sometimes resorted to Jungian archetypes to explain the appearance of certain *topoi*.[21] In the era of commercial and industrial media culture, it is increasingly important to note that *topoi* can be consciously activated and ideologically and commercially exploited.

Discursive inventions as an object of study

When we deal with *topoi* such as the one related to the stereotypical reactions of panic upon viewing a media spectacle, we deal with representations instead of actual experiences; we do not (and perhaps never will) know if any audience ever reacted to a *Fantasmagorie* or a *Cinématographe* presentation in the ways depicted in visual or literary discourses. Claiming that they did would be beside the point. The interesting thing is precisely the recurrence of the *topoi* within these discourses. It could be claimed that the reality of media history lies primarily in the discourses that guide and mold its development, rather than in the "things" and "artifacts" that, for writers like Ceram, form the core around which everything (r)evolves.

In this respect, I share Michel Foucault's determination "[t]o substitute for the enigmatic treasure of 'things' anterior to discourse, the regular formation of objects that emerge only in discourse"[22]. These "discursive objects" can, with good reason, claim a central place in the study of the history of media culture. Even though Foucault referred to media systems only casually, a related strategy has been adopted by Friedrich Kittler in his *Discourse Networks 1800/1900*, in which he traces the gradual shift from one discursive system to another, drawing on a great variety of inscriptions.[23] As David E. Wellberg has noted,

> Kittler's discourse analysis follows the Foucauldian lead in that it seeks to delineate the apparatuses of power, storage, transmission, training, reproduction, and so forth to make up the conditions of factual discursive occurrences.[24]

Instead of pursuing a systematic study of Foucauldian "discursive formations"—ideological traditions of discourses reigning in society that are based on the interplay of power and knowledge—the approach I am delineating is actually closer to the field characterized by Foucault somewhat contemptuously as the history of ideas,

> the history of those age-old themes that are never crystallized in a rigorous and individual system, but which have formed the spontaneous philosophy of those who did not philosophize. . . . The analysis of opinions rather than of knowledge, of errors rather than of truth, of types of mentality rather than of forms of thought.[25]

Registering false starts, seemingly ephemeral phenomena and anecdotes about media can sometimes be more revealing than tracing the fates of machines that were patented, industrially fabricated and widely distributed in the society—let alone the lives of their creators—if our focus is on the meanings that emerge through the social practices related to the use of technology. I agree with cultural historian of technology Carolyn Marvin when she writes that

> [m]edia are not fixed objects: they have no natural edges. They are constructed complexes of habits, beliefs, and procedures embedded in elaborate cultural codes of communication. The history of media is never more or less than the history of their uses, which always lead us away from them to the social practices and conflicts they illuminate.[26]

From such a point of view, unrealized "dream machines," or discursive inventions (inventions that exist only as discourses), can be just as revealing as realized artifacts. A case in point, the telectroscope was a discursive invention that was widely believed to exist in the late nineteenth century. It was an electro-optical device that was supposed to enable an individual to "increase the range of vision by hundreds of miles, so that, for instance, a man in New York could see the features of his friend in Boston with as much ease as he could see the performance on the stage".[27] Articles about the device were published in respected popular scientific journals such as *La Nature* and *The Electrical Review*; there were even claims that Edison had invented it. Time and again it was announced that it would be presented to the general audience at the next world's fair. Yet the telectroscope never made an appearance except in these discourses, which were widely distributed throughout the industrialized Western world.

The telectroscope can be interpreted simply as a utopian projection of the hopes raised by electricity and, particularly, by the telephone, which were realized decades later in the form of television. It should not, however, be discarded so easily. Television found its dominant form in broadcasting, which was very different from the role offered for the telectroscope as a "tele-vision machine" meant for active person-to-person communication. Jaron Lanier's utopian vision of virtual reality (VR) "as the telephone, not as the television of the future" can thus be seen as another incarnation of a *topos* well known more than a hundred years earlier.[28] It remains to be seen if Lanier's discursive version of VR will ever be realized, or if the rudimentary technology that inspired it will finally be molded into a form closer to the economically and ideologically constrained structures of broadcast television than to those of telecommunication.[29] The discursive formations that enveloped and molded the emergence of VR technology around the turn of the 1980s and 1990s would provide an appropriate subject of study for the kind of an approach I have been trying to delineate.

To sum up, it seems to me that the media-archaeological approach has two main goals: first is the study of the cyclically recurring elements and motives underlying and guiding the development of media culture. Second is the "excavation" of the ways in which these discursive traditions and formulations have been "imprinted" on specific media machines and systems in different historical contexts, contributing to their identity in terms of socially and ideologically specific webs of signification. This kind of approach emphasizes cyclical rather than chronological development and recurrence rather than unique innovation. In doing so, it runs counter to the customary way of thinking about technoculture in terms of a constant progress proceeding from one technological breakthrough to another and making earlier machines and applications obsolete along the way. The aim of the media archaeological approach is not to negate the "reality" of technological development, but rather to balance it by placing it within a wider and more multifaceted social and cultural frame of reference.

Notes

Manuscript received 28 April 1995.

Erkki Huhtamo (curator, media scholar), Yliopistonkatu 39–41 C 63, SF20100 Turku, Finland. E-mail: <erhuhta@utu.fi>.

Manuscript originally presented at the Fifth International Symposium on Electronic Art (ISEA 94) in Helsinki, Finland, 20–25 August 1994.

This article was published previously in Timothy Druckrey, ed., *Electronic Culture: Technology and Visual Representation* (New York: Aperture, 1997).

1   C.W. Ceram, *Archaeology of Cinema*, Richard Winston, trans. (London: Thames & Hudson, 1965) p. 17.
2   Ceram (n61) p.16.
3   This purpose is served much better by Franz Paul Liesegang's equally classic chronology of the prehistory of the cinema, *Dates and Sources: A Contribution to the History of the Art of Projection and to Cinematography*, Hermann Hecht, trans. and ed. (London: The Magic Lantern Society of Great Britain, 1986; originally

published in German in 1926). Another, more recent attempt at historical chronology has been made by Maurice Bessy in his *Le mystère de la chambre noire. Histoire de la projection animée* (Paris: Editions Pygmalion, 1990). Bessy's year-by-year account incorporates plenty of hard-to-find documents illuminating the "discursive" side of the prehistory of the cinema—the attitudes, fears and hopes of contemporaries.

4   Marc Bloch, *The Historian's Craft*, Peter Putnam, trans. (Manchester: Manchester Univ. Press, 1954; originally published in French, 1949).

5   Susan Buck-Morss, The Dialectics of Seeing: Walter Benjamin and the Arcades Project (Cambridge, MA: MIT Press, 1989) p. ix.

6   Tom Gunning, "Heard Over the Phone: The Lonely Villa and the de Lorde Tradition of the Terrors of Technology," *Screen* 32, No. 2, 185 (Summer 1991).

7   See Gunning (n66); Siegfried Zielinski, *Audiovisionen. Kino und Fernsehen als Zwischenspiel in der Geschichte*, Reinbek bei (Hamburg: Rowohlt, 1989); Avital Ronell, *The Telephone Book: Technology, Schizophrenia, Electric Speech* (Lincoln, NE: Univ. of Nebraska Press, 1989); Carolyn Marvin, *When Old Technologies Were New: Thinking About Electric Communication in the Late Nineteenth Century* (New York and Oxford: Oxford Univ. Press, 1988); Susan J. Douglas, *Inventing American Broadcasting 1899–1922* (Baltimore and London: The Johns Hopkins Univ. Press, 1987); Lynn Spiegel, *Make Room for TV: Television and the Family Ideal in Postwar America* (Chicago and London: The Univ. of Chicago Press, 1992); Cecelia Tichi, *Electronic Hearth: Creating an American Television Culture* (New York and Oxford: Oxford University Press, 1991); William Boddy, "Electronic Vision: Genealogies and Gendered Technologies," paper presented at the Finnish Society for Cinema Studies Conference, Helsinki, January 1993 (unpublished).

8   For a brilliant analysis of historical writing as a discursive practice, see Hayden White's *Metahistory: The Historical Imagination in Nineteenth Century Europe* (Baltimore, MD: The Johns Hopkins Univ. Press, 1973).

9   Benjamin's influence can also be detected behind this emphasis. According to Susan Buck-Morss's interpretation, in *Passagen-Werk* he aimed at writing a "'materialist philosophy of history' constructed with 'the utmost concreteness' out of the historical material itself. . . . As the 'ur-phenomena' of modernity, they were to provide the material necessary for an interpretation of history's most recent configurations." Buck-Morss (n65) p. 3.

10 Other media scholars have used this concept as well, according to their own definitions. See, for example, Siegfried Zielinski, "Medienarchaeologie. In der Suchbewugung nach den unterschiedlichen Ordnungen des Visionierens," *EIKON* No. 9 (Vienna, 1994) pp. 32–35.

11 Gunning (n66) p. 185.

12 The kaleidoscope was invented by British scientist Sir David Brewster in 1815 or 1816; his "Treatise on the Kaleidoscope" was published in 1819.

13 For a general history of stereography, see William C. Darrah, *The World of Stereographs* (Gettysburg, PA: W.C. Darrah, 1977).

14 See the anonymous stereograph dating from the 1860s reproduced on a View Master reel (Reel X, image 5) included as an annex to Wim van Keulen, *3D Imagics. A Stereoscopic Guide to the 3D Past and its Magic Images 1838–1900* (The Netherlands: AA Borger 3-D Book Productions, 1990). For another manifestation of the same motive, see the stereogram visible on the table in Ceram (n61) p. 112.

15 The film projector is basically a modified *lanterna magica* in which the transparent glass slides have been replaced by slide film. Making the film move in front of the lens required a machinery that derived from clockwork mechanisms as well as from revolvers and machine guns.

16 Two illustrations showing audience reactions, said to date from 1797 and 1798, appear in Ceram (n61) (p. 38). The reaction to the Lumière film may be a purely discursive creation. There are scattered remarks that attest to this possibility. In an article about his first viewing of a *Cinématographe* show (published in the journal *Nijegorodskilistok,* 4 July 1896), Russian writer Maxim Gorki mentioned that "it had been said that it [the train] will rush straight into the obscurity where we are," but he reported having been disappointed. The image of the train rushing towards the audience was featured in early Lumière posters and sketches. See Emmanuelle Toulet, *Cinématographe, invention du siècle* (Paris: Gallimard, 1988) pp. 11 and 14. The motif also appeared in early films about a fool who cannot tell the difference between reality and illusion in the cinema, such as *The Countryman and the Cinematograph* (R.W. Paul, 1901).

17 While paying attention to similarities, we should not try to explain away differences: *Fantasmagorie* was connected with the tradition of magic shows, with the fascination of the show being in the unexplained quality of the tricks. In the case of the Lumière screenings, the *Cinématographe* as a technical novelty was an important aspect of the appeal of the show. Thus, the projector was kept visible for the audience,

whereas Robertson's magic lanterns were hidden from sight. Yet Charles Musser's observation that "Robertson's remarks [in his Mémoires] played on the simultaneous realization that the projected image was only an image and yet one that the spectator believed was real" may apply to Lumière's (early) audiences as well. See Charles Musser, *The Emergence of Cinema: The American Screen to 1907*, Part 1 of *The History of the American Cinema* (New York: Charles Scribner's Sons, 1990) p. 24.

18   A 1993 promotional video for the Showscan Corporation, a company producing and marketing specialty cinemas, opens with a simulated theater sequence in which wind, smoke, water, fire, a fish and even a UFO are "thrown" from the screen into the audience space. The audience reactions show pleasure rather than terror.

19   Ernst Robert Curtius, *European Literature and the Latin Middle Ages*, Willard R. Trask, trans. (London: Routledge and Kegan Paul, 1979; originally published in German, 1948).

20   Curtius (n79) p. 70.

21   "[An allegorical figure in Balzac's *Jésus-Christ en Flandre* (1831)] is only comprehensible by the fact that it is rooted in the deeper strata of the soul. It belongs to the stock of archaic proto-images in the collective unconscious." Curtius (n79) p. 105.

22   Michel Foucault, *The Archaeology of Knowledge*, A.M. Sheridan Smith, trans. (London: Tavistock, 1982) p. 47.

23   Friedrich Kittler, *Discourse Networks 1800/1900*, Michael Metteer with Chris Cullens, trans. (Stanford, CA: Stanford Univ. Press, 1990).

24   David E. Wellberg, preface to Kittler (n83) p. xii.

25   Kittler (n83) pp. 136–137.

26   Marvin (n67) p. 8.

27   *Electrical Review* (25 May 1889) p. 6, cited in Marvin (n67) p. 197.

28   See John Perry Barlow, "Life in a Data-Cloud: Discussion with Jaron Lanier," *Mondo 2000* No. 2, p. 29.

29   A model for this could be the Sega Channel, an interactive all-video-game cable television channel that was to be launched in the United States in 1995 but has not yet been realized (as of February 1997). Sega may adopt its already-introduced head-mounted display for home use as an interface for both individual and collective game playing via its channel.

Chapter 6

MANUEL DE LANDA

INTRODUCTION TO *WAR IN THE AGE OF INTELLIGENT MACHINES*

I N THIS INTRODUCTION to his book on the history of warfare and automated technology the philosopher Manuel De Landa offers us a thought experiment to fundamentally rethink the relationship between human culture and technologies.

Artificial intelligence and artificial life (see **Wise**, **Kember**) are not (yet) sufficiently sophisticated to have given birth to the autonomous machines and intelligent self-acting robots familiar from science fiction. Yet, De Landa adopts a strategy that asks us to view the history of technology from a new position. He asks us to imagine a future generation of 'killer robots' emerging from ongoing military research into AI. He speculates that such an intelligent species might well wish to consider their own historical origins and technological lineage. In writing such a history, these robot historians would find a different role for the human than we human beings have given ourselves in our own narratives. Key elements in the robotic historian's account would include the way in which technological developments have not always been guided by human needs but at crucial times have, conversely, demanded changes in human forms of organisation and behaviour. Rather than inventors, designers and users of tools, with respect to the computer the human species might credibly be seen as the midwives of a new life form, or (echoing Marshall **McLuhan**) as 'industrious insects pollinating an independent species of machine flowers that simply did not possess its own reproductive organs during a segment of its evolution'. Equally, they would have a vital interest in the way that computers (themselves) have facilitated scientific enquiry into the self-organizing behaviour and deep patterns now thought to exist in non-organic matter as well as the more familiar forms of organic life studied by biology. In this manner we are introduced to Gilles Deleuze and Félix **Guattari**'s concept of the 'machinic phylum'.

Annotated bibliography for Manuel de Landa: http://www.cddc.vt.edu/host/delanda/

The image of the "killer robot" once belonged uniquely to the world of science fiction. This is still so, of course, but only if one thinks of human-like mechanical contraptions scheming to conquer the planet. The latest weapons systems planned by the Pentagon, however, offer a less anthropomorphic example of what machines with "predatory capabilities" might be like: pilotless aircraft and unmanned tanks "intelligent" enough to be able to select and destroy their own targets. Although the existing prototypes of robotic weapons, like the PROWLER or the BRAVE 3000, are not yet truly autonomous, these new weapons do demonstrate that even if Artificial Intelligence is not at present sufficiently sophisticated to create true "killer robots," when synthetic intelligence *does* make its appearance on the planet, there will already be a predatory role awaiting it.

The PROWLER, for example, is a small terrestrial armed vehicle, equipped with a primitive form of "machine vision" (the capability to analyze the contents of a video frame) that allows it to maneuver around a battlefield and distinguish friends from enemies. Or at least this is the aim of the robot's designers. In reality, the PROWLER still has difficulty negotiating sharp turns or maneuvering over rough terrain, and it also has poor friend/foe recognition capabilities. For these reasons it has been deployed only for very simple tasks, such as patrolling a military installation along a predefined path. We do not know whether the PROWLER has ever opened fire on an intruder without human supervision, but it is doubtful that as currently designed this robot has been authorized to kill humans on its own. More likely, the TV camera that serves as its visual sensor is connected to a human operator, and the intelligent processing capabilities of the robot are used at the "advisory" and not the "executive" level. For now, the robot simply makes the job of its human remote-controller easier by preprocessing some of the information itself, or even by making and then relaying a preliminary assessment of events within its visual field.

But it is precisely the distinction between advisory and executive capabilities that is being blurred in other military applications of Artificial Intelligence (AI). Perhaps the best example of the fading differences between a purely advisory and an executive role for computers may be drawn from the area of war games. In the war games of the recent past computers played the role of intelligent assistants: human players made decisions affecting the movements and actions of "troops" in the game, while computers calculated the effect of a given attack, using such concepts as a weapon's "lethality index," the rate of advance of tactical units, the relative strength of a given defensive posture or the effectiveness of a specific offensive maneuver.

Since their invention in the early nineteenth century, war games have allowed human participants to gain strategic insights and have given officers the opportunity to acquire "battle experience" in the absence of a real war. This function has become even more important in the case of nuclear war, a type of war that has never been fought and for which there is no other way of training. But in game after game human players have proven reluctant to cross the nuclear threshold. They typically attempt every possible negotiation before pushing the fateful button. This has led war-game designers to create new versions of this technology in which automata completely replace human players: SAM and IVAN, as these robots are called, do not have any problem triggering World War III. To the extent that the "insights" derived from watching automata fight simulated armageddons actually find their way into strategic doctrine and contingency plans, these "robot events" have already begun to blur the distinction between a purely advisory and an executive role for intelligent machines.

Now indeed robotic intelligence will find its way into military technology in different ways and at different speeds. Traditional computer applications to warfare (radar systems, radio networks for Control, Command and Communications, navigation and guidance devices for missiles), will become "smarter" following each breakthrough in AI. Mechanical intelligence will once again "migrate" into offensive and defensive weaponry as AI creates new ways for machines to "learn" from experience, to plan problem-solving strategies at different levels of complexity and even to acquire some "common sense" in order to eliminate irrelevant details from consideration. But we need not imagine full-fledged, human-like robots replacing soldiers in the battlefield, or robotic commanders replacing human judgment in the planning and conducting of military operations. These two technologies (autonomous weapons and battle management systems) were indeed announced by the Pentagon as two key goals for military research in the 1980s and '90s. But this announcement, made in a 1984 document entitled "Strategic Computing," was as much a public relations maneuver as it was an indication of the military roles that AI will one day come to play.

If we disregard for a moment the fact that robotic intelligence will probably not follow the anthropomorphic line of development prepared for it by science fiction, we may without much difficulty imagine a future generation of killer robots dedicated to understanding their historical origins. We may even imagine specialized "robot historians" committed to tracing the various technological lineages that gave rise to their species. And we could further imagine that such a robot historian would write a different kind of history than would its human counterpart. While a human historian might try to understand the way people assembled clockworks, motors and other physical contraptions, a robot historian would likely place a stronger emphasis on the way these machines affected human evolution. The robot would stress the fact that when clockworks once represented the dominant technology on the planet, people imagined the world around them as a similar system of cogs and wheels. The solar system, for instance, was pictured right up until the nineteenth century as just such a clockwork mechanism, that is, as a motorless system animated by God from the outside. Later, when motors came along, people began to realize that many natural systems behave more like motors: they run on an external reservoir of resources and exploit the labor performed by circulating flows of matter and energy.

The robot historian of course would hardly be bothered by the fact that it was a human who put the first motor together: for the role of humans would be seen as little more than that of industrious insects pollinating an independent species of machine-flowers that simply did not possess its own reproductive organs during a segment of its evolution. Similarly, when this robot historian turned its attention to the evolution of armies in order to trace the history of its own weaponry, it would see humans as no more than pieces of a larger military-industrial machine: a war machine. The assembling of these machines would have been, from this point of view, influenced by certain "machinic paradigms" that were prevalent at the time. The armies of Frederick the Great, for instance, could be pictured as one gigantic "clockwork" mechanism, employing mercenaries as its cogs and wheels. In a similar way, Napoleon's armies could be viewed as a "motor" running on a reservoir of populations and nationalist feelings.

Nor would robot historians need to ascribe an essential role to great commanders, for these might be seen as mere catalysts for the self-assembly of war machines. Such assemblages, the robot would say, were influenced no more by particular individuals than by collective forces, such as the demographic turbulence caused by migrations, crusades and invasions. Moreover, our historian would notice that some of its "machinic ancestors," like the conoidal bullet of the nineteenth century, resisted human control for over a hundred years. It simply took that long for human commanders to integrate rifled firepower into an explicit tactical doctrine. Since then, of course, the conoidal bullet has lived a life of its own as one of the most lethal inhabitants of the battlefield. In this sense technological development may be said to possess its own momentum, for clearly it is not always guided by human needs. As the simple case of the conoidal bullet illustrates, a given technology may even force humans to redefine their needs: the accuracy of the new projectile forced commanders to give up their need to exert total control over their men by making them fight in tight formations, and to replace it with more flexible "mission-oriented" tactics, in which only the goal is specified in advance, leaving the means to attain it to the initiative of small teams of soldiers (platoons).

When our robot historian switched its attention from weapons to computers, it would certainly also seek to emphasize the role of non-human factors in their evolution. It would, for example, recognize that the logical structures of computer hardware were once incarnated in the human body in the form of empirical problem-solving recipes. These recipes, collectively known as "heuristics" (from the Greek work for "discovery," related to the word "eureka"), include rules of thumb and shortcuts discovered by trial and error, useful habits of mind developed through experience, and tricks of the trade passed on from one generation of problem-solvers to the next. Some of the valuable insights embodied in heuristic know-how may then be captured into a general purpose, "infallible" problem-solving recipe (known as an "algorithm"). When this happens we may say that logical structures have "migrated" from the human body to the rules that make up a logical notation (the syllogism, the class calculus), and from there to electromechanical switches and circuits. From the robot's point of view, what is important is precisely this "migration" and not the people involved in effecting it. Thus, the robot would also stress the role of other such migrations, like the migration across different physical scales that carried logical structures over from vacuum tubes to transistors, and then to integrated chips of ever-increasing density and decreasing size. These two migrations would constitute an essential component of the history of the robot's body, or in the language more proper to it, of its hardware.

[. . .]

[C]omputers have not only become powerful instruments of oppression in the hands of military and paramilitary agencies: they have also opened new windows onto the creative processes of nature. In the last thirty years, for instance, computers have allowed scientists to investigate the mathematical foundations of natural processes of self-organization. These are processes in which order emerges spontaneously out of chaos. Certain natural phenomena once thought to lack any structure, like the turbulent flow of a fast-moving liquid, have now been found to possess an extremely intricate molecular organization. Because the coordination of billions of molecules needed to produce eddies and vortices in a fluid appears suddenly and without any apparent cause, turbulence is now regarded as a process of self-organization. Similarly, certain chemical phenomena once thought to be unrealizable in nature, like the spontaneous assembly of "chemical clocks" (chemical reactions that follow perfect oscillatory rhythms or cycles), have now been found to be an essential component of the machinery of the planet.

The self-organizing processes studied by the science of "order out of chaos" (or "chaos," for short) have indeed changed the way scientists view inorganic matter. While at one time only biological phenomena were considered to be relevant for a study of evolution, now inert matter has been found to be capable of generating structures that may be subjected to natural selection. It is as if we had discovered a form of "non-organic life." With this in mind, I have borrowed from the philosopher Gilles Deleuze the concept of the "machinic phylum," the term he coined to refer to the overall set of self-organizing processes in the universe. These include all processes in which a group of previously disconnected elements suddenly reaches a critical point at which they begin to "cooperate" to form a higher level entity. To provide a clearer idea of what these processes of spontaneous "cooperative behavior" are, consider a few examples: the individual spin of atoms in a metal "cooperate" to make the metal magnetic; the individual molecules in a chemical reaction "cooperate" to create the perfectly rhythmic patterns of a chemical clock; the cells making up an amoeba colony "cooperate" under certain conditions to assemble an organism with differentiated organs; and the different termites in a colony "cooperate" to build a nest. On the face of it, there would be no reason to assume that processes as different as these could be related at a deeper level. But recent advances in experimental mathematics have shown that the onset of all these processes may be described by essentially the same mathematical model. It is as if the principles that guide the self-assembly of these "machines" (e.g., chemical clocks, multicellular organisms or nest-building insect colonies) are at some deep level essentially similar.

This conclusion, that behind self-organization there is a "machinic phylum," that behind the spontaneous emergence of order out of chaos there are deep mathematical similarities, would hardly escape the notice of our hypothetical robot historian. After all, the emergence of "robot consciousness" could have been the result of such a process of self-organization. Such processes, as we will see, have in fact been observed in large computer networks (and in small neural nets). Furthermore, the notion of a machinic phylum blurs the distinction between organic and non-organic life, which is just what a robot historian would like to do. From its point of view, as we have seen, humans would have served only as machines' surrogate reproductive organs until robots acquired their own self-replication capabilities. But both human and robot bodies would ultimately be related to a common phylogenetic line: the machinic phylum.

Order emerges out of chaos, the robot would notice, only at certain critical points in the flow of matter and energy: when a critical point in the concentration of a chemical is reached, the termite colony becomes a "nest-building" machine; when available food reaches a (minimum) critical value, the amoebas self-assemble into an organism; when critical points in the rate of reaction and diffusion are reached, molecules spontaneously come together to form a chemical clock; and at a critical point in speed, the random flow of a moving liquid gives way to the intricately ordered patterns of turbulence. Robotic, or machinic, history would stress the role of these thresholds (of speed, temperature, pressure, chemical concentration, electric charge) in the development of technology. Human artisans would be pictured as tapping into the resources of self-organizing processes in order to create particular lineages of technology.

The robot historian would see a gunsmith, for instance, as "tracking" those critical points in metals and explosives, and channeling the processes that are spontaneously set into motion to form a particular weapon technology. A gunsmith must track and exploit the melting points of various metals as well as their points of crystallization. These two are critical points in temperature. He must also determine the critical point of pressure at which black powder explodes, the detonation point of fulminates and the threshold of spin after which a rotating bullet acquires coherent aerodynamic capabilities. It is as if humans (and evolution in general) selected a few of those critical points at the onset of self-organization, and channeled them into a particular (natural or artificial) technology. Just as we see the animal kingdom as the place where evolution "experimented" to create our own sensory and locomotive machinery, so our robot historian would see processes in which order emerges out of chaos as its own true ancestors, with human artisans playing the role of historically necessary "channelers" for the machinic phylum's "creativity."

Still, it is easier to say what the machinic phylum is not, than to specify precisely what it is. It is not a life-force, since the phylum is older than life, and yet it constitutes a form of non-organic life. It is not an eternal reservoir of platonic essences either, since, it will be argued, the machinic phylum is assembled piecemeal in evolutionary and historical time. Furthermore, the effects set into motion when a particular critical point is reached are not always "creative" in any obvious sense. For instance, a turbulent flow is made out of a hierarchy of eddies and vortices nested inside more eddies and vortices. This complicated organization is what allows a turbulent flow to maintain its pattern: it takes energy from its surroundings, channeling and dissipating it through this system of nested eddies. But the same processes that allow this form of internal order to emerge as if from nowhere, cause external disorder: turbulence in a flow will cause a great amount of drag on anything moving through that flow.

Similarly, the exquisite internal structure of turbulent weather phenomena (hurricanes, for example) are instances of order emerging out of chaos. But we are all familiar with the destruction that hurricanes can bring about in their surroundings. They are a form of spontaneously emerging order, created at critical points in atmospheric flow, while at the same time they are a source of apparent disorder for other systems. We find a similar situation when we move (by analogy) to other forms of turbulence affecting warfare directly: the demographic turbulence produced by migrations, invasions or crusades, for example. Critical points in the growth of the urban masses are known to have played a role in triggering wars throughout modern history. Whether we consider demographic pressures as having "creative" or "destructive" effects will depend on our point of view. They are creative to the extent that they influence the assembly of armies and of war-related technology, but destructive in their ultimate consequences. Similarly, after a certain critical point is reached in the number of computers connected to a network (a threshold of connectivity), the network itself becomes capable of spontaneously generating computational processes not planned by its designers. For instance, in many computer networks (like the ARPANET), there is not a central computer handling the traffic of messages. Instead, the messages themselves possess enough "local intelligence" to find their way around in the net and reach their destination. In more recent schemes of network control, messages are not only allowed to travel on their own, but also to interact with each other to trade and barter resources (computer memory, processing time). In these interactions, the local intelligence granted to the messages may be increased spontaneously, giving them more initiative than originally planned by the programmers. Whether these processes are viewed as "creative" or "destructive" will depend on how much they interfere with the network's original function.

[. . .]

Most of all, our robot historian would make a special effort to think of evolution as related not only to organic life (a lineage to which it clearly does not belong), but also to any process in which order emerges spontaneously out of chaos: the non-organic life represented by the machinic phylum. As I said above, it is very unlikely that robots will evolve along anthropomorphic lines to the point where they become "historians." But in a world where our future depends on establishing a "partnership" with computers and on allowing the evolutionary paths of both humans and machines to enter into a symbiotic relationship, it may prove useful to include the robot's point of view when exploring the history of war in the age of intelligent machines.

PART TWO

Models of technology, media and culture

A S WE BECAME CONSCIOUS of the sheer power and pervasion of our new media digital technologies, and dramatic differences between them and earlier mechanical technologies became apparent, a key issue arose: how, or in what way, does technological change shape culture and society? Across the twentieth century media studies had become extremely wary of granting technology a determining role in explanations of media and communications processes. As we put it elsewhere, 'The very question " does technology affect us?" was dismissed as a naïve idea.' Technology, it was argued, determines nothing. Technologies are mere tools or mute machines that we humans put to use and they are conceived and used by societies.

All the extracts collected here explicitly or implicitly articulate a model of the relations of determination between technology, human bodies and consciousness, media and culture. Is it human activity or meaning-making that shapes the technologies we use, or vice versa, or do we need to understand more complicated, non-linear circuits of shaping and effects? So, these issues run through the whole collection, but the entries in this part elucidate and exemplify models and approaches that we consider particularly significant. For most of them technology and society cannot be so easily divided into separate categories, with some going further, insisting that divisions between culture, bodies, technologies and nature must be interrogated.

As we noted, at least since the first industrial revolution of the late eighteenth and early nineteenth centuries, advanced technologies and technological systems have become highly significant aspects of culture. This is as true of media and communication processes (as key elements of modern culture) as it is of activities like banking and finance, medicine or warfare (the list could be very extensive). The term 'technoculture' points us towards those cultural phenomena in which technology is significant. 'Cyberculture', derived from cybernetics, has come to refer to the fairly recent forms of 'technoculture' in which the technologies in question are digital and networked (**Haraway** in Part Two, **Tomas** and **Kennedy** in Part Three).

The extracts in this part offer a selection of some of the main responses to the close meshing of culture and technology as it has taken place across the twentieth and twenty-first centuries. Some are specifically concerned with what this means for media and communications, others consider the state of culture more widely.

Chapter 7

KARL MARX

THE LABOUR PROCESS AND ALIENATION IN MACHINERY AND SCIENCE

THIS EXTRACT DATES FROM the mid-nineteenth century when it was drafted by the philosopher and economist Karl Marx. Here, as part of his historical analysis of the development of the means of production (the economic, social and technological ways in which people produce goods and food) and their significance for the nature of society, human labour and economic power, Marx observes how the new industrial machinery and the factory system transform men and women's relationships with technology. The pre-industrial tool is often thought of as an extension of the expert human body (think of the relationships between an artisan like a blacksmith or weaver and the tools of his or her trade), whereas in the mills and factories of the Industrial Revolution, this relationship is inverted and the human body becomes an extension or component of the machine. As Marx puts it, the individual human worker becomes like a limb of a 'powerful organism' which is the 'living' machinic system. This nightmarish image resonates with later visions of technological domination from *Metropolis* to *The Matrix*. It is an early recognition of the changing nature of technology in the industrial world, and the profound changes it wrought on people's working lives. It is important to note that Marx was not primarily concerned with technology as such. The new social relationships and working practices experienced by factory workers were not, for Marx, generated simply by the invention of new machines. Rather these new machines were the product of a new stage of capitalism, and were with capital itself, to use Marx's own gothic terms, 'dead labour', vampires sucking the blood of the workers. It is worth noting that whilst these new sociotechnical systems were doubtlessly bound up in the domination of labour by dead labour, Marx was no Luddite seeking to destroy industrial production. Rather he saw it as generative of new freedoms, if the workers could seize control of it rather than continue to be enslaved by it.

Raymond **Williams** (later in this part) develops a Marxist critique of twentieth-century media, and Tiziana **Terranova** applies neo-Marxist approaches to the contemporary structures of labour in the digital cultural economy. Marx's theories of production are a key influence on Deleuze and **Guattari**'s concept of desiring-machines and on **Baudrillard**.

http://www.marxists.org/

[. . .]

So long as the means of labour remains a means of labour, in the proper sense of the word, as it has been directly and historically assimilated by capital into its valorization process, it only undergoes a formal change, in that it appears to be the means of labour not only from its material aspect, but at the same time as a special mode of existence of capital determined by the general process of capital – it has become *fixed capital*. But once absorbed into the production process of capital, the means of labour undergoes various metamorphoses, of which the last is the *machine*, or rather an *automatic system of machinery* ('automatic' meaning that this is only the most perfected and most fitting form of the machine, and is what transforms the machinery into a system).

This is set in motion by an automaton, a motive force that moves of its own accord. The automaton consists of a number of mechanical and intellectual organs, so that the workers themselves can be no more than the conscious limbs of the automaton. In the machine, and still more in machinery as an automatic system, the means of labour is transformed as regards its use value, i.e. as regards its material existence, into an existence suitable for fixed capital and capital in general; and the form in which it was assimilated as a direct means of labour into the production process of capital is transformed into one imposed by capital itself and in accordance with it. In no respect is the machine the means of labour of the individual worker. Its distinctive character is not at all, as with the means of labour, that of transmitting the activity of the worker to its object; rather this activity is so arranged that it now only transmits and supervises and protects from damage the work of the machine and its action on the raw material.

With the tool it was quite the contrary. The worker animated it with his own skill and activity; his manipulation of it depended on his dexterity. The machine, which possesses skill and force in the worker's place, is itself the virtuoso, with a spirit of its own in the mechanical laws that take effect in it; and, just as the worker consumes food, so the machine consumes coal, oil, etc. (instrumental material), for its own constant self-propulsion. The worker's activity, limited to a mere abstraction, is determined and regulated on all sides by the movement of the machinery, not the other way round. The knowledge that obliges the inanimate parts of the machine, through their construction, to work appropriately as an automaton, does not exist in the consciousness of the worker, but acts upon him through the machine as an alien force, as the power of the machine itself. The appropriation of living labour by objectified labour – of valorizing strength or activity by self-sufficient value – which is inherent in the concept of capital, is established as the character of the production process itself – when production is based on machinery – as a function of its material elements and material movement. The production process has ceased to be a labour process in the sense that labour is no longer the unity dominating and transcending it. Rather labour appears merely to be a conscious organ, composed of individual living workers at a number of points in the mechanical system; dispersed, subjected to the general process of the machinery itself, it is itself only a limb of the system, whose unity exists not in the living workers but in the living (active) machinery, which seems to be a powerful organism when compared to their individual, insignificant activities. With the stage of machinery, objectified labour appears in the labour process itself as the dominating force opposed to living labour, a force represented by capital in so far as it appropriates living labour.

That the labour process is no more than a simple element in the valorization process is confirmed by the transformation on the material plane of the working tool into machinery, and of the living worker into a mere living accessory of the machine; they become no more than the means whereby its action can take place.

As we have seen, capital necessarily tends towards an increase in the productivity of labour and as great a diminution as possible in necessary labour. This tendency is realized by means of the transformation of the instrument of labour into the machine. In machinery, objectified labour is materially opposed to living labour as its own dominating force; it subordinates living labour to itself not only by appropriating it, but in the real process of production itself. The character of capital as value that appropriates value-creating activity is established by fixed capital, existing as machinery, in its relationship as the use value of labour power. Further, the value objectified in machinery appears as a prerequisite, opposed to which the valorizing power of the individual worker disappears, since it has become infinitely small.

In the large-scale production created by machines, any relationship of the product to the direct requirements of the producer disappears, as does any immediate use value. The form of production and the circumstances in which production takes place are so arranged that it is only produced as a vehicle for value, its use value being only a condition for this.

In machinery, objectified labour appears not only in the form of a product, or of a product utilized as a means of labour, but also in the force of production itself. The development of the means of labour into machinery is not fortuitous for capital; it is the historical transformation of the traditional means of labour into means adequate for capitalism. The accumulation of knowledge and skill, of the general productive power of society's intelligence, is thus absorbed into capital in opposition to labour and appears as the property of capital, or more exactly of fixed capital, to the extent that it enters into the production process as an actual means of production. Thus machinery appears as the *most adequate form of fixed capital*; and the latter, in so far as capital can be considered as being related to itself, is the most adequate form of capital in general. On the other hand, in so far as fixed capital is firmly tied to its existence as a particular use value, it no longer corresponds to the concept of capital which, as a value, can take up or throw off any particular form of use value, and incarnate itself in any of them indifferently. Seen from this aspect of the external relationships of capital, *circulating capital* seems to be the most adequate form of capital as opposed to fixed capital.

In so far as machinery develops with the accumulation of social knowledge and productive power generally, it is not in labour but in capital that general social labour is represented. Society's productivity is measured in fixed capital, exists within it in an objectified form; and conversely, the productivity of capital evolves in step with this general progress that capital appropriates gratis. We shall not go into the development of machinery in detail here. We are considering it only from the general aspect, to the extent that the means of labour, in its material aspect, loses its immediate form and opposes the worker materially as capital. Science thus appears, in the machine, as something alien and exterior to the worker; and living labour is subsumed under objectified labour, which acts independently. The worker appears to be superfluous in so far as his action is not determined by the needs of capital.

Thus the full development of capital does not take place – in other words, capital has not set up the means of production corresponding to itself – until the means of labour is not only formally determined as fixed capital, but has been transcended in its direct form, and fixed capital in the shape of a machine is opposed to labour within the production process. The production process as a whole, however, is not subordinated to the direct skill of the worker; it has become a technological application of science.

[. . .]

Chapter 8

MARSHALL MCLUHAN

SELECTED MATERIAL FROM *UNDERSTANDING MEDIA: THE EXTENSIONS OF MAN* ('THE MEDIUM IS THE MESSAGE', 'MEDIA AS TRANSLATORS', 'THE TYPEWRITER')

THE IDEAS OF THE Canadian media theorist Marshall McLuhan reached a wide audience in the 1960s, and have proved influential on theorists of new media in recent years too. As in the 1960s, he remains today a controversial figure, regarded by some (by **Williams** for instance) as a 'technological determinist', because his arguments about the relationships between technology, culture and society are seen as dismissive of other economic, historical and social determinants. And yet, his energetic and evocative writing, his insistence that media technologies have always been transformative of human experience and culture, and his key ideas ('the medium is the message', the global village, the extensional and environmental nature of technologies) continue to offer rich ways of thinking about contemporary digital culture.

For McLuhan then, media technologies should be understood as the 'extensions of man'. In the mechanical age, which McLuhan sees as receding as he writes, these have been extensions of the body's senses: the eye, the ear, the skin, the hand and the foot. Even the spoken word, with its origins at the very beginnings of the human race, is for McLuhan a medium, a technological extension that allowed humans to grasp their environment in new ways, beyond the immediate reach of their hands. More recently, with near-instantaneous electronic networks in mind, he sees the technological extension of the human organism to have included the human nervous system and he foresees 'the technological simulation of consciousness'. A central argument that McLuhan famously (or notoriously) makes is that 'the medium is the message'. By this he means that it is the nature of the medium through which people communicate which shapes a given society and not the particular content of the message it carries. For instance, contemporary peer to peer communication using the Internet and a broadcast television advert might both carry a similar content but they are radically different in the way that they configure relationships between the participants.

One example of this primacy of medium over message is McLuhan's insistence that we consider the electric light bulb a medium. It is, he asserts, pure information, challenging assumptions about what we mean by both 'medium' and 'information'. If a set of light bulbs spells out an advertising message, this message is still secondary to the electric bulbs; it is another, earlier, medium (written text for instance). Whereas the real 'message' is the change of scale or pace (or, perhaps, attention) brought about by the spectacular, public display of electric light (see **Marvin** who also draws on McLuhan), or the new activities it makes possible such as baseball at night or brain surgery.

McLuhan also conceives of media as constituting an environment, a view that resonates with contemporary media theory's interest in the notion of media ecologies (**Ito**). Via new media technologies the senses of the body have been externalised and distributed. Unlike the tool we hold in our hand, these technologies surround us. They become naturalised as an environment that we inhabit or, in McLuhan's phrase, they become like water to fish, imperceptible but essential to survival.

The chapters of McLuhan's book *Understanding Media: The Extensions of Man*, from which these extracts are taken, cover diverse media from the familiar (TV, radio, cinema, the press) to the less obvious (games, weapons and cars). Any of these would offer an insight into his approaches and their implications. We had to choose one medium, though, and the chapter on the typewriter epitomises McLuhan's linking together of technological and everyday change: here the new habits and new forms of dress for the new typists. It also exemplifies his understanding of the cultural effects of new technologies: poets and novelists write and think differently on typewriters, he asserts (as the German media theorist Friedrich Kittler claims, after Nietzsche, 'our writing tools are also working on our thoughts'). There are comparisons that could be made too with the contemporary keyboards of PCs and laptops, and their users (see **Poster**).

http://www.marshallmcluhan.com/

Introduction

James Reston wrote in *The New York Times* (July 7, 1957):

> A health director . . . reported this week that a small mouse, which presumably had been watching television, attacked a little girl and her full-grown cat. . . . Both mouse and cat survived, and the incident is recorded here as a reminder that things seem to be changing.

After three thousand years of explosion, by means of fragmentary and mechanical technologies, the Western world is imploding. During the mechanical ages we had extended our bodies in space. Today, after more than a century of electric technology, we have extended our central nervous system itself in a global embrace, abolishing both space and time as far as our planet is concerned. Rapidly, we approach the final phase of the extensions of man—the technological simulation of consciousness, when the creative process of knowing will be collectively and corporately extended to the whole of human society, much as we have already extended our senses and our nerves by the various media. Whether the extension of consciousness, so long sought by advertisers for specific products, will be "a good thing" is a question that admits of a wide solution. There is little possibility of answering such questions about the extensions of man without considering all of them together. Any extension, whether of skin, hand, or foot, affects the whole psychic and social complex.

Some of the principal extensions, together with some of their psychic and social consequences, are studied in this book. Just how little consideration has been given to such matters in the past can be gathered from the consternation of one of the editors of this book. He noted in dismay that "seventy-five per cent of your material is new. A successful book cannot venture to be more than ten per cent new." Such a risk seems quite worth taking at the present time when the stakes are very high, and the need to understand the effects of the extensions of man becomes more urgent by the hour.

In the mechanical age now receding, many actions could be taken without too much concern. Slow movement insured that the reactions were delayed for considerable periods of time. Today the action and the reaction occur almost at the same time. We actually live mythically and integrally, as it were, but we continue to think in the old, fragmented space and time patterns of the pre-electric age.

Western man acquired from the technology of literacy the power to act without reacting. The advantages of fragmenting himself in this way are seen in the case of the surgeon who would be quite helpless if he were to become humanly involved in his operation. We acquired the art of carrying out the most dangerous social operations with complete detachment. But our detachment was a posture of noninvolvement. In the electric age, when our central nervous system is technologically extended to involve us in the whole of mankind and to incorporate the whole of mankind in us, we necessarily participate, in depth, in the consequences of our every action. It is no longer possible to adopt the aloof and dissociated role of the literate Westerner.

[. . .]

The aspiration of our time for wholeness, empathy and depth of awareness is a natural adjunct of electric technology. The age of mechanical industry that preceded us found vehement assertion of private outlook the natural mode of expression. Every culture and every age has its favorite model of perception and knowledge that it is inclined to prescribe for everybody and everything. The mark of our time is its revulsion against imposed patterns. We are suddenly eager to have things and people declare their beings totally. There is a deep faith to be found in this new attitude—a faith that concerns the ultimate harmony of all being. [. . .]

1 The medium is the message

In a culture like ours, long accustomed to splitting and dividing all things as a means of control, it is sometimes a bit of a shock to be reminded that, in operational and practical fact, the medium is the message. This is merely to say that the personal and social consequences of any medium—that is, of any extension of ourselves—result from the new scale that is introduced into our affairs by each extension of ourselves, or by any new technology. Thus, with automation, for example, the new patterns of human association tend to eliminate jobs, it is true. That is the negative result. Positively, automation creates roles for people, which is to say depth of involvement in their work and human association that our preceding mechanical technology had destroyed. Many people would be disposed to say that it was not the machine, but what one did with the machine, that was its meaning or message. In terms of the ways in which the machine altered our relations to one another and to ourselves, it mattered not in the least whether it turned out cornflakes or Cadillacs. The restructuring of human work and association was shaped by the technique of fragmentation that is the essence of machine technology. The essence of automation technology is the opposite. It is integral and decentralist in depth, just as the machine was fragmentary, centralist, and superficial in its patterning of human relationships.

The instance of the electric light may prove illuminating in this connection. The electric light is pure information. It is a medium without a message, as it were, unless it is used to spell out some verbal ad or name. This fact, characteristic of all media, means that the "content" of any medium is always another medium. The content of writing is speech, just as the written word is the content of print, and print is the content of the telegraph. If it is asked, "What is the content of speech?," it is necessary to say, "It is an actual process of thought, which is in itself nonverbal." An abstract painting represents direct manifestation of creative thought processes as they might appear in computer designs. What we are considering here, however, are the psychic and social consequences of the designs or patterns as they amplify or accelerate existing processes. For the "message" of any medium or technology is the change of scale or pace or pattern that it introduces into human affairs. The railway did not introduce movement or transportation or wheel or road into human society, but it accelerated and enlarged the scale of previous human functions, creating totally new kinds of cities and new kinds of work and leisure. This happened whether the railway functioned in a tropical or a northern environment, and is quite independent of the freight or content of the railway medium. The airplane, on the other hand, by accelerating the rate of transportation, tends to dissolve the railway form of city, politics, and association, quite independently of what the airplane is used for.

Let us return to the electric light. Whether the light is being used for brain surgery or night baseball is a matter of indifference. It could be argued that these activities are in some way the "content" of the electric light, since they could not exist without the electric light. This fact merely underlines the point that "the medium is the message" because it is the medium that shapes and controls the scale and form of human association and action. The content or uses of such media are as diverse as they are ineffectual in shaping the form of human association. Indeed, it is only too typical that the "content" of any medium blinds us to the character of the medium. It is only today that industries have become aware of the various kinds of business in which they are engaged. When IBM discovered that it was not in the business of making office equipment or business machines, but that it was in the business of processing information, then it began to navigate with clear vision. The General Electric Company makes a considerable portion of its profits from electric light bulbs and lighting systems. It has not yet discovered that, quite as much as A.T.& T., it is in the business of moving information.

The electric light escapes attention as a communication medium just because it has no "content." And this makes it an invaluable instance of how people fail to study media at all. For it is not till the electric light is used to spell out some brand name that it is noticed as a medium. Then it is not the light but the "content" (or what is really another medium) that is noticed. The message of the electric light is like the message of electric power in industry, totally radical, pervasive, and decentralized. For electric light and power are separate from their uses, yet they eliminate time and space factors in human association exactly as do radio, telegraph, telephone, and TV, creating involvement in depth.

[. . .]

If the formative power in the media are the media themselves, that raises a host of large matters that can only be mentioned here, although they deserve volumes. Namely, that technological media are staples or natural resources, exactly as are coal and cotton and oil. Anybody will concede that a society whose economy is dependent upon one or two major staples like cotton, or grain, or lumber, or fish, or cattle is going to have some obvious social patterns of organization as a result. Stress on a few major staples creates extreme instability in the economy but great endurance in the population. The pathos and humor of the American South are embedded in such an economy of limited staples. For a society configured by reliance on a few commodities accepts them as a social bond quite as much as the metropolis does the press. Cotton and oil, like radio and TV, become "fixed charges" on the entire psychic life of the community. And this pervasive fact creates the unique cultural flavor of any society. It pays through the nose and all its other senses for each staple that shapes its life.

[. . .]

6 Media as translators

The tendency of neurotic children to lose neurotic traits when telephoning has been a puzzle to psychiatrists. Some stutterers lose their stutter when they switch to a foreign language. That technologies are ways of translating one kind of knowledge into another mode has been expressed by Lyman Bryson in the phrase "technology is explicitness." Translation is thus a "spelling-out" of forms of knowing. What we call "mechanization" is a translation of nature, and of our own natures, into amplified and specialized forms. Thus the quip in *Finnegans Wake*, "What bird has done yesterday man may do next year," is a strictly literal observation of the courses of technology. The power of technology as dependent on alternately grasping and letting go in order to enlarge the scope of action has been observed as the power of the higher arboreal apes as compared with those that are on the ground. Elias Canetti made the proper association of this power of the higher apes to grasp and let go, with the strategy of the stock market speculators. It is all capsulated in the popular variant on Robert Browning: "A man's reach must exceed his grasp or what's a metaphor." All media are active metaphors in their power to translate experience into new forms. The spoken word was the first technology by which man was able to let go of his environment in order to grasp it in a new way. Words are a kind of information retrieval that can range over the total environment and experience at high speed. Words are complex systems of metaphors and symbols that translate experience into our uttered or outered senses. They are a technology of explicitness. By means of translation of immediate sense experience into vocal symbols the entire world can be evoked and retrieved at any instant.

In this electric age we see ourselves being translated more and more into the form of information, moving toward the technological extension of consciousness. That is what is meant when we say that we daily know more and more about man. We mean that we can translate more and more of ourselves into other forms of expression that exceed ourselves. Man is a form of expression who is traditionally expected to repeat himself and to echo the praise of his Creator. "Prayer," said George Herbert, "is reversed thunder." Man has the power to reverberate the Divine thunder, by verbal translation.

By putting our physical bodies inside our extended nervous systems, by means of electric media, we set up a dynamic by which all previous technologies that are mere extensions of hands and feet and teeth and bodily heat-controls—all such extensions of our bodies, including cities—will be translated into information systems. Electromagnetic technology requires utter human docility and quiescence of meditation such as befits an organism that now wears its brain outside its skull and its nerves outside its hide. Man must serve his electric technology with the same servo-mechanistic fidelity with which he served his coracle, his canoe, his typography, and all other extensions of his physical organs. But there is this difference, that previous technologies were partial and fragmentary, and the electric is total and inclusive. An external consensus or conscience is now as necessary as private consciousness. With the new media, however, it is also possible to store and to translate everything; and, as for speed, that is no problem. No further acceleration is possible this side of the light barrier.

Just as when information levels rise in physics and chemistry, it is possible to use anything for fuel or fabric or building material, so with electric technology all solid goods can be summoned to appear as solid commodities by means of information circuits set up in the organic patterns that we call "automation" and information retrieval. Under electric technology the entire business of man becomes learning and knowing. In terms of what we still consider an "economy" (the Greek word for a household), this means that all forms of employment become "paid learning," and all forms of wealth result from the movement of information. The problem of discovering occupations or employment may prove as difficult as wealth is easy.

The long revolution by which men have sought to translate nature into art we have long referred to as "applied knowledge." "Applied" means translated or carried across from one kind of material form into another. For those who care to consider this amazing process of applied knowledge in Western civilization, Shakespeare's *As You Like It* provides a good deal to think about. His forest of Arden is just such a golden world of translated benefits and joblessness as we are now entering via the gate of electric automation.

It is no more than one would expect that Shakespeare should have understood the Forest of Arden as an advance model of the age of automation when all things are translatable into anything else that is desired:

> And this our life, exempt from public haunt,
> Finds tongues in trees, books in the running brooks,
> Sermons in stones, and good in every thing.
> I would not change it.
> AMIENS: Happy is your Grace,
> That can translate the stubbornness of fortune
> Into so quiet and so sweet a style.

(As You Like It, II, i. 15–21)

Shakespeare speaks of a world into which, by programming, as it were, one can play back the materials of the natural world in a variety of levels and intensities of style. We are close to doing just this on a massive scale at the present time electronically. Here is the image of the golden age as one of complete metamorphoses or translations of nature into human art, that stands ready of access to our electric age. The poet Stephane Mallarmé thought "the world exists to end in a book." We are now in a position to go beyond that and to transfer the entire show to the memory of a computer. For man, as Julian Huxley observes, unlike merely biological creatures, possesses an apparatus of transmission and transformation based on his power to store experience. And his power to store, as in a language itself, is also a means of transformation of experience:

> "Those pearls that were his eyes."

Our dilemma may become like that of the listener who phoned the radio station: "Are you the station that gives twice as much weather? Well, turn it off. I'm drowning."

[. . .]

Our very word "grasp" or "apprehension" points to the process of getting at one thing through another, of handling and sensing many facets at a time through more than one sense at a time. It begins to be evident that "touch" is not skin but the interplay of the senses, and "keeping in touch" or "getting in touch" is a matter of a fruitful meeting of the senses, of sight translated into sound and sound into movement, and taste and smell. The "common sense" was for many centuries held to be the peculiar human power of translating one kind of experience of one sense into all the senses, and presenting the result continuously as a unified image to the mind. In fact, this image of a unified ratio among the senses was long held to be the mark of our *rationality*, and may in the computer age easily become so again. For it is now possible to program ratios among the senses that approach the condition of consciousness. Yet such a condition would necessarily be an extension of our own consciousness as much as wheel is an extension of feet in rotation. Having extended or translated our central nervous system into the electromagnetic technology, it is but a further stage to transfer our consciousness to the computer world as well. Then, at least, we shall be able to program consciousness in such wise that it cannot be numbed nor distracted by the Narcissus illusions of the entertainment world that beset mankind when he encounters himself extended in his own gimmickry.

If the work of the city is the remaking or translating of man into a more suitable form than his nomadic ancestors achieved, then might not our current translation of our entire lives into the spiritual form of information seem to make of the entire globe, and of the human family, a single consciousness?

26 The typewriter

Into the age of the iron whim

The comments of Robert Lincoln O'Brien, writing in the *Atlantic Monthly* in 1904, indicate a rich field of social material that still remains unexplored. For example:

> The invention of the typewriter has given a tremendous impetus to the dictating habit.
> . . . This means not only greater diffuseness . . . but it also brings forward the point of view of the one who speaks. There is the disposition on the part of the talker to explain, as if watching the facial expression of his hearers to see how far they are following. This attitude is not lost when his audience is following. It is no uncommon thing in the typewriting booths at the Capitol in Washington to see Congressmen in dictating letters use the most vigorous gestures as if the oratorical methods of persuasion could be transmitted to the printed page.

In 1882, ads proclaimed that the typewriter could be used as an aid in learning to read, write, spell, and punctuate. Now, eighty years later, the typewriter is used only in experimental classrooms. The ordinary classroom still holds the typewriter at bay as a merely attractive and distractive toy. But poets like Charles Olson are eloquent in proclaiming the power of the typewriter to help the poet to indicate exactly the breath, the pauses, the suspension, even, of syllables, the juxtaposition, even, of parts of phrases which he intends, observing that, for the first time, the poet has the stave and the bar that the musician has had.

The same kind of autonomy and independence which Charles Olson claims that the typewriter confers on the voice of the poet was claimed for the typewriter by the career woman of fifty years ago. British women were reputed to have developed a "twelve-pound look" when typewriters became available for sixty dollars or so. This look was in some way related to the Viking gesture of Ibsen's Nora Helmer, who slammed the door of her doll's house and set off on a quest of vocation and soul-testing. The age of the iron whim had begun.

The reader will recall earlier mention that when the first wave of female typists hit the business office in the 1890s, the cuspidor manufacturers read the sign of doom. They were right. More important, the uniform ranks of fashionable lady typists made possible a revolution in the garment industry. What she wore, every farmer's daughter wanted to wear, for the typist was a popular figure of enterprise and skill. She was a style-maker who was also eager to follow styles. As much as the typewriter, the typist brought into business a new dimension of the uniform, the homogeneous, and the continuous that has made the typewriter indispensable to every aspect of mechanical industry. A modern battleship needs dozens of typewriters for ordinary operations. An army needs more typewriters than medium and light artillery pieces, even in the field, suggesting that the typewriter now fuses the functions of the pen and sword.

But the effect of the typewriter is not all of this kind. If the typewriter has contributed greatly to the familiar forms of the homogenized specialism and fragmentation that is print culture, it has also caused an integration of functions and the creation of much private independence. G. K. Chesterton demurred about this new independence as a delusion, remarking that "women refused to be dictated to and went out and became stenographers." The poet or novelist now composes on the typewriter. The typewriter fuses composition and publication, causing an entirely new attitude to the written and printed word. Composing on the typewriter has altered the forms of the language and of literature in ways best seen in the later novels of Henry James that were dictated to Miss Theodora Bosanquet, who took them down, not by shorthand, but on a typewriter. Her memoir, *Henry James at Work*, should have been followed by other studies of how the typewriter has altered English verse and prose, and, indeed, the very mental habits, themselves, of writers.

With Henry James, the typewriter had become a confirmed habit by 1907, and his new style developed a sort of free, incantatory quality. His secretary tells of how he found dictating not only easier but more inspiring than composing by hand: "It all seems to be so much more effectively and unceasingly *pulled* out of me in speech than in writing," he told her. Indeed, he became so attached to the sound of his typewriter that, on his deathbed, Henry James called for his Remington to be worked near his bedside.

Just how much the typewriter has contributed by its unjustified right-hand margin to the development of *vers libre* would be hard to discover, but free verse was really a recovery of spoken, dramatic stress in poetry, and the typewriter encouraged exactly this quality. Seated at the typewriter, the poet, much in the manner of the jazz musician, has the experience of performance as composition. In the nonliterate world, this had been the situation of the bard or minstrel. He had themes, but no text. At the typewriter, the poet commands the resources of the printing press. The machine is like a public-address system immediately at hand. He can shout or whisper or whistle, and make funny typographic faces at the audience, as does E. E. Cummings in this sort of verse:

In Just-
spring when the world is mud—
luscious the little
lame baloonman
whistles   far   and wee
and eddieandbill come
running from.marbles and
piracies and it's
spring
when the world is puddle wonderful
the queer
old baloonman whistles
far   and   wee
and bettyandisbel come dancing
from hop-scotch and jump-rope and
it's spring and the
goat footed
baloonman whistles
far
and
wee

E. E. Cummings is here using the typewriter to provide a poem with a musical score for choral speech. The older poet, separated from the print form by various technical stages, could enjoy none of the freedom of oral stress provided by the typewriter. The poet at the typewriter can do Njinsky leaps or Chaplin-like shuffles and wiggles. Because he is an audience for his own mechanical audacities, he never ceases to react to his own performance. Composing on the typewriter is like flying a kite.

The E. E. Cummings poem, when read aloud with widely varying stresses and paces, will duplicate the perceptual process of its typewriting creator. How Gerard Manley Hopkins would have loved to have had a typewriter to compose on! People who feel that poetry is for the eye and is to be read silently can scarcely get anywhere with Hopkins or Cummings. Read aloud, such poetry becomes quite natural. Putting first names in lower case, as "eddieandbill," bothered the literate people of forty years ago. It was supposed to.

Eliot and Pound used the typewriter for a great variety of central effects in their poems. And with them, too, the typewriter was an oral and mimetic instrument that gave them the colloquial freedom of the world of jazz and ragtime. Most colloquial and jazzy of all Eliot's poems, *Sweeney Agonistes*, in its first appearance in print, carried the note: "From Wanna Go Home Baby?"

That the typewriter, which carried the Gutenberg technology into every nook and cranny of our culture and economy should, also, have given out with these opposite oral effects is a characteristic reversal. Such a reversal of form happens in all extremes of advanced technology, as with the wheel today.

As expediter, the typewriter brought writing and speech and publication into close association. Although a merely mechanical form, it acted in some respects as an implosion, rather than an explosion.

In its explosive character, confirming the existing procedures of moveable types, the typewriter had an immediate effect in regulating spelling and grammar. The pressure of Gutenberg technology toward "correct" or uniform spelling and grammar was felt at once. Typewriters caused an enormous expansion in the sale of dictionaries. They also created the innumerable overstuffed files that led to the rise of the file-cleaning companies in our time. At first, however, the typewriter was not seen as indispensable to business. The personal touch of the hand-penned letter was considered so important that the typewriter was ruled out of commercial use by the pundits. They thought, however, that it might be of use to authors, clergymen, and telegraph operators. Even newspapers were lukewarm about this machine for some time.

Once any part of the economy feels a step-up in pace, the rest of the economy has to follow suit. Soon, no business could be indifferent to the greatly increased pace set by the typewriter. It was the telephone, paradoxically, that sped the commercial adoption of the typewriter. The phrase "Send me a memo on that," repeated into millions of phones daily, helped to create the huge expansion of the typist function. Northcote Parkinson's law that "work expands so as to fill the time available for its completion" is precisely the zany dynamic provided by the telephone. In no time at all, the telephone expanded the work to be done on the typewriter to huge dimensions. Pyramids of paperwork rise on the basis of a small telephone network inside a single business. Like the typewriter, the telephone fuses functions, enabling the call-girl, for example, to be her own procurer and madam.

Northcote Parkinson had discovered that any business or bureaucratic structure functions by itself, independently of "the work to be done." The number of personnel and "the quality of the work are not related to each other at all." In any given structure, the rate of staff accumulation is not related to the work done but to the intercommunication among the staff, itself. (In other words, the medium is the message.) Mathematically stated, Parkinson's Law says that the rate of accumulation of office staff per annum will be between 5.17 per cent and 6.56 per cent, "irrespective of any variation in the amount of work (if any) to be done."

"Work to be done," of course, means the transformation of one kind of material energy into some new form, as trees into lumber or paper, or clay into bricks or plates, or metal into pipe. In terms of this kind of work, the accumulation of office personnel in a navy, for example, goes up as the number of ships goes down. What Parkinson carefully hides from himself and his readers is simply the fact that in the area of information movement, the main "work to be done" is actually the movement of information. The mere interrelating of people by selected information is now the principal source of wealth in the electric age. In the preceding mechanical age, work had not been like that at all. Work had meant the processing of various materials by assembly-line fragmentation of operations and hierarchically delegated authority. Electric power circuits, in relation to the same processing, eliminate both the assembly line and the delegated authority. Especially with the computer, the work effort is applied at the "programming" level, and such effort is one of information and knowledge. In the decision-making and "make happen" aspect of the work operation, the telephone and other such speed-ups of information have ended the divisions of delegated authority in favor of the "authority of knowledge." It is as if a symphony composer, instead of sending his manuscript to the printer and thence to the conductor and to the individual members of the orchestra, were to compose directly on an electronic instrument that would render each note or theme as if on the appropriate instrument. This would end at once all the delegation and specialism of the symphony orchestra that makes it such a natural model of the mechanical and industrial age. The typewriter, with regard to the poet or novelist, comes very close to the promise of electronic music, insofar as it compresses or unifies the various jobs of poetic composition and publication.

The historian Daniel Boorstin was scandalized by the fact that celebrity in our information age was not due to a person's having done anything but simply to his being known for being well known. Professor Parkinson is scandalized that the structure of human work now seems to be quite independent of any job to be done. As an economist, he reveals the same incongruity and comedy, as between the old and the new, that Stephen Potter does in his *Gamesmanship*. Both have revealed the hollow mockery of "getting ahead in the world," in its old sense. Neither honest toil nor clever ploy will serve to advance the eager executive. The reason is simple. Positional warfare is finished, both in private and corporate action. In business, as in society, "getting on" may mean getting out. There is no "ahead" in a world that is an echo chamber of instantaneous celebrity.

The typewriter, with its promise of careers for the Nora Helmers of the West, has really turned out to be an elusive pumpkin coach, after all.

Chapter 9

RAYMOND WILLIAMS

THE TECHNOLOGY AND THE SOCIETY

THE INFLUENCE OF Raymond Williams on cultural and media studies is profound. Even though he may rarely be cited in current writing, his arguments and approaches are foundational and there is evidence of a resurgence of interest in his work in new media studies. Williams argues that whatever form any particular developing media technology (or, more accurately, set of technologies) may take, there is for him 'nothing in the technology to make this inevitable'.

Though the focus in this extract is television and media technologies in particular, Williams develops his argument through a consideration of the social shaping of technology in general. The key points he makes are, firstly, that technology is not autonomous, nor is it 'symptomatic'. Secondly, the role of *intention* in research and development is crucial: technological devices or systems are not the inevitable result of either clear consumer demand or their own inherent logic. For example, it is clear that television did not supersede cinema because it improved picture quality, but rather because it chimed with the broader economic and cultural move towards a more domesticated and privatised everyday life (a process Williams called 'mobile privatisation').

Williams' emphasis on the social shaping (rather than the material characteristics) of media technology is in part a reaction to, on the one hand, the crude technological determinism of the advertising and promotion of technological products, and, on the other, the considerable contemporaneous influence of Marshall **McLuhan** for whom communications technologies determined epochs in human society. For Williams, **McLuhan**'s ideas are idealist and ideological: substituting the technological products of social and economic forces for those forces themselves as the motor of historical change (see our introduction to **McLuhan** above).

Yet though Williams' argument downplays the materiality of media technologies, it is not absolutely ruled out. His account of the social shaping of television is predicated on a rich model of interactions and effects between technology, cultural form, economics and aesthetics. As communication technologies become part of wider circuits of determinations and effects (though Williams does not spell this out), the technologies themselves play an active role in these processes. A useful example is his discussion of the effect of a technical development (colour television) on programme content. Programmers, he argued, looked for particularly 'colourful' subjects and ideas to exploit this technical development. On the one hand of course the simple fact of colour technology did not inevitably cause or create new programmes or subject matter, and the operations of economic factors, and consideration of audience expectations, are clear. But, on the other hand, in a significant way this technology did have an effect in its facilitation, suggestion even, of new programme content, aesthetics and modes of presentation.

It is often said that television has altered our world. In the same way, people often speak of a new world, a new society, a new phase of history, being created – 'brought about' – by this or that new technology: the steam-engine, the automobile, the atomic bomb. Most of us know what is generally implied when such things are said. But this may be the central difficulty: that we have got so used to statements of this general kind, in our most ordinary discussions, that we can fail to realise their specific meanings.

For behind all such statements lie some of the most difficult and most unresolved historical and philosophical questions. Yet the questions are not posed by the statements; indeed they are ordinarily masked by them. Thus we often discuss, with animation, this or that 'effect' of television, or the kinds of social behaviour, the cultural and psychological conditions, which television has 'led to', without feeling ourselves obliged to ask whether it is reasonable to describe any technology as a cause, or, if we think of it as a cause, as what kind of cause, and in what relations with other kinds of causes. The most precise and discriminating local study of 'effects' can remain superficial if we have not looked into the notions of cause and effect, as between a technology and a society, a technology and a culture, a technology and a psychology, which underlie our questions and may often determine our answers.

It can of course be said that these fundamental questions are very much too difficult; and that they are indeed difficult is very soon obvious to anyone who tries to follow them through. We could spend our lives trying to answer them, whereas here and now, in a society in which television is important, there is immediate and practical work to be done: surveys to be made, research undertaken; surveys and research, moreover, which we know how to do. It is an appealing position, and it has the advantage, in our kind of society, that it is understood as practical, so that it can then be supported and funded. By contrast, other kinds of question seem merely theoretical and abstract.

Yet all questions about cause and effect, as between a technology and a society, are intensely practical. Until we have begun to answer them, we really do not know, in any particular case, whether, for example, we are talking about a technology or about the uses of a technology; about necessary institutions or particular and changeable institutions; about a content or about a form. And this is not only a matter of intellectual uncertainty; it is a matter of social practice. If the technology is a cause, we can at best modify or seek to control its effects. Or if the technology, as used, is an effect, to what other kinds of cause, and other kinds of action, should we refer and relate our experience of its uses? These are not abstract questions. They form an increasingly important part of our social and cultural arguments, and they are being decided all the time in real practice, by real and effective decisions.

It is with these problems in mind that I want to try to analyse television as a particular cultural technology, and to look at its development, its institutions, its forms and its effects, in this critical dimension. In the present chapter, I shall begin the analysis under three headings: (a) versions of cause and effect in technology and society; (b) the social history of television as a technology; (c) the social history of the uses of television technology.

a. Versions of cause and effect in technology and society

We can begin by looking again at the general statement that television has altered our world. It is worth setting down some of the different things this kind of statement has been taken to mean. For example:

(i)   Television was invented as a result of scientific and technical research. Its power as a medium of news and entertainment was then so great that it altered all preceding media of news and entertainment.

(ii)   Television was invented as a result of scientific and technical research. Its power as a medium of social communication was then so great that it altered many of our institutions and forms of social relationships.

(iii) Television was invented as a result of scientific and technical research. Its inherent properties as an electronic medium altered our basic perceptions of reality, and thence our relations with each other and with the world.

(iv)   Television was invented as a result of scientific and technical research. As a powerful medium of communication and entertainment it took its place with other factors – such as greatly increased physical mobility, itself the result of other newly invented technologies – in altering the scale and form of our societies.

(v)   Television was invented as a result of scientific and technical research, and developed as a medium of entertainment and news. It then had unforeseen consequences, not only on other entertainment and news media, which it reduced in viability and importance, but on some of the central processes of family, cultural and social life.

(vi)   Television, discovered as a possibility by scientific and technical research, was selected for investment and development to meet the needs of a new kind of society, especially in the provision of centralised entertainment and in the centralised formation of opinions and styles of behaviour

(vii) Television, discovered as a possibility by scientific and technical research, was selected for investment and promotion as a new and profitable phase of a domestic consumer economy; it is then one of the characteristic 'machines for the home'.

(viii) Television became available as a result of scientific and technical research, and in its character and uses exploited and emphasised elements of a passivity, a cultural and psychological inadequacy, which had always been latent in people, but which television now organised and came to represent.

(ix)   Television became available as a result of scientific and technical research, and in its character and uses both served and exploited the needs of a new kind of large-scale and complex but atomised society.

These are only some of the possible glosses on the ordinary bald statement that television has altered our world. Many people hold mixed versions of what are really alternative opinions, and in some cases there is some inevitable overlapping. But we can distinguish between two broad classes of opinion.

In the first – (i) to (v) – the technology is in effect accidental. Beyond the strictly internal development of the technology there is no reason why any particular invention should have come about. Similarly it then has consequences which are also in the true sense accidental, since they follow directly from the technology itself. If television had not been invented, this argument would run, certain definite social and cultural events would not have occurred.

In the second – (vi) to (ix) – television is again, in effect, a technological accident, but its significance lies in its uses, which are held to be symptomatic of some order of society or some qualities of human nature which are otherwise determined. If television had not been invented, this argument runs, we would still be manipulated or mindlessly entertained, but in some other way and perhaps less powerfully.

For all the variations of local interpretation and emphasis, these two classes of opinion underlie the overwhelming majority of both professional and amateur views of the effects of television. What they have in common is the fundamental form of the statement: 'television has altered our world'.

It is then necessary to make a further theoretical distinction. The first class of opinion, described above, is that usually known, at least to its opponents, as *technological determinism*. It is an immensely powerful and now largely orthodox view of the nature of social change. New technologies are discovered, by an essentially internal process of research and development, which then sets the conditions for social change and progress. Progress, in particular, is the history of these inventions, which 'created the modern world'. The effects of the technologies, whether direct or indirect, foreseen or unforeseen, are as it were the rest of history. The steam engine, the automobile, television, the atomic bomb, have *made* modern man and the modern condition.

The second class of opinion appears less determinist. Television, like any other technology, becomes available as an element or a medium in a process of change that is in any case occurring or about to occur. By contrast with pure technological determinism, this view emphasises other causal factors in social change. It then considers particular technologies, or a complex of technologies, as *symptoms* of change of some other kind. Any particular technology is then as it were a by-product of a social process that is otherwise determined. It only acquires effective status when it is used for purposes which are already contained in this known social process.

The debate between these two general positions occupies the greater part of our thinking about technology and society. It is a real debate, and each side makes important points. But it is in the end sterile, because each position, though in different ways, has abstracted technology from society. In *technological determinism*, research and development have been assumed as self-generating. The new technologies are invented as it were in an independent sphere, and then create new societies or new human conditions. The view of *symptomatic technology*, similarly, assumes that research and development are self-generating, but in a more marginal way. What is discovered in the margin is then taken up and used.

Each view can then be seen to depend on the isolation of technology. It is either a self-acting force which creates new ways of life, or it is a self-acting force which provides materials for new ways of life. These positions are so deeply established, in modern social thought, that it is very difficult to think beyond them. Most histories of technology, like most histories of scientific discovery, are written from their assumptions. An appeal to 'the facts', against this or that interpretation, is made very difficult simply because the histories are usually written, consciously or unconsciously, to illustrate the assumptions. This is either explicit, with the consequential interpretation attached, or more often implicit, in that the history of technology or of scientific development is offered as a history on its own. This can be seen as a device of specialisation or of emphasis, but it then necessarily implies merely internal intentions and criteria.

To change these emphases would require prolonged and cooperative intellectual effort. But in the particular case of television it may be possible to outline a different kind of interpretation, which would allow us to see not only its history but also its uses in a more radical way. Such an interpretation would differ from technological determinism in that it would restore *intention* to the process of research and development. The technology would be seen, that is to say, as being looked for and developed with certain purposes and practices already in mind. At the same time the interpretation would differ from symptomatic technology in that these purposes and practices would be seen as *direct*: as known social needs, purposes and practices to which the technology is not marginal but central.

b. The social history of television as a technology

The invention of television was no single event or series of events. It depended on a complex of inventions and developments in electricity, telegraphy, photography and motion pictures, and radio. It can be said to have separated out as a specific technological objective in the period 1875–1890, and then, after a lag, to have developed as a specific technological enterprise from 1920 through to the first public television systems of the 1930s. Yet in each of these stages it depended for parts of its realisation on inventions made with other ends primarily in view.

Until the early nineteenth century, investigations of electricity, which had long been known as a phenomenon, were primarily philosophical: investigations of a puzzling natural effect. The technology associated with these investigations was mainly directed towards isolation and concentration of the effect, for its clearer study. Towards the end of the eighteenth century there began to be applications, characteristically in relation to other known natural effects (lightning conductors). But there is then a key transitional period in a cluster of inventions between 1800 and 1831, ranging from Volta's battery to Faraday's demonstration of electromagnetic induction, leading quickly to the production of generators. This can be properly traced as a scientific history, but it is significant that the key period of advance coincides with an important stage of the development of industrial production. The advantages of electric power were closely related to new industrial needs: for mobility and transfer in the location of power sources, and for flexible and rapid controllable conversion. The steam engine had been well suited to textiles, and its industries had been based on local siting. A more extensive development, both physically and in the complexity of multiple-part processes, such as engineering, could be attempted with other power sources but could only be fully realised with electricity. There was a very complex interaction between new needs and new inventions, at the level of primary production, of new applied industries (plating) and of new social needs which were themselves related to industrial development (city and house lighting). From 1830 to large-scale generation in the 1880s there was this continuing complex of need and invention and application.

In telegraphy the development was simpler. The transmission of messages by beacons and similar primary devices had been long established. In the development of navigation and naval warfare the flag-system had been standardised in the course of the sixteenth and seventeenth centuries. During the Napoleonic wars there was a marked development of land telegraphy, by semaphore stations, and some of this survived into peacetime. Electrical telegraphy had been suggested as a technical system as early as 1753, and was actually demonstrated in several places in the early nineteenth century. An English inventor in 1816 was told that the Admiralty was not interested. It is interesting that it was the development of the railways, themselves a response to the development of an industrial system and the related growth of cities, which clarified the need for improved telegraphy. A complex of technical possibilities was brought to a working system from 1837 onwards. The development of international trade and transport brought rapid extensions of the system, including the transatlantic cable in the 1850s and the 1860s. A general system of electric telegraphy had been established by the 1870s, and in the same decade the telephone system began to be developed, in this case as a new and intended invention.

In photography, the idea of light-writing had been suggested by (among others) Wedgwood and Davy in 1802, and the *camera obscura* had already been developed. It was not the projection but the fixing of images which at first awaited technical solution, and from 1816 (Niepce) and through to 1839 (Daguerre) this was worked on, together with the improvement of camera devices. Professional and then amateur photography spread rapidly, and reproduction and then transmission, in the developing newspaper press, were achieved. By the 1880s the idea of a 'photographed reality' – still more for record than for observation – was familiar.

The idea of moving pictures had been similarly developing. The magic lantern (slide projection) had been known from the seventeenth century, and had acquired simple motion (one slide over another) by 1736. From at latest 1826 there was a development of mechanical motion-picture devices, such as the wheel-of-life, and these came to be linked with the magic lantern. The effect of persistence in human vision – that is to say, our capacity to hold the 'memory' of an image through an interval to the next image, thus allowing the possibility of a sequence built from rapidly succeeding units – had been known since classical times. Series of cameras photographing stages of a sequence were followed (Marey, 1882) by multiple-shot cameras. Friese-Greene and Edison worked on techniques of filming and projection, and celluloid was substituted for paper reels. By the 1890s the first public motion-picture shows were being given in France, America and England.

Television, as an idea, was involved with many of these developments. It is difficult to separate it, in its earliest stages, from photo-telegraphy. Bain proposed a device for transmitting pictures by electric wires in 1842; Bakewell in 1847 showed the copying telegraph; Caselli in 1862 transmitted pictures by wire over a considerable distance. In 1873, while working at a terminal of the Atlantic telegraph cable, May observed the light-sensitive properties of selenium (which had been isolated by Berzelius in 1817 and was in use for resistors). In a host of ways, following an already defined need, the means of transmitting still pictures and moving pictures were actively sought and to a considerable extent discovered. The list is long even when selective: Carey's electric eye in 1875; Nipkow's scanning system in 1884; Elster and Geitel's photoelectric cells in 1890; Braun's cathode-ray tube in 1897; Rosing's cathode-ray receiver in 1907; Campbell Swinton's electronic camera proposal in 1911. Through this whole period two facts are evident: that a system of television was foreseen, and its means were being actively sought; but also that, by comparison with electrical generation and electrical telegraphy and telephony, there was very little social investment to bring the scattered work together. It is true that there were technical blocks before 1914 – the thermionic valve and the multi-stage amplifier can be seen to have been needed and were not yet invented. But the critical difference between the various spheres of applied technology can be stated in terms of a social dimension: the new systems of production and of business or transport communication were already organised, at an economic level; the new systems of social communication were not. Thus when motion pictures were developed, their application was characteristically in the margin of established social forms – the sideshows – until their success was capitalised in a version of an established form, the motion-picture *theatre*.

The development of radio, in its significant scientific and technical stages between 1885 and 1911, was at first conceived, within already effective social systems, as an advanced form of telegraphy. Its application as a significantly new social form belongs to the immediate post-war period, in a changed social situation. It is significant that the hiatus in technical television development then also ended. In 1923 Zworykin introduced the electronic television camera tube. Through the early 1920s Baird and Jenkins, separately and competitively, were working on systems using mechanical scanning. From 1925 the rate of progress was qualitatively changed, through important technical advances but also with the example of sound broadcasting systems as a model. The Bell System in 1927 demonstrated wire transmission through a radio link, and the pre-history of the form can be seen to be ending. There was great rivalry between systems – especially those of mechanical and electronic scanning – and there is still great controversy about contributions and priorities. But this is characteristic of the phase in which the development of a technology moves into the stage of a new social form.

What is interesting throughout is that in a number of complex and related fields, these systems of mobility and transfer in production and communication, whether in mechanical and electric transport, or in telegraphy, photography, motion pictures, radio and television, were at once incentives and responses within a phase of general social transformation. Though some of the crucial scientific and technical discoveries were made by isolated and unsupported individuals, there was a crucial community of selected emphasis and intention, in a society characterised at its most general levels by a mobility and extension of the scale of organisations: forms of growth which brought with them immediate and longer-term problems of operative communication. In many different countries, and in apparently unconnected ways, such needs were at once isolated and technically defined. It is especially a characteristic of the communications systems that *all were foreseen − not in utopian but in technical ways − before the crucial components of the developed systems had been discovered and refined*. In no way is this a history of communications systems creating a new society or new social conditions. The decisive and earlier transformation of industrial production, and its new social forms, which had grown out of a long history of capital accumulation and working technical improvements, created new needs but also new possibilities, and the communications systems, down to television, were their intrinsic outcome.

c. The social history of the uses of television technology

It is never quite true to say that in modern societies, when a social need has been demonstrated, its appropriate technology will be found. This is partly because some real needs, in any particular period, are beyond the scope of existing or foreseeable scientific and technical knowledge. It is even more because the key question, about technological response to a need, is less a question about the need itself than about its place in an existing social formation. A need which corresponds with the priorities of the real decision-making groups will, obviously, more quickly attract the investment of resources and the official permission, approval or encouragement on which a working technology, as distinct from available technical devices, depends. We can see this clearly in the major developments of industrial production and, significantly, in military technology. The social history of communications technology is interestingly different from either of these, and it is important to try to discover what are the real factors of this variation.

The problem must be seen at several different levels. In the very broadest perspective, there is an operative relationship between a new kind of expanded, mobile and complex society and the development of a modern communications technology. At one level this relationship can be reasonably seen as causal, in a direct way. The principal incentives to first-stage improvements in communications technology came from problems of communication and control in expanded military and commercial operations. This was both direct, arising from factors of greatly extending distance and scale, and indirect, as a factor within the development of transport technology, which was for obvious reasons the major direct response. Thus telegraphy and telephony, and in its early stages radio, were secondary factors within a primary communications system which was directly serving the needs of an established and developing military and commercial system. Through the nineteenth and into the twentieth century this was the decisive pattern.

But there were other social and political relationships and needs emerging from this complex of change. Indeed it is a consequence of the particular and dominant interpretation of these changes that the complex was at first seen as one requiring improvement in *operational* communication. The direct priorities of the expanding commercial system, and in certain periods of the military system, led to a definition of needs within the terms of these systems. The objectives and the consequent technologies were operational within the structures of these systems: passing necessary specific information, or maintaining contact and control. Modern electric technology, in this phase, was thus oriented to uses of person to person, operator and operative to operator and operative, within established specific structures. This quality can best be emphasised by contrast with the electric technology of the second phase, which was properly and significantly called *broadcasting*. A technology of specific messages to specific persons was complemented, but only relatively late, by a technology of varied messages to a general public.

Yet to understand this development we have to look at a wider communications system. The true basis of this system had preceded the developments in technology. Then as now there was a major, indeed dominant, area of social communication, by word of mouth, within every kind of social group. In addition, then as now, there were specific institutions of that kind of communication which involves or is predicated on social teaching and control: churches, schools, assemblies and proclamations, direction in places of work. All these interacted with forms of communication within the family.

What then were the new needs which led to the development of a new technology of social communication? The development of the press gives us the evidence for our first major instance. It was at once a response to the development of an extended social, economic and political system and a response to crisis within that system. The centralisation of political power led to a need for messages from that centre along other than official lines. Early newspapers were a combination of that kind of message – political and social information – and the specific messages – classified advertising and general commercial news – of an expanding system of trade. In Britain the development of the press went through its major formative stages in periods of crisis: the Civil War and Commonwealth, when the newspaper form was defined; the Industrial Revolution, when new forms of popular journalism were successively established; the major wars of the twentieth century, when the newspaper became a universal social form. For the transmission of simple orders, a communications system already existed. For the transmission of an ideology, there were specific traditional institutions. But for the transmission of news and background – the whole orienting, predictive and updating process which the fully developed press represented – there was an evident need for a new form, which the largely traditional institutions of church and school could not meet. And to the large extent that the crises of general change provoked both anxiety and controversy, this flexible and competitive form met social needs of a new kind. As the struggle for a share in decision and control became sharper, in campaigns for the vote and then in competition for the vote, the press became not only a new communications system but, centrally, a new social institution.

This can be interpreted as response to a political need and a political crisis, and it was certainly this. But a wider social need and social crisis can also be recognised. In a changing society, and especially after the Industrial Revolution, problems of social perspective and social orientation became more acute. New relations between men, and between men and things, were being intensely experienced, and in this area, especially, the traditional institutions of church and school, or of settled community and persisting family, had very little to say. A great deal was of course said, but from positions defined within an older kind of society. In a number of ways, and drawing on a range of impulses from curiosity to anxiety, new information and new kinds of orientation were deeply required: more deeply, indeed, than any specialisation to political, military or commercial information can account for. An increased awareness of mobility and change, not just as abstractions but as lived experiences, led to major redefinition, in practice and then in theory, of the function and process of social communication.

What can be seen most evidently in the press can be seen also in the development of photography and the motion picture. The photograph is in one sense a popular extension of the portrait, for recognition and for record. But in a period of great mobility, with new separations of families and with internal and external migrations, it became more centrally necessary as a form of maintaining, over distance and through time, certain personal connections. Moreover, in altering relations to the physical world, the photograph as an object became a form of the photography of objects: moments of isolation and stasis within an experienced rush of change; and then, in its technical extension to motion, a means of observing and analysing motion itself, in new ways – a dynamic form in which new kinds of recognition were not only possible but necessary.

Now it is significant that until the period after the First World War, and in some ways until the period after the Second World War, these varying needs of a new kind of society and a new way of life were met by what were seen as specialised means: the press for political and economic information; the photograph for community, family and personal life; the motion picture for curiosity and entertainment; telegraphy and telephony for business information and some important personal messages. It was within this complex of specialised forms that broadcasting arrived.

The consequent difficulty of defining its social uses, and the intense kind of controversy which has ever since surrounded it, can then be more broadly understood. Moreover, the first definitions of broadcasting were made for sound radio. It is significant and perhaps puzzling that the definitions and institutions then created were those within which television developed.

We have now become used to a situation in which broadcasting is a major social institution, about which there is always controversy but which, in its familiar form, seems to have been predestined by the technology. This predestination, however, when closely examined proves to be no more than a set of particular social decisions, in particular circumstances, which were then so widely if imperfectly ratified that it is now difficult to see them as decisions rather than as (retrospectively) inevitable results.

Thus, if seen only in hindsight, broadcasting can be diagnosed as a new and powerful form of social integration and control. Many of its main uses can be seen as socially, commercially and at times politically manipulative. Moreover, this viewpoint is rationalised by its description as 'mass communication', a phrase used by almost all its agents and advisers as well, curiously, as by most of its radical critics. 'Masses' had been the new nineteenth-century term of contempt for what was formerly described as 'the mob'. The physical 'massing' of the urban and industrial revolution underwrote this. A new radical class-consciousness adopted the term to express the material of new social formations: 'mass organisations'. The 'mass meeting' was an observable physical effect. So pervasive was this description that in the twentieth century multiple serial production was called, falsely but significantly, 'mass production': mass now meant large numbers (but within certain assumed social relationships) rather than any physical or social aggregate. Sound radio and television, for reasons we shall look at, were developed for transmission to *individual* homes, though there was nothing in the technology to make this inevitable. But then this new form of social communication – broadcasting – was obscured by its definition as 'mass communication': an abstraction to its most general characteristic, that it went to many people, 'the masses', which obscured the fact that the means chosen was the offer of individual sets, a method much better described by the earlier word 'broadcasting'. It is interesting that the only developed 'mass' use of radio was in Nazi Germany, where under Goebbels' orders the Party organised compulsory public listening groups and the receivers were in the streets. There has been some imitation of this by similar regimes, and Goebbels was deeply interested in television for the same kind of use. What was developed within most capitalist societies, though called 'mass communication', was significantly different.

There was early official intervention in the development of broadcasting, but in form this was only at a technical level. In the earlier struggle against the development of the press, the State had licensed and taxed newspapers, but for a century before the coming of broadcasting the alternative idea of an independent press had been realised both in practice and in theory. State intervention in broadcasting had some real and some plausible technical grounds: the distribution of wavelengths. But to these were added, though always controversially, more general social directions or attempts at direction. This social history of broadcasting can be discussed on its own, at the levels of practice and principle. Yet it is unrealistic to extract it from another and perhaps more decisive process, through which, in particular economic situations, a set of scattered technical devices became an applied technology and then a social technology.

A Fascist regime might quickly see the use of broadcasting for direct political and social control. But that, in any case, was when the technology had already been developed elsewhere. In capitalist democracies, the thrust for conversion from scattered techniques to a technology was not political but economic. The characteristically isolated inventors, from Nipkow and Rosing to Baird and Jenkins and Zwyorkin, found their point of development, if at all, in the manufacturers and prospective manufacturers of the technical apparatus. The history at one level is of these isolated names, but at another level it is of EMI, RCA and a score of similar companies and corporations. In the history of motion pictures, capitalist development was primarily in production; large-scale capitalist distribution came much later, as a way of controlling and organising a market for given production. In broadcasting, both in sound radio and later in television, the major investment was in the means of distribution, and was devoted to production only so far as to make the distribution technically possible and then attractive. Unlike all previous communications technologies, radio and television were *systems primarily devised for transmission and reception as abstract processes, with little or no definition of preceding content*. When the question of content was raised, it was resolved, in the main, parasitically. There were state occasions, public sporting events, theatres and so on, which would be communicatively distributed by these new technical means. *It is not only that the supply of broadcasting facilities preceded the demand; it is that the means of communication preceded their content*.

The period of decisive development in sound broadcasting was the 1920s. After the technical advances in sound telegraphy which had been made for military purposes during the war, there was at once an economic opportunity and the need for a new social definition. No nation or manufacturing group held a monopoly of the technical means of broadcasting, and there was a period of intensive litigation followed by cross-licensing of the scattered basic components of successful transmission and reception (the vacuum tube or valve, developed from 1904 to 1913; the feedback circuit, developed from 1912; the neutrodyne and heterodyne circuits, from 1923). Crucially, in the mid-1920s, there was a series of investment-guided technical solutions to the problem of building a small and simple domestic receiver, on which the whole qualitative transformation from wireless telegraphy to broadcasting depended. By the mid-1920s—1923 and 1924 are especially decisive years — this breakthrough had happened in the leading industrial societies: the United States, Britain, Germany and France. By the end of the 1920s the radio industry had become a major sector of industrial production, within a rapid general expansion of the new kinds of machines which were eventually to be called 'consumer durables'. This complex of developments included the motorcycle and motorcar, the box camera and its successors, home electrical appliances, and radio sets. Socially, this complex is characterised by the two apparently paradoxical yet deeply connected tendencies of modern urban industrial living: on the one hand mobility, on the other hand the more apparently self-sufficient family home. The earlier period of public technology, best exemplified by the railways and city lighting, was being replaced by a kind of technology for which no satisfactory name has yet been found: that which served an at once mobile and home-centred way of living: a form of *mobile privatisation*. Broadcasting in its applied form was a social product of this distinctive tendency.

The contradictory pressures of this phase of industrial capitalist society were indeed resolved, at a certain level, by the institution of broadcasting. For mobility was only in part the impulse of an independent curiosity: the wish to go out and see new places. It was essentially an impulse formed in the breakdown and dissolution of older and smaller kinds of settlement and productive labour. The new and larger settlements and industrial organisations required major internal mobility, at a primary level, and this was joined by secondary consequences in the dispersal of extended families and in the needs of new kinds of social organisation. Social processes long implicit in the revolution of industrial capitalism were then greatly intensified: especially an increasing distance between immediate living areas and the directed places of work and government. No effective kinds of social control over these transformed industrial and political processes had come anywhere near being achieved or even foreseen. Most people were living in the fall-out area of processes determined beyond them. What had been gained, nevertheless, in intense social struggle, had been the improvement of immediate conditions, within the limits and pressures of these decisive large-scale processes. There was some relative improvement in wages and working conditions, and there was a qualitative change in the distribution of the day, the week and the year between work and off-work periods. These two effects combined in a major emphasis on improvement of the small family home. Yet this privatisation, which was at once an effective achievement and a defensive response, carried, as a consequence, an imperative need for new kinds of contact. The new homes might appear private and 'self-sufficient' but could be maintained only by regular funding and supply from external sources, and these, over a range from employment and prices to depressions and wars, had a decisive and often a disrupting influence on what was nevertheless seen as a separable 'family' project. This relationship created both the need and the form of a new kind of 'communication': news from 'outside', from otherwise inaccessible sources. Already in the drama of the 1880s and 1890s (Ibsen, Chekhov) this structure had appeared: the centre of dramatic interest was now for the first time the family home, but men and women stared from its windows, or waited anxiously for messages, to learn about forces, 'out there', which would determine the conditions of their lives. The new 'consumer' technology which reached its first decisive stage in the 1920s served this complex of needs within just these limits and pressures. There were immediate improvements of the condition and efficiency of the privatised home; there were new facilities, in private transport, for expeditions from the home; and then, in radio, there was a facility for a new kind of social input – news and entertainment brought into the home. Some people spoke of the new machines as gadgets, but they were always much more than this. They were the applied technology of a set of emphases and responses within the determining limits and pressures of industrial capitalist society.

The cheap radio receiver is then a significant index of a general condition and response. It was especially welcomed by all those who had least social opportunities of other kinds; who lacked independent mobility or access to the previously diverse places of entertainment and information. Broadcasting could also come to serve, or seem to serve, as a form of *unified* social intake, at the most general levels. What had been intensively promoted by the radio manufacturing companies thus interlocked with this kind of social need, itself defined within general limits and pressures. In the early stages of radio manufacturing, transmission was conceived before content. By the end of the 1920s the network was there, but still at a low level of content-definition. It was in the 1930s, in the second phase of radio, that most of the significant advances in content were made. The transmission and reception networks created, *as a by-product*, the facilities of primary broadcasting production. But the general social definition of 'content' was already there.

This theoretical model of the general development of broadcasting is necessary to an understanding of the particular development of television. For there were, in the abstract, several different ways in which television as a technical means might have been developed. After a generation of universal domestic television it is not easy to realise this. But it remains true that, after a great deal of intensive research and development, the domestic television set is in a number of ways an inefficient medium of visual broadcasting. Its visual inefficiency by comparison with the cinema is especially striking, whereas in the case of radio there was by the 1930s a highly efficient sound broadcasting receiver, without any real competitors in its own line. Within the limits of the television home-set emphasis it has so far not been possible to make more than minor qualitative improvements. Higher-definition systems, and colour, have still only brought the domestic television set, as a machine, to the standard of a very inferior kind of cinema. Yet most people have adapted to this inferior visual medium, in an unusual kind of preference for an inferior immediate technology, because of the social complex – and especially that of the privatised home – within which broadcasting, as a system, is operative. The cinema had remained at an earlier level of social definition; it was and remains a special kind of theatre, offering specific and discrete works of one general kind. Broadcasting, by contrast, offered a whole social intake: music, news, entertainment, sport. The advantages of this general intake, within the home, much more than outweighed the technical advantages of visual transmission and reception in the cinema, confined as this was to specific and discrete works. While broadcasting was confined to sound, the powerful visual medium of cinema was an immensely popular alternative. But when broadcasting became visual, the option for its social advantages outweighed the immediate technical deficits.

The transition to television broadcasting would have occurred quite generally in the late 1930s and early 1940s, if the war had not intervened. Public television services had begun in Britain in 1936 and in the United States in 1939, but with still very expensive receivers. The full investment in transmission and reception facilities did not occur until the late 1940s and early 1950s, but the growth was thereafter very rapid. The key social tendencies which had led to the definition of broadcasting were by then even more pronounced. There was significantly higher investment in the privatised home, and the social and physical distances between these homes and the decisive political and productive centres of the society had become much greater. Broadcasting, as it had developed in radio, seemed an inevitable model: the central transmitters and the domestic sets.

Television then went through some of the same phases as radio. Essentially, again, the technology of transmission and reception developed before the content and important parts of the content were and have remained by-products of the technology rather than independent enterprises. As late as the introduction of colour, 'colourful' programmes were being devised to persuade people to buy colour sets. In the earliest stages there was the familiar parasitism, on existing events: a coronation, a major sporting event, theatres. A comparable parasitism on the cinema was slower to show itself, until the decline of the cinema altered the terms of trade; it is now very widespread, most evidently in the United States. But again, as in radio, the end of the first general decade brought significant independent television production. By the middle and late 1950s, as in radio in the middle and late 1930s, new kinds of programme were being made for television and there were very important advances in the productive use of the medium, including, as again at a comparable stage in radio, some kinds of original work.

Yet the complex social and technical definition of broadcasting led to inevitable difficulties, especially in the productive field. What television could do relatively cheaply was to transmit something that was in any case happening or had happened. In news, sport, and some similar areas it could provide a service of transmission at comparatively low cost. But in every kind of new work, which it had to produce, it became a very expensive medium, within the broadcasting model. It was never as expensive as film, but the cinema, as a distributive medium, could directly control its revenues. It was, on the other hand, implicit in broadcasting that given the tunable receiver all programmes could be received without immediate charge. There could have been and can still be a socially financed system of production and distribution within which local and specific charges would be unnecessary; the BBC, based on the licence system for domestic receivers, came nearest to this. But short of monopoly, which still exists in some state-controlled systems, the problems of investment for production, in any broadcasting system, are severe.

Thus within the broadcasting model there was this deep contradiction, of centralised transmission and privatised reception. One economic response was licensing. Another, less direct, was commercial sponsorship and then supportive advertising. But the crisis of production control and financing has been endemic in broadcasting precisely because of the social and technical model that was adopted and that has become so deeply established. The problem is masked, rather than solved, by the fact that as a transmitting technology – its functions largely limited to relay and commentary on other events – some balance could be struck; a limited revenue could finance this limited service. But many of the creative possibilities of television have been frustrated precisely by this apparent solution, and this has far more than local effects on producers and on the balance of programmes. When there has been such heavy investment in a particular model of social communications, there is a restraining complex of financial institutions, of cultural expectations and of specific technical developments, which though it can be seen, superficially, as the effect of a technology is in fact a social complex of a new and central kind.

[. . .]

Chapter 10

BRUNO LATOUR

THE PROLIFERATION OF HYBRIDS

IN THIS SHORT INTRODUCTION Latour deftly and good-naturedly kicks the legs out from underneath the academic fields of the humanities and social sciences. These disciplines' humanist orientation means that they almost exclusively concern themselves with human activity and agency, with the cultural, social and linguistic construction of *meanings*. These would-be critical frameworks then cannot ask questions about what non-human things (or humans as things, as embodied and material entities) *are* and how they circulate, and have effects, in the world. Latour illustrates this through reading a daily newspaper. The pages of a newspaper bring together a tremendously heterogeneous range of entities, events, forces and agencies, phenomena that are at best kept separate in the social sciences, but more often ignored altogether. One article in Latour's newspaper, for example, makes connections between the hole in the ozone layer, industrial change in response to political pressure, everyday technologies implicated in environmental damage, international treaties, the Third World's right to development and so on. At the very least, he says, it mixes together political and chemical reactions. This heterogeneity is evident in articles throughout the paper, except in the cultural and literary review pages, which are reassuring, 'soothing', in their cosy ignorance of the new and proliferating hybrids documented elsewhere. The analogy with academic versions of cultural criticism is left implicit.

Latour's work, and that of others in the connected fields of science studies, science and technology studies, and Actor-Network Theory, takes these connections, hybridities and networks as their starting point, following the diverse actors (technologies, humans, chemicals, policies, environments, etc.) through the networks that they constitute. Adopting these approaches to the study of media technologies and cultures would entail finding ways of studying new media technoculture that do not dwell only on what people say in chat rooms, social networking sites or MMORPGs, but also on what they do, on what other actors are in play from computer hardware, software and networks outwards – and how all these come together as hybrids to constitute any particular activity or event.

Central to Latour's work is an insistence that agency does not rest solely (or even predominantly) in human thought and activity alone, but always already within technologies and technosocial assemblages. This is a theme that runs across many of the extracts in this book. See Part Three for a longer essay by **Latour** that explores these issues in more detail.

http://www.bruno-latour.fr/   http://www.lancs.ac.uk/fass/centres/css/ant/antres.htm

I Crisis

1.1 The proliferation of hybrids

On page four of my daily newspaper, I learn that the measurements taken above the Antarctic are not good this year: the hole in the ozone layer is growing ominously larger. Reading on, I turn from upper-atmosphere chemists to Chief Executive Officers of Atochem and Monsanto, companies that are modifying their assembly lines in order to replace the innocent chlorofluorocarbons, accused of crimes against the ecosphere. A few paragraphs later, I come across heads of state of major industrialized countries who are getting involved with chemistry, refrigerators, aerosols and inert gases. But at the end of the article, I discover that the meteorologists don't agree with the chemists; they're talking about cyclical fluctuations unrelated to human activity. So now the industrialists don't know what to do. The heads of state are also holding back. Should we wait? Is it already too late? Toward the bottom of the page, Third World countries and ecologists add their grain of salt and talk about international treaties, moratoriums, the rights of future generations, and the right to development.

The same article mixes together chemical reactions and political reactions. A single thread links the most esoteric sciences and the most sordid politics, the most distant sky and some factory in the Lyon suburbs, dangers on a global scale and the impending local elections or the next board meeting. The horizons, the stakes, the time frames, the actors – none of these is commensurable, yet there they are, caught up in the same story.

On page six, I learn that the Paris AIDS virus contaminated the culture medium in Professor Gallo's laboratory; that Mr Chirac and Mr Reagan had, however, solemnly sworn not to go back over the history of that discovery; that the chemical industry is not moving fast enough to market medications which militant patient organizations are vocally demanding; that the epidemic is spreading in sub-Saharan Africa. Once again, heads of state, chemists, biologists, desperate patients and industrialists find themselves caught up in a single uncertain story mixing biology and society.

On page eight, there is a story about computers and chips controlled by the Japanese; on page nine, about the right to keep frozen embryos; on page ten, about a forest burning, its columns of smoke carrying off rare species that some naturalists would like to protect; on page eleven, there are whales wearing collars fitted with radio tracking devices; also on page eleven, there is a slag heap in northern France, a symbol of the exploitation of workers, that has just been classified as an ecological preserve because of the rare flora it has been fostering! On page twelve, the Pope, French bishops, Monsanto, the Fallopian tubes, and Texas fundamentalists gather in a strange cohort around a single contraceptive. On page fourteen, the number of lines on high-definition television bring together Mr Delors, Thomson, the EEC, commissions on standardization, the Japanese again, and television film producers. Change the screen standard by a few lines, and billions of francs, millions of television sets, thousands of hours of film, hundreds of engineers and dozens of CEOs go down the drain.

Fortunately, the paper includes a few restful pages that deal purely with politics (a meeting of the Radical Party), and there is also the literary supplement in which novelists delight in the adventures of a few narcissistic egos ('I love you . . . you don't'). We would be dizzy without these soothing features. For the others are multiplying, those hybrid articles that sketch out imbroglios of science, politics, economy, law, religion, technology, fiction. If reading the daily paper is modern man's form of prayer, then it is a very strange man indeed who is doing the praying today while reading about these mixed-up affairs. All of culture and all of nature get churned up again every day.

Yet no one seems to find this troubling. Headings like Economy, Politics, Science, Books, Culture, Religion and Local Events remain in place as if there were nothing odd going on. The smallest AIDS virus takes you from sex to the unconscious, then to Africa, tissue cultures, DNA and San Francisco, but the analysts, thinkers, journalists and decision-makers will slice the delicate network traced by the virus for you into tidy compartments where you will find only science, only economy, only social phenomena, only local news, only sentiment, only sex. Press the most innocent aerosol button and you'll be heading for the Antarctic, and from there to the University of California at Irvine, the mountain ranges of Lyon, the chemistry of inert gases, and then maybe to the United Nations, but this fragile thread will be broken into as many segments as there are pure disciplines. By all means, they seem to say, let us not mix up knowledge, interest, justice and power. Let us not mix up heaven and earth, the global stage and the local scene, the human and the nonhuman. 'But these imbroglios do the mixing,' you'll say, 'they weave our world together!' 'Act as if they didn't exist,' the analysts reply. They have cut the Gordian knot with a well-honed sword. The shaft is broken: on the left, they have put knowledge of things; on the right, power and human politics.

1.2 Retying the Gordian knot

For twenty years or so, my friends and I have been studying these strange situations that the intellectual culture in which we live does not know how to categorize. For lack of better terms, we call ourselves sociologists, historians, economists, political scientists, philosophers or anthropologists. But to these venerable disciplinary labels we always add a qualifier: 'of science and technology'. 'Science studies', as Anglo-Americans call it, or 'science, technology and society'. Whatever label we use, we are always attempting to retie the Gordian knot by crisscrossing, as often as we have to, the divide that separates exact knowledge and the exercise of power – let us say nature and culture. Hybrids ourselves, installed lopsidedly within scientific institutions, half engineers and half philosophers, 'tiers instruits' (Serres, 1991) without having sought the role, we have chosen to follow the imbroglios wherever they take us. To shuttle back and forth, we rely on the notion of translation, or network. More supple than the notion of system, more historical than the notion of structure, more empirical than the notion of complexity, the idea of network is the Ariadne's thread of these interwoven stories.

Yet our work remains incomprehensible, because it is segmented into three components corresponding to our critics' habitual categories. They turn it into nature, politics or discourse.

When Donald MacKenzie describes the inertial guidance system of intercontinental missiles (MacKenzie, 1990); when Michel Callon describes fuel cell electrodes (Callon, 1989); when Thomas Hughes describes the filament of Edison's incandescent lamp (Hughes, 1983); when I describe the anthrax bacterium modified by Louis Pasteur (Latour, 1988b) or Roger Guillemin's brain peptides (Latour and Woolgar, [1979] 1986), the critics imagine that we are talking about science and technology. Since these are marginal topics, or at best manifestations of pure instrumental and calculating thought, people who are interested in politics or in souls feel justified in paying no attention. Yet this research does not deal with nature or knowledge, with things-in-themselves, but with the way all these things are tied to our collectives and to subjects. We are talking not about instrumental thought but about the very substance of our societies. MacKenzie mobilizes the entire American Navy, and even Congress, to talk about his inertial guidance system; Callon mobilizes the French electric utility (EDF) and Renault as well as great chunks of French energy policy to grapple with changes in ions at the tip of an electrode in the depth of a laboratory; Hughes reconstructs all America around the incandescent filament of Edison's lamp; the whole of French society comes into view if one tugs on Pasteur's bacteria; and it becomes impossible to understand brain peptides without hooking them up with a scientific community, instruments, practices – all impedimenta that bear very little resemblance to rules of method, theories and neurons.

'But then surely you're talking about politics? You're simply reducing scientific truth to mere political interests, and technical efficiency to mere strategical manœuvres?' Here is the second misunderstanding. If the facts do not occupy the simultaneously marginal and sacred place our worship has reserved for them, then it seems that they are immediately reduced to pure local contingency and sterile machinations. Yet science studies are talking not about the social contexts and the interests of power, but about their involvement with collectives and objects. The Navy's organization is profoundly modified by the way its offices are allied with its bombs; EDF and Renault take on a completely different look depending on whether they invest in fuel cells or the internal combustion engine; America before electricity and America after are two different places; the social context of the nineteenth century is altered according to whether it is made up of wretched souls or poor people infected by microbes; as for the unconscious subjects stretched out on the analyst's couch, we picture them differently depending on whether their dry brain is discharging neurotransmitters or their moist brain is secreting hormones. None of our studies can reutilize what the sociologists, the psychologists or the economists tell us about the social context or about the subject in order to apply them to the hard sciences – and this is why I will use the word 'collective' to describe the association of humans and nonhumans and 'society' to designate one part only of our collectives, the divide invented by the social sciences. The context and the technical content turn out to be redefined every time. Just as epistemologists no longer recognize in the collectivized things we offer them the ideas, concepts or theories of their childhood, so the human sciences cannot be expected to recognize the power games of their militant adolescence in these collectives full of things we are lining up. The delicate networks traced by Ariadne's little hand remain more invisible than spiderwebs.

'But if you are not talking about things-in-themselves or about humans-among-themselves, then you must be talking just about discourse, representation, language, texts, rhetorics.' This is the third misunderstanding. It is true that those who bracket off the external referent – the nature of things – and the speaker – the pragmatic or social context – can talk only about meaning effects and language games. Yet when MacKenzie examines the evolution of inertial guidance systems, he is talking about arrangements that can kill us all; when Callon follows a trail set forth in scientific articles, he is talking about industrial strategy as well as rhetoric (Callon et al., 1986); when Hughes analyzes Edison's notebooks, the internal world of Menlo Park is about to become the external world of all America (Hughes, 1983). When I describe Pasteur's domestication of microbes, I am mobilizing nineteenth-century society, not just the semiotics of a great man's texts; when I describe the invention-discovery of brain peptides, I am really talking about the peptides themselves, not simply their representation in Professor Guillemin's laboratory. Yet rhetoric, textual strategies, writing, staging, semiotics – all these are really at stake, but in a new form that has a simultaneous impact on the nature of things and on the social context, while it is not reducible to the one or the other.

Our intellectual life is out of kilter. Epistemology, the social sciences, the sciences of texts – all have their privileged vantage point, provided that they remain separate. If the creatures we are pursuing cross all three spaces, we are no longer understood. Offer the established disciplines some fine sociotechnological network, some lovely translations, and the first group will extract our concepts and pull out all the roots that might connect them to society or to rhetoric; the second group will erase the social arid political dimensions, and purify our network of any object; the third group, finally, will retain our discourse and rhetoric but purge our work of any undue adherence to reality – *horresco referens* – or to power plays. In the eyes of our critics the ozone hole above our heads, the moral law in our hearts, the autonomous text, may each be of interest, but only separately. That a delicate shuttle should have woven together the heavens, industry, texts, souls and moral law – this remains uncanny, unthinkable, unseemly.

[. . .]

Chapter 11

JEAN BAUDRILLARD

THE VANISHING POINT OF COMMUNICATION

THE INFLUENCE OF Baudrillard's work on the study of new media and technoculture is clear. Even those who profess to profoundly disagree with his diagnoses of contemporary reality are often seduced by his evocative and provocative writing. Indeed it is often his aphoristic style and ostensibly bleak vision of hyperreality that is evident, rather than any sustained engagement with his ideas and influences. His assertions that along with the rise of mass media, reality (as it is commonly understood) has disappeared to be fully replaced by a simulacral world, should not be taken to mean that lived reality in an anthropological sense has disappeared, but rather that it is of a very different order to earlier realities. Hyperreality is more-than-reality, and in later work Baudrillard talks of 'integral' or proliferating reality. We might read this as suggestive for the study of the proliferating realities of mediated and networked worlds, or even as echoing **Haraway**'s interest in the new realities of artifice and synthesis from new media to biotechnology.

From the start of this talk, Baudrillard renders the terms 'communication' and 'information' problematic. When we use the term 'media' we are generally talking about *communication* or *information* media (not least in the term ICT, or information and communication technology). He overthrows the commonsense assumption that, since the evolution of language, humans have always communicated. Speech and other social practices in ancient, tribal or village life, he argues, were *not* communication as we understand it today. Communication was invented with communication technologies and this technologised, mediated interaction has now eclipsed the 'communion' of pre-modern societies. No-one, he asserts, needed to 'communicate' when they could just talk to each other. He isn't clear about precisely when this radical change occurred, nor which technologies he has in mind, but the shift of writing from ritual and religious purposes to a mass medium with Gutenberg's printing press in Europe in the fifteenth century might serve us as a working example.

So, the informal 'communion of meaning' of pre-modern life and the fluid and rich character of everyday face-to-face conversation (perhaps 'communicating' nothing of significance but crucial to the establishment and sustenance of human relationships) is superseded by the institutions, bureaucracies, codes and technologies that sustain themselves through the sending of political, commercial or (with the advent of the mass media) entertainment 'messages'. A message assumes a distance between the sender and the receiver, indeed it assumes a sender and a receiver in the first place, separate in time and space. It also assumes a *direction*; the reciprocity of communion and symbolic exchange is lost in the circulation and circularity of communication.

If for Baudrillard communication was born at the beginning of the modern age, then it seems to have stepped up a gear with computer media and networks. With characteristic irony, he expresses nostalgia for the 'golden age of alienation' of the industrial era, a time when the exploitational nature of the relationship between people and machines was only too clear (**Marx**). Today, however, we are too thoroughly integrated into communication technologies to even see them as distinct. Like the player of a videogame, for example, the virtual world responds to human input, but all the player can do is explore the world as a programmed system. For Baudrillard, both freedom and alienation have withered.

The talk on which this chapter is based was delivered in 1992, a year or so before the advent of the World Wide Web (though he makes reference to Minitel, a French non-Internet-based computer communication network of the 1980s and early 1990s). However, his analysis resonates with contemporary celebrations of, and anxieties about, Web 2.0 social networking media. As avid Facebook and Twitter users know, there is 'a moral obligation to remain connected'. We might use this extract to explore whether these media and practices exemplify Baudrillard's vision of communication as a catastrophic implosion of genuine exchange, or whether they mark a reinvention or reinvigoration of 'communion', over distance of course, but in real-time, reciprocal speech in virtual proximity.

http:plato.stanford.edu/entries/baudrillard/

1 The vanishing point of communication[1]

[. . .]

Everything about communication seems to have been said, but actually nothing has been. Almost nothing except the stereotypes or the technological fantasies of the experts in the matter. Something really theoretical is lacking. Let us refer to what happened in the theoretical field of production: whereas the classical economists spoke of a natural philosophy of wealth and exchange, Marx came along and spoke of production, of productivity and mode of production – it was a theoretical revolution. The same later with the theory of consumption: whereas the ideologists of consumption spoke of human needs and pure commodities, we began to speak of consumption as a structural and differential logic of signs. This was something radically different, and initiated a totally new analysis. And now with the sphere of communication: we only hear about information, message, interaction and so on. But what is the real meaning, the real finality of all that?

At this moment we don't have the key. We didn't get the equivalent of the theoretical leap forward in the field of production and consumption, the radical viewpoint which would change the very terms of the problem, allowing us to speak of communication and information in terms other than those of evidence and apologia. If it is so difficult to abstract the logic of communication from its apologia, then this is because communication and information are first of all involved in their own operation, invested in their own effects, immersed in their own spectacle. So it is difficult to extract their reality from their simulation. The whole complex has succeeded today as a dominant system of values, and as a collective operational network at the same time. But the point is: are we really communicating or isn't it rather the problem of our whole society expanding, transcending, exhausting itself in the fiction of communication?

Other generations grew up with the myth of production. Saint-Simonian and proto-capitalistic Utopias marked out a radiant future for the human race according to this prospective conception. And a sort of political and economical mysticism continues to push us towards maximal production with the prospect [*la perspective*] of maximal wealth and social comfort – however cruelly smashed by the world crisis of 1929 and the latent crisis in all industrial countries ever since. Now we know that an excess of production may be obnoxious and fatal. Even consumption may reverse its finality. Ever-growing consumption of therapies and healthcare for example may turn out to be a catastrophe for social security and for our health itself.[2] The consumption of cultural goods, or of sexual pleasure, or of any commodity considered as a quantitative function, reveals itself to be an absurdity. The same paradoxical consequence is true for communication and information. We are at the critical limit where all effects can be reversed and communication vanishes into an excess of communication. All functions of transparency and fluidity in social relations end in a useless complexity and a collective suffocation. This vanishing point is not a prediction, it is a pure presumption, but a logical one, or rather a tautological one – describing communication and information as a great tautological operation, as a great self-fulfilling prophecy.

First of all: it isn't true that men have always communicated since they first spoke to each other and lived in society. It is not even true that there have been 'messages' and information ever since men were connected by language. This anthropological extrapolation, which tends to extend the principle of communication back through the ages and to give it an aboriginal status, is entirely misleading. It occults the very moment when communication began, in the technical sense of the word (communication is a technology), when we began to be involved and engaged in a collective need for communication. It occults the specificity of communication as a modern invention, as a new mode of production and circulation of speech, connected to the media and the technology of media. Conversely: just as it has not always existed, perhaps also communication will not exist forever; neither is information an extra-temporal notion – maybe both will last as long as the words to speak of them. The terminological point is crucial. Things exist only when there is a determination of them, a sign which testifies, a warrant of their meaning and credibility. Whoever had the idea of 'communicating' in ancient societies, in tribes, in villages, in families? Neither the word nor the concept existed, the question doesn't make any sense. People don't need to communicate, because they just speak to one another. Why communicate when it is so easy to speak to each other?

So, my presupposition is: just as the failure [*défaillance*] of the real is the basis for the reality principle, so the failure of speech and symbolic exchange is the basis for the principle of communication. So the basic status, the basic definition of communication is negative. It is just like what Apollinaire says of time: if you are talking about it, it is because it doesn't exist any more . . . When we speak of communication, it is because there is no communication any more. The social body is no longer conductive, relations are no longer regulated by informal consensus, the communion of meaning [*le sens*] is lost. That is why we must produce a formal apparatus, a collective artefact, a huge network of information that assumes the circulation of meaning. A new specific function is born, reflected in a code, in numerous institutions, and then all at once emerge the techniques of communication, and then the sciences of communication, all the sophistries, all the casuistries, all the social and political complexity of communication. The simplest exchanges must transit through multiple codes and feedback, which change their sense. Everything becomes a 'message' (according to McLuhan,[3] this pompous and ridiculous term sounds like 'massage', like manipulation). With the message, language becomes a pure 'medium' of communication, according to the structuralist and functionalist analysis. Emitter, receiver, code, context, contact, message: language is altered in its substance by this system of formalization, it is reduced to a one-dimensional function, according to the one-dimensional process of life. What was an act has become an operation. Speech was an act, communication is an operation, and along with it goes the operation of social life. Language is a form, but communication is a performance. Then it becomes more and more efficient [*performant*], easier and easier, faster and faster, but at the same time the system becomes heavier and heavier, more and more institutionalized, less and less conductive. (The very term 'communication' has a bureaucratic heaviness, it has all the beauty of a prosthetic mechanism.)

We must never forget this when confronting the structure of communication: its very essence is non-communication. Its horizon is negative, and this has consequences for the future of all human relations.

Communication became this strange structure where things (and beings) do not touch each other, but exchange their kinetic, caloric, erotic and informational energy through contiguity, just like molecules. Through contiguity, but without contact, always being at a distance from each other. Take highway cloverleaves. Nothing is more beautiful than two roads crossing each other, but it is dangerous as an accident risk – so is the crossing of glances or the exchange of words, human words, as a seduction risk. So we invented traffic infrastructures where cars can move without crossing each other, we invented structures of relations where humans can communicate without passing each other, without touching each other, without looking at each other. We are all commuters, and the condition for the fluidity of information, for the fluidity of transit, will be the abduction of all senses, of looking, of touching, of smelling, of all the potential violence of exchange.

It is the same with our mediatized and computerized human relations. We interact without touching each other, interlocute without speaking to each other, interface without seeing each other. Here is something really bizarre. The strangeness of a blank attraction, of a blank interaction, the inseparability of particles at distances of light-years. They talk about this a lot in physics. It seems that our social structure too is oriented towards this model, in a form of electronic solidarity. Just by chance we are discovering this in physics at the very moment when we are having the same experience in everyday life.

Permeability to all images, to all messages, to all networks – submission to the virality of signs, to the epidemics of value, to the multiplicity of codes – tactility, digitality, contact, contiguity, contagion, irradiation and chain reaction: what gets lost in this new ritual of transparency and interaction is both the singularity of the self, and the singularity of the other. That is, the irreducibility of the subject, and the irreducibility of the object. Interaction, communication describe the vanishing point of the subject, of its secret, of its desire, of its *Unheimlichkeit* (strangeness to itself). But it is the vanishing point of the other as well, of transfer and challenge; of strangeness and seduction – all the fascination of alterity, of the external quality of the other, all dual and dialectical forms of relationship get lost, for all these forms presuppose distance, contradiction, tension or intensity, quite the contrary of the superficial fluidity of the electronic screen of communication. Another point is the question of time, of the suspension of time as well as the suspending of words, or of activity. In an interactive field there is no place for silence, for idleness, for absence. There is no stasis, no vacation, no rest – only metastasis along the networks, ramifications of time and space. No dead time, no distraction, no dreamtime: time is no longer your enemy, nor your luxury (you cannot spend it uselessly). It is not your master or your slave: it is your partner, and it resolves itself without past or future, in exhausting instantaneity.

For it must be instantaneous in order to work. And images and messages must follow one another, without discontinuity. No break, no syncope, no silence. A text may be silent, it may absorb or produce silence in its words – images, at least media-images, cannot. Silence on television is a scandal. That is why these lapses or silences on the screen are so significant, significant of nothing maybe, except the rupture of communication, but precisely this suspense is delightful, inasmuch as it makes obvious that all these non-stop images, this intensive information, is nothing but an artificial scenario, a pure fiction that protects us from the void – the void of the screen, of course, but also the void of our mental screen. The scene of a man sitting and staring at his empty television screen, on a strike day, will be one of the most beautiful and impressive anthropological images of the end of the twentieth century.

In the interactive social life, it is prohibited to disconnect yourself; prohibited even on your deathbed to disconnect the tubes and wires. The scandal is not so much the offence against life (nobody cares) as the attack on the network, on medicine and the technological apparatus of survival, which must first take care of its own survival. The principle of communication implies the absolute moral obligation not so much to be involved as to remain connected.

This constitutes of course a possibility of being alienated by the whole system of interconnection, of being controlled even in your private life. But much more alienating, much more destabilizing is the reciprocal control given *to you* over the external world. The first danger is well known as the Big Brother story – the common fear of total control. But the second is more sophisticated and perverse. By using all the available screens and videos and telematic possibilities (including sex [*l'amour*] by telephone), it makes the external world superfluous, it makes all human presence, physical or linguistic, superfluous. All-out communication accentuates the involution into a micro-universe, with no reason to escape any more. A carceral niche with video walls. The fact that someone knew everything about you was frightening. But today, the best way of neutralizing, of cancellating someone is not to know everything about him, it is to give him the means of knowing everything about everything – and especially about himself. You no longer neutralize him by repression and control, you neutralize him through information and communication. You paralyse him much better by excess than by deprivation of information, since you enchain him to the pure obligation of being more and more connected to himself, more and more closely connected to the screen, in restless circularity and autoreferentiality, as an integrated network.

At this point, the question of liberty doesn't make sense any more. Our sovereignty is diffracted along the technical and mental lines of parasitic ramifications. For this process happens not only externally, in the operational network of institutions and programmes, but also internally, in the labyrinth of our brain and our body. To put it another way: the exoteric complex of communication, this huge apparatus deployed on the surface of our societies, goes along with an esoteric complex that rules the intimacy of each individual. Through this complex, through all techniques of introspection, through psychology, biology and medicine, man has learned to communicate with himself, to deal with himself as a partner, to interface with himself. He passed from the stage of passion and destiny to the stage of calculating and negotiating his own life, dealing with all the information about it, just like the way a computer operates.

The sexual discourse itself is an operational one. Sexual pleasure becomes an act of communication (you receive me, I receive you), we exchange it as an interactive performance. To enjoy without communication, without reciprocal feedback, is a scandal. Maybe communications machines feel pleasure [*jouissent*] too – we don't know, and we'll probably never know. But if we imagine pleasure-machines, they can only act, or interact, as computing networks. In fact, these machines exist right now: they are our own bodies, induced to feel pleasure [*jouir*] again by all the most subtle cosmetic and exultative techniques.

Exactly as, sitting in front of his computer or word-processor, he affords himself the spectacle of his brain and his intelligence, man affords himself the spectacle of his sexual fantasies as he sits in front of his 'Minitel rose' (this term refers to a computer network, connected with the telephone system, and freely available to every home – 'rose' refers to the type of messages, sweet ones). He exorcises sexual fantasies or intelligence in the interface with the machine. The other, the sexual or cognitive interlocutor, is never really face-to-face. Only the screen, which is the point of interface, is invested, and this interactive screen transforms the process of communication into a process of commutation that is in a process of reversibility between two identical things. Within the screen there is no transcendence as there is for the mirror (you cannot get beyond the screen as you can pass through the mirror), and then the Other is virtually the same – Otherness is virtually squatted by the machine. And so the archetype of modern communication would be this one of the 'Minitel rose': people make contact via the screen, then pass to talking on the telephone, then face-to-face, and then what? They return to the telephone 'We'll call each other' and then go back to the 'Minitel' exchange – so much more erotic, because esoteric and transparent, a pure form of communication, with the abstract presence of the screen and its electronic text, as a new Platonic cave, where one can watch the shadows of carnal pleasure passing by. Why speak to each other when it is so easy to communicate?

We used to live in the fantasy of the mirror, of the divided self and alienation. We now live in the fantasy of the screen, of the interface, of contiguity and networks. All our machines are screens. We too are going to be screens, and the interactivity of men has been turned into an interactivity of screens. We are images one to another, the only destiny of an image being the following image on the screen. And images don't have to be asked for their meaning, but to be explored instantaneously, in an immediate abreaction to meaning, in an immediate implosion of the poles of representation.

Exploring an image (or a text-image, for any text on the screen appears as an image) is quite different from reading a text. It is a digital exploration, where the eye moves in a capricious and sporadic way. The interface relation between interlocutors, or the interface relation to knowledge in information processing, is the same: tactile and exploratory. The voice, the computer voice or even the telephone voice, is a tactile one, a functional non-voice. Not really a voice, just as the screen is not really an object of vision any more. The whole paradigm of sensibility has changed. The tactility (see McLuhan) is not the organic sense of touch, it merely signifies the epidemic contiguity of eye and image, and then the vanishing of any aesthetic distance. We are coming closer and closer to the image, our eyes as if disseminated in the surface of the screen. And if we fall so easily into this cerebrovisual coma of the television, it is because of this perpetual vacuum of the screen, which we spontaneously fill up with our fantasies. Proximity of images, tactility of images, tactile pornography of images – though physically so close to us, the TV-image is paradoxically light-years away. It stays at a very special distance that can only be defined as insuperable by the body. The distance of the theatrical scene, of the mirror, is superable by the body, it can eventually surmount it, this is why this distance remains human. The distance of the screen is virtual, hyperreal, and therefore insuperable. It is adapted to this single form, to this single abstract form of communication. Not exactly human any more, but while using contiguity without contact, corresponding to an eccentric dimension, to a depolarization of space and a destabilization of the body.

There is no topology more beautiful than the Möbius strip to designate the contiguity of the close and the distant, of interior and exterior, of object and subject, of the computer screen and the mental screen of our brain intertwined with each other in the same spiral. In the same way, information and communication always feed back in a kind of incestuous convolution. They operate in a circular continuity, in a superficial indistinction between subject and object, interior and exterior, question and answer, event and image – a contiguity only to be solved in a loop, simulating the mathematical figure for infinity.

Exchange is reciprocity, reversibility, whereas communication means circulation and circularity. Communicational man is assigned to the network in the same way the network is assigned to him, by a refraction from one to the other. The machine does what he wants it to do, but man himself performs only what the machine is programmed to do. He is the operator of virtuality and his action is to explore all the potentialities [*virtualités*] of a programme, just as a gambler tends to explore all the potentialities of the game.

The machine confiscates alterity. When using a camera, for instance, these virtualities are no longer those of the subject framing the world according to his vision, but those of the object exploiting the virtualities of the lens. The camera is a machine that secretly distorts [*altère*] any specific will, that erases all intentionality, supporting only the pure reaction of taking pictures. The lens is substituted for vision, and then operates a reversal of it, an involution of sight. Thus the picture may be the object's insight into the subject and not, as we commonly believe, the subject's insight into the world. And what makes the magic of photography, indeed, is this involution of the subject into the black box, this devolution of his vision to the impersonal eye of the camera. In all techniques, maybe, in the entire operational world, in all these machines with integrated circuits between subject and object, the fact is that it is the object that short-circuits the subject; it is the object that imposes its own image.

That is why any image is possible today. That is why anything can be computerized, as something commutable in itself or in its own digital operation, just as any individual is self-commutable according to his genetic formula (exploring the virtualities of the genetic code will be a fundamental aspect of cognitive sciences). It means that there is no act, no event that would not be refracted on a screen or in a technical image, nor any action that would not be photographed, filmed, recorded, that would not be reproduced in the virtual eternity of the artificial memories. The compulsion is to exist potentially on all the screens and in the circumvolutions of all the programmes. That is our fantasy of communication.

What about freedom at this point? There is none any more. There is no choice, no final decision. Concerning networks, information, operating machines, all decisions are serial, partial, fragmentary, microscopic, fractal – so to speak, quantic. Willing and acting are diffracted along the dotted lines of microscopic sequences and objects. And the fascination of all this comes from the void and the vertigo of this black box, from this progressive fading of the real world, from this approach to the vanishing point of our freedom. Am I a man, am I a machine? In the relation with traditional machines, there was no ambiguity. Man is always a stranger for the machine, and therefore alienated by it. He rescues himself as an exploited individual [*comme exploité*] (that was the golden age of alienation). Whereas new technologies, interactive machines, computer screens do not alienate me at all. I am connected with them, I am integrated with them. They are a part of me, a part of myself, like contact lenses, like transparent prostheses integrated into the body to the point of becoming a genetic part of it, like pacemakers, or the famous papula of Philip K. Dick, a small advertising implant grafted onto the body at birth, which serves as a biological alarm.

All modern forms of communication are built on the same model: that of an integrated structure, where the quality of being human, as opposed to the machine, is undecidable.

Am I a man, am I a machine? There is no answer any more to this anthropological question. In a way, this is the end of anthropology, the science of man being itself confiscated by the most recent technologies. Paradoxically, this anthropological uncertainty goes along with the growing perfectibility of networks, just as sexual uncertainty (am I a man, am I a woman, what about sexual difference?) arises from sophisticated techniques of the unconscious and of the body. Sophisticating the undecidable. Just as radical uncertainty about the status of object and subject arises from the sophistication of the microsciences.

An immense uncertainty is all that remains from the sophistication of networks of communication and information – the undecidability of knowing whether there is real knowledge in there or not, whether there is any real form of exchange or not. This again is undecidable, and I defy anyone to decide it. But, in the end, the point is: does the fantastic success of artificial intelligence arise from the fact that it makes us free from real intelligence? From the fact that by hyperrealizing the operational phenomenon of thinking it makes us free from the ambiguity and singularity of thought in relation to the world? Does not the success of all these interactive technologies come from their function of exorcism, making the eternal problem of freedom quite irrelevant? What a relief! With virtual machines, no more problems! You are neither subject nor object, neither free nor alienated, no longer one or the other: you are the same, in several commutations. We have passed from the hell of others to the ecstasy of the same, from the purgatory of otherness to the artificial paradise of identity. Might that be a way to a new type of freedom? Some would say to a new type of servitude.

Now, this is the game in which we find ourselves, our crucial game, the game of uncertainty. We cannot escape it. But we are not ready to accept it, and even worse: we expect some sort of homeopathic salvation, we hope to reduce this uncertainty with more information, with more communication, thereby reinforcing the uncertainty of the whole system. Again this is quite fascinating: the pursuit-race [*course-poursuite*] of techniques and their perverted effects, the pursuit-race of man and his virtual clones on the reversible track of the Möbius Strip.

Notes

1   This text is based on a transcript of a lecture delivered in English by Jean Baudrillard to the Department of Social Sciences, Loughborough University, UK on 18 November 1992. Baudrillard's delivery appears to have been based on an English translation by an unknown translator. We have undertaken some light editing where the double displacement of the original French text rendered Baudrillard's intention unclear. We are extremely grateful to Chris Turner for the benefit of his experience in suggesting the likely original French vocabulary/turns of phrase (indicated in square brackets) and more appropriate English translations. The French phrases are of the status of best guesses and the editors take full responsibility for any inaccuracies introduced by this nonetheless necessary editing.

2   Cf. Illich, I. (1976) *Medical Nemesis: The Expropriation of Health*. New York: Pantheon.

3   McLuhan, M. and Fiore, Q. (1967) *The Medium is the Massage: An Inventory of Effects*. New York: Bantam Books.

Chapter 12

DONNA HARAWAY

SELECTED MATERIAL FROM 'A CYBORG MANIFESTO'

'The informatics of domination', 'The "homework economy" outside "the home"' and 'Women in the integrated circuit'

D ONNA HARAWAY'S 'Cyborg Manifesto' has been hugely influential since its first publication in the mid-1980s. Her cyborg is at once an allegory of life in late capitalism and cyberculture, and a set of actually existing (or soon to be realised) technosocial entities and relationships. Thus the human–machine hybrids she takes from feminist science fiction literature and cyberpunk movies of the early 1980s are not only representations of, but fully part of, a world in which clear divisions between nature and culture are dissolving.

This creature is 'a cybernetic organism, a hybrid of machine and organism' (Haraway 1990: 191). It is a deliberately ambiguous figure, though Haraway is careful to insist that her cyborg is at once an ironic fiction *and* a way of thinking about actually existing phenomena. Thus it encompasses fictional cyborgs such as RoboCop, the increasing material intimacy between human bodies and machines (in medicine, warfare or in miniaturised consumer electronics), and a conception of networks as complex systems in which categories of biology and machines blur.

This is a socialist-feminist manifesto and Haraway argues that we are seeing a fundamental shift in the exercise of class and gender power relations with cybernetics and biotechnology. It is important to note that, within the nightmarish possibilities of new forms of military power and political control, Haraway sees radically utopian possibilities for a cyborg world in its undermining of all kinds of distinctions as well as that between nature and culture. Indeed, she aims to challenge 'western either/or epistemology' as a whole:

> certain dualisms have been persistent in Western traditions; they have all been systemic to the logics and practices of domination of women, people of colour, nature, workers, animals – in short, domination of all constituted as others, whose task is to mirror the self. Chief among these troubling dualisms are self/other, mind/body, culture/nature, male/female, civilized/primitive [. . .]
>
> (Haraway 1990: 218)

These categories establish the dominant Western subject through opposition to his 'others'. Monsters, such as those in classical myth, demonstrate the ambiguities of self-definition through the other: the centaur, half human, half animal, represents 'boundary pollution'. The cyborg then is a contemporary monster, one to be celebrated.

It is also a challenge to feminist discourses that romanticise Nature as a realm separate from oppressive masculinist technocracy. The cyborg's ambiguity heralds the possibility of a 'post-gender' subject. Irreducible to either the natural or the cultural; it is therefore neither entirely male nor entirely female. Haraway cites *Blade Runner*'s heroine, the replicant Rachel, as an image of the fundamental confusion the cyborg generates around distinctions between the technical and the natural, and questions of origins, of mind and body (Haraway 1990: 219). The cyborg comes into being through 'replication' rather than organic reproduction, so it lends itself to the 'utopian tradition of imagining a world without gender' (Haraway 1990: 192). This then is an attempt to think beyond difference, beyond the dualisms that structure the modern subject, an attempt in which science and technology, and particularly information technology, are central.

The essay is widely anthologised and easily accessible online so we have chosen not to reproduce it in full here. The extracts we have chosen highlight important ideas within the manifesto that focus on the actual political, social and economic implications of the cyborg, rather than on its fictional components.

The full text is available here: http://www.stanford.edu/dept/HPS/Haraway/Cyborg Manifesto.html

Reference

Haraway, Donna (1990) *Simians, Cyborgs and Women: The Reinvention of Nature*. London: Free Association.

The informatics of domination

[. . .] Communications technologies and biotechnologies are the crucial tools recrafting our bodies. These tools embody and enforce new social relations for women worldwide. Technologies and scientific discourses can be partially understood as formalizations, i.e., as frozen moments, of the fluid social interactions constituting them, but they should also be viewed as instruments for enforcing meanings. The boundary is permeable between tool and myth, instrument and concept, historical systems of social relations and historical anatomies of possible bodies, including objects of knowledge. Indeed, myth and tool mutually constitute each other.

Furthermore, communications sciences and modern biologies are constructed by a common move – the translation of the world into a problem of coding, a search for a common language in which all resistance to instrumental control disappears and all heterogeneity can be submitted to disassembly, reassembly, investment, and exchange.

In communications sciences, the translation of the world into a problem in coding can be illustrated by looking at cybernetic (feedback-controlled) systems theories applied to telephone technology, computer design, weapons deployment, or data base construction and maintenance. In each case, solution to the key questions rests on a theory of language and control; the key operation is determining the rates, directions, and probabilities of flow of a quantity called information. The world is subdivided by boundaries differentially permeable to information. Information is just that kind of quantifiable element (unit, basis of unity) which allows universal translation, and so unhindered instrumental power (called effective communication). The biggest threat to such power is interruption of communication. Any system breakdown is a function of stress. The fundamentals of this technology can be condensed into the metaphor C31, command-controlcommunication-intelligence, the military's symbol for its operations theory.

In modern biologies, the translation of the world into a problem in coding can be illustrated by molecular genetics, ecology, sociobiological evolutionary theory, and immunobiology. The organism has been translated into problems of genetic coding and read-out. Biotechnology, a writing technology, informs research broadly.[1] In a sense, organisms have ceased to exist as objects of knowledge, giving way to biotic components, i.e., special kinds of information-processing devices. The analogous moves in ecology could be examined by probing the history and utility of the concept of the ecosystem. Immunobiology and associated medical practices are rich exemplars of the privilege of coding and recognition systems as objects of knowledge, as constructions of bodily reality for us. Biology here is a kind of cryptography. Research is necessarily a kind of intelligence activity. Ironies abound. A stressed system goes awry; its communication processes break down; it fails to recognize the difference between self and other. Human babies with baboon hearts evoke national ethical perplexity—for animal rights activists at least as much as for the guardians of human purity. In the US gay men and intravenous drug users are the 'privileged' victims of an awful immune system disease that marks (inscribes on the body) confusion of boundaries and moral pollution (Treichler, 1987).

But these excursions into communications sciences and biology have been at a rarefied level; there is a mundane, largely economic reality to support my claim that these sciences and technologies indicate fundamental transformations in the structure of the world for us. Communications technologies depend on electronics. Modern states, multinational corporations, military power, welfare state apparatuses, satellite systems, political processes, fabrication of our imaginations, labour-control systems, medical constructions of our bodies, commercial pornography, the international division of labour, and religious evangelism depend intimately upon electronics. Micro-electronics is the technical basis of simulacra; that is, of copies without originals.

Microelectronics mediates the translations of labour into robotics and word processing, sex into genetic engineering and reproductive technologies, and mind into artificial intelligence and decision procedures. The new biotechnologies concern more than human reproduction. Biology as a powerful engineering science for redesigning materials and processes has revolutionary implications for industry, perhaps most obvious today in areas of fermentation, agriculture, and energy. Communications sciences and biology are constructions of natural-technical objects of knowledge in which the difference between machine and organism is thoroughly blurred; mind, body, and tool are on very intimate terms. The 'multinational' material organization of the production and reproduction of daily life and the symbolic organization of the production and reproduction of culture and imagination seem equally implicated. The boundary-maintaining images of base and superstructure, public and private, or material and ideal never seemed more feeble.

I have used Rachel Grossman's (1980) image of women in the integrated circuit to name the situation of women in a world so intimately restructured through the social relations of science and technology.[2] I used the odd circumlocution, 'the social relations of science and technology', to indicate that we are not dealing with a technological determinism, but with a historical system depending upon structured relations among people. But the phrase should also indicate that science and technology provide fresh sources of power, that we need fresh sources of analysis and political action (Latour, 1984). Some of the rearrangements of race, sex, and class rooted in high-tech-facilitated social relations can make socialist-feminism more relevant to effective progressive politics.

The 'homework economy' outside 'the home'

The 'New Industrial Revolution' is producing a new world-wide working class, as well as new sexualities and ethnicities. The extreme mobility of capital and the emerging international division of labour are intertwined with the emergence of new collectivities, and the weakening of familiar groupings. These developments are neither gender- nor race-neutral. White men in advanced industrial societies have become newly vulnerable to permanent job loss, and women are not disappearing from the job rolls at the same rates as men. It is not simply that women in Third World countries are the preferred labour force for the science-based multinationals in the export-processing sectors, particularly in electronics. The picture is more systematic and involves reproduction, sexuality, culture, consumption, and production. In the prototypical Silicon Valley, many women's lives have been structured around employment in electronics-dependent jobs, and their intimate realities include serial heterosexual monogamy, negotiating childcare, distance from extended kin or most other forms of traditional community, a high likelihood of loneliness and extreme economic vulnerability as they age. The ethnic and racial diversity of women in Silicon Valley structures a microcosm of conflicting differences in culture, family, religion, education, and language.

Richard Gordon has called this new situation the 'homework economy'.[3] Although he includes the phenomenon of literal homework emerging in connection with electronics assembly, Gordon intends 'homework economy' to name a restructuring of work that broadly has the characteristics formerly ascribed to female jobs, jobs literally done only by women. Work is being redefined as both literally female and feminized, whether performed by men or women. To be feminized means to be made extremely vulnerable; able to be disassembled, reassembled, exploited as a reserve labour force; seen less as workers than as servers; subjected to time arrangements on and off the paid job that make a mockery of a limited work day; leading an existence that always borders on being obscene, out of place, and reducible to sex. Deskilling is an old strategy newly applicable to formerly privileged workers. However, the homework economy does not refer only to large-scale deskilling, nor does it deny that new areas of high skill are emerging, even for women and men previously excluded from skilled employment. Rather, the concept indicates that factory, home, and market are integrated on a new scale and that the places of women are crucial – and need to be analysed for differences among women and for meanings for relations between men and women in various situations.

The homework economy as a world capitalist organizational structure is made possible by (not caused by) the new technologies. The success of the attack on relatively privileged, mostly white, men's unionized jobs is deaf to the power of the new communications technologies to integrate and control labour despite extensive dispersion and decentralization. The consequences of the new technologies are felt by women both in the loss of the family (male) wage (if they ever had access to this white privilege) and in the character of their own jobs, which are becoming capital-intensive; for example, office work and nursing.

The new economic and technological arrangements are also related to the collapsing welfare state and the ensuing intensification of demands on women to sustain daily life for themselves as well as for men, children, and old people. The feminization of poverty—generated by dismantling the welfare state, by the homework economy where stable jobs become the exception, and sustained by the expectation that women's wages will not be matched by a male income for the support of children—has become an urgent focus. The causes of various women-headed households are a function of race, class, or sexuality; but their increasing generality is a ground for coalitions of women on many issues. That women regularly sustain daily life partly as a function of their enforced status as mothers is hardly new; the kind of integration with the overall capitalist and progressively war-based economy is new. The particular pressure, for example, on US black women, who have achieved an escape from (barely) paid domestic service and who now hold clerical and similar jobs in large numbers, has large implications for continued enforced black poverty with employment. Teenage women in industrializing areas of the Third World increasingly find themselves the sole or major source of a cash wage for their families, while access to land is ever more problematic. These developments must have major consequences in the psychodynamics and politics of gender and race.

Within the framework of three major stages of capitalism (commercial/early industrial, monopoly, multinational)—tied to nationalism, imperialism, and multinationalism, and related to Jameson's three dominant aesthetic periods of realism, modernism, and postmodernism—I would argue that specific forms of families dialectically relate to forms of capital and to its political and cultural concomitants. Although lived problematically and unequally, ideal forms of these families might be schematized as (1) the patriarchal nuclear family, structured by the dichotomy between public and private and accompanied by the white bourgeois ideology of separate spheres and nineteenth-century Anglo-American bourgeois feminism; (2) the modern family mediated (or enforced) by the welfare state and institutions like the family wage, with a flowering of a-feminist heterosexual ideologies, including their radical versions represented in Greenwich Village around the First World War; and (3) the 'family' of the homework economy with its oxymoronic structure of women-headed households and its explosion of feminisms and the paradoxical intensification and erosion of gender itself.

This is the context in which the projections for world-wide structural unemployment stemming from the new technologies are part of the picture of the homework economy. As robotics and related technologies put men out of work in 'developed' countries and exacerbate failure to generate male jobs in Third World 'development', and as the automated office becomes the rule even in labour-surplus countries, the feminization of work intensifies. Black women in the United States have long known what it looks like to face the structural underemployment ('feminization') of black men, as well as their own highly vulnerable position in the wage economy. It is no longer a secret that sexuality, reproduction, family, and community life are interwoven with this economic structure in myriad ways which have also differentiated the situations of white and black women. Many more women and men will contend with similar situations, which will make cross-gender and race alliances on issues of basic life support (with or without jobs) necessary, not just nice.

The new technologies also have a profound effect on hunger and on food production for subsistence world-wide. Rae Lessor Blumberg (1983) estimates that women produce about 50 per cent of the world's subsistence food.[4] Women are excluded generally from benefiting from the increased high-tech commodification of food and energy crops, their days are made more arduous because their responsibilities to provide food do not diminish, and their reproductive situations are made more complex. Green Revolution technologies interact with other high-tech industrial production to alter gender divisions of labour and differential gender migration patterns.

The new technologies seem deeply involved in the forms of 'privatization' that Ros Petchesky (1981) has analysed, in which militarization, right-wing family ideologies and policies, and intensified definitions of corporate (and state) property as private synergistically interact.[5] The new communications technologies are fundamental to the eradication of 'public life' for everyone. This facilitates the mushrooming of a permanent high-tech military establishment at the cultural and economic expense of most people, but especially of women. Technologies like video games and highly miniaturized televisions seem crucial to production of modern forms of 'private life'. The culture of video games is heavily orientated to individual competition and extraterrestrial warfare. High-tech, gendered imaginations are produced here, imaginations that can contemplate destruction of the planet and a sci-fi escape from its consequences. More than our imaginations is militarized; and the other realities of electronic and nuclear warfare are inescapable. These are the technologies that promise ultimate mobility and perfect exchange—and incidentally enable tourism, that perfect practice of mobility and exchange, to emerge as one of the world's largest single industries.

The new technologies affect the social relations of both sexuality and of reproduction, and not always in the same ways. The close ties of sexuality and instrumentality, of views of the body as a kind of private satisfaction- and utility-maximizing machine, are described nicely in sociobiological origin stories that stress a genetic calculus and explain the inevitable dialectic of domination of male and female gender roles.[6] These sociobiological stories depend on a high-tech view of the body as a biotic component or cybernetic communications system. Among the many transformations of reproductive situations is the medical one, where women's bodies have boundaries newly permeable to both 'visualization' and 'intervention'. Of course, who controls the interpretation of bodily boundaries in medical hermeneutics is a major feminist issue. The speculum served as an icon of women's claiming their bodies in the 1970s; that handcraft tool is inadequate to express our needed body politics in the negotiation of reality in the practices of cyborg reproduction. Self-help is not enough. The technologies of visualization recall the important cultural practice of hunting with the camera and the deeply predatory nature of a photographic consciousness.[7] Sex, sexuality, and reproduction are central actors in high-tech myth systems structuring our imaginations of personal and social possibility.

Another critical aspect of the social relations of the new technologies is the reformulation of expectations, culture, work, and reproduction for the large scientific and technical work-force. A major social and political danger is the formation of a strongly bimodal social structure, with the masses of women and men of all ethnic groups, but especially people of colour, confined to a homework economy, illiteracy of several varieties, and general redundancy and impotence, controlled by high-tech repressive apparatuses ranging from entertainment to surveillance and disappearance. An adequate socialist-feminist politics should address women in the privileged occupational categories, and particularly in the production of science and technology that constructs scientific-technical discourses, processes, and objects.[8]

This issue is only one aspect of enquiry into the possibility of a feminist science, but it is important. What kind of constitutive role in the production of knowledge, imagination, and practice can new groups doing science have? How can these groups be allied with progressive social and political movements? What kind of political accountability can be constructed to the women together across the scientific-technical hierarchies separating us? Might there be ways of developing feminist science/technology politics in alliance with anti-military science facility conversion action groups? Many scientific and technical workers in Silicon Valley, the high-tech cowboys included, do not want to work on military science.[9] Can these personal preferences and cultural tendencies be welded into progressive politics among this professional middle class in which women, including women of colour, are coming to be fairly numerous?

Women in the integrated circuit

Let me summarize the picture of women's historical locations in advanced industrial societies, as these positions have been restructured partly through the social relations of science and technology. If it was ever possible ideologically to characterize women's lives by the distinction of public and private domains—suggested by images of the division of working-class life into factory and home, of bourgeois life into market and home, and of gender existence into personal and political realms—it is now a totally misleading ideology, even to show how both terms of these dichotomies construct each other in practice and in theory. I prefer a network ideological image, suggesting the profusion of spaces and identities and the permeability of boundaries in the personal body and in the body politic. 'Networking' is both a feminist practice and a multinational corporate strategy—weaving is for oppositional cyborgs.

So let me return to the earlier image of the informatics of domination and trace one vision of women's 'place' in the integrated circuit, touching only a few idealized social locations seen primarily from the point of view of advanced capitalist societies: Home, Market, Paid Work Place, State, School, Clinic-Hospital, and Church. Each of these idealized spaces is logically and practically implied in every other locus, perhaps analogous to a holographic photograph. I want to suggest the impact of the social relations mediated and enforced by the new technologies in order to help formulate needed analysis and practical work. However, there is no 'place' for women in these networks, only geometries of difference and contradiction crucial to women's cyborg identities. If we learn how to read these webs of power and social life, we might learn new couplings, new coalitions. There is no way to read the following list from a standpoint of 'identification', of a unitary self. The issue is dispersion. The task is to survive in the diaspora.

Home: Women-headed households, serial monogamy, flight of men, old women alone, technology of domestic work, paid homework, re-emergence of home sweatshops, home-based businesses and telecommuting, electronic cottage, urban homelessness, migration, module architecture, reinforced (simulated) nuclear family, intense domestic violence.

Market: Women's continuing consumption work, newly targeted to buy the profusion of new production from the new technologies (especially as the competitive race among industrialized and industrializing nations to avoid dangerous mass unemployment necessitates finding ever bigger new markets for ever less clearly needed commodities); bimodal buying power, coupled with advertising targeting of the numerous affluent groups and neglect of the previous mass markets; growing importance of informal markets in labour and commodities parallel to high-tech, affluent market structures; surveillance systems through electronic funds transfer; intensified market abstraction (commodification) of experience, resulting in ineffective utopian or equivalent cynical theories of community; extreme mobility (abstraction) of marketing/financing systems; inter-penetration of sexual and labour markets; intensified sexualization of abstracted and alienated consumption.

Paid Work Place: Continued intense sexual and racial division of labour, but considerable growth of membership in privileged occupational categories for many white women and people of colour; impact of new technologies on women's work in clerical, service, manufacturing (especially textiles), agriculture, electronics; international restructuring of the working classes; development of new time arrangements to facilitate the homework economy (flex time, part time, over time, no time); homework and out work; increased pressures for two-tiered wage structures; significant numbers of people in cash-dependent populations world-wide with no experience or no further hope of stable employment; most labour 'marginal' or 'feminized'.

State: Continued erosion of the welfare state; decentralizations with increased surveillance and control; citizenship by telematics; imperialism and political power broadly in the form of information rich/information poor differentiation; increased high-tech militarization increasingly opposed by many social groups; reduction of civil service jobs as a result of the growing capital intensification of office work, with implications for occupational mobility for women of colour; growing privatization of material and ideological life and culture; close integration of privatization and militarization, the high-tech forms of bourgeois capitalist personal and public life; invisibility of different social groups to each other, linked to psychological mechanisms of belief in abstract enemies.

School: Deepening coupling of high-tech capital needs and public education at all levels, differentiated by race, class, and gender; managerial classes involved in educational reform and refunding at the cost of remaining progressive educational democratic structures for children and teachers; education for mass ignorance and repression in technocratic and militarized culture; growing anti-science mystery cults in dissenting and radical political movements; continued relative scientific illiteracy among white women and people of colour; growing industrial direction of education (especially higher education) by science-based multinationals (particularly in electronics- and biotechnology-dependent companies); highly educated, numerous elites in a progressively bimodal society.

Clinic-Hospital: Intensified machine–body relations; renegotiations of public metaphors which channel personal experience of the body, particularly in relation to reproduction, immune system functions, and 'stress' phenomena; intensification of reproductive politics in response to world historical implications of women's unrealized, potential control of their relation to reproduction; emergence of new, historically specific diseases; struggles over meanings and means of health in environments pervaded by high technology products and processes; continuing feminization of health work; intensified struggle over state responsibility for health; continued ideological role of popular health movements as a major form of American politics.

Church: Electronic fundamentalist 'super-saver' preachers solemnizing the union of electronic capital and automated fetish gods; intensified importance of churches in resisting the militarized state; central struggle over women's meanings and authority in religion; continued relevance of spirituality, intertwined with sex and health, in political struggle.

The only way to characterize the informatics of domination is as a massive intensification of insecurity and cultural impoverishment, with common failure of subsistence networks for the most vulnerable. Since much of this picture interweaves with the social relations of science and technology, the urgency of a socialist-feminist politics addressed to science and technology is plain. There is much now being done, and the grounds for political work are rich. For example, the efforts to develop forms of collective struggle for women in paid work, like SEIU's District 925,* should be a high priority for all of us. These efforts are profoundly deaf to technical restructuring of labour processes and reformations of working classes. These efforts also are providing understanding of a more comprehensive kind of labour organization, involving community, sexuality, and family issues never privileged in the largely white male industrial unions.

The structural rearrangements related to the social relations of science and technology evoke strong ambivalence. But it is not necessary to be ultimately depressed by the implications of late twentieth-century women's relation to all aspects of work, culture, production of knowledge, sexuality, and reproduction. For excellent reasons, most Marxisms see domination best and have trouble understanding what can only look like false consciousness and people's complicity in their own domination in late capitalism. It is crucial to remember that what is lost, perhaps especially from women's points of view, is often virulent forms of oppression, nostalgically naturalized in the face of current violation. Ambivalence towards the disrupted unities mediated by high-tech culture requires not sorting consciousness into categories of 'clear-sighted critique grounding a solid political epistemology' versus 'manipulated false consciousness', but subtle understanding of emerging pleasures, experiences, and powers with serious potential for changing the rules of the game.

There are grounds for hope in the emerging bases for new kinds of unity across race, gender, and class, as these elementary units of socialist-feminist analysis themselves suffer protean transformations. Intensifications of hardship experienced world-wide in connection with the social relations of science and technology are severe. But what people are experiencing is not transparently clear, and we lack sufficiently subtle connections for collectively building effective theories of experience. Present efforts—Marxist, psychoanalytic, feminist, anthropological—to clarify even 'our' experience are rudimentary.

[. . .]

To recapitulate, certain dualisms have been persistent in Western traditions; they have all been systemic to the logics and practices of domination of women, people of colour, nature, workers, animals—in short, domination of all constituted as others, whose task is to mirror the self. Chief among these troubling dualisms are self/other, mind/body, culture/nature, male/female, civilized/primitive, reality/appearance, whole/part, agent/resource, maker/made, active/passive, right/wrong, truth/illusion, total/partial, God/man. The self is the One who is not dominated, who knows that by the service of the other, the other is the one who holds the future, who knows that by the experience of domination, which gives the lie to the autonomy of the self. To be One is to be autonomous, to be powerful, to be God; but to be One is to be an illusion, and so to be involved in a dialectic of apocalypse with the other. Yet to be other is to be multiple, without clear boundary, frayed, insubstantial. One is too few, but two are too many.

[. . .]

High-tech culture challenges these dualisms in intriguing ways. It is not clear who makes and who is made in the relation between human and machine. It is not clear what is mind and what body in machines that resolve into coding practices. In so far as we know ourselves in both formal discourse (for example, biology) and in daily practice (for example, the homework economy in the integrated circuit), we find ourselves to be cyborgs, hybrids, mosaics, chimeras. Biological organisms have become biotic systems, communications devices like others. There is no fundamental, ontological separation in our formal knowledge of machine and organism, of technical and organic. The replicant Rachel in the Ridley Scott film *Blade Runner* stands as the image of a cyborg culture's fear, love, and confusion.

[. . .]

There are several consequences to taking seriously the imagery of cyborgs as other than our enemies. Our bodies, ourselves; bodies are maps of power and identity. Cyborgs are no exception. A cyborg body is not innocent; it was not born in a garden; it does not seek unitary identity and so generate antagonistic dualisms without end (or until the world ends); it takes irony for granted. One is too few, and two is only one possibility. Intense pleasure in skill, machine skill, ceases to be a sin, but an aspect of embodiment. The machine is not an it to be animated, worshipped, and dominated. The machine is us, our processes, an aspect of our embodiment. We can be responsible for machines; they do not dominate or threaten us. We are responsible for boundaries; we are they. Up till now (once upon a time), female embodiment seemed to be given, organic, necessary; and female embodiment seemed to mean skill in mothering and its metaphoric extensions. Only by being out of place could we take intense pleasure in machines, and then with excuses that this was organic activity after all, appropriate to females. Cyborgs might consider more seriously the partial, fluid, sometimes aspect of sex and sexual embodiment. Gender might not be global identity after all, even if it has profound historical breadth and depth.

The ideologically charged question of what counts as daily activity, as experience, can be approached by exploiting the cyborg image. Feminists have recently claimed that women are given to dailiness, that women more than men somehow sustain daily life, and so have a privileged epistemological position potentially. There is a compelling aspect to this claim, one that makes visible unvalued female activity and names it as the ground of life.

But the ground of life? What about all the ignorance of women, all the exclusions and failures of knowledge and skill? What about men's access to daily competence, to knowing how to build things, to take them apart, to play? What about other embodiments? Cyborg gender is a local possibility taking a global vengeance. Race, gender, and capital require a cyborg theory of wholes and parts. There is no drive in cyborgs to produce total theory, but there is an intimate experience of boundaries, their construction and deconstruction. There is a myth system waiting to become a political language to ground one way of looking at science and technology and challenging the informatics of domination—in order to act potently.

One last image: organisms and organismic, holistic politics depend on metaphors of rebirth and invariably call on the resources of reproductive sex. I would suggest that cyborgs have more to do with regeneration and are suspicious of the reproductive matrix and of most birthing. For salamanders, regeneration after injury, such as the loss of a limb, involves regrowth of structure and restoration of function with the constant possibility of twinning or other odd topographical productions at the site of former injury. The regrown limb can be monstrous, duplicated, potent. We have all been injured, profoundly. We require regeneration, not rebirth, and the possibilities for our reconstitution include the utopian dream of the hope for a monstrous world without gender.

Note

*Service Employees International Union's office workers' organization in the US.

1. For progressive analyses and action on the biotechnology debates: *GeneWatch, a Bulletin of the Committee for Responsible Genetics*, 5 Doane St, 4th Floor, Boston, MA 02109; Genetic Screening Study Group (formerly the Sociobiology Study Group of Science for the People), Cambridge, MA; Wright (1982, 1986); Yoxen (1983).
2. Starting references for 'women in the integrated circuit': D'Onofrio-Flores and Pfafflin (1982), Fernandez-Kelly (1983), Grossman (1980), Nash and Fernandez-Kelly (1983), Ong (1987), Science Policy Research Unit (1982).
3. For the 'homework economy outside the home' and related arguments: Gordon (1983); Gordon and Kimball (1985); Stacey (1987); Reskin and Hartmann (1986); *Women and Poverty* (1984); S. Rose (1986); Collins (1982); Burr (1982); Gregory and Nussbaum (1982); Piven and Coward (1982); Microelectronics Group (1980); Stallard *et al.* (1983) which includes a useful organization and resource list.
4. The conjunction of the Green Revolution's social relations with biotechnologies like plant genetic engineering makes the pressures on land in the Third World increasingly intense. AID's estimates (*New York Times*, 14 October 1984) used at the 1984 World Food Day are that in Africa women produce about 90 per cent of rural food supplies, about 60–80 per cent in Asia, and provide 40 per cent of agricultural labour in the Near East and Latin America. Blumberg charges that world organizations'

agricultural politics, as well as those of multinationals and national governments in the Third World, generally ignore fundamental issues in the sexual division of labour. The present tragedy of famine in Africa might owe as much to male supremacy as to capitalism, colonialism, and rain patterns. More accurately, capitalism and racism are usually structurally male dominant. See also Blumberg (1981); Hacker (1984); Hacker and Bovit (1981); Busch and Lacy (1983); Wilfred (1982); Sachs (1983); International Fund for Agricultural Development (1985); Bird (1984).

5   See also Enloe (1983a, b).

6   For a feminist version of this logic, see Hardy (1981). For an analysis of scientific women's story-telling practices, especially in relation to socio-biology in evolutionary debates around child abuse and infanticide, see this vol., ch. 5.

7   For the moment of transition of hunting with guns to hunting with cameras in the construction of popular meanings of nature for an American urban immigrant public, see Haraway (1984–5, 1989b), Nash (1979), Sontag (1977), Preston (1984).

8   For guidance for thinking about the political/cultural/racial implications of the history of women doing science in the United States see: Haas and Perucci (1984); Hacker (1981); Keller (1983); National Science Foundation (1988); Rossiter (1982); Schiebinger (1987); Haraway (1989b).

9   Markoff and Siegel (1983). High Technology Professionals for Peace and Computer Professionals for Social Responsibility are promising organizations.

Chapter 13

FÉLIX GUATTARI

BALANCE PROGRAM FOR DESIRING-MACHINES

T HE QUESTIONING OF CLEAR AND FIXED distinctions between humans and technologies is a persistent theme across this book, from **Haraway**'s cyborg to **Latour**'s networks of humans and non-humans. **Wiener**'s cybernetic insistence on connections between animals (including humans) and machines links together the biological and the artificial (also **Galison** and **Tomas**). In this extract Gilles Deleuze and Félix Guattari introduce the most radical model of technoculture in this book, a model that in fact goes beyond 'techno-*culture*' per se, describing a world of technology and nature in which humans are not an equal or even necessarily a significant part.

Guattari's collaboration with the philosopher Gilles Deleuze included two books, *Anti-Oedipus* (this extract is an afterword in the French edition of this book) and *A Thousand Plateaus*, that have influenced thought on technoculture and new media. Their concepts of the 'machinic phylum' and 'desiring-machines' run through these books and are set out here. Like the books, this article is a challenging read, but is full of energy, ideas, and examples from the history of technology, philosophy, psychoanalysis, art and films.

Before attempting to introduce the reader to these concepts, it might be helpful to pull out one of Guattari's recurring examples to help orient ourselves. In battle, Ancient Greek hoplite warriors would group together side by side into a phalanx, each soldier's shield also protecting his neighbour. Thus the men and their weapons become more than a set of individual warriors with their individual weapons, but rather an assemblage of people *and* weapons/tools in a larger technics of warfare. There are resonances here with Actor-Network Theory's insistence on the conjoined agencies of human and non-human actors (**Latour**). Importantly for Guattari and the notion of the machinic phylum, however, is the fact that the hoplite phalanx was part of, and made possible by, the broader sociotechnical formation (or machine) of the Greek city-state. Deleuze and Guattari define a machine as (1) a systematic functional interrelation of parts, i.e., anything that *works*; and (2) these parts and wholes are at the same time the products of the machine's functioning.

So, any entity contained in the machinic phylum is always part of a larger machine, and composed of smaller ones. The term *phylum* is more commonly used as a broad biological classification, below that of 'kingdom' but above 'species'. Thus the animal kingdom is made up of phyla such as the arthropods, which include spiders, scorpions, crustacea and insects.

These are creatures that share a form or a set of characteristics (they are invertebrate, with segmented exoskeletons) but not the hereditary links or genotype of individual species. The *machinic* phylum, then, groups together organisms that share machinic characteristics. Though Guattari doesn't discuss it here, the desiring-machines extend down to the molecular level of nature: think of DNA's coding of genetic information and its role in the manufacture of proteins and hence of biological life. The 'desire' of desiring-machines is not then an individual human's yearning or lust for another or an object (the basis for psychoanalysis and much cultural theory), but the impulsion driving all levels of natural and artificial connections, production and reproduction: 'these are the machine processes underlying all things' (*New Media: A Critical Introduction*: 387). In this, Deleuze and Guattari are influenced by **Marx**'s theories of production.

In another example Guattari describes the criss-crossing of distant voices and machine-generated sounds that are audible when a telephone connection fails. This soundscape indicates a technological environment functioning more or less autonomously, an emergent phenomenon not intended by human design and that goes well beyond any notion of technologies as tools or extensions of individual humans or even social groups.

This essay continues Deleuze and Guattari's sustained critique of psychoanalysis, and particularly the key Freudian concept of the Oedipus complex. Against psychoanalysis, therefore, Deleuze and Guattari maintain that desire is capable of constructing many more kinds of machines, not only Oedipal ones. However, the details of, and motivations for, this assault on psychoanalysis and psychiatry fall outside the scope of this *Reader* and so we have cut out some of the larger sections of this material. This of course does not do justice to Guattari's arguments and expertise, so we recommend that readers interested in learning more turn to their books cited above.

For a more detailed explanation of the machinic phylum and its application to cybernetic culture, see *New Media: A Critical Introduction*: 386–8. The concept has influenced the work of Manuel **De Landa** and is discussed in his extract in Part One.

1. How desiring-machines differ from gadgets—from phantasies or imaginary projective systems—from took or real projective systems—from perverse machines, which however put us on the track of desiring-machines

Desiring-machines have nothing to do with gadgets, or little homemade inventions, or with phantasies. Or rather they are related, but from the opposite direction, because gadgets, improvised contraptions, and phantasies are the residue of desiring-machines; they have come under the sway of specific laws of the foreign market of capitalism, or of the home market of psychoanalysis (it is a function of the psychoanalytic "contract" to reduce the states lived by the patient, to translate them into phantasies). Desiring-machines cannot be equated with the adaptation of real machines, or fragments of real machines, to a symbolical process, nor can they be reduced to dreams of fantastic machines operating in the Imaginary. In both instances, one witnesses the conversion of an element of production into a mechanism of individual consumption (phantasies as psychic consumption or psychoanalytic breast-feeding). It goes without saying that psychoanalysis feels at ease with gadgets and phantasies, an environment in which it can develop all its castrating Oedipal obsessions. But that tells us nothing of consequence about machines and their relation to desire.

The artistic and literary imagination conceives a great number of absurd machines: whether through the indeterminate character of the motor or energy source, through the physical impossibility of the organization of the working parts, or through the logical impossibility of the mechanism of transmission. For example, Man Ray's *Dancer-Danger*, subtitled "impossibility," offers two degrees of absurdity: neither the clusters of cog-wheels nor the large transmission wheel are able to function. Insofar as this machine is supposed to represent the whirl of a Spanish dancer, it can be said that it expresses mechanically, by means of the absurd, the impossibility for a machine to execute such a movement (the dancer is not a machine). But one can also say: there must be a dancer here who functions as a part of a machine; this machine component can only be a dancer; here is the machine of which the dancer is a component part. The object is no longer to compare humans and the machine in order to evaluate the correspondences, the extensions, the possible or impossible substitutions of the ones for the other, but to bring them into communication in order to show how *humans are a component part* of the machine, or combine with something else to constitute a machine. The other thing can be a tool, or even an animal, or other humans. We are not using a metaphor, however, when we speak of machines: *humans constitute a machine* as soon as this nature is communicated by recurrence to the ensemble of which they form a part under specific conditions. The human-horse-bow ensemble forms a nomadic war machine under the conditions of the steppe. Men form a labor machine under the bureaucratic conditions of the great empires. The Greek foot-soldier together with his arms constitute a machine under the conditions of the phalanx. The dancer combines with the floor to compose a machine under the perilous conditions of love and death . . . We do not start from a metaphorical usage of the word machine, but from a (confused) hypothesis concerning origins: the way in which heterogeneous elements are determined to constitute a machine through *recurrence and communications*; the existence of a "machinic phylum." Ergonomics comes close to this point of view when it sets the general problem, no longer in terms of adaptation or substitution—the adaptation of man to the machine, and of the machine to man—but in terms of recurrent communication within systems made up of men and machines. It is true that just as ergonomists become convinced that they are confining themselves in this way to a purely technological approach, they raise the problems of power and oppression, of revolution and desire, with an involuntary vigor that is infinitely greater than in the adaptive approaches.

There is a classic schema that is inspired by the tool: the tool as the extension and the projection of the living being, the operation by means of which man progressively emerges, the evolution from the tool to the machine, the reversal in which the machine grows more and more independent of man . . . But this schema has many drawbacks. It does not offer us any means to apprehend the reality of desiring-machines and their presence throughout this circuit. It is a biological and evolutive schema, which determines the machine as an event occurring at a given moment in the mechanical lineage that begins with the tool. It is humanistic and abstract, isolating the productive forces from the social conditions of their exercise, involving a man-nature dimension common to all the social forms, to which are thus lent relations of evolution. It is imaginary, phantasmal and solipsistic, even when it is applied to real tools, to real machines, since it rests entirely on the hypothesis of projection (Róheim for example, who adopts this schema, shows the analogy between the physical projection of tools and the psychic projection of phantasies). We believe on the contrary that it is necessary to posit, *from the outset*, the difference in nature between the tool and the machine: the one as an agent of contact, the other as a factor of communication; the one being projective, the other recurrent; the one referring to the possible and the impossible, the other to the probability of a less-probable; the one acting through the functional synthesis of a whole, the other through real distinctions in an ensemble. Functioning as a component part in conjunction with other parts is very different from being an extension or a projection, or being replaced (an instance where there is no communication). Pierre Auger shows that a machine is constituted from the moment there is communication between two portions of the outside world that are really distinct in a system that is possible although less probable. One and the same thing can be a tool or a machine, according to whether the "machinic phylum" takes hold of it or not, passes or does not pass through it. Hoplite weapons existed as tools from early antiquity, but they became components of a machine, *along with* the men who wielded them, under the conditions of the phalanx and the Greek city-state. When one refers the tool to man, in accordance with the traditional schema, one deprives oneself of any possibility of understanding how man *and* the tool *become or already are* distinct components of a machine in relation to an actual machinic agency. And we believe moreover that there are always machines that precede tools, always phyla that determine at a given moment which tools, which men will enter as machine components in the social system being considered.

Desiring-machines are neither imaginary projections in the form of phantasies, nor real projections in the form of tools. The whole system of projections derives from machines, and not the reverse. Should the desiring-machine be defined then by a kind of introjection, by a certain perverse use of the machine? Let us take the example of the telephone exchange: by dialing an unassigned number, connected to an automatic answering device ("the number you dialed is not in service . . .") one can hear the overlay of an ensemble of teeming voices, calling and answering each other, crisscrossing, fading out, passing over and under each other, inside the automatic voice, very short messages, utterances obeying rapid and monotonous codes. There is the Tiger; it is rumored that there is even an Oedipus in the network; boys calling girls, boys calling boys. One easily recognizes the very form of perverse artificial societies, or a society of Unknowns. A process of reterritorialization is connected to *a movement of deterritorialization that is ensured by the machine* (groups of ham radio transmitters afford the same perverse structure). It is certain that public institutions are not troubled by these secondary benefits of a private use of the machine, in fringe or interference phenomena. But at the same time there is something more here than a simple perverse subjectivity, be it that of a group. The normal telephone may be a machine for communication, but it functions as a tool as long as it serves to project or extend voices that are not as such a part of the machine. But in our example communication attains a higher degree, inasmuch as the voices enter into the make-up of the machine, become components of the machine, distributed and apportioned in chance fashion by the automatic device. The less probable is constructed on the basis of the entropy of the set of voices that cancel each other out. It is from this perspective that there is not only a perverse use or adaptation of a technical-social machine, but the superposing of a true objective desiring-machine, the construction of a desiring-machine within the technical social machine. It may be that desiring-machines are born in this way in the artificial margins of a society, although they develop in a completely different way and bear no resemblance to the forms of their birth.

[. . .]

2. The desiring-machine and the Oedipal apparatus: recurrence versus repression regression

Desiring-machines constitute the non-Oedipal life of the unconscious—Oedipus being the gadget or phantasy. By way of opposition, Picabia called the machine "the daughter born without a mother." Buster Keaton introduced his house-machine, with all its rooms rolled into one, as a house without a mother, and desiring-machines determine everything that goes on inside, as in the bachelors' meal (*The Scarecrow*, 1920). Are we to understand that the machine has but a father, and that it is born like Athena fully armed from a virile brain? It takes a lot of goodwill to believe, along with René Girard, that paternalism is enough to lead us out of Oedipus, and that "mimetic rivalry" is really the complex's *other*. Psychoanalysis has never ceased doing just that: fragmenting Oedipus, or multiplying it, or on the other hand dividing it, placing it at odds with itself, or sublimating it, making it boundless, elevating it to the level of the signifier. We have witnessed the discovery of the pre-Oedipal, the post-Oedipal, the symbolic Oedipus, none of which helps us to escape from the family any more than the squirrel from its turning cage. We are told: "But see here, Oedipus has nothing to do with daddy-mommy, it is the signifier, it is the name, it is culture, it is mortality, it is the essential lack which is life, it is castration, it is violence personified . . ." All of which is enough for a good laugh, at least, but it only carries on the ancient task, by cutting all the connections of desire the better to map it back onto sublime, imaginary, symbolic, linguistic, ontological, and epistemological daddy-mommies. Actually, we haven't said a fourth, or even a hundredth of what needed to be said against psychoanalysis, its *ressentiment* towards desire, its tyranny, and its bureaucracy.

What defines desiring-machines is precisely their capacity for an unlimited number of connections, in every sense and in all directions. It is for this very reason that they are machines, crossing through and commanding several structures at the same time. For the machine possesses two characteristics or powers: the power of the continuum, the machinic phylum in which a given component connects with another, the cylinder and the piston in the steam engine, or even, tracing a more distant lineage, the pulley wheel in the locomotive; but also the rupture in direction, the mutation such that each machine is an absolute break in relation to the one it replaces, as, for example, the internal combustion engine in relation to the steam engine. Two powers which are really only one, since the machine in itself is the break-flow process, the break being always adjacent to the continuity of a flow which it separates from the others by assigning it a code, by causing it to convey particular elements. Hence the fact that the machine is motherless does not speak for a cerebral father, but for a collective *full body*, the machinic agency on which the machine sets up its connections and produces its ruptures.

The machinic painters stressed the following: that they did not paint machines as substitutes for still lifes or nudes; the machine is not a represented object any more than its drawing is a representation. The aim is to introduce an element of a machine, so that it combines with something else on the full body of the canvas, be it with the painting itself, with the result that it is precisely the ensemble of the painting that functions as a desiring-machine. The induced machine is always other than the one that appears to be represented. It will be seen that the machine proceeds by means of an "uncoupling" of this nature, and ensures the deterritorialization that is characteristic of machines, the inductive, or rather the transductive quality of the machine, which defines recurrence, as opposed to representation-projection: *machinic recurrence versus Oedipal projection*. These opposing terms mark a struggle, or a disjunction, as can be seen, for example, in *Aeroplap(l)a*, or *Automoma*, and again in Victor Brauner's *Machine à connaître en forme Mère*. In Picabia's work, the finished design connects up with the incongruous inscription, with the result that it is obliged to function with *this* code, with *this* program, by inducing a machine that does not resemble it. With Duchamp, the real machine element is directly introduced, either standing on its own merits or set-off by its shadow, or, in other instances, having its place in the ensemble determined by an aleatory mechanism that induces the still-present representations to change roles and statuses: *Tu m'* for example. The machine stands apart from all representation (although one can always represent it, copy it, in a manner however that is completely devoid of interest), and it stands apart because it is pure Abstraction;

it is nonfigurative and nonprojective. Léger demonstrated convincingly that the machine did not represent anything, itself least of all, because it was in itself the production of organized intensive states: neither form nor extension, neither representation nor projection, but pure and recurrent intensities. It sometimes happens, as in Picabia, that the discovery of the abstract leads to the machinic elements, while at other times, as in the example of many a Futurist, the opposite road is traveled. Consider the old distinction drawn by the philosophers of the Enlightenment, the distinction between representative states and affective states that do not represent anything. The machine is the affective state, and it is false to say that modern machines possess a perceptive capacity or a memory; machines themselves possess only affective states.

[. . .]

All these machines are real machines. Hocquenghem is right in saying, "Where desire is active, there is no longer any place for the Imaginary," nor for the Symbolic. All these machines are already there; we are continually producing them, manufacturing them, setting them in motion, for they are desire, desire just as it is—although it takes artists to bring about their autonomous presentation. Desiring-machines are not in our heads, in our imagination, they are *inside the social and technical machines themselves.* Our relationship with machines is not a relationship of invention or of imitation; we are not the cerebral fathers nor the disciplined sons of the machine. It is a relationship of peopling: we populate the social technical machines with desiring-machines, and we have no alternative. We are obliged to say at the same time: social technical machines are only conglomerates of desiring-machines under molar conditions that are historically determined; desiring-machines are social and technical machines restored to their determinant molecular conditions. Schwitters' Merz is the last syllable of Komerz. It is futile to examine the usefulness or uselessness, the possibility or impossibility of these desiring-machines. Their impossibility and their uselessness become visible only in the autonomous artistic presentation, and there very rarely. Don't you see that they are possible because they are; they are there in every way, and we function with them. They are eminently useful, since they constitute the two directions of the relationship between the machine and man, the *communication* of the two. At the very moment you say, "this machine is impossible," you fail to see that you are making it possible, by being yourself one of its parts, the very part that you seemed to be missing in order for it to be already working, the dancer-danger. You argue about the possibility or the usefulness, but you are already inside the machine, you are a part of it, you have put a finger inside, or an eye, your anus, or your liver (the modern version of "You are in the same boat . . .").

It almost appears as though the difference between social technical machines and desiring-machines were primarily a question of size, or one of adaptation, desiring-machines being small machines, or large machines suited to small groups. It is by no means a problem of gadgets. The current technological trend, which replaces the thermodynamic priority with a certain priority of information, is logically accompanied by a reduction in the size of machines. In another very joyful text, Ivan Illich shows the following: that heavy machines imply capitalist or despotic relations of production, involving the dependence, the exploitation, and the powerlessness of men reduced to the condition of consumers or servants. *The collective ownership of the means of production* does not alter anything in this state of affairs, and merely sustains a Stalinist despotic organization. Accordingly, Illich puts forward the alternative of *everyone's right to make use of the means of production,* in a "convivial society," which is to say, a desiring and non Oedipal society. This would mean the most extensive utilization of machines by the greatest possible number of people, the proliferation of small machines and the adaptation of the large machines to small units, the exclusive sale of machinic components which would have to be assembled by the users-producers themselves, and the destruction of the specialization of knowledge and of the professional monopoly. It is quite obvious that things as different as the monopoly or the specialization of most areas of medical knowledge, the complicated nature of the automobile engine, and the monstrous size of machines do not comply with any technological necessity, but solely with economic and political imperatives whose aim is to concentrate power or control in the hands of a ruling class. It is not a dream of a return to nature when one points out the extreme machinic uselessness of automobiles in cities, their archaic character in spite of the gadgets attached to them for show, and the potentially modern character of the bicycle, in our cities as well as in the Vietnam War. And it is not even on behalf of relatively simple and small machines that the desiring "convivial revolution" has to be made, but on behalf of machinic innovation itself, which capitalist or communist societies do everything in their economic and political power to repress.

One of the greatest artists of desiring-machines, Buster Keaton was able to pose the problem of an adaptation of the mass machine to individual ends, or to those of a couple or small group, in *The Navigator*, where the two protagonists "have to deal with housekeeping equipment generally used by hundreds of people (the galley is a forest of levers, pulleys, and wires)." It is true that the themes of reduction or adaptation of machines are not sufficient by themselves, and stand for something else. This is shown by the demand that everyone be able to make use of them and control them. For the true difference between social technical machines and desiring-machines obviously is not in the size, nor even in the ends they serve, but in the regime that decides on the size and the ends. *They are the same machines, but it is not the same regime.* This is not to say, by any means, that we should counter the present regime, which submits technology to the aims of an economy and a politics of oppression, with the notion of a regime in which technology presumably would be liberated and liberating. Technology presupposes social machines and desiring-machines, each within the other, and, by itself, has no power to decide which will be the engineering agency, desire or the oppression of desire. Every time technology claims to be acting on its own, it takes on a fascist hue, as in the techno-structure, because it implies not only economic and political investments, but libidinal investments as well, and they are turned entirely towards the oppression of desire. The distinction between the two regimes, as the regime of antidesire and that of desire, does not come down to the distinction between the collectivity and the individual, but to two types of mass organization, in which the individual and the collective do not enter into the same relationship. There exists the same difference between them as between the microphysical and the macrophysical—it being understood that the microphysical agency is not the machine-electron, but molecular machinizing desire, just as the macrophysical agency is not the molar technical object, but the antidesiring, antiproductive, molarizing social structure that currently conditions the use, the control and the possession of technical objects. In our present social order, the desiring-machine is tolerated only in its perverse forms, which is to say, on the fringes of the serious utilization of machines, and as a secondary benefit that cannot be avowed by the users, producers, or antiproducers (the sexual enjoyment experienced by the judge in judging, by the bureaucrat in stroking his files . . .). But the desiring-machine's regime is not a generalized perversion, it is rather the opposite, a general and productive schizophrenia that has finally become happy. What Tinguely says of one of his own works applies to desiring-machines: *a truly joyous machine, by joyous I mean free.*

3. The Machine and the full body: the investments of the Machine

Nothing is more obscure, as soon as one considers the details, than Marx's propositions concerning productive forces and relations of production. The broad outline is clear enough:

from tools to machines, the human means of production imply social relations of production, which however are external to these means and are merely their "index." But what is the meaning of "index"? Why does Marx project an abstract evolutive line meant to represent the isolated relationship of man and nature, where the machine is apprehended starting from the tool, and the tool in terms of the organism and its needs? It then necessarily follows that social relations appear external to the tool or to the machine, and impose on them from the outside another biological schema while breaking up the evolutive line according to heterogeneous social organizations (it is among other factors this interplay between productive forces and relations of production that explains the strange idea that the bourgeoisie was revolutionary at a given moment). It seems to us on the contrary that the machine has to be directly conceived in relation to a social body, and not in relation to a human biological organism. If such is the case, one cannot regard the machine as a new segment that succeeds that of the tool, along a line that would have its starting point in abstract man. For man and the tool *are already* components of a machine constituted by a full body acting as an engineering agency, and by men and tools that are engineered (*machinés*) insofar as they are distributed on this body. For example, there is a full body of the steppe which engineers man-horse-bow, a full body of the Greek city-state which engineers men and weapons, a full body of the factory which engineers men and machines . . . Of the two definitions of a manufacture given by Ure, and cited by Marx, the first relates machines to the men who tend them, while the second relates the machines *and* the men, "mechanical and intellectual organs," to the manufacture as the full body that engineers them. It is in fact the second definition that is literal and concrete.

It is not through metaphors nor by extension that we consider public places and community facilities (*les lieux, les equipements collectifs*) the means of communication, and the social bodies as machines or machine components. On the contrary, it is by virtue of a restriction and a derivation that the machine will cease to designate anything but a technical reality but precisely under the conditions of a quite specific full body, the body of money-Capital, insofar as it gives the tool the form of fixed capital, which is to say, distributes the tools on the surface of an autonomous mechanical representative, and gives man the form of variable capital, which is to say, distributes men on an abstract representative of labor in general. An interlocking of full bodies all belonging to the same series: the full body of capital, that of the factory, that of mechanisms . . . (Or indeed the full body of the Greek city-State, that of the phalange, that of the two-handed shield). The question we ought to ask is not how the technical machine follows after simple tools, but how the social machine, and which social machine, instead of being content to engineer men and machines, makes the emergence of technical machines both possible and necessary. (There were many technical machines before the advent of capitalism, but the machinic phylum did not pass through them, precisely because it was content to engineer men and tools. In the same way, there are tools in every social formation which are not engineered, because the phylum does not pass through them while the same tools are engineered in other social formations: hoplite weapons, for example.)

The machine understood in this manner is defined as a desiring-machine: the ensemble composed of a full body that engineers, and men and tools engineered on it. Several consequences follow from this view of the machine, but we can only plot them here in a programmatic way.

Firstly, desiring-machines are indeed the same as technical and social machines, but they are their unconscious, as it were: they manifest and mobilize the investments of desire that "correspond" to the conscious or preconscious investments of interest, the politics, and the technology of a specific social field. To correspond does not at all mean to resemble; what is at stake is another distribution, another "map," that no longer concerns the interests established in a society, nor the apportionment of the possible and the impossible, of freedoms and constraints, all that constitutes a society's *reasons*. But, beneath these reasons, there are the unwanted forms of a desire that invests the flows as such, and the breaks in these flows, a desire that continually reproduces the aleatory factors, the less probable figures, and the encounters between independent series that are at the base of this society, a desire that elicits a love "for its own sake," a love of capital for its own sake, a love of bureaucracy for its own sake, a love of repression for its own sake, all sorts of strange things such as "What does a capitalist desire from the bottom of his heart?" and "How is it possible that men desire repression not only for others but for themselves?" and so on.

Secondly, the fact that desiring-machines are the internal limit, as it were, of the technical social machines is more easily understood if one bears in mind that the full body of a society, its engineering agency, is never given as such, but must always be inferred from terms and relations coming into play in that society. The full body of capital as a proliferating body, Money that produces more Money, is never given in itself. It implies a movement to the limit, where the terms are reduced to their simple forms taken in an absolute sense, and where the relations are "positively" replaced by an absence of ties. Consider the capitalist desiring-machine, for example, the encounter between capital and labor force, capital as deterritorialized wealth and labor capacity as the deterritorialized worker, two independent series or simple forms whose chance meeting is continually reproduced in capitalism. How can the absence of ties be positive? One meets again with Leclaire's question stating the paradox of desire: how can elements be bound together by the absence of any ties? In a certain sense, it can be said that Cartesianism, in Spinoza and Leibniz, has not ceased to reply to this question. It is the theory of real distinction, insofar as it implies a specific logic. It is because they are really distinct, and completely independent of each other, that ultimate elements or simple forms belong to the same being or to the same substance. It is in this sense, in fact, that a substantial full body does not function at all as an organism. And the desiring-machine is nothing other than a multiplicity of distinct elements or simple forms that are *bound together* on the full body of a society, precisely to the extent that they are "on" this body, or to the extent that they are really distinct. The desiring-machine as a movement to the limit: the inference of the full body, the eliciting of simple forms, the assigning of absences of ties. The method employed in Marx's *Capital* takes this direction, but its dialectical presuppositions prevent it from reaching desire as a part of the infrastructure.

Thirdly, the relations of production that remain outside the technical machine are, on the contrary, internal to the desiring-machine. Admittedly, they no longer exist as relations, but as parts of the machine, some being elements of production, and others elements of antiproduction. J.J. Lebel cites the example of certain sequences of Genet's film that form a desiring-machine of the prison: two prisoners locked in adjoining cells, one of whom blows smoke into the other's mouth through a straw that passes through a little hole in the wall, while a guard masturbates as he watches. The guard is both an element of antiproduction and a voyeur component of the machine: desire is transmitted through all the parts. This means that desiring-machines are not pacified; they contain dominations and servitudes, death-carrying elements, sadistic parts and masochistic parts that are juxtaposed. Precisely in the desiring-machines, these parts assume, as do all the others, their strictly sexual dimensions. This is not to say, as psychoanalysis would have it, that sexuality has at its disposal an Oedipal code that would supplement the social formations, or even preside over their mental genesis and organization (money and anality, fascism and sadism, and so forth). There is no sexual symbolism, and sexuality does not designate another "economy," another "politics," but rather the libidinal unconscious of political economy as such. The libido, the energy of the desiring-machine, invests every social difference as being a sexual difference, including class differences, racial differences and so on, either in order to guard the wall of sexual differentiation in the unconscious, or, on the contrary, in order to blow this wall to pieces, to abolish it on behalf of nonhuman sex. In its very violence, the desiring-machine is a trial of the whole social field by desire, a test whose outcome can just as well be desire's triumph as its oppression. The test consists in the following: given a desiring-machine, how does it make a relation of production or a social difference into one of its component parts, and what is the position of this part? What about the millionaire's stomach in Goldberg's drawing, or the masturbating guard in Genet's film image? Isn't a captive factory boss a component of a factory desiring-machine, a way of responding to the test?

Fourthly, if sexuality as an energy of the unconscious is the investment of the social field by the desiring-machines, it becomes apparent that a social attitude vis-à-vis machines in general in no way expresses mere ideology, but the position of desire in the infrastructure itself, the mutations of desire in terms of the breaks and the flows that pervade this field. That is why the theme of the machine has a content that is so emphatically, so openly sexual. The epoch of the First World War was the meeting ground of the four great attitudes centering around the machine: the great molar exaltation of Italian Futurism, which counts on the machine to develop the national productive forces and to produce a new national man, without calling in question the relations of production; that of Russian Futurism and Constructivism, which conceive the machine in terms of new relations of production defined by collective appropriation (the tower-machine of Tatlin, or that of Moholy-Nagy, expressing the famous party organization as a democratic centralism, a spiral model, with a summit, a driving belt, and a base; the relations of production continue to be external to the machine, which functions as an "index"); the Dadaist molecular machinery, which, for its part, brings about a reversal in the form of a revolution of desire, because it submits the relations of production to the trial of the parts of the desiring-machine, and elicits from the latter joyous movements of deterritorialization that overcome all the territorialities of nation and party; and lastly, a humanist antimachinism, which wants to rescue imaginary or symbolic desire, to turn it back against the machine, standing ready to level it onto an Oedipal apparatus (Surrealism versus Dadaism, or Chaplin versus the Dadaist Buster Keaton).

And precisely because it is not a matter of ideology, but of a machination that brings into play an entire group unconscious characterizing a historical epoch, the tie between these attitudes and the social and political field is complex, although it is not indeterminate. Italian Futurism clearly sets forth the conditions and the organizational forms of a fascist desiring-machine, with all the equivocations of a nationalist and war-hungry "left." Russian Futurists attempt to slip their anarchist elements into a party machine that crushes them. Politics is not the strong point of the Dadaists. Humanism effects a withdrawal of the investment of desiring-machines which nonetheless continue to operate inside it. But the problem of desire itself was posed in the confrontation of these attitudes, the problem of the position of desire, i.e., that of the relationship of respective immanence between desiring-machines and social technical machines, between those two extreme poles where desire invests paranoiac fascist formations, or, on the contrary, revolutionary schizoid flows. The paradox of desire is that it always requires such a long analysis, an entire analysis of the unconscious, in order to disentangle the poles and draw out the nature of the revolutionary group trials—for desiring-machines.

PART THREE

Bodies and agents

A S DAVID **TOMAS** POINTS OUT in this part, throughout history there have been repeated attempts to understand nature, and the human body, according to the working of whatever technology was dominant at the time. One of the clearest examples is that of clockwork during the seventeenth and eighteenth centuries (*New Media: A Critical Introduction*: 248–355). Since at least the 1950s it is not clockwork or the nineteenth-century steam-driven mechanisms but the computer and information technology that have come to occupy this role, driving operative research programmes and theories based upon analogies between the computer and the human brain, and between information in communications systems and human biology and genetics. This computational model for conceiving of the nature of life moves in two directions. Firstly, the steady invasion or permeation of the human body by chemical, biological, medical, social and prosthetic technologies has had a number of radical implications for how the human body, intelligence, consciousness and 'life' itself have and are being understood. The concept of the cyborg epitomises this augmentation and extension of the human body and mind. Secondly, as **Haraway** puts it, 'our machines are increasingly lively'. Automation, automata, AI and ALife as well as the increasingly dynamic and processual nature of even the most everyday technologies (self-diagnosing photocopiers, PC interfaces, non-player characters in videogames) undermine long-held assumptions that human physical, cognitive and social agency and action are the only significant drivers of history and culture. In this part we concentrate on some of the main theories of technocultural agency and offer some vivid examples of it in action. The extracts here, as in the rest of this book, move between the wider developments in technology, science, engineering, and social theory and media, especially the computer game. The 'bodies' of this part's title are not necessarily (only) human bodies.

The acknowledgement of new everyday intimacies with, and automatic behaviour of, digital machines, networks and worlds has profound implications for cultural and media studies' investments in concepts of subjectivity and identity. **Haraway**'s work is particularly influential in this regard. Helen **Kennedy**'s essay in this part argues that in the gendered cyborgian popular technoculture she is studying, bodies in play, media consumption (and production) and collective activity cannot be separated from technical aptitude, experience and materiality; she writes of *technicity* rather than 'identity'.

Chapter 14

BRUNO LATOUR

WHERE ARE THE MISSING MASSES?
The sociology of a few mundane artifacts

BRUNO LATOUR IS A sociologist of science and technology. In this essay he takes an everyday and banal occurrence as the launching pad for an entertaining and playful enquiry into what he calls the 'missing masses'. These are the innumerable nonhuman devices and objects that, he asserts, make up the 'dark matter' of society – unobservable using established sociological lenses, but necessary to the existence of human relationships and activities. He sometimes refers to these nonhumans as *lieutenants* (from the French – holding the place of, or for, another). He argues that the idea that society is made up only of human agents is as bizarre as the idea that technology is determined only by technological relations. In its insistence on the agency of nonhuman entities, this model of technosocial relations mounts a fundamental challenge to many underlying assumptions of the humanities and social sciences, from sociology and cultural studies to economics and history.

For the purposes of his argument Latour takes at face value the wry anthropomorphism of a notice on a faulty door. The sign notes that the 'groom' (the sprung arm that automatically closes the door) is 'on strike', so Latour imagines a world in which humans and nonhumans work (or refuse to work) together. He asks the reader to think about the hinged door as an invention, inviting them to compare the effort of getting through a wall with and without a door. The hinged door is then an elegant solution to the 'hole-wall dilemma', a way of getting through a wall with minimal effort, yet preserving the wall's qualities or function as security or shelter (i.e. once the door is closed again). This is a simple illustration of Latour's key term 'delegation' (or displacement, translation, shifting), a 'transformation of a major effort into a minor one'. So, the human effort of getting through the wall (presumably of knocking a hole in a wall and then bricking it up again) is delegated to the hinged door. A human activity is delegated to a nonhuman and is, in the process, transformed. As he puts it, 'every time you want to know what a nonhuman does, simply imagine what other humans or other nonhumans would have to do were this character not present'.

Latour points out that this particular delegation is characteristic of reciprocal delegations in the configuring of users by technologies. When it is working, a door-closer efficiently stops draughts, but it also replaces a human concierge, and, depending on the power or speed of the spring it may 'discriminate' against some groups of humans, the disabled or children for example. Behaviour then is imposed back onto the human by nonhuman delegates, and this imposition can be moral or political, 'the nonhumans take over the selective attitudes of those who engineered them'.

http://www.bruno-latour.fr/

http://www.lancs.ac.uk/fass/centres/css/ant/antres.htm

[...]

Description of a door

I will start my inquiry by following a little script written by anonymous hands.[1] On a freezing day in February, posted on the door of La Halle aux Cuirs at La Villette, in Paris, where Robert Fox's group was trying to convince the French to take up social history of science, could be seen a small handwritten notice: "The Groom Is On Strike, For God's Sake, Keep The Door Closed" ("groom" is Frenglish for an automated door-closer or butler). This fusion of labor relations, religion, advertisement, and technique in one insignificant fact is exactly the sort of thing I want to describe[2] in order to discover the missing masses of our society. As a technologist teaching in the School of Mines, an engineering institution, I want to challenge some of the assumptions sociologists often hold about the social context of machines.

Walls are a nice invention, but if there were no holes in them there would be no way to get in or out—they would be mausoleums or tombs. The problem is that if you make holes in the walls, anything and anyone can get in and out (cows, visitors, dust, rats, noise—La Halle aux Cuirs is ten meters from the Paris ring road—and, worst of all, cold—La Halle aux Cuirs is far to the north of Paris). So architects invented this hybrid: a wall hole, often called a *door*, which although common enough has always struck me as a miracle of technology. The cleverness of the invention hinges upon the hinge-pin: instead of driving a hole through walls with a sledgehammer or a pick, you simply gently push the door (I am supposing here that the lock has not been invented—this would overcomplicate the already highly complex story of La Villette's door); furthermore—and here is the real trick—once you have passed through the door, you do not have to find trowel and cement to rebuild the wall you have just destroyed: you simply push the door gently back (I ignore for now the added complication of the "pull" and "push" signs).

So, to size up the work done by hinges, you simply have to imagine that every time you want to get in or out of the building you have to do the same work as a prisoner trying to escape or as a gangster trying to rob a bank, plus the work of those who rebuild either the prison's or the bank's walls. If you do not want to imagine people destroying walls and rebuilding them every time they wish to leave or enter a building, then imagine the work that would have to be done to keep inside or outside all the things and people that, left to themselves, would go the wrong way.[3] As Maxwell never said, imagine his demon working *without* a door. Anything could escape from or penetrate into La Halle aux Cuirs, and soon there would be complete equilibrium between the depressing and noisy surrounding area and the inside of the building. Some technologists, including the present writer in *Material Resistance, A Textbook* (1984), have written that techniques are always involved when asymmetry or irreversibility are the goal; it might appear that doors are a striking counterexample because they maintain the wall hole in a reversible state; the allusion to Maxwell's demon clearly shows, however, that such is not the case; the reversible door is the only way to trap irreversibly inside La Halle aux Cuirs a differential accumulation of warm historians, knowledge, and also, alas, a lot of paperwork; the hinged door allows a selection of what gets in and what gets out so as to locally increase order, or information. If you let the drafts get inside (these renowned "courants d'air" so dangerous to French health), the paper drafts may never get outside to the publishers.

Now, draw two columns (if I am not allowed to give orders to the reader, then I offer it as a piece of strongly worded advice): in the right-hand column, list the work people would have to do if they had no door; in the left-hand column write down the gentle pushing (or pulling) they have to do to fulfill the same tasks. Compare the two columns: the enormous effort on the right is balanced by the small one on the left, and this is all thanks to hinges. I will define this transformation of a major effort into a minor one by the words *displacement* or *translation* or *delegation* or *shifting*;[4] I will say that we have delegated (or translated or displaced or shifted down) to the hinge the work of reversibly solving the wall-hole dilemma. Calling on Robert Fox, I do not have to do this work nor even think about it; it was delegated by the carpenter to a character, the hinge, which I will call a *nonhuman*. I simply enter La Halle aux Cuirs. As a more general descriptive rule, every time you want to know what a non-human does, simply imagine what other humans or other nonhumans would have to do were this character not present. This imaginary substitution exactly sizes up the role, or function, of this little character.

Before going on, let me point out one of the side benefits of this table: in effect, we have drawn a scale where tiny efforts balance out mighty weights; the scale we drew reproduces the very leverage allowed by hinges. That the small be made stronger than the large is a very moral story indeed (think of David and Goliath); by the same token, it is also, since at least Archimedes' days, a very good definition of a lever and of power: what is the minimum you need to hold and deploy astutely to produce the maximum effect? Am I alluding to machines or to Syracuse's King? I don't know, and it does not matter, because the King and Archimedes fused the two "mini-maxes" into a single story told by Plutarch: the defense of Syracuse through levers and war machines.[5] I contend that this reversal of forces is what sociologists should look at in order to understand the social construction of techniques, and not a hypothetical "social context" that they are not equipped to grasp. This little point having been made, let me go on with the story (we will understand later why I do not really need your permission to go on and why, nevertheless, you are free not to go on, although only *relatively* so).

Delegation to humans

There is a problem with doors. Visitors push them to get in or pull on them to get out (or vice versa), but then the door remains open. That is, instead of the door you have a gaping hole in the wall through which, for instance, cold rushes in and heat rushes out. Of course, you could imagine that people living in the building or visiting the Centre d'Histoire des Sciences et des Techniques would be a well-disciplined lot (after all, historians are meticulous people). They will learn to close the door behind them and retransform the momentary hole into a well-sealed wall. The problem is that discipline is not the main characteristic of La Villette's people; also you might have mere sociologists visiting the building, or even pedagogues from the nearby Centre de Formation. Are they all going to be so well trained? Closing doors would appear to be a simple enough piece of know-how once hinges have been invented, but, considering the amount of work, innovations, sign-posts, and recriminations that go on endlessly everywhere to keep them closed (at least in northern regions), it seems to be rather poorly disseminated.

This is where the age-old Mumfordian choice is offered to you: either to discipline the people or to substitute for the unreliable people another delegated human character whose only function is to open and close the door. This is called a groom or a porter (from the French word for door), or a gatekeeper, or a janitor, or a concierge, or a turnkey, or a jailer. The advantage is that you now have to discipline only one human and may safely leave the others to their erratic behavior. No matter who it is and where it comes from, the groom will always take care of the door. A nonhuman (the hinges) plus a human (the groom) have solved the wall-hole dilemma.

Solved? Not quite. First of all, if La Halle aux Cuirs pays for a porter, they will have no money left to buy coffee or books, or to invite eminent foreigners to give lectures. If they give the poor little boy other duties besides that of porter, then he will not be present most of the time and the door will stay open. Even if they had money to keep him there, we are now faced with a problem that two hundred years of capitalism has not completely solved: how to discipline a youngster to reliably fulfill a boring and underpaid duty? Although there is now only one human to be disciplined instead of hundreds, the weak point of the tactic can be seen: if this *one* lad is unreliable, then the whole chain breaks down; if he falls asleep on the job or goes walkabout, there will be no appeal: the door will stay open (remember that locking it is no solution because this would turn it into a wall, and then providing everyone with the right key is a difficult task that would not ensure that key holders will lock it back). Of course, the porter may be punished. But disciplining a groom—Foucault notwithstanding— is an enormous and costly task that only large hotels can tackle, and then for other reasons that have nothing to do with keeping the door properly closed.

If we compare the work of disciplining the groom with the work he substitutes for, according to the list defined above, we see that this delegated character has the opposite effect to that of the hinge: a simple task—forcing people to close the door—is now performed at an incredible cost; the minimum effect is obtained with maximum spending and discipline. We also notice, when drawing the two lists, an interesting difference: in the first relationship (hinges vis-à-vis the work of many people), you not only had a reversal of forces (the lever allows gentle manipulations to displace heavy weights) but also a modification of *time schedule*: once the hinges are in place, nothing more has to be done apart from maintenance (oiling them from time to time). In the second set of relations (groom's work versus many people's work), not only do you fail to reverse the forces but you also fail to modify the time schedule: nothing can be done to prevent the groom who has been reliable for two months from failing on the sixty-second day; at this point it is not maintenance work that has to be done but the *same* work as on the first day—apart from the few habits that you might have been able to *incorporate* into his body. Although they appear to be two similar delegations, the first one is concentrated at the time of installation, whereas the other is continuous; more exactly, the first one creates clear-cut distinctions between production, installation, and maintenance, whereas in the other the distinction between training and keeping in operation is either fuzzy or nil. The first one evokes the past perfect ("once hinges had been installed . . ."), the second the present tense ("when the groom is at his post . . ."). There is a built-in inertia in the first that is largely lacking in the second. The first one is Newtonian, the second Aristotelian (which is simply a way of repeating that the second is nonhuman and the other human). A profound temporal shift takes place when nonhumans are appealed to; time is *folded*.

Delegation to nonhumans

It is at this point that you have a relatively new choice: either to discipline the people or to *substitute* for the unreliable humans a *delegated nonhuman character* whose only function is to open and close the door. This is called a door-closer or a groom ("groom" is a French trademark that is now part of the common language). The advantage is that you now have to discipline only one nonhuman and may safely leave the others (bellboys included) to their erratic behavior. No matter who they are and where they come from—polite or rude, quick or slow, friends or foes—the nonhuman groom will always take care of the door in any weather and at any time of the day. A nonhuman (hinges) plus another nonhuman (groom) have solved the wall-hole dilemma.

Solved? Well, not quite. Here comes the deskilling question so dear to social historians of technology: thousands of human grooms have been put on the dole by their nonhuman brethren. Have they been replaced? This depends on the kind of action that has been translated or delegated to them. In other words, when humans are displaced and deskilled, nonhumans have to be upgraded and re-skilled. This is not an easy task, as we shall now see.

We have all experienced having a door with a powerful spring mechanism slam in our faces. For sure, springs do the job of replacing grooms, but they play the role of a very rude, uneducated, and dumb porter who obviously prefers the wall version of the door to its hole version. They simply slam the door shut. The interesting thing with such impolite doors is this: if they slam shut so violently, it means that you, the visitor, have to be very quick in passing through and that you should not be at someone else's heels, otherwise your nose will get shorter and bloody. An unskilled nonhuman groom thus presupposes a skilled human user. It is always a trade-off. I will call, after Madeleine Akrich, the behavior imposed back onto the human by nonhuman delegates *prescription*.[6] Prescription is the moral and ethical dimension of mechanisms. In spite of the constant weeping of moralists, no human is as relentlessly moral as a machine, especially if it is (she is, he is, they are) as "user friendly" as my Macintosh computer. We have been able to delegate to nonhumans not only force as we have known it for centuries but also values, duties, and ethics. It is because of this morality that we, humans, behave so ethically, no matter how weak and wicked we feel we are. The sum of morality does not only remain stable but increases enormously with the population of nonhumans. It is at this time, funnily enough, that moralists who focus on isolated socialized humans despair of us—us meaning of course humans and their retinue of nonhumans.

How can the prescriptions encoded in the mechanism be brought out in words? By replacing them by strings of sentences (often in the imperative) that are uttered (silently and continuously) by the mechanisms for the benefit of those who are mechanized: do this, do that, behave this way, don't go that way, you may do so, be allowed to go there. Such sentences look very much like a programming language. This substitution of words for silence can be made in the analyst's thought experiments, but also by instruction booklets, or explicitly, in any training session, through the voice of a demonstrator or instructor or teacher. The military are especially good at shouting them out through the mouthpiece of human instructors who delegate back to themselves the task of explaining, in the rifle's name, the characteristics of the rifle's ideal user. Another way of hearing what the machines silently did and said are the accidents. When the space shuttle exploded, thousands of pages of transcripts suddenly covered every detail of the silent machine, and hundreds of inspectors, members of congress, and engineers retrieved from NASA dozens of thousands of pages of drafts and orders. This description of a machine—whatever the means—retraces the steps made by the engineers to transform texts, drafts, and projects into things. The impression given to those who are obsessed by human behavior that there is a missing mass of morality is due to the fact that they do not follow this path that leads from text to things and from things to texts. They draw a strong distinction between these two worlds, whereas the job of engineers, instructors, project managers, and analysts is to continually cross this divide. Parts of a program of action may be delegated to a human, or to a nonhuman.

The results of such *distribution of competences*[7] between humans and nonhumans is that competent members of La Halle aux Cuirs will safely pass through the slamming door at a good distance from one another while visitors, unaware of the local cultural condition, will crowd through the door and get bloody noses. The nonhumans take over the selective attitudes of those who engineered them. To avoid this discrimination, inventors get back to their drawing board and try to imagine a nonhuman character that will not *prescribe* the same rare local cultural skills to its human users. A weak spring might appear to be a good solution. Such is not the case, because it would substitute for another type of very unskilled and undecided groom who is never sure about the door's (or his own) status: is it a hole or a wall? Am I a closer or an opener? If it is both at once, you can forget about the heat. In computer parlance, a door is an exclusive OR, not an AND gate.

I am a great fan of hinges, but I must confess that I admire hydraulic door closers much more, especially the old heavy copper-plated one that slowly closed the main door of our house in Aloxe-Corton. I am enchanted by the addition to the spring of a hydraulic piston, which easily draws up the energy of those who open the door, retains it, and then gives it back slowly with a subtle type of implacable firmness that one could expect from a well-trained butler. Especially clever is its way of extracting energy from each unwilling, unwitting passerby. My sociologist friends at the School of Mines call such a clever extraction an "obligatory passage point," which is a very fitting name for a door. No matter what you feel, think, or do, you have to leave a bit of your energy, literally, at the door. This is as clever as a toll booth.[8]

This does not quite solve all of the problems, though. To be sure, the hydraulic door closer does not bang the noses of those unaware of local conditions, so its prescriptions may be said to be less restrictive, but it still leaves aside segments of human populations: neither my little nephews nor my grandmother could get in unaided because our groom needed the force of an able-bodied person to accumulate enough energy to close the door later. To use Langdon Winner's classic motto (1980): Because of their prescriptions, these doors *discriminate* against very little and very old persons. Also, if there is no way to keep them open for good, they discriminate against furniture removers and in general everyone with packages, which usually means, in our late capitalist society, working- or lower-middle-class employees. (Who, even among those from higher strata, has not been cornered by an automated butler when they had their hands full of packages?)

There are solutions, though: the groom's delegation may be written off (usually by blocking its arm) or, more prosaically, its delegated action may be opposed by a foot (salesmen are said to be expert at this). The foot may in turn be delegated to a carpet or anything that keeps the butler in check (although I am always amazed by the number of objects that *fail* this trial of force and I have very often seen the door I just wedged open politely closing when I turned my back to it).

Anthropomorphism

As a technologist, I could claim that provided you put aside the work of installing the groom and maintaining it, and agree to ignore the few sectors of the population that are discriminated against, the hydraulic groom does its job well, closing the door behind you, firmly and slowly. It shows in its humble way how three rows of delegated nonhuman actants[9] (hinges, springs, and hydraulic pistons) replace, 90 percent of the time, either an undisciplined bellboy who is never there when needed or, for the general public, the program instructions that have to do with remembering-to-close-the-door-when-it-is-cold.

The hinge plus the groom is the technologist's dream of efficient action, at least until the sad day when I saw the note posted on La Villette's door with which I started this meditation: "The groom is on strike." So not only have we been able to delegate the act of closing the door from the human to the nonhuman, we have also been able to delegate the human lack of discipline (and maybe the union that goes with it). On strike . . . .[10] Fancy that! Nonhumans stopping work and claiming what? Pension payments? Time off? Landscaped offices? Yet it is no use being indignant, because it is very true that nonhumans are not so reliable that the irreversibility we would like to grant them is always complete. We did not want ever to have to think about this door again—apart from regularly scheduled routine maintenance (which is another way of saying that we did not have to bother about it)—and here we are, worrying again about how to keep the door closed and drafts outside.

What is interesting in this note is the humor of attributing a human characteristic to a failure that is usually considered "purely technical." This humor, however, is more profound than in the notice they could have posted: "The groom is not working." I constantly talk with my computer, who answers back; I am sure you swear at your old car; we are constantly granting mysterious faculties to gremlins inside every conceivable home appliance, not to mention cracks in the concrete belt of our nuclear plants. Yet, this behavior is considered by sociologists as a scandalous breach of natural barriers. When you write that a groom is "on strike," this is only seen as a "projection," as they say, of a human behavior onto a nonhuman, cold, technical object, one by nature impervious to any feeling. This is *anthropomorphism*, which for them is a sin akin to zoophily but much worse.

It is this sort of moralizing that is so irritating for technologists, because the automatic groom is already anthropomorphic through and through. It is well known that the French like etymology; well, here is another one: *anthropos* and *morphos* together mean either that which *has* human shape or that which *gives shape* to humans. The groom is indeed anthropomorphic, in three senses: first, it has been made by humans; second, it substitutes for the actions of people and is a delegate that permanently occupies the position of a human; and third, it shapes human action by prescribing back what sort of people should pass through the door. And yet some would forbid us to ascribe feelings to this thoroughly anthropomorphic creature, to delegate labor relations, to "project"—that is, to translate—*other* human properties to the groom. What of those many other innovations that have endowed much more sophisticated doors with the ability to see you arrive in advance (electronic eyes), to ask for your identity (electronic passes), or to slam shut in case of danger? But anyway, who are sociologists to decide the real and final shape (*morphos*) of humans (*anthropos*)? To trace with confidence the boundary between what is a "real" delegation and what is a "mere" projection? To sort out forever and without due inquiry the three different kinds of anthropomorphism I listed above? Are we not shaped by nonhuman grooms, although I admit only a very little bit? Are they not our brethren? Do they not deserve consideration? With your self-serving and self-righteous social studies of technology, you always plead against machines and for deskilled workers—are you aware of *your* discriminatory biases? You discriminate between the human and the inhuman. I do not hold this bias (this one at least) and see only actors—some human, some nonhuman, some skilled, some unskilled—that exchange their properties. So the note posted on the door is accurate; it gives with humor an exact rendering of the groom's behavior: it is not working, it is on strike (notice, that the word "strike" is a rationalization carried from the nonhuman repertoire to the human one, which proves again that the divide is untenable).

Built-in users and authors

The debates around anthropomorphism arise because we believe that there exist "humans" and "nonhumans," without realizing that this attribution of roles and action is also a *choice*.[11] The best way to understand this choice is to compare machines with texts, since the inscription of builders and users in a mechanism is very much the same as that of authors and readers in a story. In order to exemplify this point I have now to confess that I am *not* a technologist. I built in my article a made-up author, and I also invented possible readers whose reactions and beliefs I anticipated. Since the beginning I have many times used the "you" and even "you sociologists." I even asked you to draw up a table, and I also asked your permission to go on with the story. In doing so, I built up an inscribed reader to whom I prescribed qualities and behavior, as surely as a traffic light or a painting prepare a position for those looking at them. Did you *underwrite* or *subscribe* this definition of yourself? Or worse, is there anyone at all to read this text and occupy the position prepared for the reader? This question is a source of constant difficulties for those who are unaware of the basics of semiotics or of technology. *Nothing in a given scene* can prevent the inscribed user or reader from behaving differently from what was expected (nothing, that is, until the next paragraph). The reader in the flesh may totally ignore my definition of him or her. The user of the traffic light may well cross on the red. Even visitors to La Halle aux Cuirs may never show up because it is too complicated to find the place, *in spite* of the fact that their behavior and trajectory have been perfectly anticipated by the groom. As for the computer user input, the cursor might flash forever without the user being there or knowing what to do. There might be an enormous gap between the prescribed user and the user-in-the-flesh, a difference as big as the one between the "I" of a novel and the novelist.[12] It is exactly this difference that upset the authors of the anonymous appeal on which I comment. On other occasions, however, the gap between the two may be nil: the prescribed user is so well anticipated, so carefully nested inside the scenes, so exactly dovetailed, that it does what is expected.[13]

The problem with scenes is that they are usually well prepared for anticipating users or readers who are at close quarters. For instance, the groom is quite good in its anticipation that people will push the door open and give it the energy to reclose it. It is very bad at doing anything to help people arrive there. After fifty centimeters, it is helpless and cannot act, for example, on the maps spread around La Villette to explain where La Halle aux Cuirs is. Still, no scene is prepared without a preconceived idea of what sort of actors will come to occupy the prescribed positions.

This is why I said that although *you* were free not to go on with this paper, *you* were only "relatively" so. Why? Because I know that, because you bought this book, you are hard-working, serious, English-speaking technologists or readers committed to understanding new development in the social studies of machines. So my injunction to "read the paper, you sociologist" is not very risky (but I would have taken no chance with a French audience, especially with a paper written in English). This way of counting on earlier distribution of skills to help narrow the gap between built-in users or readers and users- or readers-in-the-flesh is like a *pre*-inscription.[14]

The fascinating thing in text as well as in artifact is that they have to thoroughly organize the relation between what is inscribed in them and what can/could/should be pre-inscribed in the users. Each setup is surrounded by various arenas interrupted by different types of walls. A text, for instance, is clearly *circumscribed*[15]—the dust cover, the title page, the hard back— but so is a computer—the plugs, the screen, the disk drive, the user's input. What is nicely called "interface" allows any setup to be connected to another through so many carefully designed entry points. Sophisticated mechanisms build up a whole gradient of concentric circles around themselves. For instance, in most modern photocopy machines there are troubles that even rather incompetent users may solve themselves like "ADD PAPER;" but then there are trickier ones that require a bit of explanation: "ADD TONER. SEE MANUAL, PAGE 30." This instruction might be backed up by homemade labels: "DON'T ADD THE TONER YOURSELF, CALL THE SECRETARY," which limit still further the number of people able to troubleshoot. But then other more serious crises are addressed by labels like "CALL THE TECHNICAL STAFF AT THIS NUMBER," while there are parts of the machine that are sealed off entirely with red labels such as "DO NOT OPEN–DANGER, HIGH VOLTAGE, HEAT" or "CALL THE POLICE." Each of these messages addresses a different audience, from the widest (everyone with the rather largely disseminated competence of using photocopying machines) to the narrowest (the rare bird able to troubleshoot and who, of course, is never there).[16] Circumscription only defines how a setup itself has built-in plugs and interfaces; as the name indicates, this tracing of circles, walls, and entry points inside the text or the machine does not prove that readers and users will obey. There is nothing sadder than an obsolete computer with all its nice interfaces, but no one on earth to plug them in.

Drawing a side conclusion in passing, we can call *sociologism* the claim that, given the competence, pre-inscription, and circumscription of human users and authors, you can read out the scripts nonhuman actors have to play; and *technologism* the symmetric claim that, given the competence and pre-inscription of nonhuman actors, you can easily read out and deduce the behavior prescribed to authors and users. From now on, these two absurdities will, I hope, disappear from the scene, because the actors at any point may be human or nonhuman, and the displacement (or translation, or transcription) makes impossible the easy reading out of one repertoire and into the next. The bizarre idea that society might be made up of human relations is a mirror image of the other no less bizarre idea that techniques might be made up of nonhuman relations. We deal with characters, delegates, representatives, lieutenants (from the French "lieu" plus "tenant," i.e., holding the place of, for, someone else)—some figurative, others nonfigurative; some human, others nonhuman; some competent, others incompetent. Do you want to cut through this rich diversity of delegates and artificially create two heaps of refuse, "society" on one side and "technology" on the other? That is your privilege, but I have a less bungled task in mind.

A scene, a text, an automatism can do a lot of things to their prescribed users at the range—close or far—that is defined by the circumscription, but most of the effect finally ascribed[17] to them depends on lines of other setups being aligned. For instance, the groom closes the door only if there are people reaching the Centre d'Histoire des Sciences; these people arrive in front of the door only if they have found maps (another delegate, with the built-in prescription I like most: "*you* are here" circled in red on the map) and only if there are roads leading under the Paris ring road to the Halle (which is a condition not always fullfilled); and of course people will start bothering about reading the maps, getting their feet muddy and pushing the door open only if they are convinced that the group is worth visiting (this is about the only condition in La Villette that is fulfilled). This gradient of aligned setups that endow actors with the pre-inscribed competences to find its users is very much like Waddington's "chreod":[18] people effortlessly flow through the door of La Halle aux Cuirs and the groom, hundreds of times a day, recloses the door—when it is not stuck. The result of such an alignment of setups[19] is to decrease the number of occasions in which words are used; most of the actions are silent, familiar, incorporated (in human or in nonhuman bodies)— making the analyst's job so much harder. Even the classic debates about freedom, determination, predetermination, brute force, or efficient will—debates that are the twelfth-century version of seventeenth-century discussions on grace—will be slowly eroded. (Because *you* have reached this point, it means I was right in saying that you were not at all free to stop reading the paper: positioning myself cleverly along a chreod, and adding a few other tricks of my own, I led you *here* . . . or did I? Maybe you skipped most of it, maybe you did not understand a word of it, o you, undisciplined readers.)

[. . .]

The distinctions between humans and nonhumans, embodied or disembodied skills, impersonation or "machination," are less interesting than the complete chain along which competences and actions are distributed. For instance, on the freeway the other day I slowed down because a guy in a yellow suit and red helmet was waving a red flag. Well, the guy's moves were so regular and he was located so dangerously and had such a pale though smiling face that, when I passed by, I recognized it to be a machine (it failed the Turing test, a cognitivist would say). Not only was the red flag delegated; not only was the arm waving the flag also delegated; but the body appearance was also added to the machine. We road engineers (see? I can do it again and carve out another author) could move much further in the direction of figuration, although at a cost: we could have given him electronic eyes to wave only when a car approaches, or have regulated the movement so that it is faster when cars do not obey. We could also have added (why not?) a furious stare or a recognizable face like a mask of Mrs. Thatcher or President Mitterand—which would have certainly slowed drivers very efficiently.[20] But we could also have moved the other way, to a *less* figurative delegation: the flag by itself could have done the job. And why a flag? Why not simply a sign "work in progress?" And why a sign at all? Drivers, if they are circumspect, disciplined, and watchful will see for themselves that there is work in progress and will slow down. But there is another radical, nonfigurative solution: the road bumper, or a speed trap that we call in French "un gendarme couché," a laid policeman. It is impossible for us not to slow down, or else we break our suspension. Depending on where we stand along this chain of delegation, we get classic moral human beings endowed with self-respect and able to speak and obey laws, or we get stubborn and efficient machines and mechanisms; halfway through we get the usual power of signs and symbols. It is the complete chain that makes up the missing masses, not either of its extremities. The paradox of technology is that it is thought to be at one of the extremes, whereas it is the ability of the engineer to travel easily along the whole gradient and substitute one type of delegation for another that is inherent to the job.[21]

[. . .]

From nonhumans to superhumans

The most interesting (and saddest) lesson of the note posted on the door at La Villette is that people are not circumspect, disciplined, and watchful, especially not French drivers doing 180 kilometers an hour on a freeway on a rainy Sunday morning when the speed limit is 130 (I inscribe the legal limit in this article because this is about the only place where you could see it printed in black and white; no one else seems to bother, except the mourning families). Well, that is exactly the point of the note: "The groom is on strike, *for God's sake*, keep the door closed." In our societies there are two systems of appeal: nonhuman and superhuman—that is, machines and gods. This note indicates how desperate its anonymous frozen authors were (I have never been able to trace and honor them as they deserved). They first relied on the inner morality and common sense of humans; this failed, the door was always left open. Then they appealed to what we technologists consider the supreme court of appeal, that is, to a nonhuman who regularly and conveniently does the job in place of unfaithful humans; to our shame, we must confess that it also failed after a while, the door was again left open. How poignant their line of thought! They moved up and backward to the oldest and firmest court of appeal there is, there was, and ever will be. If humans and nonhuman have failed, certainly God will not deceive them. I am ashamed to say that when I crossed the hallway this February day, the door *was* open. Do not accuse God, though, because the note did not make a direct appeal; God is not accessible without mediators—the anonymous authors knew their catechisms well— so instead of asking for a direct miracle (God holding the door firmly closed or doing so through the mediation of an angel, as has happened on several occasions, for instance when Saint Peter was delivered from his prison) they appealed to the respect for God in human hearts. This was their mistake. In our secular times, this is no longer enough.

Nothing seems to do the job nowadays of disciplining men and women to close doors in cold weather. It is a similar despair that pushed the road engineer to add a golem to the red flag to force drivers to beware—although the only way to slow French drivers is still a good traffic jam. You seem to need more and more of these figurated delegates, aligned in rows. It is the same with delegates as with drugs; you start with soft ones and end up shooting up. There is an inflation for delegated characters, too. After a while they weaken. [. . .]

Students of technology are never faced with people on the one hand and things on the other, they are faced with programs of action, sections of which are endowed to *parts* of humans, while other sections are entrusted to parts of nonhumans. This is the only thing they can *observe*: how a negotiation to associate dissident elements requires more and more elements to be tied together and more and more shifts to other matters. We are now witnessing in technology studies the same displacement that has happened in science studies during the last ten years. It is not that society and social relations invade the certainty of science or the efficiency of machines. It is that society itself is to be rethought from top to bottom once we add to it the facts and the artifacts that make up large sections of our social ties. What appears in the place of the two ghosts—society and technology—is not simply a hybrid object, a little bit of efficiency and a little bit of sociologizing, but a *sui generis* object: the collective thing, the trajectory of the front line between programs and anti-programs. It is too full of humans to look like the technology of old, but it is too full of nonhumans to look like the social theory of the past. The missing masses are in our traditional social theories, not in the supposedly cold, efficient, and inhuman technologies.

Notes

This paper owes to many discussions held at the Centre de Sociologie de l'Innovation, especially with John Law, the honorary member from Keele, and Madeleine Akrich. It is particularly indebted to Françoise Bastide, who was still working on these questions of semiotics of technology a few months before her death.

I had no room to incorporate a lengthy dispute with Harry Collins about this article (but see Collins and Yearley 1992, and Callon and Latour 1992).

Trevor Pinch and John Law kindly corrected the English.

1   Following Madeleine Akrich's lead (this volume), we will speak only in terms of *scripts* or scenes or scenarios, or setups as John Law says (this volume), played by human or nonhuman actants, which may be either figurative or nonfigurative.
2   After Akrich, I will call the retrieval of the script from the situation *description*. They define actants, endow them with competences, make them do things, and evaluate the sanction of these actions like the *narrative program* of semioticians.
3   Although most of the scripts are in practice silent, either because they are intra- or extrasomatic, the written descriptions are not an artifact of the analyst (technologist, sociologist, or semiotician), because there exist many states of affairs in which they are *explicitly* uttered. The gradient going from intrasomatic to extrasomatic skills through discourse is never fully stabilized and allows many entries revealing the

process of translation: user manuals, instruction, demonstration or drilling situations, practical thought experiments ("what would happen if, instead of the red light, a police officer were there"). To this should be added the innovator's workshop, where most of the objects to be devised are still at the stage *of projects* committed to paper ("if we had a device doing this and that, we could then do this and that"); market analysis in which consumers are confronted with the new device; and, naturally, the exotic situation studied by anthropologists in which people faced with a foreign device talk to themselves while trying out various combinations ("what will happen if I attach this lead here to the mains?"). The analyst has to empirically capture these situations to write down the scripts. When none is available, the analyst may still make a thought experiment by comparing presence/absence tables and collating the list of all the actions taken by actors ("if I take this one away, this and that other action will be modified"). There are dangers in such a counterfactual method, as Collins has pointed out (Collins and Yearley 1992), but it is used here only to outline the semiotics of artifacts. In practice, as Akrich (this volume) shows, the scripts are explicit and accountable.

4   We call the translation of any script from one repertoire to a *more durable* one transcription, inscription, or encoding. This definition does *not* imply that the direction always goes from soft bodies to hard machines, but simply that it goes from a provisional, less reliable one to a longer-lasting, more faithful one. For instance, the embodiment in cultural tradition of the user manual of a car is a transcription, but so is the replacement of a police officer by a traffic light; one goes from machines to bodies, whereas the other goes the opposite way. Specialists of robotics have abandoned the pipe dream of total automation; they learned the hard way that many skills are better delegated to humans than to nonhumans, whereas others may be taken away from incompetent humans.

5   See Authier 1989 on Plutarch's Archimedes.

6   We call prescription whatever a scene presupposes from its *transcribed* actors and authors (this is very much like "role expectation" in sociology, except that it may be inscribed or encoded in the machine). For instance, a Renaissance Italian painting is designed to be viewed from a specific angle of view prescribed by the vanishing lines, exactly like a traffic light expects that its users will watch it from the street and not sideways (French engineers often hide the lights directed toward the side street so as to hide the state of the signals, thus preventing the strong temptation to rush through the crossing at the first hint that the lights are about to be green; this prescription of who is allowed to watch the signal is very frustrating). "User input" in programming language is another very telling example of this inscription in the automatism of a living character whose behavior is both free and predetermined.

7   In this type of analysis there is no effort to attribute forever certain competences to humans and others to nonhumans. The attention is focused on following how *any* set of competences is *distributed* through various entities.

8   Interestingly enough, the oldest Greek engineering myth, that of Daedalus, is about cleverness, deviousness. "Dedalion" means something that goes away from the main road, like the French word "bricole." In the mythology, science is represented by a straight line and technology by a detour, science by *epistémè* and technology by the *métis*. See the excellent essay of Frontisi-Ducroux (1975) on the semantic field of the name Daedalus.

9   We use *actant* to mean anything that acts and *actor* to mean what is made the source of an action. This is a semiotician's definition that is not limited to humans and has no relation whatsoever to the sociological definition of an actor by opposition to mere behavior. For a semiotician, the act of attributing "inert force" to a hinge or the act of attributing it "personality" are comparable in principle and should be studied symmetrically.

10   I have been able to document a case of a five-day student strike at a French school of management (ESSEC) to urge that a door closer be installed in the student cafeteria to keep the freezing cold outside.

11   It is of course another choice to decide who makes such a choice: a man? a spirit? no one? an automated machine? The *scripter* or designer of all these scripts is itself (himself, herself, themselves) negotiated.

12   This is what Norman (1988) calls the Gulf of Execution. His book is an excellent introduction to the study of the tense relations between inscribed and real users. However, Norman speaks only about dysfunction in the interfaces with the final user and never considers the shaping of the artifact by the engineer themselves.

13   To stay within the same etymological root, we call the way actants (human or nonhuman) tend to extirpate themselves from the prescribed behavior *de-inscription* and the way they accept or happily acquiesce to their lot *subscription*.

14   We call *pre-inscription* all the work that has to be done upstream of the scene and all the things assimilated by an actor (human or nonhuman) before coming to the scene as a user or an author. For instance,

how to drive a car is basically pre-inscribed in any (Western) youth years before it comes to passing the driving test; hydraulic pistons were also pre-inscribed for slowly giving back the energy gathered, years before innovators brought them to bear on automated grooms. Engineers can bet on this predetermination when they draw up their prescriptions. This is what is called "articulation work" (Fujimura 1987).

15 We call *circumscription* the organization in the setting of its own limits and of its own demarcation (doors, plugs, hall, introductions).

16 See Suchman for a description of such a setting (1987).

17 We call *ascription* the attribution of an effect to one aspect of the setup. This new decision about attributing efficiency—for instance, to a person's genius, to workers' efforts, to users, to the economy, to technology—is as important as the others, but it is derivative. It is like the opposition between the primary mechanism—who is allied to whom—and the secondary mechanism—whose leadership is recognized—in history of science (Latour 1987).

18 Waddington's term for "necessary paths"—from the Greek *creos* and *odos*.

19 We call *conscription* this mobilization of well-drilled and well-aligned resources to render the behavior of a human or a nonhuman predictable.

20 Trevor Pinch sent me an article from the *Guardian* (2 September 1988) titled "Cardboard coppers cut speeding by third."

A Danish police spokesman said an advantage of the effigies, apart from cutting manpower costs, was that they could stand for long periods undistracted by other calls of duty. Additional assets are understood to be that they cannot claim overtime, be accused of brutality, or get suspended by their chief constable without explanation. "For God's sake, don't tell the Home Office," Mr. Tony Judge, editor of the *Police Review Magazine* in Britain, said after hearing news of the [Danish] study last night. "We have enough trouble getting sufficient men already." The cut-outs have been placed beside notorious speeding blackspots near the Danish capital. Police said they had yielded "excellent" results. Now they are to be erected at crossings where drivers often jump lights. From time to time, a spokesman added, they would be replaced by real officers.

21 Why did the (automatic) groom go on strike? The answers to this are the same as for the question posed earlier of why no one showed up at La Halle aux Cuirs: it is not because a piece of behavior is prescribed by an inscription that the predetermined characters will show up on time and do the job expected of them. This is true of humans, but it is truer of nonhumans. In this case the hydraulic piston did its job, but not the spring that collaborated with it. Any of the words employed above may be used to describe a setup at any level and not only at the simple one I chose for the sake of clarity. It does not have to be limited to the case where a human deals with a series of nonhuman delegates; it can also be true of relations among nonhumans (yes, you sociologists, there are also relations among things, and *social* relations at that).

Chapter 15

DONNA HARAWAY

CYBORGS, COYOTES AND DOGS
A kinship of feminist figurations

THERE ARE ALWAYS MORE THINGS GOING ON THAN YOU THOUGHT!
Methodologies as thinking technologies

THIS SET OF INTERVIEWS with Donna Haraway provides an accessible insight to the development and motivation of her ideas. Please also refer to our introductions to other extracts from **Haraway**'s work in Part Two above. It sets out in general terms what we see as the significance of her work and its centrality to new media and technocultural studies (see also another **Haraway** extract and introduction in Part Five below). We have placed these interviews in Part Three because they highlight specific questions about the objects and subjects of study in new media and technocultural studies. As well as the now-familiar cyborg, the discussion here introduces us to Haraway's more recent work on human–non-human relationships in which the 'non-human' is animal and natural rather than technical and artificial. The discussion also explores how Haraway sees her relationship to other strands of science and technology studies, notably that of Actor-Network Theory (**Latour**, this part), and the significance of feminist ideas and politics in all her work.

This extract bristles with links to other texts in this book, from her ambivalent fascination with cybernetics, communication and control (**Wiener**, **Galison**, **Tomas**, **Kember**), the machinic connections between humans and nature (**Latour**), economies (**Terranova**, **Kember**) and the unconscious (**Guattari**), art / activist practices (**Lovink**), technology and gender (**Kennedy**).

Finally, the interviews also cover Haraway's writing methods and style. It is rarely acknowledged in the published output of new media studies that the books themselves and the processes by which they are produced are also technical, a 'black box' in a flow of activities and techniques that include the technologies of print, the economies of academia and publishing, the mediation of digitised text and images, methodological and intellectual techniques and the human–non-human relationship between writer and typewriter or keyboard (**Poster**).

An interview with Donna Haraway conducted in two parts by Nina Lykke, Randi Markussen, and Finn Olesen.

Part I: Cyborgs, coyotes and dogs: a kinship of feminist figurations

Interviewer: Let us start with the Cyborg Manifesto.[1] Many women have been fascinated by the idea that the cyborg could be a woman. Why did you insist on the femaleness of the cyborg?

Donna Haraway: For me the notion of the cyborg was female, and a woman, in complex ways. It was an act of resistance, an oppositional move of a pretty straightforward kind. The cyborg was, of course, part of a military project, part of an extraterrestrial man-in-space project. It was also a science fictional figure out of a largely male-defined science fiction. Then there was another dimension in which cyborgs were female: in popular culture, and in certain kinds of medical culture. Here cyborgs appeared as patients, or as objects of pornography, as "fem-bots"—the iron maiden, the robotised machinic, pornographic female. But the whole figure of the cyborg seemed to me potentially much more interesting than that. Moreover, an act of taking over a territory seemed like a fairly straightforward, political, symbolic technoscientific project.

From my point of view, the cyborg was a figure that collected up many things, among them the way that post-World War II technoscientific cultures were deeply shaped by information sciences and biological sciences, by the implosion of informatics and biologics that was already well under way by the end of World War II, and that has only deepened in the last fifty years, that transformed conditions of life very deeply. These are not matters of choice, neither are they matters of determinism. These are deep materializations of very complex sociotechnical relations. What interested me was the way of conceiving of us all as communication systems, whether we are animate or inanimate, whether we are animals or plants, human beings or the planet herself, Gaia, or machines of various kinds. This common coin of theorizing existence, this common ontology of everything as communication-control-system was what interested me. It made me very angry and anxious, but interested me in more positive ways, too. Among other things I was attracted by an unconscious and dreamlike quality, and I was interested in affirming not simply the human-machine aspect of cyborgs, but also the degree to which human beings and other organisms have a kind of commonality to them in cyborg worlds. It was the joint implosion of human and machine, on the one hand, and human and other organisms, on the other, within a kind of problematic of communication that interested me about the cyborg. There were many levels in this, for example labor process issues: the particular ways that women—working-class women, women of color, women in Third World countries with export processing zones that would attract international capital for micro-electronics manufacture—were implicated in the labor process of cyborg production, as scientists, too, although in relative minorities. Women occupied many kinds of places in these worlds, in biomedicine, in information sciences, but also as a preferred workforce for transnational capitals. Strategies of flexible accumulation involved the productions of various kinds of gender, for men and for women, that were historically specific. The cyborg became a figure for trying to understand women's place in the "integrated circuit"[2]—a phrase produced by feminist socialists.

Moreover, the cyborg was a place to excavate and examine popular culture including Science Fiction, and, in particular, feminist Science Fiction. A novel like *Superluminal* by Vonda McIntyre[3] made a strong use of cyborg imagery in complex, interesting ways that were quasi-feminist. Joanna Russ' clone sister fiction of the mid-1970s[4] and, certainly, Octavia Butler's work[5] intrigued me a lot. There was a great deal of feminist cultural production, which was working with the cyborg in fascinating ways.

Also, the cyborg seemed to me a figuration that was specifically hard for psychoanalysis to account for. But in contrast to what a lot of people have argued, I do not think of the cyborg as without an unconscious. However, it is not a Freudian unconscious. There is a different kind of dreamwork going on here; it is not ethical, it is not edenic, it is not about origin stories in the garden. It is a different set of narrations, figurations, dreamwork, subject formations, and unconscious work. These sorts of figurations do not exclude many kinds of psychoanalytic work, but they are not the same thing. It was important to me to have a way of dealing with figurations in technoscience that were not quite so hegemonized by psychoanalysis as I found it developed around me in really lively places of feminist cultural work such as film theory. Some marvellous work has been done with Freudian or post-Freudian tools here, but they did not seem right for the analysis of technoscience. So I turned to literature as well as biology and philosophy, and questions of figurations interested me a lot.

Cyborgs are also places where the ambiguity between the literal and the figurative is always working. You are never sure whether to take something literally or figuratively. It is always both/and. It is this undecidability between the literal and the figurative that interests me about technoscience. It seems like a good place to inhabit. Moreover, the cyborg involves a physicality that is undeniable and deeply historically specific. It is possible to extend the cyborg image into other historical configurations, allegorically or analogically, but it seems to me that it had a particular historical emergence. You can use it to inquire into other historical formations, but it has a specificity.

In a way, you know, I am doing this analysis of the meanings attached to the cyborg retrospectively. I cannot imagine that I thought all these things in 1983 [laughter]. It is a funny thing to look back at something I actually began writing seventeen years ago . . .

Interviewer: Please, tell us about the intriguing history of the Cyborg Manifesto, which has taken on a life of its own in a way that academic papers seldom do.

Donna Haraway: I began writing the manifesto in 1983. *Socialist Review* in the United States wanted socialist feminists to write about the future of socialist feminism in the context of the early Reagan era and the retrenchment of the left that the 1980s was witnessing. Barbara Ehrenreich and I, and many other American socialist feminists, were invited to contribute. Moreover, Frigga Haug and the feminist collective of the West German socialist journal *Das Argument* wanted me to write about reproductive technologies, and the cyborg is an obvious place for making reflections on the technologification of reproduction. Almost at the same time, a left democratic group in the former Yugoslavia was holding a conference and I was designated as one of the American representatives from *Socialist Review*. I wrote a version of the Cyborg Manifesto for this occasion, although I actually did not deliver my paper at the conference. Instead, a small group of us made a demonstration about the division of labor at the conference, where the women were invisibly doing all the work, while the men were not so invisibly doing all the propounding! So in the beginning the Cyborg Manifesto had a very strong socialist and European connection.

Interviewer: Where did you read the word, cyborg, the first time? Do you remember that?

Donna Haraway: I do not remember. I tried to remember it, and it felt like I made the word up, but I cannot have made it up. I read Norbert Wiener, but I do not think I got it there. I did not read Clynes and Kline[6] until way after I had written the Cyborg Manifesto. I did not know about Clynes and Kline and that fabulous connection of the psychiatrist, the systems engineer, and the mental hospital. It was a graduate student of mine, Chris Gray,[7] who told me about the cyborg article of Clynes and Kline from 1960.

Interviewer: How do you yourself look upon the remarkable history of the Cyborg Manifesto? How do you evaluate the reception, in terms both of positive and negative responses?

Donna Haraway: I am astonished . . . But to answer your question, I can tell you that the reactions, right from the beginning, were very mixed. At *Socialist Review* the manifesto was considered very controversial. The *Socialist Review* East Coast Collective truly disapproved of it politically and did not want it published. But the Berkeley *Socialist Review* Collective did, and it was Jeff Escoffier, a very interesting gay theorist and historian, who was my editor at the Berkeley Collective, and he was very enthusiastic about the paper. So from the beginning the manifesto was very controversial. There were some who regarded it as tremendously anti-feminist, promoting a kind of blissed-out, techno-sublime euphoria. Those readers completely failed to see all the critique. They would read things that for me are highly ironic and angry, a kind of contained ironic fury—they would read these things as my literal position, as if I was embracing and affirming what I am describing with barely restrained fury.

The reading practices of the Cyborg Manifesto took me aback from the very beginning, and I learned that irony is a dangerous rhetorical strategy. Moreover, I found out that it is not a very kind rhetoric, because it does things to your audience that are not fair. When you use irony, you assume that your audience is reading out of much the same sort of experiences as you yourself, and they are not. You assume reading practices that you have to finally admit are highly privileged and often private. The manifesto put together literacies that are the result of literary studies, biology, information sciences, political economy and a very privileged and expensive travel and education. It was a paper that was built on privilege, and the reading practices that it asks from people are hard. I learned something about that from certain receptions of the manifesto. On the other hand, most of my readers shared the same privileges [laughter].

There were also readers who would take the Cyborg Manifesto for its technological analysis, but drop the feminism. Many science studies people, who still seem tone-deaf to feminism, have done this. It is generally my experience that very few people are taking what I consider all of its parts. I have had people, like *Wired Magazine* readers, interviewing and writing about the Cyborg Manifesto from what I see as a very blissed-out, techno-sublime position.

But I have also had this really interesting reception from young feminists—a reception which I love. They embrace and use the cyborg of the manifesto to do what they want for their own purposes. They have completely different histories from mine, from this particular moment of democratic socialism and socialist feminism, the transition of the 1980s which I just narrated. This is not their history at all. They have a totally different relationship to cultural production, to access to media, to use of computers for performance art and other purposes, to technomusic. They have, to my pleasure and astonishment, found the Cyborg Manifesto useful for queer sexuality work, and for certain kinds of queer theory that take in technoscience. I found myself to be an audience here. In this context, I am one of the readers of the manifesto, not one of the writers. I did not write that manifesto, but I love reading it [laughter]. These young feminists have truly rewritten the manifesto in ways that were not part of my intention, but I can see what they are doing. I think it is a legitimate reading, and I like it, but it really wasn't what I wrote. So sometimes people read the manifesto in ways that are very pleasant surprises to me, and sometimes it is really distressing to be confronted with the reading practices. But, anyway, it is a hard paper to read. Difficulty is an issue. On the other hand, I swear, I meet people without academic training who read the manifesto and who do not give up. They read it for what they want, and they just do not care about the difficulty issue.

Interviewer: I have been teaching gender and technoculture to registered nurses, and for many of them, the manifesto was a revelation. It helped them to see their practice as nurses in a new light and to avoid being caught in the dilemma between a humanistic and partly technophobic concept of care, on the one hand, and, on the other, the powerful and uncritically self-glorifying visions of progress, embedded in the discourses of medical science. Your cyborg was for them a critical tool, a position from which they could think their professional identity differently.

Donna Haraway: This is very interesting. I think that part of the feminist argument of the manifesto is exactly in line with this. It is neither technophobic, nor technophilic, but about trying to inquire critically into the worldliness of technoscience. It is about exploring where real people are in the material-semiotic systems of technoscience and what kinds of accountability, responsibility, pleasure, work, play, are engaged, and should be engaged.

[. . .]

Interviewer: You have recently included a new member in your kinship of potential critical figurations: the dog. Why?

Donna Haraway: Dogs are many things. They occupy many kinds of categories: breeds, populations, vermin, figures, research animals, pets, workers, sources of rabies, the New Guinea singing dog, the Dingoes, etc. Dogs are very many kinds of entities. The ontology of dogs turns out to be quite big, and there are all those names for dogs that are about various kinds of relationalities. Dogs engage many kinds of relationality, but one kind that is practically obligatory is with humans. It is almost part of the definition of a dog to be in relationship with humans, although not necessarily around the word "domestication." Though "domestication" is a very powerful word, it is not altogether clear. In fact, it is probably not true that humans domesticated dogs. Conversely, it is probably true from an evolutionary and historical point of view that dogs took the first steps in producing this symbiosis. There are a lot of interesting biological-behavioural stories that have a certain evidential quality. These are partly testable stories, partly not testable stories. So dogs have this large array of possible ontologies, that are all about relationship and very heavily about relationships with humans in different historical forms. For people, dogs do a tremendous amount of semiotic work. They work for us not only when they are herding sheep; they also work as figures, and dogs figure back very important kinds of human investments.

For me, there are many, many ways in which I am interested in dogs. I am interested in the fact that dogs are not us. So they figure not-us. They are not just cute projections. Dogs do not figure mirror-of-me. Dogs figure another species, but another species living in very close relationship; another species in relation to which the nature/culture divide is more of a problem than a help, when we try to understand it. Because dogs are neither nature, nor culture, not both/and, not neither/nor, but something else.

Interviewer: The notion of companionship becomes important here, I assume?

Donna Haraway: Yes, although the notion of companionship is a very modern way of seeing the dogs. The notion of the companion animal is a quite recent invention. Seeing dogs as companion animals, but not pets, is a rather recent contestation. We have necessarily to be in an ethical relationship with dogs, because they are vulnerable to human cruelty in very particular ways, or to carelessness, or stupidity. So dogs become sites of meaning-making and sites of inquiry: ethical inquiry, ontological inquiry, inquiry about the nature of sociality, inquiry about pedagogy and training and control, inquiry about sadism, about authoritarianism, about war (the relationship between the infantry and the war dog as tools in military history), etc.

Dogs become good figures to think with—in all sorts of circumstances. There is the development of service dogs, for example, the seeing-eye dogs and other sorts. There are all the different ways that dogs are brought into relationship with human need, or human desire. There are dogs as toys, toy dogs, dogs as livestock guardians in charge of protecting sheep against wolves, bears, coyotes, and so on. Working dogs interest me a lot and so does the relationship of a human being and a dog in the sports world. There are also dependency issues, but dogs are not surrogate children. Dogs are adult. Adult dogs should not be infantilized! When you live with a dog you live with another adult who is not your species. I find this cross-species companionship and the questions of otherness that are involved really interesting. Dogs confront us with a particular kind of otherness that raises many questions, ethical, ontological, political, questions about pleasure, about embodiment etc.

Interviewer: How does the dog relate to the cyborg and the coyote? Is it an in-between figure in the kinship of figurations?

Donna Haraway: It is, and in that sense, you know, I feel like I have written about many sorts of entities that are neither nature, nor culture. The cyborg is such an entity, and the coyote; and the genetically engineered laboratory research animal OncoMouse(tm)[8] is also in this odd family—this queer family that is neither nature, nor culture, but an interface. The family includes, for me, in terms of what I have written about, personally, the cyborg, the coyote, the OncoMouse(tm), the FemaleMan,[9] the feminists, the history of women within feminist analysis, the dogs in my new project, and, of course, the non-human primates.[10] All these are entities that require one to be confused about the categories of nature and culture.

Interviewer: Are they all on the same level, or do you consider the cyborg to be a kind of metacategory?

Donna Haraway: Well, sometimes the cyborg functions as a metacategory, but I am actually much happier to demote it to one of the litter. Sometimes I do end up saying these are all cyborg figures, but I think that is a bad idea. I like to think of the cyborg as one of the litter, the one that requires an awful lot of intervention in order to survive [laughter]. . . . It has to be technically enhanced in order to survive in this world.

Part II: There are always more things going on than you thought! Methodologies as thinking technologies

Interviewer: I would like to start the second part of the interview with a question about your writing style. When I teach feminist theory, I often advise the students to focus not only on the line of argument of your texts, but also to read them in a literary way, i.e., to give attention to the metaphors, images, narrative strategies and to study how you make the literary moves explicit. I think that you, in a very inspiring way, practice your tenet about "scientific practice" as a "story-telling practice" (Haraway 1989: 4). Your deconstructions of the barriers between theory and literature make your texts extremely rich; theoretical content, methodology, style and epistemology go hand in hand. How did you come to this kind of theory writing?

Donna Haraway: Well, there are lots of ways of talking about this. First of all, it is not altogether intentional. Writing does things to the writer. Writing is a very particular and surprising process. When I am writing, I often try to learn something, and I may be using things that I only partly understand, because I may have only recently learned about them from a colleague, a student, a friend. This is not altogether a scholarly proper thing to do. But I do that from time to time, and it affects style. It is like a child in school learning to use a new word in a sentence.

Interviewer: Would you compare this to a literary intuitive way of writing?

Donna Haraway: Yes. My texts are full of arguments, it must be said [laughs jokingly]. But my style of writing is also intuitive. It absolutely is. And I like that. I like words. They are work, but they are also pleasurable.

Interviewer: This means that it is possible to keep going back to your texts and still find new inspiring layers of meaning like in literary texts.

Donna Haraway: Yes, in a sense, I do think that they are literary texts.

Interviewer: Your efforts to transgress the barriers between theory and literature make me think of other scholars within the feminist tradition, for example Luce Irigaray, and the ways in which she deliberately links writing strategies and epistemology. Could you tell us, how you look upon these links as far as your own work is concerned?

Donna Haraway: Well, my style is not only intuitive, but also the result of deliberate choice, of course. Sometimes people ask me "Why aren't you clear?" and I always feel puzzled, or hurt, when that happens, thinking "God, I do the best I can! It's not like I'm being deliberately unclear! I'm really trying to be clear!" But, you know, there is the tyranny of clarity and all these analyses of why clarity is politically correct. However, I like layered meanings, and I like to write a sentence in such a way that—by the time you get to the end of it—it has at some level questioned itself. There are ways of blocking the closure of a sentence, or of a whole piece, so that it becomes hard to fix its meanings. I like that, and I am committed politically and epistemologically to stylistic work that makes it relatively harder to fix the bottom line.

[. . .]

Interviewer: In a video, "Donna Haraway reads the *National Geographies of Primates*" (Paper Tiger Television, #126, 1987) you visualize your analytical method pedagogically by untangling a ball of yarn. You are pulling out the threads, metaphorically demonstrating a deconstructive move, I guess, critically going back to where things are coming from. How would you compare this to the Latour-inspired "follow-the-actors" approach that I think you are very committed to, as well?

Donna Haraway: Well, I see the "pulling-out-the-threads" on the video and the "follow-the-actors" approach as closely related. In my recent book *Modest Witness* (Haraway 1997), I have this family of entities, these imploded objects: chip, gene, cyborg, seed, foetus, brain, bomb, ecosystem, race. I think of these as balls of yarn, as gravity wells, as points of intense implosion or as knots. They lead out into worlds, you can explode them, you can untangle them, you can somehow loosen them up. They are densities that can be loosened, that can be pulled out, that can be exploded, and they lead to whole worlds, to universes without stopping points, without ends. Out of the chip you can in fact untangle the entire planet, on which the subjects and objects are sedimented. Similarly, you do not have to stay below the diaphragm of the woman's body when dealing with the foetus. It leads you into the midst of corporate investment strategies, into the midst of migration patterns in northeastern Brazil, into the midst of little girls doing caesarean sections on their dolls, into the midst of compulsory reproductivity and the question: What is it that makes everybody want a child these days? Who is this "everybody"?

Interviewer: How would you describe the relationship between the research subject and the figures that perform in the analysis? What is, for example, your relationship to the figures or imploded knots, chip, gene, cyborg, foetus, brain, bomb, ecosystem, race?

Donna Haraway: Figures are never innocent. The relationship of a subject to a figure is best described as a cathexis of some kind. There is a deep connection between the writing subject and the figure. It is not just about picking an entity in the world, some kind of interesting academic object. There is a cathexis that needs to be understood here. The analyst is always already bound in a cathectic relationship to the object of analysis, and s/he needs to excavate the implication of this bond, of her/his being in the world in this way rather than some other. Articulating the analytical object, figuring, for example, this family or kinship of entities, chip, gene, foetus, bomb, etc. (it is an indefinite list), is about location and historical specificity, and it is about a kind of assemblage, a kind of connectedness of the figure and the subject.

Interviewer: I would like to know about your relationship to science and technology studies, the STS-tradition. There are, for example, some obvious parallels between your work and the work of Bruno Latour, and he is, in a sense, leaving science studies now. What about you? How do you look upon science studies today? And which role does feminism play here?

Donna Haraway: Well, science studies is a kind of indefinite signifier, and that is what has made it a good place to locate oneself. It is professionalized in various ways, and that is useful. I will sometimes use science studies as a signifier for myself, and at other times I will not use it. It is a professional and strategic location, but it is not a life-long identity. Even though in some other ways it is, because there are institutional realities connected to it. People like Susan Leigh Star, and Bruno Latour, and Andy Pickering, and many others, read each other. So we end up being both deliberately and unconsciously in conversation. But this conversation and reading of each other's texts do not refer to a kind of shared origin story or genealogy. I have a very different genealogy in science studies than, say, Andy Pickering or Bruno Latour do. People like Susan Leigh Star and I share more of a genealogy in science studies that roots it, for example, in the women's health movement and in technoscientific issues related to women's labor in the office, or to Lucy Suchman's work. You know, we share a genealogy of science studies that, among other things, situates it in relation to the history of the women's movement at least as much as it connects it to a history of a strong program, to a history of actor-network-theory (ANT), or to a history of a rejection of actor-network-theory. You know, all of those end up becoming interesting little events in the neighborhood, but not the main line of action. So in that sense, I have a kind of annoyed relationship with some of the canonized versions of the history of science studies which go like this: "Well, there was this in Edinburgh, there was that in Paris, and whatever." You know, in that narrative of science studies people like me and my buddies are always hard to incorporate. Even by people of great goodwill, such as Andy Pickering, whom I both admire and read with great pleasure, and like as a human being. Nonetheless, read his preface to *Science as Practice and Culture* (Pickering 1992) and watch the absolute indigestibility of Sharon Traweek and me. We are as the angels with the twelve trumpets. Literally. Every other figure in that introduction got a paragraph or so of analysis, in terms of what was contributed, and what he liked or objected to. But we were like blasts from John's Apocalypse [laughter]. Literally! That is the figure he used. Because we are not part of that other story in that way of telling it, and they do not know our story. They do not know it as an academic story, and they do not know it as a political story. It is a different history. So after I was already doing what I now call feminist technoscience studies, I read people like, for example, Bruno Latour. So Latour and other authors, which figure prominently in the canonized version of the history of STS, were not the origin in my story; they came after other events. And they do not get this! That there is a whole other serious genealogy of technoscience studies. So I remain irritated! [Laughter] Because we do know their genealogies, very well. And they do not know ours, even though they exist in writing; they are certainly not inaccessible! On the other hand, this does not mean that I would call myself an outsider. That would be silly of me. But I think it remains true in most academic locations, including science studies, that most feminists are both insiders and outsiders in the sense that Patricia Hill Collins theorized this insider/outsider location for African American women. Sometimes we are forced into this location, and sometimes we choose to inhabit it.

Interviewer: And I suppose the reason is the issue of feminism. . . .

Donna Haraway: Yes, we are a little hard to digest. And I think that is a good thing. On the one hand, we are so normalized, and disciplinized, and comfortable, you know, and to call ourselves outsiders is a kind of lie. But, you know, from another point of view, we are still outsiders.

[. . .]

Notes

The interview took place when Donna Haraway visited Denmark as keynote speaker at the conference "Cyborg Identities—The Humanities in Technical Light," October 21–22, 1999, arranged by Randi Markussen and Finn Olesen, Institute of Information and Media Sciences, Aarhus University, as part of the initiative "The Humanities at the Turn of the Millennium," Centre for Cultural Studies, Aarhus University. The interview was taken as part of a special event with Donna Haraway, organized by the FREJA research project "Cyborgs and cyberspace—between narration and sociotechnical reality"; the three interviewers are all members of the FREJA research group.

1   D. Haraway, "A Cyborg Manifesto: Science, Technology, and Socialist-Feminism in the Late Twentieth Century," in D. Haraway, *Simians, Cyborgs and Women* (London: Free Association Books, 1991).
2   Cf. Haraway, "A Cyborg Manifesto," p. 170.
3   V. McIntyre, *Superluminal* (Boston: Houghton Mifflin, 1983).
4   J. Russ, *The Female Man* (New York: Bantam Books, 1975).
5   O. Butler, *Dawn* (1987), *Adulthood Rites* (1988), *Imago* (1989), all published by Warner Books, New York.
6   M. E. Clynes and N. S. Kline, "Cyborgs and Space," *Astronautics* (September 1960). Reprinted in C. H. Gray et al., *The Cyborg Handbook* (London and New York: Routledge, 1995), pp. 29–33.
7   Ibid.
8   Cf. D. Haraway, *Modest_*Witness@Second_Millennium.FemaleMan©_Meets_Onco-Mouse™: Feminism and Technoscience* (London and New York: Routledge, 1997).
9   Cf. n. 8.
10 Cf. D. Haraway, *Primate Visions: Gender, Race, and Nature in the World of Modern Science* (London and New York: Routledge, 1989).

References

Haraway, Donna. 1989. *Primate Visions: Gender, Race and Nature in the World of Modern Science*. New York and London: Routledge.

———. 1991. *Simians, Cyborgs and Women. The Reinvention of Nature.* London: Free Association Books.

———. 1992. "The Promises of Monsters: A Regenerative Politics for Inappropriate/d Others." In *Cultural Studies*, L. Grossberg, C. Nelson, and P. Treichler, eds. London and New York: Routledge: 295–338.

———. 1997. *Modest_Witness@Second_Millenium. FemaleMan*™_*Meets_OncoMouse*™: *Feminism and Technoscience.* New York and London: Routledge.

———. 2000. *How Like a Leaf. An Interview with Thyrza Nichols Goodeve.* London, New York: Routledge.

Lykke, Nina. 1996. "Kyborg eller gudinde? Feministiske dilemmaer i det sene 20. århundredes øko- og teknokritik." *I:Kvinder, køn og forskning* 5 nr. 4 (1996). pp. 31–45.

Lykke, Nina. 1999. "Posthumane visioner: En postkønnet eller kvindelig cyberkultur?" *I: Kvinder, køn og forskning* 2: 43–53.

Lykke, Nina, Finn Olesen og Randi Markussen. 2000.

Pickering, Andrew, ed. 1992. *Science as Practice and Culture.* Chicago: University of Chicago Press.

Chapter 16

DAVID TOMAS

FEEDBACK AND CYBERNETICS
Reimaging the body in the age
of the cyborg

IN THE MID 1990S CULTURAL, media and film theory and philosophy saw a remarkable number of essays and books tackling ideas and instantiations of cyborgs, cybernetic and virtual computer technologies in popular film (*The Terminator, Blade Runner*) and SF literature (nearly always quoting William Gibson's cyberpunk novel *Neuromancer*), and futurological claims for impending virtuality. In *New Media: A Critical Introduction* we refer to this phenomenon as cybercultural studies. This essay by David Tomas is of particular interest in its tracing of the scientific origins and technological reality of the terms 'cyborg' and 'cybernetics' as well as their fictional and theoretical appearance. In tracing the history of the term 'cybernetics' in **Wiener**'s ideas and work in, and immediately after, the Second World War, Tomas recounts that the human body has been reconceptualised over history according to dominant technological paradigms from mythical golems to eighteenth-century clockwork, to the power engineering of the Industrial Revolution. With cybernetics, the 'science of control and communication' from the 1940s and 1950s, we see a new figuration of the human body as a system of communication and feedback both within itself as an organism and with and through other organisms (not necessarily human) and its environment. The human body's nervous system, rather than its skeleto-muscular mechanisms or digestive and respirative power generation, becomes primary as it is reimaged as patterns of information. Tomas explains Wiener's expansive notion of 'organism' as a body or even pattern of organisation (the etymological link between the words is deliberate) in the context of overall cosmic entropy. That is, organisms organise themselves and others through communication and feedback whilst the overall trajectory of the universe is towards heat death. These organisms or automata (self-moving organisms) can be biological (animals, plants, etc.), technological (artificial cybernetic systems) or, by implication, natural but not 'living' in the commonly accepted sense of the word (geological organisation perhaps). Moreover, if organisms are conceived of in terms of their informational behaviour, then their material differences (of species or substrate for instance) are much less important than the connections between them, and thus their *collective* organisation, environmentally or globally, is accentuated: 'the human body [can] be radically reimaged, its identity [becomes] an organizational singularity and its intelligence simply a pattern among many such patterns'.

Tomas refers directly to **Wiener**'s work and to **Haraway**'s 'Cyborg Manifesto'. He points out the influence of cybernetics on **McLuhan**, and on **Wiener**'s conception of 'life' as encompassing all processes of negentropic organisation, including the non-biological. This latter conception could be seen as resonant with Deleuze and **Guattari**'s notion of the machinic phylum. **Galison** addresses Wiener's work and ideas in further historical and conceptual detail, and **Kennedy** describes the everyday technoculture of videogame play as cybernetic.

Words have frightening power.

(Colin Cherry, 1980: 68)

The *cyborg* or 'cybernetic organism' represents a radical vision of what it means to be human in the western world in the late 20th century. Although the word has an official history that dates from 1964, when it was coined to describe a special union of human organism and machine system, over the last decade it has gained a certain notoriety in both popular film culture and specialized academic circles. Films such as *Blade Runner* (1982), the *Alien* trilogy, the *Terminator* series (1984, 1991), the *RoboCop* series (1987, 1990) and the British cult classic *Hardware* (1990) present a vision of the cyborg that ranges from pure machine-based military model to genetically tailored human simulation. These models and simulations are often designed to function in hostile, dystopic, futuristic worlds governed by various kinds of renegade military/industrial or corporate activity, or the consequences of such activity. More benign protocyborg models of a less imaginary, but no less militarized form, are to be found prefigured in the kinds of revisions of masculinity that were explored in the context of the American space program's shift in emphasis from test pilot to astronaut in Tom Wolfe's 1979 bestseller *The Right Stuff* and the film of the same name. On the other hand, alternative cyborg models have been explored in a more speculative vein, and from a more cloistered academic viewpoint, in 'A Cyborg Manifesto: Science, Technology, and Socialist-Feminism in the Late Twentieth Century', Donna Haraway's seminal 1985 meditation on oppositional uses of the cyborg concept.

The success of cyborg-based films and the influence of Haraway's cyborg manifesto suggest that the word 'cyborg' has functioned throughout the 1980s, in one form or another, as a keyword in Raymond Williams's sense of 'significant binding words in certain activities and their interpretation' (Williams, 1983: 15).[1] There are, however, a number of other words that paved the way for 'cyborg' and its particular 'hybrid' mode of reimaging the human body under the sign of the machine. These words, some of which have existed for decades, others for a number of centuries, include 'automaton', 'automation' and 'automatic', 'android' and 'robot'; while others like 'bionic' appeared at about the same time cyborg was coined.

Lately, we have been introduced to another word, *cyberspace*, also known as 'virtual reality', which has also begun to circulate in popular and academic discourses on the future of the human body, often in the company of the word 'cyborg' or its images. Whether in the guise of 'cyberspace', a word first coined by William Gibson in his award winning science fiction novel *Neuromancer* (1984), or in the form of 'virtual reality', the idea of a new computer-based digital mode of articulating and, indeed, of reimaging the human body has been explored in novels, including Gibson's own *Count Zero* (1986) and *Mona Lisa Overdrive* (1988), films (such as *Brainstorm* [1983] and *The Lawnmower Man* [1992]), as well as in a host of academic and popular texts.[2]

It is not hard to imagine, therefore, that words such as 'automaton', 'automation', 'automatic', 'android', 'robot', 'bionic', 'cyborg' and 'cyberspace' might constitute a Williamsian *cluster* of keywords inasmuch as they form a 'set of . . . interrelated words and references' (1983: 22) that plot ever-changing thresholds in the history of the human body. With the

appearance of each new word, a new threshold is crossed in the perception and social construction of the human body, between conceptions of the organic and inorganic, the body and
technology, the human and non-human; and, indeed, of machines themselves insofar as they
can also '*be considered as organs of the human species*' (Canguilhem, 1992: 55, emphasis in the
original).

There are two principal ways to explore the most recent cyborg and virtual reality thresholds
in the history of the body/machine interface. The first is through the word *cybernetics*. Although
it was not a new word when it was introduced in 1947, 'cybernetics' was considered to be a
neologism that best described a new interdisciplinary science of control and communication.
Reconceptualization can, in this case, be traced through the reasons given for the choice of
this particular word, its attributed meanings and, finally, its evocative powers as an analogical
tool.

The second way to explore the human body's reconceptualization is to trace cybernetics'
subsequent history and, in particular, its impact on how researchers reimaged the human/machine
interface in the early 1960s when the word 'cyborg' was coined. From there, one can trace
the reverberations of cybernetics' initial impact as *word* and 'universal' discipline (Bowker,
1993) to the mid-to-late 1980s and Haraway's socialist-feminist oppositional cyborg. Finally,
there is the question of virtual reality technology or cyberspace, which must be addressed,
however briefly, since it represents the potential site and, as such, the promise, as most recent
and perhaps quintessential of cyborg interfaces, for new or more developed kinds of human
organism/machine system interactions.[3]

Identity into pattern: Norbert Wiener, cybernetics and the 20th-century automaton

Norbert Wiener, a founding figure of the science of cybernetics, provides a useful overview
of different phases in the development of automata. His periodization is of interest because of
its focus on shifts in motive force and the way that these shifts are related to a parallel history
of the body. In his classic 1948 manifesto on a new science of cybernetics, *Cybernetics: or Control
and Communication in the Animal and the Machine*, Wiener presented a history of automata that
was divided into four stages: a mythic Golemic age; the age of clocks (17th and 18th centuries);
the age of steam, originator of the governor mechanism itself (late 18th and 19th centuries);
and, finally, the age of communication and control, an age marked by a shift from power
engineering to communication engineering, from, in other words, an 'economy of energy' to
an economy rooted in 'the accurate reproduction of a signal' (Wiener, 1948a: 51, 50).

Wiener noted, on the other hand, that these stages generated four models of the human
body: the body as a malleable, magical, clay figure; the body as a clockwork mechanism; the
body as a 'glorified heat engine, burning some combustible fuel instead of the glycogen of the
human muscles'; and, most recently, the body as an electronic system (Wiener, 1948a: 51).
Wiener's two-fold periodization is significant because it reveals an awareness, by one of the
principal founders of cybernetics, of important disciplinary phases in a machine-based history
of the western body. It is also significant because it draws attention to *parallel phases* in the
body's functional reimaging as a fundamental element in a machine culture.

While the 19th century was characterized by an *engineered* body, a body considered 'to be
a branch of power engineering', a model whose influence had extended well into the 20th
century, Wiener argued (1948b: 15) 'we are now coming to realize that the body is very far
from a conservative system, and that the power available to it is much less limited than was
formerly believed'. In place of a 19th-century model, he suggested that

we are beginning to see that such important elements as the neurones – the units of the nervous complex of our bodies – do their work under much the same conditions as vacuum tubes, their relatively small power being supplied from outside by the body's circulation, and that the bookkeeping which is most essential to describe their function is not one of energy. (1948b: 15)

In its place, cybernetics proposed that the body be conceived as a communications network whose successful operation was based on 'the accurate reproduction of a signal' (1948b: 15).

For Wiener, writing in the late 1940s, the 'newer study of automata, whether in metal or in the flesh, [was] a branch of communication engineering, and its cardinal notions [were] those of message, amount of disturbance or «noise» . . . quantity of information, coding technique, and so on' (1948a: 54). He went on to argue, 'in such a theory, we deal with automata effectively coupled to the external world, not merely by their energy flow, their metabolism, but also by a flow of impressions, of incoming messages, and of the actions of outgoing messages' (1948a: 54). This new way of conceiving of automata was, in theory and practice, coupled to a new kind of feedback mechanism: the servomechanism.[4] Wiener went so far as to argue that 'the present age is as truly the age of servo-mechanisms as the nineteenth century was the age of the steam engine or the eighteenth century the age of the clock' (Wiener, 1948a: 55).

The difference between servomechanisms and earlier forms of clockwork-based automata, or even systems of automatic machinery which were governed by a steam engine's governor, did not reside in their fundamental operational logic (since the earlier automata were also governed by a feedback-based logic) but rather in their ability to penetrate, through a wide variety of forms, the *social* as opposed to the industrial fabric of a nation.[5] Instead of being limited to clockwork mechanisms or prime movers such as steam engines, the new servomechanisms were designed for a wide range of applications. These included 'thermostats, automatic gyro-compass ship-steering systems, self-propelled missiles – especially such as seek their target – anti-aircraft fire-control systems, automatically controlled oil-cracking stills, ultra-rapid computing machines, and the like' (1948a: 55). Although Wiener conceded that 'they had begun to be used long before the war – indeed, the very old steam-engine governor belongs among them', he nevertheless pointed out that 'the great mechanization of the second world war brought them into their own, and', he prophesied, 'the need of handling the extremely dangerous energy of the atom will probably bring them to a still higher point of development' (1948a: 55). Thus, what feedback and other inventions such as the vacuum tube 'made possible [was] not the sporadic design of individual automatic mechanisms, but a general policy for the construction of automatic mechanisms of the most varied type'. Wiener went on to argue that such developments, in conjunction with a 'new theoretical treatment of communication, which takes full cognizance of the possibilities of communication between the machine and machine . . . now renders possible the new automatic age' (Wiener, 1954: 153).

As Wiener pointed out, the new study of automata was emerging in tandem with a new science of communications and control – Cybernetics – a science that proposed a completely new vision of the human body, its relationship to the organic world and the world of machines. A new set of analogies was not only establishing connections, through a series of formal correspondences, between the human body conceived as a nervous system and the machine conceived as a communicating organism, but it was also mapping out the means for the automatic linking of machine to machine by way of a common communications language.

As usual, Wiener gives us a good picture of the power and austere elegance of cybernetics' logic of analogies and its new brand of anthropomorphism when he argued:

While it is impossible to make any universal statements concerning life-imitating automata in a field which is growing as rapidly as that of automatization, there are some general features of these machines as they actually exist that I should like to emphasize. One is that they are machines to perform some definite-task or tasks, and therefore must possess effector organs (analogous to arms and legs in human beings) with which such tasks can be performed. The second point is that they must be *en rapport* with the outer world by sense organs, such as photoelectric cells and thermometers, which not only tell them what the existing circumstances are, but enable them to record the performance or nonperformance of their own tasks. This last function . . . is called *feedback*, the property of being able to adjust future conduct by past performance. Feedback may be as simple as that of the common reflex, or it may be a higher order feedback, in which past experience is used not only to regulate specific movements, but also whole policies of behavior. Such a policy-feedback may, and often does, appear to be what we know under one aspect as a conditioned reflex, and under another as learning.

For all these forms of behavior, and particularly for the more complicated ones, we must have the central decision organs which determine what the machine is to do next on the basis of information fed back to it, which it stores by means analogous to the memory of a living organism. (Wiener, 1954: 32–3)

Wiener's cybernetic automaton was conceived as an active, hierarchically governed, self-regulated and goal-oriented machine, which was bound through a particular time/space logic – the adjustment of future conduct through a comparative assessment of past actions – to its environment. This automaton marked a new threshold of intelligence, which extended beyond that which had been previously established on the basis of automated, factory based machine systems.

The particular power of cybernetics' analogical logic resided in the fact that it was able to redefine the concept of 'life' itself in order to bring it in line with a *cybernetic* automaton's operational characteristics. As Wiener noted in its connection: 'now that certain analogies of behavior are being observed between the machine and the living organism, the problem as to whether the machine is alive or not is, for our purposes, semantic and we are at liberty to answer it one way or another as best suits our convenience' (1954: 32).

If we wish to use the word 'life' to cover all phenomena which locally swim upstream against the current of increasing entropy, we are at liberty to do so. However, we shall then include many astronomical phenomena which have only the shadiest resemblance to life as we ordinarily know it. (Wiener, 1954: 32)

Instead, Wiener championed a different and far more radical point of view when he argued that it was

best to avoid all question-begging epithets such as 'life', 'soul', 'vitalism', and the like, and say merely in connection with machines that there is no reason why they may not resemble human beings in representing pockets of decreasing entropy in a framework in which the large entropy tends to increase. (1954: 32)

The claim to have side-stepped the thorny issue of 'life' went well beyond the abstract level at which it was proposed. It implied a new systemic model for the structure of organisms that was in keeping with a demise, in the 20th century, of a simple mechanistic or taxanomic view of plant or animal organization. In their place, an organism was conceived as 'a multilevel system of elaborate complexity, buffered in several dimensions so as to maintain its metabolic stability in the face of changes in its environment, and equipped with a repertoire of behaviours to ensure necessary intake of energy, materials, etc' (Pratt, 1987: 180). In other words, an organism was now conceived as if structured according to 'sophisticated systems of control' with its brain serving as a 'top-level co-ordinator' (Pratt, 1987: 180).

The model of an organism structured according to a nest of control mechanisms was also embraced by cyberneticians (Pratt, 1987: 190,194–6). In fact, one might argue that cybernetics operationalized the question of 'life' by displacing the concept of organism from biology to engineering, thus effectively transforming it into a hardware problem. According to its new existential parameters, Wiener's cybernetic automaton was 'organic' and 'alive' precisely because it was *operationally* active, that is, it was 'effectively coupled to the external world, not merely by [its] energy flow, [its] metabolism, but also by a flow of impressions, of incoming messages, and of the actions of outgoing messages'. A logic of cybernetic analogies ensured, in other words, that functional equivalence was established at the level of the sense-organs (Wiener, 1948a: 54), since these were the principal means by which an organism could maintain a stable, that is systemic, existence in a given environment through an exchange of information.

Yet another way of grasping the cybernetic automaton's organic nature was through the common temporality that it shared with the world of 'living' organisms. After noting that 'the relation of these mechanisms [the new automata] to time demands careful study', Wiener pointed out:

> It is clear of course that the relation input-output is a consecutive one in time, and involves a definite past-future order. What is perhaps not so clear is that the theory of the sensitive automata is a statistical one. We are scarcely ever interested in the performance of a communication-engineering machine for a single input. To function adequately it must give a satisfactory performance for a whole class of inputs, and this means a statistically satisfactory performance for the class of input which it is statistically expected to receive. Thus its theory belongs to the Gibbsian statistical mechanics rather than to the classical Newtonian mechanics. (Wiener, 1948a: 55)

It was on the basis of these observations that Wiener went on to argue that 'the modern automaton exists in the same sort of Bergsonian time as the living organism; and hence there is no reason in Bergson's considerations why the essential mode of functioning of the living organism should not be the same as that of the automaton of this type' (1948a: 56). As this argument suggests, it was no longer a question of machines functioning *as* organisms, or of organisms functioning *as* machines. Instead, the machine and organism were to be considered as two functionally equivalent states or stages of cybernetic organization.

Wiener's cybernetic automaton marks an important threshold in the history of the human body. By the late 1940s confusions arising from competing images of the human body as thinking organism were effectively exorcized through an anti-mimetic shift in the history of automata. Perhaps cybernetics' greatest achievement in this direction was to consummate the transformation which the Industrial Revolution had inaugurated in the case of automatic machinery. The cybernetic automaton's mirroring of the human body was not established on the basis of conventional mimicry, as in the case of androids and their internal parts, so much as on a common understanding of the similarities that existed between the control mechanisms and communicational organizations of machine systems and living organisms. As a result, the principle of cybernetic embodiment extended well beyond prime movers and factories to infiltrate into the sinews of the most humble piece of technology which could accommodate a servomechanism.

Previously, mimetic automata had provided visually based mechanical models for reflection on the nature of the human organism and its social, political and cultural identities. With the appearance of the cybernetic automaton, the sociologic of human identity was transformed into an abstract product of cybernetic organization. In the case of Čapek's pre-cybernetic 1920s robots, for example, identity was ultimately predicated on traditional categories for the representation of difference in the products of social and industrial organizations, categories such as factory marks, color and language. In short, it was a question of National & Ethnic Robots (Čapek and Čapek, 1961: 57). Cybernetics, on the other hand, proposed a radically different solution to the fundamental nature of the human organism by proposing that its Being be reduced to an organizational *pattern*[6] whose operational logic was also coextensive with other organisms and types of machine systems. As Wiener emphasized at the beginning of his penultimate chapter on 'Organization as the Message' in *The Human Use of Human Beings*:

> The metaphor to which I devote this chapter is one in which the organism is seen as message. Organism is opposed to chaos, to disintegration, to death, as message is to noise. To describe an organism, we do not try to specify each molecule in it, and catalogue it bit by bit, but rather to answer certain questions about it which reveal its pattern: a pattern which is more significant and less probable as the organism becomes, so to speak, more fully an organism. (Wiener, 1954: 95)

Machine and human organism exhibited the signs of life insofar as each managed to increase their level of organization. The process of functional equivalence or analogy would know no bounds since it too was defined in terms of an abstraction: organization (based on feedback) and pattern (a consequence of negentropy). By the early 1960s, the influence of this cybernetic model would reach mystic proportions in Marshall McLuhan's writings when he proposed that a 'current translation of our entire lives into the spiritual form of information' might 'make of the entire globe, and of the human family, a single consciousness' (McLuhan, 1964: 67). As an introductory text on cybernetics would later claim: 'Feedback is Universal' (Porter, 1969: 8).

[. . .]

From cybernetic automaton to cyborg: shifting thresholds in the human/machine interface

Wiener would state, as the opening sentence in a 1948 *Scientific American* article, that 'cybernetics is a word invented to define a new field in science' (1948b: 14). His optimism was based, as we have seen, on this field's potential range and depth of interpretation. For the word and field to which it referred was designed to encompass the human mind, the human body and the world of automatic machines and reduced all three to a common denominator: 'control and communication' (1948b: 14).

As we have also seen, the root metaphor for this enterprise was the feedback mechanism, a mechanism, moreover, which 'governed' the traffic in ideas between the domain of communications theory, with its concrete parallel world of mechanical or electronic switches and circuits, the human body's neural pathways and, ultimately, its brain. In short, cybernetics theory and its system of analogies was in a position to inject a new type of engineering language into the living human body's nervous system, a language that could pave the way for the human body's reimaging in relation to a history of automata.

It was the concept of feedback, in particular, that provided the means for a more extended process of reimaging since it opened the way for the electrical and, ultimately, the electronic *collectivization* of the human body – a collectivization that would reach planetary proportions in McLuhan's metaphor of a global village and its information-based consciousness. Access to this extended model of a cybernetic body was guaranteed by the 'ubiquity of feedback' – an ubiquity that signified that 'interaction [was] everywhere'. For it was this kind of ubiquity that could inaugurate a shift of 'attention away from an individualism that had highlighted [a] noncircular cause-and-effect [world-view] and from the individual person – as if he or she could be independent of others and even independent of chance events occurring in the environment' (Heims, 1993: 271–2). Translated into McLuhanesque terms, feedback was a privileged gateway to a collective electrically-based global consciousness (McLuhan, 1964: 64, 311), not only because it erased the distinction between automated machines and living organisms, but also because it marked, from a communications point of view, 'the end of the lineality that came into the Western world with the alphabet and the continuous forms of Euclidean space' (McLuhan, 1964: 307). It was on the basis of such a logic and world-view that cybernetics and its attendant vocabulary could disseminate the image of a new kind of body to a wider disciplinary field and, further, to a non-specialized general public.

In fact, it was a short step from invoking a functional analogy between machine and human organism in the 1940s to the 1960s and Marshall McLuhan's influential notion of a technology that functioned as 'an extension or self-amputation of our physical bodies', a technology that produced 'new ratios or equilibriums among the other organs and extensions of the body' (McLuhan, 1964: 54). Since they were clearly based on a cybernetic model, McLuhan's ideas were a belated acknowledgement of the fact that the human body had already been irrevocably transformed in the context of cybernetics. Even McLuhan's evocation of an extended nervous system (1964: 64) retains a metaphoric resonance which is lacking in the cybernetic concept of organism as 'local enclave in the general stream of increasing entropy' (Wiener, 1954: 95). Hence, it is no wonder that by the time these ideas had reached a wider public through McLuhan's writings, consciousness had long since taken the radical form of a ratio between the senses (McLuhan, 1964: 67). Wiener's first book, *Cybernetic: or Control and Communication in the Animal and the Machine*, had been published in 1948, and his popular account of cybernetics, *The Human Use of Human Being*, in 1950. These books had already proposed to a general public that the human body be radically reimaged, its identity to become an organizational singularity and its intelligence simply a pattern among many such patterns.

In 1962, two years before the publication of *Understanding Media*, McLuhan's influential introduction to the post-war world of Western media, and 14 years after the introduction of the word 'cybernetics', two American scientists introduced an important corruption of that word. They did so in order to identify a new kind of human/machine interface, a new type of 'organism'. Since that time, this organism has had a powerful hold on the way the body is imaged, imagined and constructed at the outer limits of western science, technology and industry, as well as at the outer limits of its military and aerospace industries. This hold has even extended to university-based as well as non-university-based intellectual and artistic speculations on the future of the human body. Moreover, this organism's fundamental impact on the construction of a Western Imaginary can, one suspects, be traced to the fact that it reintroduces mimesis in the shape of anthropomorphism back into the history of automata.

The neologism 'cyborg' (from cybernetic organism) was proposed by Manfred E. Clynes and Nathan S. Kline in 1960 to describe 'self-regulating man–machine systems' and in particular an 'exogenously extended organizational complex functioning as an integrated homeostatic system unconsciously' (Clynes and Kline, 1960: 27). The technical density of the definition was a function of its proposed sphere of operations: the application of cybernetic controls theory to the problems of space travel as they impinged on the neurophysiology of the human body. In fact, a special kind of 'artifact organism' – the cyborg – was posited as a solution to the question of 'the altering of bodily functions to suit different environments' (Clynes and Kline, 1960: 26). For these researchers, alteration of the body's ecology was to be effected primarily by way of sophisticated instrumental control systems and pharmaceuticals. Thus, 'the purpose of the Cyborg, as well as his own homeostatic systems' was, according to these early pioneers, 'to provide an organizational system in which such robot-like problems [as the body's "autonomous homeostatic controls"] are taken care of automatically and unconsciously, leaving man free to explore, to create, to think, and to feel' (Clynes and Kline, 1960: 27). And as the references to 'his' and 'man' indicate, this problematic was gender specific.

In its most extreme form, Wiener's cybernetic organism could take the form of pure information – 'human information' (Wiener, 1954: 104) – nothing more than a given 'pattern maintained by . . . homeostasis, which [was] the touchstone of [a] personal identity' to be transmitted as a message because it was in the first place a message (1954: 96). In contrast, the Clynes/Kline cyborg represented a different, more immediate and practical solution to the one that was envisioned by the early cyberneticians inasmuch as it was designed to withstand the rigors of space travel, while nevertheless adopting cybernetics' fundamental principles, in particular feedback and homeostasis.

Although initially designed for space travel, the transformative implications of this new type of cybernetic organism were far-reaching. As Clynes subsequently pointed out in a Foreword to *Cyborg – Evolution of the Superman*, a popular account of the cyborg phenomenon published by D.S. Halacy in 1965: 'a new frontier is opening which . . . is not merely space, but more profoundly the relationship of "inner space" to "outer space" – a bridge being built between mind and matter, beginning in our time and extending into the future'. He went on to argue that the cyborg was more flexible than the human organism because it was not bound throughout a lifetime by heredity. Indeed, the cyborg was a reversible entity precisely because it was a 'man–machine combination' (Halacy, 1965: 7). This reversibility, combined with the fact that 'man-made devices' could 'be *incorporated* into the [human body's] regulatory feedback chains', produced a stage of evolution that was *participatory* (Halacy, 1965: 8). Hence, if automatic machines held the promise of another form of human intelligence, then cybernetics redefined that intelligence in such a way that the Clynes/Kline cyborg could become its most perfect embodiment: 'a new and . . . better being' (Halacy, 1965: 8).

In 1985, 'cyborg' was appropriated, as a consequence of its polysemic resonances, by a socialist-feminist historian of biology, Donna Haraway. It was used in this case for a different social purpose, 'rhetorical strategy and . . . political method' (Haraway, 1991: 149). For Haraway the cyborg was not only a 'hybrid of machine and organism', it was also a 'creature of social reality as well as a creature of fiction' (Haraway, 1991: 149). Within a new semantic context provided by socialist-feminist discourses on the gendered body, she argued that this word could function as 'a fiction mapping . . . social and bodily reality and as an imaginative resource suggesting some very fruitful couplings' (Haraway, 1991: 150).

In contrast to the Clynes/Kline cyborg, which was conceived as a 'superman' capable of surviving hostile non-earth environments, Haraway's cyborg was a product of late-capitalist earth. In keeping with its traditional ecology, it was refashioned along the lines of an entity that could transgress earth-bound social/symbolic boundaries between human and animal, animal–human (organism) and machine, and the physical and non-physical (Haraway, 1991:

151–3). Transgression was, moreover, negotiated (in keeping with its late 20th-century context) both in terms of science fiction and the everyday cultural worlds of postmodernism and post-colonial multinational capitalism.

Haraway's cyborg exhibited two other characteristics which distinguished it from the Clynes/Kline cyborg and more recent popular cyborg images, such as those presented in the *RoboCop* and *Terminator* series. As an offspring of *feminist* science fiction, Haraway's cyborg was conceived to be 'a creature in a post-gender world'; and inasmuch as it was conceived as a social and political mentor, it was pictured (in keeping with its 'illegitimate' origins) as 'oppositional, Utopian, and completely without innocence' in the sense that it was 'resolutely committed to partiality, irony, intimacy, and perversity' (Haraway, 1991: 150, 151). It was in these multiple senses that Haraway suggested that the cyborg could become 'our ontology' and that it could give 'us our politics' (Haraway, 1991: 150). For its transgressive ontology and politics ensured that it was able to effectively circumvent, in spirit if not in name, its military/industrial origins (Haraway, 1991: 150).

The immediate origins of the word 'cybernetics' can be traced, as Wiener suggested, to military research coupled with a specific post-war interdisciplinary university-based research programme (Heims, 1993; Bowker, 1993). 'Cyborg' exhibited a similar genealogy with, however, a different inflection since it was the hybrid product of the United States' space programme and a medical research laboratory (both Clynes and Kline were at the time [1960] researchers at Rockland State Hospital, Orangeburg, New York). On the other hand, Haraway's socialist-feminist cyborg was the joint creation of mid-1980s political activism and academic radicalism. The distinction between the two categories of cyborg can be traced to their authors' respective backgrounds. While the body's physiological ecology ('the body–environment problem' (Clynes and Kline, 1960: 26) determined its early semantic field, Haraway's academic socialist-feminist background was the determining factor in her rearticulation of the cyborg's politics and gender.

Haraway's cyborg was, as such, a perfectly crafted image for a 1980s vision of a late 20th-century oppositional consciousness, especially since it embodied all of the contradictory characteristics of a decade which defined its cultural and political practices, in the context of radical academic theory, in terms of postmodernist and post-colonial criteria of partiality, hybridity, pastiche and playful irony. As one cultural theorist would later note in its connection, 'transgressed boundaries, in fact, define the cyborg, making it the consummate postmodern concept' – or, from a reverse perspective, 'uncertainty is a central characteristic of postmodernism and the essence of the cyborg' (Springer, 1991: 306, 310). Indeed, as an oppositional cyborg's multiple articulations suggested, and as Clynes had already suggested in 1965, this most recent of reconceptualizations in the domain of automata was symptomatic of the body's uncertain future in the mid to late 20th century.

A hardware-based cyborg integrates or interfaces, in its most extreme and evocative form, a human body with a pure technological environment (machine elements, electronic components, advanced imaging systems). Clearly, under such circumstances technology becomes the determining factor in the definition of the body's physical rearticulation, the material foundations for its sense of performed identity. Although traditional domains of bodily differences such as those that are subsumed under the rubrics of ethnicity and gender are still operating in the case of popular cyborg imagery (Springer, 1991), one can imagine, as Haraway has done, that these differences might eventually be eclipsed by a technologically-based system of similarities and differences. Instead of describing this body primarily in terms of age, ethnicity or gender, or even in Haraway's hybrid post-ethnic or post-gendered terms, a more accurate description is perhaps to be obtained by treating a reimaged cyborg body as a *technological* entity whose definitive characteristics are to be plotted according to a system of technicity (Tomas, 1989). Such a system would not only have to take account of the plasticity of the cyborg's politics and identity, it would also have to account for its operating principles, such as those of speed, manoeuvrability and force, as well as its participatory logic, rooted as it is in a trinity of cybernetic adaptability: communication, information and feedback.

Postface: virtual reality and the cyborg as pure data construct

Wiener's evocation of the human body conceived as pure information brings to mind virtual reality technology with its promise of a common global digital space – a kind of second atmosphere, whether one models it after McLuhan's extended consciousness whose embodiment was to be found in the 'spiritual form of information' (1964: 67), or William Gibson's often quoted definition of cyberspace: a 'consensual hallucination' experienced by 'billions' of computer operators (Gibson, 1984: 51).

The bridge of cybernetics and its living organism-as-pure-information paradigm links the worlds of cyborgs and virtual reality. In doing so it also serves as a juncture that marks an important division or, more accurately, a branching in the history of automata. One path from this juncture leads into outer space, while the other route leads into a kind of meta-atmosphere composed of a pure digitalized electronic information. The human body is, in this latter context, reimaged and reimagined to be an inconsequential historical residue, a kind of chimera, or puppet (Walser, 1991), an *automatonic* image which is subject to almost infinite manipulation. Thus the 'basic job of cyberspace technology, besides simulating a world, is', as one researcher has noted, 'to supply a tight feedback loop between patron and puppet, to give the patron the illusion of being literally embodied by the puppet (i.e., the puppet gives the patron a virtual body, and the patron gives the puppet a personality)' (Walser, 1991: 35).

It is therefore not surprising, given the possibility for an almost perfectly transparent sense of manipulation, that 'the possibilities of virtual realities' are considered by some to be 'as limitless as the possibilities of reality' – a distinction and conjunction which is founded on this technology's potential power to provide a 'doorway to other worlds' which is based on a 'human interface that disappears' (Fisher, 1991: 109). As these comments and those on the role of feedback in binding a human patron and cybernetic puppet suggest, virtual reality is, in fact, a manifestation of a cybernetician's ultimate dream: a pure information space which can be populated by a host of pure cybernetic automatons or, in Gibson's more precise and less anthropomorphic terms, data constructs.

It is in the context of this seamless boundary between the body and technology that we now return to the figure of the automaton and note, as one researcher has recently pointed out, that:

> the craftsman of the last century shaping the motion of the elaborate clockwork characters by painstakingly filing cams is much like the programmer iterating toward an algorithm for animating computer graphic human motion, or defining plastic deformations of facial expression. (Lasko-Harvill, 1992: 226)

If the Clynes/Kline cyborg offered a participatory solution to the problem of survival in hostile environments, then it did so through a radical fusion of the human/machine interface as first proposed in the context of classical mimetic automata. The astronaut/cyborg and later science fiction models were and are conceived as post-Industrial Revolution androids that embody the power of prime movers coupled with sophisticated sensory and control systems. These hardware-based cyborgs exhibit android form, robot power and cybernetic intelligence and are designed to function in extremely hostile environments. At one point in *The Human Use of Human Beings*, for example, Wiener had suggested that 'we have modified our environment so radically that we must now modify ourselves in order to exist in this new environment' (1954: 46). In retrospect, it is easy to see that the Clynes/Kline cyborg was a hardware-based solution to this kind of problem. While the first cyborg was initially designed for space travel, modification and adaptation can take as many forms as are needed for the conquering and colonization of non- or anti-human environments. Indeed, Haraway's post-gendered oppositional cyborg suggests that such environments extend to the conflicting and hostile worlds of ideas.

Perhaps conquest provides the most appropriate frame of reference through which to view the cyborg's most recent computer-based transformations since its new form is the product of a special problem in human adaptation: namely, how to exist *in* an environment that consists of pure information. The answer is, as Wiener first pointed out, provided by cybernetics: one transforms the human organism into a pattern of pure digital information. Adaptation is, as a result, perfect and complete since organism and environment are conceived in similar terms.

This most extreme of all cybernetic visions, a final and radical solution to the problem of environmental mutations and ensuing adaptation, provides a kind of 'terminal' answer to the question of the direction of the human organism's 'evolution' in the late 20th century. Insofar as 'the interface between the user and the computer may be the last frontier in computer design' (Foley, 1987: 127), then this interface may also be the last frontier in the design of human beings and, as such, the key to the diversity of cybernetic patterns that can colonize and populate virtual reality in the name of one of western modernity's root metaphors – the feedback mechanism – and in the name of one of its keywords: cybernetics.

Notes

This paper is part of book-length work that examines the relationships between the cyborg concept and late 20th-century imaging systems, including virtual reality. Its orientation is towards a critical investigation of current cultural practices and specifically oppositional practices in the arts. Earlier versions of this paper were presented at a conference on 'Body Images, Language & Physical Boundaries', University of Amsterdam, Amsterdam, in July 1993, and at the University of Windsor, Windsor, Ontario, in November 1993. A working version of this paper was published as a chapter in Murray (1994). I would like to thank all those who commented on the paper in its various versions.

1   For an extended discussion of this practice see Williams (1983: 15, 22–5).
2   A recent sampling would include the (Richards et al., 1991) collection of texts in *Bioapparatus*, Lasko-Harvill (1992), Balsamo (1992), Stone (1991, 1992). Balsamo (1993: 135 fn. 13) contains a list of recent publications in the popular press devoted to virtual reality.
3   In this connection, I stress my use of the word 'promise', since at each stage exclusions are as important as inclusions in the ongoing construction of actual and possible histories.
4   A servomechanism is a form of automatic feedback control system 'in which the motion of an output member . . . is constrained to follow closely the motion of an input member, and in which power amplification is incorporated' (Porter, 1969: 55).
5   I deal with earlier forms of automata more fully in an earlier version of this paper (Tomas, 1994).
6   'It is the pattern maintained by this homeostasis, which is the touchstone of our personal identity' (Wiener, 1954: 96).

Bibliography

Ampère, André-Marie (1843) *Essai sur la Philosophie des Sciences, ou Exposition Analytique d'une Classification Naturelle de toutes les Connaissances Humaines.* Paris: Bachelier.
Bakhtin, M.M. (1981) 'Forms of Time and of the Chronotope in the Novel', pp. 84–258 in M. Holquist (ed.) *The Dialogic Imagination: Four Essays by M.M. Bakhtin*, trans. C. Emerson and M. Holquist. Austin: University of Texas Press.

Balsamo, Anne (1993) 'The Virtual Body in Cyberspace', *Research in Philosophy and Technology* 13: 119–39.

Bowker, Geof (1993) 'How to be Universal: Some Cybernetic Strategies, 1943–70', *Social Studies of Science* 23(1): 107–26.

Canguilhem, Georges (1992) 'Machine and Organism', pp. 45–69 in J. Crary and S. Kwinter (eds) *Incorporations*, Zone 6. New York: Zone.

Čapek, Karl and Josef Čapek (1961) *The Brothers Čapek: R.U.R. and The Insect Play*, trans. P. Selver. Oxford: Oxford University Press.

Cherry, Colin (1980) *On Human Communication: A Review, a Survey, and a Criticism*, 3rd edn. Cambridge, MA: MIT Press.

Clynes, Manfred E. and Nathan S. Kline (1960) 'Cyborgs and Space', *Astronautics* September: 26–7, 74–6.

Feher, Michel, Ramona Naddaff and Nadia Tazi (eds) (1989) *Fragments for a History of the Human Body*, Part 1. New York: Zone.

Fisher, Scott S. (1991) 'Virtual Environments: Personal Simulations and Telepresence', pp. 101–10 in S.K. Helsel and J.P. Roth (eds) *Virtual Reality: Theory, Practice, and Promise*. Westport, CT: Meckler.

Foley, James D. (1987) 'Interfaces for Advanced Computing', *Scientific American* 257(4): 126–35.

Gibson, William (1984) *Neuromancer*. New York: Ace Books.

Halacy, D.S. (1965) *Cyborg: Evolution of the Superman*. New York: Harper & Row.

Haraway, Donna (1991) 'A Cyborg Manifesto: Science, Technology, and Socialist-Feminism in the Late Twentieth Century', pp. 149–81 in *Simians, Cyborgs, and Women: The Reinvention of Nature*. New York: Routledge.

Heims, Steve Joshua (1993) *Constructing a Social Science for Postwar America: The Cybernetics Group, 1946–53*. Cambridge, MA: MIT Press.

Lasko-Harvill, Ann (1992) 'Identity and Mask in Virtual Reality', *Discourse* 14(2): 222–34.

McLuhan, Marshall (1964) *Understanding Media: The Extensions of Man*. New York: Mentor.

Porter, Arthur (1969) *Cybernetics Simplified*. London: The English Universities Press.

Pratt, Vernon (1987) *Thinking Machines: The Evolution of Artificial Intelligence*. Oxford: Basil Blackwell.

Reichardt, Jasia (1968a) 'Introduction', *Studio International*: 5–7.

Reichardt, Jasia (ed.) (1986b) 'Cybernetic Serendipity', *Studio International* Special Issue.

Richards, Catherine, Mary Ann Moser and Nell Tenhaff (eds) (1991) *Bioapparatus*. Banff: The Banff Centre for the Arts.

Simon, Herbert A. (1981) *The Science of the Artificial*, 2nd edn. Cambridge, MA: MIT Press.

Springer, Claudia (1991) 'The Pleasure of the Interface', *Screen* 32(3): 303–23.

Stone, Allucquère Roseanne (1991) 'Will the Real Body Please Stand Up?: Boundary Stories about Virtual Cultures', pp. 81–118 in M. Benedikt (ed.) *Cyberspace: First Steps*. Cambridge, MA: MIT Press.

Stone, Allucquère Roseanne (1992) 'Virtual Systems', pp. 609–21 in J. Crary and S. Kwinter (eds) *Incorporations*, Zone 6. New York: Zone.

Tomas, David (1989) 'The Technophilic Body: On Technicity in William Gibson's Cyborg Culture', *New Formations* 8: 113–29.

Tomas, David (1994) 'Cybernetics and Feedback: Reimaging the Body in the Age of the Cyborg', pp. 53–103 in J. Murray (ed.) *Technology and Culture*, Working Papers in the Humanities 2. Windsor: Humanities Research Group/University of Windsor.

Walser, Randal (1991) 'The Emerging Technology of Cyberspace', pp. 35–40 in S.K. Helsel and J.P. Roth (eds) *Virtual Reality: Theory, Practice, and Promise*. Westport, CT: Meckler.

Wiener, Norbert (1948a) *Cybernetics: or Control and Communication in the Animal and the Machine*. New York: John Wiley.

Wiener, Norbert (1948b) 'Cybernetics', *Scientific American* 179: 14–19.

Wiener, Norbert (1954) *The Human Use of Human Beings: Cybernetics and Society*, 2nd edn. New York: Doubleday Anchor.

Williams, Raymond (1983) *Keywords: A Vocabulary of Culture and Society*. London: Flamingo.

David Tomas teaches in the Department of Visual Arts at the University of Ottawa. His recent publications include 'Virtual Reality and the Politics of Place', *History and Anthropology* (1995); 'An Identity in Crisis: The Artist and New Technologies' (in J. Berland et al. [eds], *Theory Rules*, YYZ Books/University of Toronto Press, 1995); and 'Art, Psychasthenic Assimilation, and the Cybernetic Automaton' (in Chris Gray et al. [eds], *The Cyborg Handbook*, Routledge, 1995).

Chapter 17

SARAH KEMBER

CREATURES ON THE INTERNET

I N 'CREATURES', A CHAPTER from her book *Cyberfeminism and Artificial Life*, Sarah Kember carefully negotiates the grounds for and the nature of 'life' in the computer game of the same name. We are introduced to the 'species' ('norns', 'grendels' and 'ettins') which inhabit a virtual online world as autonomous agents which exhibit elements of lifelike behavior as they evolve and interact with one another and with the player of the game. Designed to have a 'simulated neural network' and a basic biochemistry, these creatures behave, '"as though" they were alive because they "almost" are'. In her chapter, Kember raises some of the ethical, political and economic dimensions of these developments.

Historically, theoretical analogies, later to become operative research programmes, between biology and computation emerged within the work of early cybernetics and related science. This, in turn, gave rise to the ambition to create intelligent machines by literally programming intelligence into computers. Based upon the premise that the human brain might be understood as a kind of machine, then it might be analysed as such and the resulting understanding of the brain's cognitive and processual operations transferred, via programming, to a computer. HAL 9000, the computer in Kubrick's film *2001*, can be seen as a fictional example of such a project (and its failure). Dubbed the 'top-down' model, this approach was latterly criticised as too rigidly programmatic and replaced by the view that intelligent life should be under-stood as the result of complex, non-linear and dynamic processes arising through the interaction of elements within an environment. In this sense, instead of intelligence being programmed into software, the aim became one of providing the conditions in which something like intelligent life or behaviour might arise. Instead of the 'computational paradigm' of artificial intelligence research which entertained the idea that intelligence could be 'modelled' by the computer, ALife research sees the computer as a medium, analogous to the incubators and culture dishes of traditional laboratories within which 'life', albeit silicon rather than carbon-based, might be synthesised. The notion of 'emergence' is key here: the bottom-up nature of ALife is based on complex and unpredictable patterns and behaviour emerging from simple rules.

These *Creatures* however are not denizens of virtual worlds in computer science labs, but in the popular media form of the computer game. Kember is careful to insist that this game is not a representation of ALife (as we might see in a science fiction film) but is constructed from actual ALife evolutionary algorithms. Networked playful popular culture provides an unexpectedly productive new environment for these artificial creatures. The game's producers anticipated both user participation in modding the game and online debate with players about the philosophical implications of ALife and genetic engineering. Unexpected activities emerged though. On online forums players tended to discuss the practicalities of engineering their creatures rather than ethics. Players certainly modified the software, but in ways that surprised the game producers: splicing virtual genes and creating mutants or hybrids from distinct species for example.

Here the virtual environment and emergent behaviour of ALife are expanded to include game producers, fan/player activities and Internet media.

In the full version of this chapter, Kember explains the relationships between game players/ consumers and producers, between capital and labour, by drawing on the essay by Tiziana **Terranova** included in Part Five. For further discussion of online gameplay see **Kennedy** in this part, and **Taylor** in Part Five.

[. . .]

Creatures

Put some life into your PC!

(*Creatures* publicity slogan)

Norns have no mental lives and hence cannot be conscious . . . but they are alive.

(Steve Grand, interview 1999)

In 'Creatures: An Exercise in Creation' Steve Grand (1997a) describes his design for producing lifelike autonomous agents whose biology and biochemistry is sufficiently complex as to be believable. Grand's agents are designed with a large simulated neural network and a basic biochemical model which creates diffuse feedback in the network and represents reproductive, digestive and immune systems. Moreover, the structure and dynamics of the neural network, the structure of the biochemical model and numerous morphological features of the agents are defined by a simulated genome. The genome is of variable length and appropriate for open-ended evolution. The article is presented from a practical viewpoint and goes on to state that the design has been implemented in the form of a commercial computer game product. Underlying Grand's practical description are clear assertions about the value of biological metaphors and the importance of emergent behaviour in creating intelligent agents.

The design for *Creatures* is based on Grand's point of view as a computer engineer rather than a scientist, and for him, this entails a rejection of reductionism in favour of a holistic approach to generating artificial intelligence and artificial life. 'Why', he asks, 'do we create neural networks that have no chemistry' when organisms are heterogenous rather than homogenous systems? Most attempts to generate intelligent or lifelike agents are based on single mechanisms, and while there are good reasons for this (from a scientific or research perspective it is often necessary to simplify the object of study in order to learn in detail how it works), there is also the risk that this methodology 'will fail to deliver the emergent richness that comes from the interactions of heterogenous complexes' (Grand 1997a: 19). Put more simply, 'the fact that organisms are combinations of many different processes and structures suggests that most of those systems must be necessary, and we should heed this in our attempts to mimic living behaviour' (19). What follows is a complicated description which captures the complexity of simulating a biologically whole organism complete with its own genome. The design specifies a class of 'gene' for each kind of structure in the organism, and determines whether it applies to males, females or both. It also controls when, in the creature's life cycle, a specific gene (for example, governing the reproductive system) switches on. Creatures may then experience puberty, although it is noted that 'genes do not code for behaviour, but for deep structure – the behaviour is an emergent consequence of this structure' (23). Genes are assembled into a single 'chromosome' and when creatures mate, chromosomes are crossed over to produce offspring that inherit their complete definition from both parents. 'Mutations' and 'cutting errors' (involving dropped or duplicated copies of genes) produce variations in the gene pool, allowing 'our creatures' to 'truly evolve' (23).

Grand's design for an autonomous intelligent creature capable of learning, and situated in an artificial 'world' is completed by the addition of a simple speech mechanism. It is realised in the *Creatures* computer program 'that allows people to keep small communities of little, furry, virtual animals as "pets" on their home computer' (24). Creatures can be taught to speak, rewarded with a 'tickle' or punished with a 'smack'. They eat, play, travel and 'learn how to look after themselves' (24). Users care for their creatures and diagnose and treat illness when it occurs. Eventually, creatures get old and die, but if they live to puberty, users can encourage them to breed and reproduce: 'He or she can then swap those offspring with other *Creatures* enthusiasts over the World Wide Web' (24). From this, relatively early description of the program, it is already possible to identify quite a range of roles for the prospective user: pet owner, parent (of an anthropomorphised creature), medical scientist, breeder/genetic engineer, trader and computer (games) enthusiast. An important aim of this chapter is to highlight the dynamics of user involvement as a means of challenging the effects model of new media communications, and more significantly of science (producers) and culture (consumers).

The first *Creatures* computer game was released on CD-ROM in Europe in November 1996. In 'The *Creatures* Global Digital Ecosystem', Dave Cliff and Steve Grand state that more than 100,000 games were sold within a month and that they attracted a great deal of media attention (1999: 77). Later releases in the US and Japan in 1997 produced global sales of over 500,000 games by 1998. *Creatures 2* was released globally in 1998 with an initial shipment of 200,000. The technology in *Creatures* is directly drawn from ALife research, and the official guide to *Creatures 2* contains a brief justification of bottom-up (ALife) as opposed to top-down (AI) programming (Simpson 1998). The working definition of ALife offered here is as follows: 'Artificial Life concerns itself with capturing lifelike behaviour by creating small systems (called autonomous agents) and allowing these small systems to interact with each other to create more complex emergent behaviour that none of the individual systems are aware of. Because it is lifelike behaviour we are after, we call it artificial life' (Simpson 1998: 155). The emphasis is on a quest for emergent (intelligent) behaviour, and where other examples are offered (John Conway's *Game of Life* and Craig Reynold's *Boids*) the *Creatures* producers (CyberLife) are quick to claim that their product is leading the quest:

> All life is fundamentally biochemical, and CyberLife believes that to capture human-level intelligence inside a machine, you should create a complete functioning human. This could be achieved by modelling the individual cells and arranging them in the same way that they are arranged in a real human. The result should be a human that is a human, brain and all. There is still a long way to go, but *Creatures* and *Creatures 2* are substantial steps in the right direction. (Simpson 1998: 159)

From this it is clear that CyberLife is interested in more than commercial success in the computer games market. This is perhaps simultaneously an end in itself and a means to an end of realising one of the key aims of ALife research. There is then a reciprocal relationship between ALife science and engineering in this context that belies the separation of these categories.

Creatures involves a virtual 'world' (Albia) populated by 'species' of autonomous agents which, in the second version of the game, include norns, grendels and ettins. Norns are the focal species with which the player is encouraged to interact, and they possess artificial neural networks, biochemistry, genes and organs. A norn's behaviour 'is generated by its "brain", an artificial neural network that coordinates the norn's perceptions and actions, according to a set of behavioural "drives and needs"' (Cliff and Grand 1999: 79). There are a total of seventeen drives (ranging from hungry and thirsty to amorous and lonely) all of which can be monitored during the game (Simpson 1998). There is a short-cut in the simulated neural network in as far as it 'is not *directly* involved in either perceiving the environment or generating actions' (Cliff and Grand 1999: 79). The task of accurately modelling the physics of sound, vision, smell, taste and touch is currently considered to be too technologically complicated and advanced. Similarly, it is not possible to compute a neural network with individual neurons controlling individual 'muscles' in the norn's 'body'. In place of this, 'there are a fixed number of predefined action scripts (e.g., "move left", "push object"), written in a higher-level language' (79). These action scripts (and the drives) correlate with the simple language which norns can learn with the aid of 'learning machines' (artificial computers) situated in their environment. Using two separate machines, norns learn the words for drives and concepts expressed, respectively, through adverbs and adjectives ('intensely hungry') followed by verbs and nouns ('get food') (Simpson 1998: 69, 70). The game player, or user, must encourage the norns to learn language and 'talk' to them by positioning a virtual hand near an object and typing the object category on the keyboard. Apparently, 'Norns can distinguish only between categories; they can't distinguish between the specific objects within those categories' (Simpson 1998: 76). Users must then familiarise themselves with the norn system of classification. Because norns inhabit a virtual environment, they are referred to as 'situated' autonomous agents. Their autonomy is figured in their capability of coordinating actions and perceptions over extended periods of time without external (human) intervention: 'Interactions with the human user may alter the norns' behaviour, but the human can only *influence* a norn, not control it' (Cliff and Grand 1999: 79). The virtual hand of the user (operated by a mouse) can be used to reward (tickle) or punish (slap) a creature and to pick up and drop certain objects. It cannot be used to pick up a norn unless it is in the process of drowning, but it can be used to push it away from (or indeed towards) danger. The virtual hand can be made visible or invisible to the creatures (Simpson 1998: 64). Each individual norn's neural network is affected by its biochemistry. Specific actions such as eating 'can release reactive "chemicals" into the norn's "bloodstream", where chain reactions may occur' feeding back and altering the performance of the network. Norns may eat toxic foods in their environment, and will therefore need medical intervention and care from the user. The interaction between neural network and biochemistry also 'allows for modelling changes in motivational state such as those that occur when a human releases hormones or ingests artificial stimulants such as caffeine or amphetamines' (Cliff and Grand 1999: 80). Norn behaviour is, in other words, biologically and biochemically produced, albeit emergent rather than directly programmed. Albia contains 'bacteria' which can harm the norn's 'metabolism' and be counteracted by eating some of the available 'plant life'. The way in which bacteria affect norns and are affected by certain plants is genetically encoded for each strain of bacterium, 'so there is an opportunity for coevolutionary interactions between the bacteria and their hosts' or between the environment and the individual (80). Artificial genes govern the norns' brains, chemistry, morphology (physical appearance) and stages of development from birth, childhood, adolescence, adulthood to death. Genes are passed on through sexual reproduction (sex is represented by a 'kisspop' in the game and is strictly 'behind closed doors' and heterosexual) and are indirectly related to behaviour: 'the net effect is that new behaviour patterns can evolve over a number of generations' (80).

The creature's brain, organ system, genetics, immune system, respiration and cardiovascular system, digestive system and reproductive system are all modelled and described in detail. They can be monitored and (in most cases) manipulated by the user through the provision of 'applets' or kits such as the Health Kit (basic health care including a selection of medicines), the Owner's Kit (used to name norns, take photographs of them and study their family tree), the Breeder's Kit (covering reproductive systems and providing aphrodisiacs if needed), and the advanced Science Kit (detailed monitoring of organs, DNA, biochemistry and complete with syringe and chemical mixtures for treating illness and injury) and Neuroscience Kit (for experimenting with brains). The Science Kit and the Neuroscience Kit are 'pick-ups' which can be accessed only by persuading one of the norns to activate them. There is also an Observation Kit (to monitor population figures and details such as age, gender, health status), an Ecology Kit (to monitor the environment), a Graveyard and an Agent Injector which allows new objects into the environment. These objects include norns imported from Internet websites. The main aim of the game, or 'toy' as *Creatures* is also referred to, is 'to give birth to some Norns, explore Albia, and breed your Norns through as many successive generations as you can' (Simpson 1998: 19). However, it is clear that there are advanced features and users, different levels of involvement, and a variety of user roles.

Playing the game

The virtual world in *Creatures* is called Albia and this has both a mythology and a colonial history. Albia is a rich natural and technological environment originally inhabited by the ancient race of Shee who left behind a temple and laboratories for engineering plant and animal life. Grendels are the Shee's monstrous mistake and norns are their crowning achievement. Having created life on Albia, they set off in a rocket to colonise space. The tropical volcanic island then experienced a natural disaster necessitating the resurrection of the Shee's favoured species among the remnants of bamboo bridges, forts and intact underground laboratories. Albia has a balanced ecology with plentiful natural resources and danger in the form of poisonous plants, violent disease-carrying grendels and oceans deep enough to drown unsuspecting creatures in. In keeping with traditional Western technoscientific perspectives, nature is constructed as a resource for exploration, observation, experimentation and exploitation. The presence of both danger and biological potential is seen to justify and reward technological intervention. Albia has its own geography of east and west (as a disk it has no meaningful north and south) but its landscape of exotic plants, animal life and buildings encodes it as being Eastern, oriental, other. The technoscientific and colonial enterprises are therefore conventionally associated. The flourishing underground terrariums and laboratories of the Shee represent a technological Eden, or tamed, enhanced nature where norns can be safe and enjoy life (at least until the user discovers the genetic splicing machine). Above ground, the barren volcanic area remains an untamed and hellish realm of molten lava fit only for the uncivilised grendels to inhabit. In Albia, the next generation of biotechnological scientists are the direct descendants of the ancient Gods of Shee.

Game playing begins in the hatchery area, 'a warm, cosy, friendly place' (Simpson 1998: 10) with an incubator. The player selects one of six male and female eggs, 'each of which contains its own unique digital DNA' (22) and places it in the incubator. Some 5 to 10 seconds later ('depending on the complexity of the DNA') a norn is 'born'. The player is informed that 'baby norns are a little like two-year old toddlers' and advised to name and track them prior to teaching them to speak and eat (25). The naming of norns is a fairly emotive experience (especially when they reciprocate) and from here onwards, drowning them through lack of adequate supervision can be quite upsetting. It is also very easy to do since the player has no direct control over these cute but wilful creatures. It is possible to spend too much time placing photographs on headstones in the graveyard or making futile attempts at resuscitation at this stage of the game. The parent-educator role of the player quickly gives way to that of general medical practitioner and trainee medical specialist. This is due to the norns exploring their environment and encountering natural hazards, and to an increase in numbers which makes them even more difficult to control ('the most interesting objects in Albia to Norns are other Norns') (Simpson 1998: 81). This is despite a whole barrage of monitoring and surveillance technology and the player's overall panoptic perspective on the world. One interesting feature is the Creature's View option which 'lets you see what the selected creature is looking at' (53). As well as being a necessary mechanism for naming objects, this ability to adopt the creature's point of view is perhaps a further expression of kinship and a displacement of the surveiller-surveilled dichotomy. Surveillance offers no guarantee of control in Albia and this is most evident in the context of reproduction. The Breeder's Kit allows the user to monitor the reproductive system of individual creatures and displays their sex, age, image, life stage and estimated fertility (using a graph of hormone levels). Since 'female Norns are fertile for several minutes, whereas males are capable of getting a female Norn pregnant most of the time' (43) it follows that close monitoring of female reproduction may be necessary. In a somewhat familiar scenario, if a female becomes pregnant 'the picture of the Creature's body is zoomed in, and it shows a little egg that grows gradually over time' (47). Norns are blessed with a 20 minute pregnancy after which time 'the cycle resets and a little baby egg is hatched!' (47). Just like that. The player-programmer's eyes are shielded from this rather effortless process which is signalled by the appearance of an egg in the bottom right hand corner of the screen. Once the player has reached the stage at which norn eggs begin to appear the 'natural' way rather than via the hatchery, the role of parent gives way to that of breeder and ultimately overseer of an evolutionary process which can be influenced but not controlled. Norns will breed without intervention, and naturally occurring eggs do not need to be placed in the incubator. Despite a default setting of sixteen creatures, the population of Albia may start to escalate, making further interventions (such as birth control and the exportation of norns) necessary. The breeding of successive generations of norns (complete with their digital DNA) leads of course to evolution which is – given the underlying ALife philosophy – the true agent of the game and more powerful than the god-like Shee and their player-programmer descendants.

Creatures is by no means simply about interacting with virtual pets. Rather, the player is ultimately positioned as the overseer of a process of evolution involving artificial life forms with which he or she has a degree of kinship. Norns are like children: a new generation. The introductory tutorial to the original game states quite clearly that 'our new-born Norn is alive and like any child she has her own personality'. More than that, as representatives of the ALife project, norns are the next stage in evolution – a new species. It is clear, within the narrative of the game, that 'we', the players, have responsibility for this new species, but as overseers of the evolutionary process we are evidently not in control of it. We may observe, interact, participate and intervene in the process, but ALife carries forward a firm belief in the sovereign power of evolution. Human agency is at best secondary to the primary force of nature. The role of the player in *Creatures* is god-like in so far as it involves bringing a new, genetically engineered species into existence. But the power of the creator is compromised by the fact that neither the individual creatures nor the process of their evolution are controllable. In contrast with conventional video and computer games, the player does not play a character on the screen and does not control their actions. Creatures appear to make their own decisions about what to do and where to go. They learn how to behave and how to survive, and the player can only attempt to teach them through punishment, reward and communication. It is necessary to activate a surveillance camera in order to track the whereabouts of the creatures and the only real control players have is the pause button or exit option which places the whole game in suspended animation. The overseer of *Creatures* is a kind of parent-god whose omnipotence is exchanged for kinship. Kinship is represented on the level of narrative and interactivity and is underlined by a deeper level or principle of connection. The game is based on the principle that norns, as artificial life-forms, are alive or possess the same essential life criteria as humans, including autonomy, self-organisation and evolution. As an example of ALife, *Creatures* represents the connection between organic and artificial life-forms, and through the role of the overseer it loosens the relationship between vision and control which characterises technological forms of visualisation in science and at the intersections between science, art and entertainment.

Kinship with creatures, or the connection between organic and artificial life-forms, is something which is simultaneously underlined and disavowed in the game which encourages players to play with the idea of it through increasingly enhanced genetic engineering features. The most basic level of genetic engineering is breeding. Then comes the genetic splicing machine, a 'great gadget' that 'allows you to breed creatures together that don't normally match – such as a Grendel and a Norn' (Simpson 1998: 203). The device for creating such 'half breeds' is 'essential for any budding Dr. Frankenstein' (142). Creatures must be lured into the room, locked into the machine and both donors will be 'lost' in the transformation. The appeal is that 'you never quite know what will come out' (143). Interest in these transgenic organisms is enhanced by a feature which allows them to be exported and imported via the Internet. Users can swap or trade their monsters and – through demand – can download a Genetics Kit which 'lets you view each and every gene in a Creature's genome and edit its properties . . . You can even create a whole new genome from scratch!' (203).

Creatures on the Internet

Using a phrase coined by Thomas Ray, Cliff and Grand (1999) claim that what distinguishes *Creatures* from other ALife games (apart from the combination of simulated neural network and biochemistry) or products based on autonomous agents, is the occurrence of 'digital naturalism' in communities of users and the possible occurrence of culture in communities of artificial agents (1999: 81–83). *SimLife* is mentioned as 'one of the first pieces of entertainment software explicitly promoted as drawing on alife research' (81). But *SimLife* deals with digital organisms which are nowhere near as advanced as those in *Creatures* (82). Similarly, '*Dogz, Catz, Fin-Fin* and *Galapagos* are all presented as involving ALife technologies, but none of them (yet) employ genetically encoded neural network architectures or artificial biochemistries as used in *Creatures*' (83). Neither (as a consequence) do they allow for the possibility of culture emerging in communities of artificial creatures. Cliff and Grand argue that it is likely that 'rapid and productive evolution' will occur in CyberLife systems and that, although it is 'highly unlikely' in the current (second) version of *Creatures* it is 'tempting to speculate' about the emergence of social structures:

Given that the norns can communicate with one another, and that supplies of some environmental resources (such as food or 'medicine') can sometimes be limited or scarce, it is not inconceivable that simple economic interactions such as bartering, bargaining, and trade occur between norns, allowing for comparison with recent work in simulated societies such as that by Epstein and Axtell. (Cliff and Grand 1999: 85)

Epstein and Axtell's (1996) work will be discussed in the following chapter, as will the development of artificial societies in environments governed solely by the principles of genetic determinism and evolution. Given the relatively advanced organisation of game 'users' rather than 'agents' it seems more appropriate at this stage to look more closely at the idea of 'digital naturalism' in *Creatures* on the Internet.

Cliff and Grand compare *Creatures* with Ray's *Tierra* but, again, claim that the agents are significantly more complex: 'In colloquial terms, if the agents in *Creatures* are similar to animals in their complexity of design and behaviour, then the agents in Tierra are similar to bacteria or viruses' (Cliff and Grand 1999: 85). Yaeger's *PolyWorld* is considered to be the closest comparable program in so far as it, like *Creatures*, 'attempts to bring together all the principle components of real living systems into a single artificial (manmade) living system' (85). Cliff and Grand point out relatively small differences in technology but larger differences in the aims of the projects since *PolyWorld* is primarily a tool for scientific inquiry into the issues addressed in *Tierra* and a test-bed for theories in evolutionary biology, behavioural ecology, ethology or neurobiology (86). *Creatures* is clearly an entertainment application with technology designed to be adapted in industrial engineering. It bears greater comparison with Ray's *NetTierra* which has been in development since 1994. A development of *Tierra*, *NetTierra* is intended to run on the entire Internet rather than on a single computer. It would run on spare processor time and on as many machines as possible, migrating organisms across the network in search of idle computers: 'typically on the dark side of the planet, where the majority of users are asleep' (Cliff and Grand 1999: 86). Ray argues that the program will create a 'digital ecosystem' supporting diversity and self-organising evolutionary processes. Industrial applications of *NetTierra* are possible and it would be necessary, according to Ray, for 'digital naturalists' to observe and experiment with the evolving life-forms 'possibly removing promising-looking "wild" organisms for isolation to allow "domestication" and subsequent "farming"' (Cliff and Grand 1999: 86). Cliff and Grand maintain that, 'without any prompting', the sizeable community of *Creatures* users with their independent newsgroups and some 400 websites, 'appear to be engaging in exactly the kind of digital naturalism that Ray foresaw the need for in *NetTierra*' (87).

The original producers of *Creatures* anticipated a slightly different response to their product than the one they received and, according to Steve Grand, its appeal stems from the producers' receptiveness not just to user opinion, but to user involvement in the design and development of the product. It had been thought that the major issue for game players and observers would be 'the philosophical question of whether the norns are truly alive' (Cliff and Grand 1999: 87), but the major issue appears to have been the practice rather than the philosophy (or ethics) of genetic engineering. Interest in breeding and exchanging norns exceeded initial expectations, but the 'rapid appearance of users *reporting the results* [my emphasis] of "hacking" genomes, producing new "genetically engineered" strains of creatures' took the producers of the game by surprise (87). When asked about the extent to which *Creatures* was designed to create a community of users on the Internet, Steve Grand reveals how the design was adapted to accommodate a community of technically astute users which had formed semi-autonomously:

The practical key to making it work was to make the program open, so that people could alter it and add to it. Partly by design, and partly because of the building-block nature of biological systems, there turned out to be a number of ways that people could enhance the product and hence their enjoyment of it. Within a few days of launching the game, there was a new species of creature and also a couple of freeware add-ons available over the Web. People had developed these by hacking into the code and working out how parts of the genetics and script languages worked. In fact they were so good at this that I decided to save them the trouble of working it all out for themselves, and simply published the necessary documentation so that they could get on with it. (Interview, September 1999)

Computer hacking plays an interesting and perhaps novel role in the ownership of software in this case in so far as it is not, strictly speaking, an example of either theft or subversion. It is noted that the results of hacking genomes was 'reported' – not just to other users but also back to the producers who, in turn, responded by making an 'open' program still more accessible. The stereotype of the hacker is of an isolated asocial or antisocial computer 'criminal' (Ross 1991) who is probably between the ages of 13 and 30 and almost certainly male. The users represented in *Creatures* user groups are predominantly of school or college age and include both men and women. The question of gender might stimulate an analysis of potentially different types of use, but the focus here – and arguably the more pertinent focus – is on the dynamic interplay between CyberLife producers and consumers as they embody one index of the continuum between science and culture. Hacking is generally associated with subcultural or countercultural activity (Ross 1991) which does not appear to be relevant here. Hackers do not generally share their spoils with targeted groups or individuals. While the economic and copyright ownership of *Creatures* is not in question, the sole ownership of the technology and of successive 'generations' of the product is. While crediting CyberLife's web design team and developers' forum initiative (set up to support individuals producing 'add-ons' or new elements of the game), Steve Grand also acknowledges that *Creatures* products have been moulded 'not only through suggestions but also through direct help from some very experienced and smart Creatures users' (1999).

[. . .]

For Cliff and Grand, the main indicator of digital naturalism is the emergence of unexpected user activity. The first example they give explains the presence of the genetic splicing machine in *Creatures 2*. The creation of hybrid 'Grenorns' was a user initiative – 'we didn't think this was possible, since grendels had been deliberately made sterile . . . to prevent them from overrunning the world' (Cliff and Grand 1999: 88). Users initially tampered with the norn eggs by manually inserting a genome from a grendel in place of one 'parent'. The result was a random cross between the two species and the topic of 'much newsgroup discussion' (88). Of the 'naturally' occurring mutations, one is the 'Highlander Gene' which results in an immortal agent, and another is the 'Saturn Gene' which causes norns to shiver continuously and results in a 'rather morbidly popular phenotype' (88). What Cliff and Grand refer to as 'digital genetic engineers' have modified individual genes spreading popular mutant strains via the web. One of these, the 'G-defense gene' turns the creature's fear response into an anger response, making it more aggressive (89). A pattern begins to emerge. Aspects of anthropomorphism and sentimentality, stressed by the game producers, give way to a certain amount of sadism connected with a diminishing sense of kinship. On the one hand, a 'save the grendels' campaign attracted significant support, as did a European drive to ease the language difficulties for migrating norns (unsurprisingly, by increasing standards of spoken English). Apparently, an Australian family emailed Grand a norn that was deaf, blind, insensitive to touch and generally not getting much out of life at all. Grand diagnosed a mutated brain lobe gene, and after corrective modification, rest and relaxation, the norn was sent home (90). On the other hand, there have been disturbing reports of organised norn torture and abuse by an online character named Antinorn:

> There's a guy whose pseudonym is Antinorn, and he runs a website devoted to ways of being cruel to norns. Because of his wicked sense of humour, there are plenty of 'battered norns' around, and so people have set up adoption agency sites to look after them and find them new homes! The newsgroup has several times exploded into a frenzy over this topic and I think it's very healthy. (Interview, September 1999)

The newsgroup (alt.games.creatures) was monitored at around the time of this interview (August/September 1999). Amidst some chat about school classes and extracurricular activities apart from *Creatures*, Mae, Julius, Cati, Indigo, Patrick, Dave, Kate, Freya and others discussed Bastian's problem with a dead genetically engineered norn – 'flying around my world in circles' and resisting the dead creature remover – alongside Antinorn's antics. The debate about norn torture was, in fact, linked with the question of whether or not they can be considered to be alive. Aliveness was measured against human and animal criteria and connected to an ethical debate about rights. According to Bastian, all of the 'no-torturing stuff' is based on an association between norns and human life, and the fact that humans, unlike animals, have 'mercy for the weak ones'. But Bastian thinks that 'we should not use this attitude on other creatures – especially not on digital ones' because they will weaken the evolutionary chances of our own young: 'If we are to [*sic*] merciful with our C2 norns, they take the place you could use for stronger newborns'. Norn torture is then sanctioned on the basis that it is not as bad as the kind of medical interventions often practised on people: 'if someone wants to torture norns, so let him . . . what some other players do to their norns (let them live ages with injections and then let them starve very slowly) would be even much more cruel'. The debate about what can be considered alive picks up on philosophical, biological and ALife references (including references to the life status of viruses) and there is a sense, for example from Julius and Indigo, that norns are only really 'technically' alive. Dave agrees and brings the subject back to norn torture, AN's (Antinorn's) website and the debate about whether or not this has a right to exist. Kate makes a plea for free speech and xOtix supports this by adding:

> I don't believe that simulated torture of a simulated computer-generated model of a limited low form of life (didn't we once agree on spider intelligence as the max? Remember that thread?) is 'bad' or 'evil'. I only have one concern. I wonder what engaging in this kind of activity does to the person who is doing it?

Bastian summarises the debate by agreeing that norns are not 'really' alive but then adds that there will, in future 'be much more complex digital "life forms" that will have the same rights as we . . . and therefore cannot be tortured'. This appears to constitute a closure, and the discussion wanders off course until Tom appears:

> Hi
> Does anyone know how I can 'kill' my Norn??
> I don't know what's her problem, but she suffers, is lonely. . . all the time. I've tried almost anything: I gave her food, injections, other Norns, . . . but she lies there and cries.

She doesn't listen to me anymore. Perhaps it is a genetic defect.

So I want to kill her SOFTLY. I don't want to export and delete my Norn.
Please help me.
Tom

When asked for his view on norn torture and abuse, Steve Grand replied: '1 think it's wonderful! Well, I guess I feel sorry for the norns (although not terribly sorry – it's no more cruel than stepping on an ant)'. For him the concept of cruelty demonstrates that his project has been successful and that people are engaging with the ideas on which it is based. What annoys him is the way in which US publishers censored the 'slap' and 'tickle' feature of the game for fear of a moral panic among parents and teachers. The issue of norn cruelty forced the game producers to change the original title and 'tone down the yelp' that norns emit when slapped. This feature almost had to be removed altogether. Such censorship does not appear to have deterred the dedicated, and a thriving website (run by Antinorn) entitled Tortured Norns co-exists with literally hundreds of other independent sites, and with the official Creature Labs set up by CyberLife.

[. . .]

Chapter 18

J. MACGREGOR WISE

INTELLIGENT AGENCY

WISE IS CONCERNED HERE with a new kind of software program that developed along with the Internet as a popular mass medium from the mid-1990s. These 'intelligent agents' are designed to respond to and adapt to their users' needs and preferences in, for example, online shopping. They are agents in the sense that they have 'agency', they have autonomy and act independently (though, initially at least, within the parameters they have designed into them) across digital networks. As such they could be thought of in terms of Artificial Life or in more consumerist terms as 'digital butlers' or personal assistants.

As well as drawing attention to these new entities with which we now increasingly share our everyday lives, Wise is concerned to think through the theoretical and critical implications of living with non-human agents. He draws on Bruno **Latour**'s approach and ideas to theorise agents as our non-human delegates, raising questions for media and cultural studies' conventional concentration on human activity and linguistic discourse as the sites of meaningful action and cultural/political struggle. Agents are a vivid example of how values, ideologies and effects are conveyed by technological systems as well as by language and cultural meaning. Human actions (searching, purchasing, organising, communicating) are delegated to intelligent agents, but, importantly for cultural studies, they reciprocate: both shaping the information we seek or steering us to some parts of the network rather than others, and performing other tasks such as storing our purchasing patterns in online shopping. They can be, Wise argues, 'double agents', working according to the designs of both their users and their commercial producers.

Wise also adopts Deleuze and **Guattari**'s concept of the assemblage. This radical notion of a world of intimately connected human, technological, natural, conceptual/semiotic bodies, is exemplified here by Wise's argument that the computer interface is not a mediating screen between the human or everyday physical realm and the digital realm of networks, but rather it is one part of an assemblage of all these virtual and actual entities. At the same time he criticises discourses (prevalent at the time, and still evident today) that celebrated cyberspace as the beginnings of a new world in which material realities including the human body are dwindling in the new decorporealised virtual realm. He concludes with a model of the contemporary world in which material and immaterial bodies, virtual and actual, together constitute everyday technocultural existence.

[. . .]

When analysing a social field (or space) we have to consider not just the human actors inhabiting and crossing that space but the technologies which regulate that space as well. By being social actors, technologies exhibit a type of agency, and by this I mean social effectivity (rather than seeing agency as individual will). But humans do not simply move through social space (thereby constituting it), they are in many ways constituted by it as well (Wise, 1997), as are all the actors involved. The border often delineated between human and technology is a problematic one, which I will return to below. When we ignore technologies because they disappear into the quotidian we are ignoring social actors which have effects on how we behave and the possibilities for our actions.

We are currently facing a swarm of new technological actors in the form of information and communication technologies and the interconnections between them. Most prominently, much attention has been paid to the creation of the Internet, its economic policy form as the National Information Infrastructure, and its popular form as the Information Superhighway and, more broadly, cyberspace. However, this is not the introduction of just one type of actor: we are facing a whole array of technologies which bear a formal resonance to one another (not only interactive entertainment technologies brought to us via cable or direct broadcast satellite television, but ATMs, pay-at-the-pump petrol, voice-mail, videogames, World Wide Web interfaces, and so on). What we are facing is a new technological assemblage, aspects of which are inserting themselves in many ways between us and the world. Our lives are becoming increasingly mediated by these technologies. This is not to say that our lives were somehow unmediated and authentic before these technologies came along. Humans have always been mediated by tools and language. What these new technologies do is shift the nature of that mediation; we are now mediated in a different (if not new) way. The question to ask would be: What is the nature of this mediation, what tasks are being delegated to these new technologies, and what do they impinge back on us? This article focuses on one particular set of these new technologies that illustrates the process of delegation and the reciprocal regulation of human action: intelligent agents. Agents seem to be the current screen on which fantasies of unlimited human action and possibility are projected; the latest in a long line of Utopian technological fixes. A lot of the current work on agents comes from the Artificial Intelligence community and robotics research. However, the figure of the agent has entered the popular imaginary over the past few years and it is this body of work which I will focus on here.

I

Computers are infiltrating our cars, houses, businesses, banks, toasters and social interactions, and, as MIT's Nicholas Negroponte would have it, 'Intelligent Agents are the unequivocal future of computing' (1995a: 172). Agents therefore have the potential to impact many aspects of our daily lives. But what are intelligent agents?

> The buzzword *agent* has been used recently to describe everything from a word processor's Help system to mobile code that can roam networks to do our bidding. (Wayner and Joch, 1995: 95)

Pattie Maes, an assistant professor at MIT currently exploring the development of agents, writes that 'Agent programs differ from regular software mainly by what can best be described as a sense of themselves as independent identities. An ideal agent knows what its goal is and will strive to achieve it' (1995: 85). Peter Wayner, a contributing editor to *Byte* magazine, defines an agent as 'a software program which can roam a network, interact with its host, gather information, and come home' (1995a: 12). Wooldridge and Jennings, in their Introduction to the published proceedings of an international conference on intelligent agents, write that an agent is computer hardware or software that exhibits autonomy, 'social ability' (the ability to communicate with others), reactivity to its environment, and proactiveness (1995: 2; see also Steels, 1995). Agent research takes two forms: the development of autonomous robots which can learn, develop and pass on information to others (humans and other agents), and software agents which exist solely as programs in a computer, or on the Internet. It is the latter which has been focused on more in the popular press and will be the subject of this article; so when I refer to agents, I mean software agents.

Basically, an intelligent agent is a software program tailored to an individual's needs and personality. There are generally two types of these agents.[1] One is called an interface agent and is an intelligent, adaptable interface to a program or system. Like a teller at your local bank branch or a server at a café that you frequent, such agents come to know you and your expectations, anticipating your business and even suggesting new services or products. Pattie Maes writes that 'computers are as ubiquitous as automobiles and toasters, but exploiting their capabilities still seems to require the training of a supersonic test pilot. VCR displays blinking a constant 12 noon around the world testify to this conundrum' (1995: 84). She goes on to argue that all the new technology coming up will make the gap between users and technology that much greater. 'Some accommodation must be found between limited human attention spans and increasingly complex collections of software and data' (p. 84). Agents are that accommodation. Just as graphical user interfaces such as the Macintosh desktop look and that of Windows and Windows 95 made computers friendlier and easier to use (and therefore allowed more people to take advantage of what they had to offer), agents are an adaptive, proactive, partially independent interface.

The second type of agent is more of a personal assistant. This agent would act in the individual's place in cyberspace: buying concert tickets, negotiating meetings, database searching, and so on, all while the individual was occupied with other matters. Rather than being merely the interface between a person and the computer, the agent would be able to venture out on to the Internet independently to carry out the person's wishes or anticipate his or her demands. For example, my agent might alert me that not only have tickets for a local concert of my favourite rock band gone on sale (an announcement that I may have missed if I rely on my occasional listening to the radio or reading of the newspaper), but also that the agent has already purchased tickets in my favourite seats in that venue. Agents would also be able to communicate and share information with other agents (i.e. asking for directions) and even negotiate with them (have your agent call my agent). As computer programs which independently venture out over the Internet to perform tasks, agents bear a strong resemblance to computer viruses. Indeed, Peter Wayner refers to them as 'a good virus' and as 'controlled versions of viruses' (1995a: 9), though the best agents are supposed to work *without* our control (i.e. independence is part of the definition of a true agent). Anxieties about remaining in control of our agents will be dealt with below.

Intelligent agents are also referred to as virtual agents, agent software, messaging agents, or anything ending in the suffix -bot (knobots, infobots, softbots, etc.).[2] Microsoft's 'Bob' interface for Windows is said to be agent software and products like the Apple Newton (a handheld computer also called a personal digital assistant) have agent capabilities because they adapt to the individual user. The figure of the intelligent agent seems to be the next big thing in cyberspace and has appeared with increasing frequency in popular, academic and corporate discourses.

In a 1994 issue of *Newsweek*, Barbara Kantrowitz describes agents as digital butlers, our computer becoming an electronic version of *Upstairs, Downstairs*. Her article focuses on virtual shopping in electronic malls; once an agent knows your preferences you don't even have to accompany it as it shops and so you can avoid crowded malls. Again in *Newsweek*, a year later, Katie Hafner describes a broader range of agents dealing with managing information flow: e-mail filter programs which sort, flag or delete incoming mail; personalized newspapers which are electronic clipping services providing news to you based on your interests, and so on. *Business Week* (Brandt, 1994) describes agents as a form of artificial life, programs which 'evolve', combine, split apart and pass on programming information to the next generation of agents in an electronic survival of the fittest. The computer magazine *Byte* devoted extensive coverage to the technical side of agents in a 1995 cover story (Indermaur, 1995; Wayner, 1995b; Wayner and Joch, 1995; see also Halfhill, 1996). And *Communications of the ACM* has a germinal special issue on the topic (July, 1994) that considers social and philosophical issues surrounding agents as well as technical ones. The issue calls for a 'scientific approach' to agents and not just a marketing approach. Agents have been used to help market communication and information technology companies by being featured prominently in promotional videos from AT&T, Apple Computers, Hewlett Packard, Digital, and so on. For example, in AT&T's *Connections* video (1993) a mother and daughter shop for wedding dresses together; their agents not only take care of business while they shop (negotiating deals, and so on), they also bring the dresses to them and model them. Also in the video, agents (who appear on computer screens like television news anchors directly addressing the user) arrange meetings and negotiate with other agents.

Agents seem especially important in what might be termed the 'Wired school' centred on *Wired* magazine (see Wise, 1997). *Wired* has run an interview with Pattie Maes (Berkun, 1995) and *HotWired*, the World Wide Web version of the magazine, has had Maes debating with Jaron Lanier, a pioneer in virtual reality systems, over the viability and desirability of agents (http://www.hotwired.com/braintennis/96/29/btOa.html). HardWired, *Wired*'s book publishing arm, published *Bots: The Origin of New Species* in 1997 (Leonard, 1997).

I use the term 'Wired school' not just to refer to the magazine, web site and related publications, but also to the collection of writers connected with the magazine (either directly or more philosophically) such as Nicholas Negroponte, Kevin Kelly, John Perry Barlow, and so on, and organizations such as the Electronic Frontier Foundation (EFF) which lobbies in Washington, DC regarding civil liberties in cyberspace. What is common to this at times diverse group is an underlying libertarian view of cyberspace. The libertarian position takes technology to be the extension of rational individuals (Marshall McLuhan is often invoked here as a progenitor of this position; indeed, *Wired* lists him as their 'patron saint'). The figure of the agent fits in well with this position in that it is seen as an (autonomous) extension of one's self, a symbol of the increased agency available from cyberspace. Cyberspace is seen as a free and open space, a frontier where one can 'surf the new edge' (in cyberzine *Mondo 2000*'s phrase). However, historian Richard Slotkin has argued that the myth of the frontier in American society functions 'as rationalizer of the processes of capitalist development in America' (1985: 34). Indeed, the wired brand of libertarianism appeals all too well to free market and corporate sensibilities.

Current rudimentary agent programs and those we can expect in the near future exhibit what Arjun Appadurai (discussing the global flow of images and markets) has termed the fetishism of the consumer: 'These images of agency are increasingly distortions of a world of merchandising so subtle that the consumer is consistently helped to believe that he or she is an actor, where in fact he or she is at best a chooser' (1996: 42). On this subject, Jesse Drew (1995: 75) has written:

Mass-circulation magazines like *Newsweek* and *Time* have run cover stories about the coming 'revolution' that are little more than industry PR. Lifestyle magazines like *Wired* and *Mondo 2000* stimulate consumer demand for new gadgets and informed acquiescence to governmental and corporate policies – in the name of spurious 'liberation' and 'empowerment'.

For example, is it coincidence that Thinking Machines Corporation, a prominent maker of super-computers, is testing algorithm programs similar to those which will be the basis of autonomous agents (the type exhibiting artificial life) to predict how credit cards will be used on a broad scale (Brandt, 1994: 68)? It seems clear that consumer marketing demographics is driving much of the new technology (especially when electronic shopping is being touted as the key feature of agents). In a further example, Greg Elmer (1997) has explained how the earliest of agent programs (called 'spiders') have been used to map the sprawl of the World Wide Web and even autonomously repair broken links between sites. But such spiders are also capable of tracking user activity on the Web and 'enhancing demographic and psychographic profiles'.

> Moreover, as just one more step towards instituting strategies of advertising, marketing and consumer surveillance – which for decades now have targeted particular demographic and psychographic groups with a range of products and services (through the mail, at the supermarket, on the telephone, etc.) – the advent of spiders has also facilitated the technological construction of user profiles solicited through a language of freedom, interactivity, efficiency, and choice. (Elmer, 1997: 185–6)

If the current structures of the Web and the Internet can record one's passing for marketing purposes, how will this be different when it is an agent passing through? Might not it gather (willingly or not) handfuls of electronic brochures and bumper stickers to show you as it travels on your business? On a deeper level, it should be expected that future commercially distributed agent programs will always exhibit some form of normative action, either searching only prominent commercial sites (i.e. searching only Ticketmaster for concert tickets rather than independent dealers, or searching Microsoft sites first before others), or using one's usage-profile (which adapts the agent to your needs) to alert marketers (privacy becomes a major issue with autonomous agents; see Norman, 1994). As the Web and Internet become more active (literally pushing information at us rather than waiting for the user to actively seek it out; see *Wired*'s cover story, March, 1997), agent-type programs will become an increasingly important mediary in our wired lives, both as a means of protection from unsolicited information and a source of it.

II

The notion that technology is the extension of (a liberal, humanist) self generally arises in two ways in the popular discourse on cyberspace. One is the cyberpunk literature, which I do not follow here (but see Bukatman, 1993; Dery, 1996). The second is the intriguing notion that we will *become digital*, once we delegate to electronic avatars and our actions are carried out by digital servants. So say the fervent believers of this vision of cyberspace such as Nicholas Negroponte. Negroponte and fellow MIT professor William Mitchell lead the way in abandoning the physical world of atoms to play in the City of Bits. Negroponte (1995b) explains, for example, how much easier life will be once we stop shipping around atoms and start sending bits (once we 'become digital'). He discusses the freedom, the very lightness of being, of living in a digital world and at the speed of light. In such a realm one has much more power to construct one's surroundings and control one's interactions with the world (via agents and intelligent newspapers). Mitchell (1995) explores the ways in which currently solid institutional and architectural spaces (such as museums, schools, hospitals and theatres) may be greatly transformed by the new technologies (or even vanish into thin air). Other proponents of similar views spin out scenarios where the body itself will be abandoned, our consciousnesses let free to roam the universe.[3] These discourses are often set in evolutionist or social Darwinist terms, making such changes seem positive and inevitable (on this, see Berland, 1997).[4]

The agent focuses and personifies a popular conception of individual agency in the new technological world. McLuhan and libertarianism come together: the individual is now in complete control of its extended self. But in control of what? A quote from Pattie Maes is revealing: 'we think it's important to keep the users in control, or at least always give them the impression they are in control' (quoted in Berkun, 1995: 117).

Between hyperbolic descriptions of freedom and agency we can note anxieties over this issue of control throughout discourses on agents and cyberspace generally.[5] Apple Fellow Donald Norman (1994: 69) puts it this way:

> It's bad enough when people are intimidated by their home appliances, but what will happen when automatic systems select the articles they should read, determine the importance and priority of their daily mail, and automatically answer mail, send messages, and schedule appointments?

Will we become timid in the presence of our own agents and machines? Will they begin to control us? Trust becomes a central factor in dealing with and designing agents (Indermaur, 1995).[6] For example, William J. Mitchell (1995: 146) writes,

> Even if our agents turn out to be very smart, and always perform impeccably, will we ever fully trust them? And how will we deal with the old paradox of the slave? We will want our agents to be as smart as possible in order to do our bidding most effectively, but the more intelligent they are, the more we will have to worry about losing control and the agents taking over.

Andrew Leonard worries: 'what happens when our helpers finally throw off their chains and sever their cyborg links?' (1997: 187). And Marvin Minsky, co-founder of the Artificial Intelligence laboratory at MIT, writes:

> There's the old paradox of having a very smart slave. If you keep the slave from learning too much, you are limiting its usefulness. But, if you help it to become smarter than you are, then you may not be able to trust it not to make better plans for itself than it does for you. (quoted in Riecken, 1994: 25)

The worry that we will become enslaved to our machines (or that they will rise up against us once the intelligent agents realize that we humans are slow and boring) is not unique to intelligent agents, and is far from new. Indeed, it can be traced back through a long line of writings on what Langdon Winner (1977) has termed 'autonomous technology'. The dilemma at the heart of such fears surrounding modern technology, Winner argues, is that of the master and the slave described by Hegel. In this dilemma, the master not only becomes lazy and dependent on the slave's work, but the slave becomes enlightened through working with the land and tools and (in Marx's reading of this dilemma at least) rises up against the master. This dilemma lies at the heart of the modern (for a more extensive treatment of this see Wise (1997), following in part from Grossberg, 1993). The question is one of control, control of the other, and the differentiation between self and other (Cartesian dualism, the Kantian noumena–phenomena split). Thus we have seemingly constant debates over whether we control our technologies/slaves (social determinism) or whether they control us because we have become radically dependent on them (technological determinism).

Perhaps the issue with intelligent agents, though, is not so much that agents might take over the world, but more subtly that we may begin to defer too much to machines. This is the argument of Jaron Lanier, a computer scientist and pioneer in virtual reality systems, who argues that 'the idea of "intelligent agents" is both wrong and evil' (1996: 1). His main point is that 'Agents make people redefine themselves into lesser beings. . . . You change yourself in order to make the agent look smart. Specifically, you make yourself dumb.' If an agent is said to be intelligent (or expert) we tend to defer more towards that program. We tend also to limit ourselves only to the categories and procedures that the program offers. Thus the proliferation of intelligent agents and expert systems may actually increase normativity and obedience to technocrats and systems builders rather than freeing the individual from their control. The question to ask, then, is: What are we actually accomplishing when we use an intelligent agent? Are we just following its orders and protocols or are we exhibiting our own agency?

Theorizing resistance, Michel de Certeau contrasts 'style' with 'use' (1984: 100). *Style* refers to the singular processing of symbols or practice. In this case, style would be the ability to shape most if not all of an agent's protocols, proclivities and behaviour, and to be creative in one's use of agents. *Use* is normative and refers to socially structured codes. In this case agents would be primarily pre-programmed or come with a standard set of options. Indeed, it is a worry of the few critics of the intelligent agent (such as Lanier) that users won't exert the amount of style that they could (or, alternatively, they will not be able to, given the particular design of the agent, only certain functions can be performed, and so on).

Agents do (or will) exhibit a certain amount of agency, but of what type? To what extent do agents always at some level exhibit the normativity of their programmers and the structures of cyberspace into which they are released? Normativity and structure are not necessarily bad in and of themselves, but become much more of a concern the further apart the programmer and user are socially, economically and culturally from each other. Agents are always double agents. On the one hand, agents are nothing if not our lieutenants (in Latour's term), our butlers[7] (Kantrowitz, 1994), our familiars (in the demonic sense, as sorcerer's apprentices; Dery, 1996: 60), our delegates in cyberspace, carrying out our tasks so that our minds can be occupied elsewhere. But on the other hand, these agents are not just *our* delegates because we did not create them. The program and the logic (i.e. search protocols) of the agent limit and guide their progress and capabilities. This is what I mean when I say that all agents are double agents: they work for you, but they also work for (e.g.) Microsoft. Maes has written that 'it may prove hard for people to trust an agent instructed by someone else' (1995: 85). This will be less true as we develop agents which are not preprogrammed but learn everything from experience and from sharing information with pre-existing agents (ibid.: 86). This is when agents exhibit what is called 'artificial life' (Steels and Brooks, 1995).

Artificial life is a field of study that attempts to understand and reproduce the processes of life (Langton, 1996: 40; see also Kelly, 1995); in particular it takes the knowledge and production of self-organizing entities as its central focus (Boden, 1996: 3). More than simply mimicking life (like the animatronic figures in a Disneyland ride), artificial life would be autonomous and emergent, it would change and evolve depending on its circumstances. 'Artificial life involves attempts to (1) synthesize the process of evolution (2) in computers, and (3) will be interested in whatever emerges from the process, even if the results have no analogues in the "natural" world' (Langton, 1996: 40). The artificial life approach to agents, then, would be to create rudimentary agent programs and then let them loose, allow them to explore, interact and adapt. The assumption behind this approach is a progressivist, survival-of-the-fittest view of evolution (cf. Berland, 1997). Better, more efficient agents will evolve if we simply let nature take its course. Nature, in this case, takes place in 'a complete electronic ecosystem'; 'over time, these digital life-forms will fill different ecological niches' (Maes, 1995: 86). The artificiality of such a 'natural' ecosystem is betrayed by the fact that, coincidentally, the predicted fruits of electronic evolution happen to be agents which fill historically and socially specific human needs (i.e. database searching).

The drive to produce agents which are truly autonomous (living out their lives in the electronic jungle) is actually a drive to cover over or ignore the historical, social, cultural (and so on) conditions of creation, maintenance and development of such technologies. 'Programmers seek to remove traces of their presence in order to give the program the greatest possible autonomy' (Bolter and Grusin, 1996/7: 322). The contradiction between the historical specificity of agents and their universal evolutionary a-historicism is the same tension as that between the idea that agents become better the freer (more autonomous) they are (libertarianism returns here) and the need for control (and lack of trust) of agents, which is the dilemma of the master and the slave. In terms of human agency it is the tension between whether agent programs allow an amount of freedom (style) – i.e. agents should be able to be controlled by users – or whether users simply respond to autonomous programs. What contributes to this contradiction (and to the seemingly eternal debates between technological determinism and social determinism) is a conflation of two types of agency, what could be called 'technological agency' and 'linguistic agency'; each type presents a different way of achieving effects.[8]

III

Consider the strata in a rock formation. Strata of different composition are folded together. Imagine if one of these strata consisted of technology, thought broadly as corporeal agency – the ability to achieve effects through physical means, body on body, the direct manipulation of reality (Deleuze and Guattari, 1987). A second strata, folded on to the first, we will call language, thought of as discursive agency, the ability to achieve effects incorporeally. For example, if a judge declares an accused 'guilty', that act has definite effects (the prisoner's status, his or her ability to move freely or conduct social interactions, is restricted), but those effects were carried out without physical force. Though incorporeal, the effects are still real. The combination, the articulation, of these strata together constitutes human social space. Human agency, the ability of humans to achieve effects in a society, is always both technological and linguistic. What changes from society to society, and across time, is the relative consistency and arrangement of each strata (technologies change, languages change) *and the relation between the two strata*. But we should also remember that in any social situation we are dealing with not only human actors (what Donna Haraway refers to as 'language-bearing actors' (1991: 3)) but also non-human, non-language-bearing actors as well.

Western, industrialized humans tend to place a lot of faith in the notion of a type of linguistic agency; indeed, this is the constitutive aspect of the public sphere and democracy (one can bring about changes in government and society through language alone, by voting and declaring). It is also through linguistic agency that we can control our machines since they have far surpassed our physical control. We command machines to do our bidding (cf. the current push to perfect voice-recognition systems).

With the Internet, digitalization and the rapid expansion of communication and information technologies, it would seem that linguistic agency would be even further expanded (hence the discussions of how the Internet will usher in true democracy and everyone will have more of a voice in public affairs). The reduction of the human to this stratum alone underlies the technolibertarian fantasies so prevalent around cyberspace. Negroponte's (1995b) digital being rides a swirl of information (seen as signs and language, and seen to be effective only through its representational – linguistic – functions), leaving the world of atoms far behind. Mitchell (1995) likewise focuses on the 'incorporeal' realm of cyberspace. And a similar reduction occurs when agents are not viewed contextually, as embodied, and when the task of creating and working with agents becomes that of refining programming language alone (see e.g. Varela, 1995, on embodied agents).

To assume this reduction, to claim, as Derrick de Kerckhove, chair of the Marshall McLuhan Program in Culture and Technology at the University of Toronto's St Michael's College has, that 'the Web is a new guise of language' (in Kelly, 1996: 149), is to virtually ignore the technological mediation that is occurring. Ironically, it is the mediating technologies themselves that allow this erasure. The problem with intelligent agents is a problem with all the technologies which increasingly insert themselves between us and the world; it is a characteristic of the *interface*. 'The transparent interface is one more manifestation of the desire to deny the mediated character of digital technology altogether' (Bolter and Grusin, 1996/7: 318). As Paul Virilio (1991: 52) has written,

> We can now see more clearly the theoretical and practical importance of the notion of interface, that drastically new surface that annuls the classical separation of position, of instant or object, as well as the traditional partitioning of space into physical dimensions, in favor of an almost instantaneous configuration in which the observer and observed are roughly linked, confused, and chained by an encoded language.

The interface allows us to ignore all of the social actors (including all of the non-language-bearing actors) that must be taken into account in any activity in cyberspace. With the spread of cyberspace comes the increased insertion of technological actors into the public sphere: expert programs and artificial intelligence systems take control of situations out of human hands (this is especially true in military contexts, which reveal contemporary agents' relation to smart weapons systems (Gray, 1989; de Landa, 1991)); and we are now to have our own personal agents, and so on.

What are seemingly left behind in these cyberscenarios are both the technological actors making these changes possible and the bodies of those involved. Feminist cyborg theory made the body a political battleground (Balsamo, 1996; Haraway, 1991), but the discourses we have been examining in this article abandon the body in favour of a digital, linguistic, ephemeral agent. However, given the present proliferation of both technological actors and the increasing involvement of the body in new technological systems (both positively in terms of prosthetics and new possibilities for choice regarding one's body, and negatively in terms of repetitive strain injury, chemical and radiation poisoning, and so on), perhaps the question to ask is whether the predominant agency in social space is more technological than linguistic. In other words, that the focus on decorporealization masks important changes in the corporeal realm. Let me clarify here that I am not arguing that the body is real while the digital realm is false. Both are real, both have very real effectivity. What I *am* arguing is that both realms are inseparable. We cannot abandon one in favour of the other. Therefore discourses which attempt to do so are necessarily ignoring or masking other effects.

For example, abandoning the material realm to an electronic one helps one avoid discussing the very real problems that these electronic technologies are causing both industrially and globally (i.e. in the realm of atoms). Such ontological legerdemain ignores displaced, underemployed, temporary workforces that are exploited (and expanded) by the new information economy with its flexible, just-in-time management. As James Brook and Iain Boal have written in the Preface to their edited collection, *Resisting the Virtual Life* (1995: ix):

> The wish to leave body, time, and place behind in search of electronic emulation of community does not accidentally intensify at a time when the space and time of everyday life have become so uncertain, unpleasant, and dangerous for so many. . . . [T]he flight into cyberspace is motivated by some of the same fears and longings as the flight to the suburbs: it is another 'white flight'.

This new technology poses the risk of the further balkanization of the cyberclasses, a move which parallels the increase in elite gated communities in cities such as Los Angeles (Davis, 1990). For example, Negroponte (1995b: 153) discusses intelligent newspapers which feed us according to our special interests.

Imagine a future in which your interface agent can read every newswire and newspaper and catch every TV and radio broadcast on the planet, and then construct a personalized summary. This kind of newspaper is printed in an edition of one.

And Mitchell writes: 'as networks and information appliances deliver expanding ranges of services, there will be fewer occasions to go out' (1995: 100). As this technology further distances users from the realities and politics of the body, and from the unwired transient workforce, it also displaces that workforce. The intelligent agent can be viewed as a labour-saving device. As such it necessarily displaces labour by performing the expertise and skills of labour.[9] The first victims of search engines, spiders and agents seem to be librarians. Fifteen library schools have closed since 1976 and the number of graduate degrees in library science have dropped by half in that time (Caulfield, 1997: 64). Librarians are being retrained from being public service-oriented archivists to being more corporate-inclined managers of information and databases. Agents are also poised to replace sectors of the service economy by automating features in banking (ATMs), shopping, and so on. But in addition, as with most of such devices, agents cause more labour by increasing normative expectations.[10] More can be accomplished with its help, so more *must* be accomplished. Within today's new technological assemblage we are busier than ever, and personally responsible for more information than at any other time in history. Agents become both a solution and a symptom of our information-glutted, hyperspeed world. But as agents become more efficient and fade into the woodwork, we will lose the opportunity to interrogate some of the social actors making the greatest impact on our lives.

In order for cultural studies to adequately describe and critique social and cultural life in the new wired world (a world which is geographically and economically specific despite global and universal claims), it needs to recognize and understand the changing mediation of technological agency and, more importantly, the shifting relations between technology and language, artefacts and discourse. Indeed, it is the stratification of technology and language that makes humans human (Deleuze and Guattari, 1987: 260; Wise, 1997). Technology and discourse, mediation and agency, are not somehow external to some essentialized human identity, but rather constitute it. The question we should ask shouldn't be of the human *and* technology, but of the human *as* technology.

Rather than simply focusing on a stand-off between a person and a machine (and trying to determine on which side lies the central point of agency, the fulcrum of power on which the social rocks), perhaps we need to view the situation as the creation and functioning of an assemblage, a user–interface–machine assemblage (finger–screen–chip; face–headmount–processor) where the interface doesn't stand absolutely between the user and computer but is simply one element in the assemblage. This assemblage is articulated to other assemblages (at the ATM we have a person–car assemblage on one end and an ATM–phone network–bank assemblage on the other). These assemblages are stratified with (articulated to) assemblages of language which link discourses of freedom, agency, efficiency and consumerism.

In terms of agents, perhaps what we need to do is to re-embody the disembodied agent. Indeed, some have argued that seeing agents as embodied, as acting (and thinking) in response to a particular context, is the best way to continue to develop agents (see Steels and Brooks, 1995, and esp. Varela, 1995). Seeing cognition as embodied gets us out of the modern dichotomy described by Descartes that posits a unified thinking self and separates it from the world (Varela, 1995). By *embodied*, Francisco Varela (1995: 15) means:

(a) that cognition depends on the kinds of experience that come from having a body with various sensorimotor capacities; and (b) that these individual sensorimotor capacities are themselves embodied in a more encompassing biological and cultural *context*.

This is a lesson not just for agent research and cognitive science but for cultural theory as well. Cultural studies is said to be marked by a radical contextualism (Grossberg, 1993), but we need to recognize that such contextualism implies embodiment, and the bodies that constitute the stuff of social space are technological as well as human. Further, to recognize this embodiment means to recognize that culture, power, values and ideology can be carried by material structures and technologies, and not just in the meanings we attribute to them or discourses about them, but in the ways that they bend our space and behaviour. Resistance, likewise, can reside in the negotiated style of our habits and movements in space.

Notes

1   I want to thank Phoebe Sengers for clarifying this distinction for me. Peter Wayner (1995a) lists some of the more popular roles that have been attributed to agents: a good virus, a time saver, a personal shopper, a butler, a little person, a prodigy, a power librarian, an actor and a dancing mailman (pp. 10–11). Wooldridge and Jennings (1995) list four applications of agent technology: cooperative problem solving and distributed artificial intelligence, interface agents, information agents and cooperative information systems, and believable agents (which provide the illusion of life) (pp. 21–2).

2   Agents are also referred to as 'avatars', especially following science fiction author Neal Stephenson's book *Snow Crash*. However, one's avatar in cyberspace is usually directly controlled by the user and is therefore not a true agent in the sense developed in this article (see Halfhill, 1996).

3   See Mark Dery's (1996) survey of such discourses.

4   Andrew Leonard's (1997) book, *Bots: The Origin of New Species*, is (obviously, from its subtitle) grounded in Darwinian discourse, though he sees less inherent progression than others, that survival of the fittest doesn't necessarily make things better (p. 186).

5   A related concern often brought up briefly in discussions about agents is the question of responsibility: Who is responsible for an agent's actions? For example, what if I didn't want the tickets that my agent just purchased; do I still have to pay for them? What if my agent damaged or compromised someone else's computer? Is it my fault or the agent's fault? Though these questions are raised frequently (often, it seems, to show that the essay writer is somewhat conscious of the social implications of technology), they are never answered or dealt with at any length. One attempt to do so is Krogh's (1996) discussion of agents as legal entities.

6   Anthony Giddens has argued that trust in large-scale institutions and technologies is a hallmark of the modern (1990).
7   The gendering of the term 'butler' is deliberate as most representations of intelligent agents are male. However, Sandy Stone (1995) discusses the creation of an agent at the Atari Lab that was deliberately gendered male to avoid the stereotypes of secretaries as always female.
8   I deal with technological and linguistic agency much more extensively in Wise, 1997.
9   Cf. David Noble (1986), who explores the displacement of labour on the factory floor with the introduction of numerically controlled machine tools, that is, industrial robots.
10 For a historical perspective on the paradoxes of labour-saving technology in the home, see Ruth Cowan, 1983.

References

Appadurai, A. (1996) *Modernity at Large: Cultural Dimensions of Globalization*, Minneapolis: University of Minnesota Press.
AT&T (1993) *Connections* (promotional video).
Balsamo, A. (1996) *Technologies of the Gendered Body: Reading Cyborg Women*, Durham, NC: Duke University Press.
Berkun, S. (1995) 'Agent of change' (Interview with Pattie Maes). *Wired*, April: 116–17.
Berland, J. (1997) 'Cultural technologies and the "evolution" of technological cultures', Paper presented at the International Communication Association Conference, Montreal, May.
Boden, M. (1996) 'Introduction', in M. Boden (ed.) *The Philosophy of Artificial Life*, New York: Oxford University Press: 1–35.
Bolter, J. D. and Grusin, R. (1996/published 1997) 'Remediation', *Configurations*, 4(3): 311–58.
Brandt, R. (1994) 'Agents & artificial life', *Business Week*: 64–5.
Brook, J. and Boal, I. (eds) (1995) *Resisting the Virtual Life: The Culture and Politics of Information*, San Francisco, CA: City Lights.
Bukatman, S. (1993) *Terminal Identity: The Virtual Subject in Postmodern Science Fiction*, Durham, NC: Duke University Press.
Callon, M. and Latour, B. (1981) 'Unscrewing the big Leviathan: how actors macro-structure reality and how sociologists help them do so', in K. Knorr-Cetina and A. Cicourel (eds) *Advances in Social Theory and Methodology: Toward an Integration of Micro- and Macro-sociologies*, Boston, London and Henley: Routledge & Kegan Paul: 277–303.
Caulfield, B. (1997) 'Morphing the librarians: fighting off extinction in the information age', *Wired*, August: 64.
Cowan, R. S. (1983) *More Work for Mother: The Ironies of Household Technology From the Open Hearth to the Microwave*, New York: Basic Books.
Davis, M. (1990) *City of Quartz: Excavating the Future in Los Angeles*, New York: Verso.
de Certeau, M. (1984) *The Practice of Everyday Life*, trans. S. Randall, Berkeley: University of California Press.
de Landa, M. (1991) *War in the Age of Intelligent Machines*, New York: Zone.
Deleuze, G. and Guattari, F. (1987) *A Thousand Plateaus: Capitalism and Schizophrenia*, trans. B. Massumi, Minneapolis: University of Minnesota Press.
Dery, M. (1996) *Escape Velocity: Cyberculture at the End of the Century*, New York: Grove Press.
Drew, J. (1995) 'Media activism and radical democracy', in J. Brook and I. Boal (eds) *Resisting the Virtual Life: The Culture and Politics of Information*, San Francisco, CA: City Lights: 71–83.
Elmer, G. (1997) 'Spaces of surveillance: indexicality and solicitation on the Internet', *Critical Studies in Mass Communication*, 14(2): 182–91.
Giddens, A. (1990) *The Consequence of Modernity*, Stanford, CA: Stanford University Press.
Gray, C. H. (1989) 'The cyborg soldier: the U.S. military and the post-modern warrior', in L. Levidow and K. Robins (eds) *Cyborg Worlds: The Military Information Society*, London: Free Association Books: 43–71.
Grossberg, L. (1993) 'Cultural studies and/in new worlds', *Critical Studies in Mass Communication*, 10(1): 1–22.
Hafner, K. (1995) 'Have your agent call my agent', *Newsweek*, 27 February: 76–7.
Halfhill, T. (1996) 'Agents and avatars', *Byte*, February: 69–72.
Haraway, D. (1991) *Simians, Cyborgs, and Women: The Reinvention of Nature*, New York: Routledge.
Hebdige, D. (1988) *Hiding in the Light: On Images and Things*, New York: Routledge.

Indermaur, K. (1995) 'Baby steps', *Byte*, March: 97–104.

Kantrowitz, B. (1994) 'The butlers of the digital age will be just a keystroke away', *Newsweek*, 17 January: 58.

Kelly, K. (1995) *Out of Control: The New Biology of Machines, Social Systems and the Economic World*, New York: Addison-Wesley.

—— (1996) 'What would McLuhan say?' (Interview with Derrick de Kerckhove), *Wired*, October: 148–9.

Krogh, C. (1996) 'The rights of agents', in M. Wooldridge, J. P. Müller and M. Tambe (eds) *Intelligent Agents II: Agent Theories, Architectures, and Languages: IJCAI'95 Workshop (ATAL), Montreal, Canada, 19–20 August 1995: Proceedings*, New York: Springer Verlag: 1–16.

Langton, C. G. (1996) 'Artificial life', in M. Boden (ed.) *The Philosophy of Artificial Life*, New York: Oxford University Press: 39–94.

Lanier, J. (1996) 'Agents of alienation', http://www.voyagerco.com/misc/jaron.html

Latour, B. (1988) 'Mixing humans and nonhumans together: the sociology of a door closer', *Social Problems*, 35: 298–310.

—— (1993) *We Have Never Been Modern*, trans. C. Porter, Cambridge, MA: Harvard University Press.

Leonard, A. (1997) *Bots: The Origins of New Species*, San Francisco, CA: Hardwired.

Maes, P. (1995) 'Intelligent software', *Scientific American*, September: 84–6.

—— (1996) 'Intelligent agents = stupid humans, post 2', *Hotwired: Braintennis*, 16 July, http://www.hotwired.com/braintennis/96/29/indexla.html

Mitchell, W. (1995) *City of Bits*, Cambridge, MA: MIT Press.

Negroponte, N. (1995a) '000 000 111 – Double agents', *Wired*, March: 172.

—— (1995b) *Being Digital*, New York: Knopf.

Noble, D. (1986) *Forces of Production: A Social History of Industrial Automation*, New York: Oxford University Press.

Norman, D. (1994) 'How might people interact with agents', *Communications of the ACM*, 37(7): 68–71.

Riecken. D. (1994) 'A conversation with Marvin Minsky about agents', *Communications of the ACM*, 37(7): 23–9.

Slotkin, R. (1985) *The Fatal Environment: The Myth of the Frontier in the Age of Industrialization, 1800–1890*, New York: Atheneum.

Star, S. L. (1991) 'Power, technology, and the phenomenology of conventions: on being allergic to onions', in J. Law (ed.) *A Sociology of Monsters? Power, Technology, and the Modern World*, Oxford: Blackwell: 27–57.

Steels, L. (1995) 'Building agents out of autonomous behavior systems', in L. Steels and R. Brooks (eds) *The Artificial Life Route to Artificial Intelligence: Building Embodied, Situated Agents*, Hillsdale, NJ: Lawrence Erlbaum Associates: 83–121.

Steels, L. and Brooks, R. (eds) (1995) *The Artificial Life Route to Artificial Intelligence: Building Embodied, Situated Agents*, Hillsdale, NJ: Lawrence Erlbaum Associates.

Stone, A. R. (1995) *The War of Desire and Technology at the Close of the Mechanical Age*, Cambridge, MA: MIT Press.

Varela, F. (1995) 'The re-enchantment of the concrete: some biological ingredients for a nouvelle cognitive science', in L. Steels and R. Brooks (eds) *The Artificial Life Route to Artificial Intelligence: Building Embodied, Situated Agents*, Hillsdale, NJ: Lawrence Erlbaum Associates: 11–22.

Virilio, P. (1991) *The Lost Dimension*, trans. D. Moshenberg, New York: Semiotext(e).

Wayner, P. (1995a) *Agents Unleashed: A Public Domain Look at Agent Technology*, New York: AP Professional.

—— (1995b) 'Free agents', *Byte*, March: 105–14.

Wayner, P. and Joch, A. (1995) 'Agents of change', *Byte*, March: 94–5.

Williams, R. (1974) *Television: Technology and Cultural Form*, New York: Schocken.

Winner, L. (1977) *Autonomous Technology: Technics-out-of-control as a Theme in Political Thought*, Cambridge, MA: MIT Press.

Wise, J. M. (1997) *Exploring Technology and Social Space*, Thousand Oaks, CA: Sage.

Wooldridge, M. and Jennings, N. (1995) 'Agent theories, architectures, and languages: a survey', in M. Wooldridge and N. Jennings (eds) *Intelligent Agents: ECAI–94 Workshop on Agent Theories, Architectures, and Languages, Amsterdam, Netherlands, 8–9 August 1994: Proceedings*, New York: Springer Verlag: 1–39.

Chapter 19

HELEN W. KENNEDY

FEMALE *QUAKE* PLAYERS AND THE POLITICS OF IDENTITY

V IDEOGAME PLAY exemplifies and epitomises the intimate and intense relationships of digital technoculture, and over the past few decades its circuits of player, screen and virtual world have fed into a technological imaginary of cybercultural immersion. For Kennedy, influenced by **Haraway**, videogames such as the *Quake* series not only present images of cyborgs, gameplay sessions themselves are cyborgian: cybernetic loops of response and feedback between eyes, software, fingers, keyboards, screens and nervous systems. These circuits are not closed off from the world around them however. Kennedy's interviews with female players of online *Quake* identify the wider circuits that loop through, constitute, and are brought into being by, this particular game culture. Internet forums, fan websites, game element production (e.g. 'skinning') and uneasy relationships with the games industry are all caught up in this highly gendered game culture.

Kennedy implicitly questions the concepts of 'identification' and subjectivity that are central to the study of screen media audiences (not least in feminist film and media studies). These players do not just *identify* with the on-screen cyborgs, as a viewer of the *Terminator* films might. Rather, they must develop technical competence in learning the game controls, connecting computers to LANs or the Internet, and developing software skills in image manipulation for skinning or setting up fan websites. Gravitation towards particular generic imagery and action, and affinities with screen characters, are just one aspect of this *technicity*. 'Identification' as a term and a critical approach, then, is not adequate to account for the intense embodied pleasures, frustrations and techniques of FPS culture and play.

Kennedy cites **Taylor**'s work on MMOGs (see Part Five). See also **Kember** (this part) for another example of online gameplay and production culture, and **Sudnow** (Part 4) for what could be seen as a detailed diary of the construction and training of videogame technicity. The cultural implications of cybernetics are introduced and explored in **Wiener**, **Galison**, and **Tomas**. http://www.playfulsubjects.org

This chapter considers the ways in which female *Quake* players and female *Quake* clans have developed and enunciated a particular gaming identity and technical competence within a gaming culture that is heavily coded as masculine. Videogame and computer game play *and* the cultures that have emerged around these practices in the form of web pages, websites and other means of supporting and displaying playing preferences and practices are a critical site for both the development and display of technological prowess and virtuosity. It is also clear that technical competence is a key marker for gender differentiation in a culture that increasingly privileges a playful relationship with technology. Analyses of games and gaming practices such as those which surround *Quake* – the practice of 'skinning' which is enabled through the sharing of software to produce your own 'in game' persona; the formation of clans to compete with others in multiplayer versions of the game; the creation of web pages and web rings to support and maintain the clan communities – provide rich material for examining the relationship between technological competence, gender identity and play.

These female clans and individual players are knowingly engaged in a form of gender play and technoplay which operates counter to dominant notions of femininity, female play preferences, play styles and technical prowess. Furthermore, through their clan memberships the players form strong social bonds which enable the affirmation and articulation of an individual and collective identity based on technicity,[1] pleasure and gender insubordination. A feminist perspective developed from the work of Donna Haraway and Judith Butler, alongside theories drawn from play and performance studies, is used to examine the ways in which the identities that are articulated through these online sites are both a reflection of their liminality within the dominant gaming culture and an active attempt to carve out a space for a specific female gaming subjectivity within this apparently hostile and excluding context.

There have been relatively few explicitly feminist analyses of popular videogame or computer game playing as a cultural practice and very few which engage positively with existing female players, their pleasures and their communities. The Cassell and Jenkins edited collection *From Barbie to Mortal Kombat* (1999) is still the only volume focusing on the issue of gender and computer game culture and largely deals with the issues of how to make *better* games for girls and how to improve female access to game playing rather than engaging with the games and players that already exist (or existed then). T.L. Taylor's (1999, 2003) research into female players of the highly popular massively multiplayer online role playing game (MMORPG) *Everquest* is a significant exception to this general tendency. The feminist response to female players of first person shooter games (FPS) has been either to condemn them for their adoption of masculine values (as evidenced by bell hooks (Marriott 2003)) or to largely dismiss these players as of little interest to feminism and to privilege instead the creative practices of female game artists (Flanagan 2003). However, by locating these female play practices within a technofeminist framework and by drawing on play and performance theory it is possible to see that computer games can afford many moments of the creation of oppositional meanings and further can allow for the elaboration of an oppositional identity.

In the discussion that follows I will be drawing from a case study focusing on the consumption and production practices of individual female *Quake* players, female *Quake*-playing clans, and the ways in which they have separately and collectively represented themselves to the rest of the online game-playing community that has formed around *Quake*. This case study is part of an ongoing study of female game players and the communities which have developed through their play and play related practices. Here I will be drawing from the online material produced by individual players and particular play communities (web pages, web sites and other more specifically game-related creative practices) and interviews and correspondence with individual players. This research began in 2000 and the interviews were conducted over an 18-month period between 2001 and 2003 during which time I also learnt to play the games in single player mode and played with other female players online. I also draw from earlier online archive material on specific female gamer websites such as www.grrlgamer.com. Firstly, however, it is necessary to sketch out the specific context of these practices in order to better understand the ways in which these players and producers are required to negotiate and subvert particular meanings around appropriate feminine behaviour and appropriate feminine pleasures.

Quake (and its sequels) is an enduringly popular example of the 3D first person shooter genre, making use of an innovative game engine which offered new possibilities in terms of the 3D representation space of the game and the speed of gameplay. *Quake* also offered multiplayer capabilities and eventually the possibility for it to be played online via dedicated game servers.[2] *Quake* was initially released on 24 June 1996 as a shareware version with the release of the official version following a few months later in August. The shareware ethos and the possibility of making changes to the game allowed fans access to the production and distribution of new game content for others to share (this process is known as modding – short for 'modifying') and in the process spawned an online community based around these practices.[3] These fan activities have also enabled new forms of relationship between producers and consumers where power relationships between them may become less fixed, less predictable and less easy to control.

These factors have allowed for the emergence of highly *visible* participatory cultures where there is a collapse of distinction between the dominant culture (the games industry) and the subculture (games players and modders) not typically associated with cinema-going or television viewing (Giddings and Kennedy 2006a). There are two critical aspects of this fan/subcultural activity which are important for the discussion of female *Quake* players that follows – shareware has also been a cultural driver in so far as it facilitates the display and delight in technical virtuosity that characterises and maintains certain sub-cultures which are often predominantly male. Technical expertise provides the means of exchange in communities of expert consumers, hackers and modders which are usually highly gendered. The oppositional force of the examples which are to be discussed here derive precisely from the fact that female players have often been entirely excluded from the communities that form around these practices.

Frag everything that isn't you

To play a computer game you have to master the interface in order to engage with the game at any level, from loading the game through to making the settings suit your play style. This means that at a very basic level you have to be able to make use of a mouse and operate a keyboard simultaneously – these games require that you are adept at the handling of these controls and are incredibly unforgiving of the absolute novice. The moment that you click the mouse to signal your readiness for play you are immediately thrown into a noisy, chaotic, confusing 3D environment filled with computer generated characters whose sole function is to destroy your avatar as quickly and as efficiently as possible – even on the easiest setting in the game (there are several levels of difficulty available ranging from the novice 'I Can Win', through 'Hardcore' to the hardest level 'Nightmare!') the speed and pace of the game has to be adapted to very quickly in order to make any progress. This description provided by one female player neatly captures some of this complexity:

> you have to be able to use the mouse for more than just point and click you have to sort of be able to use it around in space which is a bit different and it's easy to end up looking at the ceiling or getting stuck in corners and becoming frag bait. Oh, yeah, and your left and right hands are doing totally different things, you've got to really know where all the keys are . . . at first I couldn't get it all sorted out, changing weapons, jumping, moving around and shooting it was all a bit much and my mouse hand would be doing

one thing and I'd have to look at the keyboard to try and find the right keys . . . then after a while it all sort of clicks and you're just staring at the screen and your hands are going like crazy and you just sort of do it all on automatic and you feel like it's you in there, sneaking round corners and fragging that poor little eyeball on legs to bits . . . (Interview with author, Xena, *Quake Interviews*, December 2001)

This extends to the processes of modification which will require some facility with operating sub-programs, understanding game code and operating graphics packages. Even without engaging in modding practices, in order to play online you will have to be able to navigate through the web to find a server and choose a level to play that is active, each step requiring you to operate the computer with some skill and proficiency.

The complex technical, legal and cultural interplay between players, player/creators and developers is wonderfully exemplified by Sue Morris's account of the steps she goes through to play *Quake III: Arena* (Morris 2003). The Gamespy server which she uses to access the game engine was originally developed by Joe Powell, a *Quake* gamer, but is now a commercial portal, using voice software developed by gamers using venture capital. The latest update is downloaded from another portal developed by gamers in 1996 to organise LAN tournaments, in turn this update includes anti-cheat software originally developed by a team of gamers but now commercially deployed by a range of online game companies. Morris then finds a local server running games that may either be commercial or enthusiast-run, there she can choose from any one of 1600 player-created environments made for *Quake III: Arena*. Once there again she may choose to play as a ready-made avatar or choose a skin made by another gamer or indeed by herself. Before play commences she will choose customised configurations for her machine that 'optimise the game's performance and appearance to my liking'; these configurations might be unique to her or learnt from online player community forums.

In a multiplayer FPS game such as *Quake III: Arena*, the 'game' is not just a commercially released program that players use, but an assemblage created by a complex fusion of the creative efforts of a large number of individuals, both professional and amateur, facilitated by communication and distribution systems that have developed out of the gaming community itself. As a cocreative media form, multiplayer FPS gaming has introduced new forms of participation, which have led to the formation of community structures and practices that are changing the way in which these games are developed and played (Morris 2003).

This assertion of games as 'cocreative' is a critical one and Morris's account here helps to underscore the complexity of these processes as engagement with different kinds of technology (hardware and software). Morris also draws attention to the formation of community structures and practices around the preferences that develop through these activities.

Gameplay as masculine technoplay

Game design, content, packaging and marketing all serve to demarcate games playing as a specifically masculine activity. This remains as true today as it was in the early 1980s and this is despite the numerous attempts, both commercially and politically motivated, to undermine this notion. Brenda Laurel is one of the few female games designers to be recognized in the wider culture and she was one of the key players in the games for girls movement. Laurel confirms this gendered lineage of the computer game and computer game culture:

Computer games as we know them were invented by young men around the time of the invention of graphical displays. They were enjoyed by young men, and young men soon made a very profitable business of them, dovetailing to a certain extent with the existing pinball business. Arcade computer games were sold into male-gendered spaces, and when home computer consoles were invented, they were sold through male-oriented consumer electronics channels to more young men. The whole industry consolidated very quickly around a young male demographic – all the way from the gameplay design to the arcade environment to the retail world. (Laurel 1998)

The majority of research and writing around female computer game players has to date tended to suggest that there exists a 'feminine' set of computer game pleasures and preferences – something which is vehemently resisted by many female players:

> I keep reading about articles and studies where experts say girls don't like shooting and blasting games but instead prefer quiet, contemplative games with well-rounded characters and storylines that stimulate their imagination. I'd venture to say, however, that these studies are a reflection of how we condition girls to be passive. The image of a woman with a gun is too shocking, too disruptive and threatening to the male dominant order of things. (Aliza Sherman aka Cybergrrrl) (Cassell and Jenkins 1998: 335)

'The notion that some forms of activity and entertainment are more appropriate to men and some to women, that some genres can be called "masculine" whilst others are labelled "feminine", has a long history' (Tasker 1993: 136). Whatever the intention, these studies of 'feminine' play styles and play preferences contribute to the construction of appropriate feminine tastes and behaviours that cannot help but inform the ways individuals understand their preferences as either 'normal' or 'abnormal'. Female *Quake* players have to live with and reconcile the fact that their pleasures have been deemed unfeminine and inappropriate. The players themselves are quick to articulate a critique of normative femininity: 'People say it's not ladylike to sit in front of a computer or want to play a game where you run around with a shotgun, but why not? I get insulted a lot and told I'm like a boy, but I'm not. I'm just a different kind of girl' (Stephanie Bergman, *Quake Interviews*, January 2002).

Gameplay as cybernetic

Videogame play works through feedback between user, hardware and software. It has been argued that the circuit of game and player in the act of playing is literally (for the duration of the game at least) cybernetic. In one of the most influential works on computer games Aarseth makes two critical points which enable us to understand the game as cybernetic. The first is to offer a conceptualization of early text based adventure games (which remains analytically useful in relation to all videogames and computer games in general) as machines:

> the text is seen as a machine – not metaphorically but as a mechanical device for the production and consumption of verbal signs. Just as a film is useless without a projector and a screen, so a text must consist of a material medium as well as a collection of words. The machine, of course, is not complete without a third party, the (human) operator, and it is within this triad that the text takes place. (Aarseth 1997: 21)

The second critical point is that this relationship between text/machine and user/player is cybernetic:

> Cybertext . . . is the wide range (or perspective) of possible textualities seen as a typology of machines, as various kinds of literary communication systems where the functional differences among the mechanical parts play a defining role in determining the aesthetic process . . . cybertext shifts the focus from the traditional threesome of author/sender, text/message, and reader/receiver to the cybernetic intercourse between the various part(icipant)s in the textual machine. (Aarseth 1997: 22)

This understanding of gameplay as a cybernetic loop in which player and game are inseparable for the duration of the game is a compelling literalization of the ontology of the cyborg – a subjectivity that depends precisely on this collapse of boundary between the human and the machine. This notion of player as cyborg has taken root in many of the most recent articulations of player subjectivity but has also been present in some of the earliest work on computers generally and computer games specifically. (Lister et al. 2003; Lahti 2003; Giddings and Kennedy 2006). In the lived enactment of gameplay there is no player separate to the interface and game world, there is a fusion of the two into a cyborgian subjectivity – composed of wires, machines, code and flesh. For the duration of the gameplay 'a new physiological entity is thus constructed from this network of organic and technological parts' (Lister et al. 2003: 374) which although temporary is a meaningful embodied experience.

By understanding gameplay as cybernetic, issues of interactivity and player agency are recast in terms of networks and flows of energy which are entirely interdependent:

> we do not see here two complete and sealed-off entities: the player on the one hand and the game on the other. Rather there is an interchange of information and energy, forming a new circuit . . . Through the tactile and visual interface with the machine, the entire body is determined to move by being part of the circuit of the game, being, as it were, *in the loop*. (Lister et al. 2003: 370)

The cybernetic nature of gameplay and the interdependency of game and player is perhaps the feature that distinguishes gameplay most clearly from other kinds of textual consumption or play. Videogames and computer games produce the gameplayer *as* cyborg. This 'new physiological' entity – avatar, machine and player – 'a wholly constructed creature composed of biological and technological components is exactly what we mean by the cyborg' (Lister et al. 2003: 375). For Haraway (1991), the cyborg is a means of conceptualizing subjectivity which disrupts the myth of the concrete stable and boundaried subject of the Enlightenment tradition; we see this cast in light of the dissolution of the boundary between player and game – in gameplay there is only player *and* game inseparable and irreducible.

The complexity of the circuit of machines, code and bodies is further increased when engaging in multiplayer games whether console based or online. Playing *Quake* as a clan in multiplayer mode with shared skins developed to provide a collective in-game identity or collectively working together on a quest in *Everquest* are compelling examples of the cybernetic circuit described above. The complexity of this human/machine circuit is startling; the individual players respond to each others' actions within the game and the process of feedback through which play advances. These instantiations of gameplay invoke Haraway's (1991) notion of 'networked and collective selves' (this notion has been taken up by many feminists working specifically in the area of cyberculture – most notably Plant (1993a), an idea she offers in recognition of affiliation and collective identity developed through technological circuits). During the gameplay there is no separation of individuals and machines but only a collective process of engagement where action and reaction flow in a circuit of technologized bodies and their pleasures.

Cyborgian pleasures

Playing *Quake* is therefore a means for displaying or performing technological competence and a form of technological embodiment but is also the means through which technological competence can develop further *beyond* the game itself, as we shall see. When describing what they enjoy about *Quake*, female players (both those who have participated directly in my own research and those who have posted online) use terms such as 'athleticism', 'balance', 'coordination' and 'taking risks' in such a way as to suggest that the cyborgian nature of gameplay is experienced as a set of embodied pleasure. Although it is the avatar that performs these feats of athleticism or coordination within the game space, it is the player's skill in controlling the interface that shapes this performance. The dizzy pleasures of FPS gameplay – the racing pulse, sweating palms, the adrenalin rush and the feeling of exhaustion all suggest a set of pleasures associated with movement, abandonment and risk. The sense of agency the (competent) player experiences is doubled; the player experiences a freedom of movement and sense of authority and mastery within the game alongside a sense of empowerment through their skill in mastering the technology. These two responses indicate the double nature of their pleasure:

> I really like the way the other bots in the game respond to how well you are doing – they get really narked if you win and say things like 'lets all gang up and kill "tankgirl" next time' or the machine says 'excellent' when you frag a couple of bots in a row. I know it sounds a bit, I don't know, but it makes me feel really good and I feel like I'm really there. (tankgirl, interview with author)

> I loved the challenge with Hunter – she's so beautiful, and she says all this sort of spiritual stuff and she's really hard to beat one on one and I felt really proud when I won when playing on 'hurt me plenty' mode which is quite hard. (supergirl, interview with author)

In my own play I have taken perverse pleasure in the practice of 'camping' in a safe place and using a powerful weapon to pick off the NPCs without fear of being fragged myself. I have enjoyed observing how the NPCs articulate a disapprobrium at my behaviour in the textual version of 'their' speech. Camping in this way was also the means through which I experienced my first 'Perfect' when playing *Quake III* – 20 NPC kills without dying myself. These examples also demonstrate the delightful confusion and ambiguity of our relationships with these *other* participants – how we assign intention and emotion to characters that are wholly computer generated.[4]

Many of these women have articulated a strong sense of pleasure in surprising male players with their competence and skill when playing online or over LAN (local area networks such as those found in Internet cafes) connections. They are aware that they are not expected to be good at these games and gain enormous satisfaction in flouting convention. In this typical response, the player has first encountered *Quake* with a group of male friends at a cybercafe, become hooked, bought the game to practice at home and then subsequently had the opportunity to play against the same group of male players. 'Next time we played together over a lan connection I held up my end and I could see that the blokes were really surprised and even a bit fed up that I was "fragging" them so successfully . . . I LOVED IT!' (Amanda/Xena *Quake Interviews*, November 2001). These female players – who take pleasure in the mastery of a game which is seen as requiring skills which are clearly demarcated as masculine – are aware of the transgressive nature of their pleasure.

The figure of the cyborg as developed by Haraway (1990) offered us the idea that our new intimate connection with machines could create a space for identity affiliation and agency which would destabilize conventional relationships between body, machine and nature, challenging the 'command, control and conquer' logic of state/corporate digital domination. Instead of critiquing technology solely on the basis of its embeddedness in both a colonialist, teleological and capitalist set of processes, the dawning of the cyber age was met with a sense of new opportunities – the figure of the cyborg was offered by Haraway as a way to move beyond the potentially essentializing association of women with nature. Haraway offered the cyborg as a new metaphor for subjectivity which could potentially avoid the problematic binaries which pervade around nature/culture, male/female. In doing so she promoted the cyborg as a 'site of possible resignifications . . . to expand the possibilities [of subjectivity] . . . to enable an enhanced sense of agency' (Butler 1992: 16). Crucial to this new sense of agency was a rally call for those who were deemed to be marginalized by technoculture to embrace their affinity with technology and to offer new symbols, new uses and practices through which to 'code' this new subjectivity. Female *Quake* players, their creative practices and the community they have developed should be understood to be relevant to a technofeminist agenda that seeks to offer both new images of technologised embodiment *and* to foster an active engagement with technology amongst women. Haraway argues that 'Cyborg imagery can suggest a way out of the maze of dualisms in which we have explained our bodies and our tools to ourselves . . . [and provide] a powerful infidel heteroglossia. It is an imagination of a feminist speaking in tongues to strike fear . . . It means both building and destroying machines, identities, categories, relationships, spaces, stories' (1990: 223).

Skinning and pimping – from player to creator

> Skinning is the art of creating the images that get wrapped around 3D player character models in 3D games. These images are what give the 'mesh' a solid, realistic look. A good analogy is if you think of the skin as the paper that goes around the bamboo frame (mesh) of a Chinese lantern. You paint what you want on the paper and the game wraps it around the frame for you based on the mapping the model has with it. (Chiq/Milla, female *Quake* player and skin artist, www.chiq.net)[5]

A particularly adept skinner may eventually see her skin being included in the range of characters on offer to other players through online communities and may receive prizes and acclaim for their art (http://www.planet quake.com/polycount is a site that monitors and nominates particular skins as well as providing guides and downloads of recommended skins and mods). Skinning is not an easy process – some taking as much as 60 hours to complete – like other art forms it is a process requiring a great deal of commitment and engagement. Camilla Bennett is a skin artist whose consumption/play practices have developed into more professional/creative activities.[6] A self-taught skinner since 2000, Milla has developed a high degree of competence and has moved on from designing her own skins to a professional role as a texture artist in the development of the skin for the heroine of Betty Bad (WildTangent) a web-based game, developed skins for *Unreal Tournament* and produced artwork for the company Liquid Development. Milla has also won a number of awards for her skins, and features prominently on the key web site which operates as a trading post for 'skinners' and players (Polycount). Milla also operates as a role-model for other female *Quake* players:

I found this one skin artist 'Milla' and I thought – 'I want to do that'. Her website is the most beautiful and has this lovely front page with this line 'skin is armor' which I just loved I don't know why and she's really doing stuff and even getting awards and things for her skins. I like spent ages following all the links and there was like this whole community out there of other women producing really great images . . . and I followed up all the links on the *Quake* sites and taught myself how to download different 'skins' for me to play around with and I even tried to make some of my own – not successfully though . . . (buff-e-girl, *Quake Interviews*, January 2002)

This player is just one example among many for whom their gameplay becomes the jumping-off point for a greater engagement with technology in general:

It really made me want to learn a how to use graphics on the computer – I had never thought that I could or that I would ever be interest[ed], I'd done some online chatting, used the computer for emails and played some free web games and stuff but I had [not] thought of myself as any good with computers . . . A friend is teaching me how to use Photoshop on his computer and when I'm okay I'm going to try to do a really good skin and stick it up on the web. (supergirl, *Quake Interviews*, December 2001)

Chiq/Milla describes her own personal skin: 'Woodswoman/warrior in a post-apocalyptic context. She's flaking rust, greasy and has these damn pesky hoverblades stuck to her feet.' The imagery used draws heavily from fantasy science fiction as well as closely resembling the type of female subject that often crops up in feminist cyberpunk literature. 'Female skinners sample elements from the pre-existing female character lexicon and add new flavours into the mix, resulting in fem monsters better suited to their female inhabitants' (Schleiner 1999). These fantasy constructions of identity offer an exploration of alternative subjectivities in which being feminine does not necessarily equal being a victim or needing rescuing.

Producing skins for their own use or to 'pimp' out to others allows players to engage in the production of images and symbols through which to articulate their own identity, tastes and agency. The skins often become the means through which a player will express aspects of their identity to other members of the community either through its inclusion in a web page or during online tournaments. The material produced through these practices become resources for other players who are either entering the world of online gameplay or seeking evidence that they are not alone in their play preferences.

In her feminist analysis of women's leisure Betsy Wearing has drawn on Foucault's notion of heterotopias: '[i]n contrast to "utopias" which are fictional critiques of society, without any actual locality, "heterotopias" for Foucault can be "real" existing places of difference which act as counter-sites or compensatory sites to those of everyday activity' (1998: 146). Wearing argues the importance of these 'counter-sites' as a means of experiencing alternative subjectivities and forms of self-empowerment not readily available in other aspects of daily experience and they 'provide spaces for rewriting the script of what it is to be a woman, beyond definitions provided by powerful males and the discourses propagated as truth in contemporary societies' (1998: 147). The creative practices which surround this playful consumption allow for gender play as these gamers explore aspects of their identity which are not recognized or legitimated in other contexts. The requirement for technological competence which is so central to these activities can lead to enhanced employment prospects (as exemplified in Camilla Bennett) but can also lead to more general forms of reward and acclaim in the larger community of players.

Female *Quake* communities

The online capability of these games has allowed for the emergence of 'clans' (teams of players who compete against other teams in tournaments) who may also develop their own particular clan 'skins'.[7] A number of communities have formed through these play practices – some are clan specific, while others are more open.[8] 'Network shooters like *Quake* and *Unreal* enable social grouping into clans that coalesce both locally among friends, workers and family, and also long distance over the Internet. The female clan offers a powerful support structure to female gamers, a place where knowledge can be shared and friendship bonds strengthened that extend outside the scope of the game' (Schleiner 1999). This is particularly significant in relation to the 'offline' representations and constructions of game culture, whether this is television programmes that may feature a female presenter but clearly address a male audience, or in the numerous magazines – official and unofficial – which through their style, layout, content and tone indicate their address directly to a male (and frequently adolescent) audience. Scantily clad female bodies are used in advertising promotions for many games; games industry gatherings feature a preponderance of 'booth babes' who are there to entice the 'putatively' male professional (developer, designers, writers, reviewers). As a financially significant player in popular culture, videogames and computer games remain the most resolutely sexist in their advertising, marketing and promotions. Yet in the heterotopic world of online game culture, female gamers and game reviewers have found a context which enables them to enunciate their identity, declare their existence and to find others of their kind. Through the creation of web pages, web sites, and web rings these women are able to recognize and affirm each other's identity as 'gamer' in opposition to an offline context where they are invisible, marginalized and frequently demeaned. This is of particular significance to players who may feel isolated as a female:

> I was the only female I knew who played and then one day I went on the web and discovered all these sites and women and art and chat about games and I just thought 'wow' – there weren't just loads of other women out there playing *Quake* but they were making stuff with the game as well, new 'skins' for the female game characters, sharing them out with other women and even playing together online in what they called 'clans'. (Xena, *Quake Interviews*, November 2001)

The female *Quake* playing community demonstrates a playful use of names to demarcate a specifically oppositional female identity within the online community. This is true both of the naming of individuals and the naming of clans or communities such as Chiq, Hellchick, Supergirl, Geekgirl, Clan PMS (Psycho Men Slayers), Da Valkyries: The Women of Quake, Clan Crack Whore, Nimble Little Minxes, The Coven and Hell's Warehouse. The names appropriate female subjectivities and identities that are drawn from real or mythical monstrous female identities (these names are also evocative of the kinds of radical feminist re/mis-appropriation of previously pejorative terms). In doing so they demonstrate their perception of themselves as countering hegemonic representations of femininity as well as the masculine representation of games culture and games players in general. Female *Quake* playing personae are chimeric, cyborgian and disruptive, they appropriate the demarcation of the female body as always already monstrous and redeploy these images as a 'tactical assault' on the normative construction of this identity. The images and names clearly draw from a long history of transgressive feminist informed femininity countering notions of femininity as passive or nurturing. By foregrounding both their 'femaleness' and their skill in the game they offer a different set of meanings to computers, computer games and technological competence. By bringing their own bodies or their fantasized bodies to the play arena they disrupt the assumption of a white male heterosexual player and avatar. They also problematize the dominant image of games playing as a masculine retreat from the 'feminized' body and make the female body figure as an agentic force in this relationship with technology. In doing so they offer compelling representations of cyborg subjectivity.

> Lethal female body architecture, deft combat moves and an organized female affront in the form of female gamer clans are shifting the gender topography of the shooter. Working the keyboard and mouse behind these female fighting machines are the women players who have dared to cross a rigid gender boundary into a violent gamer culture often understood by men and women alike as a boys' world (embraced by men affirmatively, often disparaged by women) (Schleiner 1999).

This celebration and reappropriation of the monstrous feminine cannot be dismissed as simply 'aping' masculinity — as already suggested their performance of skills which have been deemed masculine can be read as undermining the assumption of a 'male body' as the site of these competences (Butler 1992).

These personae and the interventions made through the female gaming websites cannot be considered other than as a response to the very particular context in which there exists a dominant discourse within which their voice is largely silent or absent. 'Any voice within a community is heteroglossic, combining others' voices in individualized ways. In so doing, speakers position themselves relative to other voices in their communities' (Bakhtin in Morris 1994: 89). Nancy Baym in her analysis of online fan practices also draws on Bakhtin to suggest that individuality 'gets defined in and by the effects of appropriating, transforming and resisting particular discursive practices in particular ways' (Baym 2000: 182). Nikki Douglas here takes direct issue with the statements made about gendered pleasure; she is responding to the claim that *Quake* and other action games are good for male players as they are a means of relieving stress: 'Lord knows we, as women, don't need to relieve stress. We just go shopping or eat or color code our underwear drawers, right? And I want all my gaming to be . . . just like my life is, not some escape. Oh, no, why would I want to temporarily escape all the stress and problem solving that I'm faced with every day? Why would I just once like to answer some insipid question like "I thought you were going to make dinner?" with a spray of automatic gunfire? There's your dinner, baby!' (Douglas in Cassell and Jenkins 1998: 293).

Feminism *in* and *at* play in female games culture

As well as challenging dominant notions around appropriate feminine behaviour, pleasures and competences, the female *Quake* playing community has also provided the means and support through which to contest and critique sexist behaviour amongst players and discussion list contributors. In 1998 a 'green ribbon campaign' was launched in response to the harassment experienced by a British female player known in the community as Hellkitten. Images that she had posted on her website were hacked and altered to include pornographic imagery to the dismay of many within the community. The campaign involved displaying a modified (and green) version of the *Quake* logo on web pages and web sites as a symbol of support for both the individual victim of this attack and as support for tolerance and respect amongst players. The campaign served to raise awareness of the frequency of online harassment and its damaging consequences for players and for the community.[9] The campaign was not accepted wholeheartedly by all of the community, however, and it became a particular site of vociferous and visible contestation of dominant but unspoken ideas about gender and games. These moments of disagreement and debate, however fleeting, are important in challenging dominant discourses about gender and for the participants they are the hallmark of community as norms, prohibitions and sanctions emerge around particular behaviour.

In taking up space and answering back, these feisty, fearless and transgressing female gamers perform a kind of gender insubordination which may not be feminist in its intentions but may be feminist in its effect upon themselves as subjects and within the wider community. These online personae or avatars provide us with representations of performed subjectivities where the boundaries of what is acceptable are potentially different to those experienced in the offline setting. The web pages, web sites, and online personae can be viewed as enunciations of identity that are directed at particular discourses which are important to them. These performative spaces enable the living out (however temporarily) of imaginative heterotopian identities or playful representations of self which may be limited and constrained, but in very different ways to the offline context they regularly inhabit.[10] Certainly, the successful repetition of these performances appears to have direct consequences on the offline subjectivity in that in the examples given here they also achieve a different status within the culture as they access a producerly mode of engagement with technology.

The female *Quake* playing community makes no specific claims to a feminist agenda or a feminist politics, yet it is clear from the practices of the community that their activities are at least implicitly informed by issues which have been central to feminist critiques of technology and of popular culture. They have deployed a sometimes contradictory feminist discourse in the articulation of their relationship to the game culture in general; they have produced web sites, web pages and formed clans through which to enunciate their outsider status in the naming of these clans and the imagery which inspires their skins. Their activities are analogous to other kinds of feminist practice where separate space is deemed important for the critical work of developing a network and supporting other women. They make use of language derived from feminist debates through which to describe their experiences and to critique the representation and treatment of women in computer games and computer games culture. I would argue that women who take pleasure in and contribute to popular games culture contribute significantly to the democratization of technology and technological competence in a way which elitist/artist interventions can rarely hope to achieve. Popular games culture is made up of a heterogeneous range of players, practices and pleasures and it is *the* crucial site where dominant notions of technology, gender and technological competence are both constructed, negotiated and contested.

Notes

1 The concept of technicity is used here to encapsulate taste, technological competence and the use of technology as a means through which to form and express individual and group identities. For a fuller discussion of this see Dovey and Kennedy 2006.

2 (*Quake III: Arena* and *Quake III Gold* are the most popular iterations offering this online facility with *Quake IV* yet to establish a particularly large online following.)

3 For a useful account of the shareware ethos of early games distribution see King and Borland (2003). For an account of how this ethos specifically informed the practices at *id* see Kushner (2003).

4 See Giddings and Kennedy 2006b for a fuller exploration of these processes in relation to playing *Lego Star Wars*.

5 Camilla Bennett was interviewed via email over the period between January 2001 and August 2002.

6 See her work online at www.chiq.net, accessed April 2006.

7 An amusing example is The Partridge Family *Quake* Clan, www.geocities.com/Area51/Cavern/2690, accessed April 2006.

8 Planet *Quake* www.planetquake.com is perhaps the most important example of the latter.
9 I am grateful to 'Xena' for drawing my attention to this campaign and for providing links to archived responses that were sparked by the campaign. Unfortunately most of these links are broken.
10 See Taylor (2003) for a discussion of this in relation to *Everquest* players.

Works cited

Aarseth, Espen (1997) *Cybertext: Perspectives on Ergodic Literature*, Baltimore: Johns Hopkins University Press.
Baym, Nancy (2000) *Tune in, Log on: Soaps, Fandom and Online Community*, London: Sage.
Butler, Judith (1997) *The Psychic Life of Power: Theories in Subjection*, Stanford: Stanford University Press.
—(1992) 'Contingent Foundations: Feminism and the Question of "Postmodernism"', in Judith Butler and Joan Scott (eds) *Feminists Theorize the Political*, London: Routledge.
Cassell J. and H. Jenkins (eds) (1998) *From Barbie to Mortal Kombat: Gender and Computer Games*, Cambridge, MA: MIT Press.
Douglas, Nikki (2006) 'The Future of Games Does Not Include Women', April 2006, www.grrlgamer.com/article.php?t=futureofgames, accessed April 2006.
—(2000) 'Uncommon Me', in www.grrlgamer.com, available at www.grrlgamer.com/gamergrrl04.html, accessed February 2002.
Dovey, Jonathan and Helen Kennedy (2006) *Game Cultures: Computer Games as New Media*, Milton Keynes: Open University Press/McGraw Hill.
Flanagan, Mary (2003) '"Next Level": Women's Digital Activism through Gaming', in Gunnar Liestol, Andrew Morrison, Terje Rasmussen (eds) *Digital Media Revisited: Theoretical and Conceptual Innovations in Digital Domains*, Cambridge, MA: MIT Press.
Giddings, Seth and Helen Kennedy (2007 forthcoming) '"Little Jesuses" and "Fuck-off Robots": Aesthetics, Cybernetics, and Not Being Very Good at *Lego Star Wars*', in M. Swalwell and J. Wilson (eds) *Gameplay: Pleasures, Engagements, Aesthetics*, Jefferson, NC: McFarland & Co.
—(2006) 'Digital Games as New Media', in Jason Rutter and Joanne Bryce (eds) *Understanding Digital Games*, London: Sage.
Haraway, Donna (1992) 'Ecce Homo, Ain't (Aren't) I a Woman and Inappropriate/d Others: The Human in the Post Humanist Landscape', in Judith Butler and Joan Scott (eds) *Feminists Theorize the Political*, London: Routledge.
—(1991) 'Situated Knowledges: The Science Question in Feminism and the Privilege of Partial Perspective', in Haraway (ed.) *Simians, Cyborgs and Women: The Reinvention of Nature*, London: Free Association Books.
—(1990) 'A Manifesto for Cyborgs: Science, Technology, and Socialist Feminism in the 1980s', in Linda J. Nicholson (ed.) *Feminism/Postmodernism*, London: Routledge.
—(1987) 'Contested Bodies', in Maureen McNeil (ed.) *Gender and Expertise*, London: Free Association Books.
King, Brad and John Borland (2003) *Dungeons and Dreamers: The Rise of Computer Game Culture from Geek to Chic*, San Francisco, CA: McGraw Hill/Osborne.
Kushner, David (2003) *Masters of Doom: How Two Guys Created an Empire and Transformed Pop Culture*, London: Piatkus.
Lahti, Martti (2003) 'As We Become Machines: Corporealized Pleasures in Video Games', in Mark J.P. Wolf and Bernard Perron (eds) *The Video Game Theory Reader*, London: Routledge.
Laurel, Brenda (1998) Keynote Address given at CHI 98 conference 'New Players New Games', available online at www.Tauzero.com, accessed 20 March 2004.
Lister et al. (eds) (2003) *New Media: A Critical Introduction*, London: Routledge.
Marriott, Michel (2003) 'Fighting Women Enter the Arena, No Holds Barred', *New York Times*, 15 May 2003.
Morris, Pam (ed.) (1994) *The Bakhtin Reader: Selected Writings of Bakhtin, Medvedev and Voloshinov*, London: Edward Arnold.
Morris, Sue (2003) 'Wads, Bots and Mots: Multiplayer FPS Games as Co Creative Media', *Level Up – Digital Games Research Conference Proceedings*, Utrecht: University of Utrecht/DIGRA (CD ROM).
Plant, Sadie (1993) 'The Future Looms: Weaving, Women and Cybernetics', *Broad Sheet*, 22:3, 12–16.
Schleiner, Anne-Marie (1999) 'An Underworld Game Patch Router to Female Monsters, Frag Queens and Bobs whose First Name is Betty', available at www.opensorcery.net/mutetext.html, accessed 11 September 2003.

Tasker, Yvonne (1993) *Spectacular Bodies: Gender, Genre and the Action Cinema*, London: Routledge.
Taylor, T.L. (2003) 'Multiple Pleasures: Women and Online Gaming', *Convergence*, 9:1, 21–46.
—(1999) 'Life in Virtual Worlds: Plural Existence, Multimodalities, and Other Online Research Challenges', *American Behavioral Scientist*, 43:3, 436–449.
Wearing, Betsy (1998) *Leisure and Feminist Theory*, London: Sage.

Games

Quake (1996), id Software.
Quake II (1997), id Software, Activision.
Quake III: Arena (1999), id Software, Activision.
Unreal Tournament (1999), Epic Games, GT Interactive.

PART FOUR

Texts, forms, codes

THE WORK OF MEDIA STUDIES and related disciplines such as film studies could be roughly split into three main modes of attention: towards media audiences through various forms of theoretical and ethnographic research; towards the political economy of media production and the culture industry; and towards media texts – films, television programmes, newspapers – through textual or discourse analysis. The first of these modes, audiences and the contexts of new media consumption, is addressed in Part Six, the second, political economy and media production, is touched on in this part (**Consentino**, **Klein**, and see also Part 3 of *New Media: A Critical Introduction*). The concern of Part Four is the challenges new media make to this third mode of enquiry, the study of new media texts. For, whilst popular new media remediate the 'old' media on which media and film studies were based, and hence their established analytical approaches still have some purchase, they are in important ways quite different and require different critical resources.

Each of the extracts in this part is in some way concerned with the aesthetic, textual or formalist characteristics of the media they are analysing. These media include film, computer games, digital music and photography. Each however, in different ways, foregrounds the specificity of these new media as digital, computer-based media, connecting their formal and aesthetic elements with technical and material considerations. In the extract by Lev **Manovich** it is the shift in the production and construction of the moving image from the century-old basis in narrative to one in the computer logic of the database. For Mark **Katz**, the experience of listening to recorded music is transformed by its digitization, portability and the networked culture of sharing and download. Whereas for David **Sudnow**, the analysis of the animated screen images on his television set generated by a videogame console is not motivated by media studies' ideology critique or issues of representation, but by an embodied imperative to decode the game as an interactive system and to develop the cognitive skills and dexterity to compete adequately with the machine.

If media studies has historically been primarily concerned with what images and sounds *mean*, how they mediate political information, represent or challenge dominant cultural worldviews and ideologies, then the media analyses in this part, it could be argued, are more concerned with what these images and sounds *do*, and how they do it. Espen **Aarseth**'s concept of cybertext is a clear example of this. By demanding of its reader (or player) 'non-trivial work', the cybertext, such as a work of hypertext fiction or a text-based computer game, demands at least an implicit acknowledgement of its machinic structure and operations, before any questions about its particular 'content' or message can be addressed. Structures, and forms integral to the material functioning of digital media, and concepts that account for them, such as interactivity (**Lévy**) and virtuality (**Woolley**, **Marks**), originate in computer science rather than in the techniques and processes of popular media production. So, conceptual frameworks and modes of analysis need to be adapted and developed.

We could go further and argue that the emphasis within the dominant discourses of cultural and media studies on a linguistic or textual model of culture and communication is key to the shortcomings of their attention to new media and technoculture. The model of communication as one of encoding a message (at the moment of production of a media 'text') and of its decoding (at the moment of consumption) that underpins mainstream cultural and media studies, is inadequate for the analysis of popular digital media and software. This emphasis on the textual tends to elide the fundamentally *material* nature of culture and communication in general, and doesn't allow for an understanding of digital media use as irreducibly technological and embodied.

Chapter 20

BENJAMIN WOOLLEY

VIRTUALITY

L IKE ALL THINGS 'cyber-', the word 'virtual' has been very widely and loosely applied to pretty much anything to do with computers and computer culture. At the time that Benjamin Woolley's book was published, the early 1990s, there was a great deal of excitement and rather frenzied speculation about the possibilities of virtual reality technologies to transform media, media experience and everyday life. The vision of new worlds into which we could step when equipped with datagloves and head-mounted displays was extolled in popular film (*The Lawnmower Man, Johnny Mnemonic*), and by journalists and academics. It was a vivid and intense example of a technological imaginary, shaping ideas about new media and promising radical transformations of media and everyday life.

We have selected this extract because of Woolley's attention to the *reality* of virtual technologies, their histories in computer research and development, and his charting of the connections between these actual existing technologies and the ideas, concepts and mathematics that attended them. Whilst the fevered dreams of fully immersive technologies or even of the abandonment of the body as we 'upload' our consciousness into computer networks may seem ridiculous today, virtual realities have become commonplace everyday media experiences. Millions of people play online games such as *World of Warcraft*, exploring 3D immersive worlds and constructing virtual communities with geographically remote players and NPCs (see **Kember** and **Kennedy**). Millions or billions connect daily through the mundane cyberspaces of Internet media such as email, chat and social networking (**Katz**, **Slater**). The notion of the virtual, as that which is nearly but not quite real or as a reality that is distinct from, but thoroughly entwined with, a reality that is physical or actual, is crucial to understanding the synthetic and everyday worlds of new media use and play.

See also: N. Katherine Hayles 'Virtual Bodies and Flickering Signifiers': http://www.english. ucla.edu/faculty/hayles/Flick.html

'IBM launched a product/concept called "virtual memory" way back in the '70s with panoramic ads showing the silhouette of a city skyline with the caption "a new day is dawning"', wrote a one-time salesman for the electronics company Ferranti in 1991. 'This irritated me because 11 years previously Ferranti had brought out the same idea of swapping pages of memory out of store and disk and had called it "paging."'[1] If it was my choice, I know which word I would prefer. 'Paging' is what bellboys do in hotel foyers. 'Virtual' was and remains a much grander word, scandalously underused, a huge vessel of semantic vacuity waiting to have meaning poured into it. Computing has provided some of that meaning, initially a quite modest meaning, but increasingly a cargo worthy of its carrier.

IBM introduced 'virtual memory' with two new mainframe computers, the 370/158 and 370/168 systems, introduced in August 1972. By the stage of their launch, IBM had established itself as the dominant supplier of the world's computing power. The 360 range of machines, introduced in 1964, had become a symbol of American corporatism, the foundation of centralized, mechanized, depersonalized multinational companies and state utilities, the purveyors of payrolls and bills. The '360' designation was, according to evidence submitted to one of the many antimonopoly suites brought against IBM, a reference to the number of degrees on the compass, reflecting the machine's all-encompassing nature – which, at least in terms of global market penetration, it certainly achieved.[2] The 370 range would, by the same logic, suggest an all-encompassing ambition beyond even IBM. In a sense, however, 'virtual memory' was designed to perform just such a trick. The idea, as the disgruntled Ferranti salesman suggested, was not new; it had been explored as a method of overcoming one of the main constraints of computer design.

The constraint was memory. 'Memory' is the rather grand, perhaps misleadingly anthropomorphic, term for the technology used to store information for computer processing. There are two sorts of memory, sometimes simply known as fast and slow. Fast memory is the sort accessed by the computer's processor, the electronics that perform the computations, directly. Slow memory is for keeping information that is not needed immediately and for which there is not enough room in fast memory. Fast memory tends to be electronic, once an array of magnetic 'cores' (some diehard computer users still call it 'core memory'), now a tiny silicon chip. Slow memory tends to be electro-mechanic, taking the form of disks and tape.

At the time IBM was developing its 370 range, fast memory suffered from two main constraints: it was expensive and bulky. This limited its capacity and, in turn, limited the size of computer programs and amount of data the computer could process at any one time. The aim of virtual memory was to create more room in fast memory than was actually provided by the computer's physical memory circuits. The system would then make up the difference by invisibly swapping segments or 'pages' (hence the alternative term 'paging') of information from slow into fast memory as and when they are needed. It is a system familiar in other walks of life. A shop, for example, does not have its entire stock behind the counter, but 'swaps' goods in and out of the stockroom in accordance to customer demand. Of course, such a system has its limitations: there will be unanticipated requests for slower-moving goods not usually stored on the shop's shelves, forcing the shopkeeper either to disappoint the customer or rummage around in the stockroom. Similarly a program running in virtual memory will occasionally be caught by an unexpected request for some information that has not been moved into fast memory, forcing a delay in the system while the program attempts to collect the appropriate page of information from disk. But at least such a system means the shopkeeper can sell more goods than will physically fit on the shop's shelves, and the computer program can manipulate more information than will fit into the system's fast memory. The term 'virtual' cleverly captured the status of paged memory. The fact that virtual memory is not real memory is a mere technicality; from the point of view of the computer and its user, virtual memory is just as real as actual memory. It is a simulation of a physical system that is perfect in every detail, except that it might be slower than 'real' memory.

'Virtual' has a respectable pedigree as a technical term, going right back to the origins of modern science. It was used in optics at the beginning of the eighteenth century to describe the refracted or reflected image of an object. By the beginning of the nineteenth century, physicists were writing of a particle's 'virtual velocity' and 'virtual moment'. The word is still used in physics to describe the exotic behaviour of subatomic particles that appear so fleetingly they cannot be detected. It has come a long way from its original use as the adjectival form of 'virtue', in the days when virtue itself meant to have the power of God. Echoes of that early meaning, however, survive in the excitable claims of virtual realists to have the power to create their own worlds. And it is appropriate that the word should resonate with a certain amount of divine significance, because the computing concept of 'virtual' is much more than a matter of mere technology. It means something that goes to the scientific heart of reality.

Every computer is virtual, each one a shadow of one machine, a machine specified, though not built, in 1936 by the British mathematician Alan Turing in a paper entitled 'On computable numbers'.[3] The temptation is to say that Turing's paper was a turning point in the intellectual history of our times, but it was published in a period when every point was being turned. A reliable, scientific basis of knowledge was simultaneously being constructed and destroyed. Turing's paper was part of this process, helping to reinforce breakthroughs that had left much broken.

The foundations of mathematics seemed pretty secure after Isaac Newton had demonstrated their ability to describe the machinery of the universe. They needed no underpinning when, at the beginning of the nineteenth century, the French mathematician Pierre Laplace proclaimed that, given adequate knowledge about the state of 'all the forces by which nature is animated and the respective situations of the beings who compose it – an intelligence sufficiently vast to submit these data to analysis – it would embrace in the same formula the movements of the greatest bodies and those of the lightest atom; for it, nothing would be uncertain and the future, as the past, would be present to its eyes'.[4] Poor old Pierre has since had to take the rap for excessive scientific hubris – 'Laplacian', it is called. No one now believes, of course, that such a perfect knowledge of the universe would be possible. His timing could have been better, too. At around the same time he was proclaiming that the scientific theorists could pack up and leave the job to the measurers and quantifiers, Carl Friedrich Gauss, a mathematician ranked by some alongside Archimedes and Newton,[5] published his *Disquisitions*, which demonstrated a method for constructing shapes that could not be described using Euclid's geometry, the first sign that classical and undisputed laws stretching back to the third century BC might not be the end of the matter.

By the beginning of the twentieth century, mathematics had changed out of all recognition. It was no longer just a branch of science, a means of measuring and counting physical phenomena. It had become an apparently self-contained system for manipulating its own symbols, one that operated quite separately from the real world. As Andrew Hodges, a mathematician and biographer of Alan Turing, put it: 'A rule such as "x + y = y + x" could be regarded as a rule for a game, as in chess, stating how the symbols could be moved around and combined legitimately. The rule might possibly be *interpreted* in terms of numbers, but it would not be necessary nor indeed always appropriate to do so.'[6]

Peeling away mathematics from physical reality was liberating on the one hand – it meant that it was no longer the servant of science but the master of itself – but robbed it at the same time of its authority. If it was no longer a means of describing physical reality, what was it for? What truth did it tell?

* * *

Our language betrays an uncomplicated attitude to space. Space is two-dimensional: we have revolutions, go round in circles, get straight to the point, square up. The most sophisticated geometric shape to make it into everyday language is, thanks to the US military, the pentagon.

Spheres of influence are rare examples of a linguistic acknowledgement of the third dimension. In mathematics, however, space is treated very differently. Physical space is merely one three-dimensional (four, if you count time) version of it. Mathematical space is more like a graph, but a multidimensional one in which there are as many axes as there are properties to be plotted. Chess, for example, can be thought of as the universe of all legal chess moves, and a particular game a path through that space.

It was David Hilbert who formalized this concept of abstract space. In the process, as though almost by accident, he provided a means of explaining the very unreal phenomena displayed by newly discovered subatomic particles such as electrons. Such particles behave very strangely, at least as mapped in physical space. But, the Hungarian-American mathematician John von Neumann, the man credited with developing the basic design principles of all modern computers, noticed that a far clearer picture of how these particles behaved resulted from putting them, so to speak, in Hilbert space. It was as though they belonged more comfortably there than they did in physical space.

Von Neumann's discovery was an astonishing vindication of the power of abstract mathematics. It seemed to demonstrate that abstract mathematics underlay physical reality, not the other way round. What, then, underlay abstract mathematics? What gave it the right to claim access to the truth?

In 1900, David Hilbert gave a speech to the International Congress of Mathematicians in Paris. Equal to the moment and location, Hilbert challenged his peers to solve the outstanding problems in mathematics – indeed, being the mathematician he was, he even enumerated them, counting 23 in all. The second of these was concerned with the basis of mathematics itself. The Italian logician Guiseppe Peano had worked out what he saw as the foundations of mathematics by formulating them as a series of laws or 'axioms' based on logic. Hilbert asked how anyone could be sure that such axioms did not produce an inconsistency. They had failed to reveal one so far – mathematics was apparently 'clean' – but there was no proof, no guarantee that there might not be some inconsistency which might be operating hidden in the background, or which might emerge in the future as mathematics became yet more complex.

The importance of this problem lay not only in its concern for consistency. It also raised the issue of the nature of mathematics itself. Was it 'axiomatic'? In other words, are there a set of basic principles from which all mathematics is derived? And if so, where do those principles come from? At the turn of the century, the proposed answer to the last question was that the principles came from logic.

Being a branch of philosophy, the purpose of logic is the subject of some debate. At its most confident, it is claimed to be about establishing the structure of knowledge and reasoning. It established, for example, that statements of the form 'if p and q then q' (as in 'if it is true to say that it is hot and sunny, then it is true to say that it is sunny') are always true. Like mathematics, logic is abstract and uses symbols. The idea of using it to provide the basis of mathematics was too tempting to ignore, and at the turn of the century, a number of philosophers, notably Bertrand Russell and Alfred North Whitehead, worked away feverishly to achieve this, in the hope of thereby creating a complete, consistent system of pure knowledge.

The aim of making mathematics 'pure', purging it of the uncertainties of physical reality, intensified in the churning wake of the First World War. In the early 1930s, a group of France's finest young mathematicians set up a secret club to publish a mathematical treatise under the collective nom de plume Nicolas Bourbaki, a name of obscure origins, perhaps in part a black joke about the French general Charles Bourbaki who led a disastrous campaign in the Franco-Prussian War that resulted in the death of 10,000 men. Among the club's founding membership were some important names of twentieth-century mathematics, including one Szolem

Did this after thousands of math ppl died from war

Mandelbrojt who, as we shall later see, also had close ties with a mathematician who probably represents the polar opposite of Bourbakist purity.

Mourning the loss of a generation of mathematicians killed by the war, impatient with the older professors who were left to instruct them, the Bourbakists decided to embark on a project to produce a definitive text of mathematical knowledge, the *Eléments de Mathématiques*, that would survive any future cataclysm. They no longer wanted their beloved subject to rely for its record on the frailty of human memory. They wanted to provide an indestructible account of mathematical knowledge relying on abstract principles and formal proofs.

The same motives underlay Hilbert's restatement at the 1928 International Congress of Mathematicians of the need for some eternal, undeniable validation. As well as being consistent, maths, he demanded, must be 'complete' and 'decidable': every mathematical statement must be provable or disprovable, it should admit of no 'don't knows', and there must be a definite procedure – an algorithm – for establishing whether or not it is true.

Hilbert only made such demands because he confidently expected that they could be met. 'There is no such thing as an unsolvable problem.'[7] Unfortunately, fate yielded to the temptation. Just three years later, the Czech-born mathematician Kurt Gödel published a paper entitled 'On formally undecidable propositions of *Principia Mathematica* and related systems'. The title said it all, or at least most of it: by 'related systems', Gödel meant all those that Hilbert was calling upon his colleagues to develop, indeed any system that attempted to fulfil Hilbert's criterion of completeness.

Gödel's method for puncturing Hilbert's optimism was itself a brilliant exercise in abstraction. He developed a 'theorem' demonstrating that any usable axiomatic system – the sort of system that was supposed to give mathematics its power over truth and falsehood – would not be able to prove or disprove every statement it could express. As a test case, he began by examining ways of formulating the axioms of arithmetic as a set of numbers, so the axioms themselves became part of the system they underpinned. What he discovered was that such a system would generate statements that referred to themselves, including statements of the form 'this statement is unprovable' (only, of course, the statement would be a set of symbols, a formula, not a sentence), which is false if proved true, and true if proved false. This discovery destroyed at a stroke all hopes of creating a self-sustaining mathematical system. Gödel had shown that, to establish the 'truth' of such a system, there had, at some point, to be an appeal to an outside authority, human, divine, whatever.

Argued – against Hilbert

* * *

In 1928, Bertrand Russell wrote: 'Machines are worshipped because they are beautiful, and valued because they confer power; they are hated because they are hideous, and loathed because they impose slavery.'[8] In 1936, Charlie Chaplin's *Modern Times* was released. It was a film that captured the ambiguous attitude to the 'machine age' of the prewar years, an attitude that has persisted well into the latter part of the century. Chaplin both submitted to technology – it was his first talkie – and attacked its dehumanizing influence. That same year saw the publication of 'On computable numbers'. In it, Turing disposed of the last of Hilbert's original criterion for establishing the validity of a mathematical system, that of decidability.

Turing against Hilbert

His technique was to construct a hypothetical machine, one very like a typewriter, but with a strip of paper replacing the ribbon, a mechanism for moving the strip in both directions one space at a time, a print head for printing marks on the strip and a scanner for reading marks off it. The machine could perform what sounded like quite sophisticated functions, such as recognizing particular patterns of marks, and looking up the pattern in a 'table of behaviour' to see what it should do next. In fact, the actual mechanisms needed to perform such functions could easily be implemented using standard mechanics – it would not be necessary even to use electronics. A fully operational Turing machine, were one to be built based on the design specification outlined in his original paper, would be of the same order of complexity as a typewriter or a chiming clock.

The 'table of behaviour', rather than the particular design of any components, was the key to the machine; indeed, it was the machine. For example, Turing showed that there was a table of behaviour that would turn the machine into an adding machine. Similarly, it could be turned into a machine that performed any of the basic operations of arithmetic. It followed, therefore, that there was a table, or set of tables, that could be drawn up to calculate any number that was calculable or, in Turing's chosen terminology, 'computable'. This table would perform the work without the need for any human intervention using a purely mechanical, 'algorithmic' procedure that would eventually yield a result. It was this hypothetical machine that enabled Turing to show that not all numbers could be computed, which in turn meant Hilbert's last criterion could not be met: there was no definite method that could solve every mathematical problem.

Strangely, even though Hilbert's project had been well and truly destroyed, and the work of logicians like Bertrand Russell had been abandoned, the underlying faith in the foundations of mathematics, the idea that it was somehow a pure expression of truth, persisted. It was more than just a 'game', because it submitted itself to the judgement of the most fundamental principles of logic. Gödel and Turing based the validity of their arguments on logical principles: they had shown up contradictions, and logic does not allow such things.

Ludwig Wittgenstein, the Cambridge philosopher whose ideas were as wild as his eyes, was not impressed by this reliance on the tenets of a formal logic system. Three years after the publication of 'On computable numbers', Turing attended a series of lectures given by Wittgenstein on the philosophy of mathematics, in which the latter set about undermining Turing's faith in the necessity to discover 'hidden contradictions'. Hilbert had said: 'No one is going to turn us out of the paradise which Cantor has created', the paradise of mathematical purity. Wittgenstein responded: 'I wouldn't dream of trying to drive anyone out of this paradise. I would do something quite different; I would try to show you that it is not a paradise.'[9]

Turing, however, was convinced he was in Eden, which was why his mathematics had to remain uncontaminated from even the possibility of contradiction. Wittgenstein, on the other hand, wondered what damage contradiction could do. 'You cannot be confident about applying your calculus until you know there is no hidden contradiction there', said Turing. Wittgenstein replied that all contradiction would do would be to stop you applying the calculus, because it would simply fail to work. It would not produce a wrong result, it would not produce any result at all. The two kept up this ding-dong debate until Turing finally stopped attending. The fact that the issues they argued over were never resolved – or even, one could argue, clearly defined – was a symptom of a growing impatience with the need to consider the foundations or philosophy of mathematics. The debate seemed no longer to matter, and it dropped from the mathematical agenda. Only in the 1990s was it to return as a matter of significance, restored to its former position by the emergence of virtual reality.

In 1939, it was the world that mattered, not paradise. Turing's ideas were revealing themselves to have very practical significance. The idea of the Turing machine's tables of behaviour suggested that there was a way of formally describing any machine that could perform any computation: in other words, every computer is, in the end, a Turing 'table of behaviour'. This both put formal limits on what could be computed (there will never be the invention of some supercomputer that can compute the uncomputable) and, on the positive side, showed that it was possible to construct a machine to perform any computation.

The discovery that there could be a computer that could compute any computable number does not sound like the most shattering intellectual advance. But that is because we have got used to the idea of the computer. In 1936, it meant a person. Following Turing's insight, it meant a machine: he had proved, in other words, that it was possible to mechanize what had previously only been possible by means of mental effort. The machine had crossed a critical barrier. Before, machines had taken over the body, now they threatened to take over the mind.

What, though, did this machine produce? Nothing of material significance; just numbers. What use was a machine that just produced numbers? Obviously, it could be used to perform calculations. But the development of calculating machines had no need of Turing's theoretical designs. All the mechanisms required to perform any basic arithmetical function were well known by the late 1930s, so the building of a machine capable of computing any computable number was already a practical possibility. Turing had shown that some numbers were uncomputable, which was interesting, maybe even useful, but unlikely to change the course of technological history. Turing's insight, however, did much more than just establish the limits of mechanical calculation. It introduced the idea of the universal machine, a machine that can be lots of different machines; in fact, a machine that is capable of being any machine capable of performing a computation.

The idea of an abstract, immaterial machine is a difficult one, as paradoxical now as it must have seemed when it was first introduced. A mechanism needs moving parts, cogs and wheels, components, in order to work. So, it was perhaps unsurprising that when personal computers were first introduced to the shops, no one could quite work out what they would do. Writers, for example, started to express an interest in buying a 'word processor', by which they meant a machine for writing, editing and printing text that would replace their typewriter. They did not want a computer, even one that would run a word processing software package. So, to ease the confusion, a number of manufacturers started marketing computers as high-tech typewriters called word processors, even though they were, in fact, standard personal computers and could, like other personal computers, run other software turning them into different sorts of machines: machines for compiling and maintaining business accounts, for example. Such confusion was not the result of a lack of computer 'literacy'. No amount of IT training and hands-on experience can help. It was the result of what the philosopher Gilbert Ryle called a 'category mistake', a mixing up of things belonging to incompatible logical categories, like saying 'the universe is bigger than the number three'.

Category mistakes, though basic, are easy to make. A visitor to Oxford who, having been shown all the college buildings, asks where the university is, has made one. Ryle's aim in identifying this sort of mistake was, as we shall see, to exorcise what he famously described as the dogma of the 'ghost in the machine'. He wanted to show that the concept of 'mind' had the same confused relation to the body as the visitor's concept of 'university' had to the buildings he visited. Calling a piece of physical machinery a 'word processor' – or even a 'computer' – could be described as just such a category mistake. For practical purposes, it is a mistake that can be patched over, because any conceptual problems it might produce can be sidestepped by adopting the distinction between hardware and software. Hardware is the physical object, we are told, and software the list of commands that tell it what to do. Hardware determines certain characteristics, like speed, while software determines others, like function.

But the hardware/software distinction does not work all that well when applied with any theoretical rigour. A Turing machine, for example, can be simulated on another computer using software. But it can also be built (quite easily: all you need is some tape, a little circuitry and a couple of lamps) in hardware. And there is no difference between what the software and the hardware versions can do, they will be functionally identical. Neither would be very effective computers, but computers they would nevertheless both be.

There is a solution to this conceptual confusion, and it lies in the adoption of that word 'virtual'. A computer is a 'virtual' machine – a virtual Turing machine, to be precise. It is an abstract entity or process that has found physical expression, that has been 'realized'. It is a simulation, only not necessarily a simulation of anything actual.

Using a computer gives some experience of what 'virtual' really means. Personal computer users generally become comfortable with the idea of the system being at once a word processor, a calculator, a drawing pad, a reference library, a spelling checker. If they pulled their system apart, or the disks that contain the software, they would find no sign of any of these things, any more than the dismemberment of an IBM 370 would reveal all that extra memory provided by the virtual memory system. They are purely abstract entities, in being independent of any particular physical embodiment, but real nonetheless. 'Virtual', then, is a mode of simulated existence resulting from computation. Computers are virtual, not actual, entities.

Some readers may have noticed that in my attempts to reach down to the conceptual principles of computing, the one idea that remains unexamined is that of 'information'. Since computing is sometimes called 'information technology', this may seem to be a rather perverse omission. Much is made of the idea of information in discussions about the origins of computing. Specifically, Claude Shannon's and Warren Weaver's 1949 book *The Mathematical Theory of Communications* is cited. In developing his communications theory, Shannon used the concept of information to mean any communicated message, regardless of its meaning. This was an important insight, because it meant that it was possible to examine the problems of communicating a message, of distinguishing 'signal' (the original message) from 'noise' (interference), without resorting to semantics – what the sender of the message meant, and what the receiver of the message understood by it.

In *Mind Tools*, a book about the 'mathematics of information', Rudy Rucker wrote: 'the concept of information currently resists any really precise definition. Relative to information we are in a condition something like the condition of 17th century scientists regarding energy. We know there is an important concept here, a concept with many manifestations, but we do not yet know how to talk about it in exactly the right way'.[10] There is another possible explanation. Widened out by Shannon's definition, the word is communicating less and less – we have lost the signal. There is information 'space', information 'anxiety', information 'overload', even an information 'age'. In the first, we seem (this is just a rough guess) to be talking about something a bit like Hilbert space, in the second, a concern that we cannot deal with the amount of information from TV and newspapers, in the third the result of failing to heed our information anxiety, in the fourth, the observation that people talk about 'information' a lot these days. Money, phone calls, an architectural model, the smell of rose petals, pi, 'Stairway to heaven' by Led Zeppelin, DNA and the light of a distant star are all information. What does that tell us about them? Lumping them together in this way tends to serve more to hide than reveal important distinctions. For that reason, I suspect that information will not yield to definition because its meaning has become so indefinite. 'Information', wrote Theodore Roszak,[11] 'has taken on the quality of that impalpable, invisible, but plaudit-winning silk from which the emperor's ethereal gown was supposedly spun.' Look, and you find nothing there.

This is why I prefer words like 'virtual', 'abstract', 'mathematical' and 'computable'. We have to understand that a computer is a machine that performs a very precise function – mathematical computation. It can do no more. But that is a great deal, because there seems to be an underlying mathematical structure to everything that has been successfully analysed by science. 'Philosophy is written in that great book which ever lies before our eyes, I mean the universe,' wrote Galileo in 1623, 'but we cannot understand it if we do not first learn the language and grasp the symbols in which it is written. This book is written in the mathematical language, and the symbols are triangles, circles, and other geometrical figures, without whose help it is humanly impossible to comprehend a single word of it.'[12] This language is more than just information. It has the important and unique quality of being computable; it can be written by a machine. Maybe the universe is not a book so much as a computer, everything that exists within it the product of some algorithm. If so, this would mean that Turing's universal machine would truly be universal: given the right table of behaviour, and sufficient time, it could reproduce an entire virtual universe. Never mind flight simulators; how about world simulators?

Notes

1 Richard Sarson, 'A nominal way to achieve greatness', *PC Week*, 30 April 1991, p. 9.
2 Richard Thomas DeLamarter, *Big Blue: IBM's use and abuse of power*, London: Macmillan, 1987, p. 59.
3 Alan Turing, 'On computable numbers with an application to the entscheidungs problem', *Proceedings London Mathematical Society*, July 1937, 42, pp. 230–65.
4 Pierre Simon Laplace, *Essai sur les probabilitiés*, in Andrew Hodges, *Alan Turing: the enigma of intelligence*, London: Unwin Paperbacks, 1985, p. 64.
5 Stuart Hollingdale, *Makers of Mathematics*, London: Penguin, 1989, p. 312.
6 Hodges, 1985, p. 81.
7 In Hodges, 1985, p. 92.
8 Bertrand Russell, *Sceptical Essays*, 1928, in Tony Augarde (ed.) *The Oxford Dictionary of Modern Quotations*, Oxford: Oxford University Press, 1991.
9 Ray Monk, *Ludwig Wittgenstein*, London: Jonathan Cape, 1990, p. 416.
10 Rudy Rucker, *Mind Tools*, London: Penguin, 1988, p. 26.
11 Theodore Roszak, *The Cult of Information*, Cambridge: Lutterworth, 1986, p. ix.
12 In John D. Barrow, *The World Within the World*, Oxford: Oxford University Press, 1988, p. 8.

Chapter 21

PIERRE LÉVY

INTERACTIVITY

'INTERACTIVITY' HAS PROVED to be one of the most widely and vaguely used words in the description, criticism and marketing of new media. Though dismissed by some critics precisely because of this analytical vagueness and commercial taint, it could be argued that it persists because it, however loosely, points to a significant characteristic distinguishing key digital media from earlier popular or communication forms. In this short extract, Pierre Lévy offers what he calls a *problematic* approach to the concept of interactivity, and tabulates different types according to the temporal dimension of the mode of interactive communication and the hierarchical relationship between the communicators. Whilst his table does not exhaust the possible configurations of interactive processes (and its assumption of the higher value of human over non-human participants could be questioned), it allows us to think about the differences and continuities between analogue and digital communication media. For example, mail, the telephone and virtual worlds are all situated on the axis of *dialogue* and *reciprocity* but differ according the temporal organisation of, and possibilities for material involvement in, their respective communication systems. The table also opens up the concept of interactivity according to its actual uses and operations rather than ideological assumptions of new modes of activity (or passivity).

[. . .]

Interactivity as problem

Because interactivity is so often misrepresented, as if everyone knew exactly what it was about, in this short chapter I'd like to offer instead a *problematic* approach to the concept.

The term "interactivity" generally refers to the active participation of the beneficiary of an information transaction. Indeed, we would be hard-pressed to demonstrate that an information receiver—unless dead—is ever passive. Even seated in front of a television without a remote control, the recipient decodes, interprets, participates, and mobilizes her nervous system in a hundred different ways, and always somewhat differently than the person sitting next to her. Satellites and cable provide access to hundreds of different channels. Linked to a VCR, this enables the viewer to put together a video library and define a televisual system that is obviously more "interactive" than a single TV channel alone. The possibility of material reappropriation and recombination of the message by a receiver is a significant factor in evaluating the degree of interactivity of a device. The same is true of other media: can we add nodes and links to a hyperdocument? Can we connect this hyperdocument to others? With television, digitization could further enhance the opportunities for reappropriating and personalizing the message by shifting editorial functions to the user: choice of camera, use of zoom, shifting between image and commentary, selection of commentators.

Does this mean that in an interactive environment, the communications channel operates in both directions? In this case, the paragon of an interactive medium would unquestionably be the telephone. It supplies dialogue, reciprocity, and real communication, whereas television, even digital TV, which can be navigated and recorded, provides only entertainment. Even a classic video game is more interactive than television, although the game doesn't really provide reciprocity or communication with another person. Far from an uninterruptible stream of images rolling across the screen, the video game reacts to the player's actions, and the player reacts in turn to the images before him: interaction. The TV viewer zaps and selects; the player acts. Yet the ability to interrupt an information sequence and accurately reorient the information flow in real time is not just a characteristic of video games and digital hyperdocuments; it's also a characteristic of the telephone. Only in one case we're speaking to another person, and in the other with an information matrix, a model capable of generating an almost infinite number of "parties" or different paths (all of which are coherent). In this case, interactivity is a lot like virtuality.

Let's look at the differences between games and the telephone from another angle. To compare apples with apples, I'll assume that a networked game enables two adversaries to play against each other. This arrangement maximizes the similarity between the game and the telephone. In the video game, each player, equipped with a joystick, data gloves, or some other device, modifies *his own image in the game space*. The character tries to dodge a shell, move toward a goal, explore a passage, win or lose weapons, powers, "lives." It is this modified image of the reactualized character that then modifies, in logical time, the game space itself. The player isn't fully involved in the game unless he projects himself into the character that represents him and, therefore, into the field of danger, force, and opportunity in which he exists, within the shared virtual world. With each "move," the player transmits to his partner a different image of himself and a different image of their shared world, images the partner receives directly (or can discover through exploration) and is immediately affected by. The message is a doubled image incorporating the situation and the player.

During a telephone call, however, speaker A transmits to speaker B a message that is supposed to help B construct, through inference, an image of A and the situation shared by A and B. B does the same with respect to A. The information transmitted during the ebb and flow of communication is much more limited than it is in a virtual reality game. The equivalent of the game space, that is, the context or situation comprising the respective position and identity of the partners, is not shared by A and B as an explicit representation, a complete and explorable image. The reason is that the context is here unlimited a priori, whereas it is circumscribed in the game, something that is also a function of the difference in the nature of the communications devices themselves. With the telephone, the reactualized image of the situation must constantly be reconstructed by the speakers, separately and individually. The videophone doesn't alter this in the slightest, since the true context, the universe of signification, the pragmatic situation (resources, the field of forces, threats, and opportunities, everything that can affect the plans, identities, or survival of the participants), is not shared to any greater extent simply by adding an image of the physical appearance of the person and the immediate physical environment. Systems that provide shared, remote access to documents, sources of information, or work spaces begin to approximate communication in a virtual world, until we reach systems that incorporate one or more active images of the person (filtering software agents, information trackers, personalized profiles, etc.).

Communication through a virtual world is in one sense more interactive than telephone communication because it implies within the message the image of the person and the situation—nearly always the key elements of communication. Yet in another sense, the telephone is more interactive, because it puts us in touch with the *body* of the speaker. Not an image of her body but her voice, an essential dimension of her physical manifestation. The voice of the person I'm speaking with is truly present wherever I happen to be talking to her. I'm referring not to an image of her voice but to her voice itself. Through this physical contact, an entire affective dimension is "interactively" transported during a telephone call. The telephone is the first telepresence medium. Today a number of R&D projects are attempting to extend and popularize telepresence to other physical dimensions: remote manipulation, three-dimensional images of the body, virtual reality, augmented reality environments for videoconferences, and others.

We see from this brief overview that the degree of interactivity of a medium or communications system can be measured using several different criteria:

- the ability to appropriate and *personalize* the received message, regardless of the nature of the message
- *reciprocity* of the communication (a one-to-one or many-to-many communications system)
- *virtuality*, here understood in terms of the processing of the message in real time based on a model and input data
- the *incorporation* of the image of the participants in the message (see table 2)
- *telepresence*

In table 3, for example, only two axes intersect among the many we could have used to highlight the concept of interactivity.

Through the virtualization of information, progress in interface design, and increased computing power and bandwidth, hybrid and mutant media proliferate. Each individual communications system must be subject to precise analysis, which is itself based on an updated theory of communication or, at the very least, a more detailed map of the modes of communication. The preparation of such a map has become increasingly urgent as political, cultural, aesthetic, economic, social, educational, and even epistemological issues become ever more dependent on the ways in which communication systems are configured. Interactivity has more to do with finding the solution to a problem, the need to develop new ways to observe, design, and evaluate methods of communication, than it does with identifying a simple, unique characteristic that can be assigned to a given system.

Table 3

Communication system	Linear message, not modified in real time	Interruption and reorientation of the information stream	Involvement of the participant in the message
One-way distribution	• press • radio • television • cinema	• multimodal database • static hyperdocuments • simulation without immersion or the ability to modify the model	• single-participant video games • simulation with immersion (flight simulators) but without possible modification of the model
Dialogue, reciprocity	• mail correspondence between two people	• telephone • videophone	• dialogues that take place through virtual worlds, cybersex
Multilogue	• correspondence networks • publication systems in a research community • e-mail • electronic conferences	• multiparticipant teleconference or video conference • open hyperdocuments accessible on-line, written and read by a community • Simulation (with the ability to act on the model) as a medium for community debate	• multiuser role playing in cyberspace • multiparticipant video games in "virtual reality" • communication through virtual worlds, continuous negotiation of participants with their image and the image of their shared situation

Chapter 22

ESPEN AARSETH

THE ADVENTURE GAME

ESPEN AARETH'S BOOK *Cybertext: Perspectives on Ergodic Literature* has proved influential in the study of new media, particularly in the fields of interactive fiction, web media and in game studies. A cybertext is a work of literature that requires what Aarseth calls 'non-trivial effort' on the part of its reader. Non-trivial means effort beyond that of turning the pages of the book or scanning the lines of text with one's eyes. Rather the cybertext has a mechanical nature that must be engaged with. It is by no means limited to computer media and includes ritual/game texts such as the *I Ching* (which requires readers to cast coins or sticks to generate a random number to determine which section of the book to read), and avant-garde experiments with layout and meaning such as Surrealist poetry. The cyber- prefix is meant in the specific context of **Wiener**'s cybernetics, i.e. it is concerned with feedback and control, not necessarily with computer media. This said, Aarseth is particularly concerned with computer-based interactive fiction and early text-based computer games.

The implications for digital media are significant. Traditional models of literary or media communication assume the transmission of meaning from an author or sender via a message or text, to a receiver or reader. Whilst this transmission may not be straightforward, and subject to ideological shaping and contestational reading, it does not ascribe any particular significance or influence to the technology of the medium or text itself. A cybertext differs, Aarseth argues, in that it shifts this linear relationship to a set of cybernetic circuits between a variety of participants, both human and mechanical, none of whom is clearly identifiable as the originator or ultimate receiver of a message.

We have chosen the following analyses of text-based computer games from *Cybertext* because, firstly, they identify these cybernetic participants, the distinctive characteristics or elements (Aarseth uses the technologically apt 'components') of computer media. Secondly, they force our attention to the newness and difference of cybernetic communicational media. Aarseth's amused recording of the weird world of *Deadline* notes the familiarity of the country house murder strand of detective fiction, whilst tracing the alien glitches and loops of artificially generated behaviour and intelligence. Whilst to many readers the text-based adventure game may seem archaic, Aarseth's account should resonate with contemporary experiences of the strangeness of software worlds and agents, from non-player characters in videogames to the increasing number and types of bots and other intelligent agents in everyday encounters with digital networks and services (see **Wise**).

See **Taylor**, **Kennedy**, **Dixon and Weber**, and **Sudnow** for explorations of more recent game cultures.

The introductory chapter of *Cybertext* is online: http://www.hf.uib.no/cybertext/default.html

[. . .]

The model presented here does not represent any particular cybertext system, nor does it pretend to describe all features shared by all such systems. It is not a realistic model, with a one-to-one mapping of actual components. It should instead be seen as a generalized conceptualization of the functionality of a typical, but advanced, adventure game.

The internal design of cybertexts has come a long way since the original *Adventure*, which "required about 300K of computer memory to play" (Gerrard 1984, 3). Later, more advanced cybertexts have managed on a lot less, catering to the limitations of the early home computers. With the development of *Zork* came the idea of an adventure interpreter (the Z-machine, in Infocom's case), an independent program module that could be used in more than one cybertext, like a database engine for several databases. Later, several specialized computer languages for cybertext construction appeared, such as Graham Nelson's Z-machine-compatible compiler, Inform, and also more high-level construction systems that did not require programming skills, such as Bill Appleton's World Builder.

In figure 5.1, the "ideal components" and information flow (arrows) of a cybertext is shown. The model is not limited to single-user adventure games or text-based games but can also describe multi-user dungeons and graphical games such as *Doom*. Notice the four groups of components: the data, the processing engines, the front-end medium (interface), and the users; and note the way information flows in feedback loops among them: going left on the upper level and then right on the lower, with the two middle layers like an artificial heart pumping information between the user and the database. This model is best suited to describe indeterminate cybertext. In determinate cybertext (e.g., *Adventure*), the three functions—simulation, representation, and synthesis—might be better described as a single component.

In the first of the four functional layers (the database), the data is of two kinds, static or dynamic. Some cybertexts, especially the early ones, had mostly static information, with only a few dynamic data items (the variables containing the position and status of the user's character

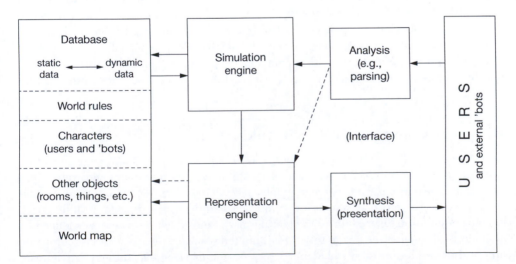

Figure 5.1 The components of a generalized, role-playing cybertext

and a few other objects), while the rest (topology, descriptions, the other characters' behavior) was read-only. Contradistinctively, in a multi-user dungeon, there are in principle no static data, although the basic topology (e.g., the links between the most common "rooms") tends to remain unchanged.

The second layer, the processing engines, represents the core of the cybertext. In the simulation engine, the course of action is decided, based on the user's input, the cybertext's idiosyncratic rules, and the current state of the simulated world. Here the events of the simulation are calculated and passed on to the representation engine. There can be two types of events: the ones generated by user input (user events) and those generated by the simulation itself (system events), normally caused by certain conditions coming true, for example, the passing of a specified period of time. Typically, the early adventure games were driven by user events only, and time was measured by counting the number of user moves. If the user did nothing, time stood still.

The representation engine presents the results of the event to the user by providing a personal perspective on the simulated world. It shows only those events that directly relate to the user's character and its surroundings, such as actions observed by, or participated in, by the user's character. In a user-configurative cybertext, the representation engine also handles the user's configurative commands (the dashed arrows), such as changing information "owned" by the user (e.g., the user's character's description).

The third layer, commonly known as the interface, consists of an input and an output component. The input component analyzes the user's commands and translates them into a semantic code that can be digested by the simulation engine. The type of input component depends on the channel, which can be text, static graphics, a combination of these two, or sound and animated graphics. The same is true of the output component, which transforms the semantic information it gets from the representation engine into the type of expression specified by the channel.

There is an obvious benefit in keeping the data base layer separate from the processing layer and this again separate from the input-output layer: when better technologies arrive, an individual component can be replaced without major changes in the others.

The fourth layer of the model, the user, is of course external to the design of the cybertext but not to its strategy. In the early adventure games, this strategy assumed an ideal reader, who would solve all the riddles of the text and thereby extricate the one definite, intended plotline. Eventually, this strategy changed, and now the reader's role is becoming less ideal (both in a structural and a moral sense) and more flexible, less dependable (hence more responsible), and freer. The multiuser, programmable cybertext instigates a more worldwise, corruptible reader; a Faust, compared to the Sherlock Holmes of the early adventure games.

[. . .]

The autistic detective agency: Marc Blank's *Deadline*

Marc Blank's *Deadline* (1982), published by Infocom, is a classic from the golden age of adventure games, just after the genre's establishment as a successful new textual medium and well before its commercial decline due to the migration to graphics. *Deadline* is a traditional detective mystery adapted to adventure game format: a mansion, a murder, and the usual suspects. It differs from the episodic paradigm of treasure hunt, bewildering maze, and tough monsters introduced by *Adventure* and instead confines the action to a closed, limited space (some 50 locations, compared to *Adventure*'s 140) with almost no hidden rooms, no mazes, less than fifteen, all human, characters (if human is the right word), and an intratextual time span of twelve hours.

As the investigating inspector, it is up to you—the player's character (the puppet)—to find out what happened to Marshall Robner, the wealthy businessman who was found dead on the floor of his library. In the house live his wife, Leslie, his black-sheepish son, George, and his thirty-something secretary, Ms. Dunbar. There are two servants, the gossipy housekeeper, Mrs. Rourke, and the rose-obsessed gardener, Mr. McNabb. In addition, there is the family lawyer, Mr. Coates; Mrs. Robner's secret lover, Steven; and a junior business associate, Mr. Baxter. To assist you is trusty Police Sergeant Duffy, and to breathe down your neck is the pushy Chief Inspector Klutz, who won't even let you work overtime to solve the murder but takes you off the case at precisely 8:00 P.M., after only twelve hours at the scene (hence the title of the game). The time passes by a minute each move you make, and you may also wait for specific times or events (e.g., "wait for mcnabb"). When you feel you have uncovered enough evidence, you arrest the suspected murderer.

Personal relations and habits in an adventure game like *Deadline* might best be described as autistic. The *Encyclopaedia Britannica* defines *autism* as "a neurobiological disorder that affects physical, social, and language skills." Further, "it may be characterized by meaningless, noncontextual echolalia (constant repetition of what is said by others) or the replacement of speech by strange mechanical sounds. Inappropriate attachment to objects may occur. There may be underemphasized reaction to sound, no reaction to pain, or no recognition of genuine danger, yet autistic children are extremely sensitive" (*Britannica Online*, "Autism").

The characters you meet in *Deadline* appear to be living in their own private worlds. When questioned, they often repeat themselves without making sense, and you may stand next to them for hours without any sign that they know you are there. Intelligent conversation is exceedingly difficult and breaks down after at most a few exchanges. And your own behavioral range is not much better, as you try to guess the word combinations that will unlock the mystery. Even moving around in the house or garden can be a pain, as the very limited commands for movement (south, west, northwest, up, etc.) will not always get you where you want to go. Most random words you try to use will result in rebuttals.

PLAYER: Stroll around.
VOICE: The word "stroll" isn't in your vocabulary.
PLAYER: Go for a walk.
VOICE: The word " 'walk' " can't be used in that sense.

Sometimes the answers are pure nonsense:

PLAYER: Fingerprint me.
VOICE: Upon looking over and dusting the me you notice that there are no good fingerprints to be found.
PLAYER: Talk to Duffy.
VOICE: You can't talk to the Duffy!

As for "inappropriate attachment to objects," to solve an adventure game, you must collect and examine as many objects as possible, because you never know what you might need later. In *Adventure*, most objects have a function, while in *Deadline*, only six objects are needed to solve the case (unless we count Sergeant Duffy as an object, as the game apparently does). In case of violence (e.g., when the detective is shot by the murderer), the pain of your character means nothing to the player, and it/you may die suddenly before you have recognized the danger. And yet, since solving an adventure game is usually very difficult, it requires extreme sensitivity to details. The contract between user and text in "interactive fiction" is not merely a "willing suspension of disbelief" but a willing suspension of one's normal capacity for language, physical aptness, and social interaction as well. It is of course not autism in a clinical, or even a fictional sense, but functionally it seems very close.

In her reading of *Deadline*, Sloane (1991, 66) suggests that the adventure game genre is characterized by three main features: "multiple point of view, nonlinearity, and second-person address." While the latter two are unproblematic and characterize all works in the genre, the first one, multiple viewpoint—by which Sloane presumably refers to the distance between the game text and the secondary texts, accompanying materials that Infocom packaged with the game diskette (maps, lab reports, transcripts of interviews, instructions for the player, etc.; see Sloane 1991, 68–69)—strikes me as extrinsic, since additional textual perspectives are not a required ingredient for all games of this kind. (It is rather a clever marketing trick, whereby Infocom made it harder for those with pirate copies to enjoy the game.) Neither is multiple viewpoint an integrated component of the game itself but is, rather, what we might call a set of paratexts, accompanying texts that refer to the game in some way, like the reviews of a theater play or its program brochure. The paratexts are of course not limited to the official Infocom package but may include comments and solutions made by players for each other. A common unofficial paratext is the "walkthru," a step-by-step recipe that contains the solution, and "walks" the user through the game. This is of course cheating, but sometimes it is the only way for a novice player to get to the end of a difficult game.

Following Genette's critique of the concept of point of view (1980, 185f.), we might profit from discussing this problem in his alternative terms of *voice* and *perspective*. The game itself is characterized by a singular perspective, which coincides with the user's symbolic presence in the game. In the case of *Deadline* the perspective is limited to that of the investigating detective, a simulated body who obeys the rules of *Deadline's* simulated world. In a superficial sense, this perspective is what we might call realist, as it contains no fantastic or supernatural elements. There are a few meta-fictional moments in the game, such as the self-referential book in the living room: "This is a novelization of DEADLINE, a classic work of computer fiction. . . . You start to read it, and it seems oddly familiar, as if you had lived it." Reading the end will depress "you" into committing suicide, and the program quits! This must be one of the more brutal types of metalepsis yet invented, or perhaps *dyslepsis* is a better word for it. But these elements are not representative of *Deadline's* intrigue and merely serve to lighten what can be a frustrating experience for a novice player. However, because of the negotiating nature of the adventure game's discourse, this perspective of "realism" is constantly interrupted by the conflict between intrigue and intriguee in terms of language problems, physical-world problems, and "intriguingly incorrect" behavior—that is, when the player tries to act outside of the intrigue's event space. We might refer to this last type of conflict as pushing the intrigue envelope.

The voice, as the narrating go-between that expedites the user's requests and commands and reports the resulting action, is not a reliable entity and may mess things up for the player because of its limited understanding. In addition, it is tiresomely tireless in repeating itself and often presents its messages with a stinging irony and sarcasm. For instance, in *Deadline*, when the player misspells the command "go upstairs" as "up stairs," the voice suggests, "Perhaps it's time for you to rest." This "mischievous spirit" is the intrigant's irritating, unseen agent among the intriguees, a kind of Puck to the intrigant's Oberon. As a negotiator it often makes mistakes or cracks jokes at the player's expense and is usually less than reliable as the servant of the intrigant. But is it really a person, even a simulated one? After talking to players of *Adventure*, Buckles concludes that their interpretations of who or what the "narrator" (as she calls it) is are too individual to form a consensus. "Whether the narrator should be considered the author's voice, their own mind's voice, the game itself, or some type of character—a witness, a participant, one of the protagonists, or an antagonist—depends in the end on the reader" (1985, 147). It also depends on the game in question, of course, but the diegetic, negotiating voice function is one of the most constant and striking elements in adventure game engineering, so a generalization seems legitimate.

Usually, the voice follows the player's instructions and merely reports the resulting action:

PLAYER: Get teacup and saucer.
VOICE: Cup: taken. Saucer: taken.

Or

PLAYER: Analyze teacup for ebullion.
VOICE: Sergeant Duffy walks up as quietly as a mouse. He takes the cup from you. "I'll return soon with the results," he says, and leaves as silently as he entered.

Or again,

PLAYER: Go south.
VOICE: End of hallway.

But even here, the voice's curious mixture of styles is noticeable, to the extent that we might want to describe it as two different voices: the curt, minimalist, camera eye style (or nonnarration) in "Cup: taken," and the direct, covert narration in "Sergeant Duffy walks up as quietly as a mouse." The second voice, typically engaged in the long descriptive passages, relates what are usually called canned sentences—prefabricated scriptons that are identical to their textons, with minimal modification at the time of playing. The first voice is used for the ergodic aspects.

In *Adventure*, the voice does feature an overt personality—an "I" that performs subjective acts, such as reincarnating the player-puppet in a magic ritual including orange smoke! (Buckles 1985, 143),—but the voice in *Deadline* never admits to any self-awareness. Even when the player asks directly "Who are you," the oracular reply is, "That question cannot be answered." Only at one point in the game, at the successful ending, does it use the personal pronoun *we:* "You have solved the case! If you would like, you may see the author's summary of the story. We would advise you to come up with your own first!" If the answer is yes, the "story" that follows is not the events of the successful game session but a retrospective exposition, the synopsis of the events that took place before the action began: why Robner was murdered, how, by whom. This "we," coming as it does at the successful end of the intrigue, and referring to "the author" in the third person, seems, if anything, to be coming directly from the (implied) publisher or from a similar extradiegetic position.

To sum up, what I here refer to as voice seems not to be identifiable as a singular speaker but, rather, as a composite, mechanical chorus coming from both inside and outside of the intrigue envelope. To classify this group as a narrator seems to be inappropriate, because the most narrating voice is also the least dynamic one and also because the voices do not fit together as one whole person nor even as several individuals. Instead, they are perhaps an imperfect simulacrum representing the intrigant and speaking with several tongues. Furthermore, the relationship between this chorus and the intrigant does not match that of a narrator and an implied author. There are parallels, but in the adventure game it is the intrigant, rather than the impartial voice positions, who schemes for successful development of the intrigue and who is the opponent of the intriguee. This implied being is not identical to the implied author or programmer of the game. As Per Aage Brandt notes, "the user cannot but feel guided by an already instantiated, implemented intentionality" (1993, 133); but Brandt assigns this symbolic entity to the "*designer* of the machine," in other words, to the implied programmer and, thus, not to the intrigant as an emergent, immanent position.

To illustrate this difference with a more nearly universal example, consider the imaginary being we invoke when we address our (ill-behaving) computers as "him" or "it" (e.g., "Oh no, he crashed again"). We are not referring to the person who wrote the program we are using (the implied programmer) nor to the voice that informs us that things have gone wrong ("Bad sector reading drive A:")—because often there is no such report, just the bad news itself—but to that eternal whoever-it-is who ultimately controls every program we use and who is, quite deliberately, driving us crazy with its irrational behavior. This is the intrigant: an unwelcome devil in real life but a pleasure-giving Mephistopheles in the cybertext.

When it comes to perspective, there seems to be an unclear boundary between the voice and the player's puppet, which indicates that the puppet's subject position (or what Aristotle referred to as *dianoia*, the thoughts of a character) is a contested site in the unfolding of the intrigue. "I'll be your eyes and hands," says the voice in *Adventure* (see Buckles 1985, 141), but sometimes the voice also takes control of the thoughts and will of the puppet, often to the great annoyance of the player, as this example from *Deadline* shows:

PLAYER: Drink scotch.
VOICE: You take a small swig of the golden fluid, which burns as it goes down.
PLAYER: Again.
PLAYER: It's one thing to take a bracer on occasion, but you must resist the temptation to indulge too often.

The intrigue in *Deadline* does not include a drunk puppet, so the player is allowed a small virtual taste, and only once.

Other times, the player's persistence eventually pays off but not the way one expected:

PLAYER: Hit leslie with roses.
VOICE: You rethink your planned action.
PLAYER: Hit leslie with roses.
VOICE: You rethink your planned action.
PLAYER: Hit leslie with roses.
VOICE: With a lethal blow of your hand, Mrs. Robner falls dead. Your mind becomes confused amidst strange screaming, yelling, and the pangs of your conscience. "How could I have done it?" you ask yourself, as you hear the distant sound of police sirens. Sergeant Duffy and two other officers enter and grab you rather unceremoniously. They take you to a waiting car, where, forlorn and disgusted, you begin to ponder prison life. "Perhaps," you think, "I shouldn't have done that."

Here we can observe how, to punish the noncooperative intriguee, the intrigant must break the illusion of free interaction and instate first thought control, then narrative control. This makes it look like the player's fault, for persisting in disobeying, but in reality it is the intrigant who has broken the ergodic contract, as the return to a narrative mode shows. Ironically, noncooperation and free play result in narrative punishment, which equals the end, death. The model intriguee, in other words, is a good puppet, which indicates that the intrigant of *Deadline* is not the autonomous ruler of the simulated world but something of an impostor and a hypocrite, an old-fashioned author dressed up in the latest technology. As Stuart Moulthrop writes about hypertext, "The text gestures toward openness—*what options can you imagine?*—but then it forecloses: some options are available but not others, and someone clearly has done the defining. The author persists, undead presence in the literary machine, the inevitable Hand that turns the time" (1991b, para. 21).

But even (and especially) the most authoritative texts include the means of their own deconstruction, and *Deadline* is no exception. Sometimes, the intrigant can be too clever for its own good. The simulated people that the player encounters in the game are all quite wooden, half-living, and as we saw when we tried to talk to Duffy ("You can't talk to the Duffy!"), sometimes more of an object than a person. "Sergeant Duffy" is actually implemented differently from the other nonplaying characters in *Deadline*; he seems to be without a location of his own but is always hovering quietly in the background, ready to assist. His even more than usually inanimate nature is revealed when we treat him like a normal nonplaying character and try to ask him questions (which normally results in the reply quoted above). But sometimes the intrigant gets it right without trying, as when we say, "accuse Duffy," and are told, "What a detective! Quick, Sergeant! Arrest that Sergeant Duffy!" This seems to be a lucky coincidence, because exactly the same canned ironic reply is given when we accuse other objects ("Quick, Sergeant! Arrest that saucer!").

Many absurd events result from this kind of mistake (bug) in the intrigue, for example, when you try to sit on a chair and are given the reply, "This isn't the kind of thing to sit on!" Examining the obstinate object yields the message, "There's nothing special about the chair"— but indeed there is. And while you may carry the ladder all over the garden, "get the chair" results only in ridicule: "You can't be serious!" Sitting on beds and sofas, on the other hand, works just fine. A more general bug is the nonplaying characters' failure to reflect on what is going on. After one of them has just been killed, Mrs. Rourke, who is "tidying up" in the hallway outside, doesn't know anything about it: "I haven't seen her today."

But if Sergeant Duffy and the other nonplaying characters in *Deadline* aren't quite alive, there is one person who is less dead than he's supposed to be. By coincidence I discovered that the clockwork world wasn't running quite on time and that there was a very literal ghost in the machine, as the following log shows.

PLAYER: North.
VOICE: Library.

Beside the desk is a large collapsible tray. Sitting on the tray is a bowl containing a white powdery substance. Alongside the desk is a wicker wastepaper basket. The wastepaper basket contains: A bunch of crumpled papers. Lying on the floor, overturned, is a beautiful saucer. There is a bottle of Ebullion here.

PLAYER: Question Mr. Robner.
VOICE: Mr. Robner is listening.
PLAYER: Show saucer to Mr. Robner.
VOICE: Mr. Robner lets out a loud yawn.
PLAYER: Accuse Mr. Robner.

VOICE: Robner shrugs off your suggestion.

PLAYER: Kiss Mr. Robner.

VOICE: Section 204D, Paragraph 7.6 of the Connecticut Police Code of Conduct specifically prohibits kissing suspects.

PLAYER: Squeeze marshall.

VOICE: It's unclear how Mr. Robner would take this, so you defer until after hours.

PLAYER: Arrest Mr. Robner.

VOICE: You realize that you don't have enough evidence to convict Mr. Robner, so you resolve to continue the investigation.

PLAYER: Ask Mr. Robner about Mrs. Robner.

VOICE: Mr. Robner isn't here!

PLAYER: Wait for Mr. Robner.

VOICE: That person is already here!

PLAYER: Throw saucer at Mr. Robner.

VOICE: Mr. Robner, puzzled by your unorthodox methods, ducks as the saucer flies by.

PLAYER: Kill Mr. Robner.

VOICE: With a lethal blow of your hand, Mr. Robner falls dead. Your mind becomes confused amidst strange screaming, yelling, and the pangs of your conscience. "How could I have done it?" you ask yourself, as you hear the distant sound of police sirens. Sergeant Duffy and two other officers enter and grab you rather unceremoniously. They take you to a waiting car, where, forlorn and disgusted, you begin to ponder prison life. "Perhaps," you think, "I shouldn't have done that." The case has ended. Would you like to start your investigation over from scratch? (Y/N)

This scene is a fine example of the potential for absurd theater that the adventure game genre has so far not exploited, and it is all the better for being completely unintentional. Not only is Mr. Robner back from the dead to haunt the scene of his murder, he is also one of the suspects! (Which makes a bizarre kind of sense, since suicide is one of the working theories.) The final irony, that the policeman ends up as the killer in his own investigation, is a masterpiece of the cybertextual aesthetics of autonomy and the closest we can get to a proof that the intrigant is not the same as the implied programer, even when the cybertext is determinate. It also supports my conclusion in chapter 2, that the possibility of unintentional sign behavior makes cybernetic media creatively emergent and, therefore, not subsumable by the traditional communication theories.

[. . .]

Chapter 23

LEV MANOVICH

SELECTED MATERIAL FROM
THE LANGUAGE OF NEW MEDIA
'The database', 'Data and algorithm' and 'Navigable space'

L EV MANOVICH IS A new media artist as well as a theorist of new media. This informs his interest in the 'cultural form' of digital media, that is, he addresses the dominant technical and aesthetic structures and conventions of software and the media objects and texts produced with it. As film theorists of the twentieth century were concerned with the narrative structure of a Hollywood movie, or its assembling of plot, mise-en-scène and character through the manipulation of shots in the edit suite, Manovich identifies the 'new' cultural forms that shape and are shaped by new media applications and processes. His book, *The Language of New Media*, covers many aspects of cultural software; for example, he identifies a number of key tools or processes (he calls them 'operations') that underpin commercial software from word processing to video editing programs. These include the conventions of 'cut and paste', copy, find, delete, transform, etc.

The extracts we have chosen highlight significant 'new' aspects of the new media Manovich is concerned with. He is often concerned with visual culture and especially with moving image media, so the first sections, 'The Database' and 'Database and Algorithm', explore something of the distinct ways in which computers store and manipulate information (here, for example, moving image footage). He compares this with traditional techniques of manipulating and editing film stock.

The 'Navigable Space' extract is also concerned with the moving image, but this is the moving image as a mapping or modelling of virtual space. From architectural 'fly-throughs' to the visceral and violent pleasures of exploring the corridors of the videogame *Doom*, virtual space is discussed as a significant new cultural form that draws on pre-digital visual and cinematic culture.

The database

After the novel, and subsequently cinema, privileged narrative as the key form of cultural expression of the modern age, the computer age introduces its correlate—the database. Many new media objects do not tell stories; they do not have a beginning or end; in fact, they do not have any development, thematically, formally, or otherwise that would organize their elements into a sequence. Instead, they are collections of individual items, with every item possessing the same significance as any other.

Why does new media favor the database form over others? Can we explain its popularity by analyzing the specificity of the digital medium and of computer programming? What is the relationship between the database and another form that has traditionally dominated human culture—narrative? These are the questions I will address in this section.

Before proceeding, I need to comment on my use of the word *database*. In computer science, *database* is defined as a structured collection of data. The data stored in a database is organized for fast search and retrieval by a computer and, therefore, it is anything but a simple collection of items. Different types of databases—hierarchical, network, relational, and object-oriented—use different models to organize data. For instance, the records in hierarchical databases are organized in a treelike structure. Object-oriented databases store complex data structures, called "objects," which are organized into hierarchical classes that may inherit properties from classes higher in the chain.[1] New media objects may or may not employ these highly structured database models; however, from the point of view of the user's experience, a large proportion of them are databases in a more basic sense. They appear as collections of items on which the user can perform various operations—view, navigate, search. The user's experience of such computerized collections is, therefore, quite distinct from reading a narrative or watching a film or navigating an architectural site. Similarly, a literary or cinematic narrative, an architectural plan, and a database each present a different model of what a world is like. It is this sense of database as a cultural form of its own that I want to address here. Following art historian Ervin Panofsky's analysis of linear perspective as a "symbolic form" of the modern age, we may even call database a new symbolic form of the computer age (or, as philosopher Jean-François Lyotard called it in his famous 1979 book *The Postmodern Condition*, "computerized society"),[2] a new way to structure our experience of ourselves and of the world. Indeed, if after the death of God (Nietzsche), the end of Grand Narratives of Enlightenment (Lyotard), and the arrival of the Web (Tim Berners-Lee), the world appears to us as an endless and unstructured collection of images, texts, and other data records, it is only appropriate that we will be moved to model it as a database. But it is also appropriate that we would want to develop a poetics, aesthetics, and ethics of this database.

Let us begin by documenting the dominance of the database form in new media. The most obvious examples are popular multimedia encyclopedias, collections by definition, as well as other commercial CD-ROM (or DVD), that feature collections of recipes, quotations, photographs, and so on.[3] The identity of a CD-ROM as a storage media is projected onto another plane, thereby becoming a cultural form in its own right. Multimedia works that have "cultural" content appear to particularly favor the database form. Consider, for instance, the "virtual museums" genre—CD-ROMs that take the user on a tour through a museum collection. A museum becomes a database of images representing its holdings, which can be accessed in different ways—chronologically, by country, or by artist. Although such CD-ROMs often simulate the traditional museum experience of moving from room to room in a continuous trajectory, this narrative method of access does not have any special status in comparison to other access methods offered by CD-ROMs. Thus narrative becomes just one method of accessing data among many. Another example of a database form is a multimedia genre that does not have an equivalent in traditional media—CD-ROMs devoted to a single cultural figure such as a famous architect, film director, or writer. Instead of a narrative biography, we are presented with a database of images, sound recordings, video clips, and/or texts that can be navigated in a variety of ways.

CD-ROMs and other digital storage media proved to be particularly receptive to traditional genres that already had a database-like structure, such as the photo album; they also inspired new database genres, like the database biography. Where the database form really flourished, however, is the Internet. As defined by original HTML, a Web page is a sequential list of separate elements—text blocks, images, digital video clips, and links to other pages. It is always possible to add a new element to the list—all you have to do is to open a file and add a new line. As a result, most Web pages are collections of separate elements—texts, images, links to other pages, or sites. A home page is a collection of personal photographs. A site of a major search engine is a collection of numerous links to other sites (along with a search function, of course). A site of a Web-based TV or radio station offers a collection of video or audio programs along with the option to listen to the current broadcast, but this current program is just one choice among many other programs stored on the site. Thus the traditional broadcasting experience, which consists solely of a real-time transmission, becomes just one element in a collection of options. Similar to the CD-ROM medium, the Web offered fertile ground to already existing database genres (for instance, bibliography) and also inspired the creation of new ones such as sites devoted to a person or a phenomenon (Madonna, the Civil War, new media theory, etc.) that, even if they contain original material, inevitably center around a list of links to other Web pages on the same person or phenomenon.

The open nature of the Web as a medium (Web pages are computer files that can always be edited) means that Web sites never have to be complete; and they rarely are. They always grow. New links are continually added to what is already there. It is as easy to add new elements to the end of a list as it is to insert them anywhere in it. All this further contributes to the anti-narrative logic of the Web. If new elements are being added over time, the result is a collection, not a story. Indeed, how can one keep a coherent narrative or any other development trajectory through the material if it keeps changing?

Commercial producers have experimented with ways to explore the database form inherent to new media, with offerings ranging from multimedia encyclopedias to collections of software and collections of pornographic images. In contrast, many artists working with new media at first uncritically accepted the database form as a given. Thus they became blind victims of database logic. Numerous artists' Web sites are collections of multimedia elements documenting their works in other media. In the case of many early artists' CD-ROMs as well, the tendency was to fill all the available storage space with different material—the main work, documentation, related texts, previous works, and so on.

As the 1990s progressed, artists increasingly began to approach the database more critically.[4] A few examples of projects investigating database politics and possible aesthetics are Chris Marker's "IMMEMORY," Olga Lialina's "Anna Karenina Goes to Paradise,"[5] Stephen Mamber's "Digital Hitchcock," and Fabian Wagmister's ". . . two, three, many Guevaras." The artist who has explored the possibilities of a database most systematically is George Legrady. In a series of interactive multimedia works ("The Anecdoted Archive," 1994; "[the clearing]," 1994; "Slippey Traces," 1996; "Tracing," 1998) he used different types of databases to create "an information structure where stories/things are organized according to multiple thematic connections."[6]

Data and algorithm

Of course, not all new media objects are explicitly databases. Computer games, for instance, are experienced by their players as narratives. In a game, the player is given a well-defined task—winning the match, being first in a race, reaching the last level, or attaining the highest score. It is this task that makes the player experience the game as a narrative. Everything that happens to her in a game, all the characters and objects she encounters, either take her closer to achieving the goal or further away from it. Thus, in contrast to a CD-ROM and Web database, which always appear arbitrary because the user knows additional material could have been added without modifying the logic, in a game, from the user's point of view, all the elements are motivated (i.e., their presence is justified).[7]

Often the narrative shell of a game ("You are the specially trained commando who has just landed on a lunar base; your task is to make your way to the headquarters occupied by the mutant base personnel . . .") masks a simple algorithm well-familiar to the player—kill all the enemies on the current level, while collecting all the treasures it contains; go to the next level and so on until you reach the last level. Other games have different algorithms. Here is the algorithm of the legendary *Tetris*: When a new block appears, rotate it in such a way so that it will complete the top layer of blocks on the bottom of the screen, thus making this layer disappear. The similarity between the actions expected of the player and computer algorithms is too uncanny to be dismissed. While computer games do not follow a database logic, they appear to be ruled by another logic—that of the algorithm. They demand that a player execute an algorithm in order to win.

An algorithm is the key to the game experience in a different sense as well. As the player proceeds through the game, she gradually discovers the rules that operate in the universe constructed by this game. She learns its hidden logic—in short, its algorithm. Therefore, in games in which the game play departs from following an algorithm, the player is still engaged with an algorithm albeit in another way: She is discovering the algorithm of the game itself. I mean this both metaphorically and literally: For instance, in a first-person shooter such as *Quake* the player may eventually notice that, under such and such conditions, the enemies will appear from the left; that is, she will literally reconstruct a part of the algorithm responsible for the game play. Or, in a different formulation of the legendary author of Sim games, Will Wright, "playing the game is a continuous loop between the user (viewing the outcomes and inputting decisions) and the computer (calculating outcomes and displaying them back to the user). The user is trying to build a mental model of the computer model."[8]

This is another example of the general principle of transcoding discussed in the first chapter—the projection of the ontology of a computer onto culture itself. If in physics the world is made of atoms and in genetics it is made of genes, computer programming encapsulates the world according to its own logic. The world is reduced to two kinds of software objects that are complementary to each other—data structures and algorithms. Any process or task is reduced to an algorithm, a final sequence of simple operations that a computer can execute to accomplish a given task. And any object in the world—be it the population of a city, or the weather over the course of a century, or a chair, or a human brain—is modeled as a data structure, that is, data organized in a particular way for efficient search and retrieval.[9] Examples of data structures are arrays, linked lists, and graphs. Algorithms and data structures have a symbiotic relationship. The more complex the data structure of a computer program, the simpler the algorithm needs to be, and vice versa. Together, data structures and algorithms are two halves of the ontology of the world according to a computer.

The computerization of culture involves the projection of these two fundamental parts of computer software—and of the computer's unique ontology—onto the cultural sphere. If CD-ROMs and Web databases are cultural manifestations of one half of this ontology—data structures—then computer games are manifestations of the second half—algorithms. Games (sports, chess, cards, etc.) are one cultural form that require algorithm-like behavior from players; consequently, many traditional games were quickly simulated on computers. In parallel, new genres of computer games such as the first-person shooter came into existence. Thus, as was the case with database genres, computer games both mimic already existing games and create new game genres.

It may appear at first sight that data is passive and algorithms active—another example of the passive-active binary categories so loved by human cultures. A program reads in data, executes an algorithm, and writes out new data. We may recall that before "computer science" and "software engineering" became established names in the computer field, this was called "data processing"—a name which remained in use for the few decades during which computers were mainly associated with performing calculations over data. However, the passive/active distinction is not quite accurate because data does not just exist—it has to be generated. Data creators have to collect data and organize it, or create it from scratch. Texts need to be written, photographs need to be taken, video and audio material need to be recorded. Or they need to be digitized from already existing media. In the 1990s, when the new role of the computer as a Universal Media Machine became apparent, already computerized societies went into a digitizing craze. All existing books and videotapes, photographs, and audio recordings started to be fed into computers at an ever-increasing rate. Steven Spielberg created the Shoah Foundation, which videotaped and then digitized numerous interviews with Holocaust survivors; it would take one person forty years to watch all the recorded material. The editors of the journal *Mediamatic*, who devoted a whole issue to the topic of "the storage mania" (Summer 1994) wrote: "A growing number of organizations are embarking on ambitious projects. Everything is being collected: culture, asteroids, DNA patterns, credit records, telephone conversations; it doesn't matter."[10] In 1996, the financial company T. Rowe Price stored eight hundred gigabytes of data; by the fall of 1999 this number rose to ten terabytes.[11]

Once digitized, the data has to be cleaned up, organized, and indexed. The computer age brought with it a new cultural algorithm: reality→media→data→database. The rise of the Web, this gigantic and always changing data corpus, gave millions of people a new hobby or profession—data indexing. There is hardly a Web site that does not feature at least a dozen links to other sites; therefore, every site is a type of database. And, with the rise of Internet commerce, most large-scale commercial sites have become real databases, or rather front-ends to company databases. For instance, in the fall of 1998, Amazon.com, an online bookstore, had three million books in its database; and the maker of the leading commercial database *Oracle* has offered *Oracle 8i*, fully integrated with the Internet and featuring unlimited database size, natural-language queries, and support for all multimedia data types.[12] Jorge Luis Borges's story about a map equal in size to the territory it represents is rewritten as a story about indexes and the data they index. But now the map has become larger than the territory. Sometimes, much larger. Porno Web sites exposed the logic of the Web at its extreme by constantly reusing the same photographs from other porno Web sites. Only rare sites featured the original content. On any given date, the same few dozen images would appear on thousands of sites. Thus, the same data would give rise to more indexes than the number of data elements themselves.

[. . .]

Navigable space

Looking at the first decade of new media—the 1990s—one can point at a number of objects that exemplify new media's potential to give rise to genuinely original and historically unprecedented aesthetic forms. Among them, two stand out. Both are computer games. Both were published in the same year, 1993. Each became a phenomenon whose popularity has extended beyond the hard-core gaming community, spilling into sequels, books, TV, films, fashion, and design. Together, they define the new field and its limits. These games are *Doom* (id Software, 1993) and *Myst* (Cyan, 1993).

In a number of ways, *Doom* and *Myst* are completely different. *Doom* is fast paced; *Myst* is slow. In *Doom* the player runs through the corridors trying to complete each level as soon as possible, and then moves to the next one. In *Myst*, the player moves through the world literally one step at a time, unraveling the narrative along the way. *Doom* is populated with numerous demons lurking around every corner, waiting to attack; *Myst* is completely empty. The world of *Doom* follows the convention of computer games: it consists of a few dozen levels. Although *Myst* also contains four separate worlds, each is more like a self-contained universe than a traditional computer game level. While in most games levels are quite similar to each other in structure and look, the worlds of *Myst* are distinctly different.

Another difference lies in the aesthetics of navigation. In *Doom*'s world, defined by rectangular volumes, the player moves in straight lines, abruptly turning at right angles to enter a new corridor. In *Myst*, the navigation is more free-form. The player, or more precisely, the visitor, slowly explores the environment: She may look around for a while, go in circles, return to the same place over and over, as though performing an elaborate dance.

Finally, the two objects exemplify two different types of cultural economy. With *Doom*, id software pioneered the new economy that critic of computer games J. C. Herz summarizes as follows: "It was an idea whose time had come. Release a free, stripped-down version through shareware channels, the Internet, and online services. Follow with a spruced-up, registered retail version of the software." Fifteen million copies of the original *Doom* game were downloaded around the world.[13] By releasing detailed descriptions of game formats and a game editor, id software also encouraged the players to expand the game, creating new levels. Thus hacking and adding to the game became an essential part of the game, with new levels widely available on the Internet for anyone to download. Here was a new cultural economy that transcended the usual relationship between producers and consumers or between "strategies" and "tactics" (de Certeau): *The producers define the basic structure of an object, and release a few examples as well as tools to allow consumers to build their own versions, to be shared with other consumers.* In contrast, the creators of *Myst* followed an older model of cultural economy. Thus *Myst* is more similar to a traditional artwork than to a piece of software—something to behold and admire rather than take apart and modify. To use the terms of the software industry, it is a closed, or proprietary, system, something that only the original creators can modify.

Despite all these differences in cosmogony, gameplay, and underlying economic model, the two games are similar in one key respect. Both are spatial journeys. Navigation though 3-D space is an essential, if not the key, component of the gameplay. *Doom* and *Myst* present the user with a space to be traversed, to be mapped out by moving through it. Both begin by dropping the player somewhere in this space. Before reaching the end of the game narrative, the player must visit most of it, uncovering its geometry and topology, learning its logic and its secrets. In *Doom* and *Myst*—and in a great many other computer games—narrative and time itself are equated with movement through 3-D space, progression through rooms, levels, or words. In contrast to modern literature, theater, and cinema, which are built around psychological tensions between characters and movement in psychological space, these computer games return us to ancient forms of narrative in which the plot is driven by the spatial movement of the main hero, traveling through distant lands to save the princess, to find the treasure, to defeat the dragon, and so on. As J. C. Herz writes about the experience of playing the classic text-based adventure game *Zork*, "You gradually unlocked a world in which the story took place, and the receding edge of this world carried you through to the story's conclusion."[14] Stripping away the representation of inner life, psychology, and other modernist nineteenth-century inventions, these are the narratives in the original ancient Greek sense, for, as Michel de Certeau reminds us, "in Greek, narration is called 'diagesis': it establishes an itinerary (it 'guides') and it passes through (it 'transgresses.')"[15]

In the introduction to this chapter, I invoked the opposition between narration and description in narratology. As noted by Mieke Bal, the standard theoretical premise of narratology is that "descriptions interrupt the line of fabula."[16] For me, this opposition, in which description is defined negatively as absence of narration, has always been problematic. It automatically privileges certain types of narrative (myths, fairy tales, detective stories, classical Hollywood cinema), while making it difficult to think about other forms in which the actions of characters do not dominate the narrative (for instance, films by Andrey Tarkovsky, or Hirokazu Kore-eda, the director of *Maborosi* and *After Life*).[17] Games structured around first-person navigation through space further challenge the narration-description opposition.

Instead of narration and description, we may be better off thinking about games in terms of *narrative actions* and *exploration*. Rather than being narrated to, the player herself has to perform actions to move narrative forward—talking to other characters she encounters in the game world, picking up objects, fighting enemies, and so on. If the player does nothing, the narrative stops. From this perspective, movement through the game world is one of the main narrative actions. But this movement also serves the self-sufficient goal of exploration. Exploring the game world, examining its details and enjoying its images, is as important for the success of games such as *Myst* and its followers as progressing through the narrative. Thus, while from one point of view, game narratives can be aligned with ancient narratives that are also structured around movement through space, from another perspective they are exact opposites. Movement through space allows the player to progress through the narrative, but it is also valuable in itself. It is a way for the player to explore the environment.

Narratology's analysis of description can be a useful start in thinking about exploration of space in computer games and other new media objects. Bal states that descriptive passages in fiction are motivated by speaking, looking, and acting. Motivation by looking works as follows: "A character sees an object. The description is the reproduction of what it sees." Motivation by acting means that "the actor carries out an action with an object. The description is then made fully narrative. The example of this is the scene in Zola's *La Bête* in which Jacques polishes [strokes] every individual component of his beloved locomotive."[18]

In contrast to the modern novel, action-oriented games do not have that much dialog, but looking and acting are indeed the key activities performed by a player. And if in modern fiction looking and acting are usually separate activities, in games they more often than not occur together. As the player comes across a door leading to another level, a new passage, ammunition for his machine gun, an enemy, or a "health potion," he immediately acts on these objects— opens a door, picks up ammunition or "health potion," fires at the enemy. Thus narrative action and exploration are closely linked together.

The central role of navigation through space, both as a tool of narration and of exploration, is acknowledged by the games' designers themselves. According to Robyn Miller, one of the two codesigners of *Myst*, "We are creating environments to just wander around inside of. People have been calling it a game for lack of anything better, and we've called it a game at times. But that's not what it really is; it's a world."[19] Richard Garriott, designer of the classic RPG *Ultima* series, contrasts game design and fiction writing: "A lot of them [fiction writers] develop their individual characters in detail, and they say what is their problem in the beginning, and what they are going to grow to learn in the end. That's not the method I've used . . . I have the world. I have the message. And then the characters are there to support the world and the message."[20]

Structuring the game as a navigation through space is common to games across all genres. This includes adventure games (for instance, *Zork*, *7th Level*, *The Journeyman Project*, *Tomb Raider*, *Myst*); strategy games (*Command and Conquer*); role-playing games (*Diablo*, *Final Fantasy*); flying, driving, and other simulators (*Microsoft Flight Simulator*); action games (*Hexen, Mario*); and, of course, first-person shooters following in *Doom*'s steps (*Quake, Unreal*). These genres obey different conventions. In adventure games, the user explores a universe, gathering resources. In strategy games, the user engages in allocating and moving resources and in risk management. In RPGs (role-playing games), the user builds a character and acquires skills; the narrative is one of self-improvement. The genre conventions by themselves do not make it necessary for these games to employ a navigable space interface. The fact that they all consistently do, therefore, suggests to me that navigable space represents a larger cultural form. In other words, it is something that transcends computer games and in fact, as we will see later, computer culture as well. Just like a database, navigable space is a form that existed before computers, even if the computer becomes its perfect medium.

Indeed, the use of navigable space is common to all areas of new media. During the 1980s, numerous 3-D computer animations were organized around a single, uninterrupted camera move through a complex and extensive set. In a typical animation, a camera would fly over mountain terrain, or move through a series of rooms, or maneuver past geometric shapes. In contrast to both ancient myths and computer games, this journey had no goal, no purpose. In short, there was no narrative. Here was the ultimate "road movie," where navigation through space was sufficient in itself.

In the 1990s, these 3-D fly-throughs have come to constitute the new genre of postcomputer cinema and location-based entertainment—the motion simulator.[21] By using first-person point of view and by synchronizing the movement of the platform housing the audience with the movement of a virtual camera, motion simulators recreate the experience of traveling in a vehicle. Thinking about the historical precedents of a motion simulator, we begin to uncover some places where the form of navigable space has already manifested itself. They include *Hale's Tours and Scenes of the World*, a popular film-based attraction that debuted at the St. Louis Fair in 1904; roller-coaster rides; flight, vehicle, and military simulators, which have used a moving base since the early 1930s; and the fly-through sequences in *2001: A Space Odyssey* (Kubrick, 1968) and *Star Wars* (Lucas, 1977). Among these, *A Space Odyssey* plays a particularly important role; Douglas Trumbull, who since the late 1980s has produced some of the best-known motion-simulator attractions and was the key person behind the rise of the motion-simulator phenomenon, began his career by creating ride sequences for this film.

Along with providing a key foundation for new media aesthetics, navigable space has also become a new tool of labor. It is now a common way to visualize and work with any data. From scientific visualization to walkthroughs of architectural designs, from models of a stock market performance to statistical datasets, the 3-D virtual space combined with a camera model is the accepted way to visualize all information. It is as accepted in computer culture as charts and graphs were in a print culture.[22]

[. . .]

Notes

1 "Database," *Encyclopædia Britannica Online*, http://www.eb.com:180/cgi-bin/g?DocF=micro/l60/23.html.

2 Jean-François Lyotard, *The Postmodern Condition: A Report on Knowledge*, trans. Geoff Bennington and Brian Massumi (Minneapolis: University of Minnesota Press, 1984), 3.

3 As early as 1985, Grolier, Inc. issued a text-only *Academic American Encyclopedia* on CD-ROM. The first multimedia encyclopedia was *Compton's MultiMedia Encyclopedia*, published in 1989.

4 See *AI and Society* 13.3, a special issue on database aesthetics, ed. Victoria Vesna (http://arts.ucsb.edu/~vesna/AI_Society/); *SWITCH* 5, no. 3, "The Database Issue" (http://switch.sjsu.edu/).

5 http://www.teleportacia.org/anna.

6   George Legrady, personal communication, 16 September 1998.

7   Bordwell and Thompson define motivation in cinema in the following way: "Because films are human constructs, we can expect that any one element in a film will have some justification for being there. This justification is the motivation for that element." Here are some examples of motivation: "When Tom jumps from the balloon to chase a cat, we motivate his action by appealing to notions of how dogs are likely to act when cats are around"; "The movement of a character across a room may motivate the moving of the camera to follow the action and keep the character within a frame." Bordwell and Thompson, *Film Art*, 5th ed., 80.

8   McGowan and McCullaugh, *Entertainment in the Cyber Zone*, 71.

9   This is true for a procedural programming paradigm. In an object-oriented programming paradigm, represented by such computer languages as Java and C++, algorithms and data structures are modeled together as objects.

10 *Mediamatic* 8, no. 1 (Summer 1994), 1860.

11 Bob Laird, "Information Age Losing Memory," *USA Today*, 25 October 1999.

12 http://www.amazon.com/exec/obidos/subst/misc/company-info.html/, http://www.oracle.com/database/oracle8i/.

13 J. C. Herz, *Joystick Nation*, 90, 84.

14 Ibid., 150.

15 Michel de Certeau, *The Practice of Everyday Life*, trans. Steven Rendall (Berkeley: University of California Press, 1984), 129.

16 Bal, *Narratology*, 130. Bal defines *fabula* as "a series of logically and chronologically related events that are caused or experienced by actors" (5).

17 In *Understanding Comics*, Scott McLoud notes how, in contrast to Western comics, Japanese comics spend much more time on "description" not directly motivated by the narrative development. The same opposition holds between the language of classical Hollywood cinema and many films from the "east," such as the works of Tarkovsky and Kore-eda. Although I recognize the danger of such a generalization, it is tempting to connect the narration-description opposition to a much larger opposition between traditionally Western and Eastern ways of existence and philosophies—the drive of the Western subject to know and conquer the world outside versus the Buddhist emphasis on meditation and stasis. Scott McLoud, *Understanding Comics: The Invisible Art* (Harper Perennial, 1994).

18 Bal, *Narratology*, 130–132.

19 McGoman and McCullaugh, *Entertainment in the Cyber Zone*, 120.

20 Quoted in J. C. Hertz, *Joystick Nation*, 155–156.

21 For a critical analysis of the motion-simulator phenomenon, see Erkki Huhtamo, "Phantom Train to Technopia," in Minna Tarkka, ed., *ISEA '94: The 5th International Symposium on Electronic Art Catalogue* (Helsinki: University of Art and Design, 1994); "Encapsulated Bodies in Motion: Simulators and the Quest for Total Immersion," in Simon Penny, ed., *Critical Issues in Electronic Media*.

22 See www.cybergeography.com.

Chapter 24

LAURA U. MARKS

INVISIBLE MEDIA

U NDERLYING LAURA MARKS' exploration of the 'invisible' media behind or within the very visible images and screens of contemporary commercial and information culture is an updating and extension of the kind of critique of capitalist social relations Karl **Marx** developed in the industrial nineteenth century. For Marks, capitalism and information are inseparable, and 'information capitalism' is not the liberatory consumerist heaven presented by Microsoft, Google and Amazon. Rather, it is exploitative and deathly.

The visibility of commercial interfaces and Internet services is countered by 'invisible media', counter-information or everyday experiences that are repressed or ignored, *enfolded* by information capitalism and its media. These enfolded experiences, media objects and practices can be, she argues, temporarily but subversively *unfolded* to disrupt our taken-for-granted familiarity with dominant information media. She adopts Hakim Bey's notion of temporary autonomous zones (TAZs) to discuss these cultural-political possibilities. Whereas Marx expected a sudden revolutionary overthrowing of capitalism, Bey and Marks see, for the time being, the possibility for only momentary guerrilla disruptions.

Marks' examples of TAZs and unfoldings in information capitalist culture are mainly taken from the overlapping area between the malicious or mischievous practices of computer hackers and virus designers on the one hand and new media/Internet art and activism on the other. Through interruption and sabotage or through new kinds of interfaces and modes of visualising (unfolding) the invisible (enfolded) information, these TAZs 'mimic the invisible processes of information capitalism in order to render its operations material, and to make manifest things that information capitalism would like to keep buried'.

See **Marx** in Part Two, and for other approaches to the radical politics of new technologies see **Haraway**, **Kidd**, **Terranova** and **Lovink** in Part Five. The extract from **Lovink** in this part also addresses new media art.

With the revolution of mass photographic and electronic media production, the twentieth century was celebrated as the century of visual media. Twentieth-century visual artists and humanities scholars devoted themselves to a critical analysis of mass-media images, in laudable undertakings such as subversion, reflexivity, and deconstruction. Prudent academia inaugurated programs in visual studies in the last decade of the century. But the visible, as Marshall McLuhan predicted, is no longer the lively and productive arena of struggle it has been. In terms I will explain below, the image is merely the selectively unfolded surface of enfolded information.

I propose that the most interesting and urgent areas of communication to study now are *invisible* media; invisible, but not immaterial. The media of the military, science, financial institutions, and mass communications are increasingly invisible, as advances in chemical and biological warfare, nanotechnology, the corporate-driven decoding of the human genome, quantum and other nondigital computing, data encryption, and other "small-scale" research areas attest. To engage these invisible media on their own territory, more rebellious media adopt similar strategies of invisibility. More precisely, they adopt strategies of enfoldment. These are waiting, hiding, latent media, coiled up like vipers or jacks-in-the-box. Invisible media constitute what Hakim Bey calls the temporary autonomous zone (TAZ): "a guerilla operation which liberates an area (of land, of time, of imagination) and then dissolves itself to re-form elsewhere/elsewhen, *before* the State can crush it."[1] The TAZ does not achieve permanent revolution but a mercurial liberation; it is defined by stealth and liquidity. After laying out the hiding places in between material experience, information/capital, and image, I will suggest that "temporarily autonomous media" can follow certain strategies of invisibility: these include making visible; sabotage; latency; and hiding in plain sight. My examples will mainly include computer-based media, though cinema, the refuge of the visible, will appear as well.

Enfolding/unfolding

A good way to understand the materiality of invisible media is to think of them as enfolded or implicate.[2] Communication entails a material connection between the utterer and the listener.[3] We may think of those communications that haven't happened yet as enfolded, or (in the latinate word for the same phenomenon) *implicate*, while those communications that take place are unfolded, or *explicate*. Physicist David Bohm used the term *explicate*, or unfolded, for that which is apparent in a given system, and *implicate*, or enfolded, for that which is latent in the same system. His elegant illustration is a model of two airtight glass cylinders, one inside the other, with a layer of viscous fluid, like glycerin, between them. When a drop of ink is put in the liquid and the inside cylinder revolves, the ink drop is drawn out into a thread; when it is revolved in the other direction, the thread of ink is enfolded back to a dot. The line is implicate in the dot.

War and invisibility

Two recent wars offer an index of the shift of power from visibility to invisibility. The Persian Gulf War, Paul Virilio argues, was the first realtime war, in which military intelligence could be transmitted and acted upon in an immediate feedback loop.[4] Military information bypassed the mediation by an image, or at least bypassed the delay that translation and transmission previously required. We could say information was potent to the degree that it remained invisible. If the Vietnam War was the media war, the war of extreme visibility, the Gulf War was the first in a new era of invisible warfare. Images from the Gulf War indexed information, not concrete events; the concrete events—the actual deaths—remained enfolded.

John Greyson's film *Law of Enclosures* (2001; based on the novel by Dale Peck), set in Sarnia, Ontario, during the Gulf War, graphically demonstrates how the military-media complex selectively enfolds and unfolds information. For the characters attempting to watch the war on television, poor rural reception further clouds the sketchy images relayed by "smart bombs" of their Iraqi targets. Myra struggles with her satellite dish and shoots her remote in frustration at her TV: "Show us the fucking war! We want to see the fucking *war*!" One character is an American soldier, Stanley, serving in the ground troops. When he returns he refuses to tell his friends what he did in Iraq. Later we learn that Stanley took part in the attack upon fleeing Iraqi soldiers after the cease-fire, part of which came to be called the "Highway of Death."[5] Barely reported during the war, the concealment of this massacre behind the rhetoric of a "clean war" set a precedent for the separation of image and information. Greyson unfolds this doubly concealed information in a stunning montage sequence. An image of the heads of hundreds of Iraqis at a rally dissolves into an overhead shot of contestants at the annual Sarnia kiss-a-thon; the latter release thousands of colored balloons, which dissolve into the black-and-white snow of a television receiving no signal (or too many signals). The true image of the Gulf War, the film suggests, is the image of the disturbed signal: Myra need not adjust her television, because war now is invisible. The war images indexed nothing because the reality of the war remained enfolded.

If the Gulf War was a war whose invisibility benefited the Western allies, then the recent and supposedly ongoing "war on terrorism" was a struggle to define the terms of invisibility. For a while in November 2001 the war seemed to be going horribly wrong. It looked like Osama bin Laden and his cohorts had a kind of invisibility on their side that the Americans and their allies did not. As Britain's Admiral Sir Michael Boyce told the *New York Times*, "This is not like Kosovo. . . . It's not like Desert Storm," he noted, "where you had very clearly defined phases and relatively straightforward objectives. This is a much more murky area in which to work, obviously because the prime element is not actually visible—Osama bin Laden and the Al Qaeda—in the same way that Milosevic and the Serbs were or the Iraqis were. This is something much more intangible."[6] For a while the Taliban seemed to defeat the technically superior Americans because it had the invisibility not of smart weapons (information) but of clandestine networks and caves (caves!)—materiality. Material reality was imperceptible to a military that refused to put soldiers on the ground. Of course, the "war on terrorism," manifest in the bombing of Afghanistan, turned out in the end to be just as ugly in its materiality as the Gulf War: at least as many Afghans were killed as were the innocent workers at the World Trade Center.[7] Meanwhile, as of this writing, the man supposed to be the center of Taliban terror evanesced like a particle of antimatter. As I write, "terror" still retains its power of enfoldment. The global powers of visibility remain daunted by the power of the invisible.

Everybody was trying to unfold the paths traveled by Taliban funds. U.S.-based global capitalism celebrates "transparency" as the basis of fair financial exchange and the smooth transfer of capital. Opacity, in the form of unsanctioned cash flows through fake charities, drug money, trade in diamonds, counterfeiting, tax havens, and the "primitive" Hawala money transfer system, is a slap in the face of global capital.[8] These alternative financial routes were successful because they occurred *far below* the speed of light. In a sort of purloined-letter strategy, the Taliban cash flow remained material, unencoded, and thus resisted detection. It was an affront, a scandal that this money did not flow along the recognized pathways of global capital: How could they do this to us?

Experience : information/capital : image

One more concept and we're ready to go. The world of computer-mediated capitalism is well summed up by a triadic relationship of enfolding—experience : information/capital : image.[9] By *experience* I mean the full complexity of material life. Experience enfolds, or holds in latent form, *information* and *capital*. Thus, information and capital selectively unfold experience. In turn, information and capital enfold images. Thus, in the digital world, images (or other palpable expressions, such as sound; computer music is the unfolding of digital information) selectively unfold information and capital. *Image*, being the third term, can also immediately enfold experience. Some photographs, whose images are too specific or banal to be useful as information or for capital, remain the direct index of experience.

Like all Peircean triads, the relationship among these three terms is very fluid. Images, information, and capital become part of *experience*, the first term in the triad. So we can understand the material world of experience to encompass images (not just visual), as well as the abstractions *information* and *capital*. In the rest of this essay, I will look at ways TAZ media can work with properties of invisibility of latency at the three levels I've described.

Level 3: image

As I am not very optimistic about the ability of visible images to produce TAZs, I will begin with this third term. As the triadic relationship implies, there are two kinds of image: images of material experience, and images as manifestations of information/capital. Unfortunately for the first kind, as soon as an image is born from the world of experience it gets taken up in the service of something else. Recall a few years back when the clothing designer Benetton piqued consumer interest by appending its logo to the photograph of a boatload of Albanian refugees.

The second kind of image is the skin or visible manifestation of information and capital. It is only a skin. George W. Bush's multicultural cabinet may be understood as the canny deployment of an image that indexes nothing: the image of U.S. state power is different; its function is exactly the same. The relationship of interface : database is a subset of the image : information/capital relationship, and recently the colon between them has become perceptibly loose. Interfaces can unfold information in many ways: they need not be visual.[10] The arbitrary nature of the visual interface is especially apparent in recent digital blockbusters like *Star Wars: Phantom Menace* and *The Lord of the Rings*, where the impossibly spectacular image denotes nothing but information. With digital media, Jean-Luc Godard's dictum, "Money is the film within the film," is truer than ever: the vast onscreen canyons populated by extrahuman hordes quickly become a mental image for costly proprietary software and powerful hardware; these in turn denote megabucks and invisible armies of laboring humans. Aware of the new possibilities of building new interfaces to existing databases, global corporate media have been researching the art of creative unfolding, as in the fountain at the Xerox Palo Alto Research Center, where the strength of the water stream reflects the behavior of the stock market.[11] Unfolding reveals only another surface.

TAZ media can unfold information and capital as well, though we must understand the effects of such manifestation to be temporary. Plenty of activist websites investigate the poor information disclosure (inadequate unfolding) of corporate and state media and create possibilities for radical coalition building. Here are a couple of films that visualize the hidden operations of global capital: *BIT Plane* (1999) by the Bureau of Inverse Technology is an aerial observation of Silicon Valley by a tiny (50-centimeter) remote-controlled plane equipped with mini-camera and transmitter. It sees housing, think-tank buildings, the antlike bodies of engineers and cheap/illegal laborers. It sees only the surface, but this is the unfolded surface of the labor and material infrastructure of military-industrial software and hardware development. *The Subconscious Art of Graffiti Removal* (2000) by Matt McCormick is a faux art-history documentary from Portland, Oregon, home of an anti-graffiti ordinance. The film's thesis is that the inherent impulse to make art is suppressed in our society to such a degree that it is manifested unconsciously in the various creative expressions of graffiti *removal* (blocky, free-form, expressionist). *The Subconscious Art of Graffiti Removal* unfolds the anarchic power of creativity— not only in graffiti, but also among the minimum-wagers hired to paint over it.

Level 1: material experience

I've written that experience is encoded only insofar as it is deemed useful, as information or as money. Thus, the first strategy is to be invisible by staying out in plain view, too material to be encoded. Bey is optimistic that the material world is studded with potential infinities, "hidden enfolded immensities," multiplying fractally such that they can never be accounted for, much less put to use, by corresponding "information." I experience such immensities along slush-gray Bronson Avenue in Ottawa, where the squeegee operators work their aggressive dance among the cars waiting at the red light, a jerry-rigged tangle of red and yellow cables decorates the side of the Olympia Meat Market, and a gamely hand-drawn "Smile for the Camera" indicates that we're under surveillance outside Leslie's Garage. I also experience such immensities in conversations that happen for their own sake, such as one in a class on October 5, 2000 where spontaneously the group imaginatively designed a device that would harness live cockroaches to move in a glass box through which we would slide film, emulsion side up, to make a cockorayographic movie. Experience is infinite! Its apparent uselessness (comparable to "junk DNA") is what makes it immune to the encoding will of information capital. But as Bey points out, this apparent uselessness is also the seed of creative insurrection:

> If we were to imagine an *information map*—a cartographic projection of the Net in its entirety—we would have to include in it the features of chaos, which have already begun to appear, for example, in the operations of complex parallel processing, telecommunications, transfers of electronic "money," viruses, guerrilla hacking, and so on.
>
> Each of these "areas" of chaos could be represented by topographs similar to the Mandelbrot Set . . . [which] might prove to be useful in "plotting" (in all senses of the word) the emergence of the counter-Net as a chaotic process, a "creative evolution" in Prigogine's term. If nothing else the M Set serves as a *metaphor* for a "mapping" of the TAZ's interface with the Net as a *disappearance of information*. Every "catastrophe" in the Net is a node of power for the Web, the counter-Net.[12]

The Mandelbrot set to which Bey refers is a fractal number set. Fractals are suggestive models of insurrectionary activity because they are complex at both large and small scales, suggesting the interdependency of local and global activity.

Writing in 1990, Bey did not mean by *the Net* only that skein of pallid digital information that so entangles and wastes the time of first-world people now. And by *counter-Net* he did not mean only the aggressive and creative use of the Internet to germinate counterinformation, viruses, and the like, although he anticipated them. Analog hindsight usefully reminds us of the many kinds of invisible media that predate digital applications: happenings, ephemeral performances, pranks, mail art,[13] loitering, and the many "useless" and ephemeral activities— often the work of women—that make life better.

At the level of experience, invisibility sometimes manifests as inactivity, undetectible on the radar. Loitering indexes disenfranchisement from the flows of power. In two movies from poor countries, loitering indicates a kind of enfolded or potential energy. Abderrahmane Sissako's *La vie sur terre* (1999), commissioned by European television for the millennium series "2000 vue par . . .," is set in Sokolo, Sissako's father's village in Mali. The major activity in this film consists of waiting for information. Nana, a young woman from the next village, waits in vain for a call from her lover on the town's one, malfunctioning, telephone. As the golden daylight moves over the village, time is marked by the row of old men who occasionally shift their chairs to stay within the shadow of a house. They listen on a transistor radio to Radio France Internationale, where live commentators breathlessly describe the millennial festivities at the Eiffel Tower. In a nub of space-time forgotten by the former colonizer, Sokolo marks the difference between visibility and invisibility, mattering to the flow of global capital and not mattering. *La vie sur terre* unfolds the enfolded infinity of the village, heart-breaking in its "useless" beauty.

Loitering also marks the time in Elia Suleiman's film *Chronicle of a Disappearance* (1996) made shortly after the disastrous Oslo Accord but before the second intifada: in other words, during a time in which Palestinian political will was enfolded. The protagonist, like Suleiman a Palestinian living in Nazareth, is invisible to the Israeli police who search his apartment. His friend's tourist shop is invisible to the few camera-toting tourists that still come through. The protagonist and his friend loiter outside the latter's "Holy Land" shop, which remains unvisited all day, the only disturbance being the minute squeaking of the postcard rack. In the stillest, most tentative of movements, the film asks whether there might still be hope for images to unfold—temporarily autonomous images that won't immediately be pulled into the deathly service of signification and surveillance.

Level 2: information/capital

One level down in the triad are powers that are invisible except in their effects. Information and capital are infinitely recodable because they have no true nature except for mercurial liquidity. Power now is the ability to toggle information into either a latent or a manifest state.[14] Thus, another goal of TAZ media in the age of invisibility is the time-honored Marxist strategy of concretizing false abstractions. There are many ways for activists to do this in the digital world, including determining the sources of servers, storage, backbones, and other material sites upon which information media rely. The collective Consume.net invites others to collaborate in building a broadband telecommunications infrastructure that provides a cheap alternative to commercial internet service providers.[15] Other concretizers include programmers who offer their software for free, such as those writing the Unix-compatible GNU (a self-referential acronym for Gnu's Not Unix) software system.[16] These programmers sabotage a system that relies not on quality programming but on copyright, licensing, and expiry dates.

For military, marketing, and surveillance purposes, information is compiled into databases, which lie dormant until they are accessed through interfaces. The kind of interface you use determines what sort of information the database will yield; it unfolds a given database in a specific way. Commercial interfaces pretend to fully unfold the data at their disposal. Search engines, for example, pretend to give access to all the information on the World Wide Web, but (with the apparent exception of Google[17]) they are really just giant Yellow Pages with paid advertisers. Similarly, graphical interfaces to the web, such as Netscape or Microsoft's Internet Explorer, obscure information sources and machine processes. Webstalker, an experimental browser released by the artist/programmers I/O/D in 1997, bypasses the obfuscatory interface. Webstalker graphs the file contents and links of a given webpage, unfolding for users the underlying code of the web.[18]

In the new genres of database art, the work's audiovisual manifestation is secondary to its status as an enfolder of information. Database artists, working with information architectures rather than images, mimic the strategies of the information economy.[19] Many forgo the Flash-y visibility available to web design and work at the level of machine code, making visible (in some cases, imitating the look of) the guts of information. They build interfaces to databases that unfold the choices implicit in the design of information platforms. These include Emmanuel Lamotte (e_rational), "Netochka Nezvanova" (m9ndfukc.com), Marek Walczak and Martin Wattenberg's project *Apartment*, which translates sentences into objects, organized according to linguistic filters; and the famous jodi.org. Often opaque and frustrating, these artists' web works make explicit that an interface is a selective unfolding of data.

A more radical, indeed terroristic, strategy is to bury TAZs within the world of sanctioned corporate and state information. The shadowy collective RTMark deploys the mimic interface for direct purposes of sabotage. Its subsidiary Etoys.com mimics the official site of the company eToys.com. Etoys.com, which appears to sell evil and nasty plastic figures that make explicit the aggression and gender stratification implicit in real children's toys, successfully brought down the stock of the real eToys over Christmas 1999. RTMark's gatt.org mimics the official site of the General Agreement on Tariffs and Trade but unfolds material relations that the real GATT prefers to leave implicit. Gatt.org mimics the drab professionalism of the actual organization's site, but its articles celebrating the advance of global capital link to activist sites that reveal its dark side: for example, "The Bright Side of Efficiency," lauding automated food production, links to Food First's "Twelve Myths about Hunger." These sites are *temporary* autonomous zones because pretty soon users cotton on to the fact that these are fake sites and RTMark is instructed to cease and desist. But they are just those nodes of chaos in the Net that Bey envisioned, causing actual economic damage and giving visitors a taste of anarchy.

Above I suggested that loitering is a form of strategic invisibility. Software can loiter, too. Viruses and worms exist typically in a dormant state but spring into action, making manifest the material connectedness of computers and users. Viruses are not so different from the "cookies" that commercial websites deposit on our hard drives in order to survey our patterns of information usage. Most browsers are initialized with the command "Enable all cookies," presuming computer users' consent. As artist Ardele Lister says, the name connotes the benign invitation that opens an abusive relationship—"Here little girl, have a cookie."[20] Viruses, on the other hand, do not presume the consent of their victim. Virus "art," in making visible the processes of infiltration and co-optation, questions who is allowed such access and what kinds of surveillance are considered acceptable.

The Biennale virus, biennale.py, appears to be the first virus produced as a work of art. Produced for the Slovenian pavilion at the 2001 Venice Biennale by a group of artists and hackers, 0100101110101101.org and EpidemiC,[21] the virus is quite benign. Written in the Python language, it can only attach itself to other files in this currently rare language; in addition, the artists provided antivirus companies with the epidemic.py. Biennale is more interesting in that it draws attention to the mutual implication of all computer users. This sense of interrelationship is the focus of another of 0100101110101l0l.org's projects, life_sharing. The anagram of "file sharing" describes accurately the project of making the artists' entire hard drive open to any online visitor.

Arguably more creative—or at least more TAZ-like—than Biennale are viruses designed without such careful restraints. Recently a virus called "Creative" infected computers with an activist message for nonproprietary software. The virus does not damage files but moves files with .zip or .jpg extensions to the root directory of the drive, adding to the file's name the admonishment "change at least now to LINUX."[22] Of the thousands of viruses out there, I am especially fond of Joshi. Reported to have originated in India and first identified in 1990, Joshi takes a common Indian surname, perhaps that of its programmer. Every January 5, the virus freezes the systems of infected computers and instructs users to type "Happy birthday Joshi!" in order to liberate them.[23] Joshi indicates its potential power with an annual flex of the claws, commands the ritual obeisance, then returns to dormancy.

A brilliant example of an invisible medium that explicates power relations was the Love Bug virus of 2000. Its perpetrator, Onel de Guzman, failed to graduate from AMA Computer College of the Philippines after the school rejected his thesis proposal involving a software program that steals the Windows passwords of Internet users. The Love Bug was released on May 4, 2000, the date Guzman's class graduated without him. It caused worldwide damages estimated to be $10 million (although the value attributed to hours of work lost is itself a symptom of encoding experience in capital, and probably overestimated).[24]

Guzman's quite reasonable rationale for this illegal program was "to spend more time on Internet without paying." Internet access is prohibitively expensive in the Philippines, where it is common to visit Internet cafés. One of the main purposes of Internet commerce in the Philippines is the mail-order-bride market or, euphemistically, the dating service. North American and European men, drawn by fantasies of demure, submissive Asian brides, advertise for what they want and are answered by women seeking to emigrate. The potential suitors send money with which the women log on at Internet cafés.[25] Perhaps Guzman was protesting the phenomenon of women selling themselves on the international market, a not-ridiculous prospect in a country where teachers' wages are below poverty level. Maybe "I Love You" was an ironic comment on the international, Internet love market: an unfolding of the neocolonial trafficking in women.

I've given several examples of ways that temporarily autonomous media can mimic the invisible processes of information capitalism in order to render its strategies material, and to make manifest things that information capital would like to keep buried. But given the brief life of TAZ media before they are incorporated into the chain of instrumentalization, I celebrate those media that remain latent, viruslike. Invisible media remain enfolded within information, refusing to become an image. Or they remain enfolded within experience, refusing to become information. Bey's examples of poetic terrorism include all-night dancing in the vestibules of ATMs[26]: an activity that is invisible because it is useless, and for the same reason, a source of life against the deathful encoding machine. Just a shade further into visibility are those acts of temporary autonomy that remind people that material life is infinitely richer and more chaotic than the poor bonds of information and capital. I suggest, then, that temporarily autonomous media might work at levels just under the radar of information capitalism: media that are less appropriable, less encodable, less "meaningful," and more potentially disruptive. I suggest we think of invisibility as a kind of degree zero: images and information that are always ready to spring forth but refuse to; refuse to be born.[27]

Notes

My hearty thanks go to the participants in the wartime conference for which I initially assembled these thoughts: Blowing the Trumpet to the Tulips: an Exchange on Experimental Media, organized by Gary Kibbins and Susan Lord and held at Queen's University, Kingston, Ontario, October 18–21, 2001. I also thank my smart artist friends Ardele Lister, Eric Rosenzweig, and Benton Bainbridge for their input; Jim Dean for research assistance; Mike Bellemare for information on Mao's Long March, a strategy of disappearance that resides invisibly in the essay; Jukka Sihvonen for a reminder of the "dark matter" of which the universe is primarily and invisibly composed; and Grahame Weinbren, as always a most perceptive and demanding reader, for helping me argue that materiality comprises everything.

1   Hakim Bey, "The Temporary Autonomous Zone," in *T.A.Z.: The Temporary Autonomous Zone, Ontological Anarchy, Poetic Terrorism* (Brooklyn, N.Y.: Autonomedia, 1991), 101. Bey's playful model of the TAZ

echoes Guy DeBord's view of revolution as festival, though his focus on the *temporary* nature of autonomous zones precludes revolution in toto.

2   I discuss the strategy of enfoldment in computer-based media in great detail in "How Electrons Remember," *Millennium Film Journal* 34 (1999): 66–80; updated in *Touch: Sensuous Theory and Multisensory Media* (Minneapolis: University of Minnesota Press, 2002). Bohm's illustration is borrowed from that essay.

3   Charles Sanders Peirce, quoted in Vincent M. Colapietro, *Peirce's Approach to the Self: A Semiotic Perspective on Human Subjectivity* (Albany: State University of New York Press, 1989), 18.

4   Paul Virilio, "My Kingdom for a Horse: The Revolutions of Speed," *Queen's Quarterly* 108, no. 3 (2002): 337.

5   See Joyce Chediac, "The Massacre of Withdrawing Soldiers on 'The Highway of Death,'" in Ramsey Clark et al., *War Crimes: A Report on United States War Crimes against Iraq* (Washington, D.C.: Maisonneuve Press, 1992); http://www.deoxy.org/wc/wc-index.htm.

6   Michael R. Gordon, "Allies Preparing for Long Fight as Taliban Dig In," *New York Times*, October 29, 2001, <http://www.nytimes.com/2001/10/28international/asia/28STRA.html>.

7   Seumas Milne, "The Innocent Dead in a Coward's War: Estimates Suggest US Bombs Have Killed At Least 3,767 Civilians," *The Guardian*, December 20, 2001, <http:/www.guardian.co.uk/print/0,3858,4323335,00.html>.

8   "Customs Service goes after terrorist funding," CNN, October 25, 2001. At http://www.cnn.com/2001/US/10/25/inv.terrorist.funding/. Rachel Ehrenfeld, "Funding Terrorism," talk at Aviation Week Homeland Security and Defense Conference, Washington, D.C., November 27, 2001. At <http://public_integrity.org/publications11.htm>.

9   The model of the iterative triadic relationship, so wonderfully useful, is borrowed from Charles Sanders Peirce.

10 Lisa Cartwright demonstrates that in many visual interfaces to nonvisual data, such as ultrasound and other kinds of medical imaging, the visual image is simply a by-product of the data and represents a virtual, rather than physical, object; Cartwright, "Film and the Digital in Visual Studies: Film Studies in the Era of Convergence," *Journal of Visual Culture* 1, no. 1 (2002): 18–20.

11 Lev Manovich, *The Language of New Media* (Cambridge, Mass.: MIT Press, 2001), 330.

12 Bey, "The Temporary Autonomous Zone," 112–13. Note the similarity between Bey's comparison of the dominating Net and the liberating web and Donna Haraway's comparison of the power-serving "informatics of domination" with the liberating, cyborg web in "A Cyborg Manifesto: Science, Technology, and Socialist-Feminism in the Late Twentieth Century," in *Simians, Cyborgs and Women: The Reinvention of Nature* (New York: Routledge, 1991), 149–81.

13 Tilman Baumgärtel traces the prehistory of web art in mail art, teleconferences, and other analog communications works; Baumgärtel, "On the History of Artistic Work in Telecommunications Media," in *Net_condition: Art and Global Media*, ed. Peter Weibel and Timothy Druckrey (Cambridge, Mass.: MIT Press, 2001), 152–61. For the precomputer history of communications and software art, see also Peter Lunenfeld, "In Search of the Telephone Opera," *Afterimage* 25, no. 1 (1997): 8–10; and Florian Cramer and Ulrike Gabriel, "On Software Art," Rhizome.org, September 20, 2001, at <http://rhizome.org/object.rhiz?2848>.

14 As I write, it's being discovered that executives of the failed Enron energy corporation "toggled" their soon-to-be-worthless stocks into personal millions of cool cash before the company declared bankruptcy. Global capital, state interests, and elite shareholders already have the power of selective disclosure.

15 See <www.consume.net>.

16 See <www.gnu.org>.

17 At this writing the stocks of major search engines Ask Jeeves, Lycos, LookSmart, and Yahoo! were exhibiting a sharp decline in 2001 over the previous year, possibly as a result of Google's success. Google does not release financial information.

18 See <http://www.backspace.org/iod/>.

19 Lev Manovich, "The Database," in *The Language of New Media*, 218–43.

20 Ardele Lister, personal communication, January 12, 2002.

21 Web artists are hard to identify and their names do not always index real people: 0100101110101101.org includes Moscow artist Olia Lialina; EpidemiC, based in Italy, includes Gaetano La Rosa.

22 Michelle Delio, "Wild Worm With Pro-Linux Message," Wired.com, December 1, 2000. <http://www.wired.com/news/technology/0,1282,40457,00.html>.

23 Julian Dibbell, "Viruses Are Good for You," *Wired* 3.02 (1995): <http://www.wired.com/wired/archive/3.02/viruses.html>.

24 Associated Press, "Love Bug Indictment Coming This Week," *USA Today*, June 13, 2000, at <http://www.usatoday.com/life/cyber/tech/cti087.htm>.

25 L. Clare Bratten, "Cyber Cherry Blossoms: Online Mail Order Brides," talk at the conference Console-ing Passions: Television, Video, Feminism; Notre Dame University, May 13, 2000.

26 Hakim Bey, "Poetic Terrorism," in *T.A.Z.*, 4.

27 Independent media remains practically invisible due to an old-fashioned lack of access to the means of production. Here are distributors for films and videos described herein:

> *BIT Plane:* Video Data Bank, <www.vdb.org>.
> *Chronicle of a Disappearance:* Independent Television Service, <www.itvs.org>; Aska Films, <askafilm@login.net>.
> *The Law of Enclosures:* Alliance Atlantis Pictures International, (416) 967–1141, Fax: (416)967–1226.
> *The Subconscious Art of Graffiti Removal:* Matt McCormick, <matt@rodeofilmco.com>.
> *a vie sur terre:* California Newsreel, <www.newsreel.org>.

Chapter 25

GEERT LOVINK

THESES ON DISTRIBUTED AESTHETICS

A S WITH THE OTHER ESSAY by Geert **Lovink** included in this book, 'Theses on Distributed Aesthetics' is of interest both in its historical specificity and in its more general critical insights. Historically then, Lovink is concerned with questions of new media art and aesthetics at the moment (the first decade of the twenty-first century) at which the net.art movement seems to be eclipsed by locative media and Web 2.0 platforms and networks. More generally he poses questions of the aesthetics of new media networked art. The kinds of projects he has in mind are rarely motivated by the creation of visually beautiful screen images, rather they are often concerned with the mobilisation of networks themselves, or the mapping of data flows and lines of communication and connectivity. Contemporary media communication, he points out, is more often tactile and manual than visual (in SMS for instance) or predicated on machine sensing and mapping rather than human optical perception (GPS).

He proposes the notion of 'distributed aesthetics' as one of a number of possible entry points, 'radical and imaginative concepts that enable us to describe what is happening around us' in network culture. With 'distribution' Lovink is referring to both new media technologies and networks and to the new social/creative/activist phenomena that have arisen with networked and mobile technologies. As well as the more familiar organisation of artist and activist groups, these include (online) blogs and wikis and (offline) flash mobs, crowds and multitudes. 'Distributed aesthetics' then, insists that these new creative activities must be understood more as technosocial events and networks, rather than as institutionally distinct and formal objects and practices. Throughout, this article refuses to separate art media and communication or information media, art and activist practices, aesthetic and everyday experience of new media culture. Distributed aesthetics is as much about constructing the social as depicting it.

On new media art, see **Marks** above, and **Kidd** (Part Five) on media activism. http://www.networkcultures.org/geert

This chapter examines a concept that emerged within the Australian Fibreculture group.[1] During the preparation of the *Fibreculture Journal* issue on distributed aesthetics, editor Anna Munster and I wrote a number of theses on this matter. These formed the basis of a workshop that was organized by Anna Munster and me on May 11–12, 2006 at the Wissenschaftskolleg/Institute of Advanced Study in Berlin.[2] The theses presented here were initially written together with Anna Munster, around mid-2005, and then rewritten after the Berlin workshop. This text may be considered a classic example of multiple authorship.

There was a wish to open up a new field of inquiry after the demise of net.art and the rise of Web 2.0, locative media, and various mapping efforts. During the roaring 1990s net.art opened up spaces, brought people together, and provoked interesting work and collaborations. This creative and subversive energy dissipated later on when the (failed) attempt was made to seek recognition of the museum and gallery world. Floating dotcom money went to MBAs, not to net.artists. In the end, it was "art" that divided people. However, many of the issues and desires remained. How can aesthetics in a network society be defined beyond the question of if this or that site, blog, or application is, or is not, art? These days, there are still a lot of interesting individual artists and groups that produce sublime and provocative work. But that is not the point. The crucial point is how, and where, the works connect. This collection of ideas proposes a new consolidated thinking through of the (sensual) experience—the "aesthesia"—of networked events. How do we experience the current wave of blogs, podcasts, and mobile phone games? What network theory is used and is it adequate to the task of engaging networks on their own terms?

Obviously, we are not concerned about "eternal beauty." Neither would it be useful to define "aesthesis" as perception of the eyes. There is no need to privilege the visual. Communication is something people do with their hands as much as with their eyes and ears. The manual aspect of, for instance, texting needs to be stressed. Writing an SMS is as much a manual exercise as it is textual, and it all occurs on a screen. Sensing presence through GPS does not have to culminate in an image. There is no necessity to, again, reproduce or question visual domination. We should reject attempts to reduce media and the arts to *Bildwissenschaften*. We are not talking about screen culture as a way to talk only about painting, film, and television. It is the abstract, the conceptual, the unseen, and the immanent that the distributed brings into play. Let's face it, we have passed the aesthetic turn, and there is no way back. There is a link to be made to Nicolas Bourriaud's relational aesthetics, of judging artworks because of the inter-human relations they represent, produce, or prompt. However, we must time and again spoil such a humanistic, subject-centered approach with machinic logic. Seminar participant Warren Sack argues for a nonvisual, conceptual, art-based understanding of artistic work in information visualization. He relies on what Benjamin Buchloh, writing about conceptual art practices, called an "aesthetic of administration."[3] What we need are new entry points, radical and imaginative concepts that enable us to describe what is happening around us. Distributed aesthetics is one such attempt. What is "sensual recognition" in the age of networks and what critical terms need to develop in order to describe properly our mediated experiences?

Another entry point for distributed aesthetics could be the longstanding discontent in interface design as if it were a static image. How can blogs, wikis, and social network sites become more interesting in terms of design, while not giving away the critical mass that many such sites have managed to create? In other words, how can usability be granted in a time when users no longer want to be fooled by quasi-interesting tricks? How can we lose track, wander around, get lost, while still being able to find that telephone number, e-mail, or postal address? Do useful information and the "link to Lorelei" sirens that lure us away from functional tasks have to be contradictory? The codeword, distributed aesthetics, expresses the wish to move on from the virtual and the visual toward an integrated approach—an approach that no longer highlights technology as something revolutionary or disruptive, but focuses on the overall architecture of flows and disruptions; be it immaterial, mechanical, aerodynamic, or static. It is in the art of distribution that we can trace new possibilities of use that go beyond techno-determinist readings that only stress the limitations that we, the trash users, have.

The distributed element not only refers to decentralized and parallel computing, in the sense of "using two or more computers communicating over a network to accomplish a common objective or task" (Wikipedia). It also points to social formations that mobile technologies provoke, such as groups, mobs, crowds, multitudes, and swarms. The distribution over a network of objects, power, work, and people not only caters to diversity and freedom, but also leads to anonymity and isolation. The difficulty of how to transform distant collaboration, solidarity, and friendship into actual situations and social change has increased to such an extent that the social has become fetishized into an exotic entity. No one would even remotely associate it with The Social Question, much less matters of class struggle or socialism. During the Berlin seminar, Brian Holmes commented that institutions have the function to discipline crowds into citizenry with predictable norms. He argued that there is something prepolitical and unruly about the crowd, the mob, and the multitude. The idea of the masses has been associated with citizen formation. In any crowd there are individuals who write its algorithm. The power is with those who are able to set the terms of the debate.[4] This is why the manufacture of concepts is such a strategic undertaking. Instead of borrowing terms from the dead discipline of mass psychology, it would be better to come up with descriptions for what we actually witness, like Warren Sack, who called the networked dialogs on lists, newsgroups, chat rooms, and blogs "very large-scale conversations," as they are often a form of conversation that involves many more people in far more complicated social and semantic dynamics compared to previous eras.[5]

Form, forming, format

The premise here is that we are moving from living, analyzing, and imaging contemporary culture as an information society technically underwritten by the computer, to inhabiting and imagining relays of entwined and fragmented techno-social networks. New media is increasingly distributed media and it requires a rethinking of aesthetics beyond the twinned concepts of form and medium that continue to shape analysis of the social and the aesthetic.[6] It requires *distributed aesthetics*. Distributed aesthetics must deal simultaneously with the dispersed and the situated, with asynchronous production and multi-user access to artifacts (both material and immaterial) on the one hand, and the highly individuated and dispensed allotment of information/media on the other. The aesthetics of distributed media, practices, and experience cannot be located in the formal principles of their dispersal. This only provides us with the conditions for serving information via a network to end-users and reduces it to a simplistic schema, one that echoes all the problems of a communications systems transmission model: server-network-users. Nor can we simply derive distributed aesthetics from the viewpoint of use. There is no singular or end use of information but rather the endless relaying of media, practices, and experience as successive dispersals. Distributed aesthetics might be better characterized as an emergent project, situated between the drift away from coherent form on the one hand, and the drift of aesthetics into relations with the social and networked formations on the other.

Networks cannot be fully studied if seen only as mere tools with schematizations and diagrams. They need to be apprehended as complex environments, within the complex networked ecologies in which they are forming. This can easily become an empty statement. By complex, we mean unpredictable, often poor, harsh, and not exactly rich expressions of the social. To project positive predictions, hopes, and desires onto networks is deceptive as it often distracts by focusing solely on the first, founding, and euphoric phase of networks. Consequently, this positivism is ill equipped to deal with the conflict, boredom, confusion, stagnation, and other expressions of our playfully nihilistic culture, which turn up in unmoderated channels such as lists, blogs, and chat rooms. If we call for distributed aesthetics, it needs to account for those experiences of stagnation within network formations. It also needs to couple these networked experiences with a network's potential to transform and mutate into something not yet fully codified. It is not enough to celebrate networks as social realities. What we call for is a systematic reflection on the formats of distribution we use. What counts are cultures of use that understand enough to alter the given software, interfaces, and content into something unprecedented. Can the user really become a network architect and not just a subject that merely leaves traces? How do users turn into developers? And, importantly, how do they develop the critical skills to resist responding at crucial moments? Besides this capacity, we also have to study the consumption of technical distribution (as Sebastian Lütgert suggested at the Berlin seminar), sitting quietly watching the P2P files being downloaded. There is not much left of the autonomy of the user, and Western subjectivity in general. It is important to reassess the status of user, as Pit Schultz has done in his essay "The Producer as Power User."[7]

The map is not the network

A concrete instance of distributed aesthetics can be found in the widespread eagerness to produce maps. What is so fascinating about mapping?[8] If we began first with a question and now follow with a gesture of negation, this is precisely because the network—so opaque, so ubiquitous and non-formal—is recruited to serve various strategies of representation. Maps of networks abound. Software for visualizing criminal networks such as PatternTracer are easily available online; an entire discursive field—social network analysis—has arisen around the mapping of networks from corporate to terrorist; and the noncartographic specialist can now log on to an entire map of the Internet, drop in, and link his or her own computer address as a 3D-visualization in the network of all other addresses.[9] Richard Rogers suggests that mapping networks, especially as an intelligence task, carries with it more than just an aesthetic outcome; we are in the midst of a techno-epistemological impulse in which the form(at) of the map has a structuring effect on how we understand the organization (structure) and dynamics (movement) of networks.[10]

Theorizing networks (as opposed to direct network visualization) must struggle with the abstraction of dispersed elements—elements that cannot be captured into one image. The very notion of a network is in conflict with the desire to gain an overview. Mapping software, the technological answer to this problem, by its own nature reduces complexity in order to produce a limited amount of general categories, which then can be applied to the map and linked. The art of network visualization deals with several limitations, those of the screen, algorithms, and the boundaries of human perception. We can read—and understand—only so many linked elements. In order to understand and appreciate network maps, we have to familiarize ourselves with "cloud thinking" in which we zoom out from relational levels in order to obtain a bigger picture. Having moved away from a chaotic cluster, we can then move into the cloud again and look for specific links between items.

Maps make visible what we have already sensed. Maps provoke a sense of recognition. Network maps may also organize our perception of a social object in formation without being forthright about the premises upon which this organizing impulse rests. Network mapping exposes a desire to be in the know, "a way of coming to know and making particular claims only with a technological apparatus that desires to grow to satisfy its cravings for 'really knowing' and, especially 'really knowing what our' intelligence also knows or should know," as Richard Rogers sees it.[11] Mapping information—the aesthetics of contemporary visualization—provides a sense of relief that the twisted and unstructured info-bits that roam around in our cognitive unconscious are finally laid out and put to rest. A beast is tamed. Against today's presumed transparency of the maps, Nils Röller, speaking at the Berlin seminar, emphasized its traditional secrecy. Often the ownership of maps gave the explorer unprecedented access to resources and power. Why would one need a map if one knows where to go, Röller asked. Instead, he proposed the use of the term *compass*. The factors that determine computational environments are too often perceived as being merely oriented on the interface level. Is it the exclusion mechanism that further fuels the open access movement? Is it still relevant to ask what information is revealed and what is hidden? Obviously today's capture devices, from satellites to handy cameras, contain other limits. What to make of Archive.org's wild claim that it provides "universal access to human knowledge?" What if the interfaces are becoming too complex and the databases overgrown with nonsense data? The drive to have a complete overview at that point collapses into madness or resentment.

Network mapping underwent a significant shift in geometry and visualization in the late 1990s.[12] As we moved from the superimposition of flows onto geo-political space, toward the abstraction of topology, similarly our understandings of what comprised networks shifted. We became interested in relations, dynamics, and sociability as opposed to traffic, connections, and community. This change in network mapping visualization has had advantages and disadvantages—we are now aware that networks are different kinds of formations that cannot be understood according to the old distinctions between society (*Gesellschaft*) and community (*Gemeinschaft*). But the increasingly abstract topological visualization of networks removes us from an analysis of the ways in which networks engage and are engaged by current political, economic, and social relations.

At any rate, maps reveal the ways in which we perceive things to be at a given historical time. The Mercator Map (circa 1569), now analyzed from a moment "post" its particular partitioning of perception along a colonial set of axes, reveals what was at stake politically and economically in making the world run according to a north–south cartography. Perhaps network mapping will similarly reveal the logic of its own will to tame complexity, to make the flows of a network society traceable. It could be more interesting, then, to not simply look at the map but at what desires network mapping is trying to satisfy. If in the past cartography has been linked to imperial conquests of space, what space is there left to conquer today? The space between the nodes or even the space of all potential connections and links? Just as network formations are indications that an unstable reshuffle of the categories for understanding the social is playing itself out, mapping this rearranging sociality indicates an aesthetic at work to order more rampant and mutant forms of emergent social relations. It is not surprising that the impetus for network mapping arrives today from the social sciences on the one hand and from the analysis, tracking, and tracing of crime on the other.[13] We ought to be suspicious of the pervasive will to network mapping as well. For Brian Holmes, on the other hand, there is no reason to downgrade the importance of making maps. For Bureau d'Etudes, their maps are tools among others, used within workshops on specific topics.[14]

The fu code

Over the past two decades, aesthetics has been extended, stretched, and turned upside down from a discipline dealing with the interpretation of the meaning and structure of the object of beauty into a philosophical praxis investigating the very conditions of contemporary life.

Aesthetics is not the science of eye-candy, in which taste is reduced to a matter of mere statistics and samples of information. Instead, we must investigate the "aesthesia" of today's networked experience. How do we perceive the socially invisible, yet all too real, relationships that are accumulating around us? Distributed aesthetics, as a project, needs to be understood as a participatory journey of network users, aiming to capture the not-yet-described and the not-yet-visualized, and to go beyond poles such as real–virtual, new–old, offline–online, and global–local. We should forget about exposing the links that are already there and, with our capacity to engage a networked logic, forge links to what is *in* the network but not yet *of* the network. By this we mean to invoke a project more akin to social aesthetics or aesthesia in which we engage in and with the collective experiences of being embroiled in networks and being actively part of their making. We can contrast this with the abstracted activity of simply mapping quantities of data such as social network maps, which is a form of production already captured by the codes and conventions of connectivity.

We do not need allegorical readings of networks. Networks are not proposals, constructions, metaphors, or even alternatives for existing social formations such as the church, the corporation, the school, the NGO, or the political party. Instead, we should analyze the rise of networks as an all too human endeavor, a tragic fall, and not as posthuman machines automating connections for us. Networks are not the answer to global problems nor are they a substitute for forgotten religions or disintegrated communities. Networks are not models to be transposed from one social or political situation or conflagration to another. It is certainly the case that technology provokes networking. But then this provocation is not the be all and end all of the network. We should be wary of techno-contradictions like social software that suggest technology will glue us humans together (again).[15] Instead, we should read—and enjoy—networks as info-clouds that cover the sun and disperse the bright light of broadcasting media.

Networks act as "fragmentators." They break up strong signs and experiences into countless threads. These info-bits might in themselves be meaningless but their overall sum provides enough distraction to topple the attention monopoly of newspapers and television. This is not done through the classic activist strategy of building up parallel counterworlds. Lists, blogs, chat rooms, and social networks sites are the "long tail" of the media landscape.[16] Networks do not burn off the media, take center stage, and continue to provide the background noise of the chattering classes. It doesn't matter how big they grow. Instead of anticipating a takeover by the corporate sphere and attempting to protect networked and locative media from demise, it is more than likely that business interests will integrate selected parts of the blogosphere. The rest of the online noise will likely fade away into digital oblivion. In the meantime, blogs, wiki, podcasting, and whatever comes next will continue to run under the rubric of media diversification. Nothing is as fluid, fragile – and unsustainable – as today's network landscape.

In the meantime, we could treat the info-bits that flow our way as short-term solutions to the environmental crises brought about by the breakdown of both massified media outlets and dedicated high-end digital aesthetics. Data flows from peer to peer, in networks hardly noticed by authorities. But before the law moves in—and with it, the academics—the crowds will have already moved on to cooler pastures. Let's not invest some salvation in all of this distribution. Distributed media are both too loose and too large upon which to build a new utopia. Their fragmentary nature will have effects but we cannot link them to a cause. We may be unable to house the endless link lists, unanswered calls and e-mails, cute blogs, and stagnant conversations under the banner of complete social and media transformation. However, we will nonetheless have to find a mode of comprehending their everyday perceptual accretions—the ways in which they make small changes to our social relations with others and with broader groupings such as mainstream media.

What network theory, and with it, distributed aesthetics, needs to tackle first is the myth of seamless and perpetual growth. Once upon a time during the golden dotcom days it was an insight to present networks as dynamic, ever-growing entities. These days, we have moved to obsessively focusing upon the micro-politics of networks within networks. It is impressive but useless to know that your social network puts you in connection with 371,558 "friends." At that point, friends are simply an effect of a network, not its constituent relations.[17] The social scientists almost reveal the desires that shape their own trajectories around "social and organizational network analysis" with their talk of egocentric networks. The micro has become awash with the atomized individuals and we waste our capacity on comprehending the shapes or shaping of networks by plotting out the link lines of one node to another. In actuality, the lines that appear so connected, seamless, and smooth on network maps can never account for the human labor required to create and maintain the link or the sudden death and change of direction for a network in which strong lines give way. Rhizomes, in fact, have odd shapes and are actually small roots that die off at some point in their lifeline. So do trees. The problem with a naïve cloning of Deleuze and Guattari's botany in the networked context lies with an unreconstructed commitment to growth. This involves a blinding by the potentialities that the network-as-dream-machine would seem to offer. Here the network and info-capital converge rather than produce friction, complications, or even poisonings. Instead, we could say that growing could mean not simply expansion but maturing. There is plenty of quantity in the mediascape and so to grow without changing or dying only multiplies or clones more networks of connected atomized units. Networks need ideas and aesthetic projects directing how they might mature and transform. The distribution concept, for instance, does not automatically imply seamless expansion.

Let's draw a difference here between growth and persistence. Growth feeds the lifecycle of capital and capital loves any kind of growth—upward, downward, or outward. Persistence, on the other hand, comprehends that something doggedly survives but that its growth or decay depends on other forces, conditions, and effort. Bits of the network break off and wither and it may be that something can endure elsewhere because of this little death. But maybe the whole damn patch of grass just ups and dies one day, and there is no longer a network in your backyard. Online social formations are more like these small tendrils of growth that shoot and die—the list, for example, lives for a while as its members try to feed it. They work to shape and develop it, providing it with new impetus while the overall form just lumbers along. But then its energy burns out and there is no more growing left to do. Something endures between some of the participants or another effort starts up elsewhere but then that something, that network, has changed too. These processes are not all part of the same growing organism or self-organizing system. Attempts to homogenize or sustain processes as a singular drive toward growth are endemic to capital. The processes are instead lateral, cumulative, and de-energized modes of labouring; also endemic to capital but, for the most part, the unpaid arc of its cycle.

Against biologism

Networks do not simply emerge. They are cybernetic constructs that, once founded and installed, erupt and then slumber, decline, go on and on, fall asleep and wake up again before they die a sudden death or face an entropic decline. Networks do not follow the simplistic models of linear mechanics or of evolutionary growth. A critical theory of scalability and sustainability has to go beyond the biological metaphors that speak of contagion, copy-paste epidemics and memes. We have to make a distinction between real existing patterns, behaviors within technical networks, and the wet dreams (or nightmares) of marketing departments trying to give a positive spin on the unpredictable moves of their blogging customers.

Complexity—of data, of connectivity—has been rolled out as an excuse for technical and cultural phenomena being too hard to comprehend. Subsequently, it figures that we have to feed all of this complexity back into the machine to be analyzed. Numbers are too hard so we get a picture instead. Complexity should not be an excuse for deferring the work of human thought and human creation—theoretical and aesthetic—to network software. Complexity is difficult and arduous but not aesthetically unmanageable. Let's not cede the complexity of networked life to procedures. If we want suggestions as to how this complex networked aesthetics might be rendered, then let us look less to maps and more to sketches and roughs that infer a category of "the relational" comprised of potentialities. This would be somewhat different from framing relations within reductive models of utility or connectivity. Let's look instead to work such as Graham Harwood's software research NetMonster.[18] Here variable keywords related to a user's current image interests or obsessions are used to initialize a crawl for sites that contain text or images related to the keywords. The crawl returns these sites as stripped text and pictures, rearranging them around an image mask based upon the user's current image obsession, collaging and redrawing the information so that it butts up in convoluted lines of connection against itself.

The links that connect the text and image together in NetMonster s collage of information arise out of a differential between what is prelinked online—the image's "mediated causes of its own existence"—and the variables a user introduces into these connections via the mask and the keywords. There are other aspects to this software in which the crawler automatically attempts to spam the phone numbers and e-mails from the garnered sites, alerting people to ways in which their information has participated in a link or connection against common sense. There is an anti-navigational and irresolvable aesthetic oscillation that results from this work. Its informatic rendering is monstrous, rampant, and pathological rather than friendly or sociable. As Harwood suggests, the image functions in the unimaginable spaces and indeterminate relations of distributed information. "The picture acts as a proposition—frustrated—oscillating between a picture's ability to say and show."[19]

We need a more complex conception of network sociality than the concept of social software that is currently attached to descriptions of networks of friends or lovers in an online dating database. We need a more complex understanding of the visual plane of information than the pictorial map of the network. Networks are not glued together by software and software does not make us social. Networks are not resolvable into zoomable details of landscapes that must fit the window of a browser. But equally we cannot take the social out of software; in fact, what we need is to be more specific about how the social and its myriad aesthetics are operating through and in software. How is a network really being sustained—computationally and through creative labor? How is the network experience to be thought and felt? Whose labor—creative, manual, skilled, disorganized—keeps it moving along? What intrusions of rhetoric from other images of neo-liberal democratic theory and its dreams of customized participation, for example, break into and intrude upon the fragile links that tentatively form within networked experience?

Where are you going?

Networks should not be defined by the visible links they place on display. Getting "linked in" a network is not materialized through (digital) information. This is what makes it so fake to ask a computer to visualize a network or to believe in link lists. Putting a link in is work, a tedious activity that requires precision and dedication. Only a few of us develop a routine that leads us to the "felt experience" of actual linking in the network. Today's networked existence hops from one medium to the next and then demands that we return back to our links in order to put in the work of connecting again and again.

What constitutes linking and how could we describe its mirror phantom, or rather, its shadow? The link as a reference to another informational object only comes into being as a conscious act. There is no automated process of putting links. And there is no unconscious or subliminal linking either. These could all be worthy scientific propositions but as of yet they do not exist. Linking is tedious work. It is an effort and should be considered extra work. There is no routine in linking. It is a precise job that needs constant control. The opposite of the conscious link is not the broken but the absent link.

We are in search, instead, of an aesthetic that comes to terms with conflict, boredom, confusion, and stagnation—one that includes social complexity (as opposed to biocomplexity). At the same time, we are dealing with a nonvisual aesthetic with respect to networks or at least a visual that is not pictorial and cannot be depicted as such. What kind of aesthetics then does the network herald? We should not forget that our debates are not entirely out of the blue and respond to certain software configurations, which can be changed. A future generation of blogs may not have the option to externally respond to postings. Due to spam, wikis could lose their capacity to alter texts. At the same time, we could see impressive new incorporations of data flow now circling around inside mobile communication space. These configurations are not merely technical innovations or developments. Software-wise they are easy to write and implement. Their innovative power is not in the complexity of code but in the simplicity of their techno-social implementations. This simplicity comes from many directions and forces at once—efficiency, standardization, and commercial viability, and from user circumvention and invention. We are not merely reflecting, imaging, or imagining when we engage distributed aesthetics. We are configuring and remaking.

Social networks should not be seen as separate entities that float out there, as a parallel reality. Rather, they reflect—and accelerate—tendencies that already exist. This is important to keep in mind if we discuss the narcotic and depressive culture of social networks like Orkut, Friendster, and MySpace. Sadness management is a key activity in this Prozac society. Social anxiety, gadget addiction, and attention deficit disorder have to be seen as one complex set of phenomena. Electronic solitude and frantic networking are nowhere near opposite phenomena. Networks can bring us down and should by no means be presented as a solution for the ruling state of mind. In that sense, distributed aesthetics can also be seen as a medicine to cheer us up. Concepts should not just cover but create tensions. What distributed aesthetics has proven is its ability to overcome suburban isolation. Let's overcome the sorrows of the young blogger. Instead of pinning down people by asking, "Where are you?" we may as well map out desired directions: "Where are you going?" Let's draw matrices of the possible and get into a "state of readiness" as Jordan Crandall described it: "It is a state that operates at the level of both perception and corporeality, where one is not only cognitively but affectively engaged. A form of alertness on the edge of action, where the vigilant and optimized machine-body is roused and poised to act."[20]

Technologically informed network theory needs to overcome the limited canon found in popular network literature. How the Medici ran their empire and how certain school groups later turned out to rule powerful corporations are all interesting examples, but they tell surprisingly little how the contemporary online world functions. In brief, the stability of the old boys network stands in contrast to the instability of large social networks that migrate from one service to the next in no time. It is easy to blame American culture for the extraordinary inflation of the term *friends*. Against the manic collection of friends on Orkut and MySpace (but also the business network LinkedIn), we can talk about what real friendship is and quote

Foucault. We may as well leave such obvious responses and admit that in that Internet context friendship lacks any romantic connotation. What the friends option does is design one's social environment and homogenize relationships. The social is not a given, defined by family, school, church, work, or society, but is something that has to be constructed in a personal manner.

Distributed aesthetics can be a catchword, critical concept, and project. Repeatedly it has proven productive to use philosophical terms and put them to work as metaphors, assisting us in the journey from here to there. It is high time to invite art historians, art critics, and many others into the field and confront them with the networked condition. It may be depressing that many of the efforts are not going beyond appropriation of commodities and services that were developed many years ago. Even for those taking up the most advanced positions, it must be a sober realization that all we do is investigate yesterday's consumer products. The gap between innovative applications in use by business and government on the one side, and the cultural rearguard on the other is wider than ever. Distributed aesthetics is one among many projects calling for a radical investigation of today's technology platforms. The least we can do is catchup.

Notes

1 See *Fibreculture Journal*, no. 7, Distributed Aesthetics, http://journal.fibreculture.org/issue7/issue7_munster_lovink.html. The term "distributed aesthetics" came into being during the preparations of the Distributed Difference day that the Fibreculture network convened as part of the BEAP conference in Perth, Australia on September 10, 2004. See Ingrid Richardson's report on Fibreculture list, posted on September 14, 2004. This one-day event and the following *Fibreculture Journal* issue were organized by Lisa Gye, Anna Munster, and Ingrid Richardson.

2 The workshop was organized by Geert Lovink and Anna Munster. Participants: Giselle Beiguelmann, Brian Holmes, Richard Rogers, Warren Sack, Mercedes Bunz, Sebastian Lütgert, Nils Röller, Judith Rodenbeck, Clara Völker, Sabine Niederer, Linda Wallace, Trebor Scholz, and Olga Goriunova. See Trebor Scholz's report of the seminar, http://www.collectivate.net/journalisms/2006/5/16/distributed-aesthetics.html.

3 Warren Sack, "Aesthetics of Information Visualization," in *Context Providers*, Christiane Paul, Victoria Vesna, and Margot Lovejoy, eds. (Cambridge, MA: The MIT Press, forthcoming).

4 Taken from Trebor Scholz's seminar report.

5 Warren Sack, "What Does A Very Large-Scale Conversation Look Like?" *Leonardo: Journal of the International Society for Arts, Sciences, and Technology*, 35, 4 (2002), 417–426.

6 The most complete contribution of a formalist analysis of new media is made by the work of Lev Manovich. This is evident in his book *The Language of New Media* (Cambridge, MA: MIT Press, 2001) where he proposes a set of formal principles for the analysis of new media, but also in more recent texts, such as "The Shape of Information" (http://www.manovich.net, 2005). Although Manovich does not maintain that new media can be analyzed through a universal form or aesthetics, the question of emerging forms of culture driven by information as process and flow drive the theoretical trajectory of his work. The medium specificity approach is best exemplified in a text such as Janet Murray's essay "Inventing the Medium," her introduction to *The New Media Reader*, Noah Wardruip-Fruin and Nick Montfort, eds. (Cambridge, MA: MIT Press, 2003), 3–29.

7 Pit Schultz, "The Producer as Power User," nettime, June 20, 2006. In this essay, Schultz describes the power user as someone who is "neither professional nor amateur, neither hobbyist nor self-employed, between sofa and kitchen table, sometimes expert, sometimes dilettante, leaving the suburbs and moving to the city centers or the countryside, using trains and airplanes but not owning a car. Living from project to project and shifting between unemployment and immediate wealth, the power user has left the factories and office buildings long ago to stay home and be the post-industrial anti-hero."

8 For further debates on this issue, see Janet Abrams and Peter Hall, eds., *Else/where: Mapping New Cartographies of Networks and Territories* (Minneapolis, MN: University of Minnesota Design Institute, 2006).

9 PatternTracer is a software package for professional crime investigators that analyses and maps telephone call data to "quickly and automatically uncover clusters and underlying patterns," Product Overview–i2:

Investigative Analysis Software, http://www.i2inc.com/Products/Pattern_Tracer/default.asp. Valdis Krebs is the most obvious example of recent work being conducted in the field of social network analysis and was responsible for mapping the network of pilots and hijackers involved in the World Trade Center attacks on September 11th. The Web site for the map of the Internet is at http://mapoftheinternet.com/.

10 Richard Rogers, "Why Map? The Techno-Epistemological Outlook2, http://pzwart.wdka.hro.nl/mdr/pubsfolder/whymap/.

11 Ibid.

12 M. Dodge and R. Kitchin, *Atlas of Cyberspace* (London: Routledge, 2000), 107–128.

13 See Mark Granovetter, "The Strength of Weak Ties," *The American Journal of Sociology* 78.6, 1360–1380, 1973 and Phil Williams, "Transnational Criminal Networks," in *Networks and Netwars: The Future of Terror, Crime, and Militancy*, J. Arquilla and D. Ronfeldt, eds. (Santa Monica, CA: RAND Corporation, 2001).

14 More on networks and maps, see Janet Abrams and Peter Hall, eds., *Else/where: Mapping, New Cartographies of Territories* (Minneapolis, MN: University of Minnesota Design Institute, 2006).

15 There is no standardized usage or understanding of the term "social software." It is deployed by marketing executives and radical software analysts to categorize two polarized vectors in networks—the social and collective understanding and production of distributed software and the deployment of software to produce social ties between individualized subjects. Our concern with a use and elaboration of the socio-technical is with this latter deployment. See, for example, the article by Stowe Boyd, "Are You Ready for Social Software?" *Darwin: Information for Executives*, May 2003, http://www.darwinmag.com/read/050103/social.html.

16 Chris Anderson, "The Long Tail," *Wired*, 12.10, October 2004, http://www.wired.com/wired/archive/12.10.tail.html.

17 See particularly the Friendster network, which aims to "make the world a smaller place by bringing the power of social networking to every aspect of life, one friend at a time." "About Friendster," http://www.friendster.com/info/index.php?statpos=footer.

18 http://www.scotoma.org/notes/index.cgi?NetMonster.

19 Graham Harwood, NetMonster research site: HowItWorks, wiki located at http://www.scotoma.org/notes/index.cgi?HowItWorks. Plus research site Description, wiki located at http://www.scotoma.org/notes/index.cgi?NetMonsterDescription.

20 Jordan Crandall, "War, Desire, and the 'State of Readiness'," nettime, June 21, 2005.

Chapter 26

GABRIELLE CONSENTINO

'HACKING' THE IPOD
A look inside Apple's portable music player

T HIS EXTRACT COMPLEMENTS the essays by **Katz** and **Bull** in this book. Its account of the political economy of Apple's development, design and marketing of its iPod digital music player and the iTunes online shop for music files provides a critical backdrop to **Bull**'s ethnographies of iPod use and **Katz**'s detailed exploration of music file-sharing practices and technologies.

As well as recounting the story of the commercial and cultural dominance of iPod and iTunes, Gabrielle Consentino addresses the aesthetic seductions of the iPod, critical issues of 'the co-optation of countercultural practices and symbols', and the fraught and complex intertwining of legality, technology, software and everyday practices in the struggles over copyright and intellectual property in digital-rights management (DRM).

> "*Rip, mix and burn. After all it's your music*"
> Ad campaign introducing iTunes

> "*Don't steal music*"
> Sticker on the iPod box

White lines and bottom lines

New York City, summer 2004. The relative proportion of business suits to stickers protesting the Republican National Convention might vary according to the demographics of each neighborhood, but there is one peculiarly consistent element noticeable across the population of Manhattan: bright white headphone wires linking people's ears to their pockets, purses, and backpacks. These white lines signify the most popular physical embodiment of the digital musical revolution, Apple's iPod.

Since its first introduction on the market in November 2001, the white, 5.6 ounce portable digital music player has gained an iconographic status that few other branded technological devices, with the possible exceptions of Sony's Walkman and PlayStation, have previously attained. The iPod sales figures, about 10 million units sold in the first three and a half years of production, have yet to match the Walkman's, more than 200 million since its first introduction. However, according to an analyst report, the iPod adoption rate is faster than it was for the Sony tape player (Marsal 2004), and the iPod impressive 900% sales growth in 2003, coupled with the four million iPods sold during the 2004 holiday quarter, indicate that Apple's device, which has yet to show its full market potential on a global scale, is something more significant than just a fad.

Media coverage of the iPod, fueled by Apple's notorious marketing savvy, has ranged from columns on tech-forum Slashdot.org to appearances on *Oprah*, from reviews on the *New York Times* to rap music videos, from financial analysts reports to fashion industry catwalks. The imposing sales figures and ubiquitous media coverage have not only made the iPod synonymous with the larger phenomenon of digital music, but might even reflect the birth of a new demographic: the iPod generation.[1] As with similar technologies combining entertainment and fashion, the overall profile of this social segment is for the largest part young, affluent, and urban, thus very profitable for marketing ends. Even traditional institutions such as universities have become aware of the iPod appeal, particularly among youths. In 2004, Duke University gave a free iPod to every new freshman, claiming that it had a significant potential for academic use, on top of being an unbeatable marketing tool to attract new students.

Thus, the iPod seems to have entered popular culture to a degree that adds weight to claims about its revolutionary impact, which is affecting both the consumer electronics and the digital music markets. As with other pop phenomena, language is the domain most receptive to change. The word "iPod" is replacing "Walkman" as a catchall term for "portable audio player," an indication that the power dynamics in the field of consumer electronics, a market long dominated by Sony, are changing. Also, few if any electronic gadgets have been able to develop the same blend of technological and fashion appeal as the iPod, which has become now such a fashion statement that well-known clothes manufacturers are selling garments specifically designed for carrying it (Fried 2004). Another field of significant change is the gender bias of the consumer electronics' market, traditionally male oriented. In February 2004, when Apple introduced the iPod Mini, a smaller version of the iPod available in different colors, nearly as many women as men purchased it, thus indicating that the reach of Apple's digital music player is extending to a larger demographic space.

Patterns of music listening and exchange are also evolving by virtue of the iPod physical portability, technical features and aesthetic flourishes. Users bring their iPods to parties to play music and share their files and playlists. Some even swap their iPods in public places like subways in a practice known as "jacking-in" (Kahney 2003). Professional DJs use it to carry their music collections to live gigs, and in cities like New York and London people set up parties where guests can play their favorite mixes through their iPods.

The spread of digital music, largely fostered by the availability through file-sharing networks of music files in mp3 format, has brought about a deep restructuring of the patterns of music distribution and consumption, both in quantitative and qualitative terms (Alderman 2001). While Napster expanded digital music consumption and distribution beyond the subcultural communities of audiophiles, geeks, and teenagers, it is the iPod that has become the physical embodiment of the same phenomenon. With the wide adoption of a single-branded mp3 player, digital music has taken on a more tangible cultural relevance.

Furthermore, the iPod is part of a larger all-round solution, including the jukebox software application iTunes and the iTunes Music Store (iTMS), that Apple deployed to enter the digital music market. The strong sales figures of the iTMS—200 million songs in its first two years— have proved customers' will to pay for digital music. Such encouraging sales figures could be taken as a sign of reconciliation between music listeners and the music industry, whose relationship for the past few years seemed irreparably compromised by litigation, heated debates, and mutual accusations.

Despite its undeniable success, upon better scrutiny Apple's business solution for digital music is not exempt from controversial elements that have important economic and cultural ramifications. The underlying hypothesis of this research is that Apple has been able to conquer the stagnant digital music market by skillfully walking a fine line between a carefully crafted business plan to sell its hardware and the widely common practice of sharing copyright protected digital content, which in turn creates demand for playback and storage devices. Thanks to a timely business strategy and the leverage of its heavily marketed brand image of cutting-edge company, Apple has persuaded the major record labels to trust the iPod and iTunes formula and make their catalogs available on the iTMS. Apple's music store is in fact the first online service endorsed by the major record labels that does not require a subscription or other forms of long-term engagement, which had fettered previous attempts to sell music online (Alderman 2001). Also, contrarily to previous models, iTMS also works with low digital-rights management (DRM) restrictions.

By drawing an unprecedented level of attention and customers to both iTunes and the iPod, in less than two years Apple has become the strongest player in the distribution of digital music. At the same time, while presenting iTunes as a revolutionary legal solution to digital piracy, Apple has been able to capitalize on the demand for playback and storage devices unfettered by digital-rights management restrictions, which allow for unregulated and often unlawful forms of music distribution.

To weigh such arguments, it might be helpful to consider some figures. As of January 2005, Apple has sold about 10 million iPods, while the iTMS has sold about 200 million; thus, the average iPod user might have about 20 songs on it purchased from the iTMS. Since the store sells individual songs for 99 cents, and albums for a price range of $9.99 to $11.99, very few customers are reasonably expected to be able to fill a 10,000-song capacity device with songs purchased only via iTMS. So one is left to speculate where the other 9,980 songs that can fill the 40-GB version come from, and the proportional split between backup copies of legitimately purchased CDs and, possibly, files unlawfully downloaded from file-sharing systems or other sources. It can be argued, as reported by some news sources (Kahney 2004a), that most iPod owners use it to store, and possibly even share, unlawfully downloaded files. To prevent this possibility, it could be further argued, Apple has set up the iTunes store to provide the iPod with a "legal" skin. Such allegations are further reinforced by the fact that the iTMS, despite being the most popular online music retail service, still does not generate any profit for Apple.[2] It does, however, work as an effective promotional avenue for the iPod. This is particularly interesting because Apple, which is a hardware manufacturer and not a content producer, has been able to gain the trust of the music industry despite the relatively low DRM restrictions enforced by the iPod and iTunes.

However, the main concern of the music industry is the extent to which Apple's and other hardware producers' ambivalent strategy towards intellectual property is affecting consumers' expectations and behaviors. As exemplified by the gap between the high profits generated by the iPod's sales and the low profits of music downloads, the business of digital music has so far proved more profitable for hardware producers than for the recording industry. The response of the entertainment industry, afraid that the expansion of unregulated forms of distribution will soon affect other types of content (i.e., films) has arrived promptly in the shape of a proposal for new legislation. The iPod and other digital portable devices are in fact being targeted by a new draft bill, originally dubbed the Induce Act, that threatens to ban playback devices that do not feature strong DRM protection and thus might "induce" users to infringe copyright (Dean 2004). However, the bill met with widespread hostility both on the part of the computer and the consumer electronics industries, both of which fear its potential chilling effects on technological progress, and its legislative course was stalled. For the future regulation of the still-growing and unpredictable digital music market, legislators will arguably have to acknowledge the fact that the iPod is now an established and profitable standard, and that its commercial success is significantly impacting the distribution and consumption of digital music. As a further example of its emblematic value in the digital music market, the iPod was chosen as a symbol to warn the public of the potential threats posed by the Induce Act (savetheipod.com 2004).

Furthermore, since the iPod is designed to function exclusively with Apple's iTunes digital jukebox, which lets users upload, delete, and organize song and access the online music store, the success of the iPod and iTunes formula is creating the conditions for a market lock-in. This situation has already caused the onset of disputes between Apple and competitors, such as with Real-Networks' attempt to make the songs sold through its online service, Rhapsody, playable on the iPod. Such technical restrictions have prompted critics to evoke Apple's notorious skepticism towards interoperable solutions, a protectionist attitude towards the market that in the past has had major negative effects for the company.

The issues outlined above will be addressed in more detail throughout the sections of this chapter. Specifically, the next section will focus on the development of the iPod within the context of Apple's strategy to enter the market of portable digital players. The design, brand, and marketing solutions that favored the success of the iPod will be observed in the third section. Particular attention will be dedicated to their relation with Apple's history of technological innovations and marketing strategies. The fourth section focuses on the effects that the iPod is exerting on the digital music market, particularly with respect to the role of competitors, regulators and artists.

Portrait of the iPod as a brainchild

"Hint: it's not a Mac." This was the teaser on the invitation to a press conference that Apple organized to unveil, in late October 2001, "a breakthrough digital device." According to the rumors (Wilcox 2001), the company had created a portable music player that promised to embody the idea of "digital lifestyle" envisioned by Steve Jobs with the launch of Mac OS X. That device was in fact the iPod, and in retrospect the teaser really hinted at a product that was destined to permanently change the perception of Apple as just a computer manufacturer.

At the time of the iPod introduction—just as Microsoft was lifting the veil on Windows XP—the market of digital portable music players was still in its infancy. Three years before, Diamond Multimedia System opened the market with the Rio PMP 300, 32 megabytes of storage capacity on a removable memory card and a connection to the computer for music download via the standard parallel port. The novelty of the product, coupled with the absence of competitors, accounted for a good market performance—about 400,000 units sold in its first year—but its limited memory and slow music transfer system fettered its wide adoption by the growing number of digital music users (Brown 1998a). Rio was also the target of an unsuccessful lawsuit brought against it by the Recording Industry Association of America (RIAA). At the time of the lawsuit, there was growing anxiety around digital music on the part of the music industry, and anything that dealt with music in mp3 format was considered tantamount to piracy, as eloquently expressed by former RIAA president Hillary Rosen: "We sincerely doubt that there would be a market for the mp3 portable recording devices but for the thousands of illegal songs on the Internet" (Brown 1998b). The lawsuit was brought on the grounds that the Rio mp3 player encouraged music piracy, along the same legal terms of the famous dispute known as the Betamax case, between the Motion Picture Association of America (MPAA) and some of the earliest videocassette recorder manufacturers, including Sony (Vaidyanathan 2003). The terms used by the court to rule against the RIAA lawsuit against the Rio were also similar to the famous Betamax ruling, according to which any technology that allowed for substantial non-infringing use should be considered lawful.

The court order was hailed as an important victory by the hardware and consumer electronics industry, which continued to invest in the production of technology for digital music. However, the entertainment industry and its lobbies did not give up the legal battle to prevent the unregulated flows of digital content. In 2000, as Napster was reaching about 100 million users worldwide and the RIAA, armed with a stronger and more focused legal strategy, successfully filed suit against it for copyright infringement, Creative Labs introduced the Nomad Jukebox, which pushed storage capacity to six gigabytes by virtue of a small hard drive. It was a major improvement in terms of capacity, a quality that appealed to the growing numbers of digital music collectors, but the company lacked the brand and marketing power to really make an impact. Other manufacturers soon followed, including established players in the field of consumer electronics such as Samsung, Casio, and Thomson, as well as new players lured by opportunities of the market. With the expansion of music file sharing inaugurated by Napster and the reluctance of traditional market leaders such as Sony to deal with music formats such as the controversial mp3, the market for digital music seemed to offer unprecedented business opportunities for newcomers. Prior to the iPod, however, no single music player had firmly attained market leadership. Several factors can account for the weak market performance of the digital players, such as consumers' unfamiliarity with digital music, market confusion due to the lack of software and hardware standards, small storage capacity, ineffective user interfaces, poor designs, and ultimately high prices, still considerably higher than for CD players.

At the time of the introduction of its first generation model, the iPod was the portable music player that sported the best ratio between storage capacity and physical space, coupled with an innovative design that was Apple's real signature. However, even for the iPod, the first reactions from the market were not exactly enthusiastic (Fried 2001). Initially marketed at $399, the iPod was the most expensive digital music player on the market, and critics, while acknowledging the beauty of its design and the ingenuity of the interface, ultimately categorized it as a gadget for deep-pocketed Mac lovers.

In March 2003, with the introduction of the smaller, even sleeker, third-generation model, retailing at a slightly cheaper price and featuring higher storage capacity, sales figures for the iPod started to grow. During summer 2003, right after the introduction of the iTMS, the market response started to become very positive. By the end of the year, iPod requests eventually became overwhelming. The third generation iPod was one of the best-selling items during the 2003 Christmas season, with more than 700,000 units sold in the United States alone (Levy 2004).

By early 2004, Apple had become the main player in the field of portable digital audio, with over 60% market share (Walker 2003), an outstanding result for an outsider coming from the computer field. The company's performance looked even more significant when considering its belated approach to the field of digital entertainment, particularly music. Prior to the iPod and iTunes, Apple had never been particularly adept at recognizing the business potential of digital music, largely because of the long-standing trademark dispute with Apple corporation, the Beatles' record label, which prevented it from associating its name to any commercial activity related to music (Smith 2003). Such a hesitant position towards music had significant effects also on the technological choices the company made for its computers. Apple provided its personal computers with CD burners much later than most of its competitors, and the introduction of the iTunes software for storing and organizing music collections on its computers came years after equivalent applications, such as Winamp, had already become widely popular for Windows-based systems (Walker 2003).

So exactly how did Apple, a computer manufacturer that as late as 1997 was on the brink of bankruptcy[3] and for a long time did not express any clear interest in the music business, manage to win over the competitive and uncertain field of digital music, amidst a flurry of high-profile litigations, failed business plans, and technological impasses? Apple is well known for being very protective of the development of its products and business ideas, particularly if successful. Most of the credit for the company's recent renaissance, from the iMac to the iPod, is ascribed to the entrepreneurial skills of Steve Jobs. Jobs is not short on talent for inventing technology that users find enjoyable to own and use. But, as is often the case with business success stories, the "genius" of the entrepreneur is put forth to romanticize and disguise the often bumpy and tentative path of research and development of the whole company, and ultimately to keep competitors at bay from the secrets of its business strategy.

In the wake of the iPod boom, major newspapers such as the *New York Times* and the *Wall Street Journal* investigated the secrets of its success story, to find out how the different parts had been assembled, which company developed the operating system, who gave the crucial design touches, and, most importantly, who envisioned the original business idea. The story that emerges began just a few years ago, around the end of 1999, when the computer world was in the midst of the millennium-bug hysteria and Apple was still mostly focused on video. Apple's most significant technological steps in the field of digital video were the QuickTime video format and the invention, in the mid to late 1980s, of the FireWire protocol, developed for the fast transfer of the large amounts of data required by digital video. In the late 1990s Apple started to add FireWire ports to its personal computer and developed Final Cut Pro, a video-editing software targeted to professionals. In subsequent marketing steps, Apple released iMovie, and then iPhoto, allowing Jobs' grand view of the personal computer as a "hub" for the digital life to materialize (Walker 2003). The last addition was iTunes, introduced in early 2001. The first generation iPod, which connected to computers only via FireWire ports, arrived about six months later. By 2003, with the introduction of the iTMS, Apple had developed a full-fledged solution for digital music, which included a digital music application, an online music store, and a portable music player.

Just as with Apple's overall approach to music, even the iPod was less an inspiration than a gradual assemblage of various inputs, ideas, and parts. More precisely, the iPod was assembled by virtue of hardware and software components coming from six different companies. Apple is very secretive about how the different pieces of the iPod came together, and its public relations division has successfully projected the picture of a "rabbit-out-of-the-hat" product. Aside from the spin, Apple's real strength and main contribution to the project was its ability to coordinate the different partners working on the project. By virtue of an efficient management effort, the development time was reduced to just nine months, from the first concept to the final marketing stage. Apple points out (Walker 2003) that coherence during the development process has been the key to the iPod success, and the secret to efficient technical innovation is the ability to put together the right specialists in the shortest time possible.

[. . .]

[Jobs] wanted to add specific features, such as high audio quality, a user-friendly interface, and, above all, Apple's unique design touch. Jobs was personally involved in shaping the device's look and feel, as he previously was with another Apple success story, the iMac. Jobs was mostly concerned with two factors in particular—simplicity and beauty—which had proved crucial to the success of the iMac; the final product had to be extremely simple to use and pleasant to see, use, and "wear." In particular Jobs insisted that the iPod have high storage capacity, excellent audio quality, and a fast and user-friendly interface for retrieving songs through the scroll-wheel.

As mentioned earlier, another crucial factor to the iPod's and iTMS's popularity is the low restrictions enforced through the FairPlay DRM system; Apple's copy-protection technology was built into Quicktime and embedded in the AAC files sold via the iTMS. At first Apple didn't want any DRM and did not request either Pixo or PortalPlayer to implement it in the first-generation models. A DRM system was only added to the second-generation iPods to comply with requirements of the introduction of the iTunes Music Store.

According to the current FairPlay features, the songs downloaded from the iTMS can be burned onto an unlimited number of CDs for personal use, and played on up to five authorized computers. An iTunes playlist containing protected tracks can be copied to CDs up to seven times. Also, FairPlay-protected songs can be downloaded to an unlimited number of iPods. The iPod is engineered to download protected and unprotected songs from any computer with iTunes installed, while the upload function is disabled.

A seductive design, high storage capacity, and low DRM restrictions: these are some of the main features that have made the iPod successful. The next section will focus in detail on how these have been assembled as part of a precise business and marketing strategy to enter the digital music market.

The music business, remixed

There is a common thread linking the aesthetic, technical, and marketing components of the iPod's and the iTunes's formula: Apple's ability to straddle profitable, risky business plans and edgy, alternative cultural expressions. Apple acknowledged the drastic change in consumer cultural and economic behaviors brought about by digital technology, and incorporated them into its business strategy. The successful elements of Apple's strategy are a legacy of its experience as an innovative, risk-prone, and brand-oriented company. Since the launch of the first Macintosh computer, Apple's brand has been built on the co-optation of countercultural visual and linguistic signs, to evoke a Utopian, liberating, and empowering view of technology, aesthetically translated into an original style of product design.

The most striking quality of the iPod, or its "aura" as a *New York Times* journalist described it (Walker 2003)—echoing Walter Benjamin's (1968) classic definition of artistic quality— stems in fact from its unique design. As the traditional physical support of music (LPs, tapes, or CDs) dissolve into the immaterial, infinitely replicable digital substance of music files, the aura of the work of art moves from the content to the medium—in this case, the playback device. From the elegant cardboard black packaging that stirs childish levels of excitement in even the most blasé customer, to the shiny ivory white of the front cover, the iPod is the embodiment of technological allure. The appeal of the iPod rests in its look as well as in its user-friendly interface. Among its many features, in fact, the one most often cited as the key to the product's seductiveness is the intuitive scroll wheel that allows the user to perform several different functions with just one finger.

Despite the peaks and troughs in the market performance of its products, Apple has always been able to challenge the physical and aesthetic boundaries of technology. Some of Apple's products, such as the colorful and compact iMac, were so successful and widely imitated that they have subsequently become icons of popular culture. More importantly, Apple design solutions have often proved vital for the company's survival. The iMac's successful blend of fashion and technology breathed new life into the Apple brand and prevented, in 1998, the company's share of the desktop computer market from dropping below the dreaded 5% figure.

Apple's experience with the iMac can be considered conducive to the iPod. Both are instances of Apple's emphasis on products that are able to create an emotional and aesthetic resonance with the user. Technology's steady pervasion into daily life has resulted in an increased importance of its function of expressing the user's personality, attitude, and style. Ergonomic and enjoyable devices that users can identify with are able to provide a solution to the growing anxiety about technology, thus countering the dystopian side of technology as embodied by cold and anonymous machines.

Apple's products are thus marketed not merely as high-end and reliable devices but also as expressions of style and personality that can seamlessly blend with the aesthetic and functional environment of the user. Apple has been ahead of its competitors in the computer field at understanding that technological products can be sold as fashion accessories. The basic assumption of brand-oriented companies is that as the core functionalities of products become more standardized across different companies, what now distinguishes a brand is its ability to provide consumers with values and meanings through symbolic and visual choices.

Apple's small share in the personal computer market belies the high ranking of its brand in terms of value,[4] largely thanks to the loyalty of its customer base. Since its earliest days, Apple's heavy investments in advertising, design, and product innovation have resulted in a widely recognized and trusted brand. Advertising has always been extremely important to Apple, particularly during the troubled decade of the 1990s. Under the controversial management of former Pepsi CEO John Sculley, Apple expanded its advertising budget from $15 million to $100 million, partly to the detriment of efficient marketing and product development (Kahney 2002). Despite the disproportionate budget allocation, heavy spending in advertising proved extremely valuable in maintaining customer loyalty and helped to reinforce a unique relationship of trust and identification.[5] John Sculley went so far as to describe Apple as more a marketing company than a computer manufacturer, a risky management attitude that has, however, been credited with helping the brand stay afloat in dire times.

When Steve Jobs returned to Apple as CEO in 1997, he focused more directly on product innovation and sales strategies, while continuing Apple's tradition of robust marketing spending, especially with the $100 million iMac campaign. Apple still spends considerable resources on advertising, an example being the 2002 "Switch" campaign aimed at convincing dissatisfied Windows users to defect to the other side. Conspicuous investments have also been poured on the famous iPod "silhouette" campaign. The advertising campaign, showing black silhouette over monochrome backgrounds, has recently become a hallmark of urban visual landscape, both in the U.S. and across international markets. In the U.K., iPod ads covered bus shelters, the London Underground, and railway stations. Japan was flooded by iPod television ads, while colored iPod silhouette banners hung from the ceilings in Paris's St. Lazare train station. At McGill metro terminal in Montreal, colorful iPod silhouettes were painted onto the turnstiles and stairways (Kasper 2004).

Apple's brand has been one of the essential determinants of the company's survival during the mid-1990s' financial crisis and even for its recent performance with the iMac and iPod (Kahney 2002). The success of the company, it is argued, depends more on the power of the brand than on innovative products. Apple's brand efforts have been targeted at building an emotional brand that creates a strong and intimate relationship with its customers, who are often willing to pay higher prices or overlook product flaws for the sake of the special, unique bond they have with the company. By evoking universal values such as imagination, nonconformity, freedom, and stylishness, Apple presents itself as a company based on the ethos of empowering people through technology, thus pushing the brand-customer relation beyond mere commerce into the realm of representation and identity. Apple's famous "1984" commercial, a retro-futuristic tale of a hero freeing a mass trapped in an Orwellian scenario, carried clear populist undertones and portrayed Apple as a countercultural, rebellious, freethinking company. This branding strategy helped the company to develop an almost ideological affiliation with its customers, based on a shared belief in the democratizing power of technology and communication.

One of the recurring themes in Apple's communications is the tension between alternative and mainstream cultures. Apple has always addressed its customers as an elite of independent freethinkers who don't comply with the homogenizing trends of mass culture. The "Think Different" campaign celebrated historical figures of creative misfits and rebels such as Picasso, Gandhi, John Lennon, and Einstein. Lee Clow, the mind behind the campaign, explained Apple's communication strategy as follows: "The comeback of Harley-Davidson motorcycles was a good model for Apple to emulate. Harley's advertising convinced people that they could feel its renegade spirit even if they were investment bankers rather than Hell's Angels. It rehabilitated a counterculture icon for the baby boomers who had grown up and sold out" (Deutschman 2000).

Apple's brand image of an alternative, edgy company played a crucial role in its move towards digital music. Apple acknowledged the cultural divide that existed between the music industry and digital music users. Apple approached the major record companies with an original business plan aimed at creating a balance between the industry and music listeners, and coupled it with a communication strategy that spoke the language of youth, freedom, and innovation. While keeping one eye on the click-happy peer-to-peer users, Apple was pursuing its main goal, which was to convince the record labels to license their songs to the iTMS. Such ambivalent attitude was epitomized by the controversial "Rip, Mix, Burn" campaign, which infuriated many powerful figures in the entertainment industries, including Disney CEO Michael Eisner (Cohen 2002). Eisner accused Apple of considering piracy its new "killer application" and warned potential buyers that they could engage in theft if they had bought Apple computers.

Apple strategy was grounded in the assumption that users, empowered by technologies such as file-sharing networks, had the upper hand in the transitional phase from analog to digital media, and that they should be approached in cautious and respectful terms instead of being labeled as "thieves." The aggressive approach adopted by the industry towards users of file-sharing networks hasn't proved effective in migrating audiences towards legal solutions, in fact. With the spread of file-sharing technologies, both producers and users of digital content have become very sensitive to the issue of intellectual property, albeit from opposite perspectives. While the industry has sought to maintain absolute control over distribution, users have exploited digital technology to develop new models of distribution, archiving, and content retrieval. Apple realized that to succeed in such a crowded and confusing space, it needed to strike a balance between these conflicting positions.

A crucial aspect of the iPod's success has been its placement within the overall business strategy that Apple has adopted towards the digital music market. This includes the iTunes software, originally available only for Apple computers but expanded to Windows since spring 2004. When Apple entered the market with its strategy, no other company had an integrated business system for digital music comparable to Apple's, which produced and managed the hardware, the software, and the online distribution.

As already pointed out, Apple's success in the digital music market appeared even more striking when its outsider role in the market is considered. Other large companies were much better positioned in the entertainment field than Apple. However, largely out of the fear of piracy, they were unable to devise a successful business strategy. Probably the most striking example of this failure is Sony, which was the ideal candidate for the leadership in the digital music market since it had the assets both in the field of content and consumer electronics. However, Sony fell into an innovation impasse due, in large part, to a conflict of interests within itself (Rose 2003). Sony's consumer electronic division, interested in selling digital devices for playback and storage, and Sony Music, one of the five major record labels, which has stakes in the distribution of digital content, took completely diverging positions with respect to development and marketing strategies for digital music. Only in December 2004, in a belated attempt to counter Apple's further expansion into digital audio, Sony released the NW-HD3, a portable player capable of mp3 playback (Williams 2004b). Previously, Sony had only released audio players supporting its own proprietary ATRAC format, a strict digital-rights management system that proved rather unappealing for the booming market of digital music users.

It could be argued that one of the reasons for iTunes's popularity is the fact that it was the first service to sell downloadable music à la carte from the catalog of major record labels. The single-choice system, as opposed to the subscription-based models, has proved effective because it catered to the preference models of music consumption established by file-sharing services. Also, the music industry trusted Apple as a reliable candidate to approach potential customers with a viable marketing solution for digital music, particularly with respect to the intellectual property concerns. Steve Jobs was personally involved in the process of acquiring the trust of the recording industry, a daunting endeavor for an executive of a computer manufacturer, given the past discrepancies between the two camps. Jobs qualified for the task by virtue of his strong reputation both in the computer and entertainment industry. Since the early days at the hackers' community of the Homebrew Computer Club with Apple co-founder Steve Wozniak, Jobs has long had good credibility in the computer community, both among grassroots amateurs and industry executives. Thanks to his successful move to computer animation with Pixar, Jobs also developed a strong reputation in the entertainment field. This combination made him the most qualified technology figure to establish the proper terms of agreement with main players of the recording industry.

Jobs presented prototypes of the iTMS project to record labels executives around the country, assuring them of the company's full commitment to the project and of the viability of the business plan. Above all, Jobs guaranteed that Apple would back the project with its full marketing potential, from an ambitious advertising plan to ample promotion through the strategically located and growing chain of Apple retail stores.

Apple believed that the only way to establish a market for digital music was to cater to the needs of the users in the simplest way possible, according to the distribution models initiated by file-sharing services. Apple understood that people buy music to own it, not just to rent it, as offered by other services. Also, Apple's policy towards piracy has been to frame it more as a behavioral rather than a technical issue, and insisted on giving users as much control as possible on the downloaded songs. Apple subscribed to the belief that "on the other side of a lawsuit there is a thriving industry" (Doctorow 2004), and that strict DRM technology would not serve the purpose of preventing copyright infringement. Jobs worked together with industry executives to define the technical and legal conditions that were necessary for the major labels' participation. Jobs initially wanted to sell music without restrictions, but the labels were resolute in blocking his position. He was, however, able to make them compromise on a much lower level of limitations than those granted for any previous online store. After the negotiations, Apple hyped the iPod and iTunes formula as a revolution in the music business with a large-scale advertising campaign.

As of December 2004, the iTMS had distributed more than 200 million songs. Despite some contentions that Apple's online music store doesn't generate profit, the company still intensely promotes and celebrates iTunes's popularity, since the ITMS's bottom line is still arguably to advertise the Apple brand in the digital entertainment market, both as hardware producer and as content distributor. This has significant implications in economic terms for the music business, in particular with respect to intellectual property issues. Despite the potentially infringing potential of Apple's solution, the major record labels have nonetheless trusted it as a possible remedy to counter the decline in music sales allegedly caused by file sharing (Borland 2003).

However, it could be argued that in strictly technical terms an mp3 player with 40-gigabyte storage capacity and low DRM restrictions, if used to download songs from different computers and played in private or public venues, could function as a computer connected to a p2p system downloading or distributing mp3 files. One can easily connect the iPod to a friend's computer, download the songs through iTunes or as raw data, and play them back or upload them to the other computer. Once iPod users are allowed to store and play digital files such as mp3s, which don't generally feature DRM, then the devices can be easily used for the unregulated circulation of copyright-protected material. This is currently one of the most frequently heard arguments (McCue 2004) against the low DRM restrictions imposed by the iPod. The technical characteristics of the iPod allow users to easily swap files, carry them around, organize them in personal collections, and play them in public venues.

The iPod's characteristics and the opportunities of music consumption and distribution it allows seem to correspond to the definition of a "democratic medium."[6] Technologies that empower users with alternative forms of interaction, production, and distribution, such as in recent times audio- and videotape recorders (Vaidyanathan 2003), have a history of clashing with the established economic and legal status quo: "Technology that disrupts copyright does so because it simplifies and cheapens creation, reproduction and distribution. The existing copyright businesses exploit inefficiencies in the old production, reproduction and distribution system" (Doctorow 2004).

However, after its first disruptive effects have been absorbed and mitigated by market and political forces, the new technologies tend to reinforce existing power structures or create new ones. In this respect, the iPod is no exception. The characteristics of peer-to-peer file sharing have led to prosecutions for facilitating copyright infringement, while for the iPod they have been exploited for commercial ends. Apple, like many other hardware producers, is arguably profiting from the continuous flows of illegal file sharing. As recently reported (Kanhey 2004a), some are taking this as a sign that the value chain of the digital music market might emphasize the modalities of access to the content, such as distribution services or hardware devices, rather than the actual content.

The characteristics and the fast rise to popularity of Apple's solution for digital music are meeting with contrasting reactions, ranging from the general positive response of customers to the competitors' prompt counter plans to the criticism of music activists. The next sections will focus on how the different players in the digital music business perceive the iPod and iTunes phenomena and how these reactions are in turn affecting Apple itself.

[. . .]

Conclusions

Apple's bet on digital music as an avenue of development for new business opportunities has so far proved successful. The focus of this research tried to look beyond the iPod's and iTMS's commercial success to unearth more critical issues, such as the co-optation of countercultural practices and symbols for marketing purposes, the unprecedented cross-industry agreements that Apple was able to obtain thanks to its brand appeal, and the instability of the current intellectual property regime.

As recounted in the chapter, Apple has deftly interpreted the conditions necessary to succeed in a time of rapid and disruptive technological change by adjusting its business strategy to the shifting patterns of music consumption and distribution. It has made being a risk-prone and innovation-driven company work to its advantage during a time of transition to new forms of technological and economic arrangements in the field of entertainment and consumer electronics.

Apple's rise to success in digital music has been so fast and overwhelming that the company now faces the paradoxical situation of possessing a quasi-monopolistic control on the market, a position that it reached, however, by exploiting the most controversial aspects of digital and network technology. Apple's market position appears particularly controversial considering that, aside from Apple's effective strategy and the iPod's undisputable technical qualities, a good part of the success of the iPod is due to the wide availability of music in digital content distributed through file-sharing networks and the lax Apple policy towards intellectual property.

The same users of file-sharing networks who were labeled as hackers by the RIAA are now lured by Apple's advertising into becoming iPod's legitimate customers, while their role of providers of a large part of the unlawful content that circulates through network technology is seen as instrumental to the success of the iPod. However, the economic rules that sustain the file-sharing networks are more inspired by practices of the sharing economy (Benkler 2002) or gift economy (see Giesler, this volume), where the subjectivities involved in exchange are more important than the actual product, while Apple's model is forcing the recommodification of digital music, with a peculiar protectionist approach that rules out interoperability across different software or hardware formats.

The company now faces the challenge, for the second time in its history, of maintaining control of a business territory that it has helped to grow. Today's challenge might, however, be greater than that of 20 years ago, when the company helped midwife the desktop computing market. Its position is now complicated not just by the actions of competitors but by the new forms of power seized by users and artists through digital network technologies.

Apple hailed the introduction of the iTMS as the beginning of "the digital music revolution," just as in 1984 they claimed a stake in the computer revolution. Perhaps by now people have grown skeptical of the revolution they are being sold, particularly when they can just freely access it through peer-to-peer file-sharing networks.

Notes

1   From a survey personally conducted in May 2004 on 100 participants of online forums of two websites, ipodlounge.com and macobserver.com, dedicated to Apple and the iPod, 60% of the iPod owners interviewed were between 18 and 35 years old, and 30% under 18. PC users accounted for 65%. In terms of frequency of use, 70% of the users who responded used the iPod every single day. As far as the key feature of the iPod, the majority indicated its storage capacity, while 40% mentioned both the Apple brand or the design. When asked what was the original source of the digital music that their IPod contained, the majority responded "backup of regularly purchased music," while 35% answered "digital music bought via the iTunes store," and only 20% indicated files downloaded from file-sharing programs. The survey also requested comments on how the iPod had changed the users' way of listening to music. In general, it was mostly emphasized that with the iPod music had permeated users' lives to an unprecedented extent, thus creating the condition of a very intimate, ubiquitous relation with the device.

2   After iTunes became available on Windows, Apple senior vice president Phil Schiller stated in an interview, "The iPod makes money. The iTunes Music Store doesn't. Using software to drive hardware sales is a

typical strategy for Apple, so it might accept moderate losses from the store to recover a net profit with device sales. In addition, inasmuch as Apple can require use of iTunes and Apple's Quicktime to play FairPlay files, Apple can increase the value of its brand by associating Apple with all uses of digital music" (Gasser et al. [2004]. See also Fried [2003]).

3   For a comprehensive account of Apple's history, see Malone (1999); see also Levy (2000) and Linzmayer (1999).
4   In 2004 Apple Computer gained 24% in brand value and went from number 50 to 43 of the most valuable global brands chart (http://www.businessweek.com and http://www.interbrand.com).
5   For a comprehensive investigation on the cult-like relationship between Apple and its users, see Kahney (2004c).
6   "New media tend to be decentralized in ownership, control, and consumption patterns; they offer greater potential for consumer input and interaction, and heighten the user's control over the form of consumption and over the relation to media sender. More important, they constitute a challenge to the one-way, monopolistic, homogenizing tendencies of the old media" (Manuel 1994, 2).

Acknowledgments

The author wishes to thank Siva Vaidyanathan and Sam Howard-Spink for their help and support.

References

Alderman, John. 2001. *Sonic Boom: Napster, Mp3 and the New Pioneers of Music.* Cambridge, MA: Perseus Press.

Benjamin, Walter. 1968. "The Work of Art in the Age of Mechanical Reproduction." In *Illuminations: Essays and Reflections*, edited by Hannah Arendt, 217–52. New York: Shocken.

Benkler, Yochai. 2002. "Coase's Penguin, or Linux and the Nature of the Firm." Retrieved December 14, 2004, from http://www.benkler.org/CoasesPenguin.html

Borland, John. 2003. "Music Industry: Piracy Is Choking Sales." CNET *News*, April 9. Retrieved October 13, 2004, from http://news.com.com/2100–1027–996205.html?tag=fd_top

Boyle, James. 2004. "The Apple of Forbidden Knowledge." *Financial Times*, August 12. Retrieved October 5, 2005, from http://news.ft.com/cms/s/2c04d39e-ec5a-11d8-b35c-00000e2511c8.html

Brown, Janelle. 1998a. "Blame It on Rio." *Salon.com*, October 29. Retrieved September 7, 2004, from http://archive.salon.com/21st/feature/1998/10/28feature2.html

———. 1998b. "Is Rio Grand?" *Salon.com*, December 9. Retrieved September 7, 2004, from http://archive.salon.com/21st/reviews/1998/12/09review.html

Cohen, Peter. 2002. "Disney Boss Accuses Apple of Fostering Piracy." *MacWorld*, March 1. Retrieved September 17, 2004, from http://www.macworld.com/news/2002/03/01/eisner/

Dean, Katie. 2004. "Copyright Bill to Kill Tech?" *Wired News*, July 22. Retrieved August 22, 2004, from http://www.wired.com/news/print/0,1294,64297,00.html

Deutschman, Alan. 2000. "The Once and Future Steve Jobs." *Salon.com*, October 11. Retrieved September 3, 2004, from http://dir.salon.com/tech/books/2000/10/1l/jobs_excerpt/index.html

Doctorow, Cory. 2004. *Microsoft Research DRM Talk*. June 17. Retrieved August 29, 2004, from http://www.dashes.com/anil/stuff/doctorow-drm-ms.html

Downhillbattle.org. 2004. Available at www.downhillbattle.org

Flynn, Laurie. 2004 "Profit at Apple Almost Triples on a Sharp Rise in iPod Sales." *New York Times*, April 15. Retrieved September 29, 2004, from http://www.nytimes.com

Fried, Ian. 2001. "Apple's iPod Spurs Mixed Reactions." CNET *News*, October 23. Retrieved August 20, 2004, from http://news.com.com/2100–1040–274821.html?legacy=cnet

———. 2003. "Will iTunes Make Apple Shine?" CNET *News*, August 16. Retrieved June 20, 2004, from http://news.com.com/Will+iTunes+make+Apple+shine/2100–1041_3–5092559.html

———. 2004. "Gucci Serves Up Apple iPod à la Mode." CNET *News*, April 20. Retrieved June 12, 2004, from http://news.com.com/2100–1041–5195940.html

Gasser, Bambauer, et al. 2004. "iTunes: How Copyright, Contract, and Technology Shape the Business of Digital Media—A Case Study." Green paper, vol. 1. Retrieved June 2, 2004, from http://cyber.law.harvard.edu/media/itunes

Kahney, Leander. 2002. "Apple: It's All about the Brand." *Wired News*, December 4, Retrieved June 9, 2004, from http://www.wired.com/news/mac/0,2125,56677,00.html

——. 2003. "Feel Free to Jack into My iPod." *Wired News*, November 21. Retrieved July 6, 2004, from http://www.wired.com/news/mac/0,2125,61242,00.html?tw=wn_story_related

——. 2004a. "Bull Session with Professor iPod." *Wired News*, February 25. Retrieved August 20, 2004, from http://www.wired.com/news/print/0,1294,62396,00.html

——. 2004b. "Inside Look at the Birth of the iPod." *Wired News*, July 21. Retrieved July 23, 2004, from http://www.wired.com/news/mac/0,2125,64286,00.html

——. 2004c. *The Cult of The Mac*. San Francisco, CA: No Starch Press.

Kasper, Jade. 2004. "Apple Heats Up World-wide iPod Advertising." *Apple Insider*, March 9. Retrieved July 6, 2004, from www.appleinsider.com/article.php?id=387

Kawasaki, Guy. 1990. *The Macintosh Way*. Glenview, IL: Scott Foresman.

Levy, Steven. 2000. *Insanely Great: The Life and Time of Macintosh, the Computer That Changed Everything*. New York: Penguin Books.

——. 2004. "iPod Nation." *Newsweek*/*MSNBC News*, December 26. Retrieved July 6, 2004, from http://msnbc.msn.com/id/5457432/site/newsweek/

Linzmayer, Owen. 1999. *Apple Confidential: The Real Story of Apple Computer*. San Francisco, CA: No Starch Press.

Malone, Michael. 1999. *Infinite Loop: How the World's Most Insanely Great Computer Company Went Insane*. New York: Doubleday.

Manuel, Peter. 1994. *Cassette Culture*. Chicago, IL: University of Chicago Press.

Markoff, John. 2004. "Oh Yeah, He Also Sells Computers." *New York Times*, April 25.

Marsal, Katie. 2004. "iPod Adoption Rate Faster Than Sony Walkman." *Apple Insider*, November 29. Retrieved November 30, 2004, from http://www.appleinsider.com/article.php?id=765

McCue, Andy. 2004. "'iPod Users Are Music Thieves,' Says Ballmer." *Silicon.com*, October 4. Retrieved October 5, 2004, from http://management.silicon.com/itpro/0,39024675,39124642,00.htm

Murphy, Victoria. 2004. "The Song Remains the Same." *Forbes.com*, September 6. Retrieved November 30, 2004, from http://www.forbes.com/home/global/2004/0906/030.html

Negativland. 1995. *Fair Use: The Story of the Letter U & the Numeral 2*. El Cerrito, CA: Seeland.

Rose, Frank. 2003. "The Civil War Inside Sony." *Wired Magazine*, February. Retrieved July 10, 2004, from http://www.wired.com/wired/archive/11.02/sony_pr.html

Savetheipod.com. Retrieved October 14, 2004 from http://www.savetheipod.com

Smith, Tony. 2003. "Beatles Record Label Sues Apple Computer—Again." *Register*, September 12. Retrieved September 10, 2004, from http://www.theregister.co.uk/2003/09/12/beatles_label_sues_apple_again/

Stein, Andrew. 2004. "Apple: RealNetworks Hacked iPod." *CNN Money*, July 29. Retrieved August 3, 2004, from http://money.cnn.com/2004/07/29/technology/apple_real/

Vaidyanathan, Siva. 2003. *Copyrights and Copywrongs: The Rise of Intellectual Property and How It Threatens Creativity*. New York: NYU Press.

——. 2004. *The Anarchist in the Library: How the Clash between Freedom and Control Is Hacking the Real Worlds and Crashing the System*. New York: Basic Books.

Walker, Rob. 2003. "The Guts of the New Machine." *New York Times*, November 11. Retrieved September 6, 2004, from http://www.nytimes.com

Wilcox, Joe. 2001. "Apple to Unveil Digital Music Device." *CNET News*, October 17. Retrieved August 24, 2004, from http://news.com.com/2100–1040–274566.html?legacy=cnet

Williams, Stephen. 2004a. "Apple's Latest Development iPod Photo Seems Unfocused." *LA Times*, November 14. Retrieved December 19, 2004, from http://www.latimes.com/technology/

——. 2004b. "An MP3-capable Walkman Is Set to Challenge iPod." *LA Times*, December 5. Retrieved December 20, 2004, from http://www.latimes.com/technology/

Wong, May. 2004. "HP Deal Is Latest Boost for Apple's iPod." *Information Week*, January 9. Retrieved June 20, 2004, from http://www.informationweek.com/showArticle.jhtml?articleID=17300324

Yi, Matthew. 2004. "Small Startup Pixo Lends a Hand to Apple's iPod." *Salt Lake Tribune*, June 18. Retrieved August 27, 2004, from http://www.sltrib.com/business/ci_23934511

Chapter 27

MARK KATZ

LISTENING IN CYBERSPACE

MARK KATZ'S COMMENT that mp3 music culture is both 'remarkable and mundane' succinctly illustrates the descriptive and analytical mode of many of the extracts in this volume. By the early years of the twenty-first century, many millions were routinely downloading and sharing music over the Internet. File-sharing and downloading practices as popular media technoculture are, like phonograph or radio listening before them, transforming the everyday experience of music yet their novelty, again like the earlier forms, quickly evaporates.

Digital music files are distinguished by their 'nonrivalrous, endlessly reproducible, extremely portable, and frequently free' characteristics, Katz argues. These characteristics are the basis for music-listening experience characterised by 'unparalleled accessibility', significantly different modes of choosing tracks ('search') and new possibilities for customisation (the selection of single tracks from albums, compiling playlists and so on). The differences between the virtual and the actual in everyday digital culture are here exemplified by the tactile and cultural differences between CD ownership and mp3 collection and storage.

Katz traces the experiences of mp3 users through a conventional survey, but his commentary on these experiences loops out from survey findings to factor in questions of legality and copyright, the history and technics of mp3 compression, virtual communities, the materiality of music media and packaging, and the cultural and legal implications of different network structures.

See also **Bull** for further empirical research on digital music file culture, **Consentino** on hacking the iPod; **Kennedy**, **Slater**, and **Taylor** for other forms of online community.

I'm driving down the road when a song on the radio catches my ear. It has a descending tetrachord—a particular type of recurring four-note pattern—and for reasons I can't quite explain, I collect descending tetrachords. Before it slips my mind, I take out my cell phone and call home. Since I'm not there, I have a slightly surreal conversation with my voice mail: "Hi Mark, it's Mark. Descending tetrachord. I think it's the Violent Femmes. Remember this line: 'Beautiful girl, love the dress.' Got that? OK, see you soon." When I get home, I go to my computer and search the Internet for the phrase *Beautiful girl, love the dress* and the word *lyrics*; I find that I had heard "Gone Daddy Gone," a 1983 song by, as I had suspected, the alternative rock group the Violent Femmes. Next, I open up a program that helps me find a recording of the song through the Internet. This was mid-2005, and at the time I used a file-sharing program called XFactor. (A few years earlier, I would have called on Napster or Kazaa; a few years later it might have been the iTunes Store, Amazon, BitTorrent, Lala, or an MP3 blog. I can now even identify and download songs using my cell phone. More on these later.) Upon my request, XFactor searches through the computers of several million people who have allowed others access to their digitized music collections. On this occasion I get a list of a few dozen who all have the song on their hard drives. With a double click of the mouse I start copying "Gone Daddy Gone." Moments later I'm listening to the song.

Just a few years earlier, I would not have believed such a thing possible. Imagine, practically conjuring a song out of thin air! Imagine, carrying this and thousands of other songs on a device small enough to fit in a shirt pocket! To my mind, such things qualify as magic. Indeed, as Arthur C. Clarke famously suggested, "Any sufficiently advanced technology is indistinguishable from magic." The advanced technology/magic that made this scenario possible—actually a combination of digital technologies, including MP3 and peer-to-peer networking—is bringing about what the musicologist Timothy D. Taylor has described as "the most fundamental change in the history of Western music since the invention of music notation in the ninth century."

The previous chapter considered the role of digital technology in the creation of music. Our focus here is on the listener and the ways in which the digital has shaped how listeners discover, experience, and even think about music. We will encounter an unusual set of phonograph effects, in which it is the *in*tangibility of a recording format, and its differences from older physical media, to which users are responding. Exploring this revolution will also mean delving into the conflicts among musicians, listeners, the record industry, and U.S. copyright law. This is hotly contested territory and will remain so for years to come. Although I want to be fair to the various sides of the debate, and recognize both the dangers of piracy and the desires of the listening public, I stake a clear position here. I believe that the broad exchange of digital music files over the Internet is and has been a public good, and that it should be the recording industry and copyright law that bend to accommodate listeners, not the other way around.

MP3 and P2P: partners in crime

At the center of the scene that opened this chapter is a digital technology known as MP3: the song that I downloaded from the Internet, and subsequently stored on my computer and carried around on my portable player, was in the form of an MP3 file. MP3 stands for Motion Picture Experts Group 1, Layer 3, a name that reveals little about its current use. Like the phonograph, which Edison originally saw as a dictation device for businessmen, MP3 was not conceived with music in mind. Rather, it arose out of the work of engineers and executives connected with the film industry—dubbed the Motion Picture Experts Group—who sought to establish standards for the digitization of video and audio. As Leonardo Chiariglione, the Italian engineer who convened the first meeting of the group in 1988, later said, "Nobody, I promise you, had any idea of what this would mean to music." An important goal of the group was to develop a way to compress the huge amount of data constituting video and audio files into sizes manageable for sending over the Internet and storing on computers. The group engaged a team from the Fraunhofer Institute for Integrated Circuits in Germany to assist, and in 1992 the German researchers created an audiovisual standard they called MPEG-1.

The system used a technique known as perceptual coding to remove data from the recording (typically a CD) being compressed. Perceptual coding is based on the idea that when we listen to music (or any sound, for that matter), some frequencies are "masked"—rendered more or less imperceptible—by competing sounds. For example, a loud cymbal crash in an orchestral piece will momentarily cover the sound of certain instruments playing at the same time. In perceptual coding, those masked sounds are assigned fewer bits of data than the foreground sounds. This reduction allows digital sound to be stored quite compactly, compressed to a small fraction of its original size.

Compression is necessarily a compromise because it requires the removal of data, a loss that could affect the listening experience. The sound quality of an MP3 file depends on the bit rate—the average number of bits (1s or 0s in binary code) used to represent one second of sound. For MP3s, a rate of 128 kilobits (128,000 bits) or higher produces near CD-quality sound but generates only about one-twelfth the amount of data as a CD. Lower bit rates produce lower-quality sound—which some engineers describe as "swishy" or "underwater"—but allow greater compression, while higher bit rates more closely approximate the sound quality of a CD but demand larger files.

MPEG-1 consisted of three different "layers," or levels of data compression. The first two layers were for high-performance use with state-of-the-art technology, the third a lower standard suitable for more modest systems, such as personal computers. To demonstrate MPEG-1, the Fraunhofer team created a free program out of this third layer to compress digital music files. Using as a guinea pig Suzanne Vega's 1984 song "Tom's Diner," which one of the researchers happened to be listening to on CD at the time, they created a typical "demo"—the first MP3—to give prospective industry users an idea of its potential. Hardly a high-security item, the program was stored unprotected on a computer at the University of Erlangen in Germany. Not long afterward, a Dutch programmer known as SoloH discovered the demo and downloaded it, tinkered with it, and then made it available to others to further refine. The modest demo soon spawned superior MP3 encoders that offered high-quality sound from highly compressed files. SoloH opened a box—Pandora's to some, a bottomless treasure chest to others—from which millions of files representing every conceivable type of music continue to pour forth.

MP3 did not have an immediate impact on modern musical life, however. In the early 1990s, few were aware of the format and fewer still had access to MP3 files. It was the rise of what is called peer-to-peer (P2P) networking later in the decade—most notably in the form of the Napster network—that endowed MP3 with its global influence. A P2P network is radically different from the more traditional client-server model, in which information flows from a centralized source (the server, a computer or group of computers that stores and distributes data) to its users (the clients, who request data from the server). Instead, *P2P* denotes a decentralized network in which each computer has direct access to certain designated files stored on every other computer. Every member of the network is a peer; the circulation of data among peers is known as file-sharing. If a public library is analogous to a client-server model, P2P is more like the arrangement my wife, her mother, and her aunt have to circulate their collections of mystery novels among themselves. But on the Internet, P2P networks can exist on a much grander scale, linking millions of users who can share data almost instantaneously.

Napster is the most famous example of a P2P network. Developed by two college students in 1999, it allowed users to share the MP3 files stored on their computers. At the height of its brief life, Napster is said to have had tens of millions of users sharing hundreds of millions of sound files. Its appeal was clear: it was free and easy to use, and it provided access to an immense collection of music. After downloading a simple program from napster.com, one had only to connect to the Internet, open the straightforward user interface, and type in the name of the composer, performer, composition, or album being sought. If anyone who was linked to the network had that file, it was there for the taking (or more accurately, copying, as I'll explain later). Napster, however, was not a pure P2P network. It relied on a centralized server, and although it held no actual files, it indexed them, linking those with particular songs to people searching for them. Although this made searching and downloading easy and efficient, it turned out to be Napster's downfall. Most of the music files circulating over the network were copyrighted and were being downloaded without the permission of the copyright holder. It was difficult for aggrieved parties to target any of the millions of individual network users, but it was possible to go after Napster itself, which was facilitating this illegal activity. In July 2001, after nearly a year of intense litigation brought by the record industry, Napster was shut down. (In late 2003, Napster reemerged under new ownership as a legal online service, sharing little more than its name with the original enterprise; in 2008, it was acquired by the retailer Best Buy.)

The end of the original Napster was hardly the end of file-sharing, as other networks came to take its place. Kazaa, for example, was far more heavily used in 2002 than Napster was at its peak. But, like Napster, it faced tremendous legal challenges and was eventually sold and remade into a pay service. Although some similarly centralized networks, such as Audiogalaxy and Scour, also folded under legal pressure, other file-sharing services were able to avoid disastrous litigation by being completely decentralized. Gnutella, for example, has no central server; in fact, it is not even a company, but a system, or protocol, for distributing digital files (whether of music, photos, film, or software) that exists in numerous versions and is controlled by no one person or group. One of the most popular P2P networks based on the Gnutella protocol was LimeWire, which was launched in 2000 but morphed into a subscription service in 2010. BitTorrent is, like Gnutella, a file-sharing protocol that exists in many versions, though it distributes data in a very different way. Whole files are not transferred from one peer to another; rather, they are downloaded in parts from many different network members. There is no real-world analogy—it would be as if my wife, instead of exchanging a book with her mother, collected it chapter by chapter from a dozen different relatives. But given that BitTorrent networks may boast millions of active members, large files can be transferred very quickly. Scores of BitTorrent sites operate around the world, some hugely popular, like the Swedish site Pirate Bay—which claimed in 2009 to have twenty-five million members—to smaller ones that specialize in certain types of media or music. This is just a sampling of the P2P networks that have flared up (and occasionally flamed out) in the post-Napster era. Many more will come and go, but whether or not any individual one survives, their collective influence is undeniable and unlikely to wane in the near future.

P2P networks are not the only way to obtain sound files over the Internet, and since the demise of Napster many online music services have arisen that offer paid downloads through the client-server model. Early pay services, such as MusicNet and Pressplay, were unsuccessful for a variety of reasons, whether because they offered a limited range of titles, used formats that could not be saved on one's computer, or were too expensive. Later ventures were substantially more successful. In April 2003, Apple—with the cooperation of several major record labels—launched its iTunes Music Store (which became simply the iTunes Store when it added nonmusic content, such as videos). From the beginning the iTunes Store delivered fast, reliable, permanent downloads at what was generally considered a reasonable price (99 cents per song, less than $12 for most albums). Its popularity, along with Apple's line of iPod music players, grew tremendously. The iTunes Store sold 50 million songs in its proprietary AAC file format in eleven months, 200 million within a year and a half, and six billion by the beginning of 2009, by which time it had long dominated the online music market. Rhapsody, which actually preceded the iTunes Store by more than a year but never enjoyed the same market share, offered a subscription model that allowed users to stream songs—that is, listen without downloading. Amazon.com, originally simply an online bookseller, added music downloads to its offerings in 2007; it distinguished itself from Apple by offering songs without digital rights management (DRM), which limits the ability to copy or transfer files and which many users consider an annoyance. (Apple dropped DRM in January 2009.) Lala.com, which closed in 2010 after being acquired by Apple, allowed members to stream whole tracks—as opposed to the thirty-second samples common on other services—without paying. Music lovers have also obtained legal downloads from sites such as emusic.com, legalsounds.com, magnatune.com, and mp3.com, from retailers such as Wal-Mart and Best Buy, and from the online stores of many record labels. Like the P2P networks, these services quickly come and go, though unlike the former they tend to fold because of economic rather than legal problems. It is important to remember that iTunes and the rest are *not* file-sharing networks and do not facilitate the illegal exchange of music among users. When I discuss file-sharing—largely the focus of this chapter—I will be referring only to the P2P networks and protocols like Napster and BitTorrent; *downloading* and *downloaders*, however, are broader terms and can refer to anyone who transfers or copies data from one computer to another, and any method of doing so.

A great deal of ink has been spilled in the debate over the impact of file-sharing on musicians and the music industry. Rather less attention, however, has been paid to its effect on listeners. Is listening to an MP3 different from listening to other recorded media or to live music? What distinctive possibilities does music file-sharing offer to listeners? Do users of MP3s think about music differently because of their engagement with the technology? What are the legal and ethical ramifications of listening in cyberspace? To address these questions, we will apply the concept of the phonograph effect; that is, we need to understand how users of these digital technologies respond to their distinctive characteristics. Instead of examining how listening to MP3s is different from listening to live music, however, we must turn our attention to those qualities that distinguish sound files from CDs and other physical recording media.

MP3 versus traditional recording media

The most distinctive and crucial attribute of MP3 files is their status as, in the language of economics, nonrivalrous resources. A resource is *rivalrous* if its consumption or use by one party limits its consumption or use by others. Most physical objects are rivalrous. If I eat a sandwich, no one else can eat it; if I build a house on a parcel of land, or even if I am simply standing on it, I am restricting its use by others. Traditional sound recordings are also rivalrous. In owning a copy of the Shaggs record *Philosophy of the World*, I am limiting everyone else's use of it. (Fortunately, there are plenty of copies to go around.) *Nonrivalrous* resources, in contrast, cannot be depleted by using them. Ideas are nonrivalrous. When I am done with the equation $2 + 2 = 4$, it is still there, intact and undiminished, quite unlike the grilled cheese sandwich I just ate. Or as Thomas Jefferson more eloquently explained in 1813, "He who receives an idea from me, receives instruction himself without lessening mine; as he who lights his taper at mine, receives light himself without darkening me." Digital sound files, like ideas, are nonrivalrous. The analogy with ideas is not capricious. As the law professor Lawrence Lessig maintains, "The digital world is closer to the world of ideas than the world of things"—which is why copyright and other protections of physical property map uneasily onto the world of cyberspace, a point I will return to later. Downloading a file is not like loading a shopping cart with groceries or a car with suitcases, for no object is actually being moved. To download is not to use or take someone else's song file, but to copy it. This is the same with all digital files on the Internet. When I look at an image or read a newspaper online, it is not as if I am looking at a painting in a museum or reading the paper in the library, actions that would impinge on the access of other users. I am making and using my own copy of the images and texts. Slow Internet connections, low bandwidth, and heavy network traffic can sometimes limit one's access to files; but for the most part, when I use digital files, I receive light from another's taper, neither taking nor extinguishing the flame.

It is also important to realize that when I download a song (or an image or text, for that matter), I am making a *digital* copy of that file. An MP3 is just a series of 1s and 0s that represents a given collection of sounds; when copied, the same arrangement of binary numbers is generated. It is not as if the 1s and 0s of the copy are slightly less crisp or true than the original MP3, as a second-generation cassette tape would be. This is part of the great appeal of MP3s, for the sound does not degrade when copying. (This is not to say that the sound quality of all MP3s is necessarily high, as one realizes when listening to an MP3 compressed at a low bit rate or created from a poor-sounding CD.)

The nonrivalrous nature of digital music files, moreover, has an important effect on the portability of recorded music. As I have pointed out, the tangibility of traditional recordings has made sound portable in unprecedented ways. But their very physicality places an upper limit on how easily and quickly music can be moved, even as recording media have become smaller and sturdier. Digital music files, however, are dramatically more portable than their tangible kin. Depending on the speed of one's Internet connection, a three-minute pop song can be downloaded from or e-mailed to anywhere in the world in a matter of a few seconds.

The nature of digital music files also affects cost. Throughout the history of recording, it has often been possible to hear certain kinds of music more cheaply on disc than live. The cost differential is even wider with MP3s and the like, with millions of tunes available free (and illegally) on P2P networks. MP3s are not subject to the physical control exerted over traditional recorded media—they cannot be bar-coded, price-tagged, shrinkwrapped, or sequestered on shelves or behind display cases—and millions are downloaded on decentralized networks, subject to no one's control. Digital rights management—including encryption, digital watermarks, self-implementing expiration dates, and the like—has been sought as a means to restrict the ways in which sound files can be used and copied, but so far with little success, and most online music stores have simply forsaken DRM.

Listening to MP3

Digital music files—nonrivalrous, endlessly reproducible, extremely portable, and frequently free—are clearly different from traditional recording media. How do these differences, then, affect the listening habits of users, a group comprising hundreds of millions worldwide? In responding to these differences, users may enjoy greater access to music, discover new repertoire, and exercise increased flexibility in the way they listen to music. Moreover, they may change their consumption of CDs, rethink their ideas about musical authenticity, and form virtual communities around shared musical interests. These are not theoretical possibilities, but represent the real-world experiences of a wide variety of users. My evidence comes from many sources: third-party studies, Internet discussion forums, as well as surveys on file-sharing habits I conducted in 2002 and 2009; at times I will also draw on student papers on file-sharing submitted in a variety of courses I have taught as well as my own experiences, but only insofar as they reflect common activities and attitudes. I want to stress, however, that I do not treat those who download music as if they are all of one mind; diverse and contradictory practices and attitudes abound. This was true when downloading largely meant the unauthorized sharing of files on P2P networks and is even more the case now that paid services and online music stores have broadened the demographic of MP3 users. Still, the individual phonograph effects I describe represent the practices of many and, taken collectively, help to paint a picture of musical life in cyberspace.

The clearest change that digital and networking technologies have introduced is the possibility of music's unprecedented and unparalleled accessibility. This new accessibility may be understood in terms of speed, ease, and breadth. The anecdote from the opening of the chapter illustrates the first two traits: I hear a bit of an unidentified song on the radio, and a few minutes after I get home I am listening to it. (Had this happened a few years later, I could have obtained the song while still driving. Using a music identification application such as Shazam or Soundhound on my mobile phone, I could have discovered the identity of the song and then downloaded it to my phone through any number of services.) It is hard to overestimate the magnitude of this change. Never mind that it could take decades or even a lifetime for dedicated listeners in the prephonographic age to hear, say, the collected string quartets of Beethoven. Even in the pre-Internet era of sound recording, years might elapse between hearing music and obtaining a recording of it. For example, I was first taken by the loony yodeling on the song "Hocus Pocus" by the Dutch rock group Focus sometime in the early 1980s but didn't come to own a recording of it until the early 2000s. Perhaps I didn't try hard enough (some might say I tried too hard), but such long lapses were not at all uncommon, and in fact I was unable to track down many of the songs whose snippets tantalized me on the radio in those days.

The Internet not only makes it possible to find particular pieces easily, it also allows users to explore unfamiliar territory. If one can imagine a particular type of music, it probably exists; if it exists, it can probably be found on the Internet. For example, here are two musical subgenres that, for all I know, may or may not exist: Swedish funk and Vietnamese hardcore rap. I will now try to find examples on MP3 . . .

Success! After entering "Swedish Funk MP3" into a search engine, I am directed to a fan site for the group Electric Boys, a Stockholm quartet formed in 1988. A number of their songs are posted on the site, and within moments I am listening to "Freaky Funksters" from their 1990 album *Funk-O-Metal Carpet Ride*. Now I am listening to "Around My Town," a hardcore rap from a California-based Vietnamese MC inexplicably known as Thai. Thai posted the song himself, apparently in the hope of generating enough interest to land a record contract. The song is not actually in Vietnamese, as I had expected, but the fact that it is playing only seconds after I wondered if such music even existed proves my point.

Such broadened access to music has long been noted by those who download. A June 2002 study found 29 percent of American respondents reporting that their favorite genre of music had changed since they began downloading, while 21 percent indicated that they had developed new radio listening habits. But even if their musical tastes do not fundamentally change, listeners seem to feel freer to explore unfamiliar genres. A number of downloaders have noted that they ventured or stumbled into new musical territory and were gratified by the results. A twenty-two-year-old female graduate student from North Carolina responded to my 2009 survey: "I can now easily download French Pop, Russian Folkmusic, Japanese Rap, and more, with the click of a mouse. Free downloading has definitely expanded my musical horizons. It's like listening to a 'World Radio,' instead of just whatever is popular on my car radio right now." Others reported discovering a love for classical music, country music, and various world musics, as well as for a range of performers including Bad Brains, Lil Wayne, Mastodon, and the New Pornographers. (I wonder if this last group was discovered in the search for something else entirely.) Still others looked for out-of-print recordings, concert recordings by familiar artists, and remixes or covers of their favorite songs.

A fifty-one-year-old consultant from Minneapolis answering my first survey had used P2P networks to collect more than seventy versions of the World War II-era song "Lili Marlene."

One fascinating manifestation of this new accessibility is what I would describe as a divergent approach to discovering music. Instead of seeking out particular pieces (a convergent approach), one initiates an intentionally general search in hope of broad and unfamiliar results. Entering the term *cello* in a file-sharing program not only yielded the expected (Bach's cello suites) but it also introduced me to Nick Drake's haunting "Cello Song," the works of Apocalyptica, the Danish cello quartet known for its Metallica covers, as well as to the riches of Annette Funi*cello*. What by all rights should be condemned as a poor search engine served as my trusted guide into the musical unknown. In a similar vein, one college student wrote of her use of Napster circa 2001, to search not for specific songs but for moods and emotions:

> I typed "rain" into Napster, downloaded all my finds with the word in the title, and then listened to every song capturing the experience of a rainstorm. With this entire repertoire at my fingertips, I felt mighty—for the range of emotions responding to rain was mine—and paradoxically brighter. Voltaire once said, "Anything too stupid to be spoken is sung." What felt trite to say myself somehow sounded profound and weighty when artists added a backbeat and a melody. After a bad break-up I typed "cry," "love," "hurt," "heart," etc., and found the most soppy song (in this case a Neil Sedaka) that trumped my depression and therefore somehow uplifted me. Some of the music captured my pain, and helped me as though some artists completely understood me, and then others were so hyperbolic I felt relatively fortunate and therefore calmed.

There's a certain Cagean indeterminacy about this divergent approach that allows us to transcend intentionality and achieve a salutary *lack* of musical discrimination. In his provocative 1982 article "On Being Tasteless," William Brooks espoused such an arbitrariness of musical selection, for it avoids imposing preexisting value systems and makes it possible to approach *all* music, as he said, "with interest and without prejudice." This indeterminacy was strikingly embraced in Apple Computer's 2005 ad campaign for its MP3 player, the iPod Shuffle. The player forgoes the typical controls and provides only the shuffle feature, which plays songs in random order. As Apple's Web site proclaimed: "Random is the New Order. As official soundtrack to the random revolution, the iPod Shuffle . . . takes you on a unique journey—you never know what's around the next tune. iPod shuffle adds musical spontaneity to your life."

The musical eclecticism and spontaneity I have been describing have only been enhanced by the arrival of a variety of influential sites and services since the early and mid-2000s. Music recommendation services such as Pandora and Last.fm help listeners discover new music by creating profiles based on their likes and dislikes; MySpace, a vast social-networking Web site, allows musicians to post sound files of their songs for fans and potential fans to hear; the video-sharing Web site YouTube includes countless music videos and films of every sort. What unites these sites, and distinguishes them from P2P networks and online music stores, is that they typically allow streaming—but not downloading—of content. These and similar sites are thus encouraging a different kind of exploration, one in which listeners discover new music without acquiring it. As responses to my 2009 survey suggest, many will first encounter a song on YouTube and then download or buy a recording of it, while others are satisfied simply with hearing music streamed from the Internet.

Another aspect of the accessibility downloaders enjoy is the flexibility to customize their musical experience. An oft-repeated complaint from fans of popular music is that any given album rarely has more than two or three tracks they want to hear. Many feel that they are forced to buy entire albums, and resent the record companies whom they see as foisting unwanted music on them. Over and over, survey respondents and contributors to P2P bulletin boards tout downloading music as a way to avoid the all-or-nothing dilemma of CD buying; they, not the artist, producer, or record company, pick out the music, and only the music they want to hear. Responding to my 2009 survey, a thirty-nine-year-old woman from Ohio who reported using only paid downloading services exclaimed, "It's like going to the buffet—you can get whatever you want whenever you want!" (Note the similarity to the slogan, "The music you want, whenever you want it," which appeared for decades in ads for the Victor Talking Machine Company starting in the 1920s.)

Although dissatisfaction with the album format preceded the advent of MP3s, file-sharing reinforces what might be called "singles listening." When listeners get to know an album intimately, the end of one song on the album strongly raises the expectation of the next. Beatles fans who wore out the grooves of *Sgt. Pepper's Lonely Hearts Club Band* will always anticipate "Lucy in the Sky with Diamonds" in the silence following "With a Little Help from My Friends" (even if they hear the latter on the radio), just as "Smells Like Teen Spirit" contains the seeds of "In Bloom" for initiates of Nirvana's *Nevermind*. For better or for worse, downloaders often miss out on the gestalt of the commercially produced album. Yet they can decide how to group songs based on their own criteria, and these personalized compilations can in turn generate their own gestalt. MP3s, so easily moved and manipulated, allow listeners greater control over their musical experience, or in the case of the shuffle feature, the paradoxical freedom to give up control as they please.

Downloaders can even go further and alter the very sound of their MP3s. Various software programs, many available free on the Internet, allow users to change pitch or tempo, add or subtract musical layers, reverse sounds, tweak frequencies, and juxtapose and combine bits of preexisting recordings [. . .]. In other words, listeners can become amateur sound engineers or musical creators. I use similar tools as a means of analysis: slowing Jascha Heifetz's performance of a Hungarian Dance lets me hear variations in rhythm and tempo, changes in vibrato, and other performance nuances much more easily than at the normal speed; isolating certain frequencies in Public Enemy's "Fight the Power" helps me to unpack its incredibly dense web of samples. MP3s allow listening to be an active pursuit.

The most controversial aspect of MP3s that distinguishes them from rivalrous relatives is their affordability. Although a variety of paid services exist, millions upon millions of MP3s are downloaded free over P2P networks. The recording industry, of course, opposes such freeloading, arguing that file-sharing is responsible for the oft-noted downturn in CD sales. One of the surprising findings of several file-sharing studies, however, is that downloaders are not buying significantly fewer CDs than they would in a world without MP3s. In a February 2002 study, 57 percent of respondents reported that they had bought the same number of CDs since starting to download, while 24 percent said that their purchases had *increased*; in a separate 2002 study, Jupiter Research found that 36 percent of "experienced file sharers" (those who have been active for more than six months) reported buying more CDs. More recent studies show that this behavior continues. "Those who downloaded an MP3 file from a free file-sharing service," notes a report on a 2009 Canadian poll, "are significantly more likely to say they will buy a CD in the next month (41 per cent vs. 34 per cent for non-file sharers), and are more likely to have gone to a concert in the past year (65 per cent vs. 52 per cent for non–file sharers)."

As this last study suggests, not only are many downloaders continuing to buy CDs, many claim to spend a great deal on concert tickets and other musical merchandise. Consider the example of this female college student from Maryland, writing in 2002:

I started listening to a punk band called Midtown. They were giving out their songs on the Internet for free, and after listening to a few songs, I went to a concert. They put on an amazing show, and I was hooked right there. I quickly bought their CD and listened to it religiously for months. It had been years since I had spent any money on any musical product, but after listening to Midtown, I was spending money left and right on concerts, t-shirts, and CDs. I never would have discovered just how amazing these guys sounded if it weren't for file swapping.

Similar responses appeared in my 2009 survey, such as this from a twenty-two-year-old man, an operations manager from North Carolina:

I have been to dozens if not hundreds of concerts over the last 8 or so years. Every single one of the musicians I have seen in concert is someone whose music I initially found online and downloaded illegally. Though I may have "stolen" a ten-dollar CD, I eventually bought a twenty-dollar concert ticket and maybe even a t-shirt which I never would have bought before.

Clearly, many downloaders treat MP3s not as ends in themselves, but as a means to decide whether to buy a particular recording or attend a live performance.

It may not be surprising to find that those who download also enjoy going to concerts since, as we've been finding throughout these pages, the live and the recorded offer different ways of experiencing music. (As one male college student explained, "There is nothing comparable to actually physically being in the atmosphere of a metal show, throwing down in the mosh pit, dancing in the circle pit, beating the crap out of people.") But it does seem unusual that those who download music also buy CDs (and, to a lesser but growing extent, vinyl records), even when they could get the same music without paying. I once wondered if perhaps the generation of listeners growing up with file-sharing would eschew such old-fashioned objects as CDs. Yet among the respondents to my 2009 survey, 68.8 percent said they continued to buy CDs, despite the fact that many had lived longer with file-sharing than without it, and despite the poor economic conditions of the time. Here are some of the reasons they cited:

I just want the experience of opening it up, looking at liner notes, photos and just having it to have. Downloading music seems sterile sometimes. Makes it hard to connect with the artist.

Something about physically owning a copy of the music brings me a certain degree of satisfaction.

object fetishification/completeness/collecting

I used to spend a lot of time in record stores. CDs make me nostalgic for when I used to get very excited about new albums or rare finds.

I have lost 5 hard drives in as many years. I don't like having my music lost en masse. Physical formats last longer. I also find I feel more attached to music I have in a tangible product than music that seems ethereal.

As these comments make clear, CDs have visual and tactile qualities that are important to their owners. CDs are more or less permanent; they are immune to computer viruses and lightning strikes, are usually glitch free, and come with handy (if small) liner notes, often with art and lyrics. As the first quotation suggests, there is even a sense of ritual attached to the acquisition of a CD. My own used to involve the following: whittling a large stack of discs to just two or three during a multihour visit to the now-defunct Tower Records; pulling the CDs out of the bright yellow plastic bag at a stoplight on the drive home to admire my new purchases; slicing the plastic wrap with the ceremonial X-Acto knife upon my return; peeling (and cursing) the adhesive strip sealing the jewel case; and then examining the jewels within. All of this took place before I heard a note of music. And all of this is connected to the tangibility of the physical sound recording, which, as I explained in the first chapter, has been a crucial factor in the modern listener's relationship with music since the earliest days of the phonograph.

It might be strange to consider the CD an object of ritual and nostalgia. Not long ago CDs were derided as cold, inhuman, and unattractively small—the antithesis of the LP, with its comforting tactility and oft-cited warmth of sound. Yet LPs were flimsy compared to the thicker, more substantial 78s; and to extend this further, many listeners preferred the "warm" sound of acoustic 78s to those made by the electrical process beginning in 1925. And of course, recording itself can be considered inauthentic compared to live music making. Authenticity is clearly a moving target. Often something is authentic to the extent that it has been replaced by something newer, less familiar, and more convenient, which is why CDs can now be thought of as "the real thing."

MP3 and P2P are still young technologies and may one day become naturalized to the point that we will develop nostalgia for mouse-clicking and carpal tunnel syndrome. For now, however, the intangibility of MP3s means not only that they are free but that, ironically, they will not replace their rivalrous and often costly ancestors.

The social aspects of file-sharing and downloading

There might seem to be nothing more solitary and unsociable than sitting in front of a computer downloading music. File-sharers, however, often defy the potentially isolating nature of the technology and interact with one another in a variety of ways. Many P2P networks allow users to communicate with one another, whether through private chats or group discussions in online forums. Conversations, even friendships, can arise when one user, interest piqued by the contents of another's music library (often displayed for all to see), initiates contact. These networks thus allow an anonymous intimacy in which users, typically identified only by aliases, bare their musical souls to one another. The sharing of music has also fostered the development of distinct online communities, outside the large P2P networks, formed around common musical tastes and interests. These communities are in some ways radically new, in some ways traditional. Unlike bowling leagues and book clubs, Internet listening communities do not congregate in the same physical space, and members typically never even see or meet one another. Yet members hold common interests and often feel a close connection with one another. In fact, such communities may address needs that no off-line group could meet. Physical distance collapses, so that the geographically isolated can come together; distinctions of age, class, gender, and race may fade (though not completely), allowing a freedom of interaction unlikely in any other way.

Let's consider a few examples of virtual communities that have arisen around the trading of MP3s. Indaba Music describes itself as "an international community of musicians, music professionals, and fans exploring the creative possibilities of making music with people in different places." On Indaba, musicians living hundreds or thousands of miles apart collectively compose in cyberspace, contributing parts, tinkering with the whole, and discussing the results. ZPoc is a P2P network dedicated to Christian music and its fans. As its welcome page explains, it is "a file sharing software for the 'Christian' community to share Jesus, through songs, with your friends." Network members can chat with one another, read a daily scripture passage, and trade MP3s of their favorite Christian rock artists. Or consider the Internet opera club that came to light in my 2002 survey. Two opera fans using Napster, one in the United States and one in Israel, discovered that they had complementary MP3 collections. The two men decided to trade complete operas by downloading entire works to a separate server to which both had access. (For the most part, they could only collect them piecemeal on Napster.) A man from the Netherlands soon joined in, and he subsequently brought along two Swedish women. This private club continued to grow and quickly became much more than a way to trade MP3s. Members posted opera quizzes and debated the merits of recordings, and even became friends outside of music, sharing the details of their personal lives and occasionally visiting one another. Whether convened because of a creative drive, a common religion, or an interest in a genre, the members of these communities find meaning in their associations and activities far beyond an interest in free music. They are sharing files, beliefs, ideals, and lifestyles.

It is worth observing that its practitioners typically call their activity file-*sharing*. The term is not (or not simply) a coy way to deflect accusations of theft; as used, the term suggests a sense of generosity, selflessness, and mutual concern among the members of a group. As a thirty-nine-year-old female respondent to my 2002 survey wrote, "File sharing is also about community. I have found file-sharers to be amongst the most sharing, friendly, compassionate and helpful, knowledgeable people on the Internet." Whether file-sharers are friendlier than average is hard to say, but more to the point is that music is a social phenomenon; it's hardly surprising then, that file-sharers would look for ways to engage with one another. A twenty-one-year-old female college student from Illinois made this point when answering my 2009 survey: "Whenever I hear a new song that I like, I try to share it with other people, because I usually listen to music in social settings."

Online musical communities have arisen in other ways as well. The massive Web sites MySpace and YouTube allow users to interact, most often by commenting on songs or music videos others have posted. A YouTube video of a baseball-cap-wearing teen playing an arrangement of Pachelbel's *Canon* was viewed more than sixty *million* times between 2005 and 2009, eliciting 276,000 comments. The site has also spawned a more YouTubian form of communication. Instead of just posting comments, many respond to videos by creating their own. In March 2006, for example, a young woman posted a video of herself playing the music to the video game Tetris on her out-of-tune parlor piano. It generated several thousand comments and a few dozen answer videos. Some tried to upstage the original poster, known as Cutiemish, by playing the music more adeptly and on better instruments; others showed their creativity by performing arrangements on guitar. Cutiemish shot back with another version, playfully closing her performance by sticking out her tongue at her rivals. Perhaps what we are seeing is a kind of sui generis form of communication and community, one that adapts to and exploits the distinctive possibilities of video and Internet technologies.

Another post-Napster phenomenon that encourages social interaction through music is the MP3 blog. *Blog*—short for *Web log*—denotes an Internet site, typically run by a single person or small group, that variously serves as a diary, scrapbook, soapbox, or op-ed page. One way to think of the MP3 blogger is as the virtual version of that friend in high school or college who was always pushing albums, mixtapes, or CD compilations on you. Instead of physically handing you a recording, however, the blogger posts music files with accompanying commentary. Blog readers are also afforded the opportunity to post their comments, and many blogs generate vigorous discussion. MP3 blogs offer yet another way to discover, share, and discuss music.

In mentioning MySpace, YouTube, and MP3 blogs, I may seem to be straying from the issue of file-sharing. These and similar sites, however, would not exist without peer-to-peer networking, whose popularity is closely tied to the growth of music file-sharing. It was the novel idea that computer users could obtain content from one another rather than through a corporate entity, and the socialization and community-building that followed from these peer-to-peer interactions, that paved the way for the social-networking phenomenon that has changed the way people use the Internet. Lawrence Lessig, in his 2004 book *Free Culture*, went even further, suggesting that the Internet might not have caught on as it did without the Napsters of the world: "The appeal of file-sharing music was the crack cocaine of the Internet's growth. It drove demand for access to the Internet more powerfully than any other single application."

The comparison to crack is crude but apt because it suggests both the powerful attraction of file-sharing as well as the lawlessness that opponents believe it encourages. The metaphor also offers a counterbalance to the utopianism my discussion of file-sharing may suggest. I readily admit that I am hardly a disinterested party, for as a scholar, teacher, musician, and music lover, my life and work have been tremendously enriched by my ability to hear and study the broadest array of music with such ease. Yet I do not believe that file-sharing will lead to a more cultured, civilized, and peaceful society [. . .]. File-sharing cures no ills; on the contrary, it can transform the merely curious into the obsessive, the fan into the fanatic. And as every user knows, file-sharing can be an exercise in frustration—the unpleasant and ever-present realities include an often high failure rate when attempting to download, incomplete and corrupted files, incorrectly labeled songs, and occasionally computer-crippling viruses. Moreover, the intangibility of MP3s and the ease with which they are obtained, disseminated, and deleted may encourage the sense that music is just another disposable commodity, an attitude I personally find worrisome.

There is also, of course, the contentious matter of the legal status of file-sharing, an issue that has driven a wedge between much of the listening public and the recording industry and one that may undermine the potential benefits the technology can offer. I want to devote the remainder of the chapter to this divisive subject.

The legal debate surrounding MP3 and P2P

Although there is nothing illegal about MP3 and P2P technology per se, it is illegal to download or distribute digital files of copyrighted recordings without the permission of the copyright holder. The Recording Industry Association of America (RIAA), the trade group that heads the effort to stop illegal downloading, points out that in the United States there are both civil and criminal penalties for such infringement, the latter including up to $250,000 in fines, five years' imprisonment, or both. And violations are occurring around the clock, throughout the world, in the open, and by the millions.

Individual record companies and the RIAA have tenaciously fought illegal file-sharing on several fronts. The most public avenue has been litigation. Perhaps the best-known case is *A&M Records, Inc., et al. v. Napster*, in which nine record companies sued the file-sharing network for copyright infringement. In July 2000, a U.S. district court enjoined Napster from "engaging in, or facilitating others in copying, downloading, uploading, transmitting, or distributing plaintiffs' copyrighted musical compositions and sound recordings." Napster finally lost on appeal in February 2001 and ceased its file-sharing service in July of that year. In June 2002, Audiogalaxy, another centralized service, capitulated to legal pressure brought by the RIAA and blocked users' access to copyrighted files. With these victories in hand, the record industry then began to target the decentralized file-sharing services, which had largely replaced those based on the Napster model. In June 2005, the industry prevailed in the Supreme Court case *MGM v.*

Grokster, which held that Grokster was legally liable for the copyright infringements of their customers, even though it did not store or index the illegal files itself. Similar file-sharing services were soon brought low as well: eDonkey, Kazaa, OiNK, and WinMX joined the ever-growing list.

Industry lawyers kept busy by simultaneously pursuing litigation against individual users. Tens of thousands of lawsuits were filed, many of them exciting media attention. Some of the more notorious were those filed in September 2003 against a twelve-year-old girl and a sixty-six-year-old grandmother; these proved a public relations disaster for the industry, which was widely depicted as bullying and vindictive. (The suit against the grandmother was dropped when it was discovered that her computer was incapable of downloading music files, illegal or otherwise.) The industry was clearly—and literally—sending a message to downloaders: in 2003, the RIAA sent millions of electronic letters to users of the Kazaa and Grokster services. "DON'T STEAL MUSIC," the message exhorted. "Distributing or downloading copyrighted music on the Internet without permission from the copyright owner is ILLEGAL. It hurts songwriters who create and musicians who perform the music you love, and all the other people who bring you music." The RIAA changed its strategy and stopped suing individuals in December 2008, though many cases remained in court after that time. One closely followed case involved a Minnesota woman, Jammie Thomas-Rasset, accused in 2007 of illegally downloading twenty-four pop songs. After a mistrial, a second jury decided against her in June 2009, announcing a penalty of $1.92 million, or $80,000 per song, one of which—appropriately—was Destiny Child's "Bills, Bills, Bills."

On a different front, the industry has also engaged in what is collectively known as "denial-of-service attacks," all intended to disrupt and discourage file-sharing. "Spoofing" is the act of supplying P2Ps with corrupt or bogus MP3s, typically files consisting of silence or of continuous loops of a song's chorus. "Flooding" creates a network traffic jam with phony queries and signals. "Forcing" aims to shut down particularly active network members by sending more queries than their computers can handle. The purpose of the industry's activities is unambiguous. As one record company executive explained, "We're doing this simply because we believe people are stealing our stuff and we want to stymie the stealing." The anger emanating from industry representatives is palpable. Referring to the Napster cofounder Shawn Fanning, a former lawyer with Sony Music once told me, "We weren't about to let some little shit tell us how to run our business."

The success of the industry's lawsuits and denial-of-service attacks is unclear. A thirty-five-year-old woman wrote this in response to my 2009 survey: "I am afraid of the RIAA. And viruses." "Having been threatened with a suit," explained a twenty-one-year-old male college student answering the same survey, "I can definitely say that this method is effective. Since then, I have not downloaded illegally." Another student told of quitting Napster and Kazaa because of "computer problems." Comments such as these were much more common than in my 2002 survey, distributed before the onslaught of lawsuits. On the other hand, the aggressive tactics and uncompromising stance of the industry have incurred tremendous ill will. Consider just a few of the sentiments file-sharers expressed to me in 2009: "The recording industry is a big sham," "It's all about Corporate greed," "Cease and desist letters are a shake down," and "I want the RIAA to die." Over and over, on Internet forums, in letters to newspapers and magazines, and in survey responses, this rhetoric recurs. There are even entire Web sites, such as Boycott RIAA and Recording Industry vs. the People, devoted to giving voice to anti-industry sentiment; another site, RIAA Radar, helps visitors avoid supporting the RIAA by providing information on which artists, albums, and record labels are formally connected with the trade group. When file-sharing first came on the scene, few had even heard of the RIAA;

in the years since then, it has become an object of intense hatred among legions of music lovers, some of whom even see illegal downloading as a form of protest.

So we find ourselves at an impasse, one that has lasted more than a decade. The industry has the law on its side and has fought illegal downloading with every available means, while many of those who share files either see nothing wrong with their activities or are unwilling to stop. Moreover, file-sharing simply cannot be stopped. Eric Garland, the CEO of Big Champagne, a firm that tracks Internet usage, explains: "Ultimately there is no real hope of eradicating copyright-infringing technology. You can push piracy around, discourage people from doing it in this or that venue, but I don't think in even the most Orwellian scenario you could reduce massive infringement in a comprehensive way."

Even if such a thing were possible, I believe that file-sharing should not be exterminated, but rather should be allowed and encouraged to evolve. Given the illegality of much file-sharing, defending it may seem perverse. In a seminal 1994 article, "The Economy of Ideas," John Perry Barlow, a cofounder of the Electronic Frontier Foundation, provides a starting point for my defense: "Whenever there is such profound divergence between law and social practice, it is not society that adapts. . . . To assume that systems of law based in the physical world will serve in an environment as fundamentally different as cyberspace is a folly for which everyone doing business in the future will pay."

Barlow makes two important points here. The first is that human laws are typically crafted out of social practice and must be broadly accepted to have any force. Moreover, they have to be enforceable. As Barlow later wrote, "No law can be successfully imposed on a huge population that does not morally support it and possesses easy means for its invisible evasion." Think of Prohibition and the national fifty-five-mile-per-hour speed limit in the United States; both failed spectacularly, despite the fact that both drinking and speeding (especially in combination) are patently unhealthy and cause innumerable deaths every year. Given that file-sharing is (as far as we know) physically harmless and that the public will to download is strong, stopping it seems a very unlikely prospect. Barlow's second assertion is one I have already stressed, namely, that the physical world and cyberspace are fundamentally different. CDs and MP3s are not the same, and people treat them differently. Thus, Barlow's two points are connected: people often feel free to flout copyright law in cyberspace because it is a fundamentally different environment from the physical world. On some level, file-sharers are aware of this difference. A twenty-three-year-old female graduate student spoke for many when, in response to my 2009 survey, she explained, "[illegal downloading] doesn't feel like the type of stealing that you are brought up to know is wrong. I would never, ever steal something from a store or another person, but I spent many years 'stealing' music through illegal file sharing."

The RIAA has taken great pains to change this attitude, and insists that unauthorized file-sharing is theft, the legal and moral equivalent of shoplifting a CD. (Actually, in the United States the penalty for file-sharing is *much* harsher than it is for shoplifting. The maximum civil fine for violating copyright is $150,000 per downloaded *song*, while in many states shoplifting a ten-song CD will cost a convicted thief no more than $1,000.) But downloading is not theft in the traditional sense, precisely because of the fundamental differences between the virtual and the physical. Theft involves physically taking property from another without right or permission. But MP3s are nonrivalrous, meaning that when I download something, I am copying, not taking. No one is being deprived of any previously held property. If, as Lawrence Lessig maintains, entities in cyberspace are more like ideas than things, then perhaps downloading is like stealing someone's ideas. But one cannot literally steal another's idea; moreover, ideas are not copyrightable. Figuratively, we say an idea is stolen if someone other than its originator takes credit for it or profits from it without acknowledging its source. It is highly unlikely, however, that anyone downloading the latest pop song is claiming credit for it, and there is little evidence that they sell MP3s. So if neither property nor credit is being taken, what is being violated?

The answer is control—the essence of copyright. This control means that a copyright holder is entitled to sell that copyrighted work, to reproduce it and authorize others to reproduce it, to generate derivative works from it (translations, remixes, etc.), to perform the work publicly, and to seek legal remedies when these rights are violated. Thus creators are given an incentive to create, for they have some guarantee that they will be allowed to profit from their work and determine to a certain extent how it is used by others. So when copyright is violated, isn't an artist being deprived of potential revenue? And isn't this equivalent to theft?

The matter is not so simple, for several reasons. First, practically speaking, it is often *not* the composer or performer but a record or publishing company who holds the rights to a song. Typically, creators transfer copyright (or elements of that right) to a corporation in exchange for manufacturing, promoting, and distributing the work. Copyright, therefore, does not necessarily protect creators. As Siva Vaidhyanathan claims, the creator is a straw man in copyright debates: "Copyright has in the twentieth century really been about the rights of publishers first, authors second, and the public a distant third." In fact, due to industry practices, recording musicians often fail to make money (and may even lose money) even on highly successful albums that generate huge sums for the record companies. This reality blunts the moral force of the industry's argument that file-sharers are only hurting their favorite artists, and in turn helps to explain why many who share files feel so strongly about the rightness of what they do.

A second point is that copyright is not simply a means of granting control to copyright holders. In the United States, it was originally intended as a means of establishing a *balance* between control and access. As article I of the U.S. Constitution states, the purpose of copyright is "to promote the progress of science and useful arts, by securing for limited times to authors and inventors the exclusive right to their respective writings and discoveries." Creators were given control of their works as an incentive to create—but only for a limited time; after that, the public could have unfettered access to these creations. This was meant to perpetuate the cycle of creativity, since the conception of new works often depends on access to existing ones. But for well over a century, copyright has become increasingly unbalanced. In the early history of the United States, a copyright expired after only fourteen years; but owing to numerous revisions over the past two centuries copyrights now hold for the life of the author plus seventy years. In this case, whom exactly is copyright intended to serve? Since copyrighted material can now be protected for 150 years or more, it certainly cannot be primarily the creators who benefit. Typically, it is long-lived corporations who profit. Critics of the 1998 Copyright Term Extension Act point to corporate influence as the driving force behind the change. As Lawrence Lessig has noted, "Each time, it is said, with only a bit of exaggeration, that Mickey Mouse [owned by the Walt Disney corporation] is about to fall into the public domain, the term of copyright . . . is extended."

My third point is that file-sharing does not always deprive copyright holders of income. Not every act of illegal downloading results in a lost sale. As we have seen, many file-sharers buy CDs of the MP3s they download. Others interested in just one or two tracks from a CD would not have bought the album in the first place. And yet another portion download MP3s of out-of-print recordings that they could not buy even if they wanted to. Moreover, as the economist Karen Croxson has suggested, file-sharing can serve a promotional function. Music sales are often driven by word of mouth, and valuable buzz can be generated both by those who paid for a song and by those who did not. "To the extent that piracy raises consumption," she writes, "consumption fuels hype, and hype in turn boosts future demand, a seller may tolerate illegal copies, even at some risk to current sales." The aptly named Web site the Hype Machine (http://hypem.com) demonstrates Croxson's point. The site posts links to scores of MP3 blogs that post free music downloads, some of which have been sanctioned by the artists or their labels, but many of which have not. Given that these sites openly allow anyone to download copyrighted MP3s without paying, they would seem an easy target for litigation. Yet the labels and the RIAA largely leave them alone. The reason, according to the Hype Machine founder Anthony Volodkin, is that the industry recognizes that these sites provide free advertising for their artists and a credibility that comes from *not* being associated with the corporate world. Furthermore, nearly all of the blogs also provide links to online retailers, making it easy to buy the albums from which the sites sample.

In making these observations I am not suggesting that illegal downloading is harmless. In 2002, the economics professor Stan Liebowitz conducted a study of thirty years of record sales and determined that a modest but real percentage of the downturn in record sales can only be attributed to illegal file-sharing; in his more recent work he has made stronger claims, notably that "file-sharing is responsible for the entire decline in record sales that has occurred." Significantly, however, he has refuted what he calls the "Annihilation Hypothesis"—the idea that file-sharing will destroy the record industry. Other researchers have also found a correlation between file-sharing and the decline in record sales, though never quite to the extent that the RIAA claims. There are some dissenters, however, including the authors of the Canadian study I cited earlier and the economists Felix Oberholzer-Gee and Koleman Strumpf, who, in a leading economics journal, made this stunning assertion: "Downloads have an effect on sales that is statistically indistinguishable from zero." Liebowitz has repeatedly attacked the team's findings as faulty and has criticized them for not sharing their data; they have defended themselves and countered that Liebowitz's research has been financially supported by the RIAA. My own inclination is to doubt the most extreme claims on both sides and to accept the general consensus that file-sharing causes at least some harm to the record industry. Even if fairly modest, this translates into fewer and less lucrative contracts for recording artists, a decline in royalties, and lost jobs, not just for executives, but for producers, engineers, and others.

Nevertheless, it is possible to acknowledge all this and still regard the industry's stance toward file-sharing as unproductive and wrongheaded. P2P file-sharing has not abated—it continues to grow. The RIAA's abandonment of its five-year campaign to stanch the flow of illegally downloaded MP3s clearly acknowledged its failure to stop the bleeding. Nor has the industry succeeded in convincing the public of a moral imperative against unauthorized downloading; even if users of LimeWire or BitTorrent sense that their actions are somehow wrong, they likely perceive their file-sharing to be a minor sin, more akin to jaywalking than to shoplifting.

In the first edition of *Capturing Sound*, which I finished researching in late 2003, I predicted that listeners could be convinced to pay for MP3s and would simultaneously continue to buy physical recordings even in a world flooded with nonrivalrous sound files. Paid downloading, I wrote, would be attractive if doing so were easy, fast, and reliable, and if files were plentiful, glitch free, and nonexpiring. I also believed that consumers would still buy CDs because of their tangibility, visuality, and permanence, and if they were enhanced with accompanying music videos or other "bonuses." And indeed, in the intervening years online music stores have thrived and proliferated, and despite predictions of its imminent death, the CD is still far more popular than the MP3 in terms of sales.

The first decade of the millennium was a time of perhaps unrivaled tumult in modern musical life. Listeners downloaded billions of dollars worth of music without paying; the industry responded with an all-out war against them and their P2P enablers. A once-symbiotic relationship had broken down, replaced by mutual antagonism. Although online music stores independent of the record labels stepped into the breach, the enmity remains, the industry continues to suffer, and the paid downloading services still offer only a portion of what is available on P2P networks. The disaffection with the current climate seems to be so widespread that even the most uncompromising representatives of the various sides agree: we must find a way out of a situation in which everyone seems to lose. What then, might the future of file-sharing hold?

The future of file-sharing

It is likely that the situation will *not* change immediately. The recording industry, though shrinking, remains a behemoth with all the nimbleness and inertia of an oil tanker. Yet, whether this tanker is gradually changing course, sinking, or both simultaneously, change will eventually come. Two broad types of change are likely: legal and economic, and the future of file-sharing depends on how these changes play out.

Legal change, if it comes, would likely arrive as copyright reform. Some believe that copyright and even the notion of intellectual property should be abolished, but this is almost certainly a noneventuality, given the centuries-long expansion of copyright and the strength of will of the deep-pocketed corporations that support it. A more reasonable goal is the restoration of copyright as a balance between access and control, between public and private rights and interests. This is the goal Siva Vaidhyanathan puts forward in his persuasive study *Copyrights and Copywrongs*. "American culture and politics would function better," he proposes, "under a system that guarantees 'thin' copyright protection—just enough protection to encourage creativity, yet limited so that emerging artists, scholars, writers, and students can enjoy a rich public domain of 'fair use' of copyrighted material."

How would copyright slim down to become the system Vaidhyanathan envisions? One avenue is the courts. In 2003, the U.S. Supreme Court heard *Eldred v. Ashcroft*, a case that challenged the constitutionality of the 1998 Copyright Term Extension Act, which added another twenty years onto copyright terms. *Eldred* plaintiffs included several publishing companies; amicus briefs on their behalf were filed by dozens of law and economics professors, fifteen library associations, and the corporate giant Intel. In 2005, *MGM v. Grokster* attracted similar briefs for the defendant, the file-sharing network Grokster, from twenty-seven different groups. One was filed by nearly two dozen prominent musicians, including Chuck D., Brian Eno, and Ann and Nancy Wilson of the group Heart. Noting that many musicians "do not perceive sharing of copyrighted works over peer-to-peer networks as a threat," they held that "file-sharing currently provides substantial opportunities to musicians to distribute their work." Another brief, signed by twenty-one professors who study media and technology (myself included), focused on the educational uses of file-sharing and argued for an expansion of "users' rights." With the backing of famous musicians, large corporations, and academics from across the disciplines, both cases demonstrated broad support for copyright reform and for P2P file-sharing. Yet these supporters lost in both cases, suggesting that overhauling copyright through the courts is perhaps a quixotic venture.

Copyright reform, however, need not require overturning laws or tilting with well-funded opponents. Lawrence Lessig, the lead counsel for the plaintiffs in *Eldred v. Ashcroft*, fought the law and lost. But at the same time he was also helping to develop an alternative system of copyright that promotes a closer balance between creators and the public. The Creative Commons (CC), a nonprofit corporation that he and a group of intellectual property experts, artists, and others established in 2001, offers copyright licenses that allow creators to specify exactly which rights they want to retain and which they give to the public. The goal is to replace the restrictive regime of "all rights reserved" with a more flexible and permissive practice of "some rights reserved." For example, when the musician Trent Reznor, the creative force behind Nine Inch Nails, released the album *Ghosts I–IV* in 2008, he did so with a license that allows anyone to share, distribute, and remix the music as long as they do so for noncommercial purposes and attribute the source material to Reznor. This is just one of several permutations of CC licenses, 130 million of which had been granted by 2008, and which are recognized by legal jurisdictions around the world. The growing popularity of these licenses suggests that musicians and creators of all types do not necessarily want to restrict the public's use of their work as much as current law makes possible. CC licenses still make up a tiny minority of the copyrights in existence, but they suggest a possible future in which the interactions between copyright holders and the public no longer resemble the antagonistic zero-sum relationship witnessed in the first decade of the millennium.

As promising as CC licensing may be, it does nothing to stop the unauthorized downloading of traditionally copyrighted music. And given that attempts to reform copyright through the courts have yet to succeed, the legal realm is unlikely to drive change in file-sharing. More important will be the economic arena.

The economic challenge that file-sharing presents is clear: how to monetize an activity that currently costs nothing. One approach is to follow the lead of broadcast radio. Listeners pay nothing for the music they hear, yet artists are still compensated when their music receives airplay. The money comes from fees that radio stations pay to various performing rights organizations such as ASCAP, BMI, and SESAC, which then distribute these fees to their member songwriters. These fees are what make it possible for stations to legally play music to the public without requesting permission. The idea could be applied to file-sharing in a variety of ways. One possibility is that Internet service providers (ISPs)—the companies such as AT&T, Comcast, TimeWarner, and countless others that connect users to the Internet and P2P networks—would add a surcharge of perhaps five to ten dollars to monthly subscription rates and contribute some portion of this money to a fund that would be distributed to artists. In exchange, subscribers could then download all the music they want—legally—from the source of their choice. Universities could do the same by adding a small fee and then allowing students to download music as they please. Details of the various proposals vary. The money could be generated through a compulsory license—essentially a tax—imposed on ISPs, or it could be voluntary; the entity collecting the fees could be governmental or private; or money could also be collected by taxing MP3 players. But why would such a system—whatever the details—discourage free file-sharing? For one thing, under a compulsory licensing system, most file-sharers would have no choice but to pay if their ISPs made the extra fee obligatory. But even those who could find ways to avoid paying might be happy to pay, safe in the knowledge that their actions are legal and that their money is supporting their favorite artists.

Proposals have been floated since at least as early as 2001, and as of 2010 no one system has been found acceptable to all the affected parties. This is, unfortunately, to be expected, given the inertial tendencies of the recording industry and the raw animosity that persists on the various sides. Nevertheless, the general idea is being taken more seriously and is the subject of increasing discussion. It is not unduly optimistic to think that file-sharing will become monetized and legalized sometime before the twentieth anniversary of Napster's demise.

A more unorthodox solution to the question of monetizing sound files is to make them, well, free. The most vocal proponent of this contrarian notion is Chris Anderson, the editor of *Wired* magazine and author of the 2009 book *Free: The Future of a Radical Price*. Music, he holds, is now so cheap to make and distribute that it should simply be given away as a means to promote concerts and merchandise, which make more money for artists than recordings. "Free music," he claims, "is just publicity for a far more lucrative tour business." There is sense in Anderson's proposal, for we know that music files generate valuable hype, and it is already common practice for artists and labels to provide free downloads or streams on their Web sites. Anderson also rightly points out that for many artists "music is not a moneymaking business. It's something they do for other reasons, from fun to creative expression. Which, of course, has always been true for most musicians anyway." If it is more important to a musician to be heard than to be paid, free is the obvious choice. The countless amateur musicians who post videos on YouTube, or the mashup artists we encountered in the previous chapter who share their work with one another, are cases in point. But for many working musicians, free is not a viable option. Pablo Aslan, a professional bass player and producer active in jazz and tango, points out that there are irreducible costs involved in being a professional musician. "If information wants to be free, creating a recording, which costs money, is a losing proposition. And no, you can't make a good record at home." Touring, too, can sap the finances of those musicians not supported by a label: "we can't propose that every musician go on the road to subsidize their recordings," Aslan explains. Factor in the cost of buying and maintaining instruments and equipment and other not so incidental expenses, and it turns out that for many artists, free comes at a high price. Although free will likely not become the accepted model for music across the board—it may simply be *too* radical a price—the artist- and industry-approved gratis download will certainly come to play an ever more important function in the economy of music.

Alone, no one of the scenarios I have described—whether copyright reform, the subsidization of downloading through increased ISP subscription rates, or free music—will be the future of file-sharing. They will all operate simultaneously. As it happens, this coexistence is also the past and present of file-sharing. Therefore, the only way the future will be significantly different—and better—is if the coexistence becomes less antagonistic and more focused on the interests of listeners.

My own experience with file-sharing—which I believe is not unusual—suggests a trajectory from which we might extrapolate. I began with Napster in 1999, and then after its downfall in 2001 moved on to a series of other P2P networks, none of which was nearly as good as the original. Apple's iTunes Store went online in 2003, and because it provided the quality and convenience P2P networks could not guarantee, it became my first stop when seeking out music. At the same time, MP3 blogs were becoming better known, and I began to download the music they championed as a way to expand my horizons. Similarly, I started dabbling with Pandora, essentially a personalized Internet radio service that recommends music based on the listener's tastes. YouTube arrived in 2005, and drew me to its copious and ever-expanding collection of professional and amateur music videos. Amazon started offering DRM-free downloads in 2007 and so I patronized its music store, and when in 2008 Lala allowed whole songs to be streamed free, I added it to my list of frequented sites. Meanwhile, I was also using what cheekily came to be known as Sneakernet, simply the practice of exchanging files with others in person through the use of very small, high-capacity portable hard drives. And all the while, I continued to spend time on file-sharing networks and I continued to buy CDs, though in both cases less than in the past.

I draw two larger points from my own experience. One is to reiterate the reality and necessity of technological coexistence. Like countless others, I paid for MP3s through online music stores but also downloaded them illegally on P2P networks; I bought some CDs and copied others; I listened to music on computers, stereos, and MP3 players, as well as in clubs and concert halls. This is not especially remarkable; most of us are quite used to living with both old and new technologies. As I look at my desk I see an iPod and a laptop computer, both new technologies filled with another new technology—MP3s. But I also see pencils and books, paper clips and a telephone, all of which have been with us for at least a century. The second point comes from a clear pattern in my music consumption. Over the years I have been file-sharing, I went from paying for rather little of the music I heard to paying for a much higher percentage; I went from being a frequent violator of copyright to an infrequent one. This trend was not encouraged by the RIAA, either through its attempt to bully listeners or to "educate" them or, I must admit, from a gradually developing moral compass. (I may be unusual in that I can reasonably excuse my file-sharing because I do research on the topic. But to be honest, I would have used Napster anyway.) No, the reason for my change in habits, the reason I don my pirate hat less often, is because over the years I have been provided with more and better alternatives to file-sharing, and thus more and better ways to experience the widest array of music.

My experience suggests what a possible—and positive—future for file-sharing might look like. It would be one in which the various means of disseminating music continue to coexist, but operate more efficiently and in mutually beneficial ways. In this future, the RIAA serves the best interests of its members *and* the fans who make their business possible. In this future, the P2P networks flourish, both because they generate money for musicians and the labels and because, with the industry no longer undermining them, their services improve. In this future, ever cleverer marketing encourages audiences not to be satisfied with the plenitude of free, high-quality sound files, but to demand—and pay for—physical recordings and live performances. In this future, the kudzu-like growth of copyright terms slows, as more and more artists decide that a looser grip on their creations is good for everyone. I must admit that "good for everyone" is an optimistic scenario and thus, unfortunately, not the most probable one. Given, however, that such a future will serve the interests of listeners, artists, and the industry alike—and even provide much-needed respite for all those overworked lawyers—I hold out hope.

File-sharing is neither plague nor panacea. MP3 and P2P are influential not because they are good or bad, but because they provide radically new ways to disseminate and experience music. They are influential, too, because of the constellation of phonograph effects they have birthed, whether collective composition over the Internet, online communities of music lovers, changes in listening habits, or the growing eclecticism of musical tastes. Given the daily twists and developments in technology, law, and culture, further phonograph effects are sure to arise. Just watch. And listen.

Chapter 28

NORMAN KLEIN

HYBRID CINEMA
THE MASK, MASQUES AND TEX AVERY

TO DATE, MUCH OF THE critical attention to Computer-Generated Imagery (CGI) in popular cinema has been concerned with the 'realism' of synthetic imagery. That is, firstly, the extent to which this imagery replicates the look and conventions of conventional cinematography (and/or the perceivable world that this cinematography purports to capture). Secondly, the aesthetics and techniques of stitching these images as special effects into conventionally photographed sequences, and thirdly, the implications for both popular cinema and its mediation of our engagement with the world.

These are all of concern to Klein, but he also delves into the genealogy and contemporary production context for what he calls 'hybrid cinema'. Hybrid because, as he demonstrates, CGI is to all intents and purposes *animation*, cinematic images manipulated at the level of the frame, and as such it results in a fusion of photographed and animated sequences quite different in scale and intent from earlier modes of special effects. Moreover Klein demonstrates that recent CGI-heavy blockbusters are characterised by animation conventions and aesthetics as well as techniques. *The Mask* explicitly draws on Looney Tunes cartoons of the 1940s, but Klein explains how even the apparent 'realism' of the animated dinosaurs in *Jurassic Park* was generated by animators schooled in the chase cartoon and who brought to the simulated movement a deep understanding of the timing and editing of classic cartoon animation.

There is something of **Huhtamo** and **Marvin**'s media archaeology in Klein's method, and his genealogy includes spectacular Baroque theatre as well as the histories of cinematic forms. However, Klein also explores the contemporary industrial production of this hybrid cinema as a key factor in its make-up, tracing links between animation studios and live-action production, as well as the economics and industrial relations of movie production. See also Part 2.6 (Digital Cinema) of *New Media: a Critical Introduction*.

After his groundbreaking work for Warner Bros. in *Porky's Duck Hunt* (1937), *The Isle of Pingo-Pongo* (1938), *Detouring America* (1939), and *A Wild Hare* (1940), Tex Avery hoped that someone would give him a shot at writing and directing a live-action feature during his tenure at MGM (1942–1955). He imagined Red Skelton comedies, even chatted with and suggested gags to live-action directors. This faint itch to try writing or directing a live-action comedy probably increased after the success of Frank Tashlin's films *The Girl Can't Help It* (1956) and *Will Success Spoil Rock Hunter?* (1957). However, Tashlin was an anomaly among animators. With very few exceptions, animators were classified in the industry as craftspeople, incapable of making a movie ninety minutes long. With the fusion of animation and live-action cinema in the past twenty years, this rule has changed, particularly with animator-directors like Tim Burton, Terry Gilliam, and even the Brothers Quay, but also in borrowings from cartoons since *Star Wars* (1977) or *Who Framed Roger Rabbit?* (1988); and with experimental animation transformed into feature films: *The City of Lost Children* (1995), *Institute Benjamenta* (1996).

The Mask (1994) is a classic case in point: it was made and marketed very much with Tex Avery in mind. According to the press release, "a hundred" gags were lifted directly from cartoons by Avery and by Robert Clampett, in what the special-effects team called "animation takes." That included the famous Avery double takes: eyes bulging priapically; the shriek while body parts explode; the jaw dropping like cement.

From the first scene, Avery's cartoons are the signature of the film. Stanley Ipkiss (Jim Carrey) runs a video of *Red Hot Riding Hood* (1943) on his VCR, while he suffers the humilities of the hapless schlemiel. Then, with Avery on the brain, he puts on the mask and whipsaws into cartoon medleys reminiscent of Carl Stalling's musical samplings for Looney Tunes. With Dionysian enthusiasm, he howls like Wolfie, whirs like the Tasmanian Devil, bounces like early Daffy.

Many reviews of the film cited the influence of Avery or the Warner Bros. chase cartoon on *The Mask*. Stanley was as "cocky as Bugs Bunny, as frenetic as Daffy Duck," "styled after the cartoon great Tex Avery"; the "cartoon style"; "cartoon boldness"; "textbook cartooning." Jim Carrey's elastic body made him a "biological cartoon of himself," "proud to have achieved a personal career goal by becoming a living cartoon." Then, like Daffy, or even Betty Boop, he zipped through an arpeggio of celebrity impressions, from Desi Arnez as Cuban Pete to Schwarzenegger in *Commando* (1985).

The distributor of *The Mask*, New Line Cinema, promoted this cartoon look, in the press kit, in print ads, in every interview I found. Industry news columns before its release suggested a very strong "word of mouth," the next hit in the subgenre of "cartoony" movies—films that borrow from Warner Bros. animation or by way of comic books. Since *Who Framed Roger Rabbit* or even *Star Wars*, practically every special-effects hit had Warner Bros. "takes" buried somewhere, either as a comic-book gag, or a blackout aside, or a roller-coaster effect, which, as I will explain later, originates with the same branch of entertainment as animation.

Also, Warner Bros. gags had become essential to the nostalgic look of many special-effects films. As the candy-box version of forties "screwball noir," these films featured nightclubs and Nazis; men in porkpie hats; women dressed like Rita Hayworth or Veronica Lake; bawdy chases reminiscent of wartime cartoons like *Red Hot Riding Hood*.

Of course, I am talking about applied animation: those effects that appear in postproduction. These have come to resemble animation increasingly, starting with computerized motion control in *Star Wars*, then much more layered compositing, and finally much enhanced 3-D animation: quicktime software, computerized flythroughs, texture mapping—a sculptural and architectonic update of cel animation, cartoon layout, and the chase. Today, essentially everyone working in special effects is expected to understand techniques from the chase cartoon. Knowing cartoon cycles and extremes helps the artist time an action sequence or splice in surprises in midaction: the offbeat aside, the wink to the audience.

But with so many levels of slapstick—more collisions and overreactions—the composition tends to get more congested, again like an Avery cartoon. Effects artists are usually asked to add objects or gimmicks, rather than clean up or thin out. Effects enliven the shot, from blue-screen effects to garbage mattes. That means much more visual throwaway than in the usual live-action film. Avery was, of course, a genius at visual throwaway. He littered the corners of the screen with tiny posters, novelty caricatures on the shelf, puns on the walls. And yet, despite the clutter, he made his chase gags hit like a sledgehammer. His timing was minutely exact. He might cut as little as a single frame, between the top of the screen, from where the object appears, to the point of impact farther down—slam! He was certain that for action sequences, the audience can sense the absence of one twenty-fourth of a second.

Chuck Jones disagrees. He thinks the threshold is more like five frames, perhaps a quarter of a second. Avery and Jones were much like the masters of action films: they knew the rhythm of gleeful violence supremely well; for example, they would add pauses to make the collision stronger, to have characters look less prepared. Only the audience suffers anticipation. The character is caught short by at least one frame.

Special-effects master Donna Tracy has confronted many of the same problems while working on dozens of effects films, from *Star Wars* to *Independence Day* (1996). She often will cut only a few frames from a chase and knows how to add zany cartoon elements where necessary, for contrast—the "balloony" contours (rubbery, too round, less natural), the anarchic use of scale, the upside downness. The slightest alteration, a frame or two, can ruin the movement (the effect), make it wobbly, or suggest a different mass. This is very similar to animation. It requires the same time-consuming minutiae. The computer does not shorten the work, only makes it more thorough. At the same time, a certain anarchy is required for a good action sequence. Like a cartoon chase, it requires the collision of the unlikely, such as mixing media and mood, with surprise pauses, and sudden lurches forward once the final volley begins. All these contraries are then synchronized balletically, to look like a magic act, thanks to the computer.

But beyond techniques in postproduction that resemble cartoon work, there is the subtle influence of the digital work environment itself. Special-effects crews are even more isolated from the studio than cartoon animators were. This breeds a strange ennui, not unlike film editors going thirty hours straight—but at a much slower pace. The result of weeks, even months, might be three seconds of film; five hundred hours to digitally engineer the texture of a tornado or the fidgety ears of alien reptiloids. This is managed without seeing the director much, except through notes brought by the effects supervisor for the film. Indeed, it is *applied* animation. Even more than cartoon work, where at least the actors were animated, the effects team works far away from the hustle and tactile presence of actors and live production.

This distanced milieu tends to enhance a movie plot that often is distanced already—dehumanized—where the dramatic characters tend to be hosts in trouble, elements whose main job is to introduce the tornado or the alien war strikes. As each abstracted shape is harvested slowly on a screen, one cannot help but feel disengaged from the political or social buzz outside, a kind of sensory deprivation. "After working for weeks on an effect," says Tracy, "all I want to do is smell a real tree."

At the same time, there is the illusion of a bigger cyber universe. Other screens nearby may be on utterly different projects, not for cinema at all. Effects artists have skills that allow them to work in many media: on malls, casinos, theme parks, Web sites, virtual chat lines, TV commercials, music videos, animated features, kid-vid, and incidentally live-action cinema. Therefore, inside an effects studio, one witnesses animation as muscle tissue for a hundred different industries, on a global scale. For a moment this bank of screens seems as exciting as a fully packed world—like a special-effects action ride. But in fact, it is emptied as well, highly undifferentiated. Anything from a bomb to a cyber toy looks the same—detached, innocent—a computer wire frame or a miniature.

This is a workplace far more fetishistic even than the "fun factories" on a movie lot, more like staring at Barbie dolls for months at a time, perfecting the tilt of her breasts or the angle of her smile. The work seems very independent of factory rules. And yet, it is utterly contingent. I would compare it to a crafts environment in the nineteenth century. People work in small teams, as in a shoe factory in 1870 (only without the toxic smells, and with overtime pay, and much more cybernetically polite). It is not Fordist, not an assembly line, perhaps less alienated from the means of production, seemingly more autonomous. And yet, the result is fundamentally industrial—repetitive action, based on severely restricted options, a chain of production controls, including contracts that say the studio owns whatever "creative" ideas are generated. Beneath the ergonomics and cheery carpeting, it is still a factory.

Beside obvious comparisons to Disney in the thirties, one can see similarities to Termite Terrace as well, to worker complaints in the stream of gags about Leon Schlesinger, about contracts, from *You Out to Be in Pictures* (1940) to *Duck Amuck* (1953). Perhaps the model is more a plantation than an assembly line—paternalistic, scattered, but severely controlled.

The mood of the plantation animator will influence the look of special-effects films, much as it adds a pungent irony to Warner Bros. cartoons. Even the plot and structure of special-effects films reflect this mood. Increasingly, the action-ride movie has insular gags, mostly about watching other movies by way of television. The antidramatic structure, with pieces of epic narrative, folkloric narrative, and various magic acts thrown in, resembles the interhierarchical, layered, nonlinear form of production. The seeming immobility of many of the characters suggests a feudalistic world where power is fluid but vast—diffuse—where individual initiative seems possible mostly as a form of caricature.

Consider the similarity of plots in so many of these action films, including *The Mask* and *Independence Day*. They center on disaster as conflict, where an unprepared world is invaded by special-effects forces of nature, from tornadoes to dinosaurs to digitally enhanced serial killers, or capitalist terrorists with foreign accents, alien warships from an intergalactic economy.

They always have a fetish, like a comic metonym, that stands in for the effects themselves. Would it be a stretch to identify the mask that Stanley wears as the place (metonym) where special effects enter? The device stands in for the cartoon process. It is a special-effects costume, a virtual-reality headset; or a time-travel chute that you wear, like sliding through an MRI at the hospital. The metonym erases your identity, but you wear it like clothing, to generate a few Dionysian gags, then take it off. Clearly, identity is a kind of accessory one wears, like a tattoo or a pierced ear, nose, stomach.

This is not to say that such fetishes/metonyms have not operated as entertainment before. They have been fundamental to how animation has worked for centuries, even before cinema. The effects industry is drawing from the same well as animation. No wonder it relies so heavily on the chase cartoons of Avery, Clampett, Jones, and others.

Brief background

Briefly, what do I mean by centuries of narrative theory and techniques common to both chase cartoons and effects movies? Obviously, these roots are not at all postmodern. They are closer to preindustrial. Most effects before the computer (and now being rediscovered digitally) borrowed heavily from theatrical devices already old in the nineteenth century. They are animation in real space, very architectural illusions. For example, the trick films of Méliès rely on music-hall gimmickry dating back to medieval carnival, also puppet theater, magic lantern effects since the Counter Reformation, the wizardry of Renaissance theatrical machines, as well as mannerist trompe l'oeil and anamorphosis. Many of these already had entered the home as well, through popular illustration since Dürer, then mass illustration with the steam engine, along with trick gizmos like zoetropes. That is why I am convinced that special effects in casinos, baroque churches, and the movies have a common heritage.

Another crucial point to remember is that both special effects and animation have been part of the same industry for generations. Special effects simply emphasize that precinematic architectural aspect of animation, as in trick entertainment, circuses, magic acts, music halls, and costume masque—again, animation in real space, as in Méliès's shorts or even McCay's vaudeville act with Gertie the dinosaur.

In the United States, Willis O'Brien became the key figure in the emergence of special effects, first in the feature *The Lost World* (1925) and then of course with *King Kong* (1933). He transferred what was called "trick work" (as in trick photography and double exposure) into a genre of Hollywood filmmaking.

But the transition was inevitable anyway. After 1927, with the coming of sound more film was shot indoors. The need for in-camera effects grew enormously, particularly for very elaborate glass mattes and rear projection. These crafts were supposed to be "below the line" generally, hidden rather than exaggerated. They came to be classified within the industry as "animation" because the mattes used techniques similar to cartoon watercolor background, to layout. Similarly, by the midthirties, models became more essential, not only for live action but also for tabletop animation in Fleischer cartoons, or as visual aids for Disney animators, to help them draw their characters turning. However, since many of these live-action effects were not designed to be perceived, applied animation was barely noticed until the last twenty years— after *Star Wars* essentially. Except for the occasional book on masters of the stop-motion miniature (O'Brien or Ray Harryhausen), special effects were relegated to chapters in how to books for amateurs or manuals for professionals, mostly on cinematography.

But that has irrevocably changed. Applied animation has been retooled as software, for interactive entertainment across the media, even in malls, theme parks, a year-round consumerist carnival. It is simply the architectural version of the animated, more about the shopper as spectator, more about rides than conflict.

Like an amusement park in 1900, or even like the Vatican in 1510 for that matter (illusionistic masterpieces of Michelangelo and Raphael), animation-in-real-space is once again an interactive journey where the audience is a central character. Character animation is simply a variant of this interactive form.

Special-effects environments, what we today call "interactive," were essential to the urban plan of Renaissance and baroque cities, in the design of plazas, in the domed interiors, even the illusions painted on the walls. To repeat, then, this form of "architectonic" story appears in theater, illustration, circus, any number of entertainments that feed into what we now call animation.

Animation has always been fundamentally an "interactive," not a dramatic form of story; the characters are dominated by, or at cartoon war with, the effects. It is more like an epic form, about worlds rising and falling, characters as types within the whole, or as elements like machine parts designed to move the spectacle along. These spectacles are narratives about environments, not characters, at risk; about folklore, carnival, the caricature of community in commedia dell'arte. For example, one source that continues to fascinate me is the Renaissance machines used for effects in theaters (similar to the gears and levers used in fortifications). They cranked up illusions from below stage and through the ceiling. Inside such a machinelike magic, the characters remain more stylized, even with comic masks on their faces or dancing in masques. Centuries later, cartoon characters are stylized in similar ways; they are masks with bionic or rubbery bodies—anarchic phantasms, more like revelers in a masque than dramatic characters, ducks amuck.

That means if you work with animation (as in *Duck Amuck*, where Daffy is lost in the apparatus of the movie), you are drawing on an architectural mode of story quite different from Bazinian space, not simply illusionistic but a caricature of the stage (movie staging). This anarchic architectural illusion is littered with self-reflexive, intertextual gags; they speak to the audience the way a stand-up comedian does, or a TV talk show does, or a TV commercial. Much on TV, therefore, derives from roots similar to animation, to the navigated "epic" journey of the audience through a special-effects space.

The Warner Bros. chase is an accelerated version of this journey, developed from 1937 to 1958. The contract player (represented by Bugs) is prey to Elmer (dumb boss). Bugs is hunted and haunted, then cheerfully takes his revenge, in alliance with the audience, who are brought into the story with direct address, signs, and winks. In *Red Hot Riding Hood*, the contract players complain to their boss that they are sick and tired of their scripts. They refuse to do painfully sentimental "mellerdrammer." Instead, they want a masque on Hollywood Boulevard. Then, from a special-effects point of view, Avery navigates the audience through a madly improvised space, very upside down, where gravities meet and are made to collide. But it is also similar to trompe l'oeil domes where the sky appears to be collapsing on the spectator—a special-effects masque.

Here is how Steve Williams, the special-effects supervisor on *The Mask*, saw this Avery gimmick: First, he called the project "an animation acting model rather than a visual effects model," more like making cartoon comedy flat, rather than mixing an animated element inside a story closer to dramatic structure, as they had with *Jurassic Park* (1993) immediately before. *The Mask* apparently was a relief after the tedium of building T-Rex.

In other words, animation as a story form felt freer, but also truer to the potential of visual effects, if allowed to mature into its own aesthetic.

Director Chuck Russell set a new standard in that he allowed us to play with cut lengths of scenes in order to improve the flow of the animation once it was composited (timing like a chase cartoon essentially) . . . This was not commonplace before *The Mask*, but now it is. . . . [After hoping for years to try Avery gags on an f/x film:] For ten years I've wanted to make someone's, ANYONE'S, eyes bulge.

Beyond our love of chase cartoons, what makes elemental stories emotionally captivating when they appear as live action? What is the vocabulary? We understand that there is not much time for dramatic development between characters, except as stock pantomime; or as dramatic shorthand, a quick "Hello, what's my conflict?" and on to the chase. That is what passes for dramatic structure in *The Mask*, in many of the best special-effects films—as in the best fairy tales, the best chase cartoons.

However, despite the pubescent spirit or thudding redundancy in many of these films, their sheer impact can be breathtaking. Most critics isolated Carrey as the good cartoon ("smokin'"), and the rest as the *blague* or blah of the story. Reviewers identified with Carrey inside his appliances, makeup, and computer enhanced body, but not as a man in dramatic conflict. Donna Tracy says much the same. 'The cartoony look of Jim Carrey in *The Mask* brings feelings to us about our own lives, not about his life in the story. We feel the exclusion of our own emotions. We feel ourselves hiding our emotions and content so much, as he does.'

Stanley's "character" is a shell, controlled by outside forces, as if animation stood in for an ancient special-effects machine. He is trapped inside an apparatus that forces him to explode like an animated cartoon, a parodic allegory about determinism. His frenzy under the cartoon mask is not so much about intimacy as it is about being trapped inside an apparatus. The mask is a container, like all animated effects really, another allegory about determinism.

Dramatic narrative, by contrast, is very much about free will, about individualism. If Stanley were in a dramatic story, it might be "Dr. Jekyll and Mr. Hyde," though this story also reprises regularly in special effects, most recently in *The Nutty Professor* (1996).

To sharpen this distinction, I will pause for a few sentences on Jekyll/Hyde, clearly a trope that is almost mythic for many "dark metamorphosis" stories in graphic novels and comics. What does Robert Louis Stevenson's dramatic narrative suggest? Clearly it is a tale about the moral dilemma of releasing selfcontrol, as in Edgar Allan Poe, Mary Shelley's *Frankenstein*, and dozens of others from popular English literature. But it is also a response to the burgeoning growth of London in the 1890s, to slums, prostitution, the flammable mixing of classes, the invading proletariat, the revenge of the declining gentry. Let us say that Jekyll's torment is an allegory about the end of the myths of the entrepreneur: the cowboy who cannot head west; the detective going alone down mean streets; Stevenson's pirates killing for gold; Jekyll the scientist overextending his reach. The hero makes mistakes out of free will or even out of greed, refusing to take an honest profit or to stop before breaking God's law.

Drama, in its nineteenth-century variant, is often a businessman's idea of predestination and salvation; that soon it will be too late for free enterprise, that the proletariat will overwhelm the natural order of profit and loss. To stretch the point, as a matter of contrast with animation today: dramatic narrative, as we in the West have developed it since 1820 or so, revolves around capitalist myths about the individual struggling to survive as an entrepreneur.

Animation, even in its preindustrial forms, tends toward stories about the reification of the apparatus itself, the mechanized leviathan beyond the individual. Again, this is a feudal model more than an industrial one. Characters, like folk heroes, tend to be more *elemental* within the apparatus, and less dramatic, not necessarily dimmer or shallower, simply different. Their relationship to the magic effect, to the gag, the magic potion, reminds the audience that this is a journey into developmental moments in their own life. The character is supposed to be empty, to be filled by the audience's sensibility.

To avoid overstating my case—overclassifying—let me add that all this is a matter of degree.

A: The dramatic story exaggerates the internal dialectic of character.
B: The elemental story emphasizes the conflict around the apparatus itself; it is much more about power, spectacle, and presence.

Special effects are a hybrid of the two. However, in the mix, each tends to erase the other, leading to a very diminished sense of character. Perhaps this amounts to an allegory about diminished individualism, that the self, as an industrial myth about freedom, cannot survive the effects of the electronic workplace.

The need for new theory about hybrid cinema

Critics, and, I must admit, film theorists, as a rule still ignore the elemental form of story that is inherent to animation, and therefore, they often get flustered by the special-effects film. For example, let us sort through some of the reviews of *The Mask* at the time of its release.

> *The Mask* underscores the shrinking importance of conventional storytelling in special-effects-minded movies, which are happy to overshadow quaint ideas about plot and character with flashy up-to-the-minute gimmickry.
>
> —Janet Maslin, *New York Times*

Some of the shocks are amazing: like pinpricks on your hand, only fun. There's no script to speak of, and the other characters hardly matter.

—David Denby, *New York*

The plot's throwaway. You've got to get on board, or move out of the way.

—Jeff Giles, *Newsweek*

The responses were much the same with *Independence Day*, which indeed was a bit blunt, a very cynical film, filled with all the hot-button effects, but at least making run on itself. Still I saw it from the first row and wasn't bored, no more than if I had been dragged five miles by a runaway bus—which brings me back to a recurring theme: one of the most common terms used in production of these films is "the ride." As Donna Tracy explains: "The ride is more important than the story. The ride is the story."

What we need to understand is that the ride is an allegory about the audience, about the shocks of globalized economic arrangements, about new forms of visuality, and fundamentally about the collapse of private and public space—all of these wrapped into a cartoon *bildung*, without any interior life, in fact bluntly displaying characters incapable of interiors.

In other words, we see a simulation of self as a movie effect. Forget Baudrillard's nostrums for a moment. Simulation (copies without originals) as a device in moviemaking merely announces the folkloric or elemental use of character; then enables the immersive journey, where we, the audience, cannot distinguish between inside and outside, where our identity is invaded by special effects; yet, in some ergonomic way, we are comfortable with our self-erasure (or are we?). It is a grim allegory indeed. No wonder critics resent it. Beneath the blithe and thrilling, there is a warning, the invasion of self, loss of intimacy, loss of private boundaries.

But we must take these films more seriously, even though they are so misanthropic in the way they hawk their hype. I could sidestep the entire problem by taking the high road and using experimental animation as the model, for example: stop-motion masterpieces by Starevich, Borowczyk, Rybczynski, Svankmejer, and then the ambient journeys by the Brothers Quay. By Hollywood standards, these films are systematically antidramatic, simply outside the range of pop dramatic narrative. But that approach, a lofty formalism, would do no good. It avoids more than it defends. Animated "action" films like *The Mask* present a very different set of parameters. Unlike a Quay film, they are a category fundamental to the mainstream, immensely popular, even dominant in the nineties. They are built out of a new form of cinematography that has taken the global film market by storm, led to glittery articles on the animation industry in the *New York Times*, the *Wall Street Journal*, and a buzz in the art world that amazes me. This buzz has become a windfall to film schools and dozens of new animation programs in colleges, even in high schools now. Every major studio is investing hundreds of millions of dollars to ramp up for more special-effects films like *The Mask, Forrest Gump* (1994), *Independence Day*, and *The Lion King* (1994). That means effects above and below the line, for lighting, stunts, locations. The gold mine for licensing special effects in toys, games, clothing, and virtual-reality malls is greater than what animated films have earned before, very much like cartoon licensing, but on an astronomical level. *The Lion King* alone earned over $1 billion in clear profit, the most lucrative consumer object ever made. What do you think Henry Ford would have done?

Nevertheless, I am convinced that we are not witnessing the collapse of movie culture as we know it—dramatic structure—but the gaudy birth of a hybrid form. And animation, particularly the chase cartoon, is the key to understanding how this hybrid can mature (one hopes). We need to outgrow our postmodern cynicism and concentrate more on inventing a modernist poetics for the computer era.

The glamour of special effects reminds us that consumerism has matured. It is now integrated as a partner in the industrial economy. Disney is on the DOW. Time Warner has absorbed Turner. Not since the late feudal era that gave birth to animation, has power, entertainment, and salvation been concentrated in precisely the same place—the same screen, so diffuse yet so omnipotent. Indeed, hybrid cinema is merely reminding us that in the "New World Order," public and private, work and leisure, capital and information are being hybridized.

What's more, this electronic feudalism is allegorized by the mood inside a special-effects studio. Something as fissionable as the industrial revolution of the nineteenth century is upon us, promising us cable, remote control, and special effects in return for declining real income in the "New World Order." What presence and engagement, what fresh films and books, do we intend to make of this trade-off?

These flashy special-effects films will be teaching the future what we thought of our mess, just as trick cinema teaches us today about the impact of electricity and locomotives in 1900. In other words, one could argue that films like *The Mask* speak more directly, or at least more problematically, about the impact of computer capitalism than CD-ROMs or the Internet, than the entire telephonic, hypercard boosterism that is called cyberspace.

In 1994, Richard Corliss wrote of *The Mask*: "By obeying the insane pace, wild exaggeration, mock cheerful tone and inside references that today define much of a movie and TV entertainment, Avery practically invented pop culture's Postmodernism." While I'm not comfortable with the overripe term "postmodernism" (I'm more a modernist, I suspect), Corliss is on the right track. Movies that hark back to the televisual, like *The Mask*, rely on vocabulary developed by Avery and the chase cartoon; I find that cartoons help explain a great deal about the semiotics of television narrative, since cartoons have their roots in theater, which leads to television as well. Animation has always been hybridized, in its marketing, scripting, production, and reception. And now, live-action cinema is turning into a kind of animation.

Recently, George Lucas said that digital effects can bring assembly-line efficiency to moviemaking. Through digital libraries, like painted backdrops of New York City in studio lots of the thirties and forties, the process of building a movie can be integrated, not split off between the shoot and digitalized postproduction. There will be "no aesthetic advantage in shooting on location anymore." Digital content will become reusable, like old cartoons. The era when digital effects shift from a service industry to production has arrived.

James Cameron repeats in various interviews, as if he were a master animator at his light table: "Anything you can imagine can be done. If you can draw it, if you can describe it, we can do it." His version of the collapse of public into private has arrived—as story—on the image-capture stage that he used for *True Lies* (1994). "In Digital Hollywood you won't even be able to trust your eyes." The special-effects films, for all their gaudiness, have become the portable cathedrals for this integrated, weirdly disengaged feudal civilization.

Chapter 29

MARTIN LISTER

PHOTOGRAPHY IN THE AGE OF ELECTRONIC IMAGING

L OOKING BACK AT THE anxieties and doom-laden prophecies that attended the emergence of digital photography as popular media technology in the early 1990s, Martin Lister interrogates both obituaries for photography and its privileged status as the dominant visual medium of the modern world, and counter-claims that digital photography represents more a continuation or enhancement of this dominant medium. Anxieties over the loss of photography's 'truth status' and realism have resulted in critical attention to precisely why a photograph is seen as indexical in the first place, the direct physical result of the objects photographed. Lister points out the persistence of long-established conventions of pictorial composition and representation in digital photographic practices.

Significantly, the 'content', message or aesthetics of individual photographs are much less important to Lister's discussion than their production and reception. In terms of production, citing **Manovich**, he questions assumptions that the digital capture of an image is fundamentally different to the chemical reactions of analogue photographic film. In terms of reception, he notes that in many ways photographs still 'feel' the same in the digital age: there are clear continuities in their circulation as both evidence (on passports for example) and as personal, emotion-laden objects. A consideration of the look of photography is brought to bear on the use of CGI in cinema (see also **Klein**), where it is the faults of the photographic (film grain, shallow depth of field, lack of focus, lens flare, etc.) that must be simulated for digital images to read as 'real'.

These discussions allow Lister to move on to what he suggests might the most pressing and significant technocultural changes heralded by digital photography: changes in what it means to be human. Critiques of humanist investment in the dominant relationships between subject and object in photography and questions of what kind of 'machine eye' we are seen by today, and what else these eyes see, Lister suggests, lead to the dissolution of 'the very security of our traditional distinctions between nature and culture and human and technology'. Digital photography is bound up in current and future post-human or cyborg worlds.

We have seen in the previous pages that the earlier, and still influential, attempts to gauge the significance of digital imaging for photography focused upon the differences between the analogue and the digital image, and between practices of representation (photography) and simulation (computer graphics) as the key issues. They argued that shifts from analogue/representation to digital/simulation were the visual expression of an underlying shift from a modern to a postmodern world and the loss of the kind of world-view that photography had provided since the mid-nineteenth century. A new post-photographic era in visual culture was being ushered in, in which we could no longer cling to our fragile if tenacious belief in the truth and evidential value of photographs. At the same time a range of historical antecedents had been brought to light which pointed to cultural continuities in the uses of photography which cut across its many technological developments.

It now seems clearer than ever that the 'logic' of digital photography contains a tense relationship between continuity and discontinuity. While digital image technology may be replacing the photographic apparatus it is also playing a part in continuing and even raising the value of the photographic image so that thinking in terms of absolute differences between the two hardly makes sense. We can see a more complex interplay taking place. By any account we are faced with a situation which cannot be reduced to simply thinking in terms of the replacement of one medium or image technology by another. As Lev Manovich puts it,

> The logic of the digital photograph is one of historical continuity and discontinuity. The digital image tears apart the net of semiotic codes, modes of display, and patterns of spectatorship in modern visual culture – and, at the same time, weaves this net even stronger. The digital image annihilates photography while solidifying, glorifying and immortalizing the photographic. (Manovich 2003: 241)

On this note, the rest of this chapter will consider more recent challenges and refinements to the ideas considered in earlier sections of the chapter as it is now possible to think through what has occurred in more measured and nuanced ways. We now find a situation where the digital has:

* continued to make us puzzle over the source of photography's realism;
* renewed an interest in photography's indexical nature;
* given rise to a new interest in the identity of the viewer of 'post-photography';
* required us to think about the reception, rather than the production, of digital photographs;
* led us to question, in the light of practical experience and use, the earlier abstract thinking that was brought to bear on the analogue/digital difference;
* suggested grounds for conceiving of a 'post-human' vision (replacing an earlier preoccupation with the resonance between 'post-photography' and the postmodern).

Remembering photography's nature

It has been a remarkable aspect of the emergence of digital image technology that it has led us to reappraise how we have understood photography and to revisit old questions and debates about its realism. Sarah Kember (1998: 17) points to a conundrum which is one of the main reasons for this:

> Computer manipulated and simulated imagery appears to threaten the truth status of photography even though that has already been undermined by decades of semiotic analysis. How can this be? How can we panic about the loss of the real when we know (tacitly or otherwise) that the real is always already lost in the act of representation?

[. . .]

Why then, does computer manipulated and simulated imagery appear to threaten a practice that is already recognised as one of mediation and manipulation? In the section Digitisation and the commodification of images, we met Rosler's argument that manipulation was integral to photography as seen in the very earliest uses of multiple negatives by photographers like Oscar Rejlander and in the openly manipulative, alternative traditions of photography, represented by photomontage and the work of the Dadaists and John Heartfield. Subsequently, Manovich has asserted that 'Digital technology does not subvert "normal" photography because "normal" photography never existed' (Manovich 2003: 245). Batchen (2001: 137) also argues that photography is nothing if not a history of manipulated images.

In different ways, both Kember (1998: 17) and Batchen (2001: 139–43) have argued that a tenacious belief in photography's realism is due to a strong historical investment in the idea. We must look to the history of image making and the 'way of seeing' that it embodied that we traced earlier in this chapter (A new way of seeing and the end of the 'Cartesian dream?').

Our belief in photography's realism

We saw earlier that photography is part of a **scopic regime**[1] that is far wider and has a much longer history than itself. We must now consider the cultural identity of the 'viewer' who sees in this manner. At the centre of this history of Western visuality stands the humanist self. This is a conception of the human subject who, amongst other things, is understood to be the rational centre of the world and the prime agent in seeking its meaning and establishing its order. We described this humanist subject as one who has searched for certain and objective knowledge through a disinterested and rational method of enquiry.

In her own reflection on the question, Kember stresses that this subject and this scopic regime are part of a larger scientific system and mode of enquiry, 'fashioned in Enlightenment philosophy and by Cartesian dualism and perspectivalism' (1998: 23). It is a system in which the viewer is understood as a centred, knowing subject coaxing information from a passive supine nature. However dominant this rational-scientific system and the centred humanist subject became over a period of some 500 years she reminds us that this position was always unstable and gendered. It was gendered because typically the 'knowing subject' was figured as male and 'supine nature' as female. It was unstable, because it was a system that depended upon (and was simultaneously troubled by) a desire to exercise power and control over nature and over others. Seen in this context we can understand that our 'panic' about the computer's threat to photography's realism does not actually take place at the level of the image itself. It is cultural panic over the potential loss of our centred, humanist selves, with our 'dominant and as yet unsuccessfully challenged investments in the photographic real' (Kember 1998: 18). The perceived threat is to our subjectivity, where a more fundamental fear is triggered which concerns, 'the status of the self or the subject of photography, and about the way in which the subject uses photography to understand the world and intervene in it' (1998: 18).

Digital photography (or digital imaging) has clearly shown us that even if the mechanical camera and chemical film are no longer involved, a practice and a form of image production persists that can be called photographic (or at the very least post-photographic). We have now seen that the value of photography depends upon more than its technology or the way it 'looks' but also upon our historical, cultural and psychic investment in it as a way of seeing and knowing. It affords us a position, an identity, a sense of power, and it promises to meet our desires. So, as Batchen (2001: 140) suggests, photography is more than its machines, it is also an 'economy of photographic desires and concepts'. At the centre of this economy is a desire to be securely placed as observers in relation to objects which interest us. For over 150 years we have gone to photography to give us reports on nature, to produce knowledge of others, to arrest time, to document and remember, to bring the spatially distant closer (to travel in space). Overall, we have looked to photography to provide a picture of a reassuring world in which everything appears to stay in its time, space and place (Kember 1998: 2). As long as such interests and projects are pursued by human beings, then surely 'a photographic culture of one sort or another will (. . .) endure despite the fact that computers may replace cameras and film' (Batchen 2001: 141).

Kember's account of photographic realism as part of a long humanist investment, and Batchen's concept of a 'photographic economy' which contains a set of enduring human desires and concepts, remind us why the single most important medium in modern visual culture cannot simply be swept aside by technological change. However preoccupied we have become with the technological and signifying differences between photography and digital imaging we are also called to think about the strength of the human (humanist) values which will direct our use of either. Yet, as we shall see below, arguments are now made which suggest that a new kind of vision and new kinds of images may displace photography precisely because the old, settled concept of the human as absolutely different and other to technology is, itself, under attack.

The force of the indexical image

We dealt earlier with the over-played idea that realism is more a property of some kinds of photograph than of some kinds of digital image, an idea that was at the centre of many early estimations of their difference. Photography's indexical quality also played a part in those earlier comparisons, in that the photograph was seen to have a fixed and mechanically guaranteed link with what it depicts while the digital image tended toward the artificial, the constructed and simulacral. Much was also made of its novel 'immateriality' in the sense that a photograph could exist as an electronic file.

The value that we have traditionally placed on the indexical nature of the mechanical and chemical photograph is an important part of the 'photographic economy' we have just discussed. It is also a quality that is closely associated with beliefs in photography's realism but which needs thinking about in an entirely different way. The resources to do this have been to hand for some time (Barthes 1980) but it is the puzzles thrown up by digital image technology's relationship to photography that have sent us back to think again. A compelling feature of chemical photography is the manner in which a photograph is caused by the light travelling from an object; in other words, that it is an image that is caused by what it represents; as the footprint is to the foot. In making the same point, photographs have been described as being like stencils off the real (Sontag 1979). However, these 'stencils' or traces are ones in which any reality content or verisimilitude has been transcribed, manipulated, enhanced, suppressed or emphasised by the mediating processes of photography yet they remain traces or indexes, nevertheless. Such traces could be in fact quite minimal in terms of verisimilitude or information about what they represented, being little more than smudges and marks on paper which we struggle to decipher.

While it plays a part in forming our beliefs in photography's realism, photography's indexicality is, in fact, something quite different from realism. The indexical quality of a photograph has more to do with a sense of presence than realism. It testifies to the *being* or existence of something that was once before the camera. The photographic negative was once, as it were, in touch with the object it depicts. Clearly, this indexical quality of a photograph can coexist alongside its mediations. The *ideas* that a photograph constructs and leads us to have about some-*thing* (or person, or event) through its mediations and codes, whether they are 'true' or 'realistic' or not, can be accompanied by a powerful sense that this thing 'has been', does or did exist (Batchen 2001: 139). Hence, even given the theoretical knowledge and critical understanding we may have about the impossibility of photographic representations capturing the 'real', we nevertheless 'sense' the real in a photograph. We 'feel' the presence of the real. This indexical quality is a characteristic of the photographic image which resists and is untouched by our very understanding that what is before us in a photograph, is very far from a simple reality or truth (Kember 1998: 31).[2]

Traditional photographs are material, and usually portable objects. In considering photography's indexical proximity to the 'real', it is important also to think about this materiality. A photographic print is both like a 'stencil' and is a physical object itself. Photographs frequently take the form of small things we have and keep, which we can carry with us and look at in the absence of what they depict. Putting photographic indexicality and materiality together we get a powerful mix; we see the photograph as something which it is as important to hold, touch, feel and check for as it is to see, and which we sense has literally touched something that exists but is absent or has existed but is no more. This is the photograph as a modern kind of fetish; it stands in for or displaces something lost or unattainable but desired (Kember 1998: 210).

However, digital photographs can also be indexes in both a technical way and, possibly more importantly, in how they are received and valued. We will consider this below as part of a wider discussion of the reception of digital images.

The reception of digital images

[. . .] [I]n his book *Camera Lucida*, Roland Barthes was interested in the act of looking at photographs rather than their production. He was interested in the meaning or, indeed, the feelings we have about photographs which remain of people once known to us, after their death. In thinking about photography this way we move to consider the reception, rather than the production of photographs; and to reflect on our felt experience of images rather than the analysis of their signifying means. When we do this, the difference between the chemical and the digital photograph again ceases to be important.

The significant differences between the purely photographic and the digitally registered photograph lie in the way it was 'taken', registered or transmitted, not simply the way it looks. Hence, in thinking about 'pre' and 'post' digital photography we are not always faced with evident and visible differences in the images themselves. This is because of the capacity of the new image technologies to register, carry, mimic, or simulate photographic images in increasingly undetectable ways. Over the last decade of 'digital photography' this has become more and more clearly the case. Far from always being used to produce images of a montage-like heterogeneity, digital imaging technology is just as likely to be used to make images that are as traditionally coherent in their pictorial unity and exhibit the pictorial values of traditional, chemical photographic prints. Similarly, in the case of the impact of digitisation on archive images, picture libraries and image banks, the critical issues are ones of access, transmission and the use of images which *continue to look like photographs*.

Jay David Bolter and Richard Grusin (1999: 105–12) extend this point when they observe that digital photographs are intended to be received by their viewers as photographs. It matters not whether an image was captured by the photosensitive cells of a digital camera (clearly a form of indexical registration), or, perhaps more surprisingly, was a conventional photograph that is subsequently scanned by a computer and altered, or is a combination of two digitised photographs and computer generated elements. All of these images address us as photographs. Digital photographers want us to regard their images 'as part of the tradition of photography' (Bolter and Grusin 1999: 105). These are all images that are *advertised or presented to us as photographs*. They are all intended to *be part of the tradition of photography*. When we see any of these images we see, phenomenologically, a photograph; an image that has all the marks of a photograph and calls us to read it as a photograph, that depends for its sense on the capacity of viewers to read photographs. Further, Bolter and Grusin argue, digitising the light that comes through the lens of a digital camera is no more or less artificial then the chemical process of traditional photography. A photograph's tonal values may be altered by the algorithms contained within a piece of computer software or by the length of time it is immersed in chemicals. It is a cultural judgement to say that one of the images is more true than the other. In short, 'whether the image is mechanically or digitally produced is irrelevant' (Kember 1998: 11).

It is also the case that many photographs do not operate, or are not valued, as indexes (even if they are). It is quite possible to 'read' photographs as other than evidence of concrete things that existed in a specific time and place. As Manovich observes, 'A photograph as used in an advertising design . . . does not say . . . this hat was in a room on May 12'. Rather it simply represents 'a hat' or 'a beach' or 'a television set' without any reference to time and location (Manovich 2003: 245). Thought about this way the difference between certain kinds of photographs and paintings, let alone digital images, no longer holds.

Does digital photography exist?

Another kind of criticism of earlier ideas about the revolutionary impact of digital imaging upon photography has emerged. It again qualifies the degree of difference between them, and it flows from a continuing suspicion of arguments that are based upon abstract principles and technical differences. In the mid-1990s, Manovich and others (see Robins 1995, Lister 1995b, Kember 1998), pointed out the flaw of restricting the discussion of digital technology's effect upon photography to its technical means alone. They objected, in particular, to the habit of inferring cultural consequences directly from technological differences. In 'The Paradoxes of Digital Photography' Manovich pointed out that two key points of difference between photography and digital imaging, which were made much of by Mitchell (1992: 4–6), while correct in technical principle, have no cultural significance (Manovich 2003: 242). These differences were:

(i)   that there is no hierarchy between a digital original and its copy;
(ii) that the information encoded in a photograph is indefinite and continuous while in a digital image it is precise and definite. Enlarging a photograph reveals more information (if at the loss of resolution) while enlarging a digital image reveals none.

Neither, observes Manovich, matter in practice. In the first case, due to the file compression used in storing and sending digital images (a necessary and normal practice in digital production now central to the economy of new media), loss of data and degradation of the image routinely occur as files are copied and circulated. Practically, it makes no sense to say that digital technology makes the 'flawless replication of data' (ibid: 243) possible and that a digital image has no original or copies. In the second case, the high resolution capable by modern scanners means that the amount of information or detail contained in a digital image records, 'much finer detail than was ever possible with traditional photography' (ibid: 243). Effectively, it surpasses human interest in that detail or our cultural need for it. This is a good case of abstract theory being correct in its own terms while shedding little light on practice. Mitchell's 'differences' may be correct in principle but, 'if we consider concrete digital technologies and their uses, the difference disappears. Digital photography simply doesn't exist' (Manovich 2003: 242).

Photo-realism versus post-human vision

So far, in 'taking stock' of more recent thinking on the photodigital, we have noted a marked tendency to refute, or at least minimise the earlier claims for a radical difference. Finally, we turn to note another line of thought which, arguably, paints a more revolutionary picture than any of the thinking we have met so far in this chapter.

The computer is a kind of universal machine; it can assume the function of many other machines, including the camera, a machine that takes photographs. This capacity may be distributed across the silicon chips that compute the operations of a digital camera, which itself is connected as a 'peripheral' to the processing power in a PC, and to others such as scanners, printers and data-projectors. There may then be an optical lens trained upon the world of physical things but it is deeply enmeshed in digital technology. In the case of the simulation of photographic images by 3-D computer graphics software this optical relationship to 'things' in the world is replaced by knowledge of their physics and of photography (its optics) stored in the computer and its software. The computer knows what something in the physical world would look like if it were photographed. This last point alerts us to the fact that whatever else computer generated 'photographs' represent they also always represent or refer to the look of photographs (Batchen 2001: 140). Digital images become signs for photographs, which, as we discussed above, are themselves signs of the 'real'.

A good example of this is now found in the employment of computer graphics in contemporary cinema. 3-D computer graphics as it is used in contemporary cinema has realist goals. In many cases, the aim is to make a fantastic proposition appear realistic. The standard of realism it seeks is 'photorealism' – the look of something when photographed. As Allen (1998: 127) observes:

> In cases where a real-life equivalent is clearly impossible, such as the morphing effects in. *Terminator 2*, the pictorial quality of the effect must be sophisticated and 'photo-realistic' enough to persuade the audience that if, for example, a tiled floor transformed into a human figure in real life, it would look exactly like its screen depiction does.

To achieve the seamless integration of computer simulated scenes with cinematography of real scenes, the clinical images produced by the computer are deliberately degraded and rendered 'photographic' by closely guarded algorithms which are the industry's stock in trade (Manovich 2003: 247). These add 'noise' to the pristine computer image in the form of distinctive photographic qualities: areas of soft focus, depth of field, lens flare and halation, added to ensure the 'reality' of the image. If computer graphics succeeds in creating realist illusion it does so by borrowing 150 years of photographic history in which time we have come to accept the images of photography and film as images of the real (ibid: 246). In this aspiration of computer graphics to be photo-realistic the photographic image is newly valued as the very sign of reality at the same time as it is, in part, displaced in the technical production of the movie (ibid: 246–8).

But what of the computer simulated images themselves? If not adjusted to match the look of photographs, they are photo-unrealistic in their hyperreality, and free from the limitations of human and camera vision. '(W)hose vision is this?' asks Manovich (2003: 248). His answer is that they are representations of a cyborg vision; the vision of a hybrid human-machine. Indeed, it is argued that Manovich's 'cyborg body to come' is with us already, as Batchen recognises, when he points to digitisation, prosthetic and cosmetic surgery, cloning, genetic engineering, artificial intelligence and virtual reality as signs that the old category of 'the human' may no longer be with us in any settled way.

As such, they are representations of a future vision, when human sight will be augmented by computer graphics. Even the gaps and imperfections of computer images are not 'unreal' because they are the images of another kind of body than the organic human one – they are of a cyborg body yet to come. In the 1930s Walter Benjamin claimed that 'evidently a different nature opens itself to the (photographic) camera than opens to the naked eye' (Benjamin 1970a: 238). Now we may need to entertain that computer simulated images are not less or more real than those of photography, they are a representation of a different reality or, in Benjamin's terms, 'nature'.[3]

In considering the idea that different realities open themselves up to the human eye, the camera, and now the computer, we are yet again returned to the Cartesian or humanist scopic regime we discussed earlier in this chapter. We must now entertain the idea that we live amidst large shifts in how we understand the world and our place within it. Ones in which the very security of our traditional distinctions between nature and culture and human and technological are dissolving.

Notes

1   The concept of a 'scopic regime' is Martin Jay's. See Jay, M. (1992) 'Scopic Regimes of Modernity' in Lark, S. and Friedman, J. (eds) *Modernity and Identity*, Oxford: Blackwell.
2   This is the aspect of photography famously explored by Barthes in *Camera Lucida* – where he runs counter to his own influential, intellectual semiotic analysis of photography to ask, 'What does my body know about photography?'
3   See also: Hayles, N. Katherine (1999) *How We Became Posthuman: Virtual Bodies in Cybernetics, Literature, and Informatics*, Chicago and London: University of Chicago Press, and Lury C. (1998) *Prosthetic Culture: Photography, Memory and Identity*, London and New York: Routledge.

Chapter 30

DAVID SUDNOW

'EYEBALL' FROM *PILGRIM IN THE MICROWORLD: EYE, MIND AND THE ESSENCE OF VIDEO SKILL*

WRITTEN IN THE EARLY 1980S, this is an account by an American ethnomethodologist and piano teacher of his obsession with early videogames such as *Breakout* and *Missile Defence*. David Sudnow records the ways in which he learnt how the games work, and how his eyes, brain and fingers were trained by these new media technologies in a remarkable kind of autoethnography. He captures the moment at which the new (the new machines and software, and the new skills and reflexes needed to play them) become internalised and habitual. This in itself is a rich resource for the study of digital culture: paying attention to the cusp between the novelty and excitement of a new medium, and the taken-for-granted, mundane nature of familiarity once the medium has engineered its place in everyday life.

Though the games may seem primitive in comparison to contemporary 3D, photorealistic and networked games (**Taylor**, **Kember**, **Kennedy**), the cybernetic feedback loops between eyes, fingers, brain, controller, screen and software that Sudnow is caught up in here remain broadly the same. And this process of learning the system, of playful software training fingers and attention, and the development of technicity (**Kennedy**) has changed little.

[T]he salesman said this Breakout thing was a real good game, the TV was sitting in the backseat of the car, and rather than drive around all day looking for missiles, I figured I'd take this one home for starters. How was I to know it would become "my game," that I'd get so obsessed with it as to live out the next three months of my life almost exclusively within this nineteen-inch micro-world, heaven help me.

My next door neighbor must have seen me coming in and out, first carrying the TV up the stairs, then the box marked Atari, for no sooner was the configuration set up and ready to go than he appeared. And inside of twenty minutes versus this young San Francisco lawyer I'm in a cold sweat. Here's a snapshot of the pristine landscape:

At bottom screen there's a paddle, controlled by a steering wheel knob that comes with the unit along with the joystick you get for other games. You push a button to serve yourself a ball, which descends from just beneath the barricade strip across the screen. Then you hit it back, and every time you do an unmarked half-inch brick segment gets knocked out of the wall. Of course size is relative, the more competent you become the more these lights take on a sort of environmental density and you're pulled by the fingertips onto a full-scale playing field whose dimensions aren't found on rulers.

The immediate object is to chip through to the open space on the other side, and once you've made this Breakout the ball rebounds like crazy between the far wall and the band, moving from one side to the other and then back again to knock out bricks from above unless none obstructs its path and it therefore returns down to you:

The overall goal, fat chance, is to eliminate the entire barricade until paddle and ball are alone in empty court, victors.

The wall is composed of six differently colored strata, and if and when a ball first gets through to hit the fourth one from the bottom, it takes off fast in a sudden break slam shot and then holds at this new speed till you miss and have to serve again. You get five balls per game, can set the console to play solo or in turns with an opponent, and can of course hit the reset switch at any time to reconstitute the whole barricade and instantly get a fresh five serves.

Within about twenty minutes my neighbor had cut through the wall a few times while I couldn't even get close, and when he insisted he'd only played the game once before for an hour, my evening was decided. Some piano player. As if last night's effort to save the world wasn't bad enough, I must have now gone on for four hours by myself after I finally got him to leave. And by the time I gave up for the night, I'd broken out one lousy time. I relentlessly served that damn speck of light without intermission, couldn't pull myself away from the thing. Two hundred bucks after all.

I tried rationalizing my initial anxiety with the conviction the guy was lying. But then again, he didn't smoke, was ten years younger, who knows? Maybe some basic nervous system capacities were involved, rhythmic acuities different from what you need for jazz, say. Maybe microworld mastery varied by age, metabolic or alpha wave rates, astrological signs for all I knew. And how about cultural factors? I didn't see a TV before the age of ten, probably haven't logged a thousand hours in thirty years. Maybe he'd grown up with several hours of television a day. For all I knew extensive tube time trained micromuscles for neuroathletic competition and I was thus irrevocably consigned to the video boondocks.

At least the rudiments of slower play were easy enough for me. One of the guys at the party had created a big laugh, throwing himself back and forth while swinging his entire upper torso and arms and almost falling off the chair to hit the Breakout ball. He took the ribbing with good humor, exaggerating his incompetence for the sake of the party, but actually seemed unable to effect that transformation of sense needed to engage himself with big looking movements through little feeling ones. He couldn't project a comfortable scale of being into the confining detachment of the interface, couldn't trust the efficiency of a mere knob, but instead handled the encounter like those proverbial preliterate aborigines who respond to a photograph by looking around at its reverse side. The guy acted at the controls as if there were no video fence in the way. It probably took him a long time to get used to automatic transmissions and electric typewriters, not because the skills are so different from a technical standpoint, but because he refused to adopt the postural respect solicited by new embodied equipment The guy just wasn't a button pusher.

I didn't have his sort of quaint confusion, but automatically made the necessary shift in stance to control the paddle while sitting still in the right terminal position. And it only took a little time to transcend the physical awkwardness of the knob so I could get the racket more or less where I wanted, more or less when I wanted, without too often over- or undershooting the ball.

Line up your extended finger with the lower left corner of the TV screen a comfortable six feet away. Now track back and forth several times in line with the bottom border and project a movement of that breadth onto an imagined inch and a half diameter spool in your hands. That's how knob and paddle are geared, a natural correspondence of scale between the body's motions, the equipment, and the environs preserved in the interface. There's that world space over there, this, one over here, and we traverse the wired gap with motions that make us nonetheless feel in a balanced extending touch with things.

They had it set just right. Held by fingertips and rotated through a third of its revolution, the little paddle steering wheel afforded rapid enough horizontal movement anywhere along the backcourt to handle the pace of action without wrist or forearm aid:

Not like a very fine tuning knob to change hi-fi stations, for with such a gearing you've got to spin the dial to traverse full field, letting go with your fingers and losing all accuracy. Very fine tuning knobs are meant for slow motions, and while you can twirl these dials to reach a rough vicinity quickly, to hit Breakout balls a vicinity isn't enough. On the other hand, were the gearing too tight, the slightest motion would send the paddle right across screen. Ideally geared for travel through the terrains and tempos of a microworld, the dial had enough resistance so an accidental touch didn't send the paddle too far, but not so much that you had to exert yourself to move through the court.

I served myself a ball. It came down. I went for it and missed. I centered the fingers in relation to the knob's range so I could swing back and forth across the field with hardly any elbow play at all. I rotated some partial practice strokes, trying out each side to test the expanse and timing of the whereabouts, appraising the extent of pressure needed to move various distances at various rates.

I served again. The ball's coming down over there and my paddle's here. How fast to go? A smooth gesture knows from the outset when it'll get where it's headed, as a little pulse is established that lays out the upcoming arrival time, a compressed "ready, set, go" built into the start of the movement. The gesture then feels when to speed up and slow down to attain the target. I swing the bat back and forth to acquire its weight, establish a usable rhythm then held in reserve as I await the ball, preparing for a well-timed movement anywhere within the arc of the swing.

Within fifteen minutes I'm no longer conscious of the knob's gearing and I'm not jerking around too much. So far so good. Slow down, get rid of the neighbor, get a little rhythm going, and in no time at all you've got a Workable eye-hand partnership. The calibrating movement quickly passes beneath awareness, and in the slow phase the game is a breeze, doesn't even touch the fingering you need for "the eentsy, weentsy spider went up the water spout. . . ." Here I was lobbing away with a gentle rhythm, soon only now and then missing a shot through what seemed a brief lapse in attention rather than a defect in skill.

Then came the breakaway slam when the ball reaches the fourth layer, and the eye-hand partnership instantly dissolved. *Wooosh*, there it goes right past, coming from nowhere, a streak of light impossible to intercept. They've got to be kidding. Out of the playpen onto the Softball field. I missed every one, each time left standing with bat in hand swatting video air. The lawyer had to have been lying, had to have put in more hours than he said.

I tabled my anxiety and simply figured more delicate paddle handling skills were called for. Besides, just as the panning shot made Missile Command fun, I began getting off on the action, building control and precision in these gentle little calibrations. With slow shots my gaze could lift a bit off from the finer details of the ball's path to roam the court analytically, to glance at my paddle, then here the ball would hit the barricade, and then ahead to predict where it'd hit the side so I could position myself in advance. And I'd get there, sometimes in sync with the ball and sometimes ahead of it, just waiting. My glance took snapshots of the overall neighborhood, there was enough give in the tempo to allow for some instant geometry during play, enough casualness to the pace that looking could disengage from tracking to analyze the opponent's ways and fit the rhythm of its queries into the timing of the shots. Scrutinizing the neighborhood to learn my way around, I could still bring the paddle where needed on time.

The sounds helped. Every time you hit the ball there's a little bleep, then a differently pitched tone if you hit a side wall, and still another one for each different bandful of bricks. These recurrent bleeps helped you gear into the overall rate of action. The sights helped. The more or less steady passage of the ball painted the action's tempo in broad strokes, so when the eyes loosened their hold on it to take in a wider or different territory, that gently tracing light kept the fingers continuously alive to the whereabouts and pace of things.

At first it felt like my eyes told my fingers where to go. But in time I knew the smooth rotating hand motions were assisting the look in turn, eyes and fingers in a two-way partnership. Walking a rainy street, you identify the dimensions of a puddle in relation to the size and rate of your gait, so the stride itself patterns the style of your looking, how you scan the field's depth of focus and extent of coverage, what you see. So too with sight reading music at the piano for instance, where you never look ahead of what you can grasp and your hands' own sense of their location therefore instructs the gaze where to regard the score. So too again with typing from a text, where if your eyes move in front of where your fingers are, you'll likely make an error, and thus hands and gaze maintain a delicate rhythmic alignment. And so too here, you'd have to sustain a pulse to organize the simultaneous work of visually and tactilely grasping the ball, your hands helping your look help your hands make the shot.

I played around with slow balls, getting the first chance I'd had in years to handle Ping-Pong-type action, listening to the bleeps and feeling my way round the court. I hit a shot over to the left. Can I place the next one there as well? Of course the lights didn't obey the laws of physics governing solid objects, like billiard balls, say. But Atari had rather decently simulated a sense of solidity. The light came from a certain angle toward the side wall, and then followed out the triangulation by going in the direction you'd predict for a real ball. What about the paddle? Hit on an off-centered portion of a tennis racket or hand, a ball will deflect on a different path and you can thereby place shots. Sure enough they'd programmed the trajectories and different parts of the paddle surface to match, so the light-ball behaved rather like a tangible object, refracting and deflecting so it seemed you could at least somewhat control the ball's direction.

I watched the paddle and ball at the precise point of their contact, refining the control I could exercise over placement. Could I hit it on the left third of the paddle? How about the left fourth? Could I hit balls with the paddle's side rather than its upper surface, maybe useless in actual play but fun, and perhaps good for improving touch. I tried knocking out all the bricks of the lower band before the ball broke through to the next layer, eating corn on the cob. Virtually impossible. I tried putting more English into the shot, coming at the ball from the side and swooshing the paddle across quickly beneath it at the last moment, trying a spin. Did Atari accommodate that? I thought so, but wasn't sure.

It was here I discovered an ethically troublesome defect in the game. I'd hit a brick and the ball would come down. Taking care to line up the paddle, I knocked out an adjacent one, or even knocked out one above it, entering the open slot made by the preceding shot:

Again I aimed. The lights faked enough solid physics and the placement was tight. With still more barricade cut from the same narrow region, the ball once again dropped almost straight down as you'd expect. So I hit it square on again to further eat away that vicinity.

Poof. It veered radically to the side, a full sixty degrees off course. I went through the same sequence enough times to make sure it wasn't my mistake. And it wasn't. They'd messed with the rebounds, by God, preventing you from breaking through too fast. A few shots straight up and down to the same vicinity, and then Atari took the mathematically cheap way out. The arbitrary and sharply pitched deflection they used to get out of trouble sent the ball into a low horizontal pattern for several volleys, and I couldn't redress these returns to pursue a vertical attack, had to wade through a long drawn-out exchange until the trajectory gradually became more upright.

Three explosions on screen at Missile Command is one thing. That becomes an acceptable rule of play. But an electronic tactic to forestall your progress is another. "All right, veer off to the side. I'll wait it out. Mess with my carefully aimed shot. But if you want forgiveness for being a computer, don't put rocks in the snowballs."

I stored the disturbance like you register a lie on the first date and puzzled for a moment over the game's moral integrity. If the programmer could patch up an organizational weakness with a trivial trick like this, where else might there be monkey business? If it was their way to let you feel competent, giving you three easy placements and then veering off as if you wouldn't notice it, they were stupid. Anybody would see what was up after a few times at the controls. The tactic didn't speak well for Breakout. What if she lies all the time?

By this point I was getting pooped and needed to go for the score, to break out at least once before calling it a night. If my neighbor could do it after an hour, certainly I could after three. The slam shot had been putting me out of commission every time. Mostly, by the time I knew it was coming, it was gone. You're going along at a comfortable pace, hit the fourth band, and then *whap*, the ball goes double time on you and you're wiped out.

Now I told myself, "Concentrate." I did a little seat squirm, as when entering a freeway on-ramp and you have to hit sixty in a real hurry, peeked up to the band to get the jump on when it was coming, stiffened up and sat on the edge of the chair, and handled one. I missed the follow-up but had returned my first slam. Actually, I got myself in its way.

In a half hour of just "concentrating" I'd refined the instruction. I discovered if I told myself to "glue my eye to the ball" I could start fielding first slams much better and get some of the follow-ups as well. For about twenty minutes I sat there mesmerized, tracking the ball like my life depended on it, my entire being invested in the hypnotic pursuit of that pea-sized light. Kneading my eyeballs into the guts of its movement like following a guy in a fast crowd where a momentary diversion would lose him, I soon got to hold on to a four- or five-round volley of fast ones. Knocking out that many more bricks a hole opened on the side of the barricade, and I watched the ball break out, ricochet like crazy between the back wall and the band, eat up six or seven more bricks, then fly down right past me. Had I not been taken in by the new quickened sights and sounds, I might have fielded it back up. My first Breakout. Thank God, I could go to bed.

PART FIVE

Network culture

JUST AS, IN PART FOUR, media and cultural studies' established methods and theories of analysing popular media *texts* were questioned, in this part we are broadly concerned with shifts in *communication*. Much has been made over the past two decades of the possibilities of the Internet for the democratisation of communication, as the one-to-many hierarchies of broadcasting and the limited one-to-one network of telephony are challenged by the bottom-up, self-organising networks and communities facilitated by email, bulletin boards, chat channels, online virtual worlds and Web 2.0 media.

We can identify two broad historical approaches to network culture that have influenced media and cultural studies. The first, from the late 1980s to the late 1990s, could be called 'cybercultural studies'. Profoundly influenced by Donna **Haraway**'s cyborg, and also, like Haraway, by cyberpunk science fiction films and novels, these books and articles saw in the Internet and Virtual Reality technology (and the two are often collapsed, as 'cyberspace') the realisation of the SF dream/nightmare of alternative, virtual, realities, disembodied spaces of pure data and consciousness. In their attention to actual emerging text-based Internet media such as bulletin boards and chat channels (most of this work was conducted before the graphic interface of the World Wide Web was prevalent), much was made of the possibilities for the emancipatory potential of communities in which gender, race, bodily ability and other physical and locational markers of identity were irrelevant. Utopian claims for new fluid and experimental selves were based on the material characteristics of pre-Web media: Internet users could write to each other, but could not *see* each other. Don **Slater**'s article in this part interrogates this discourse in an ethnography of an Internet Relay Chat community.

With the transformation of Internet media by both the graphical and multimedia Web and by the rapid shift of Internet use from early adopters to its current status as a near-universal media form in the developed world, the critical and analytical paradigm of cybercultural studies has also been transformed. With accessible software tools for web page construction people could easily design and publish their own home pages, complete with personal details and photographs. This trend has accelerated markedly in recent years with the advent of Web 2.0 applications, particularly blogs and social networking sites. Moreover the facility for adding comments to blogs and Facebook pages, opening chat, messaging, Twitter and Skype channels, uploading and sharing photographs, *and* the possibilities for doing all of this through one's mobile phone and not just at the PC means that the everyday is intensely and intimately mediated by networked communication.

So, the Internet now suffuses everyday life and communication in the developed world, bringing new socioeconomic structures and ways of working (**Terranova**, this part), new forms of art production and activism (**Lovink**, **Kidd**), and realising the corporate dataspheres and metaverses imagined by William Gibson and Neal Stephenson as the commercial virtual worlds of *Second Life* and Massively Multiplayer Online Games (**Taylor**). Whilst some commentators may mourn the 'loss' of the radical, non-commercial nature of the early Internet, others grasp the new political and creative possibilities of Web 2.0 and related network media and formations, including their convergence with mobile phones (see **Lovink** in this part and Part Four).

Chapter 31

DON SLATER

TRADING SEXPICS ON IRC
Embodiment and authenticity on the Internet

T HOUGH THE INTERNET medium and practices of exchange he is studying (text-based Internet Relay Chat and the swapping of digital pornographic images) have been largely superseded by social networking sites and the thorough commercialisation of networked pornography, Don Slater's virtual ethnography offers a critical take on online relationships that offers much for the analysis of contemporary Internet culture.

Commentary on the pre-Web Internet, and the Web itself in the mid-1990s, was often characterised by a set of assumptions about the radical difference of virtual communities and relationships from offline or actual social relationships. Because Internet users knew each other only by nicknames and did not necessarily know anything about each other's age, gender, race or location, it was argued, a new meritocratic society was emerging. Free from the embodied prejudices and assumptions of the offline world, users could construct or play with their own identities, developing open and honest networked relationships.

Slater's research inverts these assumptions. Engaging with IRC sexpic trading over the course of a year, he studied the 'problematized relation between body and identity' not as a set of theoretical assumptions but as it was lived, negotiated, regulated and understood in everyday, virtual-social practices. A key term was 'authenticity'. If embodied and located identities and social positions lose their relevance then we might assume that questions of who people 'really are' become less urgent. However, Slater concluded that the IRC culture he participated in was characterised by two main attitudes. The first was a cynicism about the online world, a general assumption that virtual events and relationships were not to be trusted or believed. The second, which seems at first glance to contradict the first, is a desire to establish more authentic and meaningful relationships in cyberspace. Slater sees these two attitudes as a dialectic not a contradiction: IRC users were wary of online deception and rejection, but wanted to develop meaningful connections. In direct contradiction of cyberculturalist assumptions about freefloating identities and sexualities, the establishment of closer relationships was usually predicated on the gradual sharing of embodied and located details: full name, address, phone numbers, gender and sexual orientation.

Slater's findings do not merely debunk cyberculturalist theories and replace them with assertions of the normalcy or conservatism of online communities. Rather, his sensitive observations (like those of **Taylor** later in this part) capture something of the richness and complexities of virtual and actual everyday life, the interweaving of the established and the emergent in digital culture. For more on online communities, see **Kennedy**, **Kember**, and **Katz**.

The body – or its absence – is central to contemporary notions of 'cyberspace', 'the Internet', 'virtuality': computer-mediated communications (CMCs) are defined around the absence of physical presence, the fact that we can be interactively present to each other as unanchored textual bodies without being proximate or visible as definite physical objects. The revolutionary claims for the kinds of identities available on-line flow from this feature: if identity is performed independently of fixed bodily attributes, then who you are or can be is not limited – or falsifiable – by features of your physical body but turns rather on your resourcefulness in using tools of representation. The body itself is released – through avatars or imagination – from its traditional shapes, colours, genders, boundaries: 'With no limit to the number of names that can be used, one individual can become a population explosion on the Net: many sexes, many species' (Plant, 1997: 46).

This focus on the separation of identity from fixed physical embodiment has tended to filter our understanding of CMCs through poststructuralist hopes and concepts: cyberspace has come to be widely understood as a practical deconstruction of essentialism. Out there, bodies and identities alike may lose their connection to terrestrial limits, extending through a new range of possibilities, and in the process may reflect back upon the supposed naturalness, givenness, reification or territorialization of real life bodies and identities. In cyberspace, social identity becomes increasingly (revealed as) performative to the extent that 'real' bodies are unable to act as anchor, essence, guarantor, container of a 'true' or 'real' self. To the extent that bodies become virtual, cyberspace constitutes a virtual critique of essentialism and a practical liberation from the shackles of authenticity. (A list of conventional reference points and discussions might include Bassett, 1997; Benedikt, 1991; Butler, 1990, 1993; Dery, 1994; Featherstone and Burrows, 1995; Haraway, 1990; Plant, 1995, 1996, 1997; Porter, 1997; Shields, 1996; Springer, 1996; Stone, 1996; Turkle, 1984, 1995.)

This article is based on a year-long ethnographic engagement with one CMC setting – sexpics trading on Internet Relay Chat (IRC). The aim is to approach the above claims from the perspective of participants' routine practices rather than from the theoretical concerns and hopes projected on to them: how did participants *in practice* engage with virtual bodies and identities? The aim is not to criticize or refute contemporary critiques of essentialism or authenticity but simply to avoid assuming that participants share them. The strength of ethnographic engagement is a close focus on how participants dealt with, regulated, inhabited, understood a social setting in which the problematized relation between body and identity was the central feature of everyday life; we are not expecting them to react, or want to react, to virtual embodiment as if they were poststructuralists.

More specifically, if this virtual setting constituted a practical critique of essential bodies and identities we would expect – or hope for – at least two central features to emerge: first, we would expect the construction of new kinds of bodies, identities and connections between them, a liberation, an experimentalism or at least a diminished conventionality; second, we would expect that the notion of authenticity – a desire to determine which bodies and identities were *real* or true – would become irrelevant or marginal; that participants would be less concerned to anchor performed identities in an underlying truth or reality.

In fact, the ethnography indicates that the deconstruction of body and identity on-line is experienced by participants as a set of practical and existential *problems* that have to be dealt with and not as a field of deconstructive or Utopian possibilities; and that in everyday on-line life considerable energy may be directed into the (admittedly hopeless) project of reconnecting and re-fixing bodies and identities. First, despite inhabiting a space of apparently limitless transgression, participants structured their transgressions in fairly conventional ways (in particular, according to norms of mainstream pornography and male heterosexuality). Second, the impossibility of establishing the other's real identity did not make the notion of authenticity redundant. Rather, participants operated within a dialectic of cynicism and belief: they experienced their on-line world with a mixture of cynical detachment on the one hand (a refusal to believe anything on-line and therefore a refusal to treat events or relationships there as serious), and on the other hand a desire to trust and invest in on-line relationships which depended on pursuing strategies of authentication (and constant concern about being deceived, ripped off and otherwise hurt by others' inauthenticity). Significantly, these strategies of authentication – necessary in order to trust in a relationship, in order to credit a relationship with any ethical weight – were attempts to fix the other in a body or body-like presence, one which persists over time and is locatable in space.

Sexpics trading on IRC

Internet Relay Chat (IRC) is a medium for 'chatting' in real time to other people who are connected to an IRC network. People first connect to the Internet, as they would for email or world wide web. Instead of loading an email program or browser, they then connect to an IRC network by loading 'client' software onto their local computers [. . .]. Users may choose amongst an ever-growing number of IRC networks. The network used for this ethnography usually has around 20,000–30,000 clients simultaneously connected at peak time.

Participants can find and talk to each other in two basic ways. First, they can talk directly and privately with one other person. They make a connection which opens a window on each participant's screen; if one person types a line of text, it will appear on both screens. Conversation takes the form of a flow of text lines. These lines can be of three different sorts which cover the basics of social interaction: simple speech; actions (lines, preceded by asterisks, which describe or performatively carry out an action); and events ('real' actions performed with the basic command set of IRC: bans, invites, entering or leaving channels or networks). Second, these one-to-one chats – the private sphere of IRC – generally cluster around channels, the public spheres in which any number of participants may communicate communally. A channel window will have a section listing the nicks (nicknames) of all participants, a section for the communal chat and a section in which to type in one's own messages. Channels have names and topics which reflect their content. During the period of fieldwork, both the largest channels and the largest number of channels tended to be sex related, though these could be divided into those more oriented to trading sexpics and those more oriented to meeting others for cybersex or flirting or partying. Finally, there is no technical limit to the number of windows – chats and channels – participants can have open at any one time.

If you can transmit lines of text over IRC, you can transmit anything that is digitized, thus any kind of representation: photos, drawings, video clips, sound files, streamed sound or video, software program files. Hence the sexpics trade: 'sexpics' usually refers to any kind of sexually explicit material circulated within this scene. People meet up or advertise their wares in and around designated channels, chatting either publicly in the channel or privately. Alongside the chat, they can send files to each other (technically, this is done by a facility called DCC, direct computer to computer communication). They can also use a facility called 'fserve' (file server): someone offering an fserve allows others (usually by way of a 'trigger' word that can be typed in a channel window) to access and peruse directly the hard disk of their local computer, looking through subdirectories and lists of files, and then to select and download the files they want, usually up to a limit (a specified number of kilobytes). As discussed below, people can also set ratios (you can download x bytes for every y bytes you upload): these are like exchange rates or prices.

Fieldwork took the form of a self-consciously conventional ethnography, over approximately 18 months (July 1996 to December 1997), focused on one IRC network and revolving around a limited number of sex-related channels. The ethnography was also contextualized by following IRC links into neighbouring CMC media such as newsgroups and web-sites. Engagement with the setting took the form of participant observation in public channels and private conversations, formal and informal interviews with participants (either by way of on-line chat, telephone or email), analysis of logs of conversations sent me by informants, collection and analysis of directory structures and images. Long-term engagement with both the setting and particular informants was crucial to the research.

Disembodiment on IRC

The strength of ethnography – notably lacking from much CMC literature – is an attention to the specificity of settings that allows the researcher to disaggregate global concepts such as – in this study – cyberspace, Internet, pornography. We see rather an extraordinarily diverse and fluid world of practices, constituencies, media, technologies which can only be recovered through learning the local culture in detail. Part of understanding the specificity of 'sexpics trading on IRC' is to understand what 'virtuality' and '(dis)embodiment' mean in this particular context: both are differently constructed and understood on IRC than in other Internet settings; we might therefore expect issues of authenticity and identity to work differently here than in even ostensibly similar CMC (or indeed off-line) settings. We can summarize IRC 'disembodiment' in terms of three aspects:

First, participants have a purely textual presence for each other. In the main, they exist in and between the typed lines of text scrolling sequentially down their screens, through which speech, actions and events are accomplished. Bodies and their attributes (gender, ethnicity, age, beauty) are therefore not perceptible, and there is certainly a feeling that one can claim to be whatever one wants and that others' identity claims are not falsifiable. Participants are almost continuously aware that they are witnessing textual performances and frequently topicalize this feature, while at the same time they can find themselves deeply immersed in those performances. It is like watching realist TV or film: the experience is constituted around different levels of suspension of disbelief. Participants are vividly aware of the complexity and skill involved in textual performances, a feature which sets limits on their disbelief in others' presences (e.g. it is deemed hard to maintain a different gender identity from your own, at least over time).

These issues of textual presence, though partly shared with some other CMC and indeed non-CMC settings, are intensified by specific features of synchronous chat systems like IRC: these are real time, live encounters with other people who must actually *be there now* in order for anything to be happening, yet who are *not here* in the flesh. Ironically, although participants may know nothing or be able to authenticate nothing about the other's body, the fact that on-line identities on IRC depend *entirely* on physical presence in the present tense means that the presence and reality of the other's real, off-line body is always in the participant's mind: are they still there? Will they be there tomorrow? Who was here just now? This is also central to the eroticization of these relationships: there is a hyper-awareness that nothing could be happening here on-line unless a real body out there (whoever they 'really' are) was typing these lines to me; there must really be a body out there, but always titillatingly just out of reach.

Second, the bodies of IRC participants are not only invisible but untraceable and anonymous: it is almost impossible to track on-line presences to off-line bodies or geographical locations. Not even an email address is available unless offered. The issue is not simply that one cannot find a 'real body' in which to anchor an identity; the issue is also that one cannot hold an identity accountable for its actions because one cannot trace it to a unique and locatable *address*. Who would place trust in a spectre that can evaporate when things get serious? As we shall see, as soon as serious emotional or practical issues arise in an IRC relationship, participants have either to attach the other's identity to a unique body with a spatial address or else (lacking that) to trust in its body-like persistence over time (that the other has proved reliable in being *here* even if we could not locate it out *there* in real life).

The ontological detachment of performed identity from unique and locatable body is compounded by the fact that IRC identities are also not 'owned' by participants. People are identified by their 'nicks' (nicknames) and these can be changed at any moment by a simple command. Moreover, if someone is already on-line with 'my' nick, I simply have to choose a new one. Conversely, if someone presents themselves to me with a familiar nick, it may not be the same person I was talking to last time. Recognizing someone as the same as or different over time and tracking down unique others (in order to make them ethically responsible for emotional commitments or trading obligations) is a central practical issue which obsesses participants and centres on the obvious matter of tracing multiple presences to unique identities and bodily locations, a concern which may require considerable technical expertise.

Third, the most unique and extreme aspect of IRC disembodiment is its almost completely 'dynamic' or 'evanescent' character. 'Dynamic' means that nothing exists on IRC independently of someone's presence on-line: for example, I can call a channel into being by simply typing a command: /j#Slater ('join channel Slater'). I am then in #Slater and can invite others into it. However when the last person leaves #Slater that channel vanishes without a trace – it leaves no record, no sign of its existence. There is no way of leaving things behind in it and when I join a channel that has been ongoing before me, I merely see a blank screen: there is no record of the conversation that took place before I entered it. Similarly, my own personal on-line identity depends entirely on my on-line presence: I can leave behind no information about myself, have no ownership over my name ('nick'), and have to reconstitute my self on-line in a permanent present tense.

IRC therefore has no material culture, no objects or structures, which would allow its world and identities to be fleshed out and built up over time, to have a rich past and future. It lacks those processes of objectification through which cultural transmission is accomplished. While this might make for even greater freedom to experiment with identity and to marginalize the notion that any identity could be authentic, it actually militates against projects of either identity or community: much work has to be done to stabilize both identities and settings into ongoing social orders. Indeed some participants do devote considerable labour and expertise to maintaining IRC social structures (ongoing trading relationships, channels, leadership structures), battling to solidify their evanescence. On IRC, identity and 'community' are generally pragmatic matters rather than aims for participants; they are *problems* because they are necessary but unavailable, fragile or costly conditions of getting on with the business at hand. The situation is the reverse of Maffesoli's (1996) world in which specific interests are merely the occasion for achieving a generic sense of communality.

We can see some of the importance (and uniqueness) of IRC's lack of material culture, and its own specific brand of disembodiment, by comparing it with ostensibly similar CMC settings. The dynamism of IRC sharply distinguishes it from the CMC settings on which much of the current literature on virtuality and identity is based: MUDs and avatar-based virtual environments. The most grounded and sensitive of this literature (Bassett, 1997; Dibbell, 1994; Turkle, 1995) stresses participants' extraordinary investment and identification with highly developed on-line personae developed over time. These virtual personae are possible on MUDs not only because of the freedom from real-world bodies and selves (a feature shared with IRC) but also because MUDs (unlike IRC) allow for the construction and persistence over time of the kind of material culture which sustains identities and identity projects: one can build up descriptions of one's environment and person, and leave them behind. The ability to objectify identity and environment in a persistent material culture on MUDs allows both identification with a developing character but also a distancing: because personae are objectified, the conventionality and performativity of identity can be held up to a reflexive self-consciousness (see especially Bassett, 1997). All of this is not to say that individuals do not explore and invest in identities on IRC, but that they surely do so under quite different conditions. Participants may certainly value identities they have developed over time but they are likely to define those identities in terms of friendship and trading networks, social statuses in particular channels (e.g. as an op) and 'style'. They are less likely to see their on-line presence as a fictive or objectified character, more likely to talk about their way of being on-line simply as a mode of operating in a particular social space.

The ability to objectify identities and environments is not an independent technological variable; MUD software famously arose out of a fantasy game-playing culture which – on-line or off – involves huge personal investment in avatars and intersubjectively sustained fictional settings. Although the software structures underlying and organizing IRC are constantly being revised and rewritten, they are not being developed in the direction of MUDs. IRC participants presumably have other concerns, aims, styles: IRC participants tend to focus technically on defending (or attacking) stable social structures so that people can get on with the business at hand.

The specificity of IRC disembodiment – and its difference from other on-line settings – is important in developing a sound ethnographic sense of the setting. However, the aim in this article is definitely not to present IRC (or 'the Net', or 'cybersex') as new, unique, unprecedented or revolutionary. It is actually crucial to appreciate the ways in which it is similar to, and indeed connected to, other and older experiences of disembodied communications. For example, long-term sexpics relationships may be very like correspondence by letter or 'pen pal' relationships, in which the presence of the other is constructed out of both their textual performances and the hopes and fantasies projected into the silent spaces between their performances; short-term IRC encounters are very close to telephone chat-lines and phone-sex or citizens' band radio; possibly the closest to the experiential, sensory quality of IRC is broadcast radio. Indeed, it is no coincidence that all these other media have been associated with sexual commerce and have raised much the same ethical issues, often to the point of moral panic, as do Internet sex and pornography. For example, pen pal correspondence or telephone chat lines, like IRC, all allow for relationships and encounters which pleasurably release a complete freedom of fantasy with an interactive other, fantasy pleasures which can be treated as real. However, these engagements are considered to be extremely dangerous when participants believe them to be *really* real, rather than merely pleasurably realistic: because the identities involved are 'disembodied' – are not anchored in physically present, spatially locatable and temporally persistent bodies – they are also deemed not to be ethically (or legally) accountable for their actions and therefore as likely as not to be lying and untrustworthy.

Not only does IRC disembodiment and virtuality bear structural similarities to other communications settings, but it also has direct continuities and connections with them. For example, IRC relationships may well develop from on-line chats through letter-like correspondence (email, snail mail or both), phone conversations (either Internet or standard phone systems) or paging systems like ICQ, each of which inflects disembodiment somewhat differently. Conversely, participants may move their relationships or activities from IRC to other on-line settings not because these settings share IRC's virtuality or disembodiment, but exactly the opposite: Usenet newsgroups or web sites are far more stable and *embodied* than IRC at least in the sense of providing settings that persist dependably over time and may be more connected to off-line addresses.

Disembodiment and sexuality

IRC, then, represents an extreme point in disembodiment or virtual embodiment: purely textual, cut off from locatable real-life bodies, and lacking temporally persistent objectifications: any body, any self could be projected at any time. Indeed, the first impression of the IRC sexpics scene is generally of libertarian licence: the scene is a place of exuberant transgression in which anything is allowed and every desire that is conceivable is indulged through fantasy, conversation, representation. Above all, any and every transgression can be indulged *with others*, within a sociable and public space. In fact, most informants were clear that one of the great pleasures and attractions of the IRC sexpics scene was not so much the direct indulgence of their own desires as a fascination with the diversity of human sexuality, all of which was there to see on IRC:

> <Lash> But seriously. What do you like about trading, collecting pix [. . .]
> <Serrina> well I like to look at them, trading them u get to find out what people
>   prefer sexually, kind of like a sexual education:))

However, despite the excitement of being able to express and share transgressive desires, there is nonetheless a clear structure of desire and transgression, much of which is conventional or hyperconventional. This is not to dismiss the liberation or simple relief expressed by so many informants who said they felt able on IRC to explore desires or to escape an everyday world they considered boring or restrictive. The point is simply that the scene did not seem to produce new sexual configurations: rather, the IRC sexpics trading scene is strikingly organized and policed according to the conventions of off-line mainstream (heterosexual) pornography. We can sum this up in terms of four main features.

First, the imagery that is circulated on IRC is either scanned in from standard publications or videos, or shot by 'amateurs' according to familiar genres and conventions. I have recorded no images circulated on IRC which significantly transgress, let alone explore, those conventions. This is extraordinary given the ease of digital image manipulation which most participants routinely use to change file sizes, colour balances, contrast and so on: I have not seen anyone use these technological skills to modify represented bodies except to montage celebrity faces onto naked bodies or, occasionally, to enlarge breasts or penises. This is also confirmed by analysis of the directory structures of dozens of fserves: the directory and file names give a clear picture of the categorizations that collectors and traders use, of the sexual cosmology of the scene, as it were. These routinely organize body imagery into a conventional repertoire of sex acts (couples in action, group sex, lesbian, oral, cum shots, anal); into conventional body types (blondes, brunettes, redheads); into degrees of 'hardness' (celebrities, poses, lingerie, hard, weird, extreme); into conventional fetishes and kinks (bondage, voyeur/exhibition, mature, latex, etc.). That is to say, the images traded and their categorical organization is indistinguishable from the organization of magazines or video titles on the shelves of newsagents or sex-shops.

Second, self-representation notoriously runs according to gendered conventions (cf. Bassett, 1997): IRC appears to be populated with young blonde bombshells and well-hung dudes, both with inexhaustible drives and unfaltering performance; people routinely send others pictures, supposedly of themselves ('personals'), that conform to their ideal self-image (and spend much time wondering whether the picture they just received is 'real' – really a picture of the sender). In fact, this generalization has to be qualified in terms of participants' aims, kinds of encounter and time-horizon of their relationship: conformity to narrow convention is more likely, and possible, in the context of one-off trading or cybersex than where longer-term and more emotional contact is expected or desired. Nonetheless, it is more or less assumed that even then people are likely to leave out or falsify those bodily features they are most sensitive about in relation to conventions of desirability: age, weight, height, figure, etc. Body representation on IRC is about grounding ideal identities, not about undercutting gender conventions.

Third, although IRC sexpics trading scenes exhibit an extraordinary profusion of represented and virtually enacted sexual desires there are some well-policed deep structures that contain them and set limits. The most important of these involved norms of heterosexuality. On IRC, the gay male scene is completely separate from the heterosexual, mixed-sex scene. There is prevalent homophobia, sometimes explicit, more often covert but always routinely enforced by the heterosexual men who dominate. There seems to be little if any overlap in membership or activity between channels focused on gay men and those devoted to sexpics, cybersex and female bisexuality (to a lesser extent lesbians), all of which are significantly intertwined. There are frequent explicit declarations (in fserves, channel windows and private trades) that solo pics of men are definitely unwelcome, sometimes followed by public flare-ups when such pics have been received by someone. There are sometimes explicitly homophobic remarks, in public or private. Relationships between (self-declared) men on IRC were either strained or technical: as in most mainstream sexual representation, phalluses must never touch; their relationship must be mediated through the woman (group sex pictures and enacted scenarios were very popular) or else desexualized (channels named after the most recondite sexual practices were often filled with technical computer chat).

On the other hand, women on IRC – both women in the porn images traded and on-line women as virtual presences – are routinely assumed to be, and declare themselves to be, bisexual. This assumed bisexuality cannot be dismissed as simply male wish-fulfilment (or as men masquerading). To argue that this is entirely male-instigated would be to argue both that there are no women in these scenes and that they do not fantasize or enact bisexuality. In fact there is sufficient evidence (both in my ethnography and other research) of women wanting to explore bisexual desires (as well as a vast range of other desires) which they feel they cannot or will not explore IRL ('in real life'). Conversely, however, it is also abundantly clear that both the desires and the ways in which they are expressed, imagined and linked to particular acts and other bodies all closely fit the generic conventions of mainstream and hetero-male-oriented pornography. What is important here is not to try to establish whether particular desires are real or false, but to see that participants can treat them as simultaneously authentic attributes of (real life) people and generic conventions of systems of representation. In fact, the real interest is in how and on what terms people insert themselves or others into conventional systems of representation. What is interesting is the conventionality itself.

Finally, although the sexpics scene appears to embrace transgression, it does so in ways that reinforce rather than deconstruct 'normality'. The dominant IRC view of transgression is libertarian: 'to each their own'. This stance generally means that sexual transgressions are seen in much the same light as consumer choices and tastes, as the expressed preferences of a choosing self. Not only is the notion of self not brought under scrutiny, but most of the preferences are read as the 'real' desires of selves which cannot be expressed off-line: a simple repression model. Obviously, there is a huge difference between seeing oneself as a stable identity making choices – however extreme – and allowing one's identity to be destabilized by extreme experiences. The orientation on IRC is more consumerist than deconstructive (Rival et al., 1998).

Similarly, although the libertarian ethos is constantly defining and policing pariah sexualities (in addition to male homosexuality), it largely deals with them through exclusion ('do it somewhere else', 'not in my back yard'). The list of pariah sexualities is conventional and indistinguishable from off-line and media agendas (paedophilia, bestiality, violence, coprophilia routinely feature as grounds for banning people from channels). The exclusions are absolute and often ferocious, and repress any sense that 'normal' sexualities and 'normal' transgressions might arise in relation to the exclusions and inclusions that people operate. Again, the ethos of IRC sexpics moves in precisely the opposite direction to deconstruction, asserting a conventional notion of the sexual transgressor as well as of their transgressions.

For example, WhiteGold, a very experienced op on the largest and best-regulated sexpics trading channel:

> <WhiteGold> That's why I like #Sexpics.. We believe in LEGAL trading of legal
> pictures.. Actresses or models over 18 only etc etc.. Anything illegal as a norm
> in the world is illegal in there.

Off-line legality is here explicitly conflated with the broader embrace of conventional normativity. He later identified this normativity as a limit or line drawn in the sand: on one side of the line is absolute libertarian tolerance and on the other side is absolute exclusion (enacted by a consumerist choice to make it 'go away'):

> <WhiteGold> Whenever you have a meeting ground of this magnitude, you HAVE
> to tolerate the idiosyncracies of others or else you're lost already.. Once you get
> past that it's just a matter of nailing down what YOU think it right and wrong
> and sticking to it.
> <Lash> drawing your own limits
> <WhiteGold> The best and only way I let limits hold me;)
> <Lash> and if something is over your limits on IRC you can generally make it go
> away by clicking the x in the top right corner
> <WhiteGold> Yep.. If you don't want to see something, go away;)

Similarly, Serrina contrasts total freedom of exploration with 'ignore lists', a technical means of automatically excluding particular nicks:

> <Lash> yes – but you've said you couldn't be open about porn or being bi in real
> life till recently?
> <Serrina> 'True! but I'm talking about what i would want from someone in bed,
> life, to tell them how i feel
> <Lash> Ah, I see.
> <Lash> But do you think that in some ways the net is an easier place for women to
> be sexually free in than real life sometimes is?

<Serrina> easier and safer!!!![. . .]

<Serrina> yes i couldn't go into a bar here, and talk about the things i do on here, i would be in so much trouble, like rape, harassment [. . .]

<Lash> though there are forms of harassment out here too – I've watched when [Greta – another female informant] goes on #sex or #cybersex and you can't see the screen for all the /msgs – hundreds of guys trying to track her down. I find it intimidating!!

<Lash> And they're coming on with some pretty heavy shit!!

<Serrina> It is, that's why they invented ignore lists:)) [. . .]

<Serrina> i never talk to anyone on here, that the first thing that pops onto the screen is, "wanna fuck"?

It sometimes seems as important to make a constant *show* of heavy policing – to line up with off-line versions of ethics and identity in the most histrionic ways – as it is for the culture of a channel to be seriously normative in its own right or in its own way. This is clearly the case with the most self-evidently pariah sexuality, paedophilia. The heavy policing in this case concerns both the self-respect of members and of the community, the desire to eradicate any hint of taint or complicity in the eyes of the off-line world, and the practicalities of keeping out 'creeps' and 'assholes'. For example, IceFalcon – a very active female op in several channels, who also runs a web site and a detective operation tracking missing children – ran a very tight ship. Her fserve carried a reasonably heavy version of a standard preamble (**NOTE-I KICK Sharks/Assholes & Incest/Kid/Teen Channelers!) indicating that she would exclude from both fserve and channel not only those trading banned images, but also those who could be identified as being on another channel with a name that suggested such images. IceFalcon also checked out the wares of any new fservers in her channels, not only for content but also for *filenames* which were as solid grounds for banning as were their visual content:

<IceFalcon> I understand we're more strict. . . but I have seen some horrid shit and I have a little girl, so I err on the side of protecting children. I also do PI work on the side with missing kidnapped kids

<IceFalcon> ok I understand about the misty16 [a 'legitimate' picture whose filename could be interpreted as a 'teen pic'], just saying if some sicko saw it he might think it was a 16 yr old

That is to say, the channel must be kept clean not only of actual child pornography or paedophilic traders but of any possibility of a paedophilic thought or the taint of any association with such thoughts. The point here is obviously not to take issue with the ethical-legal line IceFalcon (and most others) have drawn, but rather to examine its absoluteness, conventionality and complete identification with off-line concepts of identity and difference. This especially needs examining since the absolute and public exclusion of 'Incest/Kid/Teen Channelers' and of filenames suggesting models under the age of 18 contrasts with the entirely ambiguous nature of most of the images they – including IceFalcon – actually traded: the very vast majority involved representing young women, whose age is obviously impossible to determine. Again, the one absolute and public exclusion contrasts with an entirely libertarian attitude to what remains, to what is not covered by the absolutized identity.

IRC conventionality does not mean that participants are not getting up to anything interesting or 'progressive' or 'liberating' on IRC. There is certainly a robust exploration of fantasies, desires, a use of freedoms to be outrageous, to be another sex and so on. The IRC sexpics scene also places sexual diversity in a generally sociable, friendly and liberally tolerant context which – unlike most of on-line sexuality and sexual representation – is relatively free of commerce and the sex industry. Moreover, participants value and enjoy (as well as worry about and criticize) their activities on-line. The point is that they do so largely on other grounds than might be expected within the current literature on identities.

It could be argued that the conventionality of representation in this ethnography is an artefact of its methodology: had the setting been less conventionally defined (for example, by including the gay scenes) then the range of bodies and identities might have been less conventional. Indeed, I am not denying that elsewhere on the Net (in particular media like MUDs, or within specific constituencies such as gays or lesbians) body and identity performance might not be more in keeping with poststructuralist expectations. However these exclusions were not an arbitrary methodological decision but a structural and indeed *constitutive* feature of the setting itself: the IRC setting that I researched is organized around exclusions which indicated that there is very little commitment to producing (or even allowing) sexual identities or processes of identification outside the conventionally pornographic ones. Crudely speaking, if virtual disembodiment of the extreme sort characteristic of IRC does not free up identities (or even body representations) in this one setting then we cannot argue that deconstructions of sexuality automatically arise from the virtuality of cyberspace.

Authenticity and ethics

If the regulation of sexual identity on IRC continues to be conventional, or at least conventionally pornographic, we might ask whether a conventional notion of identity as such persists: do concepts of real bodies and real identities continue to play a part? In fact, the sexpics scene comprises very diverse relationships in which the notion of authenticity involves different meanings, functions, strategies and practices. What I want to suggest is that IRC participants are intensely and incessantly aware of the fact that all on-line identities are textual performances: this is indeed the common sense of on-line life. However, participants only feel there is a 'real relationship' when they believe that the other is authenticated by a body-like presence, when, like a body, the other persists over time (has 'object constancy') and is locatable in space (and can therefore potentially be made ethically accountable for their actions). These conditions are rarely secured on IRC. The result is not that authenticity becomes marginalized or irrelevant but rather that on-line relationships are treated as not real, not serious, just a laugh, a matter for immediate gratification rather than as something consequential for self-identity. The predominant response, the general *modus vivendi*, is frank cynicism: you can't believe *anything* on-line (and are a dupe if you do). Hence, nothing on-line should be taken seriously. And yet, at the same time, IRC relationships, events and experiences can be extremely vivid, intense and wish-fulfilling: there is a powerful desire to believe in their reality. Being drawn by their own desires into mental states that are engrossing yet lacking 'authenticity', participants are forever wavering between a dismissive, cynical stance bolstered by defensive strategies and postures, and a trusting stance bolstered by strategies designed to authenticate the other by giving them an increasingly reliable 'body'. In sum, the problem that is practically posed to IRC participants by the performative nature of on-line identity is simply, how can I trust or believe anyone or anything? How can I accept the other, or be myself accepted, as an ethical subject?

RockDr

I would like to introduce these themes first by way of two contrasting extracts from the ethnography. First, a conversation with RockDr, a reasonably experienced male op on a channel whose members tended to be fairly long-term traders. RockDr is extremely sceptical of any on-line identities, and – talking about basic identity claims about sex and gender – states that only 'about 10–20% [at] most of the "girls" are real' on the sexpics channels, an issue which immediately leads him into questions of deception and authenticity and the perils of credulity, of taking things seriously out there. He recounts a story – one of legion – from his channel in which a lesbian falls in love with a woman on-line, only to discover that the other is really a man. She commits suicide. Aside from the high stakes the story illustrates of treating the realistic performance as if it was really real, there is the problem of the veracity of the story itself. The story, he says, is 'semi-verified':

> \<RockDr\> but I'm not sure about the suicide
> \<Lash\> I have to ask: how do you know the 'real' girl was a 'real' girl
> \<Lash\> ?
> \<RockDr\> the rest is certainly true
> \<Lash\> leaving aside the suicide?
> \<RockDr\> good question
> \<RockDr\> I don't know anything for sure
> \<Lash\> no. . .we never do
> \<Lash\> does this bother you?
> \<RockDr\> so I guess I must retract the 'certainly true'
> \<RockDr\> hmmmmmm
> \<RockDr\> it bothers me that people allow themselves to take irc seriously
> \<Lash\> yeah, that's interesting. . .
> \<Lash\> but they do, don't they?
> \<RockDr\> and it bothers me that people would allow another to take a fantasy that far
> \<RockDr\> yes people sure do
> \<RockDr\> one of my occasional 'crusades' is that none of this is real
> \<Lash\> yes, but it is also very intense
> \<Lash\> can feel very real
> \<RockDr\> it's like when someone complains that the woman who they were having great cyber sex with is a male
> \<RockDr\> my view is that a fantasy is a fantasy
> \<Lash\> . . .ie doesn't matter who it is with?
> \<RockDr\> doesn't really matter if the other party is male
> \<RockDr\> it's all fantasy anyway
> \<RockDr\> yes exactly
> \<Lash\> in the normal course of being on-line does it bother you that you can't tell the real girls from the boys?
> \<RockDr\> in normal course of events, no it doesn't
> \<Lash\> is that cos you're mainly trading and chatting rather than looking for cyber? [i.e. cybersex]
> \<Lash\> actually, let me ask that another way: can you have a long-term friendship, relationship with someone on-line without being sure of their gender, age, appearance, etc., etc.?

<RockDr> I trade pics regularly with a 'girl' in Sydney . . . I'd be surprised if she really is but I couldn't care less

<RockDr> but if I'm trying to develop a real friendship, then I like to know the truth

<RockDr> and truth is a very rare commodity in irc

<RockDr> yes to the first question

<Lash> and the second?

<RockDr> as to the second . . . I think it would be very difficult to develop a serious relationship w/o some personal knowledge of the person [. . .]

<RockDr> and their sex is prolly [probably] the least important to me

[. . .]

<RockDr> question for you . . . do you think that you can tell a real female by the way she talks in irc?

<Lash> I don't think so. . ..

<RockDr> I find that women think they can always tell

<RockDr> I don't think so either [. . .]

<Lash> do you have any tricks or tips about how to tell?

<Lash> '<RockDr> I find that women think they can always tell' – how do you know THEY are women:)

<RockDr> and I don't think women can either all the time [. . .]

<RockDr> the women I referred I know because I've either met them, talked to them on the phone or know someone who has

<RockDr> unless the 'women' meet those criteria, I assume they are male

<RockDr> but I rarely care

<RockDr> I find cyber sex pretty boring so it's not really an issue for me

RockDr – like most people who spend a lot of time on the sexpics trading scene – finds both sexpics and cybersex very boring. He, like many others, consistently claims that both are merely occasions or opportunities for other pleasures of the scene: casual chat, a generally erotic ambience, carrying out channel business and so on. For these kinds of involvement, most issues of veracity are 'not really an issue'. At the same time, this also implies – as he indicated above – that these involvements themselves are not really much of 'an issue'. In the end it is all a fantasy; to go further – and to warrant the personal danger of going further into any kind of seriousness – would mean going into more embodied encounters ('personal knowledge'). In fact, the most common descriptions of the IRC mode of experiencing relationships approximate best to the idea of 'hanging out': it has the kind of intensity that absorbs one, passes the time but can instantly evaporate, especially when viewed from any external vantage:

<Lash> can I ask: how important to you are your IRC friendships/relationships

<Lash> ?

<RockDr> hmmmmm, hard to say

<RockDr> when I'm in town and on irc a lot, they are like real friends

<RockDr> and it's easy to get upset, hurt, etc. just like irl [in real life]

<RockDr> but I notice when I'm away, I don't really think about many of them

WhiteGold – quoted earlier – put it very clearly:

> \<WhiteGold\> I like these people, but they have separate lives as well . . . I miss some who've disappeared, and I'd miss some if I disappeared, but when you left school, did you keep in touch with 1 % of the people you said you would ?
> \<Lash\> though, that 1% were pretty important
> \<WhiteGold\> Sure, but I need face-to-face relationships to allow that %1 to become real enough . . . Cyberlife is way different to me.

Crucially, both regard their blasé attitude as pre-eminently *healthy*, or at least see the alternative as dangerous and silly: only the gullible believe or get involved.

LoverGirl

At the far side of the blasé attitude is an apparently contrary but in fact complementary orientation. LoverGirl thoroughly enjoyed the casual banter of IRC, and was certainly the most virtuoso, flirtatious and charismatic on-line presence I have ever encountered. Yet she took the crossing of certain lines as boundaries into more serious relationships: as each was crossed, trust in the reality of the relationship rose and the stakes for her of finding that trust abused became considerable. These lines included such things as trading real names, email and postal addresses, phone numbers; the amount of time spent (both time shared in the present and the length of time the relationship persisted); acknowledgement and honouring of obligations (does the other come when needed, when promised, at the cost of off-line inconvenience to off-line relationships). After meeting through on-line chat, LoverGirl had been communicating with a couple, Stu and Lisa, and their friend Alli for 18 months, across several different media, when Alli confessed to her on-line that none of their names were real, that they lived in different countries than originally claimed, that Stu and Lisa had married and had a child without telling LoverGirl, that some crucial features of their lives (especially occupations) had been falsified:

> Is it silly that I'm sitting here in tears??? I feel so incredibly betrayed. I have known these people for a year and a half now . . . I thought some sort of trust would have been built by this point. Stu and I were sort of involved, before Lisa came along (Jesus these aren't even their names!!) we've shared a lot . . . and I KNOW it's just a name.
> But what an adjustment to have to make after calling them that for YEARS. . .it took me a while to adjust to "Jane" and I'd only known her as Greta for a month!
> I don't know why I feel so betrayed, but I do. It's like . . . I couldn't be trusted with the truth. That hurts so much, hon!!:((((
> I know people lie on here . . . people do it all the time, for all sorts of reasons . . . but to continue a lie like that . . . for so long . . .
> I'm just really hurt.

After all this time, LoverGirl has not been entrusted with their names, which would allow her to locate them, which gives them an address and a unique, fixed and dependable identity. Part of the problem is that it is through such tokens of trust that LoverGirl is able to internalize the relationships and live them as real, which in this case she did very intensely. LoverGirl contrasts her reaction with the RockDr-like stance of her friend Amelia who said:

> "well forget em then, who needs em . . ." which is typical Amelia. If AOL [America On-Line: some of the events shifted out of IRC to other chat spaces] people don't make themselves Real fairly quickly they seem to cease to exist for her. Maybe it's

because I live so much of my life in my head that these people seem so real (been trying to rationalize this ache I have inside and it isn't working so well . . .) I'm still pretty unstable, burst into tears at no prompting . . .

Also crucial to the real intensity of the hurt is the fact that Stu and Lisa vanished into cyberspace, disappeared in their puff of lies despite LoverGirl's attempts to contact them. The final abuse of trust was their refusal of the moral commitment to confront the issues and injured party they left behind, while LoverGirl – having lost their locatable, addressed bodies (real, unique names) could not call them to account. From bodies to nobodies. Indeed, LoverGirl measures the strength of the lost relationship precisely by the extent to which they had been physically there for each other: while LoverGirl was separated from her husband, Stu and she

> talked on the phone for hours and hours and hours . . . he helped me a LOT through the breakup [. . .], the affair . . . and I helped him get his life back together after Victoria [. . .] and I was there for him when he "met" Lisa . . . now I wonder if it was ALL a sham. Did he already KNOW her . . . were they already married?? God I don't even know . . . I don't know what to believe anymore!!

LoverGirl went on, in a series of emails and conversations with me and others – and eventually in a very long on-line conversation with Lisa, who had finally responded – to pull apart their 18-month performance: this meant first recasting the whole affair as a charade, examining every significant aspect of the relationship from the standpoint of incredulity and injury. In the end, Lisa and LoverGirl recast their past as one in which the web of 'lies' was explained as the result of Lisa, Stu and Alli being captured by a performance from which they could not escape:

> SO many lies . . . and once they got in too deep they couldn't stop and tell me. So . . . basically all was forgiven and we spent hours talking, me finding what was true and what wasn't . . . it was amazing. But I DID know them in spite of all the lies, the people they really are . . . I knew them. Still do. I would like to think that, no matter what happens here in cyberland, whatever little lies we put up to shield ourselves from . . . whatever . . . the REAL person does shine through. And eventually, given enough time, we care, we love . . . it really happens. It transcends the physical. The superficial. [. . .] and I learn, once again, in spite of all the pain, it really IS worth it. And it reaffirms my belief that people can be, and mostly are, basically good in the long run.

LoverGirl – herself a tremendous performer – fundamentally treats performances as lies when in the context of an ostensibly 'meaningful' relationship. She swore after this and various other similar disillusionments that she – like RockDr – would never believe anything anyone ever said on IRC again. Her entire on-line life sometimes seemed a battering by the twin gales of cynicism and credulity, in which a desire to commit and to believe were inseparably connected to each other and constantly winning out over a safer, lighter orientation. She kept putting her head generously on the block because the lesson of her pain was not the deconstruction of authenticity but rather a desire to track that authenticity to the ever deeper recesses of the soul where it hid: once she had calmed down and had received an apology and reaffirmed commitment from Lisa, LoverGirl asserted that 'I DID know them in spite of all the lies', that there is a deeper authenticity and goodness, a definition of the other's truth that places it beyond superficial facts about them, a truth that is accessible because the real person shines through and because LoverGirl can sense their real selves (there is constant reference on-line to intuition and 'having good antennae' (Serrina)). It is in terms of that deeper authenticity – purchased at the cost of pain and risk – that it is all worth it.

Businesses and pleasures

We can make some sense of the contrasts and deeper complementarities between RockDr and LoverGirl by relating their stances to the business at hand, to the things they are trying to do, the stakes, dangers and investments that are involved (or that they are willing to allow), and the kinds of relationships they feel themselves to be involved in in particular social and temporal contexts. Levels of belief and trust in others need to be related to specific relationships, aims and activities. Figure 2 [not reproduced] presents a typology of the kinds of relationships formed in the IRC sexpics scene. The horizontal axis registers the fact that people may be more oriented to 'business' (trading and collecting, maintaining and policing channels, solving technical problems) or more focused on 'relationships' (hanging out, chatting or chatting up, friendship and support, flirting, cybersex, romance). The vertical axis indicates that different temporalities – longer or shorter acquaintance, intense or intermittent encounter, different temporal horizons – define different kinds of social relationship and social action on-line. Different concerns about authenticity and different strategies for authenticating the other arise depending on the interest in the relationship and on its temporality.

Business

The lower right-hand quadrant of Figure 2 is typified by one-off trading between two strangers. A basic trade takes the form of a private chat involving some minimal discussion of what the two parties have and want, some agreement about what would make a fair exchange and then a flurry of file transfers with perhaps some commentary on the quality of the pics or a request for more (or less) of something. This obviously can develop into more sociable chat, cybersex or a continuing relationship. Participants themselves may find it hard to say whether they are more interested in chatting or trading. However, for as long as the encounter is treated as a trading encounter with a short time horizon it is not regarded as much of a relationship: participants might know little about each other (not even age, sex, location), but they do not *need* to know anything. They are also unlikely to believe or rely upon anything others say about themselves; there is no context or reason to trust an entirely fugitive textual presence. However, this relationship, in which concern for the other's authenticity is most minimal, is also one which participants do not regard as a significant or meaningful relationship. It is therefore not surprising that participants have produced a range of software add-ons that render this kind of trading almost completely automated and depersonalized: the software manages all aspects of fserves to the extent that the trader need not even be present. There is much unhappiness amongst IRC old-timers who feel that this migration to automation is killing off the sociability of their scene. Nonetheless, it is equally clear that automation suffices for the business at hand.

And yet underlying even the minimal sociality of one-off trading lies a normative concern that decisively requires authenticating an ethical other by locating it in a real body. This concern is with *reciprocity* in exchange: will the other return a good measure of pics (in both quantity and quality)? The expectation of reciprocity depends on some certainty that one is dealing with one other person who will persist long enough to complete the exchange. In fact, even that basic condition of embodied dependability is generally absent or unreliable. Presences will take pics and then vanish without reciprocating, will send 'any old rubbish', will use multiple nicks to 'leech' more pictures than a single contractual partner is entitled to. Despite the fact that the supply of sexually explicit pictures on IRC is entirely free and apparently inexhaustible – beyond either scarcity or value – being ripped off or 'leeched' is a matter of constant, obsessive anger and regulation. The issue is evidently ethical rather than economic (there is no scarcity): the other should be a unique ethical subject located in a unique and accountable body. Hence it is again unsurprising that automated fserve programs (for example 'Hawkee's leech proof fserve', the most popular) regulate the normative issue of reciprocity by building in exchange ratios as well as devices for detecting if several nicks share a single local host address (and therefore by sharing a single location can be presumed to be one body). That is to say, at the level of a one-off trading encounter IRC participants are concerned to define and identify something close to a legal subject, a unique and accountable person in a locatable body. It is fundamental to ethical exchange that a just measure is legitimately due to real and unique bodies, not to multiple performed identities.

Although one-off trading encounters probably account for most of the sexpics scene, in the course of 'doing business' over time identities can develop that are treated as persistent and anchored, as having a constancy that is close to having a body. This most typically takes the form of being a big, regular trader with a constant on-line presence and a reputation and standing, or of becoming a 'channel op', one responsible for managing and policing a channel. The latter assumes a considerable stake in the persistence not only of particular relationships but of the 'society', the channel as a collectivity independent of the presence of particular members: enforcing and adjudicating rules, socializing new participants into a transmittable culture, maintaining ancillary media such as web sites, protecting the channel against take-overs and flooding, sustaining endless ban and kick wars against pariah figures and miscreants. Insofar as the business dimension of sexpics trade relationships is meant to represent what participants recognize as 'real relationships' (as opposed to automated or automatable operations), the temporal consistency, reliability and presence of the other become extremely important. One is really talking about familiar 'real-life' qualities: a good op should be consistent and reliable in his or her judgements, application of rules, technical expertise and so on. The role of the op is to extend normativity over time: in a sense, to embody a normative order as well as simply to enunciate or enforce it. Good ops are credited with this ability on the basis of both personal qualities (someone is considered friendly, sensible, knowledgeable, a leader) and 'experience' (ops are seen as veterans who know the ropes, really know the scene from the inside out, socially and technically). Basehit's account of his recent rise to op status foregrounds all-round dependability, condensed into 'a good reputation'; he has been

> \<Basehit> on the channel as an active trader and "helper" for months, and I have a good reputation here [. . .]
> \<Basehit> quality pictures, fair trades, and help the channel ops when they need anything like help with scripts, sometimes I will be a guinea pig for them.

In other words, good ops are talked about as somehow 'the real thing'. By contrast, people who want to play at being an op or who have not demonstrated their leadership qualities over time, people not authenticated on the basis of qualities and experience, are seen as unreliable, dangerous or irritating. RockDr contrasts ethical stability with pure self-interest:

> \<RockDr> basically a new op has to be a regular here
> \<RockDr> not an asshole

<RockDr> know a bit about irc
<RockDr> and usually run an fserve
<RockDr> a good op is patient
<RockDr> helpful to newbies
<RockDr> encourages fun in channel
<RockDr> and enforces rules strictly
<Lash> that sounds very clear . . .
<Lash> now that raises a question I've wanted to ask: how do you define an 'asshole' on IRC?
<RockDr> an asshole is someone who is only here to satisfy his/her ego at the expense of others

Relationships

The lower left-hand quadrant of Figure 2 includes sociable chatting, of which there is plenty in IRC sexpics scenes, but also 'chatting up' and eroticizing on-line relationships. Cybersex is one possible outcome, and certainly the place is permeated with marauding male presences hoping for a convincing female presence to get off with. Explicit cybersex aside, what is most striking about the scene is that chats and trades can be eroticized at any moment; eroticism is incipient in every encounter.

However, whether the chat is loosely erotic, an explicit virtual sex act or a sociable encounter, participants are intensely aware that they are dealing with textual performances which can be gratifying or wish-fulfilling and may be highly skilled (much of the pleasure is in the performance or in watching a good performance). Moreover, IRC encounters are 'interactive': they arc texts that are built up in the moment by two or more people responding to each other's performances. This is the level of virtuality: can you conjure up an event within representation that can be imaginatively experienced as real? This is where people routinely describe cybersex as like being inside an interactively written pornographic novel. The issue in such interactive performances is, as we have already noted, much the same as in 'realism' in film or television: the ability to sustain a fictive world which is internally coherent and consistent and which therefore allows a willing suspension of disbelief which is quite compatible with both engrossed attention and an unfailing knowledge that what is going on is a performance, not a reality.

In essence, the other person and the interaction are assessed in terms of 'realism' (a way in which we evaluate representations) rather than in terms of 'authenticity' (a way in which we trust other people). As the case of LoverGirl clearly shows, people on-line are very aware – quite painfully aware – of the difference between realism and authenticity. They speak about the difference in terms of disappointments, deceptions, being let down or conned by others who seemed very real at the time. Or simply in terms of the unaccountable disappearance of the other. They are drawn into the realism because they have a huge desire for various kinds of emotional engagements, including a desire for the erotic, and for the erotic to be transferred from the pornographic images they trade to the pornography they can construct interactively with each other. But they do not *trust* that realism: they know it to be a fiction in the very process of making it ever more real. This awareness may take the form of a disbelief in anything said on IRC; or a belief that everything said on IRC is positively a lie (a male informant claimed in one sentence to have had cybersex hundreds of times and that there are absolutely *no* women at all on IRC); or a strategy – like RockDr's – of treating everything as if they were lies.

The most vivid and painful examples of the pragmatically necessary distinction between realism and authenticity involved relationships that had developed, like LoverGirl's, over time (the upper left-hand quadrant). Her story also illustrates what might be termed the dialectic of realism and authenticity, that dialectic of disillusionment in which participants might retire into a complete cynicism, a total disbelief in the authenticity of any identity claims, only to be gradually drawn into the pleasures of a new relationship with engrossing involvements that they again slowly came to treat as true or authentic, rather than simply pleasurable, performances. The virtual keeps slipping into the authentic. Although participants will often claim that 'you are what you type', or you can be whatever you want to be on-line, nonetheless the issue that preoccupies them is how to tell the difference between the real and the realistic, the authentic and the performed, a difference which they never question in principle and understand to be highly consequential in practice. Indeed, there is a somehow masochistic pleasure in unmasking performances that rivals the pleasures of enjoying performances; yet the latter pleasure involves suspending precisely those claims to authenticity which the former pleasure both assumes and perversely enjoys debunking.

In the quadrant of casual encounters, as with one-off trading, it is felt to be impossible to establish any real credibility, but it is also not particularly necessary: at stake is either a vivid experience or a pleasant chat, neither with any serious consequences. Realistic performance is sufficient to the business at hand. As relationships develop over time however these issues of authenticity become both more pressing and more capable of being dealt with in complex ways. Participants' growing sense of having a relationship – and the experiential grounds upon which participants are prepared to claim that a 'real' relationship does exist – is bound up with two strategies for authenticating the other.

The first is a strategy of 'progressive embodiment': to see the other's picture, hear their voice, get their address or phone number, exchange letters, see them on quickcam or talk on iphone, or to meet in real life. To put flesh on the texts. Embodiment actually does two things: it gives the other a fixed point or origin in space (an address) from which their actions can be mapped, to which responsibility for those actions can be traced; and it provides the kind of sensual delineation of the other and their presence that people have come to treat as incontestable in everyday life. Hence, developing an IRC relationship often means moving off IRC. However, one of the ironies of these relationships, and of this strategy, is that although moving to more embodied encounters may begin to transform realism into authenticity (I can *really* believe in a relationship with someone whose body I can both locate and see), the very opposite may be happening: that one is simply drawing the actual body of the other into an ever more realistic performance which still has no authenticity (I can use the real body of the other to make the fantasy even more realistic, credible, exciting).

Second there is a strategy of 'object constancy': to establish the consistency of the other's presence and performance over time. This strategy involves a constant testing and probing of the narrative realism of the other, a kind of falsificationist epistemology in which truth claims are always provisional and are vigorously challenged. Indeed it is something like pushing the realism of the other's representation of themselves to various breakpoints: if it passes the test, realism can be treated as authenticity, performance as real presence. At a basic level, this can simply be a matter of 'are you still there for me?' or 'where were you last night?' If you blew off a real life encounter to be with me on-line, this must be for real. At another level, this strategy takes the form of vigilance over time, of watching for inconsistencies, lapses, ruptures in the unfolding narrative of the other, something which counts as a lie or a cheat and therefore a revelation of the true falsehood of the representation. Time becomes the dimension of exposure, unmasking, nakedness. At the same time, object constancy involves assimilating an ever more complex, variegated, contradictory experience of the other to a sense of them as somehow innerly consistent and recognizably the same, if only at some deeper level than the performative. In this sense, the constancy of the other is my construction, and the most credible construction may testify to *my* performative skills and my desire to believe rather than to the other's authenticity.

In the end, of course, participants acknowledge that there is no guaranteed authentication on IRC, as anywhere else: people simultaneously trust the other while always reserving judgement, feeling niggling doubts, testing and scrutinizing – all in proportion to the degree of investment and potential hurt involved if they prove false. This dominant mode of participation – simultaneously accepting the realism and doubting the authenticity – is largely defensive rather than deconstructive. That is to say, it is about protecting a self which is seen to be coherent and absolute but potentially vulnerable to all manner of hurt, embarrassment, deception, danger. It is precisely the opposite of a critique of that self. To the contrary, the idea is to defend the solidity of this self either by establishing beyond all (situationally available and appropriate) doubt the solidity of the other, or by preventing any emotional engagement that might make one more vulnerable, to distance oneself from any sense of the relationship as significant.

Conclusion

There is obviously a connection between the conventionality of on-line sexuality and the persistent role of authenticity in structuring on-line experience: while the disembodied character of IRC – its textuality, anonymity and dynamic, present-tense character – is essential if people are to feel safe enough to transgress and explore identity, it also precludes that persistence of the other in time and that locatability of the other in space which allows commitment, trust, ethical responsibility. That is to say, the necessary conditions for treating the whole experience seriously are constantly in doubt. It could be that participants are simply retrograde in importing into IRC an older relational apparatus; in fact, their world sometimes looks post-war rather than post-human, with constant talk of fidelity and cheating, true love, an American high school romance language of dating and going steady. But this in itself is significant: it is clear that participants see transgression without ethical commitment as a recipe for something scary and dangerous. There is much talk about the crazies one has encountered, the horrible pics people have sent, the horrible fantasies thrust upon one, the harassment. One suspects that the IRC sexpics scene is a strange halfway house, a place where anything is possible but little is realized because, although the malleability of the body allows any identity to be performed, no identity can be taken seriously, trusted or even properly inhabited without the ethical weight – persistence over time and location in space – that dependable bodies are believed to provide.

References

Bassett, C. (1997) 'Virtually Gendered: Life in an On-line World', in K. Gelder and S. Thornton (ed.) *The Subcultures Reader*. London: Routledge.

Benedikt, M. (1991) *Cyberspace: First Steps*. Cambridge, MA: MIT Press.

Butler, J. (1990) *Gender Trouble: Feminism and the Subversion of Identity*. London: Routledge.

Butler, J. (1993) *Bodies That Matter*. London: Routledge.

Dery, M. (ed.) (1994) *Flame Wars: The Discourse of Cyberculture*. London: Duke University Press.

Dibbell, J. (1994) 'A Rape in Cyberspace; or, How an Evil Clown, a Haitian Trickster Spirit, Two Wizards, and a Cast of Dozens Turned a Database into a Society', in M. Dery (ed.) *Flame Wars: The Discourse of Cyberculture*. London: Duke University Press.

Featherstone, M. and R. Burrows (ed.) (1995) *Cyberspace, Cyberbodies, Cyberpunk: Cultures of Technological Embodiment*. London: Routledge.

Haraway, D. (1990) 'A Manifesto for Cyborgs: Science, Technology and Socialist Feminism in the 1980s', in L. Nicholson (ed.) *Feminism/Postmodernism*. London: Routledge.

Maffesoli, M. (1996) *The Time of the Tribes*. London: Sage.

Plant, S. (1995) 'The Future Looms: Weaving Women and Cybernetics', in M. Featherstone and R. Burrows (ed.) *Cyberspace, Cyberbodies, Cyberpunk: Cultures of Technological Embodiment*. London: Routledge.

Plant, S. (1996) 'On the Matrix: Cyberfeminist Solutions', in R. Shields (ed.) *Cultures of Internet: Virtual Spaces, Real Histories, Living Bodies*. London: Sage.

Plant, S. (1997) *Zeros and Ones: Digital Women and the New Technoculture*. London: Fourth Estate.

Porter, D. (ed.) (1997) *Internet Culture*. London: Routledge.

Rival, L., D. Slater and D. Miller (1998) 'Sex and Sociality: Comparative Ethnography of Sexual Objectification', *Theory, Culture & Society* 15(3–4): 295–321.

Shields, R. (ed.) (1996) *Cultures of Internet: Virtual Spaces, Real Histories, Living Bodies*. London: Sage

Springer, C. (1996) *Electronic Eros: Bodies and Desire in the Postindustrial Age*. Austin: University of Texas Press.

Stone, A.R. (1996) *The War of Desire and Technology at the Close of the Mechanical Age*. Cambridge, MA: MIT Press.

Turkle, S. (1984) *The Second Self: Computers and the Human Spirit*. London: Grafton Books.

Turkle, S. (1995) *Life on the Screen: Identity in the Age of the Internet*. New York: Simon and Schuster.

Don Slater is Senior Lecturer in Sociology at Goldsmiths College University of London. Recent publications include *Consumer Culture and Modernity* (Polity Press, 1997). He awaits publication of *Markets and Modern Social Theory* (with Fran Tonkiss) and *The Business of Advertising* (with Sean Nixon).

Chapter 32

TIZIANA TERRANOVA

FREE LABOUR

ALMOST FROM ITS INCEPTION, the Internet has been portrayed as a space characterised by free communication, collective intelligence and by an alternative 'gift' economy based on the free sharing of time, communication, support, advice and virtual products or services online. Some leftist commentators have celebrated the revolutionary potential of these characteristics, seeing the Internet as opening up a space within late capitalism for alternative social and economic models; whereas free market, neo-liberalist thinkers, journalists and entrepreneurs have interpreted these same phenomena as fully part of the logic and potential of capitalism to sustain or hypercharge itself. In this chapter Tiziana Terranova interrogates these assumptions and explores in detail the nature and theories of work and labour in the digital cultural economy. She argues that the post-Web Internet has always been *both* a gift economy *and* part and parcel of an advanced capitalist economy, but that the relationship between the two is not harmonious.

The notion of 'free labour' exemplifies this agonistic relationship. Though critical of the glamorisation of work and the blurring of the lines between work and non-work in everyday life in the digital economy (particularly in the 1990s and dotcom era), she recognises that 'free labour' cannot be reduced to just a new, intensified, process of extraction of surplus value from a workforce. Rather, she addresses the overlap between paid work for digital companies and the massively productive activities in a broader digital cultural economy that includes voluntary work on websites, mailing lists, shareware and freeware production and dissemination, testing and modding software, user-generated content, etc. Free labour in its ideal state would be free in the senses both of being unpaid and of being pleasurable and freely entered into. This creative, collective and affective labour is not however a straightforwardly utopian alternative to capitalism, operating within, yet oppositional to, capitalist accumulation. Capitalism, Terranova argues, both sustains and exhausts free labour — a recent example would be the attempts by marketing companies to elicit free YouTube/Flickr-style video and photographic 'content' for their advertising sites and campaigns.

Whilst not all the practices and products of free labour are directly exploited, 'they have developed in relation to the expansion of the culture industries and they are part of a process of economic experimentation with the creation of monetary value out of knowledge/culture/affect'. She draws on neo-Marxist (including reference to the same passage from **Marx** included in

Part One of this volume) and anarcho-communist ideas in a critique that recognises the dominance and operations of digital capitalism yet is alive to its internal contradictions and the possibilities for alternative economic and cultural formations.

See also Richard Barbrook's work on digital gift economies: http://imaginaryfutures.net/

Free labour[1]

> The real *not-capital* is *labour*. (Karl Marx *Grundrisse*)

Working in the digital media industry was never as much fun as it was made out to be. Certainly, for the workers of the best-known and most highly valued companies, work might have been a brief experience of something that did not feel like work at all.[2] On the other hand, even during the dot-com boom the 'netslaves' of the homonymous webzine had always been vociferous about the shamelessly exploitative nature of the job, its punishing work rhythms and its ruthless casualization.[3] They talked about '24/7 electronic sweatshops', complained about the 90-hour week and the 'moronic management of new media companies'. Antagonism in the new media industry also affected the legions of volunteers running well-known sites for the Internet giants. In early 1999, seven of the 15,000 'volunteers' of America Online rocked the info-loveboat by asking the Department of Labor to investigate whether AOL owed them back wages for the years of playing chat hosts for free.[4] They used to work long hours and love it; but they also felt the pain of being burned by digital media.

These events pointed to an inevitable backlash against the glamorization of digital labour, which highlighted its continuities with the modern sweatshop and the increasing degradation of knowledge work. Yet the question of labour in a 'digital economy' as an innovative development of the familiar logic of capitalist exploitation is not so easily dismissed. The netslaves are not simply a typical form of labour on the Internet; they also embody a complex relation to labour, which is widespread in late capitalist societies.

In this chapter, we call this excessive activity that makes the Internet a thriving and hyperactive medium 'free labour' – a feature of the cultural economy at large, and an important, yet unacknowledged, source of value in advanced capitalist societies. By looking at the Internet as a specific instance of the fundamental role played by free labour, we will also highlight the connections between the 'digital economy' and what the Italian autonomists have called the 'social factory' (or 'society-factory').[5] The 'society-factory' describes a process whereby 'work processes have shifted from the factory to society, thereby setting in motion a truly complex machine'.[6] Simultaneously voluntarily given and unwaged, enjoyed and exploited, free labour on the Net includes the activity of building web sites, modifying software packages, reading and participating in mailing lists and building virtual spaces. Far from being an 'unreal', empty space, the Internet is animated by cultural and technical labour through and through, a continuous production of value which is completely immanent in the flows of the network society at large.

Support for this argument, however, is immediately complicated by the recent history of Anglo-American cultural theory. How should we speak of labour, especially cultural and technical labour, after the demolition job carried out by 30 years of postmodernism? The postmodern socialist feminism of Donna Haraway's 'Cyborg Manifesto' spelled out some of the reasons behind the antipathy of 1980s critical theory for Marxist analyses of labour. Haraway explicitly rejected the humanistic tendencies of theorists who see the latter as the 'pre-eminently privileged category enabling the Marxist to overcome illusion and find that point of view which is necessary for changing the world'.[7] Paul Gilroy similarly expressed his discontent at the inadequacy of the Marxist analysis of labour to the descendants of slaves, who value artistic expression as 'the means towards both individual self-fashioning and communal liberation'.[8] If labour is 'the humanizing activity that makes [white] man', then, surely, this 'humanising' labour does not really belong in the age of networked, posthuman intelligence.

However, the 'informatics of domination' which Haraway describes in the 'Manifesto' is certainly preoccupied with the relation between technology, labour and capital. In the 20 years since its publication, this triangulation has become even more evident. The expansion of the Internet has given ideological and material support to contemporary trends towards increased flexibility of the workforce, continuous reskilling, freelance work, and the diffusion of practices such as 'supplementing' (bringing supplementary work home from the conventional office).[9] Advertising campaigns and business manuals suggest that the Internet is not only a site of disintermediation (embodying the famous death of the middle man, from bookshops to travel agencies and computer stores), but also the means through which a flexible, collective network intelligence has come into being.

I will not offer here a judgement on the 'effects' of the Internet on society. What I will rather do is map the way in which the Internet connects to the autonomist 'social factory'. We will look, that is, at how the 'outernet' – the network of social, cultural and economic relationships which criss-crosses and exceeds the Internet – surrounds and connects the latter to larger flows of labour, culture and power. It is fundamental to move beyond the notion that cyberspace is about escaping reality in order to understand how the reality of the Internet is deeply connected to the development of late postindustrial societies as a whole. It is related to phenomena that have been defined as 'external economies' within theoretical perspectives (such as the theory of transaction costs) suggesting that 'the production of value is increasingly involving the capture of productive elements and social wealth that are *outside* the direct productive process . . .'.[10] Cultural and technical work is central to the Internet but is also a widespread activity throughout advanced capitalist societies. Such labour is not exclusive to so-called 'knowledge workers', but is a pervasive feature of the postindustrial economy. The pervasiveness of such diffuse cultural production questions the legitimacy of a fixed distinction between production and consumption, labour and culture. It also undermines Gilroy's distinction between work as 'servitude, misery and subordination' and artistic expression as the means to self-fashioning and communal liberation. The increasingly blurred territory between production and consumption, work and cultural expression, however, does not signal the recomposition of the alienated Marxist worker. The Internet does not automatically turn every user into an active producer, and every worker into a creative subject. The process whereby production and consumption are reconfigured within the category of free labour signals the unfolding of another logic of value, whose operations need careful analysis.[11]

The digital economy

The term 'digital economy' emerged in the late 1990s as a way to summarize some of the processes described above. As a term, it seems to describe a formation which intersects on the one hand with the postmodern cultural economy (the media, the university and the arts) and on the other hand with the information industry (the information and communication complex). Such an intersection of two different fields of production constitutes a challenge to a theoretical and practical engagement with the question of labour, a question which has become marginal for media studies as compared with questions of ownership (within political economy) and consumption (within cultural studies).

We will distinguish here between the New Economy, 'a historical period marker [that] acknowledges its conventional association with Internet companies',[12] and the digital economy

– a less transient phenomenon based on key features of digitized information (its ease of copying and low or zero cost of sharing). In Richard Barbrook's definition, the digital economy is characterized by the emergence of new technologies (computer networks) and new types of worker (such as digital artisans).[13] According to Barbrook, the digital economy is a mixed economy: it includes a public element (the state's funding of the original research that produced ARPANET, the financial support to academic activities which had a substantial role in shaping the culture of the Internet); a market-driven element (a latecomer that tries to appropriate the digital economy by reintroducing commodification); and a gift economy (the true expression of the cutting edge of capitalist production which prepares its eventual overcoming into a future 'anarcho-communism').

What Barbrook proposed was that the vision of politicians and corporate leaders who linked the future of capitalism to the informational commodity involved a basic misunderstanding. Pointing to the world of discussion groups, mailing lists and the distributed learning of programmers, he suggested that the Internet was far from simply being a new way to sell commodities. The predominance of relationships of collaboration across distance and exchange without money suggested that this was a practised relationship with a viable and alternative political and economic model.

> Unrestricted by physical distance, they collaborate with each other without the direct mediation of money and politics. Unconcerned about copyright, they give and receive information without thought of payment. In the absence of states or markets to mediate social bonds, network communities are instead formed through the mutual obligations created by gifts of time and ideas.[14]

Barbrook's vision of the informational commons was only reinforced by the subsequent explosion of peer-to-peer, file-sharing networks – a huge network phenomenon that had the music and film industry up in arms.

From a Marxist-Hegelian angle, Barbrook saw the high-tech gift economy as a process of overcoming capitalism from the inside. The high-tech gift economy is a pioneering moment which transcends both the purism of the New Left do-it-yourself culture and the neoliberalism of the free-market ideologues: 'money-commodity and gift relations are not just in conflict with each other, but also co-exist in symbiosis.'[15] Participants in the gift economy are not reluctant to use market resources and government funding to pursue a potlatch economy of free exchange. However, the potlatch and the economy ultimately remain irreconcilable, and the market economy is always threatening to reprivatize the common enclaves of the gift economy. Commodification, the reimposition of a regime of property, is, in Barbrook's opinion, the main strategy through which capitalism tries to bring back the anarcho-communism of the Net into its fold.

This early attempt to offer a polemical platform from which to think about the digital economy overemphasized the autonomy of the high-tech gift economy from capitalism. The processes of exchange which characterize the Internet are not simply the re-emergence of communism within the cutting edge of the economy, a repressed other which resurfaces just at the moment when communism seems defeated. It is important to remember that the gift economy, as part of a larger informational economy, is itself an important force within the reproduction of the labour force in late capitalism as a whole. The provision of 'free labour', as we shall see later, is a fundamental moment in the creation of value in the economy at large beyond the digital economy of the Internet. As will be made clear, the conditions that make free labour an important element of the digital economy are based on a difficult, experimental compromise between the historically rooted cultural and affective desire for creative production (of the kind more commonly associated with Gilroy's emphasis on 'individual self-fashioning and communal liberation') and the current capitalist emphasis on knowledge as the main source of added value.

The volunteers for America On Line, the netslaves and the amateur web designers did not work only because capital wanted them to, but they were acting out a desire for affective and cultural production which was none the less real just because it was socially shaped. The cultural, technical and creative work which supported the New Economy had been made possible by the development of capital beyond the early industrial and Fordist modes of production and therefore is particularly abundant in those areas where post-Fordism has been at work for several decades. In the overdeveloped countries, the end of the factory has spelled out the marginalisation of the old working class, but it has also produced generations of workers who have been repeatedly addressed as active consumers of meaningful commodities. Free labour is the moment where this knowledgeable consumption of culture is translated into excess productive activities that are pleasurably embraced and at the same time often shamelessly exploited.

Management theory has also been increasingly concerned with the question of knowledge work, that indefinable quality which is essential to the processes of stimulating innovation and achieving the goals of competitiveness. For example, Don Tapscott, in a classic example of New Economy managerial literature, *The Digital Economy*, wrote about a 'new economy based on the networking of human intelligence'.[16] Human intelligence provides the much needed added value, which is essential to the economic health of the organization. Human intelligence, however, also poses a problem: it cannot be managed in quite the same way as more traditional types of labour. Knowledge workers need open organizational structures in order to produce, because the production of knowledge is rooted in collaboration; this is what Barbrook had defined as the 'gift economy'.

> . . . the concept of supervision and management is changing to team-based structures. Anyone responsible for managing knowledge workers know they cannot be 'managed' in the traditional sense. Often they have specialized knowledge and skills that cannot be matched or even understood by management. A new challenge to management is first to attract and retain these assets by marketing the organization to them, and second *to provide the creative and open communications environment where such workers can effectively apply and enhance their knowledge.*[17]

For Tapscott, therefore, the digital economy magically resolves the contradictions of industrial societies, such as class struggle: whereas in the industrial economy the 'worker tried to achieve fulfillment through leisure [and] . . . was alienated from the means of production which were owned and controlled by someone else', in the digital economy the worker achieves fulfillment through work and finds in her brain her own, unalienated means of production.[18] Such means of production need to be cultivated by encouraging the worker to participate in a culture of exchange, whose flows are mainly kept within the company but also need to involve an 'outside', a contact with the fast-moving world of knowledge in general. The convention, the exhibition and the conference – the traditional ways of supporting this general exchange – are supplemented by network technologies both inside and outside the company. Although the traffic of these flows of knowledge needs to be monitored (hence the corporate concerns about the use of intranets), the Internet effectively functions as a channel through which 'human intelligence' renews its capacity to produce.

Is it possible to look beyond the totalizing hype of the managerial literature, but also beyond some of the conceptual limits of Barbrook's gift economy model? We will look at some possible explanations for the coexistence, within the debate about the digital economy, of discourses which see it as an oppositional movement and others which see it as a functional development to new mechanisms of extraction of value. Is the end of Marxist alienation wished for by the management guru the same thing as the gift economy heralded by leftist discourse?

We can start undoing this deadlock by subtracting the label 'digital economy' from its exclusive anchorage within advanced forms of labour (we can start, then, by de-pioneering it). This chapter describes the 'digital economy' as a specific mechanism of internal 'capture' of larger pools of social and cultural knowledge. The digital economy is an important area of experimentation with value and free cultural/affective labour. It is about specific forms of production (web design, multimedia production, digital services and so on), but it is also about forms of labour we do not immediately recognize as such: chat, real-life stories, mailing lists, amateur newsletters and so on. These types of cultural and technical labour are not produced by capitalism in any direct, cause-and-effect fashion, that is they have not developed simply as an answer to the economic needs of capital. However, they have developed in relation to the expansion of the cultural industries and they are part of a process of economic experimentation with the creation of monetary value out of knowledge/culture/affect.

This process is different from that described by popular, left-wing wisdom about the incorporation of authentic cultural moments: it is not, then, about the bad boys of capital moving in on underground subcultures or subordinate cultures and 'incorporating' the fruits of their production (styles, languages, music) into the media food chain. This process is usually considered the end of a particular cultural formation, or at least the end of its 'authentic' phase. After incorporation, local cultures are picked up and distributed globally, thus contributing to cultural hybridization or cultural imperialism (depending on whom you listen to). Rather than capital 'incorporating' from the outside the authentic fruits of the collective imagination, it seems more reasonable to think of cultural flows as originating within a field which is always and already capitalism. Incorporation is not about capital descending on authentic culture, but a more immanent process of channelling of collective labour (even as cultural labour) into monetary flows and its structuration within capitalist business practices.

Subcultural movements have stuffed the pockets of multinational capitalism for decades. Nurtured by the consumption of earlier cultural moments, subcultures have provided the look, style and sounds that sell clothes, CDs, video games, films and advertising slots on television. This has often happened through the active participation of subcultural members in the production of cultural goods (independent labels in music; small designer shops in fashion).[19] This participation is, as the word suggests, a voluntary phenomenon, although it is regularly accompanied by cries of 'Sell-out!' The fruits of collective cultural labour have been not simply appropriated, but voluntarily *channelled* and controversially *structured* within capitalist business practices. The relation between culture, the cultural industry and labour in these movements is much more complex than the notion of incorporation suggests. In this sense, the digital economy is not a new phenomenon, but simply a new phase of this longer history of experimentation.

Knowledge class and immaterial labour

In spite of the numerous, more or less disingenuous endorsements of the democratic potential of the Internet, its links with capitalism have always been a bit too tight for comfort to concerned political minds. It has been very tempting to counteract the naive technological utopianism by pointing out how computer networks are the material and ideological heart of informed capital. The Internet advertised on television and portrayed by the print media seems not just the latest incarnation of capital's inexhaustible search for new markets, but also a full consensus-creating machine, which socializes the mass of proletarianized knowledge workers into the economy of continuous innovation.[20] After all, if we do not get online soon, the hype suggests, we will become obsolete, unnecessary, disposable. If we do, we are promised, we will become part of the 'hive mind', the immaterial economy of networked, intelligent subjects in charge of speeding up the rhythms of capital's 'incessant waves of branching innovations'.[21] Multimedia artists, writers, journalists, software programmers, graphic designers and activists, together with small and large companies, are at the core of this project. For some they are the cultural elite, for others a new form of proletarianized labour.[22] Accordingly, digital workers are described as resisting or supporting the project of capital, often in direct relation to their positions in the networked, horizontal and yet hierarchical world of knowledge work.

Any judgement on the political potential of the Internet, then, is tied not only to its much vaunted capacity to allow decentralized access to information, but also to the question of who uses the Internet and how. If the decentralized structure of the Net is to count for anything at all, the argument goes, then we need to know about its constituent population (hence the endless statistics about income, nationality, gender and race of Internet users, the most polled, probed and yet opaque survey material in the world). If this population is still largely made up of 'knowledge workers', a global elite with no ties to a disenfranchised majority, then it matters whether these are seen as the owners of elitist cultural and economic power or the avant garde of new configurations of labour which do not automatically guarantee elite status.

The question of who uses the Internet is both necessary and yet misleading. It is necessary because we have to ask who is participating in the digital economy before we can pass a judgement on the latter. It is misleading because it implies that all we need to know is how to locate the knowledge workers within a 'class', and knowing which class it is will give us an answer to the political potential of the Net as a whole. If we can prove that knowledge workers are the avant-garde of labour, then the Net becomes a site of resistance;[23] if we can prove that knowledge workers wield the power in informated societies, then the Net is an extended gated community for the middle classes.[24] Even admitting that knowledge workers are indeed fragmented in terms of hierarchy and status won't help us that much; it will still lead to a simple system of categorization, in which the Net becomes a field of struggle between the diverse constituents of the knowledge class.

The question is further complicated by the stubborn resistance of 'knowledge' to quantification: knowledge cannot be exclusively pinned down to specific social segments. Although the shift from factory to office work, from production to services, is widely acknowledged, it just isn't clear why some people qualify and some others do not.[25] The 'knowledge worker' is a very contested sociological category.

A more interesting move is possible, however, by not looking for the knowledge class within quantifiable parameters but by concentrating instead on 'labour'. Although the notion of class retains a material value which is indispensable to make sense of the experience of concrete historical subjects, it also has its limits: for example it 'freezes' the subject, just like a substance within the chemical periodical table – one is born as a certain element (working class metal) but then might become something else (middle class silicon) if submitted to the proper alchemical processes (education and income). Such an understanding of class also freezes out the flows of culture and money which mobilize the labour force as a whole. In terms of Internet use, it gives rise to the generalized endorsements and condemnations which I have described above and does not explain or make sense of the heterogeneity and yet commonalties of Internet users. It seems therefore more useful to think in terms of what the Italian autonomists, and especially Maurizio Lazzarato, have described as *immaterial labour*. For Lazzarato, the concept of immaterial labour refers to *two different aspects* of labour:

> On the one hand, as regards the 'informational content' of the commodity, it refers directly to the changes taking place in workers' labor processes . . . where the skills involved in direct labor are increasingly skills involving cybernetics and computer control (and horizontal and vertical communication). On the other hand, as regards the activity that produces the 'cultural content' of the commodity, immaterial labor involves a series of activities that are not normally recognized as 'work' – in other words, the kinds of activities involved in defining and fixing cultural and artistic standards, fashions, tastes, consumer norms, and, more strategically, public opinion.[26]

Immaterial labour, unlike the knowledge worker, is not completely confined to a specific class formation. Lazzarato insists that this form of labour power is not limited to highly skilled workers, but is a form of activity of every productive subject within postindustrial societies. In the highly skilled worker, these capacities are already there. In the young worker, however, the 'precarious worker', and the unemployed youth, these capacities are 'virtual', that is they are there but are still undetermined. This means that immaterial labour is a virtuality (an undetermined capacity) which belongs to the postindustrial productive subjectivity as a whole. For example, the obsessive emphasis on education of 1990s governments can be read as an attempt to stop this virtuality from disappearing or from being channelled into places which would not be as acceptable to the current power structures. In spite of all the contradictions of advanced capital and its relation to structural unemployment, postmodern governments do not like the completely unemployable. The potentialities of work must be kept alive, the unemployed must undergo continuous training in order to be both monitored and kept alive as some kind of postindustrial reserve force. Nor can they be allowed to channel their energy into the experimental, nomadic, and antiproductive lifestyles which in Britain have been so savagely attacked by the Criminal Justice Act since the mid 1990s.[27]

However, unlike the post-Fordists, and in accordance with his autonomist origins, Lazzarato does not conceive of immaterial labour as purely functional to a new historical phase of capitalism:

> The virtuality of this capacity is neither empty nor ahistoric; it is rather an opening and a potentiality, that have as their historical origins and antecedents the 'struggle against work' of the Fordist worker and, in more recent times, the processes of socialization, educational formation, and cultural self-valorization.[28]

This dispersal of immaterial labour (as a virtuality and an actuality) problematizes the idea of the 'knowledge worker' as a class in the 'industrial' sense of the word. As a collective quality of the labour force, immaterial labour can be understood to pervade the social body with different degrees of intensity. This intensity is produced by the processes of 'channelling' of the capitalist formation which distributes value according to its logic of profit.[29] If knowledge is inherently collective, this is even more the case in the postmodern cultural economy: music, fashion, and information are all produced collectively but are selectively compensated. Only some companies are picked up by corporate distribution chains in the case of fashion and music; only a few sites are invested in by venture capital. However it is a form of collective cultural labour which makes these products possible even though the profit is disproportionately appropriated by established corporations.

From this point of view, the well-known notion that the Internet materializes a 'collective intelligence' is not completely off the mark. The Internet highlights the existence of networks of immaterial labour and speeds up their accretion into a collective entity. The productive capacities of immaterial labour on the Internet encompass the work of writing/reading/managing and participating in mailing lists/websites/chat lines. These activities fall outside the concept of 'abstract labour', which Marx defined as the provision of time for the production of value regardless of the useful qualities of the product.[30] They witness an investment of desire into production of the kind cultural theorists have mainly theorized in relation to consumption.

This explosion of productive activities was undermined for various commentators by the globally privileged character of the Internet population. However, we might also argue that to recognize the existence of immaterial labour as a diffuse, collective quality of postindustrial labour in its entirety does not deny the existence of hierarchies of knowledge (both technical and cultural) which pre-structure (but do not determine) the nature of such activities. These hierarchies shape the degrees to which such virtualities become actualities, that is they go from being potential to being realized as processual, constituting moments of cultural, affective, and technical production. Neither capital nor living labour want a labour force which is permanently excluded from the possibilities of immaterial labour. But this is where their desires cease to coincide. Capital wants to retain control over the unfolding of these virtualities and the processes of valorization. The relative abundance of cultural/technical/affective production on the Net, then, does not exist as a free-floating postindustrial Utopia but in full, mutually constituting interaction with late capitalism.

Collective minds

The collective nature of networked, immaterial labour was exalted by the utopian statements of the 1990s cyberlibertarians. Kevin Kelly's popular thesis in *Out of Control*, for example, suggested that the Internet is a collective 'hive mind'. According to Kelly, the Internet is another manifestation of a principle of self-organization that is widespread throughout technical, natural and social systems. The Internet is the material evidence of the existence of the self-organizing, infinitely productive activities of connected human minds.[31] From a different perspective, Pierre Levy drew on cognitive anthropology and poststructuralist philosophy to argue that computers and computer networks enable the emergence of a 'collective intelligence'. Levy, who is inspired by early computer pioneers such as Douglas Engelbart, argues for a new humanism 'that incorporates and enlarges the scope of self-knowledge and collective thought'.[32] According to Levy, we are passing from a Cartesian model of thought based upon the singular idea of *cogito* (I think) to a collective or plural *cogitamus* (we think):

> What is collective intelligence? It is a form of *universally distributed intelligence*, constantly enhanced, coordinated in real time, and resulting in the effective mobilization of skills . . . The basis and goal of collective intelligence is the mutual recognition and enrichment of individuals rather than the cult of fetishized or hypostatized communities.[33]

Like Kelly, Levy frames his argument within the common rhetoric of competition and flexibility which dominates the hegemonic discourse around digitalization: 'The more we are able to form intelligent communities, as open-minded, cognitive subjects capable of initiative, imagination, and rapid response, the more we will be able to ensure our success in a highly competitive environment.'[34] In Levy's view, the digital economy highlights the impossibility of absorbing intelligence within the process of automation: unlike the first wave of cybernetics, which displaced workers from the factory, computer networks highlight the unique value of human intelligence as the true creator of value in a knowledge economy. In his opinion, since the economy is increasingly reliant on the production of creative subjectivities, this production is highly likely to engender a new humanism, a new centrality of man's [sic] creative potentials.

Especially in Kelly's case, it has been easy to dismiss the notion of a 'hive mind' and the self-organizing Internet-as-free market as 'Internet gold rush' rhetoric, promptly demolished by more or less unexpected events of 2001 (dot-com crash, resurgence of international terrorism and imperialism). It was difficult to avoid a feeling of irritation at such willing oblivion of the realities of working in the high-tech industries, from the poisoning world of the silicon chips factories to the electronic sweatshops of America Online, where technical work is downgraded and workers' obsolescence is high.[35] How can we hold on to the notion that cultural production and immaterial labor are collective on the Net (both inner and outer) after the belated Y2K explosion in 2001 and without subscribing to the idealistic and teleological spirit of the wired revolution?

We could start with a simple observation: the self-organizing, collective intelligence of cybercultural thought captured the existence of networked immaterial labour, but was weak in its analysis of the operations of capital overall (including the coexistence of different capitalist lobbies and their relation to institutional governance). Capital, after all, is the unnatural environment within which the collective intelligence materializes. The collective dimension of networked intelligence needs to be understood historically, as part of a specific momentum of capitalist development. The Italian writers who are identified with the post-Gramscian Marxism of Autonomia Operaia have consistently engaged with this relationship by focusing on the mutation undergone by labour in the aftermath of the factory. The notion of a self-organizing 'collective intelligence' looks uncannily like one of their central concepts, the 'general intellect', a notion that the autonomists 'extracted' out of the spirit, if not the actual wording, of Marx's *Grundrisse*. The 'collective intelligence' or 'hive mind' captures some of the spirit of the 'general intellect', but removes the autonomists' critical theorization of its relation to capital.

In the autonomists' favorite text, the *Grundrisse*, and especially in the 'Fragment on Machines', Marx argues (as summarized by Paolo Virno) that

> knowledge – scientific knowledge in the first place, but not exclusively – tends to become precisely by virtue of its autonomy from production, nothing less than the principal productive force, thus relegating repetitive and compartmentalized labor to a residual position. Here one is dealing with knowledge . . . which has become incarnate . . . in the automatic system of machines.[36]

In the vivid pages of the 'Fragment', the 'other' Marx of the *Grundrisse* (adopted by the social movements of the 1960s and 1970s against the more orthodox endorsement of *Capital*) describes the system of industrial machines as a horrific monster of metal and flesh:

> The production process has ceased to be a labour process in the sense of a process dominated by labour as its governing unity. Labour appears, rather, merely as a conscious organ, scattered among the individual living workers at numerous points of the mechanical system; subsumed under the total process of the machinery itself, as itself only a link of the system, whose unity exists not in the living workers, but rather in the living (active) machinery, which confronts his individual, insignificant doings as a mighty organism.[37]

The Italian autonomists extracted from these pages the notion of the 'general intellect' as 'the ensemble of knowledge . . . which constitute the epicenter of social production'.[38] Unlike Marx's original formulation, however, the autonomists eschewed the modernist imagery of the general intellect as a hellish machine. They claimed that Marx completely identified the general intellect (or knowledge as the principal productive force) with fixed capital (the machine) and thus neglected to account for the fact that the general intellect cannot exist independently of the concrete subjects who mediate the articulation of the machines with each other. The general intellect is an articulation of fixed capital (machines) *and* living labour (the workers). If we see the Internet, and computer networks in general, as the latest machines – the latest manifestation of fixed capital – then it won't be difficult to imagine the general intellect as being alive and well today.

However the autonomists did not stop at describing the general intellect as an assemblage of humans and machines at the heart of postindustrial production. If this were the case, the Marxian monster of metal and flesh would just be updated to that of a world-spanning network, where computers use human beings as a way to allow the system of machinery (and therefore capitalist production) to function. The visual power of the Marxian description is updated by the cyberpunk snapshots of the immobile bodies of the hackers, electrodes like umbilical cords connecting them to the matrix, appendixes to a living, all-powerful cyberspace. Beyond the special-effects bonanza, the box-office success of *The Matrix* series validates the popularity of the paranoid interpretation of this mutation.

To the humanism implicit in this description, the autonomists have opposed the notion of a 'mass intellectuality', living labour in its function as the determining articulation of the general intellect. Mass intellectuality – as an ensemble, as a social body – 'is the repository of the indivisible knowledges of living subjects and of their linguistic cooperation . . . an important part of knowledge cannot be deposited in machines, but . . . it must come into being as the direct interaction of the labor force'.[39] As Virno emphasizes, mass intellectuality is not about the various roles of the knowledge workers, but is a '*quality* and a distinctive sign of the *whole* social labor force in the post-Fordist era'.[40]

The pervasiveness of the collective intelligence within both the managerial literature and Marxist theory could be seen as the result of a common intuition about the quality of labour in informated societies. Knowledge labour is inherently *collective*, it is always the result of a collective and social production of knowledge.[41] Capital's problem is how to extract as much value as possible (in the autonomists' jargon, to 'valorize') out of this abundant, and yet slightly untractable terrain.

Collective knowledge work, then, is not about those who work in the knowledge industry. But it is also not about employment. The mass layoffs in the dot-com sector have not stopped Internet content from growing or its technologies from mutating. The acknowledgement of the collective aspect of labour implies a rejection of the equivalence between labour and employment, which was already stated by Marx and further emphasized by feminism and the post-Gramscian autonomy.[42] Labour is not equivalent to waged labour. Such an understanding might help us to reject some of the hideous rhetoric of unemployment which turns the unemployed person into the object of much patronizing, pushing and nudging from national governments in industrialized countries (accept any available work or else . . .). Often the unemployed are such only in name, in reality being the life-blood of the difficult economy of 'under the table', badly paid work, some of which also goes into the new media industry.[43] To emphasize how labour is not equivalent to employment also means to acknowledge how important free affective and cultural labour is to the media industry, old and new.

Ephemeral commodities and free labour

There is a continuity, and a break, between older media and new media in terms of their relationship to cultural and affective labour. The continuity seems to lie in their common reliance on their public/users as productive subjects. The difference lies both in the mode of production and in the ways in which power/knowledge works in the two types. In spite of different national histories (some of which stress public service more than others), the television industry, for example, is relatively conservative: writers, producers, performers, managers, and technicians have definite roles within an industry still run by a few established players. The historical legacy of television as a technology for the construction of national identities also means that television is somehow always held more publicly accountable than the news media.

This does not mean that the old media do not draw on free labour; on the contrary. Television and the print media, for example, make abundant use of the free labour of their audiences/readers, but they also tend to structure the latter's contribution much more strictly, in terms of both economic organization and moralistic judgement. The price to pay for all those real-life TV experiences is usually a heavy dose of moralistic scaremongering: criminals are running amok on the streets and must be stopped by tough police action; wild teenagers lack self-esteem and need tough love; and selfish and two-faced reality TV contestants will eventually get their come-uppance. If this does not happen on the Internet, why is it then that the Internet is not the happy island of decentred, dispersed and pleasurable cultural production that its apologists claimed it to be?

The most obvious answer to such questions came spontaneously to the early Internet users, who blamed it on the commercialization of the Internet. e-commerce and progressive privatization were blamed for disrupting the free economy of the Internet, an economy of exchange which Richard Barbrook described as 'gift economy'.[44] Indeed, the Internet might have been a different place from what it is now. However it is almost unthinkable that capitalism could have stayed forever outside of the network, a mode of communication which is fundamental to its own organizational structure.

The outcome of the explicit interface between capital and the Internet is a digital economy which manifests all the signs of an acceleration of the capitalist logic of production. During its dot-com days, the digital economy was the fastest and most visible zone of production within late capitalist societies. New products, new trends and new cultures succeeded each other at anxiety-inducing pace. It was a business where you needed to replace your equipment/knowledge, and possibly staff, every year or so.

At some point, the speed of the digital economy, its accelerated rhythms of obsolescence and its reliance on (mostly) 'immaterial' products seemed to fit in with the postmodern intuition about the changed status of the commodities whose essence was said to be meaning (or lack of it) rather than labour (as if the two could be separable).[45] The recurrent complaint that the Internet contributes to the disappearance of reality is then based *both* in humanistic concerns about 'real life' *and* in the postmodern nihilism of the recombinant commodity.[46] Hyperreality confirms the humanist nightmare of a society without humanity, the culmination of a progressive taking over of the realm of representation. Commodities on the Net are not material and are excessive (there is too much information, too many web sites, too much spam, too many mailing lists, too much clutter and noise) with relation to the limits of 'real' social needs.

It is possible, however, that the disappearance of the commodity is not a material disappearance, but its visible subordination to the quality of labour behind it. In this sense the commodity does not disappear as such; it rather becomes increasingly ephemeral, its duration becomes compressed, it becomes more of a process than a finished product. The role of continuous, creative, innovative labour as the ground of market value is crucial to the digital economy. The process of valorization (the production of monetary value) happens by foregrounding the quality of the labour which literally animates the commodity.

The digital economy, then, challenged the postmodern assumption that labour disappears while the commodity takes on and dissolves all meaning. In particular, the Internet foregrounds the extraction of value out of continuous, updateable work and is extremely labour-intensive. It is not enough to produce a good web site; you need to update it continuously to maintain interest in it and fight off obsolescence. Furthermore, you need updateable equipment (the general intellect is always an assemblage of humans and their machines), which in its turn is propelled by the intense collective labour of programmers, designers and workers. It is as if the acceleration of production has increased to the point where commodities, literally, turn into translucent objects. Commodities do not so much disappear as become more transparent, showing throughout their reliance on the labour which produces and sustains them. It is the labour of the designers and programmers that shows through a successful web site and it is the spectacle of that labour changing its product that keeps the users coming back. The commodity, then, is only as good as the labour that goes into it.

As a consequence, the sustainability of the Internet as a medium depends on massive amounts of labour (which is not equivalent to employment, as we have said), only some of which was hyper-compensated by the capricious logic of venture capitalism. Of the incredible amount of labour which sustains the Internet as a whole (from mailing list traffic to web sites to infrastructural questions), we can guess that a substantial amount of it is still 'free labour'.

Free labour, however, is not necessarily exploited labour. Within the early virtual communities, we are told, labour was really free: the labour of building a community was not compensated by great financial rewards (it was therefore 'free', unpaid), but it was also willingly conceded in exchange for the pleasures of communication and exchange (it was therefore 'free', pleasurable, not-imposed). In answer to members' requests, information was quickly posted and shared with a lack of mediation which the early netizens did not fail to appreciate. Howard Rheingold's book, somehow unfairly accused of middle-class complacency, is the most well-known account of the good old times of the old Internet, before the net-tourist overcame the net-pioneer.[47]

The free labour which sustains the Internet is acknowledged within many different sections of the digital literature. In spite of the volatile nature of the Internet economy (which yesterday was about community and portals, today is about P2P and wireless connections, and tomorrow, who knows . . .?), the notion of users' labour maintains an ideological and material centrality which runs consistently throughout the turbulent succession of Internet fads. Commentators who would normally disagree, such as Howard Rheingold and Richard Hudson, concur on one thing: the best way to keep your site visible and thriving on the Web is to turn it into a space which is not only accessed, but somehow built by its users.[48] Users keep a site alive through their labour, the cumulative hours of accessing the site (thus generating advertising), writing messages, participating in conversations and sometimes making the jump to collaborators. Out of the 15,000 volunteers which keep AOL running, only a handful turned against it, the others stayed on. Such a feature seems endemic to the Internet in ways which can be worked on by commercialization, but not substantially altered. The 'open-source' movement, which relies on the free labour of Internet tinkers, is further evidence of this structural trend within the digital economy.

It is an interesting feature of the Internet debate (and evidence, somehow, of its masculine bias) that users' labour has attracted more attention in the case of the open-source movement than in that of mailing lists and websites. This betrays the persistence of an attachment to masculine understandings of labour within the digital economy: writing an operating system is still more worthy of attention than just chatting for free for AOL. This in spite of the fact that in 1996, at the peak of the volunteer moment, over 30,000 'community leaders' were helping AOL to generate at least $7 million a month.[49] Still, the open-source movement has drawn much more positive attention than the more diffuse user-labour described above. It is worth exploring because of the debates which it has provoked and its relation to the digital economy at large.

The open-source movement is a variation of the old tradition of shareware and freeware software, which substantially contributed to the technical development of the Internet. Freeware software is freely distributed and does not even request a payment from its users. Shareware software is distributed freely, but incurs a 'moral' obligation for the user to forward a small sum to the producer in order to sustain the shareware movement as an alternative economic model to the copyrighted software of giants such as Microsoft. 'Open source' 'refers to a model of software development in which the underlying code of a program – the source code a.k.a. the "crown jewels" – is by definition made freely available to the general public for modification, alteration, and endless redistribution'.[50]

Far from being an idealistic, minoritarian practice, the open-source movement has attracted much media and financial attention. In 1999, Apache, an open-source web server, was the 'Web-server program of choice for more than half of all publicly accessible Web servers'[51] and has since then expanded to the point where Bavaria in Germany and the whole of China have recently announced a switchover to it. Open-source conventions are anxiously attended by venture capitalists, informed by the digerati that open source is a necessity 'because you must go open-source to get access to the benefits of the open-source development community – the near-instantaneous bug-fixes, the distributed intellectual resources of the Net, the increasingly large open-source code base'.[52] Open-source companies such as Cygnus convinced the market that you do not need to be proprietary about source code to make a profit: the code might be free, but technical support, packaging, installation software, regular upgrades, office applications and hardware are not.

In 1998, when Netscape went open source and invited the computer tinkers and hobbyists to look at the code of its new browser, fix the bugs, improve the package and redistribute it, specialized mailing lists exchanged opinions about the implications.[53] Netscape's move rekindled the debate about the peculiar nature of the digital economy. Was it to be read as being in the tradition of the Internet 'gift economy'? Or was digital capital hijacking the open-source movement exactly against that tradition? Richard Barbrook saluted Netscape's move as a sign of the power intrinsic in the architecture of the medium.[54] Others such as John Horvath did not share such optimism. The 'free stuff' offered around the Net, he argued,

> is either a product that gets you hooked on to another one or makes you just consume more time on the net. After all, the goal of the access people and telecoms is to have users spend as much time on the net as possible, regardless of what they are doing. The objective is to have you consume bandwidth.[55]

Far from proving the persistence of the Internet gift economy, Horvath claimed, Netscape's move is a direct threat to those independent producers for whom shareware and freeware have been a way of surviving exactly those 'big boys' that Netscape represents:

> Freeware and shareware are the means by which small producers, many of them individuals, were able to offset somewhat the bulldozing effects of the big boys. And

now the bulldozers are headed straight for this arena. As for Netscrape [sic], such a move makes good business sense and spells trouble for workers in the field of software development. The company had a poor last quarter in 1997 and was already hinting at job cuts. Well, what better way to shed staff by having your product taken further by the freeware people, having code-dabbling hobbyists fix and further develop your product? The question for Netscrape [sic] now is how to tame the freeware beast so that profits are secured.[56]

Although it is tempting to stake the evidence of crashes and layoffs against the optimism of Barbrook's gift economy, there might be more productive ways of looking at the increasingly tight relationship between an 'idealistic' movement such as open source and the venture mania for open-source companies.[57] Rather than representing a moment of incorporation of a previously authentic moment, the open-source question demonstrates the overreliance of the digital economy as such on free labour, free both in the sense of 'not financially rewarded' and of 'willingly given'. This includes AOL community leaders, the open-source programmers, the amateur web designers, mailing list editors and the netslaves who for a while were willing to 'work for cappuccinos' just for the excitement and the dubious promises of digital work.[58]

Such a reliance, almost a dependency, is part of larger mechanisms of capitalist extraction of value which are fundamental to late capitalism as a whole. That is, such processes are not created outside capital and then reappropriated by capital, but are the results of a complex history where the relation between labour and capital is mutually constitutive, entangled and crucially forged during the crisis of Fordism. Free labour is a desire of labour immanent to late capitalism, and late capitalism is the field which both sustains free labour *and* exhausts it. It exhausts it by undermining the means through which that labour can sustain itself: from the burnout syndromes of Internet start-ups to under-compensation and exploitation in the cultural economy at large. Late capitalism does not appropriate anything: it nurtures, exploits and exhausts its labour force and its cultural and affective production. In this sense, it is technically impossible to separate neatly the digital economy of the Net from the larger network economy of late capitalism. Especially since 1994, the Internet has always and simultaneously been a gift economy *and* an advanced capitalist economy. The mistake of the neoliberalists (as exemplified by the *Wired* group), was to mistake this coexistence for a benign, unproblematic equivalence.

As we stated before, these processes are far from being confined to the most self-conscious labourers of the digital economy. They are part of a diffuse cultural economy which operates throughout the Internet and beyond. The passage from the pioneeristic days of the Internet to its 'venture' and 'recession' days does not seem to have affected these mechanisms, only intensified them. Nowhere is this more evident than on the World Wide Web.

The net and the set

In the winter of 1999, in what sounded like another of its resounding, short-lived claims, *Wired* magazine announced that after just five years the old Web was dead:

> The Old Web was a place where the unemployed, the dreamy, and the iconoclastic went to reinvent themselves . . . The New Web isn't about dabbling in what you don't know and failing – it's about preparing seriously for the day when television and Web content are delivered over the same digital networks.[59]

The new Web was made of the big players, but also of new ways to make the audience work. In the new Web, after the pioneering days, television and the web converge in the one thing they have in common: their reliance on their audiences/users as providers of the cultural labour which goes under the label of 'real life stories'. Gerry Laybourne, executive of the web-based media company *Oxygen*, thought of a hypothetical show called *What Are They Thinking?* a reality-based sketch comedy show based on stories posted on the Web, because 'funny things happen in our lives everyday'.[60] As Bayers also adds, '[u]ntil it's produced, the line separating that concept from more puerile fare dismissed by Gerry, like *America's Funniest*, is hard to see'.[61]

The difference between the puerile fare of *America's Funniest* and user-produced content does not seem to lie in the more serious nature of the new Web as compared to the vilified output of 'people shows' and 'reality television'. From an abstract point of view there is no difference between the ways in which people shows rely on the inventiveness of their audiences and the web sites rely on users' input. People shows rely on the activity (even amidst the most shocking sleaze) of their audience and willing participants to a much larger extent than any other television programmes. In a sense, they manage the impossible; they create monetary value out of the most reluctant members of the postmodern cultural economy: those who do not produce marketable style, who are not qualified enough to enter the fast world of the knowledge economy, are converted into monetary value through their capacity to *affectively* perform their misery.

When compared to the cultural and affective production on the Internet, people shows and reality TV also seem to embody a different logic of relation between capitalism (the media conglomerates which produce and distribute such shows) and its labour force – the beguiled, dysfunctional citizens of the underdeveloped North. Within people shows and reality TV, the valorization of the audience as labour and spectacle always happens somehow within a power/knowledge nexus which does not allow the *immediate* valorization of the talk show participants: you cannot just put a Jerry Springer guest on TV on her own to tell her story with no mediation (indeed that would look too much like the discredited access slots of public service broadcasting). There is no real 24/7 access to reality TV, but increasing/decreasing levels of selective editing (according to the different modalities of a communication spectrum that goes from terrestrial to digital TV and the Internet). In the case of talk shows, various levels of knowledge intervene between the guest and the apparatus of valorization, which normalize the dysfunctional subjects through a moral or therapeutic discourse and a more traditional institutional organization of production. So after the performance, the guest must be advised, patronized, questioned and often bullied by the audience and the host, all in the name of a perfunctory, normalizing morality. In reality television, psychologists and other experts are also brought in to provide an authoritative perspective through which what is often a sheer voyeuristic experience may be seen as a 'social experiment'.

TV shows also belong to a different economy of scale: although there are more and more of them, they are still relatively few when compared to the millions of pages on the Web. It is as if the centralized organization of the traditional media does not let them turn people's productions into pure monetary value. TV shows must have morals, even if those morals are shattered by the overflowing performances of their subjects.

Within the Internet, however, this process of channelling and adjudicating (responsibilities, duties and rights) is dispersed to the point where practically anything is tolerated (sadomasochism, bestiality, fetishism and plain nerdism are not targeted, at least within the Internet, as sites which need to be disciplined or explained away). The qualitative difference between people shows and a successful web site, then, does not lie in the latter's democratic tendency as opposed to the former's exploitative nature. It lies in the operation, within people shows, of majoritarian discursive mechanisms of territoralization, the application of a morality that the 'excessive' abundance of material on the Internet renders redundant and, even more, irrelevant. The digital economy cares only tangentially about morality. What it really cares about is an abundance of production, an immediate interface with cultural and technical labour whose result is a diffuse, non-dialectical antagonism and a crisis in the capitalist modes of valorization of labour as such.

[. . .] [I]t would be a mistake to think of such trends as constituting an automatic process of liberation from the tyranny of capitalist exploitation. On the contrary, as we have also suggested here, this open and distributed mode of production is already the field of experimentation of new strategies of organization that starts from the open potentiality of the many in order to develop new sets of constraints able to modulate appropriately the relation between value and surplus value – or, the entanglement of emergence and control.

Notes

1   This chapter has been made possible by research carried out with the support of the 'Virtual Society?' programme of the Economic and Social Research Council (ESRC) (grant no. L132251050). I shared this grant with Sally Wyatt and Graham Thomas, Department of Innovation Studies, University of East London. The chapter has previously been published as 'Free Labor: producing culture for the digital economy' in *Social Text* volume 18, number 2 (2000), pp. 33–58.

2   See Andrew Ross's ethnography of NYC digital design company Razorfish, *No-Collar*.

3   http://www.disobey.com/netslaves/. See also Bill Lessard and Steve Baldwin's playful classification of the dot-com labour hierarchies in *Net Slaves*.

4   Lisa Margonelli 'Inside AOL's "Cyber-Sweatshop"', p. 138.

5   See Paolo Virno and Michael Hardt *Radical Thought in Italy*; and Toni Negri *The Politics of Subversion* and *Marx Beyond Marx*.

6   Negri The Politics of Subversion.

7   Donna Haraway *Simians, Cyborgs, and Women*, p. 159.

8   Paul Gilroy *The Black Atlantic*, p. 40.

9   Manuel Castells *The Rise of the Network Society*, p. 395.

10 Antonio Negri *Guide*, p. 209 (my translation).

11 In discussing these developments, I will also draw on debates circulating across Internet sites such as *nettime, Telepolis, Rhizome* and *Ctheory*. Online debates are one of the manifestations of the surplus value engendered by the digital economy, a hyperproduction which can only be partly reabsorbed by capital.

12 Ross *No-Collar*, p. 9.

13 See Richard Barbrook 'The Digital Economy'; and 'The High-Tech Gift Economy'. See also Anonymous 'The Digital Artisan Manifesto'; and Andrew Ross's argument that the digital artisan was an expression of a short-lived phase in the Internet labour market corresponding to a temporary shortage of skills that initially prevented a more industrial division of labour (Andrew Ross *No-Collar*).

14 Barbrook 'The High-Tech Gift Economy', p. 135.

15 Ibid., p. 137.

16 Don Tapscott *The Digital Economy*, p. xiii.

17 Ibid., p. 35 (my emphasis).

18 Ibid., p. 48.

19 For a discussion of the independent music industry and its relation with corporate culture, see David Hesmondalgh 'Indie'. Angela McRobbie has also studied a similar phenomenon in the fashion and design industry in *British Fashion Design*.

20 See the challenging section on work in the high-tech industry in Josephine Bosma et al. *Readme! Filtered by Nettime*.

21 Martin Kenney 'Value-Creation in the Late Twentieth Century: The Rise of the Knowledge Worker', in Jim Davis et al. (eds) *Cutting Edge: Technology, Information Capitalism and Social Revolution*; in the same anthology see also Tessa Morris-Suzuki 'Capitalism in the Computer Age'.

22 See Darko Suvin 'On Gibson and Cyberpunk SF', in *Storming the Reality Studio*, ed. Larry McCaffery (London and Durham: Duke University Press, 1991), 349–65; and Stanley Aronowitz and William

Di Fazio *The Jobless Future*. According to Andrew Clement, information technologies were introduced as extensions of Taylorist techniques of scientific management to middle-level, rather than clerical, employees. Such technologies responded to a managerial need for efficient ways to manage intellectual labour. Clement, however, seems to connect this scientific management to the workstation, while he is ready to admit that personal computers introduce an element of autonomy much disliked by management (Andrew Clement 'Office Automation and the Technical Control of Information Workers').

23 Barbrook 'The High-Tech Gift Economy'.

24 See Kevin Robins 'Cyberspace or the World We Live In'.

25 See Frank Webster *Theories of the Information Society*.

26 Maurizio Lazzarato (1996) 'Immaterial Labor' in Saree Makdisi et al. (eds) *Marxism Beyond Marxism*, p. 133.

27 The Criminal Justice Act was popularly perceived as an anti-rave legislation and most of the campaign against it was organized around the 'right to party'. However, the most devastating effects of the CJA have struck the neo-tribal, nomadic camps, basically decimated or forced to move to Ireland in the process. See Andrea Natella and Serena Tinari, eds, *Rave Off*.

28 Maurizio Lazzarato 'Immaterial Labor', p. 136.

29 In the two volumes of *Capitalism and Schizophrenia*, Gilles Deleuze and Felix Guattari described the process by which capital unsettles and resettles bodies and cultures as a movement of 'decoding' ruled by 'axiomatization'. Decoding is the process through which older cultural limits are displaced and removed as with older, local cultures during modernization; the flows of culture and capital unleashed by the decoding are then channelled into a process of axiomatization, an abstract moment of conversion into money and profit. The decoding forces of global capitalism have then opened up the possibilities of immaterial labour. See Gilles Deleuze and Felix Guattari *Anti-Oedipus*; and *A Thousand Plateaus*.

30 See Franco Berardi (Bifo) *La Nefasta Utopia di Potere Operaio*, p. 43.

31 See Kevin Kelly *Out of Control*.

32 Eugene Provenzo 'Foreword', in Pierre Levy *Collective Intelligence*, p. viii.

33 Pierre Levy *Collective Intelligence*, p. 13.

34 Ibid., p. 1.

35 See Little Red Henski 'Insider Report from UUNET' in Bosma et al. *Readme! Filtered by Nettime*, pp. 189–91.

36 Paolo Virno 'Notes on the General Intellect' in Makdisi et al. (eds) *Marxism Beyond Marxism*, p. 266.

37 Karl Marx *Grundrisse*, p. 693.

38 Paolo Virno 'Notes on the General Intellect', p. 266.

39 Ibid., p. 270.

40 Ibid., p. 271.

41 See Maurizio Lazzarato 'New Forms of Production' in Bosma et al. *Readme! Filtered by Nettime*, pp. 159–66; and Tessa Morris-Suzuki 'Robots and Capitalism' in Davis et al. (eds) *Cutting Edge*, pp. 13–27.

42 See Toni Negri 'Back to the Future' in Bosma et al. *Readme! Filtered by Nettime*, pp. 181–6; and Donna Haraway *Simians, Cyborgs, Women*.

43 Andrew Ross *Real Love*.

44 See Richard Barbrook 'The High-Tech Gift Economy'.

45 The work of Jean François Lyotard in *The Postmodern Condition* is mainly concerned with *knowledge*, rather than intellectual labour, but still provides a useful conceptualization of the reorganization of labour within the productive structures of late capitalism.

46 See Arthur Kroker and Michael A. Weinstein *Data Trash*.

47 See Howard Rheingold *The Virtual Community*.

48 See Howard Rheingold 'My experience with Electric Minds' in Bosma et al. *Readme! Filtered by Nettime*, pp. 147–50; also David Hudson *Rewired*. The expansion of the Net is based on different types of producers adopting different strategies of income generation: some might be using more traditional types of financial support (grants, divisions of the public sector, in-house Internet divisions within traditional media companies, business web pages which are paid for like traditional forms of advertising) or by generating interest in one's page and then selling the user's profile or advertising space (freelance web production); or by innovative strategies of valorization such as book publishing (e-commerce).

49 See Margonelli 'Inside AOL's "Cyber-Sweatshop"'.

50 Andrew Leonard 'Open Season', p. 140. Open source harks back to the specific competencies embodied by Internet users in its pre-1994 days. When most net users were computer experts, the software

structure of the medium was developed by way of a continuous interaction of different technical skills. This tradition still survives in institutions like the Internet Engineering Task Force (IETF), which is responsible for a number of important decisions about the technical infrastructure of the Net. Although the IETF is subordinated to a number of professional committees, it has important responsibilities and is open to anybody who wants to join. The freeware movement has a long tradition, but it has also recently been divided by the polemics between the free software or 'copyleft' movement and the open-source movement, which is more of a pragmatic attempt to make freeware a business proposition (see debates on www.gnu.org; www.salonmag.com).

51   Andrew Leonard 'Open Season'.

52   Ibid., p. 142.

53   It is an established pattern of the computer industry, in fact, that you might have to give away your product if you want to reap the benefits later on. As John Perry Barlow has remarked, '[F]amiliarity is an important asset in the world of information. It may often be the case that the best thing you can do to raise demand for your product is to give it away' (John Perry Barlow 'Selling Wine Without Bottles', p. 23). Apple started it by giving free computers to schools, an action which did not determine, but certainly influenced, the subsequent stubborn presence of Apple computers within education; MS-DOS came free with IBM computers.

54   '. . . the technical and social structure of the Net has been developed to encourage open cooperation among its participants. As an everyday activity, users are building the system together. Engaged in "interactive creativity", they send emails, take part in listservers, contribute to newsgroups, participate within on-line conferences and produce websites' (Tim Berners-Lee, 'Realising the full potential of the Web' <http//www.w3.org//1998/02/Potential.html>). Lacking copyright protection, information can be freely adapted to suit the users' needs. Within the hi-tech gift economy, people successfully work together through ' . . . an open social process involving evaluation, comparison and collaboration' (Richard Barbrook 'The High-Tech Gift Economy', pp. 135–6).

55   John Horvath 'Freeware Capitalism', posted to *nettime*, 5 February 1998.

56   Ibid.

57   Netscape started like a lot of other computer companies: its founder, Marc Andreessen, was part of the original research group which developed the structure of the World Wide Web at the CERN laboratory, in Geneva. As with many successful computer entrepreneurs, he developed the browser as an offshoot of the original, state-funded research and soon started his own company. Netscape was also the first company to exceed the economic limits of the computer industry, in as much as it was the first successful company to set up shop on the Net itself. As such, Netscape exemplifies some of the problems which even the computer industry met on the Net and constitutes a good starting point to assess some of the common claims about the digital economy.

58   Andrew Ross *Real Love*.

59   Chip Bayers 'Push Comes to Show', p. 113.

60   Ibid., p. 156.

61   Ibid.

Chapter 33

T.L. TAYLOR

GAMING LIFEWORLDS
Social play in persistent environments

A KEY CHALLENGE FOR THE study and explanation of massively multiplayer online games (MMOGs) is that for the uninitiated it is extremely difficult to grasp what is happening beyond the game screen's animated environment and plethora of buttons, icons, statistics and lines of text. Conversely the seasoned player (or inhabitant) of these multiuser Internet worlds is often oblivious to the sheer strangeness (of 'monster trains' for instance) of the sociotechnical environment in which they spend hours in the company of hundreds and thousands of other players, both human and non-human. The worlds of *EverQuest* and *World of Warcraft* combine a Tolkien-inspired swords-and-sorcery diegesis with a head-up display interface more familiar from near-future science fiction, and are supported and disrupted by surreally hybrid virtual-actual events and economies, from in-game player protests to the selling of virtual artefacts and experience for actual cash.

In this extract T.L. Taylor provides an invaluable genealogy of multiuser virtual worlds and MMOGs, from *Dungeon and Dragons* table-top role-playing games to the experimental MUDs and MOOs developed in university computing departments from the 1970s to the first domestically accessible graphical multiuser environments in the 1990s. She combines a sociologist's interest in the social structures of – and socialisation into – MMOGs as collective spaces, with a game scholar's sensitivity to the rule-bound and playful artifice of gameworlds. These gameworlds are, she argues, 'deeply social', quite different from popular prejudices of the isolated, anti-social nature of videogame play. This sociality is not confined to the time playing and the virtual space of the multiuser game and Taylor has conducted ethnographic research into the online and offline relationships that initiate, or have been initiated by, playing *EverQuest*. MMOGs are, she argues, fundamentally 'reorganizing social life'.

The complexity of the interweaving of virtual and actual domains is exemplified by an account of changing systems of exchange within the gameworld. Bazaars and auctions within the game bring together economic models, software and game design (echoing Michel Callon she points out that MMOG designers must be sociologists as well as engineers), player desires and collective action. More prosaic technical factors are also in play: Taylor explains that players with poor Internet connections or inadequate computer hardware would have to walk through busy areas with their avatar's eyes looking at the floor, keeping the processing-hungry graphics of other avatars out of view.

This extract touches on other significant aspects of network culture evident elsewhere in this collection, notably: online game communities and extra-game production (**Kennedy**), a cultural economy of the 'gift' (**Terranova**) and relationships of online trust (**Slater**). http://tltaylor.com/

After years in the making and millions of dollars in development costs *EverQuest*, one of the most popular MMOGs, purports a subscriber base of around 420,000, with peak play periods hosting 100,000 simultaneous gamers and generating sizable revenues each year (Asher 2001; Humble 2004; Marks 2003; Morrison 2001; Tedeschi 2001; Woodcock 2005).[1] Measured against the 2000 U.S. Census, the population of "*EverQuest* would be the 35th largest city in the U.S., between Long Beach, Calif., and Albuquerque, New Mexico" (Humble 2004, 25). Since being launched, 2.5 million copies of the game and its expansions have been sold and the game continues to have a team of about 50 people working with it daily, with some additional support staff in India.

Despite the seeming novelty of this game, *EverQuest* (and MMOGs in general) can be traced back to several older traditions both in gaming and virtual multiuser spaces. Tabletop gaming, most notably *Dungeons and Dragons* (*D&D*), provides some of the basic structure and underpinning of many multiuser fantasy-genre games. In *D&D*, players create characters by building from a palette of attribute types (like charisma and dexterity) and then, using dice rolls, are assigned various amounts of points to these and other skills. Character sheets detailing all the abilities of each character are used as players adventure together through scenarios laid out by a fellow player, a game master (GM, or DM for dungeon master within *D&D*). This emphasis on adventuring, group action, and characters built out of a combination of statistics and equipment was carried over to computer gaming with the creation of MUDs.

MUDs (multiuser dungeons) form a second thread in the history of *EverQuest* in that they heavily informed not only the designers of the game, but the entire genre that has emerged in MMOGs. MUDs are text-based virtual environments hosted on a computer that allows users to log in and participate in the world. Using Telnet (or any of the client programs designed specifically for MUDding),[2] the players connect to a remote computer via the Internet. The host computer can be located anywhere. Once in the space, players are given a textual description of where they are. The first MUD (known as *MUD1*), for example, began like this:

> Narrow road between lands.
> You are stood on a narrow road between The Land and whence you came. To the north and south are the small foothills of a pair of majestic mountains, with a large wall running round. To the west the road continues, where in the distance you can see a thatched cottage opposite an ancient cemetery. The way out is to the east, where a shroud of mist covers the secret pass by which you entered The Land.[3]

The player types commands such as look, say, get, north, east, and various emotive commands to interact with the game's world. They can move around in the space and, depending on the type of MUD it is, proceed on adventure-like quests, kill monsters, walk along virtual streets and shops, go into clubs, socialize, and a wide variety of other activities the various worlds might offer. The genre dates back to 1979 when, by spring of that year, MUD was being developed by the team of Richard Bartle and Roy Trubshaw, both of Essex University.[4] As Bartle describes it, "The game was originally little more than a series of interconnected locations where you could move and chat" (Bartle 1990a). This version was rewritten several times with

Bartle developing the system into *MUD1*, a "fantasy environment, i.e. a vaguely medieval world where magic works and dragons are real" (Bartle 1990b). Bartle notes that, "Most of the first generation of lookalike games stayed in the genre, partly because the authors liked that kind of game (or they wouldn't have played *MUD1*), and partly because *MUD1* could be used as a source of ideas for commands, spells, monsters and so forth" (ibid.). Indeed, what remains quite striking is how many MMOGs continue to operate in this fantasy genre and remain based in the preferences and play styles favored by the designers themselves.

Spring 1980 brought a handful of external players to MUD to test it out given the good fortune that Essex University was a part of an early packet-switching system and was connected to the ARPANet. Bartle writes, "The game was initially populated primarily by students at Essex, but as time wore on and we got more external lines to the DEC-10, outsiders joined in. Soon, the machine was swamped by games-players, but the University authorities were kind enough to allow people to log in from the outside solely to play MUD, so long as they did so between 2 am and 6 am in the morning (or 10 pm to 10 am weekends). Even at those hours, the game was always full to capacity. Thus, MUD became a popular pastime throughout the modem-using computer hobbyists of Britain. I also sent copies of the code to Norway, Sweden, Australia and the USA" (Bartle 1990a). Brad King and John Borland note in *Dungeons and Dreamers*, a fascinating account of some of the more biographical and nitty-gritty details in the computer game developer scene, "In Bartle's MUD, the people he knew were the game, and these people became one of the first communities to bond wholly inside the context of the game world" (2003, 54). The popularity of the game signaled a new turn in which multiuser spaces were to become one of the more innovative developments within Internet technologies and certainly a genre that excited many computer users. The importance of Trubshaw and Bartle's early work is not just its contribution as a game system but that it also marks the beginning of development within a broader genre—multiuser virtual worlds. The early ethic of public source-code release with the MUD development community, and the fact that it intersected with an audience often largely based in universities (who had ready access to the Internet and technology) spawned many adoptions and variations in the scene, helping fuel the growth of multiplayers in general.

In a move away from a strict gaming theme, in 1989 a Carnegie Mellon student by the name of James Aspnes built a somewhat different kind of server which he named TinyMUD. TinyMUD was a space in which the prime activity was not slaying dragons, but world building and socializing with other people (Bruckman 1999; Keegan 1997). Keegan argues that "TinyMUD revolutionised mudding, replacing combat and competition with socialisation and world building. Made such a giant leap away from (then) conventional that some didn't even consider it a 'game.'"[5] Beyond breaking the game-oriented formula of MUDs, it also served as an important precursor to MOO, yet another "flavor" of text-based world.

MOO (MUD, object-oriented) proved to be a significant development in early multiuser worlds. Released in 1990 by Stephen White, its emphasis on object-oriented classes and object creation was an important addition to the kinds of spaces available at the time. MOOs quickly became highly user-extendable environments, often geared toward social, professional, and educational themes. The ability of users to learn the language relatively easily and create objects of their own made them particularly popular. While the worlds of You are in a dark corridor are still around and gaming spaces continue to develop a sophistication all their own, the social worlds fostered by MOO, or TinyMUSH, or any of the other variants now available, mark a turning point in online virtual spaces. No longer just a playground for gamers, MUDs in the 1990s established themselves as suitable for a variety of activities, experiences, and users (for some excellent work on MUDs and graphical worlds see Cherny 1999, Dibbell 1998, Jakobsson

2002, Kolko 2000, LeValley 1999, Mortensen 2003, Pargman 2000, Reid 1996, Schaap 2002, Schroeder 2002, Schroeder, Heather, and Lee 1998, Suler 1996, Sundén 2003, and Turkle 1995). Though originally grounded in a *D&D* gameplay style, as they developed they began to more explicitly orient toward a kind of virtual "worldness" and, as such, prefigure the kinds of spaces we see in *EverQuest*-like games.

While MUDs typically figure into the histories that are told around MMOGs (indeed many of the most prominent designers of the genre come from MUDding backgrounds) it is also important to consider the ways the history of graphical social worlds intersect the story. In 1985, four years before the creation of the socially oriented TinyMUD platform, Lucasfilm Games in association with Quantum Computer Services created *Habitat*, an online graphical virtual environment for multiple users.[6] Using a home computer and modem, a person could dial into the QuantumLink computer system and access this world. Once logged on, they would see cartoon-like graphics representing the world and others in the space. Users could roam around the world, meeting others who were also logged in at the same time. They could walk, talk, and interact with people and objects in the world—much like in some MUDs, but without extensibility by users as with the MOO platform. Chip Morningstar and Randall Farmer, lead designers on the project and longtime developers of virtual worlds, describe their intent in an important early essay entitled "The Lessons of Lucasfilm's *Habitat*":

> Habitat, however, was deliberately open-ended and pluralistic. The idea behind our world was precisely that it did not come with a fixed set of objectives for its inhabitants, but rather provided a broad palette of possible activities from which the players could choose, driven by their own internal inclinations. It was our intention to provide a variety of possible experiences, ranging from events with established rules and goals (a treasure hunt, for example) to activities propelled by the players' personal motivations (starting a business, running the newspaper) to completely free-form, purely existential activities (hanging out with friends and conversing). (Morningstar and Farmer 1991, 287)

This system was a significant development in networked virtual worlds. It was one of the first online graphical spaces in which average computer users could fashion for themselves avatars and undertake living in a virtual world. While games did exist in the space, its sense of emergent "worldness" was foregrounded. The original *Habitat* closed it doors in the United States in 1990 though the technology was then licensed to Fujitsu-Japan and a Japanese version of the Habitat world called *Populopolis* was born. The technology eventually made its way back to the U.S. (now under the name *Vzones)* and has been up and running in various forms (with the *Dreamscape* world being the oldest) since 1995. These worlds operate as an environment in which users can play games, role-play, visit with friends, decorate personal homes known as "turfs," and participate in a social world. With an economy, housing system, lively social life, and emergent player culture it is an artifact that anticipates the mass virtual worlds of games like *EverQuest*

Though *Habitat* and the later *Dreamscape* were 2-D worlds using third-person perspective,[7] they spurned the development of a range of spaces. In 1995, the company Worlds, Inc. released *AlphaWorld*, the first 3-D world-building platform for multiuser environments to generate a sizable community. The first version of the product had only one avatar (the somewhat infamous "Cy," a very generic-looking faceless male) and allowed the user to assume first- or third-person perspective. People could log into the server, interact with others and, nearly as central, build homes and various structures. Users registered for "immigration numbers" and then became official "citizens" of the world, allowing them full access to building locations and objects in the space.

The mid-90s saw a boom in graphical virtual worlds with everything from the 3-D world of *Onlive! Traveler*, with its voice-enhanced talking heads, to *The Palace*, a somewhat cartoon-like space where players could create and run their own unique worlds complete with avatars, objects, and games.[8] This period was also the time of ambitious, though ultimately failed, ventures like VRML (virtual reality markup language) and standards for "universal avatars."[9] Often inspired by Vernor Vinge's influential story "True Names" and Neal Stephenson's book *Snow Crash*, many early world designers thought about and debated the possibilities for a "metaverse" in which large-scale vibrant virtual worlds, filled with numerous avatars, would coexist.

Around this period the graphical multiuser game world emerged. These spaces mixed together the long tradition of online multiplayer games (à la MUDs) with the cultures and "world" focus reminiscent of what we see in graphical social spaces. Games like 3DO Company/Near Death Studios's *Meridien59* (1996)[10] and Blizzard's *Diablo* (1996) offered players the chance to enter into a graphical space and play with others in real time. *Ultima Online* (1997) is often seen as the breakthrough game of the genre because of its popularity, world focus, and lively player culture. It fairly quickly reached the 100,000 subscriber mark, far surpassing the kinds of player populations seen in MUDs and the handful of other graphical worlds.

As Elizabeth Kolbert described it in her 2001 *New Yorker* article about the game, "*Ultima Online* is also extraordinarily detailed, down to its most banal features. Players can design clothes for their avatars; they can have pets and train them to do tricks; and they can construct elaborate houses, which, if they have the wherewithal, they can decorate with paintings and rugs and candelabra and tchotchkes" (Kolbert 2001). *Ultima Online* has become notable in the history of MMOGs not only for the ways it revolutionized multi-player gaming, but for being a frontrunner on issues still under heavy debate. It was one of the first games to confront mass player protest, not to mention the sale of virtual items for real world currency. The development and support team (a number of whom have continued to build the MMOG genre) ultimately had to tackle one of the biggest challenges to these games, mass community management.

The intent here is not to provide a complete history of these virtual worlds (which itself deserves an entire book) but to sketch out what I see as the historical context in which a game like *EverQuest* could arise. When the game launched in 1999 Internet use was continuing to accelerate and broadband services were reaching many major cities in the United States. Internet users were increasingly familiar with the notion of spending leisure time online (be it via chatrooms or surfing the Web) and combined with the popularity of gaming, *EQ* hit a fortunate window of opportunity. It piggybacked on the old culture of MUDding and tabletop gaming, as well as drawing on advances in graphics and multiuser virtual worlds.

The threads I am pulling together here are certainly not the only way to retell the history of these spaces. Indeed, they reflect my own research biography and the paths that led me to *EQ*. I came to the game in November of 1999 when I was in the final stages of a large project on MUDs and social graphical worlds. I had spent a number of years researching embodiment in virtual environments and was tapering off that project. It was then that I began to hear about "this game, *EverQuest*." As anyone who has spent time in virtual worlds can tell you, users of such spaces are often an inquisitive bunch when it comes to new places to explore. I was constantly tossed new leads on worlds to check out, and it was in this last half of 1999 that the word *EverQuest* began to appear more frequently in conversations. At the time the game had just hit somewhere around 150,000 subscribers, far more than I had ever seen in a multiuser space. I should note that the primary virtual world I was investigating at the time was not a gaming space and, not surprisingly, much of the way *EQ* was framed for me early on was as a world versus a game.

The relationship between these two categories is a fascinating one and something explored more and more by those interested in multiuser spaces. On the one hand *EverQuest* has many of the characteristics of a game: hunting monsters, pursuing quests (also for experience points), advancing a character through levels and achievements, and competing (sometimes directly, sometimes not) against fellow players. On the other hand, there is no winner. There is no obvious finish line, no point of completion, where it is clear the game has been won. While there are levels to progress through, which mark achievement, they have only a partial connection to any sense of completion. Indeed, the numerous players who continue in the game even after hitting the highest level (which the developers are always raising—from the original 50 levels to 70 at the time of this writing) are a testament to the way the game does not support closure. The game's old tagline, "You're in our world now," evokes the feeling that what you do in *EQ* is immerse yourself in a space. People create identities for themselves, have a variety of social networks, take on roles and obligations, build histories and communities. People live and, through that living, play. Certainly MUDs have a history of this kind of rich social milieu and early graphical worlds had their fair share of gaming (typically player-driven), so this is not meant to be a story of two forms marrying to produce a new genre entirely. *EverQuest* instead popularized what had been brewing on a smaller scale for a number of years—the notion of shared persistent world environments full of both instrumental and free action.

The world of *EverQuest*

Like many games in the massively multiplayer genre, *EverQuest* is made up of a fantastical land covering several continents, planets, and "planes" inhabited by numerous creatures and people, some "real" and some driven by fairly basic artificial intelligence systems. The world of *EQ* is rendered in high-resolution three-dimensional graphics complete with accompanying soundtrack.

By purchasing the game and paying a monthly fee, users are able to connect to *EverQuest* through a client program that communicates with the game servers run by Sony Online Entertainment.[11] The world of *EverQuest* exists as a persistent world environment players can connect to 24 hours a day and game together.

As I describe in chapter 1, the first step for all players is to create a character based on a variety of choices that will inform their gameplay. Once the character is created, they then enter the world and begin the process of gaining levels to progress through the game. There are currently 70 levels a player can attain, and with each level comes new skills, powers, and abilities. Players gain experience (also known as "leveling" or "gaining XP," experience points) by killing monsters (known as "mobs") that represent a challenge to them, or through quests. By working either on their own or in a group with others, players wander the virtual landscape constantly looking for new challenges.

While some servers allow for players to kill other players (termed "player versus player" or "PvP"), the majority of *EQ* users spend time on player versus environment servers (PvE) and only kill nonplayer-character (NPC) mobs, creatures not played by any live person but instead animated through the internal artificial intelligence of the game system.[12] As players progress through the levels of the game and become powerful, they are able to travel more freely throughout the fairly large world that makes up the game. The landscape of the world consists of mountain regions, oceans and lakes, grassy plains, fortresses, and dark twisty dungeons. Most zones in the world (now totaling well over 200) have an associated level, meaning that players are likely to encounter monsters of a particular strength in specific areas. There are areas for new players, known as "newbie" zones, with creatures of very low strength (though certainly still a challenge to the new level-1 character) and higher-end areas where a single monster can take upwards of 55 people to kill. As a player becomes more powerful, creatures that once threatened them may no longer do so or, if they do attack, are killed easily. Because of the growth of the player's character over time the world of *EverQuest* is notably dynamic in a way many other computer games are not. The experience of the environment, monsters, other players, and even oneself changes over the course of a character's development. Monsters that were once quite formidable become easily killed and areas that were dangerous, or completely inaccessible, become neutral territory.

Although the game, with its world of magic and mythical creatures, seems to suggest a role-playing genre, players rarely employ any kind of formal RP orientation outside of special circumstances or the one server dedicated to the play style. The lack of role-playing in the game, however, does not mean that there is no interaction or social life among the players. One of the most notable things about games like *EQ* are the ways they are deeply social. While much of what we hear about gaming in the popular press evokes images of alienation and isolation, it is often a grave misunderstanding of (or sometimes a willful bias against) the nature of these games. The sociality of the space is not simply a matter of players talking to each other but a web of networks and relationships—sometimes weaving between on- and offline life, in-game and out-game—developing, and disintegrating, over time.

Despite my first character being one that could play alone ("solo") fairly easily, I was inducted quickly into the social worlds of the game. All new players typically start out having to spend a fair amount of time in the newbie zone with other low-level characters and monsters. It is here that players learn the initial skills required for the game and the ways to coordinate with others. When I first began *EverQuest*, travel across the regions was much more difficult than it is now. Given that I did not understand how to travel the world, not to mention my character being too poor and my not knowing how the "port" system worked (instantaneous magic transport from a player who is a Druid or a Wizard), I spent quite a few levels in the Steamfont Mountains, a newbie zone outside of my "home city," the underground caverns of kingdom of the Gnomes, Ak'Anon.

During those first few weeks of play I got to know the area very well. When I venture back now I still remember the valleys and hills, the location points of many monsters I killed . . . or was killed by. Returning is not unlike going back to a real-life hometown, with all the memories the landscape and architecture evoke. It was also here that I met my first fellow players, also typically Gnomes, who, like me, were very new to the game and running around trying to figure things out themselves.[13] Despite having spent a fair amount of time in MUDs, the text-based adventure worlds that prefigure MMOGs, and having some familiarity with the genre and even game commands, the world called "Norrath" certainly captured my imagination. When I began *EQ* in November 1999, most of the people I encountered found it all as new as I did.

Becoming a player

While we sometimes imagine games as contained spaces and experiences in which a player sits down, examines the rules, and begins play, those like *EverQuest* seem to suggest a more complicated engagement. In large measure because of the multiplayer nature of the game, participants undergo a socialization process and over time learn what it means to play far beyond what the manual or strict rules articulate. To twist de Beauvoir's classic phrase, one is not born an *EverQuest* player but becomes one.[14] Constance Steinkuehler shows in her research on the MMOG *Lineage* how individual players are embedded in a "community of practice" and that through these communities they come to "understand the world (and themselves)" (Steinkuehler 2004).[15] There are then at least two levels—constantly interlinked and redefining each other—that work to acculturate players into the world and the game-play: the structure of the game itself, and the culture and practices that have emerged in and around it. These form a much broader game apparatus, a sociotechnical one, that goes well beyond the artifact contained within the off-the-shelf box the game purchaser first encounters.

Interdependence is built into the very heart of the game, and from the onset players can see the benefits of cooperation. While I spent more time than some soloing when I began, it was still often the case that as newbies we would help out each other with tips, supplies (the game requires always having some food and drink in the character's inventory), or assistance in killing a monster before being killed by it. Avoiding death is particularly important both because experience points are taken away each time the character dies and "respawns," or restarts, at the last "home" point ("bind point") in the game. Depending on where the character dies, this can result in a fairly long run back to the corpse, where all the previously accumulated items are waiting to be picked up again. The "corpse run" can be one of the most harrowing, frustrating parts of the game because it is typically performed without the benefit of any weapons or armor (which reside on the now inert corpse back at the fighting area) and often involves dangerous travel. In newbie areas nonplayer-character guards are posted to help. They will typically kill any roaming monsters, so that running to guards, generally with monsters following quickly behind, and reaching them before being killed saves the character from death. Quite often, however, the protection of city guards is too far away, and this is where a game command for assistance comes in handy. When a player types /yell (or /y), it automatically broadcasts to those nearby that help is needed. Built into the system is a very fundamental affordance for social interaction. Since gaining experience by killing challenging monsters creates often precarious situations, this command becomes an important signal for someone to jump in and lend a hand. It is not without cost however. If another player assists and does more damage to the monster than your character did, you will not gain any experience points nor be able to "loot" the creature for items.[16]

The use of the yell command to receive help is one basic building block in supporting cooperation within the game. When I began, it was not unusual to find helpful higher-level players standing on the sidelines, so to speak, watching over lower-level characters in case the trusty /y command was issued and their help needed. Even among lower-level characters it was typical for groups of people to jump in to help out a struggling player, though often only after watching at a respectful distance either until the help command was called out or it was clear the player was in serious trouble. While the underlying narrative of the game suggests that players may actually be opponents (Dark Elves, for example, are supposed to be the sworn enemy of High Elves), I have only seen a request for help turned down a handful of times.[17] Whether for altruistic reasons or to demonstrate power, players typically help out each other as much as possible in these kinds of situations.

While the /y command represents a built-in social facilitator, there are numerous examples of emergent norms around the issue of combat help and assistance that reflect the ways communities creatively negotiate social action. The player who is running to a guard for help (or to a zoneline where they cross over into another area of the game and thereby escape trouble) is typically expected to use the "shout" channel, which is heard by all in the zone, to call out that there is trouble headed that way. This is not something mentioned in detail in the game manual nor in any rule set, yet over time the player community has found ways to negotiate the collective management of danger. In places like dungeons, for example, players will shout "train" as a way of signaling that a line of monsters is following close on their heels as they run to escape. For those resting near an exit, this is invaluable. Without these kinds of informal norms many players can find themselves suddenly in the midst of a huge mob of monsters that might quickly slaughter them.

Around the issue of combat we can see a formalized mechanism for dealing with assistance (/y) and an informal norm (shouting "train"). But there is also a third layer entailing an interpretative and symbolic appropriation of such events. Truth be told, players regularly still do find themselves in these sticky positions. Trains are such a common part of life that they actually form a point of nostalgia for many. People often exchange screenshots of particularly "good" trains (ones that are very large) or nostalgically recount starting or getting caught in one. No matter what the level of the player, trains seem to form a kind of universal connection point. But the fact that there are norms regarding what to do in a train situation also gives the community methods for evaluating the player who caused the problem.

Starting trains is a not infrequent method of "griefing" other players (causing havoc), and groups of players often decide fairly quickly, sometimes through public debate, whether or not a train was unintentional but excusable, unintentional but "dumb" (caused by poor judgment and probably avoidable), or intentional and therefore a grievance. Giving other players advance warning of any trouble you have caused is certainly one point that weighs in favor of the player in the court of public opinion. A humor page on trains, for example, provides a comical "grading" table and plays on the expected norms around the situation. Instead of awarding points for the best handling of the situation, the grading is based on how spectacular, how over the top, the train you created was. The player thus gets points for things like warning *after* the train hits (+50) and loses points for "no confirmed deaths" (−200).[18]

In many ways learning how to use the /y command, and more significantly learning to call out "train," point to the socialization that occurs in a game like *EQ.* As Jackie, a woman who has played the game since its launch, told me, it has changed somewhat from its earlier emphasis on role-playing to a more formalized normative environment. As she puts it,

> A more rigid expected social structure has developed in *EverQuest* to the point now, I think a lot of people who come in they're more assimilated into the social structure. They learn the rules, how to behave and how to act in *EverQuest.* What's acceptable and what's not in the *EverQuest* society and it's less every individual defining for themselves what *EverQuest* is going to mean for them socially and asserting themselves socially.

While the game manual provides some of these basic guidelines, it is only the barest of frameworks for how to actually play the game. As Jackie suggests, new players are acculturated into the game and essentially taught not only how to play, but how to *be.* The manual can, for example, tell the player about the different kinds of "buffs"—spells that enhance or protect a player—available but it says nothing about the process of getting and giving them. There is, however, an emergent culture in the game that has, over time, formulated norms around social behavior, how favors are given out, how killing is handled, and how help is requested. One of the most important lessons a new player learns is that there is an entire culture within the game that they must accommodate. Players are socialized into the space and over time learn what it means to become a good *EQ* player.

Of course, there are certainly people who play the game with no real regard for others, who consider themselves "outlaws" and not beholden to their fellow players in any way. But these are not the norm and, in fact, succeeding in a game like *EQ* absolutely requires adapting to all kinds of social practices and relationships that go well beyond, and sometimes in opposition to, any formal game rules. Those players who continue to cause trouble in the player community often find themselves ostracized. Players sometimes keep lists of those they have found troublesome and very frequently such information is shared by word of mouth not only across guild chat channels, but on message forums and e-mail lists. Bad players can acquire a reputation that has serious effects on their ability to get groups, be invited into a guild, and by extension advance in the game. Given the deep reliance on social networks to progress, sustained bad player behavior, while it does occur, carries significant costs and is typically weeded out.

The necessity of social networks

MMOGs are by their very nature social ventures in that they involve numerous players gaming together in real time in a shared virtual environment. It is worth noting, however, the varying configurations of networks that occur and how they can change over time through the life of the game. While many players on the low- or mid-range side of the game modulate between playing alone and joining with others in small groups, at the high-end game participation in groups and collectives generally becomes the only way to gain experience and advance. Logging in for simply an hour can be quite difficult given the necessity of finding people to play with and a location to hunt in.[19] It is not uncommon for people to spend upwards of 3 hours, and in some situations 8 or more, playing the game. Instead of just blackboxing the "social," we might think of structures in the game via a kind of building block model so that you have:

The Player

Solo   The single character on its own.

several of whom make up. . .

A Group

Groups are formal teams that cooperate to kill monsters and share experience and items gained from the kills. They can range in size from 2 to 6.

Pairs   Players on a simple team consisting of the self and one other, typically a friend or complementary class (for example, Warrior and Cleric).

Pickup groups   A collection of players who do not know each other (or not very well) who have found each other by either using the game's "looking for group" tool or have advertised in the public-zone channel for additional group members.

Friend groups   A collection of players who know each other fairly well—either solely within the game or outside of it—and do not share any formal alliance (via guild membership) but are actively grouped together.

Guild and ally groups   A subset of players drawn from their larger guild group or any ally guilds they are aligned with.

Hybrid groups   Mix of several of the other forms—groups made up of friends and strangers, guildmates and friends, etc.

several of which together constitute. . .

The Raid

Raids are complex, multigroup formations required to kill some of the higher-level, more menacing monsters in the game. The current raid tool limits a single formal raid group of 72 though often dual raids are run to increase the numbers.

Guild raids   Given many guilds have memberships ranging from 10 (the minimum required to be formally recognized) to hundreds, they are often able to generate enough participants to handle more difficult areas or monsters that cannot be handled by one group of 6 alone.

Ally raids   Many guilds have "ally" or friend guilds that share public allegiances to each other. Guilds may sometimes join with their allies to undertake large raids.

Pickup raids   These are raids formed around impromptu organization through chat channels or word-of-mouth in the game. While they may operate with some regularity, they do not require any advance sign-up and typically consist of members of a variety of guilds or those who are unguilded.

Scheduled (sign-up) raids Somewhat less popular now that most players do not rely on third-party calendars (schedules hosted at non-SOE Web sites), there still remain some raids that require advance sign-up for participation (sometimes with qualification requirements) and are typically made up of people of a variety of guild affiliations.

While *EverQuest* certainly can be played alone, the solo game is only a partially realized experience. Indeed, the high-end game (where characters achieve levels 65 and higher) can in large part only be achieved via the help of others. This reliance on social networks, or communities, is an intentional aspect of the game design. As Brad McQuaid, original producer/codesigner of *EQ* and now president/CEO of Sigil Games, puts it:

> Community is relationships between players, whether it be friendly or adversarial, symbiotic or competitive. It's also a form of persistence, which is key to massively multiplayer games. Without community, you simply have a bunch of independent players running around the same environment. Players won't be drawn in and there won't be anything there to bind them. The key to creating community, therefore, is interdependence. In *EverQuest*, we forced interdependence in several ways and although we've been criticized for it, I think it's one of a couple of reasons behind our success and current lead. By creating a class-based system, players NEED each other. By creating an environment often too challenging for a solo player, people are compelled to group and even to form large guilds and alliances. All of this builds community, and it all keeps players coming back for more and more. (Aihoshi 2002)

Supporting networks through structure

To this end it is possible to identify specific mechanisms within the structure of the game that facilitate various forms of social interaction and interdependence.[20] The importance of linking design with the social life of a game cannot be overemphasized. Mulligan and Patrovsky (2003) highlight, in very concrete ways, that the role-playing tools for communication or community building form an integral part of the game and suggest that designers must be attuned to creating robust systems that support this activity. In *EverQuest* each of the forms described above is supported in varying degrees through the architecture of the system. The notion that technical choices are always already tied to social choices and values plays out at an explicit level here (Taylor 2003, 2004). At the individual-player level, there are both mechanisms to facilitate making new connections with other players as well as sustaining them. For example, the game now has introduced a tool which allows people to tag themselves as looking for a group (LFG). In the past players had to call out in zone channels or ask around to try and find partners. With the new LFG tool they are now able to submit themselves to an in-game searchable database of players who want to join together. Of course, the introduction of such a tool ends up supplanting some of the more personal touches in the process (where players, for example, try and create exciting calls to draw in other players) but also introduces the ability for players to search across the whole of the game world (and not just their specific location) for partners. At the individual level there are also commands such as /friend that allow people to keep lists of other players they deem more than simple acquaintances.[21] When issuing a special command they can then see if anyone in their list is logged on, and if so where in the game space.

Communication in the game is also a central feature of how social life is supported and in addition to public communication methods (speaking out loud so those around you can hear, or speaking on a zone-based chat channel), players are also able to send private messages ("tells") to one another across zones. In the beginning the game had a fairly rudimentary communication system. Aside from several zone-based chat channels ("shout," "auction," and "ooc"—out of character, a holdover term from role-playing) multiplayer communication was limited to those in formal groups or their guild channel. In 2002 players were given the ability to set up their own self-defined chat channels (which can work across servers), thus allowing groups of friends or family to create a private back channel for themselves. Friends who are playing at the same time but in different areas of the world can now join shared channels to talk to each other. In many instances, these systems are not primarily used to actually play together. The value can, in fact, lie in having people to talk to while off doing solo adventures, helping each other out with anything from information to equipment, and knowing that there are players for support if trouble arises. In this way characters do not have to be near each other in the game but can sustain communication across distances.

Beyond the more individual social mechanisms however, the game is particularly notable for the ways it supports collectives. Groups, for example, are formal collections in which people, once joined together, can monitor each other, use a private chat channel, and all gain experience points based on teamwork. The formal group in *EQ* also has a leader who can invite and disband members. At the guild level people are now able to bring up a tool that allows them to see all the members of their association and where they are in the world. All guild members share a "tag" on their name identifying their guild affiliation. Guilds also have automatic private-chat channels and can set "messages of the day"—broadcast messages that all guild members see when logging in.

[. . .]

For the new player who does not yet know anyone else in *EQ*, induction into the social life of the game comes first from the small, temporary connections made with other new players. As I mentioned earlier, players routinely group up with each other to progress through the game more rapidly and successfully. Groups act as a microlevel, short-term social network. By creating a group out of characters specializing in different but complementary skills, members collectively can take on and defeat opponents who are equal to or stronger than the individual characters in the group. When players join a group they also have access to a group-based chat channel for communication. Players use the channel not only to coordinate their fighting, but for small talk, joking, and general conversation. While the group functionality in the game is most narrowly intended for facilitating collaborative hunting or questing, it also becomes one of the primary methods through which players come to make new friends, learn about the world, form and learn strategies for play, and in general participate in the social life of the game.[22]

While a large portion of the game is of course focused on killing monsters, completing quests, and leveling-up your character, the mechanisms through which this occurs and the values embedded there are particularly interesting. In the example I gave earlier about trains I suggested that the player community quite often evaluates the behavior that goes on within it. People are constantly making judgments about who to trust, whether or not someone is cheating, if they want to commit themselves to a group of other players, and all kinds of other social considerations. This is not to say that players are constantly angsting over such issues, sitting at their computers consciously weighing all kinds of factors (though of course that does sometimes occur). Much like the ways we do this kind of work all the time, unconsciously, in our offline daily lives, MMOGs similarly tap into the work, evaluations, and pleasures of relationships and social networks. This kind of engagement can be seen most clearly by looking at guilds, the primary formal organization in the game.

While some players may go their whole career without having joined a guild, this is not typical given the benefits of collaboration, which become especially important in the higher end of the game. Guilds are officially sanctioned organizations of players with a hierarchical leadership structure. Membership in a guild offers players admission into a broader social network. In general two types of guilds exist: family guilds (sometimes called "social guilds") that emphasize personal connections and playful engagement with the game, and raiding guilds (sometimes called "uber guilds") marked by a very well-articulated commitment to pursuing the high-end game.[23] While social guilds involve complex social systems, raiding guilds are also heavily reliant on social mechanisms. Despite their own proclamations sometimes to the contrary—such as the guild that says. "Don't confuse ROV with a social club guild, we are a 90 MPH ultra competitive TEAM guild"—high-end guilds rely on many of the same basic social mechanisms pervasive at other levels of the game (Ring of Valor 2003). While for many hardcore players terms like "social" often evoke images of chatting, hanging out, and general undirected play, even the most ambitious, dedicated guilds rely on deeply social mechanisms to succeed. [. . .] [E]ven high-end guilds are very adept at blending instrumental action with social work. The main mechanisms at work in all guilds, to varying degrees, are reputation, trust, and responsibility.

[. . .]

Trust

With reputation comes obligation, and one of the first areas that shows this dramatically is the area of trust. Guild members are constantly risking their characters' lives for each other and, in turn, trusting each other that hunting and raids will be well planned, loot distributed fairly, and that if problems arise the group will band together to solve them. Trusting groupmates is a common theme throughout the game and it becomes even more pronounced at the high-end where venturing into dangerous zones brings heightened risk of death and potential loss of corpse (and all the hard-earned items carried on it). Advanced play involves immense coordination and cooperation, and participants trust each other to not only play their characters well but to see through group events till everyone leaves safely.

Beyond the trust that occurs in fights, there are other instances in which players rely on the honor of others. Many guilds operate banks serving as warehouses for the collective. Players are allowed to borrow equipment from the bank, which has been stocked by fellow members via donations. Typically players are trusted to only use the borrowed equipment on authorized guilded characters and to return it if they no longer need the item or leave the guild. Spells, which cannot be given back, are given out on an as-needed basis. In all these instances members are entrusted with the collective property of the guild and in turn expected to respect its status and donate back when possible.

While these types of sharing behaviors are all sanctioned, if not supported, by the game, one form of trust is explicitly prohibited. *EQ*, in its End User License Agreement, states that:

> You may not transfer or share your Account with anyone, except that if you are a parent or guardian, you may permit one child to use the Account instead of you (in which case you may not use that Account). (Sony Online Entertainment 2005)

However, it is not unusual to see players sharing accounts. Among friends and family members, it certainly is often the case that the prohibition seems to have no direct correlation to actual practice. Indeed, the ways players use and circulate accounts is quite often in clear opposition to the ways Sony wants them handled. For many players sharing accounts can seem a fundamental necessity to successfully play the game and as such constitutes a practice quite counter to the specified terms of play. This can be viewed as a practice in which "sensible use [is] developed in context" (Hine 2000, 10; see also Woolgar 1991a). In any given guild a handful of people have particularly high-level characters that are especially beneficial (Clerics being the most notable), and it is common for several guild members to have access to these prime accounts, despite the formal prohibitions.

Generally account access is rooted in friendship first and foremost but, given the way social networks operate, it is also the case that shared access simultaneously benefits a guild. For example, imagine a scenario in which a guild goes on a particularly difficult raid and the entire group is wiped out. An additional cleric is needed to resurrect all of the guildmembers, so one of the people present logs on another member's character to assist. On more than one occasion such an action has salvaged an otherwise disastrous play session. Though formally prohibited, account sharing represents one of the ultimate forms of trust in the game, one that is not taken lightly and is quite valued.

[. . .]

Offline connections

Over the years I have heard repeatedly of people coming to *EQ* because of a family member, friend, or coworker.[24] Kim, for example, met her husband in the game (something she does not tell too many people, given the stigma often attached) and now their family plays together. As she put it, "Four people, four computers, one server." Another woman, Katinka, who became a regular part of my game life and was in several guilds with me over the course of the years, began the game because her husband (who had himself been playing for a while with his friends) sat down one night and made her a character based on one of her tried-and-true *D&D* characters.[25] In the course of my research it was not at all uncommon to find that people were connected to other players through a variety of preexisting offline ties.[26] Indeed in the case of women and power gamers (which I discuss later) this is particularly notable. Besides providing an explanation for how people first are exposed to the game, however, offline ties between players also serve as an important component in the enjoyment of the game. In the following example, I am having a conversation with a young guildmember, Dargon, that turns to the subject of family.

Dargon: I only wanted to have an alt for awhile he is a STD

TL: A what darg?

Dargon: A STD super twinked dwarf

TL: Heh, ah.

Dargon: My uncle said i was that and i got laughed at by him so i stop[p]ed his moeny [sic] source for awhile

TL: Lol

TL: How many in your family play darg?

Dargon: I think 7 or 8

TL: Wow, nice

TL: Did you guys get them into it or them you?

Dargon: Both uncles on dads side sister brother and me dad and then 2 cousins

Dargon: We got my 1 of my uncles but the other got it for his B day by his wife (who now regrets it)

TL: Aw, heh. Do you guys group together a lot?

Dargon: And the cousins we got them into it

TL smiles.

Dargon: Well the one we got in to it he is lvl 9 chanter so my 10 dwarf can and the my other uncle has about a million characters on in the guild even i group with him a lot and my cousins i group with a lot but the group is different i PL [power level][27] them

TL: Ah, gotcha. still pretty cool. didn't realize you had all kinds of family in [the guild]. heh, neat:)

Dargon: We have are only little chat thing set up to wear we get on and join the chat

TL: Oh, handy:)

Here we see the way an extended family negotiates the game space. It is not unlike the stories you hear from many other players in which a kind of domino effect occurs whereby yet one more family member finds themselves picking up the game and starting her own character. One interesting aspect of this particular example is the elevated position Dargon has inside the game. When his uncle teases him about his character, he retaliates by freezing in-game monetary support. Dargon has a kind of duality to his status within the family. On the one hand because he is young he often is not in the same position of power as his parents, aunts and uncles, or cousins. But in-game this dynamic is flipped and he has opportunities to occupy the more powerful or higher status position.[28] James Gorman, in his piece in the *New York Times* entitled "The Family That Slays Demons Together," recounts a similar experience in which he found himself relying on the help—both knowledge and financial—of his son in the game *Diablo II*. He writes of one of their in-game shopping excursions:

> "This one I'll buy for you," he [his son] said, pointing out the Plated Belt of Thorns (which I now wear), "but if you go for the more expensive one, you'll have to pay yourself." I could hear my own voice, in the aisles of Toys "R" Us, urging moderation in the purchase of Beast War transformers.

These situations also point to the ways families and friends bring social capital into the game space through preexisting relationships. While it is sometimes called twinking, it is not at all unusual to find players helping newbies they know offline by giving them some money, items, or, just as important, crucial game advice and tips. Beyond game objects and knowledge, out-of-game relationships give players an instant social network in the game. Cousins can introduce a new player around, coworkers can put together groups to help the new player, and in general the existing in-game networks can be marshaled to help the new player. These offline connections also provide unique situations in which people sometimes play together in the same shared physical space, where the benefits of instant easy communication or handing off keyboards, if needed, are also apparent.

While I have so far suggested that offline connections are primarily ones that predate the players' entry into the game, it is important to note that game relationships quite often move offline and that players regularly form out-of-game relationships with each other.[29] This is something we see in other Internet spaces, as well, so it should come as no real surprise that people who form regular meaningful relationships in the game space might want to pursue them offline. This can occur in a range of different ways.

Katinka—I previously mentioned that her husband created the original character for her— was only one member of a very close extended family-and-friends group that I spent much time with over the years. In fact, I first met her through her husband, Jack, who played in the game. Both being Gnomes, we found a kind of instant playful bond that many Gnomes seem to have in the game. As I spent more time with the couple, I came to see that they negotiated a very interesting set of relationships. Quite often they were in separate guilds (though regularly with secondary characters in a common one) and had an extended friendship network that piggy-backed on many other offline relationships. Katinka's cousin, for example, was a player I also ran into with some regularity, and Katinka played with a group made up primarily of husbands, wives, cousins, and close in-game friends. Figure 2.6 is a simple map of that small group.

One of the most interesting things I saw in my time with this group was the ways partners often negotiated semi-role-played extramarital game relationships and friendship bonds. Once a character reaches level 20 in *EQ*, the player is allowed to give it a last name. Several times I spent evenings with sets of couples who shared character last names but were, I would find out in back-channel, actually married offline to other players. Katinka, for example, shared a last name with Vin, one of the other members of our guild who was not her husband. She and Vin had developed a fairly close friendship over the years and while the last name signified an in-game marriage (of several years), it was as much a marker of a deep friendship commitment. After several years they decided to meet and Vin flew from his home in Hawaii to visit Katinka and her husband (who he also knew from in the game) at their home in Texas.

> TL: How was that, meeting him for the first time?
> Katinka: Oh, God, I was a nervous wreck. I'm gonna meet my best OOC friend in real life. I hadn't slept in 24 hours. Do you remember Rianna?
> TL: Yeah, I do.
> Katinka: Well she's my cousin.[30] She was staying with me that night. She was going to go to the airport with me, because I can't find my way out of a wet paper sack without a map, a flashlight, and a Sherpa to guide me. It's like 7 in the morning, we haven't slept, because I'm rushing around the house trying to make sure everything's just right. We get to the airport, we're sitting there, and we're completely loony by this time, so we're sitting there waiting for his plane to come in. I don't have the slightest idea what he looks like really, I've seen one picture of him. He told me what he was going to be wearing, so we gotta look for this guy wearing this. And all of a sudden all these little A—cause he's Asian, all of a sudden all these Asians get off the plane and I'm like "Oh, my God," and I'm

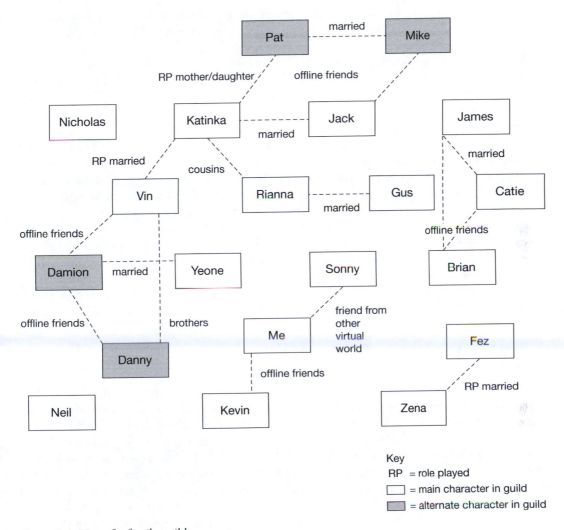

Figure 2.6 Map of a family guild

looking for him and there he is, so I'm like "okay." So we get him and we give
    him a hug and we could have knocked each other over because neither one of us
    had slept. So, it was great, ya know, being able to meet him.

TL: Was he different than you expected him to be?

Katinka: if he had been any quieter he would have been dead. He's not a very loud
    person. And being from Texas, ya know, we are just loud—you don't take us
    out in public if you can avoid it. He's a lot like how he is in the game, just quieter.
    And after the first day or two we were able to relax and act completely silly.

TL: And was that your first time meeting somebody that you had only met online?

Katinka: Yeah.

TL: Interesting. Would you do it again, do you think?

Katinka: Yeah, I think so.

TL: And did it end up changing how you guys were able to interact with each other
    online?

Katinka: not really, because we got to be really great friends before we met, and we're still really good friends now. It wasn't very different.

This ability to have relationships that might not otherwise occur without the game strikes me as one of the fundamental ways spaces like MMOGs are reorganizing social life. As children and teens occupy positions of power, as inter-generational friendships develop, as partners find new friendship networks not solely reliant on a nuclear family, as people develop deep connections with those who live far from them or whom they never meet in person, these game spaces offer interesting possibilities to undo some of the constraint produced by traditional families and localized friendship pools.

Beyond what happens in these smaller individual offline meetings, one of the most common, and most formalized, venues for players to see each other offline is the guild meet. Guild meets are much like the Fan Faire I describe in chapter 1, though they generally are much smaller and not organized through SOE but by the members themselves. Guild members physically meet up, typically for a weekend, in some geographic location often decided based on how easy it will be for most members to attend. Guild meets are generally informal and usually revolve around eating, socializing over drinks, and reminiscing and talking about the game, which often act as jumping-off points for romantic or sexual encounters. It is fairly common for people to post follow-ups in guild forums for members who could not attend, recount antics, and often post pictures.

Extending the network

My own experience of the game, and what I have seen with many others over the course of the years, is a progression from new, unaffiliated player to embeddedness in this variety of friendship and organizational webs. But it is important to note that it is not just the first-hand, real-time interpersonal relationships and groups that constitute the social world of the game, but also the collection of message boards, databases, comics, fan art and stories, and even game modifications that contribute to players feeling a bond and connection to the *EQ* world and their fellow gamers. Any discussion of game life must include a model of the distributed social sphere via groups, practices, and knowledge that exist outside of the formal bounds of the game.

The resources and communities available to players through various third-party services and Web sites is impressive. Sites such as EQAtlas[31] have provided detailed maps of the game world to the player community (long before they were integrated into the game interface), and Allakhazam[32] offers extensive searchable databases on everything from game monsters to clothing. Notably, the knowledge available at sites like Allakhazam or Graffe's Wizard Compilation[33] are built from player input and represent a kind of collective experience repository where players can benefit from the play (and work) of others. Information-gathering sites can also act as anchors for player communities. For example, one of the primary ways I learned how to be not just an *EQ* player, but a Necromancer, was through a message board/database site for the class. The site, EQNecro,[34] provided a space for people playing the Necromancer class to talk about game strategies, note new things in the world, complain about particular aspects of the game, and joke around. It offered a common meeting point with other players. As has been noted in many other Internet studies, participants often find such spaces invaluable and meaningful communities of affiliation, and this is certainly the case with *EQ* (Baym 1999; Danet 2001; Wellman and Gulia 1999). Whether it is a message board based on playing a Druid or focused on the social life of a particular server, discussion lists and Web sites expand the definition of the game world.

Another category of Web sites worth mentioning are the comic, humor, or art sites. A large number of daily comics, fan-produced humor pages, and movies have emerged around the game. These productions are particularly interesting in that while they do not have any community-communication component (no one is talking to each other and no data is being shared) they can form a powerful connection to the game for players. Relating shared experiences through art (be it comic or not) is a common way players circulate feelings about the game to others and reflect on their own experience. For example, when new fan-produced movies turn up—on all kinds of subjects including sitting at tiresome camps or, in a more poignant one I recently saw, a long-time player touring the world as a way of saying goodbye and leaving the game—links to them often circulate rapidly. While sharing information about the game or passing along a link to a favorite comic can be a way of connecting with an existing social network, it also becomes a powerful mechanism for participating in a larger game public.

From gift to commodity: how design influences social life

Because of the organic nature of the culture in games, it is quite malleable and can change over time, often in relationship to the underlying structures of the game. Two examples of this are buffing and porting. Buffing is a basic action in *EQ* in which players cast spells—either onto themselves or another—that assist them in the gameplay. Buffs can increase the number of hit points (HP) a player has (the numerical measure of health such that more HP means you can take more damage in a fight), make them stronger, hit harder, regenerate mana (a kind of reservoir of energy required to cast spells) at a quicker rate, help them be resistant to opponents' spells, and various other advantageous qualities. When a buff spell is given, the caster loses some mana, which can generally only be regained through time and, on occasion, requires an expendable component like a gem.

Buffing is an integral part of play, but how has the player community negotiated this aspect of the game? In the early years of *EQ* it was very common for people to ask for buffs with a fair amount of frequency. It was typically only done in particular environments—common areas where people gathered—and not when someone was in the middle of a battle. Generally social norms required people be polite and, in fact, this was one of the few spaces in which a role-play "voice" would often occur. So, for example, a player might approach a Druid and say "Kind sir, can I ask you please for a SoW," the Spirit of Wolf spell, which increases running speed. It was very unusual for such a request to be turned down as it was typically seen as costing the caster very little and was in some ways interpreted as part of the work associated with being a class that could bestow such spells. Casting particular spells could be seen as a public-service duty, a way of contributing to the larger player base. Sometimes the player who received the buff would try and give the caster a bit of money in return, though just as often it was refused. Players who did not stick to some basic conventions were often thought of as rude, newbies, or young and socially inexperienced. In fact, the generosity of buff-giving was such that it was also not uncommon to see higher-level characters wander through lower-level zones buffing people randomly as they went. For a lower-level character, a "drive by" buff or regeneration heal could be an enormous advantage for their hunting session and in such cases public acknowledgement of the good deed was typical via shouts of "thanx" on the zone-wide communication channel.

As the game has progressed, however, this dynamic has changed somewhat. While there are still random acts of generosity in regards to doling out spells and within formal groups it is still the norm that people do not pay for buffs, it is now more common to see buffs advertised (or requested) in zone-wide channels via calls: "Donating 100 plat for a virtue for me and my partner." This is certainly in part because the cost to the caster has risen over the years. Whereas in the past spells were typically purchased from game vendors or "dropped" off killed monsters with a fair degree of frequency, the scenario for acquiring new spells at the higher levels has changed. Spells themselves have been altered such that they do a lot more relative to what they used to but are also now much rarer to find. This has produced an expensive market, where players pay upwards of 80, 000 platinum for some of the most powerful spells. As the personal costs have become higher the social norm toward nonfriend gift-giving has decreased. Players now see charging for buffs as a way of recouping their costs. Requests to be buffed for free are met with replies about the high price of obtaining the spell. We can see in the shift from a gift to market economy around buffs how the design choices—combining very powerful, highly sought-after spells with scarcity—has produced a companion effect in social behaviors.

It is also just as likely, however, that the age of the player base in relation to the game (i.e., there are more longtime *EQ* players than new ones) has contributed. In the beginning most characters simply could not afford this kind of monetized buff system. Over time the player base has become more experienced in the game, has acquired more wealth, and in turn can sustain not only a commodity orientation, but a fairly inflated pricing structure. The social norms of politeness and gift-giving have in part morphed into a kind of capitalistic exchange in response to a combination of design and character demographics.

However, it is certainly not the case that gift-giving and acts of generosity no longer occur in the game. They certainly do. But they now operate in a much narrower sphere—tighter associations form a more central part of the game and, in turn, gift economies more closely map onto friendship and formal affiliation networks like guilds. This is in part a result of a change in mobility within the world and the advanced experience of the player base. The issue of mobility brings up the example of porting.

In the beginning *EQ* was a game in which the work, and potential peril, it took to cross the vast geographical distances was not insignificant. Aside from the risks of encountering higher-level monsters, there was at a very basic level the need to run great distances to get around. Crossing continents required running through zones to get to a dock to wait for a ship that, when you got on it, actually simulated sailing by forcing the player to wait while the character crossed a virtual sea. For members of an evil race or class that was not allowed in good-aligned cities, journeys were even more dangerous and involved hiding, sneaking, taking underground passageways, and all kinds of additional time-consuming activities. For lower-level characters, travel often necessitated companionship to avoid being caught alone having to fend off a tough monster.

Into this structure the designers gave a helper—the classes of characters known as Druids and Wizards. Both are able to instantaneously transport (known in the game as "port") other players to locations all over the game world. Each are constrained a bit in this ability in that they are granted the spells to do so only as they progress through levels in the game and can only port to specific areas. Given how valuable a resource porting is, both classes quickly realized they could make some additional in-game money through the service. In the early days of the game it was common to hear shouts such as "Porting to WC, SR, NK, Nek, BB, Toxx + SoW, just send me a tell" or "Taxi to NRo, WC, NK meet at spire." Players would then contact the porter, meet up, and receive their transport. Quite often Druids would include an additional buff like Spirit of Wolf, making receiving a port from them often preferable. What was always striking was the way this service emerged from the player community and how it regulated prices associated with it. There is certainly no outline in the game manual for how the procedure should work, nor any specification of whether it should be free or cost.

The stability, of both the price (there was very little competitive pricing around porting, and on my server the price never wavered from 10 platinum coins, for example) and the practice once again testifies to the ability of player communities to self-organize and regulate.

Landscape and mobility in *EQ* now have a different configuration. Since newbies no longer are so tightly bound to their home and adjacent zones, only a handful of people still try to make a living by porting. People are, aside from zones requiring specific porters to get in, no longer reliant on each other for mobility.[35] Indeed, even the boat that previously provided all travel from the continent of Antonica no longer runs. While the world has quantitatively grown (from 65 zones when I started to 222 now), in many ways it feels smaller. This radical change in culture occurred in large part because of two key design decisions—the introduction of a centralized transport zone with NPC porters and the inclusion of automated self-service porting. The first of these was the creation of a zone named Nexus and nonplayer-character porters as part of the *Shadows of Luclin* expansion to the game. Players were now able to visit Wizard spires (the previous sites used by actual Wizard player porters) and meet NPCs who, when asked, give a free token for travel. Every seven minutes the spire automatically transports anyone holding the token and standing in the vicinity to the Nexus zone. The Nexus zone, a centralized transportation area located on the new moon, simply provided access points not only to new Luclin locations, but to Wizard spires in other parts of the world. It instantly became a way to port all around the game without the help of another player. Of course, one could still only port to preexisting wizard spires, but this limitation was soon eroded as well.

The ability of the general population to self-port was enhanced further in 2002, as part of the *Planes of Power* expansion to the game. While the previous change had kept intact the notion of needing someone to assist in porting (even if it was an NPC), in the *Planes* expansion this work was taken over by an object, a book on a stone pillar located in various zones in the game. When a player clicked on this book they were instantly transported to another new hub—the Plane of Knowledge (PoK)—where another appropriate stone could provide transport to any other zone needed. Almost overnight the economy around porting crashed. Players who had formerly made a decent living as a kind of in-game taxi service found themselves practically out of work. Just as significantly, however, was the way this simultaneously changed the nature of the locales throughout the world that were once transportation zones. In the past people often gathered around popular porting spots. They were not only the places for picking up rides but for finding buffs, safely resting surrounded by other players likely to help out if something attacked, or simply a convenient meeting spot. With the automatization of porting and the introduction of centralized transportation zones like PoK and the Nexus, the regional gathering places died, as did the social life around them.

The shift from provincialism to cosmopolitanism

[. . .]

One of the most fundamental and indeed most powerful design choices made for the game was the creation of money, objects, and the ability to trade. It may seem a bit odd to call this a choice given how ubiquitous these things are in MMOGs, but it is certainly the case that you could build a game that includes none of them (Farmer 2004). Like many MMOGs, *EQ* has included all of these, and as a result of these basic design decisions it has an economy and culture of not only gift-giving but of buying and selling.[36] Not insignificantly, *EQ* has for many years now had a permanent zone-based auction chat channel for players to use in advertising and looking for goods.

[. . .]

This market configuration required a number of things—people had to be "physically" present in the zone to hear about items and see goods, and the seller had to be present to continually call out auction information and make the transactions. With the advent of the Bazaar zone, processes changed radically. The Bazaar, located on the new moon in the game, was built for the sole purpose of buying and selling. Players now can purchase special "trader satchels" and, if they stand in a designated area, can initiate a command putting them into vendor mode. Vendor mode allows players to set fixed prices on their goods and automates the process of selling. If a player approaches and offers the designated amount, the trade is processed automatically. This allows the player to turn on vendor mode and leave her computer, turning the character into an automated merchandise machine. While the player must remain logged in, the character no longer needs to call out auctions, haggle prices, or manually initiate trades.

On the buyers' side, they can enter into the Bazaar and do fairly complex searches on items for sale, looking for things by name, by statistics, by price, by vendor, and by many other subcategories. Buyers can comparison shop instantly among all sellers present (and it is now fairly rare to find anyone selling things outside of the Bazaar). They no longer haggle. Indeed, 99% of the vendors a player encounters in the Bazaar are simply placeholders, avatars who will automatically carry out the formal wishes of their now-absent players. In the beginning the Bazaar was an extremely "laggy" zone to be in. There were simply too many people (equating a graphics overload) engaged in too much processing-heavy activity. Anyone with a less-than-lightning-fast computer often had to walk, avatar eyes on the floor so as not to see any complex graphics (read: other people), and try to find the particular vendor he had chosen. In another interesting change, the Bazaar has now been redesigned such that all other trader graphics can be turned off when entering the space. Instead of showing all the vendors selling their goods, the screen shows only the character's avatar in a large hall, maybe with a few other shoppers, and the one vendor chosen to purchase from.

This scenario certainly recalls situations like the rise of WalMart or the mall versus Main Street. But many players feel that life is much easier now and that running around buying and selling, paying outrageous prices because there was no competition, and all the time "wasted" having to sit and sell things has been fixed.[37] It is hard to not look at the empty wizard spires and druid circles and hear echoes of the death of local culture and public space, but many players claim that waiting for ports, sitting on ships that crossed virtual oceans, and paying for help were not any meaningful part of the game.[38]

Of course, people do form social networks even though these old meeting areas are gone, and emergent culture has not simply given way to centralized systems. While there is no vibrant East Commonlands tunnel culture on my old server anymore, people still hang out and chat in places like the Plane of Knowledge. Indeed, many players simply shake their heads in the face of the nostalgic old-timers who bemoan the way the game has developed. I do think there are some losses that come, however, with the conveniences of the Bazaar or teleportation devices. One of the tricky aspects about a game like EQ is that many of the things that are seen as nuisances or difficulties are exactly the mechanisms that propel the creation of emergent cultures and social networks. The lack of easy transportation options forced people to deal with and rely on each other, to set up practices that foster and facilitate that engagement, simultaneously creating value around a set of skills. Having to deal with an actual buyer for your goods can lead to negotiations of value, moments of generosity, and even trust. Just as in offline life, the move from provincialism to cosmopolitanism, from localism to globalism, may bring with it many quality-of-life improvements, but we would be remiss to not at least be clear-eyed about the costs associated with it as well. The design and structural choices by game developers are always deeply connected to the forms not only of play, but of sociality, that participants enact. As Michel Callon notes, "Indeed engineers transform themselves into sociologists, moralists or political scientists at precisely those moments when they are most caught up in technical questions" (1991, 136). In a game like *EverQuest* where the social aspects of the game drive its success and some of the pleasures derived from playing it, the relationship between design and culture, and the importance of understanding the ways those intersections feed into the game, cannot be overstated.

Notes

1   The number of subscribers to the game peaked at somewhere around 460,000 in the summer of 2003. For extensive information on subscribers across a number of MMOGs, see Bruce Sterling Woodcock's MMOGChart.com Web site.

2   A client program is an application that mediates between the server and the user's computer. It provides a more easy-to-use interface, and for text-based worlds integrates aspects like separate input lines, word wrap, and often triggers.

3   Many thanks to Richard Bartle for providing me with the opening text.

4   The term "MUD" originally stood for this particular game, not as it generally does now, for a whole class of text-based environments. Except in this first instance, this book uses the term "MUD" to refer to the overall genre of text-based multiuser games.

5   Personal communication via e-mail, June 2005. The quote originally appeared in the interactive version of The MUD Tree online, which was a repository of information about the genre.

6   For those particularly interested in the lineage, a prior version of the software, operated under the name *Club Caribe*, experimented with many of these basic properties. See Farmer, Morningstar, and Crockford (1994) for more on *Habitat*.

7   Its designers sometimes described it as 2 1/2 D, because of its use of perspective.

8   On a side note regarding the institutional structures these worlds were embedded in, eventually *The Palace* and *OnLive!* came to be owned by Communities, Inc., a company eventually run by F. Randall Farmer, one of the key designers for the first world, *Habitat*.

9   For an almost evangelical exploration of virtual worlds during this period see Bruce Damer's *Avatars!* book (1998).

10 Available at http://www.meridien59.com/.

11 The various names that have prefaced "*EverQuest*" can be a bit confusing, so a short history is in order. Essentially the general idea that an online game should be produced originated within Sony Interactive Studios of America (SISA) under the leadership of John Smedley. In 1998, SISA changed its name to 989 Studios and, when the decision was made that it should focus on console titles, Verant Interactive emerged as a spin-off venture to continue to support online game development. Created in 1999, Verant (with the group still headed up by John Smedley) went on to develop not only *EverQuest* but several other titles. Eventually Sony Online Entertainment (SOE), Verant's primary publisher, acquired the company (in 2000) and continues to develop and manage *EverQuest*.

12 Nick Yee suggests that about half of *EQ* players have at least tried out PvP (Yee 2001).

13 This aspect of the game has changed dramatically over the years—the numbers of players who are completely new to either the genre or the game itself has significantly decreased. Low-level characters now are often longtime players starting up new characters or those migrating over from other MMOGs, and this shift in demographic has had profound changes on the game itself.

14 The reference is to Simone de Beauvoir's famous statement: "One is not born, but rather becomes, a woman" (1989/1949, 267).

15 For more on this idea of communities of practice, see Bowker and Star 1999, Lave and Wenger 1991, and Star 1983.

16 When *EverQuest 2* (*EQ2*) launched, it "locked" encounters such that players were not able to help each other out once combat had begun unless they issued a specific command for help. Many players commented on the ways this "feature" actually undermined a fairly common, and useful, practice in the original game.

17 Unfortunately I do not have data on how this dynamic operates on servers dedicated to direct oppositional play, such as the "race war" server (Humans against Trolls, for example) or PvP. I have heard anecdotally

that despite server rules, helping often occurs anyway, so I would certainly not be surprised if there is a more complex mechanism for assistance on these servers.

18 Author unknown, *EverQuest Train Grading Points*, http://www.geocities.com/rustycat3/TrainGrading Points.html.

19 The underlying time requirement continues to present one of the biggest challenges to the genre in that it is difficult for the casual player to simply pop in for a brief period of time and accomplish much.

20 Nicolas Ducheneaut and Robert Moore (2004) have done some interesting work regarding how the design of *Star Wars Galaxies* affects various modes of interactivity. They point to not only the ways social interaction has been facilitated through particular game mechanisms, but instances in which "over-design" has also occurred, producing a more rote, instrumental pattern of play. From a slightly different perspective, Jeff Dyck, David Pinelle, Barry Brown, and Carl Gutwin (2003) have examined user-interface design in computer games and the ways various innovations lend to community formation and collaboration.

21 People are not notified when they have been added to a friend list, so it is a fairly private mechanism and does not build on the kinds of mutual signals you see in Web-based networks like Friendster or Orkut (see Donath and Boyd 2004 for more on social networking software like these).

22 Each *EQ* account is allowed eight characters per server, and many players maintain several characters at once. Indeed, some players have access to multiple accounts (and computers), thus multiplying their number of characters on each server. Given that each player also has her own network of contacts, any given group extends well beyond the six characters in the group list.

23 "Uber" (from the German *über*) is a term that is commonly used by players in reference to these guilds.

24 In Nick Yee's dataset he finds 69.5% of women playing with their romantic partners (versus 16.4% of men playing with theirs), 8.1% playing with a parent or child, and 15.9% with a sibling (Yee 2001). Contrary to more negative findings typically reported in the press, a study out of the Pew Internet and American Life Project also suggests that some American college students use gaming as a way to spend time with friends, stating that 20% "felt moderately or strongly that gaming helped them make new friends as well as improve existing friendships," and 65% of respondents did not feel that gaming had taken any time away from what they might spend with family and friends (Jones 2003).

25 Among pen-and-paper players this kind of importation of character and identity is not uncommon, at least for a player's first character. It points in part to the powerful ways game histories travel across play spaces and how people approach and make sense of a game based on their past experiences.

26 One of the more entertaining examples I found of this was the baseball player Doug Glanville of the Philadelphia Phillies explaining two recent home runs against former teammate Curt Schilling. He playfully recounted the way his home runs acted as retribution for the death of his character while playing with Schilling: "I vowed to revenge on the soul of Bingbong [his character] for the negligent actions of Cylc [Schilling's Dwarf Cleric]. . . . Not enough attention is paid to the off-the-field motivators that create nasty on-field grudges. I believe video atrocities top the list. Curt Schilling assassinated my lovable Dwarf Paladin in EverQuest, happily smiling as his character stood in the safety of the town guards" (Stark 2003).

27 "Power levelling" is when a high-level character helps a low-level character progress through the game at an accelerated rate, typically by helping kill tough monsters. While this type of play is not explicitly prohibited, it is seen by some as going against the spirit of the game. Nonetheless many players rely on it as a technique for integrating new friends into the game and feel that it is a central aspect of the social networking and bonding between players.

28 The line between these two is not completely clear, however. On more than one occasion I have been surprised to learn that a character I was playing with was the child of a fellow player – a revelation frequently revealed when the parent says something to the child in the game about doing homework or lapsed bedtimes.

29 Nick Yee (2001) has found that nearly half of *EQ* players would be interested in meeting their game friends offline (though 40% answered they had "mixed feelings" about doing so). Similarly, almost half of the *EQ* players responding to his survey found "their *EQ* friendships are comparable to their real-life friendships," with 15% feeling they were better and 37.7% feeling they "do not come close to their real-life relationships" (2001, 27). This trend is also mirrored in Axelsson and Regan's (2002) work on the MMOG *Asheron's Call*.

30 She later noted that "I got her hooked. And then she got her boyfriend, who she met on *ICQ*, so they play."

31 Available at http://www.eqatlas.com/.

32 Available at http://www.allakhazam.com/.

33 Available at http:graffe.com/.

34 The original no longer exists, but some of the community eventually moved over to a new site sponsored by a major gaming portal.

35 I should note that at the time of this writing a new expansion has been recently introduced and none of those new zones support the automatic porters. Not surprisingly, there has been some resurgence in people requesting the help of those with transport spells.

36 For example, Edward Castronova, in a landmark work, detailed how much trade was occurring around game items outside of the game world. His 2001 study of the economy of Norrath proposed that the "labors of the people [players] produce a GNP per capita somewhere between that of Russia and Bulgaria" (Castronova 2001). This phenomenon is discussed more in chapter 5.

37 There were, not surprisingly, innovative attempts by the player community to manage and regulate the markets within the game even before the implementation of the Bazaar. Third-party Web sites hosted items' sales data where buyers and sellers could input their recent purchase prices. When someone then wanted to buy or sell an item in the game, he could look it up at the site and see what it had most recently been going for on a particular server.

38 There is a companion discussion I am not covering here on the development of "instanced zones" in the game. These are spontaneously created replicas of specific areas for fixed sets of players. They are one way designers try to work around the difficulty produced when many people want access to the same monsters or areas simultaneously. Instead of people competing, negotiating, and generally finding a way to handle access (something they have historically done remarkably well in a self-organized fashion in the game) instanced zones solve the competition problem by providing multiple copies of the same thing. As Mikael Jakobsson (forthcoming) notes, while this is a design choice that breaks basic virtual-world models, *EQ* provides an interesting "test bed" for design concepts.

Chapter 34

DONNA HARAWAY

TECHNOSCIENCE IN HYPERTEXT

HYPERTEXT (see **Nelson**) and hypermedia are the architecture of the World Wide Web and many other digital media applications today. In this short piece Haraway explores hypertext both as a historical software form *and* for its tendency to function as a metaphor or metonym for broader thought about knowledge and connectivity in the contemporary world. So, this account of hypertext is grounded in an understanding of its history and technical form, but refuses to see these 'basics' as separable from uses, politics and potentials.

There are echoes of Bruno **Latour**'s insistence (in Part Two) on the radical connectedness of apparently disparate objects, activities and practices. Hypertext becomes a metaphor or metonym for connections, software and information linking through all kinds of objects and bodies. In one sentence, the technoscientific webs Haraway traces link together '[o]bjects like the fetus, chip/computer, gene, race, ecosystem, brain, database, and bomb'. Her approach to science studies differs from Latour's in its more upfront insistence on political, particularly feminist, motivations. Hence, she is concerned not only with analysing networks, but rather with urgent questions about *which* links and networks we would want to make or sustain in a yearning for 'possible worlds'.

Pragmatics

Technoscience in hypertext

> Considered from the point of view of pragmatics, a linguistic structure is a system of behavior.
>
> —Charles Morris, *Foundation of the Theory of Signs*[1]

> You cannot spill coffee on this text, or glance back at an earlier chapter, or suspend judgment, or just let it wash over you: you have to interact with the thing.
>
> —Marilyn Strathern, *Knowing Oceania*

Hypertext is a useful metaphor for the reading and writing practices I want to emphasize in Part III, Pragmatics. Anthropologist Marilyn Strathern's wonderful, irritated remark about hypertext mystification (Strathern 1994) is a good place to begin my own ambivalent engagement with this problematic metaphor and technology. Computer software for organizing networks of conceptual links, hypertext both represents and forges webs of relationships. Hypertext actively produces consciousness of the objects it constitutes. Practice makes perfect, in consciousness, as in agency. As any good technology does, hypertext "realizes" its subjects and objects. In short, hypertext is an ordinary bit of the material-discursive apparatus for the production of technoscientific culture.

At its most literal and modest, hypertext is a computer-mediated indexing apparatus that allows one to craft and follow many bushes of connections among the variables internal to a category. Hypertext is easy to use and easy to construct, and it can change common sense about what is related to what. Helping users hold things in material-symbolic-psychic connection, hypertext is an instrument for reconstructing common sense about relatedness. Perhaps most important, hypertext delineates possible paths of action in a world for which it serves simultaneously as a tool and metaphor. Making connections is the essence of hypertext. Hypertext can inflect our ways of writing fiction, conducting scholarship, and building consequential networks in the world of humans and nonhumans.

Mosaic was the name for software developed at the National Center for Supercomputer Applications at the University of Illinois that allowed computer users to gain access to the cobbled-together and dispersed resources of the Internet through hypertext-based browse protocols. The university, which holds the copyright, made the software freely available to users of desktop computers in homes and offices worldwide. In late 1994, about two million copies had been downloaded, and the rate of new downloadings from the Internet was about 50,000 copies per month. Also by late 1994, major corporations such as AT&T, Digital Equipment Corporation, and Time-Warner, Inc., had obtained licenses and were commercially developing the software for a wide range of uses. Mosaic's offspring and their competition will likely be the medium for global information distribution at the heart of business, academic, and cultural action in a world where chances of life and death are systematically reshaped by "computers."

Of course, "computers" is metonymic for the articulations of humans and nonhumans through which potent "things" like freedom, justice, well-being, skill, wealth, and knowledge are variously reconstituted. "The computer" is a trope, a part-for-whole figure, for a world of actors and actants, and not a Thing Acting Alone. "Computers" cause nothing, but the human and nonhuman hybrids troped by the figure of the information machine remake worlds. Software sufficiently powerful to revolutionize how computers are used—that is, how further hybrids of humans and nonhumans take shape and act—are, unfortunately, called "killer applications." Comparable only to the importance of word-processor and spreadsheet software, Mosaic-like browsers are likely to be such "killer applications" that reconfigure practice in an immense array of domains.[2] Mosaic was about the power to make hypertext and hypergraphic connections of the sort that produce the global subject of technoscience as a potent form of historical, contingent, specific human nature at the end of the millennium. Contesting how such subjects and hybrids are put together and taken apart is a critical feminist technoscientific practice.

Because of hypertext's physical/symbolic power to inflect the way we make the associations implicated in forging new "human universals," I adopt the metaphor for the webs of consequential, contingent connections explored in Part III of *Modest_Witness@Second_Millennium*. Pragmatics is meaning-in-the-making; pragmatics is the physiology of semiotics. In the 1930s, Charles Morris, the codifier of semiotics as it was practiced in the United States, could still argue that only organisms were sign interpreters. "Since most, if not all, signs have as their interpreters living organisms, it is a sufficiently accurate characterization of pragmatics to say that it deals with the biotic aspects of semiosis, that is, with all the psychological, biological, and sociological phenomena which occur in the functioning of signs" (Morris 1938: 30). In the 1990s, when it takes resolve to avoid the experience of machines as sign interpreters, only fossils make such organicist assumptions. The myriad, daily negotiations among humans and nonhumans that make up the consensus called technology are at least as important to characterizing sign interpreters as are the life science discourses Morris lists. However, for technoscientific citizens at the end of the millennium, neither people, animals, plants, protists, environments, nor artifacts can be represented by the impoverished schemata by which Morris imagined organisms. In the 1990s, across the former divide between subjects and objects and between the living and nonliving, meaning-in-the-making—the physiology of semiotics—is a more cyborg, coyote, trickster, local, open-ended, heterogeneous, and provisional affair. Sign interpreters are ontologically dirty; they are made up of provisionally articulated, temporally dispersed, and spatially networked actors and actants. In the most literal and materialist sense, connections and enrollments are what matter.

Making connections is the kind of physiology in feminist science studies that I want to foster. I want feminists to be enrolled more tightly in the meaning-making processes of technoscientific world-building. I also want feminists—activists, cultural producers, scientists, engineers, and scholars (all overlapping categories)—to be recognized for the articulations and enrollments we have been making all along within technoscience, in spite of the ignorance of most "mainstream" scholars in their characterizations (or lack of characterizations) of feminism in relation to both technoscientific practice and technoscience studies.

However, I also adopt the hypertext metaphor to put pressure on the sore spots in my soul that this figure inflames. Located in the subject position structured for me by the Internet address that is my book title, I am condemned to follow through with the consequences of my imagery. Although the metaphor of hypertext insists on making connections as practice, the trope does not suggest which connections make sense for which purposes and which patches we might want to follow or avoid. Communication and articulation disconnected from yearning toward possible worlds does not make enough sense. And explicit purposes—politics, rationality, ethics, or technics in a reductive sense—do not say much about the furnace that is personal and collective yearning for just barely possible worlds.

Paul Edwards (1994) details the trouble in his provocative argument about the similarities of poststructuralist theories of intertextuality, where meaning does not flow from the author/subject, to theories of the social construction of science, such as actor/network theory and the role of inscription devices, where meaning and knowledge also do not flow from scientists-as-creators. Edwards argues that the laudable common efforts to devise an approach to signification that does not depend upon the subject-as-creator—a project for which the metaphor and tool of hypertext is very useful—perversely end up importing unexamined psychologistic assumptions about cognitive abilities and the structure of minds. These assumptions typically have deep roots in behaviorism and artificial intelligence research, which provide impoverished representations of cognitive and social processes for humans and nonhumans alike. These representations reach back to the beginnings of U.S. semiotics, in which communication was theorized as a problem in control systems. The fundamental task was to understand, without mentalistic assumptions, how systems of signs affect behavior patterns. Organisms and machines alike were repositioned on the same ontological level, where attention was riveted on semiosis, or the process by which something functioned as a sign. "Semiotics, then, is not concerned with the study of a particular kind of object, but with ordinary objects in so far (and only in so far) as they participate in semiosis" (Morris 1938: 4).

These assumptions are problematic for the further development of science studies, for which a more usable—that is, psychologically, technologically, and politically lively—theory of actors, agents, actants, and practice is urgently needed. Decentering the godlike, individualist, voluntarist, human subject should not require a radical temperance project mandating abstinence from the strong drugs of networked desire, hope, and—in bell hooks's (1990) provocative term for an affective and political sensibility—"yearning."

Examining the limitations of hypertext for figuring social action, where questions of comprehension and significance cannot be ignored, Edwards explores the notion of "hypertension." I am informed by his arguments. Cognition and communication need such a third term, which allows the fruitful blurring of boundaries between outside and inside, human and machine, subject and object, that poststructuralism and science studies have developed. We do not need the automatism of crypto-behaviorism to explore the boundary blurring. Both people and things are more interesting and odder than that. Both people and things have a nonreducible trickster quality that resists categories and projects of all kinds. Yearning is fed from the gaps in categories and from the quirky liveliness of signs.

So, the figure of hypertext in this book should incite an inquiry into which connections matter, why, and for whom. Who and what are with and for whom? These are practical, pragmatic, semiotic, technical questions. The figure should likewise incite our lust for just barely possible worlds outside the explicit logic of any Net. The hypertext-based World Wide Web is the package of Internet services, developed by the European Laboratory for Particle Physics (CERN) high-energy physicists for following networks of textual and graphic data, that is used by Web browsers like Mosaic and Netscape, for example. This Web is less my trope for feminist pragmatics than is bell hooks's figure of yearning translated into a worldwide tissue of coalitions for a more livable technoscience.

Informatics hybridizes with biologies in the New World Order. Thus, in order to sketch an effective pragmatics for a mutated modest witness, I must splice my hypertext trope to a figure derived from biology. Totipotent stem cells are those cells in an organism that retain the capacity to differentiate into any kind of cell. Stem cells can regenerate the whole array of cell types possible for that life form. The genome and the nongenomic apparatus of a stem cell remain unfixed, undetermined, multitalented. After irradiation, the stem cells of the hematopoietic system must be restored if the many cell types of the blood and immune system are to reappear. After wounding, stem cells in some organisms can regenerate lost organs or even whole beings. Stem cells are the nodes in which the potential of entire worlds is concentrated.

Objects like the fetus, chip/computer, gene, race, ecosystem, brain, database, and bomb are stem cells of the technoscientific body. Each of these curious objects is a recent construct or material-semiotic "object of knowledge," forged by heterogeneous practices in the furnaces of technoscience. To be a construct does NOT mean to be unreal or made up; quite the opposite. Out of each of these nodes or stem cells, sticky threads lead to every nook and cranny of the world. Which threads to follow is an analytical, imaginative, physical, and political choice. I am committed to showing how each of these stem cells is a knot of knowledge-making practices, industry and commerce, popular culture, social struggles, psychoanalytic formations, bodily histories, human and nonhuman actions, local and global flows, inherited narratives, new stories, syncretic technical/cultural processes, and more.

For example, a seed contains inside its coat the history of practices such as collecting, breeding, marketing, taxonomizing, patenting, biochemically analyzing, advertising, eating, cultivating, harvesting, celebrating, and starving. A seed produced in the biotechnological institutions now spread around the world contains the specifications for labor systems, planting calendars, pest-control procedures, marketing, land holding, and beliefs about hunger and well-being. Similarly, in Joseph Dumit's argument, a database is a technical and utopic object that structures future accessibility. A database "is an ideal place where all elements are equal in the grid—and everyone can access all of them."[3] The database is a condensed site for contestations over technoscientific versions of democracy and freedom. Both the genome and the brain are databases—literally—built in the experimental, multidisciplinary, documentary, proprietary, information-management, and other practices of the Human Genome Project and the Human Brain Mapping Project.[4]

I cannot follow here each of my stem cells, much less the much larger set that would be needed for the excessive account of technoscience that I crave. But I try to work out at least some of the knots that constitute genes, databases, chips/computers, seeds, cyborgs, races, and fetuses. My accounts are clearly not exhaustive, nor are they rigorously causal, but they are intended to be more than merely suggestive about the connective tissues, lubricants, codes, and actors in the worlds we must care about. The articulations among the stem cells, and within each of them, are links that matter in what gets affectionately called the "real world." How do technoscientific stem cells link up with each other in expected and unexpected ways and differentiate into entire worlds and ways of life? How do the differently situated human and nonhuman actors and actants encounter each other in interactions that materialize worlds in some forms rather than others? My purpose is to argue for a practice of situated knowledges in the worlds of technoscience, worlds whose fibers infiltrate deep and wide throughout the tissues of the planet, including the flesh of our personal bodies.

Notes

1   *Foundation* (Morris 1938) is the second publication in the important Chicago series, the International Encyclopedia of Unified Science, that later published Kuhn (1962).
2   My discussion of Mosaic is based on Coates (1994).
3   Joseph Dumit, personal communication, December 4, 1992. Dumit's dissertation (1995) on the development of positron emission tomography (PET) brain imaging focuses on the professional, technical, popular, legal, and industrial interactions that forge new disciplines and discourses. His project examines closely the interdisciplinary development of computer sciences and the interfacing of such specialities with neurosciences in brain-scanning research.
4   The Human Genome Project haunts many chapters in *Modest_Witness@Second_Millennium*. On genome databases at the beginning of the 1990s, see "Genome Issue: Maps and Database," *Science* 254 (October 11, 1991): 201–07. For the Human Brain Mapping Project, see Roberts (1991) and AAAS 1993. The 1990s is the "Decade of the Brain," a designation for transnational technoscience something like the United Nations' Decade of the Woman or Year of the Child. Such labels signal conferences, declarations, and high-status locations. Data from molecular neurobiology, systems neuroscience, developmental neurobiology, and genetics, as well as new graphics and data storage capacities of computers, have revolutionized brain-mapping practices, necessitating major changes in the nature of atlases and research interactions. Nonorganic "brains" also continued in the 1990s as objects of rapt technoscientific attention in artificial intelligence and robotics research. For example, see Travis 1994. In the last decade of the millennium, the action lies in the "marriage of computational models and experimentation" (Baringa 1990: 524–26).

Chapter 35

GEERT LOVINK

UPDATING TACTICAL MEDIA

G EERT LOVINK'S DISCUSSION here is bound up in a particular moment of very recent technocultural history, a history of new media art, media activism and 'hacktivism' in the late 1990s and early years of the current century. He is concerned with the relationships between this online activity and media production, Web 2.0 developments, and the 'anti-globalisation' street protests in Seattle, Gleneagles and Genoa. The term 'tactical media' encompasses the alternative journalism of Indymedia (**Kidd**) and the aesthetic and critical concerns of new media art (**Marks**), and pursues critical and creative interventions in political and social movements and actions.

These interventions are generally short-lived, hence they are *tactical* rather than attempting the sustained programmatic political *strategies* of the historical Left. Indeed, Lovink is concerned with explaining the strengths, weaknesses and challenges of tactical media activities and their networked structures. In this regard, his discussion has much broader implications for cultural and political action in the network age. Networks themselves, he points out, do not necessarily or automatically undermine centralised power structures. They are ambiguous formations, creating possibilities for openness and democracy, but always 'on the brink of collapse'. http://networkcultures.org/wpmu/portal/

Strategies for media activism

Running updates is an integral part of our technological culture. It is considered a necessary evil. To not download the necessary patches is seen as suicidal. In contemporary theory production, this practice has not yet been introduced. Within the humanities and the arts, wikis remain underutilized. Theory is still considered a terrain of the sole author who contemplates the world, preferably offline, surrounded by a pile of books, a fountain pen, and a notebook. This is of course a caricature, but where exactly is the obstacle located? Apart from a text having different versions before it is published, most writers do not take out bugs or flaws after publishing the text even though word processing and online text editing have become so easy. Instead of updating old texts, the consensus is that it is better to come up with something new altogether. This not only satisfies producers and users; newness is what the market demands. Radio maker and programmer Alexander Klosch from Weimar led me to the difference between updating and upgrading. Wikipedia continuously upgrades and downgrades its articles. Whereas updating has a time element, upgrading usually refers to quality and status. A change does not by definition result in an improvement or a disqualification. According to Klosch, the update is best placed in collaborative work. A single maintainer is often overstretched keeping a complex structure up-to-date. This is where a community or smaller group of maintainers comes into play. Thus far, online platforms are rarely used to create—and change—theoretical concepts. Theory books rarely make it to a next print run, much less are ever rewritten for a second edition. The common belief holds that outdated theories are hard to use, have bugs and limitations, and can only be read under the rubric of history. In the Change Society in which we are stuck, yesterday's concepts are not just worn out; they are by definition wrong as they are deconstructed at the time of their release.

In this chapter, I propose critical updates for the concept of tactical media. I provide a subjective overview of current debates about new media and the role they play in global social movements. In the first part, I look into the status of the tactical media meme since it embarked on its remarkable journey. Then I discuss strategies of the biggest emerging political force in decades—the so-called antiglobalization movement—and discuss some books about this topic. It has often been remarked that this movement is not one, it has many faces and names. In some instances, I speak of the global justice movement, in others of multitudes. Some call this multi-headed dragon the "movement of movements." Another name, the "other-globalization movement," expresses the desire to go beyond the anti-position of street protests in order to emphasize the common search for alternatives. Here I specifically look into strategies of critical new media culture in the postspeculative phase after dotcommania, 9/11, the big mobilizations from Seattle to Gleneagles and, in particular, inquire about the relationship between the real and the virtual. Instead of burying the tactical media concept, which could have been done years ago, we may as well celebrate its robustness. Missed the autumn of tactical media? Then join the renaissance of tactics!

Revisiting tactical media

Let's briefly look back. The term *tactical media* arose in the aftermath of the fall of the Berlin Wall as a renaissance of media activism, blending old school political work and artists' engagement with new technologies. The early 1990s saw a growing awareness of gender issues, an exponential growth of media industries, and the increasing availability of cheap DIY equipment—creating a new sense of self-awareness among activists, programmers, theorists, curators, and artists. Media were no longer seen as merely tools for the struggle, but experienced as virtual environments whose parameters were permanently under construction. This was the golden age of tactical media, open to issues of aesthetics and experimentation with alternative forms of storytelling. However, these liberating techno-practices did not immediately translate into visible social movements. Rather, they symbolized the celebration of media freedom, in itself a great political goal. The DIY media that was used varied widely—from video, DVDs, cassettes, 'zines and flyers to music styles such as rap and techno—and the content was equally diverse. A commonly shared feeling was that politically motivated activities, be they art or research or advocacy work, were no longer part of a closed and suspicious identity circuit. They could intervene in pop culture without necessarily having to compromise with the system. With everything up for negotiation, new coalitions could be formed.

The origins of tactical media go back to the Next Five Minutes (N5M) festival in Amsterdam, a new media event with a clear political angle that grew out of a coalition of cultural institutions, individuals, and groups. Around mid-1992 a name had to be chosen for an art, activism, and media festival and it became "N5M: Tactical Television." The first N5M took place in January 1993 and focused on the camcorder revolution and the events in Eastern Europe after the fall of the Berlin Wall. In March 1996, during the Internet boom, the second edition took place, and the name was changed to Tactical Media. The first systematic text on the topic, written by David Garcia and me, appeared in 1997. The third festival was held in March 1999, days before the outbreak of the Kosovo war. The post-9/11 fourth edition took place in September 2003. N5M never culminated into an organization. It did not become an annual or biannual event and never obtained a legal structure or a stable Web site. From the beginning, N5M had been a temporary coalition of individuals and institutions that came together to organize the festival—and then separate. Also remarkable is the fact that the event thus far has not resulted in a (sustainable) network. To some extent, Indymedia took over this role from 2000 onward, but Indymedia misses an imaginative and artistic agenda, mainly due to its narrow focus on news.

The current movements worldwide cannot be understood outside of the diverse and often very personal desire for digital freedom of expression. Tactical media is a short-term concept, born out of disgust for ideology. It surfs on the waves of events, enjoying the opening up of scenes and borders, on the lookout for new alliances. Curious, not afraid of difference, it is not bound to certain formats or platforms. It comes with a positive attitude toward contemporary digital technology. It is more exploratory than confrontational. It wants to make a new start for activism and reach new audiences. But, as Paul Garrin warns, "Tactical Media is not only something that Media Activists engage in. It's advertising, corporate psychological warfare of Perception Management." My critique of tactical media is not its short-lived character. By definition, tactical media is nonsustainable, always on the verge of disappearance. Its unstable nature creates situations while setting clear limits for further growth.

Let's not repeat the definitions that are floating around. Since early 2006, there has been a Wikipedia entry for tactical media. What is worth mentioning is the way in which this term has been adopted by numerous groups and individuals worldwide. Besides the tactical media scene in Brazil, one could think of Tactical Tech, an Amsterdam-based network of free software open source developers in non-Western countries, or of the Slovenian artist Marko Peljhan, whose Makrolab has been given the tactical media adjective. In his book *Protocol*, Alex Galloway mentions a few more projects, from computer viruses to cyberfeminism and games. What brings these tactical initiatives together is their carefully designed workings, their aesthetics beyond the question of taste. Being neither cute nor ugly, neither good nor bad, tactical media appears, strikes, and disappears again. Instead of the old school rituals of negation and refusal, tactical media engages makers and users, producers and viewers, into a game of appearances and disappearances. Key to tactical media is its mix of art and activism, and a shared critical awareness of style, design, and aesthetics. This is also its most vulnerable part, as most activists, journalists, and intellectuals do not necessarily subscribe to its agenda, or are even informed about its existence.

Tactical media celebrates disorganization. There is not even an electronic mailing list that brings together tactical media practitioners. Net-time, Spectre, Fibreculture, and IDC might do this, in part, but none of these lists is focused on media activists. Agreed, tactical media makers meet up every now and then, but rarely create networks among themselves, yet they are often grouped around an event or incident. Tactical media workers seem to have other identities.

[. . .]

It is not hard to see that the challenge for tactical media is no longer technical but resides in knowing how to negotiate differences within a loose and temporal network structure.

All too easily, the energy of tactical media practitioners is getting lost inside the locality called Internet, a place we all love to hate. It is tempting to get lost there and believe in the Internet as the "medium to end all media." What tactical media makers do is discourage high expectations around the liberating potential of all technologies, both old and new, while not falling into the trap of cultural pessimism. Instead, we look for ways to connect the banal with the exclusive, the popular with high art, common trash with expensive branded commodities. On a technical level this means finding ways to connect, relay, disconnect—and again reconnect—a veritable stampede of pirate radio waves, video art, animations, hoaxes, wi-fi networks, music jam sessions, Xerox cultures, performances, grassroots robotics, cinema screenings, street graffiti, and (don't forget!) computer code. There is a lot of mutual aid in building up centers and networks, up to the point when it is time to leave them to others, to history, and move on. The strength of tactical media is that it can bring people together. Its weakness is its lack of borders and programmatic statements. Tactical media has a tendency to fall apart in numerous micro swarms. There is nothing against that—that is the nature of coalitions. What actually happens goes global. There are realities that cut across borders and across the old North-South divide, says Saskia Sassen. Activists in Sao Paolo and Manila share an emergent geography of centrality that connects them, through rather unstable connections, with groups in New York or Paris. Small organizations that have little financial resources meet up with like-minded initiatives from dozens of countries, spread across the planet, from Latin America to South Asia. We see similar connections established in visual arts, music, and free software. How do we gain cultural sensitivity? How do we master the labor-intensive task of arranging visas for African participants? Think twice if you think you want to use the term *global*.

The time of the movement

Different phases of the global movement are becoming visible, all of which have distinct political, artistic, and aesthetic qualities. By the end of the 1990s, the postmodern "time without movements" had come to pass. Organized discontent began to rise against neo-liberalism, global warming, labor exploitation, and numerous other issues. Equipped with networks and arguments, backed up by decades of research, a hybrid movement—wrongly labeled as "antiglobalization"—gained momentum. One of the particular features of this movement was its apparent inability and unwillingness to answer the question that is typical of any kind of movement on the rise or any generation on the move: What is to be done? There was and is no answer, no alternative—either strategic or tactical—to the existing world order, to the dominant mode of globalization.

Moreover, maybe this is the most important and liberating conclusion: There is no way back to the twentieth century, the protective nation state, and the gruesome tragedies of the "left." It has been good to remember—but equally good to throw off—the past. The question "What is to be done?" should not be read as an attempt to reintroduce some form of Leninist principle. The issues of strategy, organization, and democracy belong to all times. We neither want to bring old policies back through the backdoor, nor do we think that this urgent question can be dismissed by invoking crimes committed under the banner of Lenin, however justified such arguments are. When Slavoj Žižek looks in the mirror he may see Father Lenin, but that's not the case for everyone. It is possible to wake up from the nightmare of the history of communism and ask: What is to be done? Can a multitude of interests and backgrounds still ask that question, or is the only agenda the one defined by the summit calendar of world leaders and the business elite?

Nevertheless, the movement of movements has spread like wildfire. At first sight, it appeared to use a traditional medium: the mass-mobilization of tens of thousands in the streets of Seattle, hundreds of thousands in the streets of Genoa. Tactical media networks played an important role in this coming into being. From now on, pluriformity of issues and identities was a given reality. Difference is here to stay and no longer needs to legitimize itself against higher authorities such as the Party, the Union, or the Media. Compared to previous decades, this is its biggest gain. There are no longer any central meaning structures. The Church has been replaced by a never-ending parade of celebrities that provide us with comfort and hope. The multitudes are not a dream or some theoretical construct, but a reality. This world is decentralized and fragmented. That is where the trouble starts: How do multitudes communicate over distances, and in what language? How do they create common ground without using traditional intermediaries? How do they operate in the market of micro-identities? And most of all, once they gather, how do they discuss and come to make decisions?

If there is a strategy, it is not contradiction but complementary existence. Despite theoretical deliberations, there is no contradiction between the street and cyberspace—one fuels the other. Protests against the WTO, neo-liberal EU policies, and party conventions have all been staged in front of the gathered world press. Indymedia centers crop up as parasites of mainstream media. Instead of having to beg for attention, protests take place under the eyes of the world media during summits of politicians and business leaders, seeking direct confrontation. Alternatively, symbolic sites are chosen. These include border regions such as in East–West Europe, South Europe–Africa, United States–Mexico, or refugee detention centers at the Amsterdam and Frankfurt airports, the centralized Eurocop database in Strasbourg, or the Woomera detention center in the South Australian desert. Rather than merely objecting to it, the global entitlement of the movement adds to the ruling mode of globalization a new layer of globalization from below.

[. . .]

Repeatedly we see that local events, not general ideas, make up the movements. In that sense the movement is "post-1989" in its refusal of ideologies, and this is an element the theorists, in particular those from Italy and France, still have yet to come to grips with. The "protestivals" have a carnivalesque militancy that has not yet been properly described—Spinoza and Heidegger may not be the adequate sources for it. Even though we read a strong sense of urgency in Kingsnorth's stories, there is no "state of exception" or even a permanent crisis. Kingsnorth rightly analyses the State of the Globe in its full potentiality. One might also read this as the naïve optimism of youth, but that easy judgment overlooks the wild social variety of participants in the protests worldwide. This is not a wave. Rather, it is a set of eruptions that have started to resonate and are transforming into something else.

During the late 1990s, the Seattle movement against corporate globalization gained momentum, both on the street and online. But, can we really speak of a synergy between street protests and online "hacktivism"? What the street and the Internet had in common was their conceptual stage. The sheer potentiality was enormous. Both real and virtual protests risk being stuck at the level of demo design, no longer grounded in actual topics and local situations. This means the movement never gets out of its beta stage. Only at an abstract level can we link struggles and events, but often this type of analysis is more of a religious nature in order to provide people with hope. There is a networked solidarity, yes, but no synergy effect. At first glance, reconciling the virtual and the real seems to be a rhetorical act. Radical pragmatists have often emphasized the embodiment of online networks in real-life society, dispensing with the real/virtual contradiction. Internet activism, like the Internet itself, is always a hybrid, a blend of old and new input and output devices, haunted by geography, gender, race, and other political factors. There is no pure disembodied zone of global communication, as the 1990s cyber-mythology claimed. Nevertheless, can we make a jump over these all too obvious statements? Instead of promoting correctness, it may be more interesting to instigate education initiatives aimed at bringing social movements into the Web 2.0 age. Instead of promoting the use of obscure free software that is still in a beta version, it may be better to install easy-to-use blogs and wikis.

Limits of tactical networks

The call of many artists and activists to return to real life does not provide us with a solution as to how alternative new media models can be raised to the level of mass (pop) culture. Yes, street demonstrations raise solidarity levels and lift us up from the daily solitude of one-way media interfaces. However, we should ask the question "What comes after the demo (design)?" of both new media and the movements. In his text *Demoradical vs. Demoliberal Regulation*, Alex Foti proposes labeling the postmovement activity The Pink Conspiracy.

Women's emancipation and the end of the patriarchal family with its unequal gender roles, feminist movements, gay mobilizations, queer politics, full civil rights for lesbian-gay-bisexual-transgender people, the assertion of reproductive rights against papist reaction and equality of access to political representation for women represent an epochal earthquake for Western politics. In a movement context, the pink carnival of rebellion was the major innovative form of political expression emerging from the Prague-Göteborg-Genoa cauldron, next to, but separate from, the white overalls and black blocs, the two other distinctive youth expressions of the anti-globalization movement. Pink collars are the present of social work and pink movements are the future of social progress.

The pink coalition, says Foti,

> would already manifest itself in the precarity movement that is at the brink of becoming a global movement. On Mayday 2006 one single, huge yell was heard from Berlin to Los Angeles: "No borders! Stop persecution! Halt discrimination! Fuck precarity! Beat inequality!" It is to me self-evident that Mondo Mayday cannot wait any longer.

Foti also admits this isn't the heady 1960s. The 1960s movements resulted in environmentalism, so where will today's movement go after its adolescence? The negative, pure, and modernist level of the conceptual has hit the hard wall of demo design as Peter Lunenfeld described it in his book *Snap to Grid*. The question thus becomes how to jump beyond the one-off event and start prototyping? What comes after the siege of yet another summit of CEOs and their politicians? How long can a movement grow and stay virtual? Or in IT terms, what comes after demo design, after the countless PowerPoint presentations, broadband trials, and Flash animations? Will Linux ever break out of the geek ghetto? The feel-good factor of the open, ever growing crowd, as conceived by novelist and theorist of crowds and power Elias Canetti, will wear out; demo fatigue will set in. We could ask, does your Utopia version have a use-by date? We cannot merely answer such questions in terms of the inevitable cycles of excitement-experience-confrontation-frustration. Kenneth Wirbin discusses another aspect of Internet activism, namely the danger of mistaking forwarding of information with activism.

People hide behind references and theories, they are also increasingly inclined, in our ever expanding open social order, to hide behind forwarding information; not taking a position one way or the other, just forwarding. In a world that favors forwarding information over personal positions, critical engagement will continue to wane and ultimately vanish, not just on listservs and blogs, but everywhere. These are the contradictions and ambiguities of living in a social order in which life is controlled through its very openness.

Rather than making up yet another concept, it is time to ask the question of how software, interfaces, and alternative standards can be installed in society. Ideas may take the shape of a virus, but society can hit back with even more successful immunization programs: appropriation, repression, and general neglect. We face a scalability crisis. Most movements and initiatives find themselves in a trap. The strategy of becoming "minor" (as in Deleuze and Guattari's concept of a "minor literature") is no longer a positive choice but the default option. Small groups are presently being catered to—what has yet to be facilitated is how to scale up and build temporary coalitions that can claim hegemony. At the moment, designing a successful cultural virus and getting thousands of visitors to your Weblog will not bring you beyond the level of a short-lived spectacle. The challenge is to use media while going beyond them. Culture jammers are no longer outlaws but should be seen as established rebel experts in guerrilla communication.

Today's movements are in danger of being stuck in self-satisfying protest mode. With access to the political process effectively blocked, further mediation seems the only available option. However, gaining more and more brand value in terms of global awareness may turn out to be like overvalued stocks: they might pay off, they might turn out to be worthless. The pride of "We have always told you so" is boosting the morale of minority multitudes, while delegating legitimate fights to the level of Truth and Reconciliation Commissions (often parliamentary or Congressional), long after the damage is done.

Instead of arguing for reconciliation between the real and the virtual, I would call for a rigorous synthesis of social movements' technology. Instead of taking the "the future is now" position derived from cyber-punk, a lot could be gained from a radical reassessment of the techno-revolutions of the last ten to fifteen years. Dotcoms invested their entire venture capital in (old media) advertisements. Their belief that media-generated attention would automatically draw users in and turn them into customers proved unfounded. This is still the case. Social networks such as Flickr, Orkut, and MySpace did not grow because of a giant television advertisement budget. To remix old and new media sounds good but is not necessarily the way to go if you want to create movements. Information forms us. However, new consciousness results less and less in measurable action. Activists are only starting to understand the impact of this paradigm. What if information merely circles around in its own parallel world? What is to be done if carnival-like demonstrations cannot transcend the level of the Spectacle and the transnational protester gets tired of summit hopping?

The hype of networks reveals a conceptual crisis of collaboration and cooperation. The confusing aspect of networking is the fact that large formations of power apparently defy networks. There is growing confusion if blogs and social networks are mainstream or remain a hobby in the fringes, placed outside of the economy where real money circulates. The same can be said of Internet-based activism, in which case it becomes unclear whether the Internet is marginal or vital in today's struggles. Habermas' Internet description as an informal public sphere that has to submit to the higher authority of formal media such as publishing houses, newspapers, and magazines is, in the end, a moral judgment as to how the world should function. Both positions are perfectly valid. The Internet can be secondary while becoming powerful at the same time. There is nothing spectacular about networking. This is exactly why leading intellectuals and theorists are not aware of the current power transformations. They still sit in front of the television, watch the news, and perhaps recently bought a DVD player. Corporations and institutions are still in the process of opening up. The introduction of computer networks within organizations over the past decade has changed workflows but has not reached the level of decision-making. In this period of transition and consolidation, we get confusing answers to the question of whether new media is part of mainstream pop culture and this puts tactical media in a difficult position of stagnation, much like new media arts (see chapter 8). Whereas it is easy to see that networks have become the dominant mode of power, this is still not the case for power in the narrow sense. This is why the call for openness, transparency, and democracy, on both micro- and macro-levels, can still contain progressive elements and should be seen as a counterpart to popular conspiracy theories that complain about closed elites, knowing that openness is the new frontier of power formation.

The classical dichotomies of public/private and global/local have become useless and even obsolete. These binaries are replaced by the flexible attitudes of managing singularities and fluid differences. Rather than challenging power, networking environments act as carriers for virtual self-management and self-control, right up to the point of crashing. Networked environments are inherently unstable and their temporality is key, much like events. Networks are dense social structures on the brink of collapse and it is questionable that there are sustainable models that can "freeze" them. Maybe it is better to understand networking as syncope of power, a temporary loss of consciousness and posture, rather than a panacea against corruption, commodification, resentment, and the general dumbness of traditional hierarchies. The result of networking often is a rampant will to powerlessness that escapes the idea of collective progress under the pretext of participation, fluidity, escapism, and over-commitment.

Many activists easily get lost in the overload of e-mail messages, Weblogs, and chat exchanges. The subjective feeling, having to swim against a tsunami of noise and random tension, can no longer be explained by a lack of media literacy. Activists no longer care about the next wave of technologies, or simply use them without bothering too much about the politics and potentials that are attached to the features. Software and interface solutions can be helpful, but often only temporarily assist users to get a handle on complex information flows. This often results in the abandoning of collective communication somewhere halfway—leaving the online participants with the unsatisfactory feeling that the online conversation got stuck or is broken and unable to reach a conclusion. After an exciting first phase of introductions and debates, networks are put to the test: either they transform into a body that is capable of acting or they remain stable on a flat line of information exchange, with the occasional reply of an individual who dares to disagree. In the meantime, street events occur—the anti-Iraq war demonstrations, the riots in the outskirts of Paris in November 2005, and the student protests in Paris in early 2006—proving that network technologies can support protests, but not necessarily ignite them.

At the same time, we are facing a backlash toward romantic and outdated forms of representation, hierarchies, and command on many terrains. Due to the conceptual wall that an online community often finds hard to cross, and unable to deal with its own democracy (let alone the one that rules society), classic, informal forms of representation fill the gap. This is part of a larger process of normalization, in which networks are integrated in existing management styles and institutional rituals. However, the progress of networking technologies are not linear nor are they irreversible, as it appears in the techno-naivety of some NGOs. It is often hard to admit that the realm of power (agenda setting, decision making) exists relatively autonomous of the techno-sphere as F2F (face-to-face) meetings. Instead, we all hang onto the idea that decentralized networks somehow dissolve power over time. Meanwhile, networking environments also create specific dispositives that are coordinating new forms of power, consisting of a variety of elements. To research these new elements—the statements, norms, standardizations, practices, and institutions as an ensemble organizing the transactions from power to knowledge and knowledge to power—goes far beyond the current talk about the information society. It also exceeds the attempts to find and replace information with knowledge, as well as any attempt to locate and identify an object of networking, let alone a purpose.

Chapter 36

DOROTHY KIDD

INDYMEDIA.ORG
A new communications commons

POPULAR POLITICAL MOVEMENTS have been generating their own alternatives to governmental and official news media forms and channels for centuries. In this essay, Dorothy Kidd examines what she calls a 'watershed in a historical continuum of radical activist media', but links it too, beyond media and news production, to historical political movements, from the late middle ages to the post-war period, that challenged private property in favour of locally organised and collective 'commons'.

This watershed in alternative media and collective action, then, is the 'grand transformation' made possible by the Internet and its facilitation of decentralised and bottom-up networks and communication, and – more recently – by cheaper digital video cameras and computers for editing and distribution. Kidd offers a brief history of the Internet and its implications for 'citizen' or 'activist' journalism and NGOs. This collective and voluntary sharing of alternative news and opinion was energised by responses to the coverage of the aftermath of September 11 2001 and the anti-globalisation protests around the same time. The convergence of these social movements, independent journalists and media producers, technology and technical expertise made IMC (the Independent Media Center) and its global reach possible.

Lovink (this part) includes Indymedia within his broader category of tactical media. http://www.indymedia.org/

On September 11, 2001, I first heard about the attacks on the World Trade Center and Pentagon from conversation with the early morning regulars at my local café in San Francisco, California. Returning home, I quickly turned to three other sources of information—network television, KPFA-FM radio, and the World Wide Web's indymedia.org, the site of the Independent Media Center (IMC).

I flipped around the TV and saw that all the major networks had canceled their regular advertising-driven programming to provide round-the-clock coverage of the attacks and their aftermath. For the following month, the networks provided more hard news about government, military, national, and especially international affairs than had been seen in decades. However, as the Project for Excellence in Journalism Report (CJR) confirms, the shift in news agenda was only in the subject in focus, and not the overall approach (2001, 1). The selection and emphasis of news content were still within the very tight framework that favors U.S. political and economic elites (Ryan, Carragee, and Meinhofer 2001; Smith et al. 2001). There was little criticism of the policies and actions of the U.S. military and the Bush administration; little discussion of alternative political views, especially of peace movements; and little talk of the international political and economic context that might help explain this crisis (Solomon 2001).

My second source, Pacifica Radio, began immediately to explore that larger context, absent in the corporate media. The morning of September 11, Berkeley's KPFA-FM interrupted their regular programming to run a live feed from New York's new program, "Democracy Now," broadcasting only blocks away from Ground Zero. The "special" team provided coverage of the impact on New York and Washington, as well as background interviews about the history of Afghanistan, and especially of U.S. relations in Afghanistan and the Middle East. For the next month, "Democracy Now" and KPFA continued the dual focus, covering stories from perspectives missing in network TV coverage: the peace protests in New York, San Francisco, and around the world, and the voices of victims' families who stood for peace; illegal immigrants lost in the Twin Towers; New Yorkers trying to reconstruct their lives amidst the environmental and fiscal devastation; individuals from the Arab and South Asian communities who were targets of discrimination, violence, and police detention in the United States; as well as journalists, activists, and scholars from around the world.

One might imagine that Pacifica would step up to provide this coverage. Started by pacifists after the Second World War, the first station, KPFA, was founded to counter the build-up of the U.S. military-industrial complex and to challenge the monopoly control and commercialization of the broadcast media. Since then, KPFA and the noncommercial listener-supported Pacifica Network it formed have modeled a communications resource that draws from "sources of news not commonly brought together" and on-air dialogue between people of widely differing political and philosophical views (Land 1999; Lasar 1999). Pacifica had been a leading independent media voice for several decades, covering the McCarthy era, the Vietnam War, and the civil rights movement, as well as the rise of the new social movements of African Americans, Native Americans, women, Latino Americans, lesbians, and gays.

However, in the 1990s, a series of disputes over the makeup of programming and leadership had precipitated a major crisis. Supporters and staff were embroiled in lawsuits, workplace disputes, and public actions with the national management. By the fall of 2001, a series of firings, bans, and strikes led to a decline in news and other programming. Amy Goodman, host of "Democracy Now," was banned from the New York Pacifica station, WBAI, and she and her staff were working as independent contractors, sharing a studio with other media activists in a local community television center. While "Democracy Now" still provided cutting-edge commentary and dissent, a new generation of social movements, organized around anti-corporate globalization, had given rise to a new critical medium of independent news and commentary.

"Don't Hate the Media—Become the Media"[1]

My third choice was to browse IMC's Web site, which I have followed through meetings, conferences, collaborations, and interviews since its beginnings. Within the first few days following September 11, the site featured street-level descriptions of peace vigils and demonstrations in the United States and internationally. On the Israeli site, I also found a strong comment from a human rights activist, condemning the attack and countering the corporate media's attempt to link it to Palestinians. All served as important correctives to the barrage of support on TV for the U.S. government's military build-up.

Indymedia is made up of over sixty autonomously operated and linked Web sites in North America and Europe, with a smaller number in Africa, Latin America, and Asia. The first IMC was started in Seattle in 1999, just before the encounter between the World Trade Organization (WTO) and the social movements opposed to its policies. Early on in the counter-WTO planning, several different groups had recognized the strategic importance of making an "end-run around the information gatekeepers" to produce their own autonomous media (Tarleton 2000, 53). They were well aware of the limitations of depending on the corporate media to provide coverage, especially the necessary analyses and context for the complex changes threatened by the WTO regime. In fact, before the event, only a handful of articles in the U.S. corporate media had discussed the implications of the WTO meetings.[2]

The IMC would not have been possible without the convergence of new levels of social movement organization and technology. In three short months in the fall of 1999, and with only $30,000 in donations and borrowed equipment, Seattle organizers created a "multimedia peoples' newsroom," with a physical presence in a renovated downtown storefront and in cyberspace on the Web (Tarleton 2000, 53). The IMC enabled independent journalists and media producers of print, radio, video, and photos from around the world to produce and distribute stories from the perspectives of the growing anti-corporate globalization movement. The IMC was the child of a collaboration between local housing and media activists; journalists, independent media producers, and media and democracy activists from national and international arenas; and local, national, and international organizations active in the burgeoning anti-corporate globalization movement.

Second, the Seattle IMC drew from the technical expertise and resources of computer programmers, many of whom came from the open-source movement. While Bill Gates of Microsoft played a major role in bringing the WTO to Seattle, Rob Glaser, who made his millions at Microsoft, donated technical support and expertise, and in particular the latest streaming technologies, to the indymedia Web site. "From the standpoint of all these independent media, the WTO couldn't have picked a worse place to hold their meeting," according to local media activist Bob Siegel. "I mean it's Seattle—we've got all the techies you'll ever want. . . . It's perfect that the WTO came here. Perfect" (quoted in Paton 1999, 3). Indymedia.org allowed real-time distribution of video, audio, text, and photos, with the potential for real interactivity through "open publishing," in which anyone with access to the Internet could both receive and send information.

In just two years, the IMC network has become a critical resource for activists and audiences around the world, providing an extraordinary bounty of news reports and commentaries, first-person narratives, longer analyses, links to activist resources, and interactive discussion opportunities from around the world. In the beginning, they focused primarily on the anti-globalization mobilizations at the multilateral summits of neoliberal governance. At each of these meetings, they provided innovative international coverage, which often included collaborative initiatives with other media and social-movement activists. In the last year, and particularly since September 11, the network has added several new member sites and widened the scope of its coverage to include local, national, and international campaigns concerning anti-corporate globalization.

In this chapter, I demonstrate how the independent media centers are a new watershed in a historical continuum of radical activist media, in which media activists have continually created new communications resources and challenged the enclosure of the communications commons.[3]

The Seattle IMC and the growing Independent Media Center Network represent a new and powerful emerging model that counters the trend toward the privatization of all public spaces by expanding our capacity to reclaim public airwaves and resources. (IMC Brochure 2001, 1)

The IMC constitutes a new commons regime, relatively autonomous from the direction of the corporate and state media, in which unpaid workers share cyber and real territories, labor time, and communications technologies, techniques, and techne.

Lessons from the commons and enclosures

The concepts of the commons and enclosures date back to a conflict in England five hundred years ago. However, the terms have recently been given new currency in the debate over globalization and development and global communication. There are broadly three sets of meanings in use, which correspond with the three sets of social actors involved in these debates—the capitalist market, the state, and social movements (Sénécal 1991). Neoliberal economists invoke the "tragedy of the commons," arguing, as did the first feudal landlords, that the resource should be enclosed under corporate control in order to stop its unregulated overuse and make it more efficient and that nonconforming practices should be criminalized (Travis 2000).[4] The second school describes the commons as a "public" resource, which should be managed by state or multilateral international institutions, or public-private partnership.

My own perspective derives from groups within the social movements opposed to corporate globalization, specifically the activists grouped loosely around the International Forum against Globalization and the radical historians and political analysts of autonomist Marxism. Both of these two schools demonstrate important parallels between the first enclosures of the English feudal commons, which led to the grand transformation to capitalism and European imperialism and the continuing colonization and exploitation of shared resources throughout the world (Caffentzis 1995; Shiva 1993; Thompson 1968). They also show a historical line of succession from the creativity, resistance, and rebellion of the English commoners throughout the various colonies and diasporas of European colonialism to contemporary campaigns for local, democratic rule of shared resources (Dalla Costa 1995; Linebaugh and Rediker 2000; Shiva 2000).

The narrative of the English commons was one of protracted and often bloody struggle over land, a mode of production, a way of life, and over history itself. After the collapse of serfdom in the mid-fourteenth century, farm labor was in demand. A new class of small farmers, or yeomen, became responsible for much of the agricultural production, working the land under a complex system of open fields and common rights. They held customary right, or "copyhold," to a part of the feudal estate, as a sort of subtenancy. They also shared the use of untitled village land, marsh, and water holdings, in common with other small and medium-sized farmers and tenants (Travis 2000, 5). Some historians have called the fifteenth century a "golden age" of English labor, as many laborers were able to sustain themselves from their work on the land without needing to purchase additional commodities, while some were even able to accumulate wealth (Travis 2000, 5).

The English commons did not exist within a democratic society, but on the margins, or interstices, between state and private domains. Many rural families were poor and were subject to the domination of the feudal landlords via rents, levies, tributes, and taxes. However, there were many significant physical, social, cultural, and psychological times and spaces where the dominant classes and the commoners did not intersect. Open to all with a shared interest in their use, their value was derived from participation and was not a tradeable commodity (Shiva 1994). Not private, they were concerned more with continuing sustenance, security, and habitat, not with producing, distributing, or circulating commodities for a growth-oriented market system (Ecologist 1993). Commons regimes were also not public resources administered by the state, but instead were a form of direct rule by individuals and groups drawn from civil society, for the most part outside the electoral franchise.

As a corrective to the mainstream history, which argued that the commons were inefficient and unorganized, E. P. Thompson (1991, 131) documented their orderly use through a "rich variety of institutions and community sanctions which . . . effected restraints and stints upon use." Obligations, bonds, and evolving customary rights were defined and regulated as people negotiated multiple uses and schedules of space, time, labor power, and technical resources (Humphries 1990; Johnson 1996; Neeson 1993; Thompson 1968, 1991). This required the development of sophisticated interpersonal and community communication, which, in part, helps explain the origin of the words "communication" and "democracy" during this period. "Communication" meant "to make common to many," and democracy originated in the sixteenth century, when it meant "the rule of the comminaltie," the popular power of the multitude, implying the suppression of rule by the rich (Williams 1976, 93).

The scope and pace of the enclosures picked up in the fifteenth century and were an integral part of the grand transformation to European global capitalism (Thompson 1968). The first stage of the enclosures involved the fencing of common lands and copy-hold properties in order to introduce capital-intensive exploitation of the land for wool production. A new class of commercial landlords brutally dispossessed the rural population from grazing, fishing, hunting, quarrying, fuel, building materials, and rights of way. Eventually the landed gentry who dominated Parliament instituted enclosure laws.[5] The restructuring of the land and the way of life was instigated through a variety of measures, including engineering and highway projects, surveillance, the imposition of new work disciplines, systems of thought and governance, as well as dispersal and criminalization of all those who resisted. The enclosures, first developed in England, were extended to Ireland, Scotland, Wales, and then overseas, in the expropriation and exploitation of lands, waterways, and indigenous laborers throughout the Americas, Africa, and Asia.

However, the enclosures were not implemented without extraordinarily widespread and diverse resistance, a diversity of tactics that parallels those in use today. These ranged from moral and legal appeals, parliamentary petitions, and lobbying to fence breaking, arson and systematic trespass, and direct uprisings and riots. Some of the resisters articulated a radical communitarian philosophy. For instance, Gerard Winstanley of the Levellers argued that the common people should share equitably in the resources of the lands and waterways, negotiating their use among themselves without intervention by lords, military might, or parliamentary dictum.

The story of the commons provides insights into the different notions of democracy of the bourgeois and popular revolutionary traditions. Linebaugh and Rediker describe the saga of four hundred years of cross-Atlantic circulation of this heritage of commoners' creativity and revolt, tracing the ideas and experiments about popular rule and social justice of this motley crew to the French and American revolutions (Linebaugh and Rediker 2000). Vandana Shiva (2000) has described the legacy of women's direct action during the 1940s against the British Empire's privatization and extraction of rent from the land in contemporary Indian laws and democratic principles. Italian Marxist feminist Maria Rosa Dalla Costa links the Zapatista challenge to land enclosures brought about by the North American Free Trade Agreement (NAFTA) to the current campaigns against corporate globalization. "The webs of relations, analyses and information interweaving" among indigenous movements, workers, ecological movement militants, women's groups, and human rights activists are bridged by the continuing struggles for the commons, whose public spaces and ecology provide the possibility of "life, of beauty and continual discovery" (Dalla Costa 1995, 13).

The Internet and the grand transformation

We are now at the center of another grand transformation, from an economy dominated by industrial production to one in which information and digital knowledge play a key role in production, distribution, and circulation. One of the principal technologies of this new mode of production and social organization is the Internet. As the Internet has developed from a publicly funded network centered among universities, research institutions, and governments to one dominated by corporate commercial exchange, there has been a widespread debate over its ownership, governance, customary operation, model of communication, and relationship to democracy. There has also been a renewal of discussion and debate about the Internet as a new commons and new enclosure.

The Internet developed through both deliberate design and unintended consequence. An odd combination of social actors—U.S. military research, academic and corporate scientists, and grassroots social movements—used public resources and a high degree of creativity and collaboration to create this globally networked communications system.[6] The role of state and corporate players in the history of the Internet is of course much better known (Murphy, forthcoming). In response to the launch of the Russian *Sputnik* in 1957, the U.S. Department of Defense formed the Advanced Research Projects Agency (ARPA) to develop superior military technologies. They commissioned scientists in a number of different think tanks throughout the United States and western Europe. Working interdependently throughout the 1960s and 1970s, the scientists created the communications system that would become the Internet. They designed a decentralized system that allowed every node on the network to operate without centralized control centers, with the capacity to send and receive packets of digitally coded information.

This research work spawned a small number of research and development units in the 1970s near Stanford University in Palo Alto, California, which manufactured silicon chips (hence Silicon Valley) and personal computers. Silicon Valley provided the capacity for U.S., Japanese, and European corporations to "globalize" their production and distribution of goods and services. They developed an extensive network of computer-based Intranets, linked through the widely available and relatively cheap publicly regulated telephone lines. Foremost among these multinational corporations were the computer firms that moved their production to Asia, where strong U.S.-backed authoritarian regimes kept labor rates low.

During the 1990s, the dominant model of cyberspace shifted from publicly funded "information sharing" to a model of private commercial space (Menzies 2001, 219–220). The majority of users are no longer the .orgs and .govs who operated among decentralized communications networks of many to many. Much of the traffic is now dominated by the .coms and the broadcast model, in which a small number of dominant global media giants control the distribution pipelines into the Net, online traffic, and much of the content, exploiting this resource through fees, advertising, and subscriptions (Raphael 2001). However, this move to fence off or enclose the Net under corporate control has not been achieved without resistance. Among many tactics, Net users have lobbied and advocated with all levels of government and corporate actors, acted deliberately to break down barriers through sabotage or hacking, or refused to accept the privatization of common code and content through massive sharing of music and movie files (Dyer-Witheford 2002).

The new commoners

The genesis of this resistance can be explored in the less celebrated history of the Internet and social movements, involving two principal sets of social movements (Murphy, forthcoming). The first group included the computer technicians who went on to develop many social communications uses for the Internet, to lobby for democratic policy, and/or develop hacking networks to fight the enclosure of cyberspace (Ludlow 2001). The next generation would become integral to the indymedia movement. The scientists and graduate students within the university research centers, and then the corporate factories of Silicon Valley, developed a communications system with the potential of allowing untold numbers of communicators to produce and distribute unlimited kinds and quantities of information with no central gatekeeping command. Operating with public money, they exchanged ideas to create software and hardware with open-source protocols that allow anyone to utilize and change the code. While some of these "geeks" or "techies" went on to become entrepreneurs, the development of the Internet, and especially the World Wide Web, owes much to this dispersed corps of individual techies, hackers, students, community-based organizations, and policy activists (Witheford 1997). By the 1990s, hundreds of individuals and groups, loosely collected in the open-source movement, were distributing information for free, sharing new software and hardware, and challenging the operating protocols of intellectual property through regulatory and entrepreneurial means. Another group was demonstrating the limits of existing corporate and state software and operating systems by sharing hacked software or warez (Pahati 2002).

This new class of knowledge workers operates in centers all over the world with a concept of collective intelligence in which they share a "common code" that is antithetical to proprietary ideas of intellectual property (Bosma et al. 1999; Castells 2001). While few would describe themselves as commoners, some speak in terms of breaking the corporate domination of the Internet and others think of themselves as contributing to democracy (Pahati 2002). Their mantra is that "information is free," that technology is a means to liberate information; their role is to allow information to circulate freely—without the gate-keepers of nation-state or corporate domain (Castells 2001, 33). Regardless of their self-definitions, the open-source movement, the hackers, and file-sharing "pirates" have had a profound impact on the global Net, challenging the new corporate enclosures and attempting to keep the open architecture and free flow of information (Dyer-Witheford, 2002; Pfaffenberger 1999).

Building networks against corporate globalization

Another group of social movements also identified with the communitarian aims of the early commoners. In the 1970s, a number of community-based groups began to use the new information technologies for social justice and social development. Several projects, such as Berkeley Community Memory, started in the Bay Area around Silicon Valley with the aim of making the information networks and communication capacity of the Internet publicly available. Other community-based organizations across North America and Europe developed a wide variety of new computer software and hardware for the Internet, including the Chicago group that developed the bulletin board system (BBS) and the movement of community nets to provide public access (Castells 2001; Gutstein 1999).[7] By the 1980s, a number of international non-government organizations had realized the potential of linked international networks.

During the late 1980s, a coalition of national and international nongovernmental organizations (NGOs) from the northern and southern hemispheres acted to develop their own linked computer networks—including Geonet, Worknet, Fidonet, Econet, Greenet, Labornet, and Peacenet—allowing social movements of labor, ecology, peace, and women to share text-based information. This network of networks "preceded and long remained parallel to the commercialized Internet" (Murphy 2001, 7). In 1990, the Association for Progressive Communications (APC) was formed to support this global network, providing the first of many services with low-cost access to extensive resources at a global reach and speed, dramatically transforming the possibilities for political organization and action (Eagleton-Pierce 2001; Smith 2001).

Many of the NGOs had been working with social movements of small farmers, women, indigenous peoples, grassroots trade unionists, and environmentalists. There had been nationalist and left-wing critiques of the World Bank (WB) and International Monetary Fund (IMF) for their role in U.S.-driven capitalist exploitation of the Third World (Cleaver 1999). During the 1980s, this critique gained power as environmentalists and indigenous rights groups disseminated information about the impact of World Bank-funded megadevelopment projects on their livelihoods and cultures. Many NGOs allied to protest the imposition of World Bank and IMF policies of free trade and structural adjustment, which had privatized public resources, depleted public services, and weakened indigenous industries and national controls (Caffentzis 1995; Cleaver 1999; Dalla Costa 1995).

Some began to draw on the discourse of the commons. Vandana Shiva (1993, 215) argued that the dominant ideology of postwar development focused on the enclosures of the national commons. Shiva (1994) and other ecologists framed debates over the uses of seeds and genetic materials as common regimes of knowledge and resources versus a corporate logic of enclosing and exploiting intellectual property.[8] *The Ecologist* magazine documented the efforts of a wide array of groups, outside the institutions of both market and state, to create or "defend open democratic community institutions that ensure people's control over their own lives" (Ecologist 1993, 175). Autonomist Marxist George Caffentzis described the privatization of the land tenure system in Africa as a "new enclosure movement" (Caffentzis 1995, 27). Maria Rosa Dalla Costa described the Zapatista revolt against NAFTA and the enclosure of commons lands as a struggle for the commons. However, the struggle was no longer local, or even national, but international in scope.

This new international movement continued to mobilize during the 1990s, as many of the NGOs and social-movement groups met face to face in international conferences and events. Some were counterconferences to multilateral organizations and strategems, including UN-sponsored meetings on the environment, women's rights, and human rights; WB, IMF, WTO, and NAFTA; the Asia Pacific Economic Conferences (APEC); and the Organization for Economic Cooperation and Development (OECD). Others, such as the *encuentros* in Mexico and Spain initiated by the Zapatistas, convened activists for exchanges and planning meetings and led to the formation of the People's Global Action (Moynihan and Solnit 2002). Seattle was to have been just one more international mobilization. However, the spotlight of the U.S. corporate media gave the movement a new level of power; Seattle was the coming-out party.

Seattle Independent Media Center

> The timing was right, there was a space, the platform was created, the Internet was being used, we could bypass the corporate media, we were using open publishing, we were using multimedia platforms. So those hadn't been available, and then there was the beginning of the anti-globalization movement in the United States. I think it was all of those pieces together. (Herndon 2001)

The roots of the IMC derive from these struggles over control of the resources of the cyber and terrestrial commons. The Seattle IMC brought together four sets of commoners: the social movements that were cooperating in "anti-globalization," local Seattle community activists, technicians from the open-source movement, and activist-media producers. While few would describe themselves as commoners, many used the discourse of commons and enclosures in their critiques of corporate privatization in general, and of the Internet and media gate-keeping in particular. They shared a vision of the IMC as an open, unbounded communications resource, whose "open publishing" innovation allows access to all. This new group of media workers are also like the early commoners, who operated their own copy-hold plot and shared the commons to sustain themselves without needing to buy commodities in the marketplace.

The indymedia commoners intend to be self-sufficient, volunteering their labor and supporting the local centers and the Net through a variety of grassroots efforts rather than depending on outside support. The Israeli site's banner, "You are your own journalist," and the Italian's "Don't Hate the Media—Become the Media," encapsulates the do-it-yourself approach. They see themselves as activists and journalists who produce their own firsthand accounts of campaigns in which they are involved and circulate the accounts of struggles from other sites all over the world.

The IMC in Seattle, and the international IMC movement, has also drawn on a legacy of organizational skills developed by earlier social movements (Herndon 2001). This process of sophisticated interpersonal and community communication is not unlike the earlier commons. One of the first things one will observe, on the Web sites and in face-to-face meetings, is the high level of democratic processing. The IMC network is based on a nonhierarchical structure that relies on highly complex processes of networked consensus. International meetings are held online. There are a wide array of listserv discussion groups that range from general discussions to finances to translation and technical issues. Meetings are conducted through highly complex processes of decision-making, using a consensus model drawn from the direct action wing of the anti-globalization movement.

Indymedia represents a new level of development of a communications commons. There had been earlier attempts among media activists to collaborate and share resources. Radical film documentarians in the 1960s and 1970s, the cable community-access movement of the 1970s and 1980s, Deep Dish TV and Free Speech TV via satellite TV, and micro-radio producers had all shared production and programming resources. Media-specific organizations of radio producers, video producers, and Web activists had been formed at the local, national, and international levels.[9] National and international conferences in San Francisco, New York, Amsterdam, Kuala Lumpur, and Delhi had convened activists interested in developing networks to promote media and democracy. However, many of these efforts had been stymied by the difficulties of sustaining long-term collaborations without stable financing, production facilities, or mechanisms for distribution; the craft separation into specific media technologies and practices; and rivalries for resources.

The Seattle IMC was able to surmount some of these barriers and move to a new level of social organization for a number of reasons. They carefully built a relationship with social-movement activists rather than distancing themselves from political organizing. They also consciously built on the experience of earlier networks, inviting many of the activists from the independent video, community radio, micro-radio, and open-source movements to participate very early on in the planning, fund-raising, and gathering of production equipment.[10] The storefront provided the personal and technological interface to bridge the rivalries between different media, different organizations, and different generations. More seasoned media activists worked together on production projects with newer producers and activists. The four-hundred-strong crew also used all the old and new media, from pens to laptops, and from inexpensive audio-tape and camcorders to the latest in digital recording technologies.

This high level of cooperation helped to break down, if not eliminate, some of the old craft and territorial divisions. Tom Poole, of Deep Dish TV, said: "In the early '90s, we all knew about each other but folks were more factionalized. Now you can see that there's a more collective effort" (quoted in Rinaldo 2000). During the WTO meetings in Doha, Qatar, in 2001, the IMC produced the "No New Rounds" radio Webcast offshore, together with Greenpeace; and in 2002, with "Democracy Now," the IMC broadcast from the protests against the World Economic Forum in New York City and the World Social Forum events in Porte Alegre, Brazil. After the World Social Forum, a caravan of media activists from several different groups covered the crisis in Argentina, reporting directly from the mass meetings in the streets.

The success of the IMC was also due to the new array of available digital technologies. As a high-tech center, Seattle was also home to the original technical support crew, and the technical crew remains an indispensable part of the IMC. Most of the Centers still operate on the same donated ISP and use open-source software. The IMC also took advantage of the advancements in digital video. The new lightweight digital cameras are cheap, easy to work with, and edit and can broadcast instantaneously, allowing much more collaboration. Eric Galatas from Free Speech TV thinks that television will change dramatically as a result. "There are so many people now picking up DV [digital video] cameras, getting their hands on iMacs or G4s and editing great videos. . . . I think we're going to look back on this period as a launch pad for an entirely new way of making and distributing television" (quoted in Rinaldo 2000).

Most important, the IMC could overcome the limited space and the distribution problems inherent in the old media. The Internet and related technologies enabled a quantum leap in time and space for other kinds of content generation as the site could accept an unlimited amount of content, including text, photos, graphics, video, and audio. While debates over how to sustain the resource continue, there are none of the space limitations, and ensuing conflicts over sharing, that led to the crisis at Pacifica and constant tensions among other older independent media. Also, the reach is potentially so much further: During the anti-WTO protests in Seattle, the site had a million and a half hits, and the entire network is now estimated to receive about four-hundred thousand page views a day (Pavis 2002).

The IMC represents a major step forward in the tactical use of autonomous media. It has brought together activists and journalists from across the different media with movements that were able to circulate their messages on a scope and scale not realized before. In many ways, they have been able to surmount the limits on the resource that always faced the land-based commons and earlier media commons. The expanded horizon for production and distribution has limited the battles over resources, but not eliminated them. The IMC is networked; highly consultative decision-making owes a lot to skills developed in the consensus-model training of the direct action wing of the anti-globalization movement. The negotiation of resources appears to operate with far fewer of the stand-offs that seemed inherent in the earlier activist media movements of which I was a part. However, in the long-term, some of the same old questions remain.

How can the IMCs sustain this resource? The decentralized network model helped share the labor and the fund-raising. However, the dependence on volunteers and the sharing of a limited number of resources will be hard to continue indefinitely. Already, those people who are able to volunteer tend to represent a small minority of young white North Americans and Europeans who can afford to share their time (Rinaldo 2000). The network is facing these problems in creative ways, sending the caravan to Argentina, sending volunteers with technical expertise to new sites in Latin America, providing constant technical and other kinds of support via the Internet itself, and circulating key personnel through the network. Nevertheless, very creative solutions are needed to overcome the huge inequality of access to media production and Internet technologies that exists among working-class communities of color in North America and Europe, and even more so in the southern hemisphere.

The success of the IMC network has not been without other challenges and costs. Its visibility has brought more attention from national and international security agencies. In Seattle, the IMC had been able to operate as witnesses, providing a thin skin of protection against greater police violence and a photographic and audio record for the legal teams fighting police actions. However, after the confrontation between demonstrators and police during the spring 2001 Free Trade Agreement of the Americas (FTAA) meeting in Quebec City, the Seattle site was raided by the FBI, based upon information from the Canadian Security Intelligence Service (CSIS). During the 2001 Genoa Meeting of the G8 in Genoa, Italy, the Italian police attacked the IMC, beating and arresting everyone inside (Halleck 2002; Starhawk 2001). What are the risks of more security intervention in IMC offices and Web sites?

Among the monocultural enclosures of the coms and media giants, indymedia is a vibrant commons. The IMC produces counterinformation to the media giants, and are able to do so using the same communication and information machinery that capital uses to ensure its own mobility (Witheford 1997, 205). The IMC has built a network from the heritage created by earlier media activists and, as importantly, has based itself within the social movements against corporate globalization, acting to make visible and circulate a multiplicity of social movements and actions.

Notes

1   A banner on the homepage of the Italian Independent Media Centre, September 2001.
2   The local daily and weekly Seattle newspapers presented a range of views about the impact of WTO free trade decisions on the environment, labor standards, and local democratic governance. However, the initial television coverage and national mainstream coverage focused on the few incidents of property damage; characterized the wide range of protesting groups as laughable and ill informed, and dismissed their critiques of the WTO and corporate globalization. One *New York Times* columnist summed up this trope about demonstrators: "a Noah's ark of flat-earth advocates, protectionist trade unions, and yuppies looking for their 1960s fix" (FAIR Media Advisory, December 7, 1999). A 2001 study in the *Columbia Journalism Review* shows how this framing leans "heavily towards the corporate side in major news organizations coverage of protests at the IMF meeting in Prague, the FTAA talks in Quebec City, the European Summit in Sweden, and the G-8 meeting in Genoa" (cited in Hyde 2002).
3   In Kidd 1998 I teased out the concept of the radio communications commons, based in the electrospace.
4   Hannibal Travis (2000) argues that enclosure includes the actual process of enclosure, and as importantly, a "recharacterization of existing entitlements as theft" (4).
5   The Houses of Parliament who enacted the Enclosure Laws were dominated by the landed gentry and noblemen in the top 1 percent income bracket (Travis 2000, 5).
6   There are many good histories of the Internet that show this complex development, propelled by very different social actors (Bosma et al. 1999; Castells 2001; Dyer-Witheford 1999; Murphy 2001).
7   This development of public-use software and hardware continues throughout the world. Most recently, Indian and Brazilian computer designers have developed cheap personal computers for mass use and have adapted open-source software for operating systems.
8   In the plenary address to the counterconference against the World Economic Forum in Melbourne, Vandana Shiva compared the struggle for farmers' control of their seed to the campaign for free computer software (Shiva 2000, 9).
9   The Newsreel Organization built national and international links among radical film producers. International video producers had convened in conferences in the 1980s and 1990s under the loose direction of Videazimut. Grassroots radio producers formed an international organization called the World Community Radio Organization (AMARC), which also facilitated collaborations among feminist and indigenous producers. The Tactical Media Conferences in Amsterdam convened activists from old and new media (Bosma et al. 1999; Halleck 2002; Kidd 1998).
10 Collaborators included Deep Dish TV; Paper Tiger TV; Free Speech TV; Whispered Media; Changing America; NY Free Media Alliance; the micro-radio producers, including Free Radio Berkeley and Prometheus Media; as well as many others.

References

Barstow, Anne Llewellyn. 1994. *Witchcraze: A New History of the European Witch Hunts*. San Francisco: Pandora Books.

Basuki, Tedjabayu. 1999. "Indonesia: The Web as a Weapon," in The Next Five Minutes 3 Public Debates List. Online. http://www.n5m.org.

Bosma, Josephine, Pauline van Mourik Broekman, Ted Byfield, Mathew Fuller, Geert Lovink, Diana McCarty, Pit Schultz, Felix Stalder, McKenzie Wark, and Faith Wilding. 1999. *Read Me! Filtered by Net Time: ASCII Culture and the Revenge of Knowledge*. Brooklyn, NY: Autonomedia.

Caffentzis, George. 1995. "The Fundamental Implications of the Debt Crisis for Social Reproduction in Africa," pp. 42–57 in *Paying the Price: Women and the Politics of International Economic Strategy*, ed. Maríarosa Dalla Costa and Giovanna Dalla Costa. London: Zed Books.

Castells, Manuel. 2000. *The Rise of the Network Society*. Oxford: Blackwell Publishers.

———. 2001. *The Internet Galaxy: Reflections on the Internet, Business and Society*. Oxford: Oxford University Press.

Cleaver, Harry. 1995. "The Electronic Fabric of Struggle." Online. http://www.eco.utexas.edu/faculty/Cleaver/zaps.html.

———. 1999. "Computer-Linked Social Movements and the Global Threat to Capitalism." Online. http://www.eco.utexas.edu/faculty/Cleaver/hmchtml-papers.html.

Curtin, Michael, and Thomas Streeter. 2001. "Media," pp. 225–249 in *Culture Works: The Political Economy of Culture*, ed. Richard Maxwell. Minneapolis: University of Minnesota Press.

Dalla Costa, Maria. 1995. "Development and Reproduction." *Common Sense* 17: 11–33.

Dyer-Witheford, Nick. 1999. *Cyber-Marx: Cycles and Circuits of Struggle in High-Technology Capitalism*. Urbana: University of Illinois Press.

———. 2002. "E-Capital and the Many-Headed Hydra," in *Critical Perspectives on the Internet*, ed. Greg Elmer. Lanham, MD: Rowan and Littlefield.

Eagleton-Pierce, Matthew. 2001, September. "The Internet and the Seattle WTO Protests." *Peace Review*. 13(3): 331–38. Special Issue: Social Justice Movements and the Internet.

Ecologist, The. 1993. *Whose Common Future? Reclaiming the Commons*. Philadelphia and Gabriola Island, B.C.: New Society Publishers.

Esteva, Gustavo. 1993. "Development," pp. 6–25 in *The Development Dictionary: A Guide to Knowledge and Power*, ed. Wolfgang Sachs. London: Zed Books.

Ford, Tamara Villarreal, and Genève Gil. 2001. "Radical Internet Use," pp. 201–34 in *Radical Media: Rebellious Communication and Social Movements*, ed. John Downing et al. Thousand Oaks, CA: Sage.

Gutstein, Donald. 1999. *e.con: How the Internet Undermines Democracy*. Toronto: Stoddart.

Halleck, DeeDee. 2002. *Hand-Held Visions*. New York: Fordham University Press.

Hardt, Michael, and Antonio Negri. 2000. *Empire*. Cambridge, MA: Harvard University Press.

Herndon, Sheri. 2001, July 20. Telephone interview.

Humphries, Jane. 1990. "Enclosures, Common Rights, and Women: The Proletarianization of Families in the Late Eighteenth and Early Nineteenth Centuries." *Journal of Economic History* 50(1): 17–42.

Hyde, Gene. 2002. "Independent Media Centers: Cyber-Subversion and the Alternative Press." *First Monday*. 7(4). Online. April. http://firstmonday.org/issues/issues_4/hyde/index.html

Independent Media Center brochure. 2001. Seattle, WA: Independent Media Center.

Johnson, Mathew. 1996. *An Archaeology of Capitalism*. Cambridge: Blackwell Publishers.

Kidd, Dorothy. 1998. "Talking the Walk: The Media Enclosures and the Communications Commons." Doctoral Dissertation. Simon Fraser University.

———. 2001, September. "Introduction." *Peace Review* 13(3): 325–30. Special Issue: Social Justice Movements and the Internet.

Kidd, Dorothy, and Nick Witheford. 1994, November 12. "Counterplanning from Cyberspace and Videoland: or Luddites on Monday and Friday, Cyberpunks the Rest of the Week." Paper presented at "Monopolies of Knowledge: A Conference Honoring the Work of Harold Innis," Vancouver.

Land, Jeff. 1999. *Active Radio: Pacifica's Brash Experiment*. Minneapolis: University of Minnesota Press.

Lasar, Mathew. 1999. *Pacifica Radio: The Rise of an Alternative Network*. Philadelphia: Temple University Press.

Lessing, Lawrence. 1999. *Code and Other Laws of Cyberspace*. New York: Basic Books.

———. 2001. *The Future of Ideas: The Fate of the Commons in a Connected World*. New York: Random House.

Linebaugh, Peter, and Marcus Rediker. 2000. *The Many-Headed Hydra: Sailors, Slaves, Commoners, and the Hidden History of the Revolutionary Atlantic.* Boston: Beacon Press.

Ludlow, Peter, ed. 2001. *Crypto Anarchy, Cyberstates, and Pirate Utopias.* Boston: MIT Press.

Menzies, Heather. 2001. "On Digital Public Space and the Real Tragedy of the Commons," pp. 217–28 in *e-commerce vs. e-commons: Communications in the Public Interest*, ed. Marita Moll and Leslie Regan-Shade. Ottawa: Canadian Centre for Policy Alternatives.

Messman, Terry. 2001. "Justice Journalism: Journalist as Agent for Social Change." *MediaFile* 20(4): 1.

Midnight Notes Collective. 1992. *Midnight Oil: Work, Energy, War 1973–1992.* Brooklyn, NY: Autonomedia.

Moynihan, Denis, and David Solnit. 2002. "From the Salt Marshes to Seattle: Direct Action's History," pp. 129–34 in *The Global Activist's Manual: Local Ways to Change the World*, ed. Mike Prokosch and Laura Raymond. New York: Thunder's Mouth Press/Nation Books.

Murphy, Brian Martin. 2001. "Propagating Alternative Journalism through Social Movement Cyberspace: The Appropriation of Computer Networks for Alternative Media Development," in *Appropriating Technology: Vernacular Science and Social Power*, ed. R. Eglash, J. Croissant, G. DiChiro and R. Fouché. Minneapolis: University of Minnesota Press.

——. 2002. "Towards a Critical History of the Internet." *Critical Perspectives on the Internet*, ed. Greg Elmer. Lanham, MD: Rowan and Littlefield.

Neeson, J. M. 1993. *Commoners: Common Right, Enclosure and Social Change in England, 1700–1820.* Cambridge: Cambridge University Press.

Pahati, Omar. 2002. "Digital Pirates and the 'Warez' Wars." Online, www. alternet.org (January 24).

Paton, Dean. 1999. "War of the Words: Virtual Media versus Mainstream Press." Online, www.csmonitor.com (December 3).

Pavis, Theta. 2002. "Modern Day Muckrakers: The Rise of the Independent Media Center Movement." Online. http://www.ojr.org/ojr/business/1017866594.php. *OnLine Journalism Review.* USC Annenberg.

Pfaffenberger, Bryan. 1999, December 13. "In Seattle's Aftermath: Linux, Independent Media, and the Survival of Democracy." www.linuxjournal.com/article.php?sid=5075 (December 13).

Project for Excellence in Journalism. 2001. "Before and After: How the War on Terrorism Has Changed the News Agenda." Network Television. June–October. Columbia University School of Journalism. Pp. 1–21.

Raphael, Chad. 2001. "The Web," pp. 209–10 in *Culture Works: The Political Economy of Culture*, ed. Richard Maxwell. Minneapolis: University of Minnesota Press.

Regan, Tom. 1999. "News You Can Use from the Little Guys." *Christian Science Monitor.* Online, www.csmonitor.com (December 9).

Rifkin, Jeremy. 2000. *The Age of Access: The New Culture of Hypercapitalism Where All of Life Is a Paid-For Experience.* New York: Jeremy P. Tarcher/Putnam.

Rinaldo, Rachel. 2001. "Pixel Visions: the Resurgence of Video Activism." Online. www.libmagazine.org/articles/featrinaldo_115_p.htm (July 9).

Ryan, Charlotte, Kevin M. Carragee, and William Meinhofer. 2001. "Theory into Practice: Framing, the News Media, and Collective Action." *Journal of Broadcasting and Electronic Media* 45: 175.

Sénécal, Michel. 1991. "The Alternative in Search of Its Identity," pp. 209–218 in *Video the Changing World*, ed. Nancy Thede and Alain Ambrosi. Montreal: Black Rose Books.

Shiva, Vandana. 1993. "Resources," pp. 206–18 in *The Development Dictionary; A Guide to Knowledge and Power*, ed. Wolfgang Sachs. London: Zed Books.

——. 1994. "The Recovery of the Commons, A Public Lecture." Alternative Radio Production.

——. 2000. Plenary address to RMIT University conference "Global Capital, Local Responses," Australian Broadcasting Corporation, Melbourne, Australia.

Smith, Jackie. 2001, Spring. "Cyber Subversion in the Information Economy." *Dissent*: 48–52.

Solomon, Norman. 2001. "When Journalists Report for Duty." Online. http://www.fair.org/media-beat/010920.html.

Starhawk. 2001. "Lifelong Activism: Finding the Courage, Tenacity, and Love," pp. 262–264 in *Global Uprising: Confronting the Tyrannies of the 21st Century*, ed. Neva Welton and Linda Wolk. Gabriola Island, B.C.: New Society Publishers.

Tarleton, John. 2000, Winter. "Protesters Develop Their Own Global Internet News Service." *Mark Nieman Reports*, 54(4): 53–55.

Thompson, E. P. 1968. *The Making of the English Working Class.* Harmondsworth, England: Penguin Books.

———. 1991. *Customs in Common*. London: Merlin Press.

Travis, Hannibal. 2000, Spring. "Pirates of the Information Infrastructure: Blackstonian Copyright and the First Amendment." *Berkeley Technology Law Journal*, 15(2): 777.

Williams, Raymond. 1976. *Keywords: A Vocabulary of Culture and Society*. New York: Oxford University Press.

Witheford, Nick. 1997. "Cycles and Circuits of Struggle in High-Technology Capitalism," pp. 195–242 in *Cutting Edge: Technology, Information, Capitalism and Social Revolution*, ed. Jim Davis, Thomas Hirschl, and Michael Stack. London: Verso.

PART SIX

Everyday media technocultures

A S WE EXPLORE IN some detail in Part 4 of *New Media: A Critical Introduction*, everyday life is a key concept in media and cultural studies and a key site for the marketing, dissemination and success or failure of new media. It is the environment where popular new communication and entertainment devices and services must find a niche, either fitting in with the existing domestic media ecology or, like an alien species with no natural predators, displacing or replacing native technologies and routines. They might mutate or hybridise, as with, for example, the new convergences of television with games consoles and the Internet. This is a harsh environment, however, and new arrivals that do not fit face rapid extinction themselves (remember laser disc players, email TV sets and the multimedia CD-ROM?), or transformation through the intense evolutionary processes of upgrade culture.

The challenge for the description and conceptualisation of new media technoculture in everyday life then is to recognise the continuity of longer histories and contexts – **Williams'** 'mobile privatisation', domestic architecture, family dynamics, existing media technologies – whilst keeping our eyes open for the innovative and transformative. Each of the extracts in this part studies digital culture not as discrete texts or technologies, but as it is *lived*. They trace the minute and incremental changes in mediated lives, technocultural practices that were novel and exciting yesterday, but mundane and familiar today. Each pays attention to the novelty within the familiar though, alive to the strangeness of technoculture: the new pleasures, channels of communication, and intimacies with others, both human and non-human. Michal **Daliot-Bul** for example traces playful patterns through Japanese mobile phone culture, from game applications to decoration to the emerging ludic practices of communication itself. For Elaine **Lally**, an emphasis on the embodied, material nature of domestic computer use leads to a reconceptualisation of the home and furniture as having always been technological, Le Corbusier's 'machines for living in'. The other extracts collected in this part all, in different ways, track movement between the actual everyday world and its new, virtual, annexes. For Shanly **Dixon** and Sandra **Weber**, like **Daliot-Bul**, moving between the virtual and the actual is now a commonplace and thoroughly playful journey for children and young people, whereas for Mizuko **Ito** it is a zone characterised by imaginative engagement and new forms of sociality.

The articles in this part are less diverse in their methods, concepts and objects of study than those in other parts. They all use ethnographic or autobiographical research as well as conceptual work, and all approach the everyday in a manner sensitive to the communicative and generative possibilities of new media forms.

Chapter 37

ELAINE LALLY

THE DOMESTIC ECOLOGY OF OBJECTS

THROUGH ETHNOGRAPHIC WORK and theoretical reflection, Elaine Lally describes computer technology in everyday domestic life and space not as a disruptive new technologisation of the home, but as the material integration and symbolic negotiation of a particular set of technologies into an environment that is always already dynamic and technological. Architecture, room layout, furniture, non-digital technologies, even space itself are all active elements of a complex set of relationships that constitute everyday life. Furniture for instance is space solidified around human activities, characteristic of a 'productive relation' between humans and objects that 'allows them to interact'. When entering this environment, new objects and technologies must find a physical and cultural space for themselves; they are adapted to, or adapt, these spaces.

This approach questions hard and fast distinctions between technological and non-technological objects. Citing the ideas of American philosopher of technology Don Ihde, Lally suggests that any artefact in use has a technological aspect, that we must speak of 'human-technology relations' not of technological objects (see many other extracts, notably **Latour** and **Haraway**). A clear example of this, and one that highlights the contingent, negotiable and emergent characteristics of everyday technoculture, is that of the fridge door. This functional component of a mundane technology was not designed to function as a family notice board, but its ferromagnetic qualities, coupled with its physical and relational position in the house (in a busy communal space), led to this widespread adaptation. There is now an industry producing fridge magnets and even, recently, new networked devices designed to attach to fridge doors to remediate the established bricolage of domestic communication and organisation.

Computers then should not be separated from their technical and material relations with space, furniture and residents. However, given their size, mode of use, necessity of proximity to power and communication sockets, and so on, they do demand distinct adaptations of the domestic environment and activities. They have to interact with other objects (rooms, furniture, cables), generate smaller, more mobile objects (disks, printouts), and require consideration of comfort and ergonomics. They must fit in with established household taste and aesthetics (through ornamentation for example), and necessitate negotiations of use, time and space between household members.

[. . .] [T]he physical presence of material objects may allow them to act as a kind of personal psychic scaffolding. Home, in particular, is a place in which the familiarity and continuity of the material environment of objects provides us with a space of 'maximal practical know-how: knowing what everything is for and when it ought to be used' (Hage 1997: 102). It is a place of embodied familiarity, where we hardly need to wake up in the middle of the night to be able to make our way to the bathroom or the fridge. For the extended self, as a self-in-relation to the objects by which it is constituted, the objects of home clearly form a privileged domain. As we have seen, however, the extended self does not simply map onto such assemblages of objects, but is constructed dynamically in interaction with them. Neither are the objects themselves disposed in static arrangements, but in their meanings and uses they are constituted by their incorporation into everyday praxis.

The artist and designer Douglas Fitch (1995) describes how contemplating Pompeii led him to think of furniture as the space solidified around human activities:

> Once, a long time ago, a mountain exploded near Pompeii and, in a single moment, everything that had been *between* suddenly *became*. All that space between people, the room in their rooms – even the space inside their mouths – was filled up with lava, and what had been merely invisible space became object . . . There are lessons from Pompeii about taking space for granted. After seeing it, I started to think about furniture as being the space solidified around human activities. The chair, for example, I suddenly saw as the result of making the space around a sitter solid. (50)

Human activity, however, is just that – it is *activity*. Even when seated we frequently change position in order to remain comfortable: the most comfortable chairs and sofas often seem to be the ones which will support a range of different positions. When Mount Vesuvius erupted and Pompeii's space solidified, all activity immediately ceased.

Furniture is therefore not simply the space solidified around human activities, but bears a more complex relation to those activities, in which the space is not a passive stage, but itself preserves the potential for interaction and particularly for flexibility in interaction. When the space between subject and object itself is filled, there can be no activity, no interaction: the existence of the space between objects (and humans and objects) establishes a productive relation between them and allows them to interact. Spatial organization is itself a modality of objectification:

> Culturally and socially, space is never simply the inert background of our material existence. It is a key aspect of how societies and cultures are constituted in the real world, and, through this constitution, structured for us as 'objective' realities. (Hillier 1996: 29)

Furniture as solidified space

Fitch also describes the task of assembling the home by bringing together objects – the bricolage of home-building – when moving into a new apartment:

> When I relocated to a two-bedroom apartment in New York City, it took me an entire year to completely move in, for various reasons. But that extended time afforded me the opportunity to explore my relationship to the space I was moving into and to study, over time, the elements I was adding. Its existing contents – appliances, cabinets,

walls, doors, room dividers, cable TV hookups – seemed like a bunch of large found objects with which I would assemble a new way of life. The challenge was in combining the existing components – detritus of previous human/object interrelationships – with new ones, including myself and a roommate. (50)

A single object, such as a home computer, needs such complex collaborations of other objects within the domestic space in order to function properly within the domestic pattern of life.

In constructing a personal 'living appliance', the components we use, as we saw above, may be more or less materially (and symbolically) resistant to adaptation. The fabric of the building itself provides little scope (in the short-term) for change, although there will be the choice of allocation of rooms to functions. New houses, for example, are frequently now built with a room designated as a 'study' or home office, while older housing does not have such spaces as formally designated, but may have other spaces (such as bedrooms) which can be allocated to this purpose. Much of the adaptation of these spaces is performed through locating furniture within them, as a means of further defining the proper use of the space and supporting those functions within the space. Indeed, in the French language the terms *mobilier* (furniture) and *immobilier* (real estate) give this sense of the home as constructed from both movable and immovable elements.

If we may think of the home computer as a kind of domestic appliance, then might we not also think of such organizations of domestic objects as having an appliance-like character? Having assembled a personal domestic environment for ourselves, it must function effectively as the locus of the practices of our everyday living, as a 'machine for living' in Le Corbusier's famous phrase. For Le Corbusier, the home as a machine for living would be an engineered, hygienic and mechanically efficient space for living, in which every element has its correct place, in tune with the advances in technology and manufacturing processes (such as the theories of F.W. Taylor) of the twentieth century. In this way it would resemble other products of industry such as ocean liners, motor cars and aeroplanes (Curtis 1986). Most importantly, such housing could be mass-produced, and indeed would provide mass-housing, in planned urban communities.

However, the image of the domestic environment as a DIY bricolage of objects found at hand in the cultural environment is rather different from the one that the father of Modernist architecture envisaged in using this phrase. The term bricolage (Lévi-Strauss 1966: 16–33) has gained broad currency to refer to cultural processes which involve creative symbolic combination and recombination. This is also the sense in which the term is used within this book, but here the usage is particularly apt, since in common French usage bricolage is used to refer to do-it-yourself construction, as opposed to more professional or engineered forms of construction. This is precisely the distinction made here between the home as a 'machine for living' which is a bricolage construction of its inhabitants, and not as an engineered product of large-scale manufacturing processes.

The home-building practices of contemporary western householders involve the translation of symbolic and material goods originating in large-scale social processes, particularly those of mass consumption, into the concrete and particular contexts of everyday domestic life. Home-building is not just, however, about the management of the affective and social relationships of home, but is also a material practice by which the physical environment of home is assembled. The process of home-building is not one in which the home is manufactured and then lived in, but its construction is more like that of [a] bird's nest: although the materials from which it is built are brought into it from outside, the home is 'modeled by fine touches', and is, in the final analysis, 'a house built by and for the body . . . in an intimacy that works physically'.

Figure 9 [not reproduced] shows the 'computer room' in Sue Kozlowski and Phillip Healey's two-bedroom apartment, which contains their four networked computers (three PCs and one Sun Sparcstation). The objects in this room – furniture, the computers themselves, and ancillary objects such as the rubbish bin, the empty coffee cup, and the large quantities of books, papers and disks – seem to form the space into a 'machine for living'. While many home offices might be thought of more functionally as 'machines for working', this one is a space for performing a range of kinds of activities, and not just for working. The couple can 'sit down together here, chat to each other, be doing different things at the same time': the chair on the right of the image is Sue's, while the workstation on the left is Phillip's.

Sue and Phillip spend a lot of their time at home in this room, much more, they say, than they spend in the living area of their apartment. Indeed, the living area looks as if they have never really finished moving in. A number of framed art-works lean against the walls, because they have never 'got around to putting them up'. The living area is likely to stay this way, since Sue and Phillip are planning to move again, partly because they would like a bigger space for the computers, and so that they can also set up Sue's electronic music equipment in the same space. The computers are used extensively for communication (email, news-group reading and posting, browsing the Internet and publishing web pages), for experimentation and learning about the technology.

Indeed, this room seems to operate for this couple as a kind of technological cocoon. Within it, although their embodied selves are physically located there, the technologies within the room give them a two-way window to the external world, particularly when their local computer network is connected to the Internet (at the time of the study they were thinking of putting in a second phone line so that they could stay connected continuously). The poster on the door says 'A World of Information': it is on the outside of the door, so that when the door is closed it seems to indicate both the room's contents and its purpose. The material objects in this room, then, structure a space for the bodies of the home's inhabitants within which the patterns of their everyday living can be enacted.

Constructing the home as inhabited space requires more than the provision of the material infrastructure as an engineered, designed space for living. As we saw in the discussion of objectification in chapter 2, it is the case with all mass-manufactured objects that they are taken up by individuals who reshape and adapt them to their own purposes. In doing so, each individual attempts to build for themselves a personalized place in the world, through adapting (or adapting to) those materials which are found at hand in the cultural environment.

Patterns of computer use, as we have seen in previous chapters, are constructed in complex ways. They do not emerge straightforwardly as a natural consequence of how its designers anticipate it will be used. Fundamentally, technologies are embedded within and in an essential way constituted by particular sets of human praxis. Any technology takes on its meanings and uses from its cultural context and environment of use, and does not necessarily take on the same roles when relocated to another cultural context (Ihde 1993).

Indeed, Ihde insists that technologies are fundamentally relational. Human-technology pairings must be considered as the units of analysis: one must speak therefore of 'a human-technology relation, rather than abstractly conceiving of them as mere objects' (1993: 34). Technologies in use are always contextual and relational, 'they "withdraw" in use and become partially transparent means by which humans relate to an environment' (1993: 108). Ihde uses the term 'technical' to refer to the physical characteristics of a technological artefact, essentially the material condition for its functional effectiveness. Functionality is not fixed once and for all by these characteristics – which 'may be designed or they may be discovered' (73) – there is the intrinsic possibility of flexibility in use. A technology is therefore, perhaps, not so much a particular kind or class of artefact, to be contrasted with objects which are not technologies. On the contrary, any artefact in use – that is, involved in human-artefact interaction – has a technological aspect.

This tool-like functionality – how the object performs the physical/material effects that it does in our interaction with it – is an aspect of many everyday objects, including such things as tables, chairs, cups, blankets and so on. The physical/material characteristics of an object do, however, predispose it to perform certain kinds of function (that is, to be involved in certain kinds of praxis): any large flat-topped surface within a range of suitable heights is potentially a table, for example. To suggest a more sophisticated example, the magnetic metal door of the contemporary fridge predisposes its use as a notice board and display area. This use, although peripheral to the fridge's main purpose of food storage, is enhanced by its role as a centre which is visited frequently by household members. As this example demonstrates, an object's physical characteristics may result in its being used in ways unforeseen by its designers (although the proliferation of fridge magnets indicates that such successes tend not to go unnoticed for long). This example also clearly shows, however, that domestic objects are not used in isolation but exist as elements in the household's total assemblage of artefacts and technologies, and are built into its patterns of activity and interaction – its 'pattern of life', as has been stressed throughout this book. As Ihde suggests, 'technologies in ensemble are probably more like cultures than like tools' (1993:42), and therefore how each element is used must be seen in the context of how this totality operates.

Sue Kozlowski and Phillip Healey's computer room is therefore a 'machine for living' in this profound sense. The material ensemble of the room – both the mundane elements like the desks and chairs and the technological ones like the computers and the room's reticulation into utility networks (telephone, electricity) – structures a space for the body of its inhabitants, which supports the praxis of their living in the room. Such technological ensembles are surely the contemporary equivalents of the earliest of human inventions, shelter and storage technologies (Sofia 1995).

As we have seen, the home computer adds certain types of functionality to the domestic ensemble. In examining the functionality of the home computer, then, and in investigating which alternative household arrangements it may be introducing or displacing, it is necessary to think outside the narrow confines of the obvious communication and information technologies which are generally indicated in discussions of technological convergence (television, telephone and VCR). The ways in which the physical space and objects of the household function as a 'machine for living' adapt to the changing functionality of the collection of objects within it (the setting aside of rooms as home offices, for example, and the appropriation by home computers of other pieces of furniture such as desks and chairs). The functionality of any one object is thus dependent on the supporting functionality of a large range of other objects, and other uses of a room will shape how the object is used.

Computers in relation to other household objects

Computers tend to be large, fairly immobile objects, and generally have a defined physical place within the household. The allocation of household space, and its segregation into rooms with different purposes, is considered in the next chapter. In general, however, the disposition of the computer within the home also involves the use of furniture such as desks and chairs at least, and often also such objects as filing cabinets, bookcases, books and large numbers of small objects such as papers and disks. The computer cannot therefore be seen simply as an independent object within the home, but is one which forms one node in a network of objects which are disposed within the household in relation to each other. It is just one element in the total ensemble of domestic objects.

Further, it is important to emphasize that the ensemble of domestic objects is not a static disposition of objects, but is one which is dynamic and active. Small portable objects, in particular, can be highly mobile, such as computer disks which travel between the home and work. The movement of small objects traces the locus of activity within the space of the household. Children's toys, for example, at times appear to adults to move around the home without human intervention. Household 'mess', which must be actively managed as a distinct domestic activity, is a reflection of and necessary concomitant to this mobility.

In relation to the home computer, for example, pieces of paper are often mediators of an activity which is partly computer-based: John Powell keeps bank statements in two sheaves held together with bulldog-clips which hang on hooks on either side of the window frame. On one side are the ones which are still to be input into his financial accounting program and on the other are the ones which have already been entered. The movement of pieces of paper between one sheaf and the other traces the progress of the activity of maintaining his financial records on the computer (Pellegram 1998 analyses paper as material culture in an office environment). Many of the images of home computers which have been reproduced in this book clearly show that the computer, rather than being an object disposed statically within the home, is the centre of many intersecting domains of activity which involve the movement of people as well as other objects.

Computers 'collaborating' with other objects

Jim Christou is a 25-year-old computer programmer who has two self-contained rooms (a sitting room/study and a bedroom) within his parents' house. He spends most of his time at home here, where he has had cable television installed for his own use (his parents and sister were not interested in it). Jim tends to have the television on most of the time, and has his sitting room set up in such a way that he can see the television easily when he is using the computer:

> Like at the moment, when the cricket's on and I'm watching that, you don't really want to watch it for seven hours straight, so I'd have it on and every now and then you'd hear something and turn away from the computer. If I'm watching like a series or a show or something then I'll leave the computer, go and watch, then come back to it.

In households with both a computer and a dedicated games machine, game-playing activity can be distributed between the two. The games machine may be used when someone is already using the computer (as we saw in the case of the Collins household), or the reverse may take place. In some households the computer becomes redefined as for 'serious' use, rather than for playing games. In the Manfredotti household, for example, the children have become bored with the games on the computer, and tend to use the Nintendo for playing games instead. While there is often, then, a complementarity between the role of the home computer and dedicated electronic games machines, there is also complementarity of the computer's relationship with other kinds of objects.

Some of the householders in the study are very aware of the ergonomics of computer workstation set up, both through employment experience, but also through the marketing of specialized computer furniture such as adjustable desks and chairs and accessories such as wrist pads and anti-glare screens. Although Hilary Lacey, for example, is generally concerned to minimize the cost of her computer, she has invested money in a good keyboard and is aware of the ergonomics of her computer set up, such as having the monitor at the right height. Jim Christou is a member of his workplace occupational health and safety committee, and has brought some of the work-based principles of ergonomics to his home set up:

> I've got pretty much an ergonomic chair, but the computer desk is sorely needed, I've just got a flat desk at the moment for the Macintosh . . . I'm considering getting some other ergonomic furniture. I slouch a lot. I do stretch and stuff, and I've got computer glasses that I don't always use, but I do try to use them. And I try to look away a lot and blink and that.

Charlotte Thompson also makes an effort to apply ergonomic principles to her workstation, although she does this by bringing together items she finds around the house, rather than by acquiring specialized furniture: 'Even if I haven't got a typist chair – like that I have at work – then I am quite conscious at least of getting it at the right height for my eye level . . . I do find the right chair in the house and usually set things up on telephone books to get the right height.'

Many of the study participants had adapted existing furniture within their homes to accommodate their computer. Laurence Harrison, however, had constructed specialized built-in furniture for the computers, modifying a built-in wardrobe by taking off the doors and building in a desktop and wall shelving.

Danielle Singleton had bought specialized computer covers to protect her computer, but at the time I interviewed her had fallen out of the habit of putting them on the computer when it was not in use, although at one stage she says that she had been quite fastidious about this. The interplay of convenience and comfort in the emergence of habits and routines is clear here, as it was in the case of Hayley Crowther's routine of studying when her daughter was sleeping, rather than using the computer.

Other participants use a variety of methods to either protect the computer or appropriate it visually and make it comply more closely with the aesthetic style of their household. Regine Vassallo drapes a crochet shawl over her computer, because 'it gets really dusty', she says. Both Ann Harrison and Gail Shaw have themselves made covers for the computer in their household, which in both cases was a kind of gift or domestic craft offering for their partner. Laurence had asked Ann to make the cover for the Commodore (shown on the left in figure 11), when it was still a 'new toy', although this request was also justified by the original location of the computer in their previous house, in a garage which could be dirty. Gail Shaw made curtains for her partner Felicity's room, and made a computer cover to match from the left-over fabric:

> A small home-maker gesture. I made her curtains for that room. Partly because I was exasperated with what she was using, and partly because I thought she'd really like some nice curtains. And I'd never tell her how much the fabric cost . . . And I thought out of the leftover bits, a cover for the computer would be really good.

Although such collaborations between domestic objects as have been described tend to have a utilitarian justification, it is not uncommon for people to decorate their computers with objects in a manner which seems more aesthetic or ironic than functional. Both the Chapman household and Margaret Paine have teddy bears on their computers as decoration:

I've got a little teddy bear on the top . . . A friend gave it to me as a gift and I sat it on top of my computer and then after a while I thought 'I like that there.' It's like a little friend sitting there looking at me and I've kept it there and I know it annoys the shit out of Hilary. She always says 'What's that teddy bear doing there?' It's really tiny and I just say 'Tess gave me that.' She says 'Yes?' I think it's fallen off once and she kind of put it on the table and I put it back on the computer. That's where I want it to be. (Margaret Paine)

The Chapman's computer is shown in Figure 12 [not reproduced]. This computer is located in the bedroom of the Chapman's eldest son, who is a university student. This computer is rarely used, however: as is clear from the photograph, the computer was unplugged at the time of the interview.

Marjorie Brennan keeps a clear white crystal on the top of her computer. This item was also given to her by a friend as a gift, and is said to bring 'clarity of thought'. Marjorie does not subscribe to a belief in the potency of such crystals herself, but thought that the top of the computer would be a suitable spot to place the crystal. (Although she was not sure whether by being there it symbolized her own clarity of thought or that of the computer.)

For Ruth Bourke aesthetics were an important element in the kind of computer she bought. She likes the compact 'look' of the portable Macintosh Classic, and also the fact that the computer is small enough that the desk can also be used to do other work: 'I just like the idea that it is small and it is compact and it doesn't dominate a room. You can shove it to the back of the desk and you can do something in front of it.'

For Margaret Paine, the look of the area the computer is in is also important: 'I just hate to think what it would look like without the proper computer tower that I've got . . . We've got a black filing cabinet which is between the two computers and we've got a black dining room table, so all charcoal and black matches.'

For Jessica Lane, whose computer is located in her main living space, the computer's styling offends her general sense of how things should look:

I don't find it aesthetically pleasing in the lounge room but that's where it is. And I've no longer got it on the workstation so it's not ergonomically set up because I do have a fairly strong sense of aesthetics so I've got it on the nice old wooden table in the lounge room and the chair that I sit on is a nice old wooden swivel chair. I have difficulty in my house – I find it easier to make things look nice than to actually make things comfortable. I can't make things comfortable but I can make them look right. So that's the way the computer's set up.

On the other hand, when Jessica's computer was in the study, it did not matter as much what it looked like: 'whereas when it was in the study it was fine, and totally ergonomic, and I wasn't looking at it all the time, purely functional'. Jessica would ideally like to be able to hide her computer away inside a piece of furniture which corresponds to a different aesthetic to the contemporary functionality of the computer's design:

I would prefer it to be something that I could put in a beautiful antique wooden cupboard that would open up into an ergonomic work station when I wanted to use it, and then it could be closed away when I wasn't using it . . . If one had the money you could have it made up but I'm limited by finances. If I had the money I could probably find a nice wooden cabinet and have it adapted or whatever, or specially made so that I could have that but I can't even afford to have the actual telephone point moved.

Incorporating the computer visually into the home environment is thus an important aspect of the domestication of the technology for many householders, and the aesthetic is a further dimension of the household's appropriation of the object. The appropriation of the object is not, however, only attributable to the human householders: as these examples make clear, the computer is also capable of appropriating other household objects to itself.

Indeed, to some extent, household objects are also able to appropriate their owners. Claire Matheson, for example, has five pairs of glasses, which are disposed around the house and used for different purposes:

> One very rarely gets used, which is that pair over there, which are just for looking at that screen [the 386] and they don't do anything else. If I'm typing in the database thing then I use these [bifocals which are around her neck, on a glasses 'chain'] so that I can see the screen through the top, and I can read my information here. Where that one there [the 486] is at a different distance, and I use my music glasses for that one. And I have one pair of music glasses for the computer, and one pair of music glasses out near the piano, so that I'm not racing from one end of the house to the other, which is a nuisance, and to me it was worth having an extra pair of glasses.

Claire's fifth pair of glasses are her reading glasses. This particular ensemble of objects and their owner is an example of the technological phenomenon of 'prescription': the need for us as human beings to behave in certain ways, because of the functions that have been built into the objects we use. In the strand of the literature on the sociology of technology which is known as actor network theory, the notion of 'actor network' is adopted as a heuristic, and the functionality of non-human artefacts is based on the delegation of human capacity for action (Akrich and Latour 1992). Having delegated potential human action to a non-human actor, however, there is often a trade-off in that the lack of flexibility in the behaviour of non-human as compared to human actors is that these artefacts often impose behaviour back onto humans (referred to as prescription). These prescriptions incorporate assumptions about the characteristics and behaviour of the human user, which complement those of the technological artefact. Users who do not display these characteristics may effectively be discriminated against by the technology (as is the case for automatic doors, which will often not open for children or for people who approach them too quickly).

Claire's need to have the right glasses available at the right time means that, although she herself has organized her domestic space in this way, her everyday praxis must now fit in with the structure she has created:

> If one is missing, I miss it dreadfully. I couldn't find these [the ones she is wearing around her neck] the other day, and half of me was thinking at that stage 'I don't think I'll get these again'. But when I couldn't find them I missed them, because I couldn't do what I wanted to do, which was putting the database in. And I had to put one of my reading glasses up to read the stuff, and then put those ones on [the computer/music glasses] so that I could see what was happening on the screen. It was a real nuisance.

The relationship between the computer and other household objects is also illustrated by competition, rather than collaboration, between the computer and other objects for their use in activities.

Computers 'competing' with other objects

A number of authors have reported that heavy computer use tends to result in less watching of television (Wheelock 1992). Among the participants in the current study, television was one activity which was said to have been displaced by computer use (although, as we saw above, some people are able to use the computer and watch or listen to television at the same time). However, a number of other kinds of activity were also mentioned.

Margaret Paine, for example, has noticed that since she bought the computer her habit of writing a daily diary has fallen off:

> I've always been fanatical about writing a daily diary. And, like, I've got diaries from the last seven or eight years that I've lived in Australia and I've got each year's diary. Since I've bought the computer I'm not writing in my diaries and I feel really heartbroken about that because it's been really important for me to keep that daily diary and I can time it as to when I got the computer to when there's slowing down in my writing habits . . . I do it much less frequently.

Friends have suggested to her that she should write the diary on the computer instead, but Margaret feels that this is not personal enough: 'My handwriting in my special diary with my special leather cover is much more personal.' The transition from handwriting to computer writing involves much more, then, than simply switching from one medium to the other. The physical praxis of handwriting engages with objects which have particular tactile qualities – the look, feel and smell of a leather cover, with their associations of luxury and history – which contrast markedly with those of the computer and its connotations of contemporary professional life.

If the presence of material objects in our environment acts at a level below that of consciousness to provide us with a kind of psychic scaffolding, and within which what I have referred to as a kind of cultural proprioception is enabled, then such changes in technology may have profound effects on the self in relation to writing. Other forms of activity with a practical outcome are also clearly affected: a number of study participants also commented on how the computer seemed to displace craft activities, such as knitting, needlework and sewing, or the playing of musical instruments. It might be suggested, therefore, that in our 'living with things' (Dant 1999) in the contemporary world, our interactions with the materials and objects we are surrounded by is increasingly becoming technologically mediated, even within the intimate locale of the domestic sphere.

Some formerly quite common domestic objects have been supplanted by the arrival of the computer. Many of the study participants had typewriters before they had computers, and Jim Christou's sister does not have a computer but does have a typewriter. As Janet Fuller puts it, there's no need for a typewriter when one has a computer: 'I have an old typewriter and it's always kind of handy to have a typewriter or now it's like a computer because it's better than a typewriter.' Ruth Bourke gave her typewriter away once she got her computer. She feels that the computer has not, however, simply taken the typewriter's place, but has given her additional possibilities and made it possible for her to start a university course, which she does not feel she would have been able to do with just the typewriter.

John Powell, in talking about whether or not to use the computer for some kinds of tasks or to do them the 'manual' way, compares the issue to that of whether or not to grate cheese in the food processor:

I sort of think of the computer a bit like I think of this thing [the food processor]. You know it can do all these sort of things, you know . . . you can grate cheese with it, but is it actually easier to sort of take this out, put in the cheese grating appliance, plug it in, grate the cheese then take this off and wash it, or would it be easier to get the grater out and just grate the cheese?

In a similar vein, Elizabeth Martin speculates on whether it is worth starting the computer up to look something up on the CD-ROM encyclopaedia:

We actually do use it on occasion for her homework. It's like 'we'll just get the encyclopaedia and look it up'. But it takes such a long time to do that sometimes, I've got to turn it on and wait until it comes up, put the CD in just to get this one bit of information and then turn it off and I'm just wondering whether it's really worth the effort.

In many households there is a sense that both the computer and dedicated electronic games machines (such as Nintendo and Sega equipment) have displaced more traditional gaming methods, such as card and board games. The Cooper household has always had a 'culture' of playing games, but is finding that the computer has displaced some of this activity:

We have always had that culture of playing games, cards or whatever. That's how I grew up. Say, like every Sunday we do a quiz that's in the paper. That's like a little thing that I did with my family and we do it now. Someone comes and they'll say 'Have you done the quiz yet?' and so I think that when we come together often it's expected that some sort of game follows. (Sylvia Cooper)

Although they do still play card and board games, particularly when the family gets together, Sylvia feels that their use of their Sega game system is an extension of this culture of communal game-playing within the family. Indeed, it has to some extent taken the place of the non-electronic types of game. In this as in many of the study households, computer or electronic game-playing is a common joint activity, either for children playing together, children playing with an adult, or adults playing together. In the Cooper household, while the children tend to prefer to play on the computer, their parents will frequently play together on the Sega:

We play Columns on the Sega and the kids play on the computer usually. We have competitions. To see who's going to make the cup of tea and things like that . . . We probably would do it at least a couple of times a week. Of a night, usually when the kids have gone to bed. (Sylvia Cooper)

This behaviour appears not to be unusual. Peter and Sarah Richards report that when they first bought an Atari games machine for their children, they themselves 'used to sit up until midnight playing it'. Perhaps the willingness to be engaged in such 'playful' pursuits is part of the constitution of the relationship of these couples.

In the Collins household, although both a computer and a games machine are owned, the computer is preferred by the children, so it tends to be a case of whoever gets to the computer first plays on that, while the other takes a turn on the Nintendo. Both the computer and the Nintendo are located downstairs from the main part of the house, in a family room which was built onto the house a couple of years before. Patricia Collins feels that the Nintendo does not get as much use as it did before the computer came into the household. Patricia feels that her son's level of use of the computer or the video games machine, particularly as a joint activity with his friends, is also related to the age group he is moving into:

> It's got a bit to do with him getting older as well. Once upon a time they would play cricket up on the road perhaps even go out and throw balls to each other. There's not much of that happening now. I don't think that he would do that now anyway, even if the computer wasn't there. I think the Nintendo would get more use if the computer wasn't there.

In the Bartlett household, where there are four sons aged between ten and nineteen, games machines also take up some of the overflow of game-playing from the computer:

> We do have the old Atari system, with joystick thing plugged into the television, and they've got Gameboys and things like that. If it's school holidays they'll alternate [between games machines and the computer] and if I drag the Atari stuff out and say here it is stick it on, they'll play that. The Gameboy is used constantly or not at all – if it happens to be in the line of fire they'll grab it to play. (Merilyn Bartlett)

If the computer may be seen to be both collaborating and competing with other household objects, we must also consider the extent to which the computer may be viewed as a space containing other 'objects' such as software and electronic documents, rather than a simple object. As a domestic space, the computer itself must be actively managed and kept organized.

Computer 'housekeeping'

In most households, computer 'housekeeping' tasks, such as backing up important files or keeping the hard drive organized and tidy, are taken on by one person in particular. In the households where there is one person who has a clear proprietorship over the computer it tends to be this person who undertakes housekeeping tasks associated with the computer. In the Turner household, for example, although the computer 'technically' belongs to the family as a whole, in practice Thomas Turner uses it most and has exerted proprietoriality over the computer. Thomas is also the one who keeps the hard drive organized. Each member of the family has their own folder:

> If you open the computer it's got the hard disk. You open the hard disk it's got 'Applications' for the software, then it's got 'Users' and then you click on 'Users' and it's got 'Jonathan', 'Michael', 'Thomas', 'Sally', and then within mine it's got other folders, 'Tax', and 'Current Jobs' and all this sort of stuff and then 'Masters'. So yes, so things are organized. (Thomas Turner)

In the Martinez household, Carlos and his eldest son do the computer housekeeping together:

> Now and then I check that everything seems to be OK and sometimes we'll get together [with Jonathan], and that is one thing that we do together is clean up the drive together. And before we do the defragmentation we'll say 'Get rid of this, this. I like it but I'm not using it' and so on. (Carlos Martinez)

Defragmenting the hard drive is a procedure that most householders would not undertake as part of their routine maintenance of the computer. Over a period of time, through successive deleting and overwriting of files on the hard drive, the information can become inefficiently stored and defragmenting the disk rearranges the information so that it can be read efficiently by the computer, resulting in some performance improvement. Making backups of the information on the computer is another kind of 'housekeeping' task, and households vary in the degree to which they do this. In the Cooper household, there is no internal organization to the computer, all the files are in together, and individuals are expected to take care of backing up their own files if they want to make sure they are kept.

While for many computer users their housekeeping of the computer's internal space reflects more general domestic patterns, Thomas Turner feels that it's possible to be more organized within the virtual space of the computer than it is in 'real' life, because the computer forces a choice about where a file will be located:

> I'm very lazy when it comes to organizing things but I find I'm really organized on a computer. And the thing I like about the computer is that you can open all these things out and then you just click on them and they all close and then you switch the computer off and when you come back to it you know it's all there. Whereas with papers, it's all over the place and I hate it.

In the Richards household, it is Peter who has oversight of the information on the hard disk. Each of the children has their own floppy disk on which they store their own data, and for which they are responsible themselves: 'I make sure that things go into folders on the hard disk. The children do all their own work on floppy disks.' If one of the children leaves something on the hard disk, Peter puts it onto their disk for them. The activity of keeping the computer organized is thus similar to that of other household space, where some members of the household may leave objects 'lying about' for other people to 'tidy up'. Indeed, Peter actively tidies the hard disk: 'I'll often tidy it up. I can't keep my office one as tidy, but I can keep this one tidy. It has to be fairly tidy because it's got various users and they have to have space to put their stuff when they come to use it.'

Peter's habit of neatness is reflected also in his general behaviour around the house. Sarah says that she can 'handle more mess' than Peter: he is often the one to tidy up and is responsible for all of the household vacuum cleaning. Peter also feels that it is easier to stay on top of things at home, since work is too busy to be able to spend time there keeping things tidy. 'It's probably also that I can't keep my office under control at work, so I think I want home to be more of a haven.' In this household, then, although there is a gendered division of household labour (Sarah does all the cooking, for example), it tends not to be the 'traditional' one in which the woman is responsible for the inside housekeeping tasks such as vacuuming while the man is responsible for 'outside' tasks such as taking out the garbage and mowing the lawn (Goodnow and Bowes 1994).

In many of the images of home computers included in this book, the computer is surrounded by the by-products of everyday domestic activity – by 'mess'. Indeed, household mess can be seen as the normal state of entropy of the household's objects, which is routinely overcome by the reverse entropic activity of 'tidying up'. People vary in the degree to which they experience stress as a result of living amongst their own or other people's 'mess', and in their responses to living with mess, and these variations are probably to some extent determined by upbringing, and by their formation within the environments of childhood. In some households, one or more people have such a low tolerance for mess that tidying is a high priority activity and the house is kept extremely tidy. In other households it seems that the disorder produced by the ongoing activities of the household's occupants is a perfectly acceptable environment. 'Tidying' is therefore one of those activities of home-building by which we make household space habitable, whatever that means to us.

What to one person will appear to be a hopelessly messy desk, for example, to its owner may be a highly efficient work space. Each item having been placed in its location as a result of its owner's ongoing activities, the desk's state at any given time is essentially an externalization (objectification, even) of ongoing processes which are also partially internal to the owner. The relationship between the owner and the desk is therefore one in which there is synchrony between the state of the desk and the owner him or herself, the objects on the desk interfacing with the owner's expectation of where to find each item. This is indeed a critical point: the owner needs to be able to find each item as and when it is needed, without having to think about it too much, or having to search for it. The purpose of tidying up, then, can be seen to also fulfil a similar purpose, and hence the adage 'a place for everything and everything in its place'.

The processes of home-building require such housekeeping activities. It is only when objects can be relied upon to stay in their places that the home's ability to provide a maximally familiar environment is fulfilled. Further, to refuse to reimpose such order may be a strategy for asserting ownership over such spaces. It is difficult to imagine that a messy desk could have more than one owner: when work space is shared (in shared offices, for example), the shared space is generally left orderly when each user leaves it available for others. To leave a desk messy is to assert one's proprietoriality over it, as if to say to passers-by, 'I haven't finished here, please leave this as it is'.

Conclusion

Home is an objectification of its members and is thus a structure in space and time made up of material objects and established patterns of activity, as well as ideas, meanings and values. Although it is created by its members, it exists outside of them but not independently of them. Nor do they live independently of it: although home is generally a structure which supports and enables the everyday life of its inhabitants, their actions and activities are also constrained by it. The computer's relationship to the other 'movable' objects of the home is, as we have seen, the result of complex dynamic processes of negotiation, involving not just its human 'owners', but also the objects themselves and their existing interactions and relationships.

Chapter 38

LARISSA HJORTH

DOMESTICATING NEW MEDIA
A discussion on locating mobile media

THE REMARKABLE RISE OF the mobile (or cell) phone over the past few decades raises many challenges for the study of new media. It was, initially at least, quite different from the technocultural forms of the PC and Internet that provided the focus of new media studies. Yet, in recent years these handheld devices have come to adopt, and even supersede, many of the functions and practices of more established computers. They carry web browsers, cameras, GPS functions, email and SMS. Newer devices such as netbooks and the iPad are hybrid computers/mobile media.

It is significant then that Larissa Hjorth's discussion here says little directly about telephony, arguing instead that mobile devices are the Swiss army knife of new media, portable and extremely multifunctional. She is, for instance, more concerned with the use of GPS-enabled devices in pervasive games, games (generally created by media artists rather than commercial media companies) that mix movement through actual space with virtual gameworlds (see also **Lovink** and **Marks** on new media art). Initially designed for handheld computers or PDAs, such games are now fully realisable with most contemporary smart phones. These games, she argues, offer ways of exploring the relationships between the virtual and the actual, between the mediated experiences of distance and intimacy, and between media immediacy and delay.

It is also significant that she is concerned with precisely *how* we might study these devices and the cultural activities that they initiate or are entangled in. In addition to the attention to new media art production, she identifies two key theoretical frameworks for the study of mobile media cultures. These are the 'domestic technologies' approach and remediation. Though different in their concerns, these two frameworks each question linear, futurological assumptions about the development and cultural impact of new technologies. Drawing on cultural studies, anthropology and sociology, a domestic technologies approach emphasises the negotiation of uses and meanings of a new device or system by consumers in the home and in everyday consumption to interrogate their social and political implications. Remediation, applied to digital media by Jay David Bolter and Richard Grusin but based on Marshall **McLuhan**'s insights, is a genealogical approach that asserts that new media always incorporate, or remediate, existing media (see also **Huhtamo**, **Marvin**, and **Klein**). Thus mobile media rework the nineteenth-century technoculture of telephony and photography, but also, Hjorth argues, texting and multimedia messaging remediate letter writing and postcard sending.

Finally, Hjorth identifies two more important aspects of mobile media culture with political and media analytical implications. Firstly, she is critical of unqualified celebrations of user-created content or UCC (sometimes called user-generated content or UGC). The creative and social work, and the pressure to produce this work, of uploading images, videos, commentary, etc. in Web 2.0 applications is often driven by the commercial interests of Internet media companies (an argument that resonates with **Terranova** in Part Five). Secondly, she argues that the emphasis on the screen and visuality in both commercial media production and in the study and criticism of popular media in the twentieth century needs to be overthrown in favour of attention to the haptic nature of mobile screens. The 'haptic' refers to the sense of touch rather than sight and is, she argues, dominant in the ubiquity of the handheld touch-screen of game devices such as the Nintendo DS and most new mobile phones.

http://www.larissahjorth.net/

Introduction

As convergence leaves its mark on this century, the ultimate alibi in the convergence rhetoric seems to be the mobile device. Convergence can occur across various levels such as technological, economic, industrial, and cultural. As Henry Jenkins observed, in the growth of the mobile phone into converging various forms of multimedia—into the ambiguous and yet ubiquitous mobile media—one could almost forget that mobile media arose from an extension of the landline telephony.[1]

Now the twenty-first century's equivalent to the Swiss army knife,[2] mobile media encompasses multiple forms of media including camera, gaming platform, MP3 player, and Internet portal. As we begin to chart the burgeoning phenomenon of mobile media, we must reassess the methodologies and frameworks being used. How do we grapple with mobile media's interdisciplinary background? Should mobile media be framed in terms of the mobile communication and material cultures traditions, fathered by British theorist Roger Silverstone, that have contextualized the sociocultural processes of media technologies in terms of the domestic technologies approach? Or should mobile media be framed by creative theories and practices of new media?

The rise of the mobile phone into mobile media has attracted scholars from various disciplines such as media studies, gender studies, cultural studies, media sociology, virtual ethnography, and new media, all bringing with them a wealth of traditions, methodologies, and approaches. One of the dominant and highly successful approaches in the field of studying mobile phone cultures is, undoubtedly, the domestic technologies approach.

As an interdisciplinary framework, the domestic technologies approach[3] draws from anthropology,[4] cultural studies,[5] and consumption studies.[6] A significant part of its lineage lies in anthropology and its commitment to analyzing the processes of material cultures in everyday life. Undoubtedly, the seduction of the domestic technologies approach is that it focuses on the symbolic dimensions of technologies in everyday life. In particular, the domestic technologies approach focuses on meanings individuals and cultural contexts give to their technologies, extrapolating on the ways in which users perceive them.

However, as the mobile phone expands into a multimedia device, how can the dimensions of social and reproductive labor—addressed by domestic technologies approaches—be incorporated into the growing realm of mobile media as new media? Domestic technologies approaches seem to fail in grasping the role of creative labor associated with mobile media beyond social and reproductive labor paradigms. In turn, new media approaches to mobile media seem unequipped to address the political dimensions of social and reproductive labor. Since both approaches have been useful in addressing the dynamic, social, creative, and procedural nature of mobile media, it seems fitting to discuss these two enveloping traditions in the context of locating mobile media within "Domesticating new media."

In this chapter I will explore the marriage between the two traditions—on the one hand, the domestic technologies approach, on the other hand, new media remediation approach—in order to conceptualize some of the paradoxes found in mobile media in terms of earlier, ongoing processes. I will outline some of the key attributes and paradoxes that have plagued both traditions' examination of mobile media. Through the example of mobile location-aware gaming, I will draw upon current discourses around mobile media and its coinhabitation in both domestic technologies and new media discourses. As this chapter will argue, through mobile media we can gain insight into some of the recurring paradoxes that run across disciplines and boundaries, continuing to haunt and limit interdisciplinary approaches to twenty-first-century new media practices. In particular, I argue that the emphasis upon visuality and screen-centric views have neglected to address one of the most important aspects of mobile media, the haptic.

Media @ mobile

Mobile media is a strange animal to tame. Part domestic technology, part new media, the phenomenon has attached much stargazing and posturing about the future. Through the portal of mobile media, we have witnessed mobility becoming conflated with futurism. The rise of the mobile phone has been marked by its shifting symbolism, usages, and adaptations.[7] When mobile phones first graced the mainstream in the 1980s they were associated with yuppies and conspicuous displays of wealth as demonstrated in the iconic 1980s film *Wall Street*. Then, as mobile phones were adopted and adapted by youth cultures, the phone shrunk into a complex creature adorned by user-created customization from phone straps to sticker faceplates and screen savers. Then, as the phone became more than *just* a phone and started to emanate this century's Swiss army knife, it expanded in size both physically and psychologically to become an integral component in visual, textual, and aural practices in contemporary everyday life.[8]

It is with this size change that we moved into an epoch of mobile multi-modality that became synonymous with contemporary mobility. The rise of mobile media as multimedia par excellence has also been accompanied by corporate smoke and mirrors around the so-called empowered user by way of user-created content (UCC) and prosumer agency. In this climate of optimistic futurism, mobile media promised a further democratization of media. But as Finnish theorist Ilpo Koskinen notes, this accessibility of multimedia often resulted in the aesthetics of banality; images and media rehearse well-known genres and themes.[9] Within the so-called banality are normalized power relations inscribed at the level of everyday practice; thus mobile media serves to remind us of the growing significance of place.

Much work has been conducted around the "banality" of mobile media practices in terms of cameraphone visual and distribution characteristics with many theorists pointing to the content of mobile media rehearsing earlier media (that is, cameraphone images reenacting analogue genres) being banal but the context in which they are shared (or not) providing much signification;[10] however, it seems that the haptic economies, so particular to mobile media, are in need of reevaluation. While Mizuko Ito and Daisuke Okabe's 3 S's—sharing, storing, and saving[11]—noted some of the particulars, we need to examine the politics of "waiting for immediacy" just outside the frame/screen. In other words, what are some of the haptic workouts occurring just outside the frame that undoubtedly affect inside the frame?

So what do I mean by haptic? Just one glance at the current models of mobile media such as iPhone and LG prada and we can see that the screen is no longer about visuality; it is about haptics—haptic screens, to be precise. The engagement of mobile media is not ocular in the case of the gaze or the glance, but rather akin to what Chris Chesher characterizes as the "glaze."[12] Drawing on console games cultures, Chesher identifies three types of glaze spaces— the glazed-over, sticky, and identity-reflective. For Chesher, these three 'dimensions' of the glaze move beyond a visual economy, deploying the filters of the other senses such as aural and haptic.

The haptic has often been undertheorized in mobile communication discourses, often left up to new media practitioners to grapple with in such projects as location-aware gaming. In the growth of mobile-media discourses, much has been discussed in terms of media such as cameraphone practices and the associated sharing and distribution methods. However, much of the rhetoric around mobile media and convergence has been focused upon the frame and visuality—as such concepts as "cross-platforming" entail. These models have discussed media in terms of twentieth-century preoccupations with the visual and the screen, neglecting to reorient frameworks around what makes mobile media so particular; whether being mobile or immobile, the logic is of the haptic. It is about the touch of the device, the intimacy of the object, that makes it so meaningful.

For new media artists such as Rafael Lazano Hemmer and his relational architecture projects, it is this very oscillation of the haptic and the cerebral that partakes in mobile media copresence that makes it such a particular vehicle for twenty-first-century new media practice. In urban spaces, it is not so much the cameraphone images that are transforming the spaces but, rather, the haptic workouts of the everyday user documenting. Much of the discussion of mobile media has encircled the important role of mobile media copresence,[13] and yet the integral notion of the haptic, apart from the hype around SMS thumb cultures, has been largely ignored.

However, the critique of normalized everyday practices and the haptic workouts outside the frame can be found in the various upsurge of experimental new media projects such as location-aware gaming, mobile gaming, or "big games." Location-aware or pervasive games often involve the use of GPS (geographic positioning systems), which allows games to be played simultaneously online and offline. As Finnish theorist (and director of DiGRA) Frans Mäyrä notes, gaming has always involved place and mobility and yet this is precisely what is missing in current games, especially single player genres.[14] Mäyrä points to the possibilities of pervasive (location-aware) gaming as not only testing our imagination and creativity but also questioning our ideas of what constitutes reality and what it means to be copresent and virtual.

The notion of "big games" does not so much relate to the gadget's gluttonous size but rather it has more to do with the role of people and the gravity of place in the navigation of copresence. These projects served to remind us of the importance of locality and its relationship to practices of copresence. The potentiality of "big games" to expose and comment on the politics of copresence—traversing virtual and actual, here and there—in contemporary media cultures has gained much attention. They highlight some of the key paradoxes of everyday life that have been exemplified in mobile-media projects such as location-aware gaming. The paradoxes include virtual and actual, online and offline, cerebral and haptic, delay and immediacy.

As Frank Lantz, a New York-based game designer who has been involved in such pivotal projects as *PacManhattan*, notes, the importance of location-aware mobile gaming—or "big games"—definitely plays an important role in the future of gaming.[15] Citing examples such as *PacManhattan*, UK's blast theory, Geocaching, and Mogi, Lantz emphasizes the importance of these projects in testing the notion of reality as mediation. As Lantz observes, the precursors to big games and the 1970s New Games Movement were undoubtedly the art movements of the 1960s such as happenings (impromptu art events) and the Situationist International (SI) tactics of Guy Debord such as *détournement*, which operated to interrupt/disrupt everyday practices and the increasing role of media and commodification. In this way, this can be paralleled with the trend in contemporary art from the 1990s that French curator and critic Nicolas Bourriaud dubs "relational aesthetics."[16] As Bourriaud observed, "relational aesthetics" dominated the international art scene from the 1990s onwards, building from an emphasis upon locality and deinstitutionalization of installation and the "international" in favor of the vernacular and local.

Locative mobile gaming illustrates the paradoxes of mobile media as part of the cyclic and dynamic processes of technology. For example, in an age of so-called immediate technologies, such projects enlighten us to the conundrum of instantaneity, that is, the inevitable poetics of delay. They highlight the price of mobility and its oscillation between freedom and leash[17] in which work and leisure boundaries are increasingly blurred.[18]

Locative mobile gaming also emphasizes other paradoxes apart from the aforementioned immediacy/delay temporal conundrum. These projects highlight the way in which mobile media can often interfere with, rather than help, face-to-face connections. For example, the tyranny of mobile media's creative labor/democratizing of media dimensions, as epitomized by UCC, sees users becoming more enslaved to the technology rather than it freeing up time to spend with intimates. Locative mobile gaming projects afford us one way in which to reflect and mediate on the paradoxes of contemporary mobile media.

Moreover, locative mobile gaming illustrates that in the face of democratizing of media, new media is still far from the understandings and interests of the everyday person. It also reflects new media artists' fears and yet curiosity about mobile media's ultimate creative conundrum: is it the rise of democratized media and mainstreaming of new media or does the "banality" represent the domination of pedestrianization of new media? Can mobile media teach new media ways to remember the histories' "shock of the new" as actually the "delay of the banal"?

As a new conflation of many techniques, traditions, and media histories, it is no easy task to outline the nebulous terrain of mobile media. In this chapter I argue that one way in which we can understand mobile media is vis-à-vis its borrowing from, and adapting of, various sociological and new media traditions. In the next section of the chapter I will address two traditions—domestic technologies and remediation, new media approaches—in the cartography of mobile media. I argue that many parallels can be found in the two traditions and that by incorporating the two genealogies we could gain much insight into mobile media.

Just as mobile media needs the rigor of domestic technologies approaches to comprehend the social dimensions of new media, it also needs the innovative approaches of new media theory in order to reconceptualize the conflations between creative and social labor in mobile media's fusion between media communication and new media practices. Through the conflation of domestic technologies and remediation of new media approaches we can begin to conceptualize mobile media as no longer just a "third screen," but, more importantly, a *third space*.

Domesticating new media: two examples of the multitraditions of mobile media

The rise of mobile media could be read as nascent. However, such a belief, propagated in global media's lauding of the new mobile revolution in consumer agency (in the form of the prosumer and Web 2.0), neglects to address the dynamic dimensions of technology as a sociotechnological process. In the case of domestic technologies approaches, in which domestication is always an ongoing and never-completed process, the dynamics of mobile media extends already existing cyclical models. So too, in the tradition of new media, in which old and new have had a dialectical and dynamic relationship that disrupts any linear or casual notion of time.

As mobile communication and media industries converge, the all-pervasive futurist rhetoric becomes stifling. And yet, if the twin histories of new media and mobile communication have taught us anything, the "new" is always remediated and mediated. Each "new" technology deploys techniques of the older technology, which in turn revises the earlier media. This cuts to the core of all communication and cultural practices implicated in intimacy. For Jay Bolter and Richard Grusin, new media are remediated with older media into a dynamic ongoing process that disrupts any causal or linear notion of old and new technologies.[19] As Margaret Morse concisely notes in the case of the Internet, all forms of intimacy are mediated—by language, gestures, and memories.[20] Emerging forms of visual, textual, and haptic mobile genres such as SMS and cameraphone practices—reenacting earlier rituals such as nineteenth-century letter writing, postcards,[21] and gift-giving customs[22]—have only served to highlight the remediated nature of the rise of mobile media.

There is much to be learnt from understanding the parallels between new media theory on remediation and mobile communication's usage of the domestic technologies approach. Like the domestic technologies approach,[23] the study of new media through the lens of remediation echoes a similar philosophical stance. As influential theorist in the field of media archaeology, Erkki Huhtamo, has argued, the cyclical phenomena of media tend to transcend historical contexts, often placating a process of paradoxical reenactment and reenchantment with what is deemed as "new."[24] For Huhtamo, media archaeology approaches are "a way of studying recurring cyclical phenomena that (re)appear and disappear over and over again in media history, somehow seeming to transcend specific historical contexts."[25] As Jussi Parikka and Jaakko Suominen note, the procedural nature of media archaeology approaches means "new media is always situated within continuous histories of media production, distribution and usage—as part of a longer duration of experience."[26]

Citing an example of the launch of Nintendo DS that heralded a new and "unique" experience for twenty-first-century entertainment, Parikka and Suominen note that much of contemporary postindustrial digital media culture is inundated by futurism that seeks to break with the past.[27] Parikka and Suominen note that this "creates the impression that, in the new media discourse, the past functions solely as something worse or less sophisticated, something that has to be left behind and practically forgotten."[28]

When Marshall McLuhan identified that the content of new media is that of the previous technology, he highlighted the nonlinear and dynamic role of new technology imbued by the specters of old technology.[29] In short, that the "new" is far from superseding or breaking with the old as modernist mythologies would have it. The fact that the notion of "new" in new media has been continuously challenged and demonstrated as a fallacy echoes the way in which technology has been approached by many mobile communication scholars (from predominantly sociological and urban anthropological traditions) through the domestic technologies approach.[30]

In the picture painted by the domestic technologies approach, domestic technologies such as the radio, TV, and mobile phone are seen as part of the cyclic and ongoing process of consumption in everyday contemporary life. As Daniel Miller notes in his coauthored study with Heather Horst on Jamaican cell-phone use, "what one has to study are not things or people but processes."[31] Much of the literature analyzing mobile communication has utilized the domestic technologies approach[32] to identify adoption and adaptation of technologies as always ongoing and never completed.[33] Like the cultures in which they inhabit, domestic technologies are always in flux. Domestication is ongoing and dynamic, and through customization practices we can domesticate domestic technologies as much as they domesticate us in a productive tension. In the case of the mobile phone, while the domestic technology device may have *physically* left the home, it *psychologically* resonates what it means to be at home and local no matter where it is located.

As David Morley has noted, the mobile phone has often been cited as a key example of domestic technologies par excellence.[34] Key scholars in this area include Leslie Haddon, Roger Silverstone, Haddon and Silverstone, Rich Ling, and Miller. As a key scholar in the field, Haddon provided decisive apparatus to comprehend the dynamic and enduring processes of the domestic technologies.[35] Often users' relationships to their domestic technologies can wax and wane, drawing feelings of ambivalence, and yet inevitably due to the prescribed need to have the technologies to be part of contemporary urbanity.

As an approach, the domestic technologies method sees the process of engagement with technologies undergoing various stages or nodes of a cycle that include "imagination, appropriation, objectification, incorporation, and conversion."[36] Consumption is seen as an ongoing process that is perpetually negotiated, way after the actual point of sales. As Rich Ling notes, "our consumption becomes a part of our own social identity. Further, others' consumption is a type of lens through which we see them and through which we interpret their social position."[37]

Mobile media represents a meeting of the crossroads between the genealogy of domestic technologies and media archaeologies of new media. In both these traditions, we see mobile media remediating and reenacting previous media cultures and modes of domestic regimes. Reminding us of our forgetting whilst harnessing the inevitable amnesia that accompanies any notion of "new," mobile media represents the conundrum of new technologies. In new media discourses we can find many examples of the content or specters of the older media. Like the domestic technologies approach, the study of new media through the lens of remediation echoes a similar philosophical stance.

According to Timo Kopomaa, the mobile phone is an extension of nineteenth-century media.[38] For Kopomaa, mobile media creates a new "third" space in between public and private space. On the one hand, the project of examining mobile media entails observing the remediated nature of new technologies and thus conceptualizing them in terms of media archaeologies.[39] On the other hand, mobile media's reenactment of earlier technologies is indicative of its domestic technologies tradition that extends and rehearses the processes of precursors such as radio and TV. It is the fact that Kopomaa draws our attention to mobile media as a third space, rather than third screen, which is significant.

Both traditions—the domestic technologies and new media remediation approaches—emphasize the cyclic and dynamic process of media technologies that cannot be simplistically divided between old and new or inside and outside the screen. Rather, the cartography of mobile media is one imbued by paradoxes. In the case of cameraphone practices—whether still or moving—mobile media demonstrates two distinctive paradoxes, that of the *reel* in the real, and the inherent poetics of *delay* in the practice of immediacy in the navigating of offline and online copresence. As Lev Manovich identified,[40] contemporary new media and digital practice are all consumed by fetishizing the real through the lens of the reel—that is, texture and skin of the analogue.

For Manovich, the way in which to understand the remediated emerging digital cultures and the haunting by the ghost of the analogue is through a series of paradoxes. These sets of paradoxes are located around the relationship between the real and the reel. As Manovich identifies, while the analogue may disappear, it will continue to haunt the digital in the form of the analogue's particular realism, the "reel." This is evident in the way in which cameraphone practices echo previous analogue norms[41] and that, in turn, make mobile media, according to Koskinen, characterized by "banality."

However, one of the most compelling examples of the real/reel phenomenon, where the tactile process of the analogue is fully felt both metaphorically and actually, is the rise of screen cultures in mobile media. In particular, the rise of such mobile-media devices as iPhone, LG prada, and Samsung Arami phone—to name a few—all incorporate one key feature, haptic screens. Here the reel/real paradox is played out in the haptic versus visual, in which the haptic is undoubtedly the more meaningful factor that "domesticates" the device into the user's everyday life. Much of the specters of the analogue reel are more about the tactical experience of image processing; and while these processes have been deleted in the rise of the digital, it is the legacy of the haptic—that has moved from the filmic developing process to the actual politics of the touch screen—that continues unabated. However, in the language set of twentieth-century media cultures, much discussion was given to visuality rather than the increasing role of the haptic.

While location-aware projects are invaluable in geocaching (such as GPS) and demonstrating the importance of place and specificity in a period of global technologies, they also served to highlight one of the greatest residual paradoxes of mobile media as a metaphor for sociotechnologies. That is, the paradoxical politics of copresence. One example can be found in the aims of twentieth-century technology to overcome difference and distance from geographic and physical to cultural and psychological. This attempt to overcome distance and difference sees the opposite result, the overcoming of closeness. Practices of copresence intimacies become fetishized, through what Misa Matsuda has characterized as "full-time intimacy."[42] This recites what Michael Arnold identified as the Janus-faced nature of mobile media that operates to push and pull us, setting us free to roam, and yet attaches us to a perpetual leash.[43]

As Arnold notes, the Janis-faced phenomenon is symptomatic of what Martin Heidegger characterized as "un-distance." The role of technology in the twentieth century has always been to overcome some form of distance—whether geographic, physical, social, cultural, temporal, or spatial. But herein lies the paradox. The more we try to overcome distance, the more we overcome closeness. This is the kernel of un-distance and its temporal and spatial tenor. Un-distance can be seen today in the practice of mobile media, particularly pervasive location-aware projects that rely on the so-called immediacy or instantaneity of the networked.

However, one could argue that un-distance has been perpetuated by the ocular-centrism of twentieth century "tele" media, a phenomenon that has been disrupted by mobile media's emphasis on the haptic. For Ingrid Richardson, mobile media needs to harness the importance of the haptic. Conducting a small ethno-phenomenological study on the use of phonegame hybrids, Richardson disavows the ocular-centrism prevalent in "new media screen technologies" to focus on "the spatial, perceptual and ontic effects of mobile devices as nascent new media forms."[44] As she persuasively observes,

> In order to grasp the epistemic, ontic and phenomenological status of screen media it is important to trace their ocularcentric legacy; by understanding this history we can then interpret how mobile screens in particular work to bewilder classical notions of visual perception, agency and knowing.[45]

Indeed, one of the compelling factors to arise from mobile media, and this links back to its fusion of remediation and domestic genealogies, is the persistence of the ontology of the reel.

However, unlike the twentieth-century "reel"—in the form of the aural modes of address embroiled in "screenness"—the mobile reel, and thus possible creative worlds and realities, is undoubtedly governed by the haptic.

The game of mobile media—whether it be partaking in cameraphone imagery and the haptic exercises outside the screen, to mobile gaming, in which interactivity and engagement are navigated by haptic mobility and immobility rather than visualities of screen cultures—is undoubtedly changing how we are thinking about domestic technologies and new media. Through the lens of paradoxes that encompass virtual and actual, online and offline, haptic and visual and delay and immediacy, some lessons about twentieth-century media practice can be learnt. For anyone that has participated in a mobile pervasive game, they will quickly identify the lack of coherence between online and offline copresence. The more we try to partake in the *politics of immediacy*, the more we succumb to the *poetics of delay*. This paradox extends beyond just mobile gaming and can be found in many of the multimedia possibilities of mobile media— from cameraphone imagery and MMS to moblogging and SMS.

In the case of the growing interest in urban screen cultures as an analogy for the twenty-first century, one could argue that it is indeed the very eruption of the twentieth century's obsession with visualities for the twenty-first century's politics of the haptic that dominates the canvas of mobile media. From the haptic screen interfaces to the various multimedia tactics such as mobile gaming that disavow the screen for the haptic and audio, mobile media revises the perceived hierarchies of the senses which, in turn, could breathe new life into new media and domestic technologies approaches.

Time after time: the never-ending concluding beginning

In modernism, the role of originality was celebrated. For the modernist avant-gardeists, such vehicles as technology served as a decisive break from the past in what art critic Robert Hughes characterized as "the shock of the new."[46] In contemporary postindustrial digital cultures, the "new" promised by mobile media is in fact "banal" and located in nostalgic politics such as the real/reel paradigm. In this chapter, I have assembled two traditions—domestic technologies and remediation—in order to show the similar cyclic debates operating across disciplines. I argue that perhaps mobile media needs to be conceptualized as the "shock of the banal," that is, its paradoxes—online and offline, virtual and actual, delay and immediacy, haptic and visual— are far from new and can be traced through various disciplinary traditions.

In my ethnographic studies into cameraphone practices in Seoul, Tokyo, Hong Kong, and Melbourne, one of the increasing features of the tyranny of the "full =N time intimacy"[47] of mobile media customization is the use of immediacy to camouflage delay. Many respondents spoke of creating their own forms of delay so that they could savor the SMS or MMS. With the immediacy of such technologies, the tactics of pretending to not see or receive a message immediately allowed respondents time—what I call "the poetics of delay." Moreover, the persistence of the reel in much of the cameraphone images, genres, and mobile movies was significant. In particular, for many respondents, mobile-media making was less about visual economies and more about aural and haptic modes of address akin to earlier "reel" domestic technologies such as the TV and radio. Thus, the conflation between domestic technologies and new media approaches could further address one of the greatest paradoxes of shifts from twentieth to twenty-first century media; that is, rather than it being a history predicated on visualities as the "screenness" would entail, it is a history of the rise of the audio and the haptic that are becoming the key indicators and characteristics of mobile media.[48]

I have chosen to focus on two traditions—one draws from media and communication and material cultures (anthropology) in the form of the domestic technologies approach; the other calls upon new media approaches of remediation and media archaeologies approaches. In these two traditions we can see various similarities—the focus on the dynamic, sociocultural processes of mobile media. While the former allows for more insight into social and reproductive labor debates, the latter affords us acuity into shifting modes of accessing creative labor and everyday life. In the case of mobile media projects such as location-aware gaming, I argue we need to draw upon the two models, incorporating them into a new framework for evaluating dimensions of mobile media, and twenty-first century screen cultures, in terms of key attributes such as the haptic. The important factor here is against the seductive and simplistic futurism prevailing in much discussion around mobile media we need to recognize that mobile media, like new media, is inevitably involved in the politics of the banal and nostalgia.

Much of the futurist posturing accompanying mobile-media discussions in global media have celebrated the potential democratization of new media. With the rise of the prosumer from the term coined by Alvin Toffler in 1980[49] to its adaptation by Don Tapscott in 1995[50] to the context of the Internet's digital economy, much of the media of late has celebrated UCC and the prosumer as part of the Web 2.0 enterprises. But behind this rhetoric is the pivotal role mobile media has played in creating and reenacting debates about technology, labor, and creativity that have long accompanied new media and domestic technology discourses. Rather than just domestic and artistic labor having little or no remuneration in the general community, now the UCC associated with mobile media could see the everyday person subject to the injustices of industry convergence whereby corporations buy and exploit social and creative labor in the form of Web 2.0 media such as SNS.

The conundrum of new mobile technologies is that they are *supposed* to free us up and yet, as a good existential crisis would have it, the freedom is a leash. Work becomes mobile; labor is on a perpetual drip. We are supposed to be available at all times, perpetually connected. Rather than free us, the "immediacy" logic of mobile technologies makes us feel like we must be quicker and must achieve more. Rather than saving time, applications such as cameraphone image making—and the attendant customizing and modes of sharing/distribution—mean users spend a lot of time sharing and editing the so-called immediate. The present gets put on hold. However, one of the features that becomes apparent in mobile media is the need to move beyond the screen-centric and ocular-centricism of twentieth-century media and reconnect with the very reason the mobile phone has grown into mobile media, its importance at the level of everyday haptics.

By engaging in the significance of the haptic in mobile media we can grasp some of the paradoxes at play. It is important to recognize that this conundrum of delay and immediacy is not new with the rise of mobile media. Rather, these paradoxes have been central in the emphasis upon screen cultures in the face of the importance of the haptic in the making sense of mobile media. As I have attempted to discuss, mobile media represents some interesting paradoxes about contemporary media and consumer cultures. In this chapter I have tried to show the ambivalences surrounding mobile media from both a new media and domestic technologies approach in order to reconceptualize the philosophical and phenomenological dimensions of mobile media. To socialize the creative media dimensions and to innovate the social, domestic dimensions.

In order to grapple with the burgeoning field of mobile media we need to comprehend the twin histories—such as the domestic technologies and remediation approach—to fully grasp the histories, contemporary and future paradoxical permutations of mobile media and not just fetishize the "new" by futurist posturings. Mobile media is undoubtedly a project involving the domesticating of new media in which old boundaries between art and life, production and consumption perpetually change and shift, repeat and pause. But it is time that we moved away from the twentieth-century preoccupations with visual cultures and screenness that deems to view mobile media as a (advertising) *third screen* and instead acknowledge its genealogy, as a *third space* that is governed by the politics and aesthetics of haptics.

Notes

1 Henry Jenkins, "Welcome to Convergence Culture," *Receiver*, 12 (2005) http://www.receiver.vodafone.com/12/articles/pdf/12_01.pdf.

2 John Boyd, "The Only Gadget You'll Ever Need," *New Scientist*, 5 (2005): 28.

3 Roger Silverstone and Eric Hirsch, eds., *Consuming Technologies: Media and Information in Domestic Spaces* (London: Routledge, 1992); Roger Silverstone and Leslie Haddon, "Design and Domestication of Information and Communication Technologies: Technical Change and Everyday Life," in *Communication by Design: The Politics of Information and Communication Technologies*, ed. Roger Silverstone and Richard Mansell (Oxford, UK: Oxford University Press, 1996): 44–74; Daniel Miller, *Material Culture and Mass Consumption* (London: Blackwell, 1987).

4 Mary Douglas and Baron Isherwood, *The World of Goods: Towards an Anthropology of Consumption of Goods* (London: Routledge & Kegan Paul, 1979).

5 Dick Hebdige, *Hiding in the Light: On Images and Things* (London: Routledge, 1988).

6 Miller, Material Culture and Mass Consumption.

7 John Agar, *Constant Touch: A Global History of the Mobile Phone* (Cambridge: Icon Books, 2003).

8 Boyd, "The Only Gadget You'll Ever Need."

9 Ilpo Koskinen, "Managing Banality in Mobile Multimedia," in Raul Pertierra, ed., *The Social Construction and Usage of Communication Technologies: European and Asian Experiences* (Manila: University of the Philippines Press, 2007), 48–60.

10 Barbara Scifo, "The Domestication of the Camera Phone and MMS Communications: The Experience of Young Italians," in Kristóf Nyíri, ed., *A Sense of Place: The Global and the Local in Mobile Communication* (Vienna: Passagen Verlag, 2005), 363–73; Mizuko Ito and Daisuke Okabe, "Camera Phones Changing the Definition of Picture-Worthy," *Japan Media Review* (2003), http://www.ojr.org/japan/wireless/1062208524.php; Mizuko Ito and Daisuke Okabe, "Intimate Visual Co-Presence," presented at *UbiComp 2005*, 11–14 September, Takanawa Prince Hotel, Tokyo, Japan, http://www. itofisher.com/mito/.

11 Ito and Okabe, "Intimate Visual Co-Presence."

12 Chris Chesher, "Neither Gaze nor Glance, but Glaze: Relating to Console Game Screens," *SCAN: Journal of Media Arts Culture*, 1(1) (2004), http://scan.net.au/journal/.

13 Ito and Okabe, "Intimate Visual Co-Presence."

14 Frans Mäyrä, "The City Shaman Dances with Virtual Wolves—Researching Pervasive Mobile Gaming," *Receiver*, 12 (2003), www.receiver.vodafone.com.

15 http://www.pacmanhattan.com/.

16 Nicolas Bourriaud, *Relational Aesthetics*, trans. Simon Pleasance and Fronza Woods (Dijon, France: Les Presses du Réel, 2002).

17 Michael Arnold, "On the Phenomenology of Technology: the "Janus-faces" of Mobile Phones," *Information and Organization*, 13 (2003): 231–56.

18 Judy Wajcman et al, "Intimate Connections: The Impact of the Mobile Phone on Work Life Boundaries," see this volume. Also see Melissa Gregg, "Work Where You Want: The Labour Politics of the Mobile Office," presented at *Mobile Media Conference* (University of Sydney, July 2007).

19 Jay Bolter and Richard Grusin, *Remediation: Understanding New Media* (Cambridge, MA: MIT Press, 1999).

20 Margaret Morse, *Virtualities: Television, Media Art, and Cyberculture* (Bloomington: Indiana University Press, 1998).

21 Larissa Hjorth, "Locating Mobility: Practices of Co-presence and the Persistence of the Postal Metaphor in SMS/MMS Mobile Phone Customization in Melbourne," *Fibreculture Journal*, 6 (2005), http://journal.fibreculture.org/issue6/issue6_hjorth.html.

22 Alex Taylor and Richard Harper, "Age-Old Practices in the 'New World': A Study of Gift-Giving between Teenage Mobile Phone Users," in *Changing Our World, Changing Ourselves* (proceedings of the *SIGCHI* Conference on Human Factors in Computing Systems, Minneapolis, 2002): 439–46; Alex Taylor

and Richard Harper, "The Gift of Gab? A Design Oriented Sociology of Young People's Use of Mobiles," *Journal of Computer Supported Cooperative Work*, 12 (2003): 267–96.

23   Douglas and Isherwood, *The World of Goods*.

24   Erkki Huhtamo, "From Kaleidoscomaniac to Cybernerd: Notes Toward an Archaeology of the Media," *Leonardo*, 30(3) (1997).

25   Erkki Huhtamo, "From Kaleidoscomaniac to Cybernerd," 222; cited in Jussi Parikka and Jaakko Suominen, "Victorian Snakes? Towards a Cultural History of Mobile Games and the Experience of Movement," *Games Studies: The International Journal of Computer Game Research*, 6(1) (2006), December, http://gamestudies.org/0601.

26   Parikka and Suominen, "Victorian Snakes? Towards a Cultural History of Mobile Games and the Experience of Movement."

27   Parikka and Suominen, "Victorian Snakes?"

28   Parikka and Suominen, "Victorian Snakes?"

29   Marshall McLuhan, *Understanding Media* (New York: Mentor, 1964).

30   Haddon and Silverstone, "Design and Domestication of Information and Communication Technologies"; Miller, *Material Culture and Mass Consumption*.

31   Daniel Miller and Heather Horst, *Cell Phone* (Oxford and New York: Berg, 2006), 7.

32   Rich Ling, *The Mobile Connection* (San Francisco: Morgan Kaufmann Publishers, 2004).

33   Leslie Haddon, *Empirical Research on the Domestic Phone: A Literature Review* (Brighton, UK: University of Sussex Press, 1997).

34   David Morley, "What's 'Home' Got to Do with It?" *European Journal of Cultural Studies*, 6(4) (2003): 435–58.

35   Leslie Haddon, "Domestication and Mobile Telephony," in *Machines That Become Us: The Social Context of Personal Communication Technology*, ed. James E. Katz (New Brunswick, NJ: Transaction Publishers, 2003), 43–56.

36   Ling, The Mobile Connection, 28.

37   Ling, The Mobile Connection, 27.

38   Timo Kopomaa, "The City in Your Pocket," in *Birth of the Mobile Information Society* (Helsinki: Gaudemus, 2000).

39   Huhtamo, "From Kaleidoscomaniac to Cybernerd."

40   Lev Manovich, "The Paradoxes of Digital Photography," in *The Photography Reader*, ed. Liz Wells (London, Routledge, 2003), 240–49.

41   Lisa Gye, "Picture This," paper presented at *Vital Signs* conference (September 2005, ACMI, Melbourne).

42   Cited in Mizuko Ito, Daisuke Okabe, and Misa Matsuda, eds., *Personal, Portable, Pedestrian: Mobile Phones in Japanese Life* (Cambridge, MA: MIT Press, 2005).

43   Arnold, "On the Phenomenology of Technology."

44   Ingrid Richardson, "Pocket Technoscapes: The Bodily Incorporation of Mobile Media," in *Continuum: Journal of Media and Cultural Studies*, 21(2) (2007): 205.

45   Richardson, "Pocket Technoscapes," 208.

46   Robert Hughes, *The Shock of the New* (London: Thames and Hudson, 1981).

47   Matsuda, cited in Ito, *Personal, Portable, Pedestrian*.

48   Richardson, "Pocket Technoscapes."

49   Alvin Toffler, *The Third Wave* (William Morrow: New York, 1980).

50   Dan Tapscott, *The Digital Economy: Promise and Peril in the Age of Networked Intelligence* (New York: McGraw-Hill, 1995).

Chapter 39

MICHAEL BULL

BERGSON'S IPOD?
The cognitive management of everyday life

M ICHAEL BULL'S ETHNOGRAPHIC research addresses the ways in which iPods (and personal digital music or mp3 players in general) are used to control or intensify their owners' cognitive and emotional states as they travel through the urban environment. He establishes two conceptual poles from which to map critical approaches to this technological mediation and 'management' of everyday experience and urban movement. These poles are personified by Henri Bergson and Theodor Adorno. It should be pointed that neither of these thinkers had anything to say directly about iPods, having died in 1941 and 1969 respectively. Rather, Bull distils from their work theoretical positions, or models of everyday experience, that mark out a range of critical positions in the study of individuals' media culture today. Bergson, he says, sees a 'world of free consciousness, a world in which consciousness is inherently mobile, fluid and in flux', uncontrollable by others. As a body moves through space it is experienced as the centre of the universe. The resonance of this worldview with iPod users' experience of shaping the world around them as they move through it by choosing (or allowing 'shuffle' technology to choose) their personal soundtrack should be clear. By contrast, Adorno's vision of modern media culture is one in which everyday life and experience are colonised and commercialised by the culture industries and their mass-produced commodities and experiences. For Adorno, popular music itself (though he was talking about jazz rather than hip hop or rock music), as well as music technologies, is industrial, fetishised and ideological. This pessimistic position has faint echoes in popular or journalistic assumptions about the 'zombie-like', alienated and anti-social nature of personal stereo use prevalent since the introduction of the Sony Walkman in the late 1970s.

The accounts of iPod use and experience that Bull has elicited through interviews would seem to sit most comfortably at the Bergsonian end of this notional spectrum, as users talk of 'freedom' in, and 'control' over, their everyday experience through their iPods, and of deliberately managing their mood or train of thought through choice of songs. However, Bull argues that a Bergsonian position does not account for the 'repetitive or compulsive behaviour associated with consumer culture'. Some of Bull's interviewees explain how they set their devices to repeat a particular song, or set of songs, to enhance or maintain a desired mood. This practice sits somewhere in the middle of the spectrum for Bull: it is evidence of everyday control of mood and thought by the individual user, yet also follows the logic of consumer culture in its repetitious, seamless and, in terms of individual experience and attention, all-encompassing consumption of media commodities.

Bull considers the differences of experience and practices between the earlier personal stereo or Walkman and contemporary iPod use (he has also conducted extensive research with Walkman users). The continuities are clear (control over one's auditory environment whilst on the move), but the differences are predicated on the digital memory and retrieval capacities of the iPod as a digital medium. On the one hand the iPod fulfils a dream inspired by the Walkman, to 'control time continually and in microseconds', whilst on the other (though Bull doesn't use these terms) it exemplifies **Manovich**'s database logic of digital culture.

[With music] one enters the 'dark world' in which language and daily structures of time and causality no longer reign supreme, and one finds the music giving form to the dim shapes in the darkness. (Nussbaum 2003: 269)

There is no state of mind, however simple, which does not change every moment, since there is no consciousness without memory, and no continuation of a state without the addition, to the present feeling, of a memory of past moments. It is this which constitutes duration. (Bergson 1998: 72)

Masses of people are concerned with their single life histories and particular emotions as never before; this concern has proved to be a trap rather than liberation. (Sennett 1977: 5)

In the morning when I first put on my iPod, I walk through a residential neighbourhood, comprised of mainly low- to middle-class homes, to the bus stop at the edge of a small public park. I like to listen to music with faster, driving beats, so my pace quickens as I walk to the bus stop. Things look clearer and my outlook for the day is more positive, even if I know I'll have an incredibly busy day at work or a long commute due to traffic. I find that listening to the iPod helps to calm me, and lets me modulate my moods according to the morning's circumstances. The same goes for walking in the streets during any point in the day: I don't mind the jostle of the city so much, and the stress I feel is dissipated. (Mia)

Tia DeNora has commented, 'the role that music plays in "the constitution of the self" has been insufficiently analysed' (DeNora 2000: 46). Music is intimately linked to our deepest strivings and most powerful emotions. iPod use appears to offer a glimpse into the internal workings and strategies engaged in by users in their management of themselves, others and urban space through engaging in a series of self-regulatory practices through which they habitually manage their moods, volitions and desires. In its inherent fluidity music appears to correlate with a Bergsonian model of consciousness based upon duration in which the notes of a tune melt into one another to produce an organic whole. iPod users appear to be embracers of a Bergsonian world of free consciousness, a world in which consciousness is inherently mobile, fluid and in flux – and, hence, ultimately uncontrollable by others, the culture industry or society in general. In a Bergsonian world the 'intuitive' and 'non-quantifiable' self stands apart from any rational and external critique.

iPod users, in describing their attentiveness to the flow of experience, appear to intuitively tune their flow of desire and mood to the spectrum of music contained in their iPods. Beyond the scrutiny of others, they believe they exist in a naturalised heterotopia (Foucault 1986). The presumption of subjective significance is supported within a Bergsonian framework. Bergson believed that as the body moved through space so it was indeed the centre of the experienced universe. This centrality of world view is replicated technologically by iPod users who experience all before them through the mediated and privatised sounds of the iPod.

> . . . It's as though I can part the sea like Moses. It gives me and what's around me a literal rhythm, and I feel literally in my own world, as an observer. It helps regulate my space so I can feel how I want to feel, without external causes changing that. (Susanna)

On a Bergsonian world view, what is essentially creative in a person resists mechanical repetition – consciousness is essentially unpredictable (Boym 2001: 50). Yet in the present age of instantaneous digital reproduction iPod users manage their flow and flux of experience precisely through the technology of the iPod. Technologically mediated behaviour increasingly becomes second nature to iPod users: habitual and unrecognised. This entails the presupposition that everyday behaviour is mediated by, and constructed through, the omnipresent sounds of the products of the culture industry in some form or other. Mediated behaviour is transformed into an ideology of directness – of transparency – like so much in consumer culture in which appearance masks the production process. Transparency is suggested by the technological enclosing of the ears by headphones, enabling music to be played directly and immediately into the ears of users.

Adorno *contra* Bergson

Bergson's understanding of the innateness of free consciousness works in direct opposition to the colonisation of consciousness thesis portrayed by Adorno, Baudrillard and others (Adorno 1991; Baudrillard 1993; Marcuse 1964). From an Adornian position the use of consumer technologies like the iPod, rather than signifying a free and uncontrolled consciousness, highlights the fetishising role of music in the management of contemporary urban experience. From this viewpoint the contemporary consumer appears increasingly unable, or at least unwilling, to organise significant portions of daily life independently or autonomously. iPod users, from this perspective, rather than being 'free', become imbued with the need for mediated experience in order to remain cognitively 'in control'. In contrast to a Bergsonian free spirit, iPod users represent a hyper-form of one-dimensionality in which they mimetically embrace the culture industry in order to remain 'free':

> They need and demand what has been palmed off on them. They overcome the feeling of impotence that creeps over them in the face of monopolistic production by identifying themselves with the inescapable product . . . The fetish character of music produces its own camouflage through the identification of the listener with the fetish. (Adorno 1991: 288)

The following comments by iPod users represent, from this perspective, a form of 'one-dimensionality' (Marcuse 1964):

> I can't overestimate the importance of having all my music available all the time. It gives me an unprecedented level of emotional control over my life. (Terry)

I love the freedom to have any music I want to listen to in my pocket, wherever I am. I find that music really helps to change my mood, so it's nice to have the ability to get a quick 'pick me up' in my pocket. (Frank)

Music represents an especially powerful ideological aphrodisiac in Adorno's analysis of commodity culture owing to his interpretation of the existence of an archaic utopian remnant of non-commodified, direct communal experience embodied in music itself. The 'happy consciousness' of the iPod user becomes, from this perspective, an intensified form of conformism in which users intuitively manage their social behaviour in tune to the increasingly sophisticated dictates of consumer culture. The fulfilment of the iPod user is increasingly administered to them through the multiple options available to them through the use of their iPod.

This contrasts with a Bergsonian world view in which consciousness, by its very nature, resists total colonisation. From a Bergsonian position the fluid nature of music itself, coupled with the structure of choice offered by digital technologies like the iPod, complements the very nature of the user's consciousness, enabling them to construct an 'individualised' relationship between cognition and the management of experience. Contra to the colonisation of consciousness thesis, the choice offered by the iPod would work to create a conceptual distance from the structural organisation of these products. In effect, iPod users become free, transcendental consciousnesses in contrast to being tethered to the fetishised products of an all-encompassing culture industry.

Whilst the idealism of a Bergsonian world view is attractive to users, and is replicated in many descriptions of use, it suffers from an historicism in which consciousness is always structurally 'free'. Much of the repetitive or compulsive behaviour associated with consumer culture sits ill at ease with a Bergsonian world view. iPod culture rather appears to sit somewhere between the parameters of freedom and those of constraint. The choices engendered in iPod users have, as we will see, potentially rebellious underpinnings as consumers distance themselves from the hyper-commodification embodied in much of the media. As they construct their individualised consumption packages there is a sense in which consumers have progressed from the Fordist tendencies of popular culture critically encoded in the work of Adorno and others. Yet this distancing strategy of the subject – the autonomous resistance to the predetermined schedules and rhythms of the mediated day – sits uneasily with the increased dependence upon the use of technologies like the iPod through which their cognitive states are managed. The following pages investigate this conundrum through an analysis of iPod cognition.

Sound cognitions

Mobility, fluidity and flux are the condition of subjectivity in contemporary urban experience. This is accompanied by a ratcheting up of the pressure, speed and demands made upon consumers (Gleik 1999). Communication technologies themselves further the experience of flux, transitoriness and fluidity whilst simultaneously providing a buttress against these tendencies. Users commonly describe themselves as bereft without the mediated auditory presence of their iPod. Experience unadorned by the immersion of experience through the intimate sound world of the iPod is often described with apprehension:

It [the iPod] removes the internal dread. For example, when I needed to do yard work I used to become depressed because my mind would wander. Now, with the iPod, yard work is a positive experience because I know I have hours of uninterrupted listening, exercise, fresh air, and no business worries . . . Sertab Erener's 'Everyway that I can' stirs me for some reason. As a consequence, when I confront larger problems, I play it several times in a row and it seems to help. Also, Coldplay's 'Clocks' has a strange, positive effect upon me when I play it. (Sam)

Non-mediated experience creates a sense of vulnerability in many users. This sense of vulnerability refers to the perceived uncontrollable nature of their own streams of consciousness and the cognitive states associated with it. Users often recognise their own sense of cognitive contingency, which the use of the iPod negates. Routine, often pleasurable activities like gardening may threaten the user's sense of cognitive control with the introduction of 'uncontrollable' thoughts, or with feelings flooding in, engulfing the subject left to their own unmediated cognitive state. Cognitive control comes with technological mediation in iPod culture. iPod use permits users to saturate periods of 'non-communication' with their own intimate, familiar and comforting sounds.

Strategies of mood maintenance

Sound loops

One strategy for mood maintenance is the repeat – the listening to a music track repeatedly in order to maintain a specific cognitive state in contrast to the ebb and flow of time. Users are often unable to articulate just why certain songs enable them to manage their experience in the desired way or why the same repeated song permits them to maintain their required mood. It is 'as if' consciousness becomes the equivalent of and, in contradiction to Bergson, a tape loop:

If I'm in a particular mood then I will repeat the same five or six songs for a very long time, basically until my mood changes or I have to go talk to someone. (Rosa)

There are times I'll listen to the same song two or three times in a row. And this relates to my mood as well as to the place I'm in. If I'm in a good mood, and I'm listening to a song that I just love, I'll repeat it. If I'm working out, and a song really gets me moving and raising my heart rate accordingly, I may well play it two or three times. (Donna)

It usually happens when I feel that I am 'in' a certain song so much that I couldn't think of listening to anything else. The song becomes sort of a mantra and I just want to hear it over and over, absorbing it. (Sean)

I often play the same song repeatedly back to back. When I do, it's more because the song strikes a chord within me, or fits the moment so perfectly, that I want to extend the feeling or moment longer. The best way to do that is to play the song again and again. (Amy)

I play the same song repeatedly – for example, the [non-traditional] song we used to walk down the aisle at our wedding – when I need to improve my mood – and lower my stress level! Also, if I'm playing it at work as background music, and I miss some of it while I'm in other parts of the office, I let it repeat. (Michelle)

The rationale for the repeating of songs varies from the maintenance of mood, the syncing of mood to place, the maintenance of a mood engendered by a specific memory, to the maintenance of body movement and rhythm. A particular song or rhythm may also act as a 'mantra' into which all experience is channelled.

Bauman has argued that the need to have time filled with sound implies that 'it is [the] fear of silence and the seclusion it implies [that] makes us anxious that our ingeniously assembled security wall fall apart' (Bauman 2003: 98). Modern consciousness is conditioned to experience daily life through the mediated sounds of the culture industry – the habitual presence of radio sounds, television and the like. The silent vistas desired by a Thoreau, who required spaces of silence in order to think clearly, is clearly not a desire possessed by iPod users. Rather, iPod users describe needing the throbbing personalised sounds of music in order to think clearly – or, alternatively, to take them away from themselves so as not to be subject to invasive and undesirable thoughts and moods. iPod use is transcendent precisely in its capacity to take users away from 'the conventional confines of time and space' (Boym 2001: xiv). This 'happy consciousness' is dependent on the technology of the iPod – contingency is invariably controlled successfully as users manage the rhythms of their mood and desires, creating a successful cognitive congruence between emotion, music, technology and experience:

> If I'm angry I'll put on something dark and angry. If I'm happy, upbeat happy music. If I don't want to be brought down from a good mood I'll avoid depressing music. If I'm not sure how I feel I'll put it on shuffle. That sometimes leads me to listen to a whole album, or I'll just skip over the tracks I'm not in the mood for until I find something that fits the way I feel that moment. Or, if I want to change the way I feel, I'll choose music accordingly. I never plan . . . My choice of music isn't determined by time of day but how I'm feeling or want to feel. (Elizabeth)

> I like being able to listen to any song, any artist, any album, and any genre that either fits my current mood or that can change my current mood. (Juno)

iPods become strategic devices permitting the user to shape the flow of experience, holding contingency at bay by either predicting future experience – the next song on the play list – or by shaping their own sound world in tune with their desire. Users are also able to adjust their privatised soundtrack whilst on the move, thus micro-managing their mood with great precision and skill. iPod users demand an instantaneous response to the nuances of their mood, signifying a ratcheting up of expectations demanded of new technologies such as the iPod.

The technology of the iPod appears to further promote the development of an 'attentive' or 'listening' self embodied in rudimentary forms in previous analogue technologies. Earlier portable-sound technologies such as the personal stereo provided less capacity for users, often requiring prior and precise planning for the day's listening. For some users this was not a problem, as they would play the same tape each day for long periods of time – forcing their environment to mimic the straitjacket of their own auditory mind set. For most users, however, a hastily bundled selection of tapes or CDs would be carried in the hope that it would contain appropriate music (Bull 2000). The development of MP3 players such as the Apple iPod provided a technological solution to the management of the contingency of aural desire. Users now habitually take large portions of their music collection with them in their iPods. As one user describes, 'It gives me the ability to carry my entire music collection in my pocket instead of a steamer trunk.'

From Walkman to iPod sounds

The iPod expands the options available to users for customising music to mood and environment. It is rare for iPod users to resort to switching off their machines for lack of appropriate music, unlike the world of Walkman users, where no music was often preferred to the 'wrong' music:

> It has completely revolutionised how I listen to music. Before it I had to decide what I felt like listening to and then be restricted to one CD at a time. Now I let the iPod choose, or use specific playlists. (Helen)

> I can now carry all my CDs with me and listen to whatever I want whenever I want. I don't even have to think about it any more – what should I bring, how do I feel today, I wish I had that one . . . Not to mention now I can bring songs that I don't particularly like, the whole CD as well. I've not had that since I used to have mixed tapes on my Walkman . . . There's no need to plan any more, because I'm bringing all my music with me all the time. I used to have to plan with the Walkman or Discman. I listen to whatever I feel like. I listen depending on mood and what I'm doing and where I am. (Susan)

John, a thirty-year-old US computer technician, points to the seamless technological infrastructure that provides the backdrop to his mobile listening habits:

> Between the iPod itself, iTunes software and the iTunes Music Store my relationship to music has been changed forever. Due to the hassle of carrying CDs around with me I had begun to lose touch with my music collection. That has all changed since I bought the iPod. For example, the Beatles are my favourite band. Sometimes, I will want to hear a particular song from the eighteen Beatles CDs I own. Now I simply reach into my pocket and the song is there. I don't need to carry a duffel bag filled with CDs.

iPod users fully embrace the ideology that 'more is better'. The carrying of large slices or perhaps all of one's musical library in a small piece of portable technology appears to liberate users from the contingency of mood – they no longer have to predict what they will want to listen to or the vagaries of potential future moods.

Whilst the personal stereo was commonly used as an 'in-between' device – from door to door – the iPod expands the possibilities of use from the playing of music through attaching it to the user's home hi-fi, plugging it into the automobile radio, and by connecting it to the computer at work, thus giving users unprecedented ability to weave the disparate threads of the day into one seamless and continuous soundtrack. In doing so, iPod use extends users' field of aspirational reorganisation to include many more segments of daily life. The dream of living one's life to music becomes for some users a reality. With the increased power of the technology comes the ratcheting up of consumer desire. What was previously acceptable for the personal stereo user is no longer acceptable for the iPod user. The iPod permits users to control time continually and in microseconds.

> I used to listen to one album at a time, or multiple albums from one artist at a time. (I'd keep an entire group's back catalogue on a single mini-disc.) Now I spend a lot more time listening to playlists I set up in iTunes. It's a painless process to create a new playlist for every conceivable mood or situation. (Kerry)

The iPod permits users to be more attentive to the vagaries and changes of mood, seeking either confirmation of mood or transformation into an alternative mood via their choice of playlist. Playlists are created precisely to cater for a wide spectrum of moods or times of the day, as the following young US user demonstrates:

> When I'm going to work I like loud, energetic music to get me going. The same for when I get off work. I want to listen to something as non-work-related as possible. Probably some rap music. A lot of times at night I go visit my boyfriend, and on my way to his house I throw in some 'get in the mood' music. Something slow and sultry that makes me feel good inside. At the gym I like high-energy music . . . I feel as though life is a movie and is playing especially for me. If I listen to sad music, which I only listen to when I'm down – boyfriend break-up, just bad news – then everything sort of has a grey shadow over it, even when it's sunny outside. Music is like a drug to me, and not just one drug that does one thing but many different drugs that magnetise your existing mood, or even sometimes the music is so powerful that it changes the mood you're in. Music can make you feel happy, horny, sad, wanting. It can do wonders. (Fali)

iPod use permits unparalleled micro-management of mood, environment and sound, permitting the successful management of the self through the contingencies of the user's day. iPod culture is a culture that habitually controls experience:

> I tailor my music and content by activity. 'Playlists' allow me to create subsets of music that I can easily call up. I create 'playlists' to tailor my music to my different moods. I label them as 'Quiet' or 'Exercise tunes' or 'Contemplative'. (Jeremy)

Digital technology, with its storage and organising potential, has enabled users to fulfil their dream of control over mood, time and surroundings, permitting them to live in a dream of auditory control:

> Music tastes are largely a function of environment and mood, both of which can be hard to anticipate when you're out and 'on the go'. Since music listening in public is essentially a form of isolation, I find that I especially depend on the iPod during phases of my life where I'm depressed or needing encouragement or energy or reinforcement. Sometimes that will mean finding a particular song that matches – or influences – my current mood and thought patterns, and putting it on repeat for an entire day. (Ivan)

> There are times where I will put on one song, and then half-way through it I will change my mind and switch to another song because my mood changed or the song wasn't capturing my mood correctly. (Heather)

The fleeting nature of cognition is often hard to manage. Moods vary in consequence of users' response both to the environment and to the internal flow of experience. The Bergsonian iPod becomes the tool used by the listening and attentive self. The expectation that there is something in the iPod to suit any circumstance becomes increasingly taken for granted:

> Mostly the sheer amount of music constantly at my fingertips changes listening habits, as access is always instant. (John)

I have lots of music that to me evokes a feeling of either peace and calm or even melancholy. I use the soundtracks to *The Piano* and *Schindler's List* for those. Both instrumental, but really emotional and powerful . . . I almost always keep the setting on 'shuffle' so that the songs come up randomly. If a song starts that doesn't suit my mood at the moment I just hit 'Next'. (Karen)

Most importantly, though, I have all my music at hand, all of the time. Essentially, it lets me change or enhance my mood however I want, whenever I want . . . . I usually listen to my iPod on my way to work, and have it set to my 'Most played' list, which ensures that I start my day in a good mood . . . Sometimes I'll just have a random song day, but then I flip songs every time I hit one I'm not in the mood to hear. If I'm on a random by artist or genre mode I usually don't flip past a song. On my way home I'll pick something that suits my mood. For example, if I'm heading out to a club I'll throw on some trance. (Ashvin)

The music on the iPod provides a stimulus for mood matching as users treat their music collection as a 'magical' prompt for cognitive management. Central to these strategies of control is the enhancement of mood.

Sound reinforcements

Music listened to on the iPod invariably enhances the experience of the user, colouring their relation to the environment passed through. The following is a description of a user moving through the city wearing their iPod:

It is usually a mood elevator or, at least, a mood intensifier. For example, if I'm wearing it on a crowded city street the crush of people seems like an obstacle course and a fun challenge to wend my way through. Without it I would be annoyed and frustrated at my lack of progress through the crowd, but with it it's almost as if I'm dancing. If I'm frustrated or angry, intense, driving music makes me feel like I have company in my mood. Pleasant weather seems that much more pleasant with music to accompany me. I am aware that, even when I'm not singing along, the way I walk and move and my facial expressions are affected by what music is playing. (Malcolm)

I commute into Paris for the week and sometimes, when a desire to hear something in particular occurs, it's to reinforce the mood of the moment, happy after a success at work, or thoughtful or depressed as per the events of the day. Having the huge song library in my pocket makes this possible. (Eric)

The mundane world of the city becomes more adventurous to privatising sound. The contingency of the street in which one moves with the others, dependent upon the ebb and flow of others, becomes manageable and potentially pleasurable. The subject is simultaneously 'passivised' and 'energised' as they wend their way through the street. Walter Benjamin, in his analysis of city life, was attentive to the role that technology played in the navigation of the urban subject through the city. iPod users become reminiscent of the urban subject whom Benjamin described as plunging 'into a crowd as into a reservoir of electric energy . . . a kaleidoscope equipped with consciousness' (Benjamin 1973: 171). The iPod user has moved on technologically, and is accompanied by music, which drives both their mood and their relationship with the spaces passed through. Enhancement relates to the mood of the user or, and sometimes also, the environment passed through, which in turn feeds back into the cognition of the user. iPod users describe the pleasure of mood reinforcement:

> I use it as a mood enhancer all the time. If I'm depressed I'll throw on some Leonard Cohen or Nick Cave to bring me down even more. If I'm happy I'll use upbeat music to put a smile on my face. And sometimes, when I just want to think, I'll use a familiar classical piece (I use Vivaldi) so I can enjoy it and still think about other things simultaneously. (Damien)

Whether subjects live in New York, London or Paris there is a similarity of description as to how the iPod functions to manage mood and experience, a similarity of desire to micro-manage experience through the use of the iPod and to construct a mediated and privatised auditory world through which experience is seamlessly filtered. This filtering aims not just at enhancement but also at mimesis, to bring the world in line with cognition through music:

> If I'm feeling depressed I'll often try to match that with suitable music, quite often to achieve an insularity. (Ryan)

Users habitually require the iPod to orchestrate their day functioning as a cognitive Sherpa, accompanying them and directing them through the cognitive and physical spaces of their day. The nature of this mediated experience varies according to the activity and purpose of the user. Whilst music is invariably listened to loudly, it is not always experienced as such. Remember the user who played music in search of peace and quiet: 'I didn't realise how much I yearn for control and probably peace and quiet. Strange, since I'm blasting music in my ears.' Music functions in this instance as a clarifier of experience, enabling users to 'clear a space' for thought:

> If I want to be with my own thoughts I'll use the iPod. (Rosa)

> If there's a specific mood I'm in, especially if it means contemplating a situation fairly deeply, I will pick music that seems conducive to that kind of thought. It's odd, because once I'm fairly well lost in my thoughts I can't really hear the music any more. I'd notice if it was gone, though. The right music can help isolate me from the things going on around me. I use the music on my iPod as a buffer between the outside world and me, giving me a more secluded environment to think about whatever needs my mind's attention. (Kerry)

> Frequently the iPod is more of a contemplative device than the actual thought 'Let's listen to music now.' Music is such a huge part of my life that it's almost imperative that I have *something* happening all the time. I have music stuck in my head almost non-stop for the same reason. In certain moods the iPod serves to extend and accentuate the mood rather than being a source of something to *listen* to. In fact, unless I'm listening to something specific, like a new artist, it's usually just there to have something playing in the background . . . to help my thoughts along. (David)

> The iPod allows me to drown out everything and everyone else. This is important for me. I am a thinker, and the iPod allows me my time to do that free of interruptions.

I pick and choose my songs in accordance with how I'm feeling. It can either bring me down or pick me up, depending on what I select. (Freedom)

Sometimes it's wonderful to have so that I can block out everything else and concentrate on the things I need to think about. (Donna)

Clearing a space is used both metaphorically and physically in the above descriptions. Users clear cognitive spaces for themselves in which music assumes the role of a clearing mechanism, providing a platform for the users' thoughts, uncontaminated by the vicissitudes of their own cognition. Equally, the privatised auditory world inhabited acts to cognitively passivise the spaces passed through.

iPod users exclude or transform their spaces of habitation, managing 'duration' in the process. All the above strategies point to the potential and powerful transcendent possibilities entailed in iPod use.

The fragility of, or contingent nature of, cognition in relation to external (the world) or internal factors (cognition) is kept at bay through iPod listening. The exclusion or transformation of the world beyond the user, coupled with the transformation of the user's 'inner space', permits a restructuring of cognition, creating a free and orderly mobile space in which the user is able to successfully manage experience. Situations of cognitive conflict are avoided through a process of compartmentalisation through which users focus upon the immediate task of control. The control of the self is managed through technological mediation in which the subject gives themselves over, albeit actively, to the technology of the iPod as a form of higher control. The iPod user resembles Lasch's 'minimal self' in which the user withdraws into a world small enough to exert total control over it.

iPod culture is also a culture in which users successfully manage the potentially oppressive nature of routine, of the day stretching ahead, of the unwanted journey, the unwanted meeting, the decisions to be made at work. In everyday life, users may not wish to think about the day ahead, the relentless routine of going to and from work. The drudgery of the everyday and the lack of freedom in the daily rhythm of consumer culture is successfully mediated, and put at a distance, through the use of iPods. The iPod delivers. It is a strategic device permitting the user to shape experience in a manner they are unable to accomplish on their own. In iPod culture, successful experience is invariably mediated experience. Structurally this micro-awareness – this listening self – constitutes both a heightened invasion by the culture industry of the auditory self and a distancing strategy through which users attempt to reinforce a sense of presence – self-mastery. Enclosing the user's world between the earphones of the iPod monumentalises the significance of users' cognitive processes, making them loom larger in the mind's eye as more immediate and pressing. With the subject's attentiveness to the micro-management of cognition comes the increasing realisation of their contingent and unpredictable nature, resulting in the mediating influence of the iPod becoming more pressing, more necessary. Users wish to remain at the centre of their universe – they do not embrace a decentred subjectivity, as postmodern thought would have us believe. They embrace a Bergsonian ideology of cognitive freedom precisely through a tethering of cognition to the auditory products of the culture industry. Yet it is the very fear of dislocation and decentring that provides a powerful motivation for continuous listening.

Chapter 40

MARK POSTER

EVERYDAY (VIRTUAL) LIFE

THIS EXTRACT IS TAKEN FROM a longer essay that addresses critical theories of everyday life and their implications for digital culture in some detail. We have chosen this short section firstly because of its object of research (the transformational nature of everyday media technoculture before and after the digital) and secondly because of its method: a rich autobiographical approach that traces the texture of everyday technocultural experience. Poster writes evocatively of the worlds of music and cultural difference that radio opened up for him as a child. His account of learning to type and the differences between mechanical typewriters and computer keyboards complements both **McLuhan**'s study of the new embodied culture of typewriting and **Sudnow**'s description of learning the manual skills and dexterity of the computer game controller. It is also a persuasive account of what Poster sees as an ontological shift between analogue and digital media technologies. The analogue typewriter is, he argues, merely an enhanced adjustment to the techniques and tools of handwriting, reinforcing a subject–object (writer–paper) relation. By contrast, the computer keyboard is a 'liminal apparatus', an interface to many possible processes from selecting music to sending emails; written text itself may never leave its digital fluidity for the fixity of paper. The subject–object relation is also transformed into, perhaps, 'symbiotic human-machines or cyborgs'. As with **Haraway**, the insistence on the reality of cyborgian subjectivity in everyday life requires radically different ways of understanding contemporary technoculture.

Autobiographical investigations: the media and me

The study of the place of media in everyday life is plagued with difficulties. Media mediate. They go between established social and cultural positions and between the categories deployed to comprehend these positions. They are machines—neither subjects nor objects, minds nor bodies, persons nor things, but both at the same time and yet different from each. They enter our lives in funny ways, obliquely, behind the back of our cultural self-understanding. The standard Western notion of machines as tools, with users as subjects and machines as objects, with a utilitarian ethic presumed for the subject and a privilege given to the subject's intentionality or consciousness—this longstanding framework for fitting tools into culture does not do justice to the complexity of the practice of humans with information machines. Since the introduction of print, each generation has confronted the issue of media, taking as given the media that existed in its youth, and responding variously with anxiety or joy to the placement of new media in society. In what follows, I analyze my relation to several media in the order I encountered them, attempting to understand how each medium altered my subject position. I include only a few of the media I encountered since a comprehensive discussion is beyond the scope of this essay.

My purpose differs from standard autobiography. I am not attempting to illuminate my singular life or to confess moral events. I am not even trying to contextualize my life, indicating its contingencies and historical determinations. Instead I hope to use my experience as a case study of the historic synergy of human and information machine. By demonstrating how profound and extensive has been the role of media in my life, I offer a model to further the conceptualization of everyday life.[1]

The example of radio illustrates a fundamental feature of all media: that they bring diverse cultures into close contact, a degree of proximity not possible without them. In this way, media accentuate greatly the tendency of daily city life to mix populations from different ethnic or racial origins. Media enact this mixing in ways different from the urban topography. Juxtaposing cultures in media is often haphazard and instantaneous, whereas cities feature neighborhoods with particular ethnic groupings. Media tend in this respect to destabilize local customs, to extend awareness of other ways of life, and to add complexity to the process of socialization.

A boy of six or seven in the mid- to late 1940s, living in the Flatbush area of Brooklyn, I was introduced to new cultures through the radio. I remember clearly being in bed with a cold and turning the radio dial in boredom until tuning in a country-and-western music station, music I had never heard before that was foreign to the culture of my upbringing. The whining plaintive sounds from throats and violins that emanated from the small speaker were a revelation to me. I had never heard anything like it and could not imagine the cultural context from which it sprang (I had not yet seen western movies or television shows). There I was, alone in the bedroom, listening to the strange sounds and being fascinated by them. The radio brought me a new culture. At the same time, it opened my sensorium to music: I would continue to love music to this day. I learned the saxophone and clarinet, playing in high school bands and ROTC bands. I also love recorded music. But more of that later.

Perhaps of greater interest than my experience of the radio was that of my schoolmate a few years later in Queens, Paul Simon. He reported in a TV interview in the late 1990s having heard rhythm and blues, rock and roll, and other black music on the radio in Kew Garden Hills, an area with few African Americans. In both his case and mine, the radio allowed the introduction of other cultures in a manner outside the control of parents, although admittedly the consequences were far greater of his listening than of mine. Children could discover cultures through music that otherwise would remain unavailable to them. The youth culture and popular music of the 1960s were deeply affected by the radio, and in turn they contributed significantly to other forms of popular culture that would take by storm not only the United States but the world.

During the years of my youth, the radio was a fixture in my family's home. I did not regard it as special in any way. When I listened to country-and-western music that day, I did not appreciate the radio itself, had no sense of its ability to overcome geographic and social distance. My focus was totally on the music. Yet I had made a bond with the radio. Mark-radio could now enjoy this music at any time. Unlike Radio Raheem in Spike Lee's film, *Do the Right Thing* (1989), I could not take the radio with me through the streets. But I could come back to it after a day at school, back to its fixed place in my home, and turn the dials to connect with a culture remote from the middle-class Jewish world that I knew. In fact, when I began to hear Jewish music, mostly at summer camps, I regarded it as exotic and strange compared with radio music.

The radio I heard in Brooklyn came from the culture industry, the media corporations that had controlled the airwaves since the onset of broadcasting in the 1920s. In Britain in the 1970s, the Anglo-African community refunctioned radio to suit the needs of their community.[2] Pirate radio, as it was known in mainstream media, enabled the local community to hear music unavailable on the commercial and public stations. In addition, the disc jockeys employed the newer cassette technology to compose music with bits and pieces from the culture and politics of the day. Inexpensive radio transmitters along with cheap cassette recorders formed an assemblage that empowered the Anglo-African community and enriched their daily lives with the music of their choice. The question of control in everyday life arises from the examples of British pirate radio and my listening. Shall we understand the dissemination of information machines in everyday life under the sign of democratization?

My experience of radio was isolated. I listened usually alone in a room to a station of my choice. Radio did not intercede between me and my family but substituted for other activities I might do without any company. Not so with television. Television was watched by the family as a whole, displacing conversation, parlor games, and other forms of conviviality. Television introduced into the home a collective popular culture, one beyond the family.[3] Since there were, in the 1950s, few stations, everyone with televisions tended to watch the same programs.[4] In my experience, radio simply brought to my attention alternatives to my immediate cultural surroundings; television introduced into the home a new national culture, one with which the family could not compete.[5]

My father, I later realized, was an early adopter of information technologies. He was an accountant whose busy season was tax time. He insisted I help him at these times and I recall the early copy machines and primitive adding machines he used. The copy machines were messy affairs, with specially coated paper and liquids of all sorts. The world of work, I learned, was also saturated with information machines.

But in 1949, shortly after the introduction of nationally broadcast television shows, he purchased a TV. Aside from images of Howdy Doody and Milton Berle my clearest memory is of neighbors filling our modest-sized living room to watch and listen in awe to our nine-inch Admiral television set, a large free-standing object with lots of polished wood encasing the tube. In these early days, television created a community of sorts. My family and neighbors all marveled at the technical feat of broadcast moving images and sound. Here was something new and important. Yet to my young eyes television was interesting but not astonishing. It was easy to accept its novelty; it did not seem extraordinary. I suppose this is a basic difference between adults and children in the reception of new media.

Television's greatest emotional effect on me was through sporting events. I remember distinctly my profound disappointment and frustration when in September 1951, Bobby Thompson hit a home run against the Dodgers to give the Giants the pennant. I was alone in front of the television with no one to share this depressing event, just the tube, which disgusted me deeply.

These media—radio and television—impacted my life in important ways. I recall that the technical feats they accomplished did not surprise me in the least. I simply accepted that text, images, and sound could appear from outside my small world. While the wonders of these media affected me deeply at times, my life was concentrated mostly on sports and friends. Playing baseball, stickball, basketball, and football were the really important occasions of my life. The rest was supplementary (broadcast sports events) or marginal (country-and-western music, sci-fi films and novels). In my youth, activities with others took priority over mediated experience. Nonetheless, radio and television entered into my life and altered significantly the contours of everyday experience.[6] I learned skills of shifting registers from face-to-face relations to information machines and back. Growing up in the 1940s and 1950s, I was moving increasingly toward a culture of multiplicity. If the ethnic mix I encountered in these early years was limited, the ontological mix of human and machine was rich and diverse. Multiculturalism began for me through the mediation of information machines and only later extended to street life.

In junior high school in 1953 students were required to take a course in typing. I had little interest in the machine at the time, but learning to touch type has proven to be an invaluable skill. When I went off to college in 1958, I received as a gift a Royal portable electric typewriter which I used for years, and even wrote my dissertation on it. Even though typing was considered a menial skill beneath the dignity of a future "professional," I accepted it and grew to enjoy using the machine. When I arrived in California, having never traveled west of Philadelphia, on September 2, 1969, to take an assistant professorship at the University of California at Irvine, my office equipment consisted of a dictionary and a typewriter.

A good portion of my work life has consisted since then in using a keyboard. For any reader of my generation, I need not belabor the difference between an electro-mechanical keyboard and a computer keyboard. The former, Friedrich Kittler and William Burroughs notwithstanding,[7] was a miserable affair. Changing text required messy liquids and powders. Multiple copies, with carbon papers which inevitably left stains on clothing and hands, were truly bothersome. On these machines, the transfer of the life of the mind into material form was difficult work. Often this work was subcontracted (as we now say) to full-time typists. Because of the limits of the typewriter, writers did not produce texts in an edited form, but instead yielded manuscripts and typescripts almost unreadable with erasures, crossed out passages, marginal revisions, and scribbling of all kinds.

The electro-mechanical typewriter was truly a tool of the older kind. It required skill. It was a tool that resisted the subject's intentionality, demanding some physical force to produce markings on paper. The object that emerged from it bore the traces of labor—of the imperfections in the keys, the uneven spread of ink on the ribbon, and the variable force of the typist across the QWERTY. Computer keyboards, by contrast, elide these markings of the body. Word processing files appear to inscribe directly the intellect of the writer, obeying with precision the author's intentions. There are indeed experiments with disabled computer users in which the brain directly transposes its will to the screen, bypassing entirely the work of writing.[8] Information machines have clearly transformed the domain of work, constructing symbiotic human-machines or cyborgs in the process.[9]

The shift from the typewriter keyboard to the computer keyboard is ontological: the former instantiates and reinforces a subject-object relation. The paper page receives the mechanical blows of the keys as the writer presses on the machine to produce the inked page. The typewriter merely improves the legibility of the page over the hand-manipulated quill, ink pen, or pencil, where one scratches inscriptions into the paper. The computer keyboard, by contrast, sends digital signals to the central processing chip through the word processing program, producing letters on the screen that lack the material properties of the typed paper page. The letters on the screen are fluid, easily changeable and movable. No more scratching out and brushing of white liquids. The words appear on the screen almost as quickly as they are thought or revised. Spelling and grammar are instantly checked. A thesaurus is only a few keystrokes away. Other files on one's machine are also ready to be marked, copied and pasted into the text. Bibliographical annotations are just as available not only from information existing in one's database but from other databases anywhere in the world. The same keyboard serves many functions not limited to word processing. Switching between programs magically transforms the keyboard into a calculator, an input system for a database, a music selector, a telegraph-like communication system, and so forth.

The keyboard is a liminal apparatus. It sutures the consciousness of the writer to the vast stores of information on the Net and the compelling facilities of the programs on one's machine. There is no opposition of creative mind to dumb (typewriting) machine, but rather interaction between writer, keyboard, computer program, and network, each having considerable cognitive abilities. The mind moves with the aid of the keyboard into the screen, merging with global information systems through the interface. Writing is no longer an isolated activity but one that affords simultaneous connections to others through chat rooms, E-mail, and instant messaging. And the keyboard, perhaps a collapsible one, moves with the user through everyday life far more easily than a portable typewriter, accompanying the user wherever she happens to be. The keyboard user is thus always, for better or worse, ready to write.

As a hi-fi snob, I was uninterested in portable cassette players introduced by Sony as the Walkman. My children were not so restricted, and quickly adopted the media. In the early 1980s, in a mall in Mission Viejo with my wife and daughters, I was bored by shopping. My younger daughter offered me her Walkman with a U2 cassette in it. I was astonished. Standing in the same position in the midst of clothing stores and the like, I was enveloped by the gorgeous, bleating sounds of *Joshua Tree*, literally displacing me from my surroundings. A simple audio device transported my consciousness to the musical "space." If radio commingles cultures, shifting spatial arrangements, the Walkman blends in the same body different senses from divergent locations, in this case, sight from the mall with sound from U2's recording studio. Such alterations in the spatial and temporal configuration of the everyday urge us finally to consider the question that has been haunting these analyses: the control of daily culture.[10]

[. . .]

Notes

1 For a discussion of the role of the personal case history or anecdote in social and cultural analysis see Mike Michael, *Reconnecting Culture, Technology, and Nature: From Society to Heterogeneity* (New York, 2000), pp. 14–16.

2 Dick Hebdige, *Cut 'N' Mix: Culture, Identity, and Caribbean Music* (New York, 1987).

3 Lynn Spigel, *Make Room for TV: Television and the Family Ideal in Postwar America* (Chicago, 1992).

4 In *Reconnecting Culture, Technology, and Nature: From Society to Heterogeneity*, Mike Michael contrasts television with the Internet and other media regarding the ability of each to promote a common culture. This is increasingly characteristic of television studies; that is, finding an advantage to broadcast systems where the same signal is transmitted to millions of receivers.

5 For the change in the public/private relation wrought by television, see Joshua Meyrowitz, *No Sense of Place: The Impact of Electronic Media on Social Behavior* (New York, 1985).

6 For an excellent analysis of the impact of television in places outside the home see Anna McCarthy, *Ambient Television: Visual Culture and Public Space* (Durham, 2001).

7 See Friedrich A. Kittler, *Discourse Networks 1800/1900*, tr. Michael Metteer (Stanford, 1990), and William Burroughs, *Naked Lunch* (New York, 1959).

8 This work is still in the formative stages but there is some progress. See for example Jennifer Kahn, "Let's Make Your Head Interactive," *Wired*, August 2001, 106–15.

9 Shoshana Zuboff, *In the Age of the Smart Machine: The Future of Work and Power* (New York, 1988).

10 For a subtle investigation of this question see Rayford Guins, "'Now You're Living': The Promise of Home Theater and Deleuze's 'New Freedoms,'" *Television & New Media*, 2 (2001), 351–65.

Chapter 41

MICHAL DALIOT-BUL

JAPAN'S MOBILE TECHNOCULTURE
The productions of a cellular playscape and its cultural implications

MICHAL DALIOT-BUL'S research on young Japanese people's uses of, and play with, their mobile phones (*keitai*) complements **Hjorth**'s enquiry in its exploration of the diverse creative communication practices that mobile devices make possible. However, she is concerned with mobile culture within popular, everyday use, rather than in professional artistic and creative contexts (which resonates with **Ito**'s essay below). She views practices of *keitai* use as inherently playful, both in the decoration of the device itself with stickers and charms or through customising wallpapers and ringtones, and in the non-instrumental communicative practices developed by young phone users. *Keitai*-mediated communication is at least as often about 'maintaining social contact and conveying feelings' as about arranging meetings or passing on information. It constructs and sustains 'a playful and emotional connectedness among friends'.

Because of the sheer omnipresence of mobile phones, this play-dimension effects significant changes in everyday life more generally. 'Keitai blurs the distinctions between the private and public, leisure and work, here and there, and virtual cyberspace and reality.' The boundaries between play and non-play in the everyday are also blurred.

In 2005, KDDI-au, the second largest mobile carrier in Japan, opened to the public a first of its kind, mobile technology funland: the KDDI Designing Studio. According to Natsuko Kimura,[1] general manager of the KDDI Designing Studio, after much debate it was decided that the perfect location for this centre would be Harajuku, Tokyo's busiest and probably best-known urban laboratory of youth popular cultures. The five-storied cylindrical glass building was conceived as an amazing and dynamic space that offers spectacular imagery of a technology integrated into cultural practices – a 'technoculture' (Green, 2002). Beyond the expected hands-on examining of sleek handsets, 3D games, mobile TV, mobile manga and mobile books with special effects, visitors are invited, for example, to create a personal card featuring their photo as well as their contact information and favorite mobile content sites. The latter are encrypted in Quick Response codes (known as QR codes) that can be deciphered by handsets equipped with a QR code reader.[2] In another 'ride', by merging their photo with an animated cartoon template, visitors create their own personalized graphic representation, their 'avatar', which can be downloaded to a cell phone and sent to friends.

Three mobile carriers were the main players in Japan's thriving mobile communications market in 2005, the year I conducted most of the research on which this article is based: KDDI-au, Vodafone-live[3] and NTT-DoCoMo, which revolutionized the mobile communication industry when it introduced the first mobile internet in 1999, and which is still, in 2007, leading the market in number of customers, mobile data users and subscribers to third-generation technology services.[4] The KDDI Designing Studio is a technocultural centre built to create the KDDI-au brand name, and it signals KDDI's determination to compete for market leadership in Japan. More importantly for this article, it reflects the dominant market positioning of *keitai*, the Japanese term for cellular phones, as a mass consumer product that is framed by cultures of gadget fetishism, technofashion and technofuturism (Ito, 2005: 9) and is consumed as experimental play. In marketing keitai, the main mobile carriers in Japan are producing an image of a product that not only makes users' lives easier and more convenient in highly sophisticated ways, they are also selling a product that 'stimulates the banal everyday life' (*mainichi wo shigeki suru kētai*).[5] Keitai are presented as opening up possibilities to challenge grinding everyday routines, over which people have only limited control, by offering an interactive, spectacular *playscape* that increasingly merges with real life.

The impact of keitai on Japanese culture and society is drawing increasing academic and popular interest in Japan and around the world (e.g. Gottlieb and McLelland, 2003; Ito et al., 2005; Ohara, 2002; Okada and Matsuda, 2002; Rheingold, 2002). In this article, I would like to contribute to this area of research by looking into a hitherto neglected focus of inquiry, that of the keitai playscape that developed as soon as mobile phones in Japan became a mass consumer commodity. In the following, I reconstruct the developmental trajectory of keitai from a technological device into a little friend that is an intensely personal part of users' lives and is an outlet for fun and play-thrills (Daliot-Bul, 2002). Keitai technology started in Japan, as in other places, as a business-oriented technology, but was soon 'hijacked' by youth popular cultures (Fujimoto, 2005; Ito, 2005: 9). The social reception of keitai communication and the internet by Japan's youth has oriented the shaping of the keitai eco-system, and thus its present and future, reflecting a larger cultural context in which youth have become the new cultural avant-garde of urban lifestyles in Japan. A process of social construction and negotiation of mobile technologies among carriers, handset manufacturers, content providers and young people (see Bijker, 1990: 18) has transformed keitai from a technological product into something playful, a 'toy-box' (Kohiyama, 2005a). Producers of the keitai technoculture are thus adopting play as a favorite interface for the convergence of widely circulating youth cultural forms, cutting-edge technologies and consumerism.

Beyond the packaging of keitai as something cool and playful, and the redirecting of keitai uses and content toward entertainment applications, the idealization of play within the keitai environment turned out to be a strategy with significant sociocultural implications.[6] By looking at keitai as a product 'deeply embedded in the contexts of Japan' (Matsuda, 2005: 38), I argue that the keitai playscape was constructed by specific sociocultural circumstances, that it came to be constructive of the keitai environment and practices and is ultimately transcending the keitai technologies, uses and contents, becoming a mechanism of cultural change. The ubiquity of cellular phones in Japan, and the way they have become for many 'an extension of the self' (see McLuhan, 1994 [1964]), is bringing about the merging of play into everyday life. The cultural borders between play and non-play blur, introducing and spreading new modes of relating to the social, the technological and the urban environments.

From a technological device to a mass consumer product: keitai as a platform of play promoting self-expression

The mid-1990s was a pivotal period in the history of cellular phones in Japan. Until then, keitai was strongly linked with professional organizations; it was a luxury item owned by high executives, professional team leaders and the well-to-do. In 1996, however, the costs of keitai ownership were greatly reduced (Kohiyama, 2005b: 64), and keitai was gradually transformed into a personalized medium that connects individual users. The social reception and popularization of keitai communication was closely related to the embrace of this medium by youth. Before the keitai boom, personal pagers were enthusiastically adopted by Japanese youth as a favorite medium for peer communication. In 1996, several competing keitai carriers introduced a mobile text-transmission application, thereby transforming keitai into a technologically advanced and – more than ever before – reasonably priced alternative to pagers. The recently created pager texting culture was carried over into keitai usage (Okada, 2005: 50–1). Market studies soon pointed out that youth-driven mobile texting picks up at around 10:00 pm, when for most people the day is over (Matsunaga, 2000: 153). Beyond coordinating social life, mobile texting is based on short, phatic communication used for maintaining social contact and conveying feelings rather than exchanging information or ideas. It creates a playful and emotional connectedness among friends. It is about *feeling* and *reaffirming* the connection.

The huge potential in the positioning of mobile telecommunication as a form of play was tapped in 1998 by the advertising campaign of TU-KA, one of Tokyo's local mobile carriers at the time. The company launched an aggressive campaign to promote several of its new services, using as a catchword the English verb 'play', which was sometimes interchanged with its Japanese equivalent, *asobu*. The different ads included variations on the following messages:

1. MOTE ASOBE.[7] PLAY TU-KA.
   Play and have even more fun.
   Get even more thrills.
   TU-KA's communication is not merely about talking. TU-KA expands the means of transmitting one's thoughts.
   Your life will be different from what it was yesterday.
   From now on, you will be able to communicate your feelings as they are.

2. Own a voice dial, and play. **MOTE ASOBE. PLAY TU-KA.**

3. Have mail friends and play. Have more friends with TU-KA.
   Mail Friends Campaign. MOTE ASOBE. PLAY TU-KA.

The explicit identification of communication technologies with play emphasized interpersonal relations and social bonding. Already in the 1980s, 'play' had become a favored aphorism for self-fulfillment through consumption that was often evoked by advertising, the media and retailing industries (Kinsella, 1995: 248). The identification of mobile communication with play was now hinting at a wealth of new possibilities for interpersonal communication. According to a Japanese proverb, 'In one match ten years of friendship are earned' (*Ikkyoku shiai – jūnen no chiko wo eru*). In Japan, play, or *asobi*, has long been conceived as the perfect cultural space for verbal and non-verbal communication. According to this cultural conceptualization, play enables interpersonal communication that may not otherwise be possible.[8] With the popularization of interpersonal communication and multimedia industries during the 1990s, play has come to be identified as the preferred strategy for overcoming the Japanese cultural tendency for restraint in social interactions.

As keitai became a personalized medium, an extravagant range of matching accessories filled entire stores. With a variety of hand straps; cute, attachable mini-dolls and cartoon characters; funny, illuminating antennae; carrying bags; 3D stickers to cover up the mouthpiece; full-body stickers; screen holograms; and handmade painting on customer demand, mobile phones became a fashion item of complex and excessive signs play. As early as 1996 ring tones (*chakumero*) came to be a particularly popular feature of keitai. Originally, users could use the keypad to input hit songs of their choice note by note. Ring-tone composition books became bestsellers and, before it became possible to digitally sample and replay live music on one's keitai, sound chips able to produce complex chords and sound combinations were developed (Okada, 2005: 55). Choosing keitai accessories and a ring tone were the forerunners of keitai customization practices. Although the forming keitai consumption practices were youth driven, the crowd queuing to buy keitai accessories was heterogeneous. It included not only teens and university students, but urban strollers of all age groups.

According to one advertisement for mobile telephone full-body stickers from 1998, it was time to 'change clothes!' (*kigaeyou!*) and 'get some personality!' (*kōsei wo get shiyō!*). It was indeed often an individualistic self that would reveal itself in the consumption practices of keitai. In the words of Wireless Watch Japan reporter Gail Nakada,[9] 'back in the 1990s a "salaryman" [white collar employee in a large corporation] who bought for his keitai a Hello Kitty charm was also making a statement. It was his little anti-establishment rebellion, his "Che Guevara Hello Kitty."' Between 1998 and 1999 the industry experimented with different handset designs. In 1999, the first keitai models with colour display were introduced. Japanese keitai became an emblem standing at the forefront of Japanese consumerism.

This trajectory of keitai consumption reflects larger cultural processes in which youth culture forms and images have come to be powerful forces at work in the recession-stricken urban Japanese culture. As other industries grew sluggish during the 1990s, playful teen-centric products and services became the fastest-growing components of Japan's economy (Machiyama, 2004: 15, Rheingold, 2002: 7), reaching a crowd far larger than youth only. Popular youth culture, with its dominant unorthodox styles of playful excessiveness, cuteness and fantasy, has been commodified and reproduced to the point it has become a marked feature of Japan's urban public culture. There are numerous reasons for this contemporary idealization of youth culture. During Japan's recession, urban youth became the most affluent social sector, thus also becoming key players in Japan's consumer culture. Furthermore, many of today's adults in urban Japan were youths during the 1980s, a decade that saw an unprecedented proliferation of youth popular cultures, providing them with the prerequisite aesthetic sensitivities and nostalgic disposition to youth popular culture forms. Some scholars have also interpreted the contemporary popularity of youthful consumer play merchandise in Japan by pointing to their social and psychological merits of relieving loneliness and stress in this moment of economic and cultural anxieties (Allison, 2003: 391). On an even more latent level, youth-oriented consumer play merchandise offers an outlet for expressing in a small and personal way a disenchantment with Japan's post-war conservative institution- and production-oriented values, echoing 'a narrative of recession [that] began to supersede that of [economic] success' in the late 1990s (Ivy, 2000: 820). Japan's urban public culture celebrates alternative cultural forms and lifestyles readily available in Japan's late-consumer culture, which were until recently considered subcultural and even countercultural youth forms.

As befitting every cultural avant-garde, while many cultural forms and styles previously defined as youth-only are becoming mainstream or adapted to fit other age-groups of the population, youth cultural separatist 'avant-gardeisme' is renegotiated and redefined among the media, consumer industries and youths. As is clear from observing the keitai technoculture, new youth-only applications and practices, some of which are gender-specific and all of which can be characterized as having a consumer 'play-value' (see Clammer, 1997: 107), are continuously produced, propelling the keitai industry to new technological frontiers and setting the keitai technoculture agenda.

The production of mobile internet as an outlet of play

Probably the most memorable technological and business breakthrough in the history of mobile telecommunication in Japan was the inauguration in February 1999 of NTT-DoCoMo's mobile internet service, known as i-mode. Labeled as 'Japan's Wireless Tsunami' (Beck and Wade, 2003), i-mode's high rate of acquisition of subscribers surpassed all of the most optimistic forecasts (Kridel, 2000) and made internet access an established element of keitai ownership in Japan (Kohiyama, 2005b: 68). While i-mode has been much applauded for its successful technological and business models (e.g. Kunii and Baker, 2000), not as much has been written on the successful marketing design of Japan's first mobile internet as an intensely personalized and enjoyable tool. In her book on the making of i-mode, Mari Matsunaga – who was recruited by DoCoMo specifically to develop Japan's first mobile internet content and whose name has since been often associated with the success of i-mode[10] – describes how i-mode was designed to become a 'digital concierge', a service constructed to help coordinate life and make it more pleasurable (Matsunaga, 2000: 83–5). It turned out that the concierge concept ended up directing the use of wireless data in Japan, rather than a more practical business-oriented concept (Beck and Wade, 2003: 156). For Matsunaga, who came up with the brand name 'i-mode', the 'i' in it stands obviously for 'internet', 'interactivity' and 'information', but also for signaling the centrality and individuality of the keitai owner (Matsunaga, 2000: 124). This is an image that reverberates with the late consumer culture advertising ideology of romantic authenticity and emotional fulfillment found in narcissistically pleasing oneself (Featherstone, 1991: 27).

From early on, the wireless industry in Japan was looking for ways to transform keitai and mobile internet services into an indispensable part of daily life (see Hakuhōdō seikatsu sōgō kenkyūjo [Hakuhodo Research Institute of Everyday Life], 2001). But the initial key interaction between the new technology and users in Japan that led to the industry formation and that still plays a crucial role was the interaction between entertainment content and young people. At the turn of the millennium, market research showed that Japanese youth expenditure on entertainment had considerably dropped because many young people preferred to spend their pocket money or their wages on their mobile phone bills (Auckerman, 2001). The marketing image of cellular phones as an arena of play and entertainment was aimed, however, at a much larger audience than youth only. An advertisement from 2001 promoting a business partnership between i-mode and PC internet access provider AOL shows Yamazaki Tsutomu[11] as a serious-looking middle-aged Japanese man wearing pink-dotted pajamas and holding a sign saying 'playing only when away from home will not do . . . one should also be able to play after returning home . . .', suggesting that even the most serious segments of Japanese society should by now have embraced mobile internet as an outlet of play. According to NTT-DoCoMo's publications, in 2002, 79 percent of i-mode content access was for fun applications, ranging from ring tones and screen savers to horoscopes, sport, games and more (Funk, 2003).

Since 2000 a growing number of monthly magazines devoted to keitai have been published. Besides introducing new keitai models and comparing prices and technological features, these magazines are structured as guidebooks to 'time killing' (*hima tsubushi*) content. Starting in 2001 *MediaWork* has been publishing monthly a comprehensive NTT-DoCoMo i-mode official guidebook, titled *Let's Play with i-mode!* (*i-mode de asobō!*), which focuses on the possibilities of using i-mode services as a platform for gaming and playing. Occasionally, a free supplement to this magazine is distributed, introducing new keitai models and favorite content sites for wallpaper, animated screen savers, ring tones, fortune telling, matchmaking (*deai*), games and mail rooms organized by animated cartoon characters, as well as convenient sites for weather reports, sports news, public transport and so forth. Most information and news sites also come in more fun customized versions, hosted by an animated interactive cartoon character ranging from Sanrio's Hello Kitty to Mobile Suit Gundam.

Choosing the hosting character for these sites (and also resisting them) reflects the user's taste (Hjorth, 2003) and often becomes part of her self-presentation (her 'Front', in Goffman, 1976: 93–4). It also domesticates and humanizes the technology (Horjth, 2005) by giving it a personality. According to the hosting character of choice the cell phone becomes cute, feminine, manly, funny, morbidly sarcastic and more. It has been noted that when machines display emotions, like an animated interactive cell phone does, they provide a rich and satisfying interaction with people (Norman, 2004: 194). Users respond by nurturing and caring for this kind of anthropomorphic creature, regardless of whether it has consciousness or intelligence or is simply a toy.

The initial developments in Japan's mobile internet content were informed by an understanding of the basic characteristics of mobile technology, a technology that is personal and time/location specific. The user interface cannot be as complex as in a PC-accessed internet portal, and the content needs to be of the sort to provide quick gratification. The users have to be able to get on a train, push a few buttons on their cell phone, and get what they were looking for before getting off the train at the next station. In 1999, for example, Dwango, a mobile entertainment company, released the mobile fishing game Tsuribaka Kibun (In the mood for silly fishing). In this game, the player sends a message to the server that he would like to begin fishing at a certain location with a certain type of lure. After a while, when 'the fish starts to bite', the keitai vibrates and the player can handle the controls until the fish is caught. The game became so popular, especially among young salarymen, that next the company developed a mobile internet fishing community around it. A web forum offers lists of the largest fishes caught, statistics, fishing-aficionado chat rooms and the possibility of betting on the type of fish the player might catch (Kontio, 2004).

Also in 1999, Imahima (literally meaning 'Are you free now?') launched its first product: an application for a mobile instant messaging service that allows users to share their current personal status (location, activity, mood) publicly with all the service subscribers, or privately with only their restricted list of buddies. The potential of Imahima as a matchmaking site for strangers attracted much attention (e.g. Rheingold, 2002: 166). However, according to Neeraj Jhanji,[12] founder and CEO of Imahima, the service was mostly used between friends, being particularly popular among unmarried young people. The marketing vision behind Imahima was 'to celebrate human relationships and communication, by introducing some joy to people's busy lives'.[13] The Imahima business has been creating and managing media and user communities ever since.

The Imahima community and the Tsuribaka Kibun community were relatively early forms of mobile communities. These communities have become another way of enhancing the user's experience, by merging different technologies and creating a service that explores the boundaries of the potential property of mobile phones as means to carve new groups out of the masses. Rheingold (2002) emphasizes the potential of these new mobile networks in inducing different forms of social activism. I would like to point to the way this fragmentation of the masses into groups induces a paradigm of being in which people come together in temporary play communities that offer a shared experience of intense moments of ecstasy and affectual immediacy. Mobile play communities are temporary, and often inclusive, heterogeneous groups distinguished by their members' shared interests and lifestyles, bringing to mind sociologist Maffesoli's (1996 [1988]) description of the formation of 'postmodern tribes' in late modernity's mass society. These groups network to enjoy 'the power of the life-affirming, Dionysian quality of the transcendent warmth of collectivity' (Shields, 1996 [1988]: x).

Whether an entertaining technology that is used to retrieve information and play games, an emotional, interactive technological device, or a technological means to network with temporary play communities, the Japanese mobile internet emerged as a playscape quite different from its PC-accessed counterpart. The popularity of Japan's mobile internet evolved through its colonization of the in-between moments of everyday life, and their transformation into enjoyable, pleasurable breaks.

Emotions as social practice in the keitai playscape

According to Matsunaga (2000: 153), an important feature that contributed to the raging popularity of i-mode was the way the i-mode email service was constructed to enhance the mobile texting experience. While mobile texting has many applications for both the business and private sectors, Matsunaga was targeting youth. At the height of the youth-driven pager boom, the bestselling pager model was one that had the ability to send a cute 'heart mark'. The heart mark feature reverberated in a metonymic way with an already well-established tendency among Japanese youth to adopt stylistically cute (*kawaii*) forms as means of self-expression (Kinsella, 1995). This inspired Matsunaga to introduce several pictorial icon-marks, known as *emoji* (pictograms), which allow more expressiveness in short messages. The popularity of *emoji* has since been so huge that i-mode and its competitors have kept on introducing new *emoji* in new models, and publishing instructions on how to become an '*emoji* master' (*emoji masutā ni narō*) and 'enjoy *emoji* ever more' (NTT-DoCoMo i-mode official guidebook, i-mōdo de asobo! supplement, summer 2002).

Until quite recently, although mobile texting between different keitai carriers was possible, sending and receiving *emoji* was restricted to communication between same keitai-carrier phones. Japan's *kōgyaru* – street-savvy high school girls who are the heaviest users of mobile texting – overcame this obstacle by the ongoing creation of *kaomoji* (emoticons, literally 'face letters'), which they invent by playfully combining punctuation, alphanumerics and other special marks. *Kaomoji* imitate facial expressions and transmit emotions in a world of plain text. Yasuko Nakamura, founder and CEO of Boom Planning, a Tokyo-based marketing company that has employed, since its establishment in 1986, high school girls as informants and sales promoters, conducts much of her communication with her teen employees through mobile text messages. In her fascinating book on the culture of contemporary Tokyo high school girls, Nakamura (2004: 32–3) lists over 50 (!) *kaomoji* that are in current use and their meanings, such as:

> *Gomennasai* (X^X ;) (Sorry (X^X ;))
> *Otanjōbi omedetō* V(^o^)V (Happy Birthday V(^o^)V)

High school girls, in order to create messages that transmit even better their feelings and personalities, have also developed their own encrypted *gyarumoji mērukomi* (girls' writing mail communication). In *gyarumoji mērukomi*, whole messages are written by uninhibitedly combining *kaomoji* with alphanumerics, the indigenous hiragana, katakana and kanji characters, and interchanging what should be written as full-size katakana or hiragana letters with half-size ones, mimicking graphically girlish prosody – pauses, rhythm, intonation – as in the following example (Nakamura, 2004: 34–5):

Gyarumoji mērukomi:

えゐ～！け゛㊉きレ二Uてゑ? (∧○∧)♪

Standard Japanese with emoticons:

えみ～！げんきにしてる?(ˆ0ˆ) ♪

English translation with emoticons:
Emi! How are you? (^ 0 ^) ♪

It is thus not surprising that one of the earliest versions of a mobile mail room hosted by an animated character in Japan was most successful in targeting high school girls. The PostPets – eight cute, animated characters that starred in a 1997 email software program designed for PCs – became an instant hit among desktop email users in Japan. In 2000, the same software was adapted to pastel-colored pocket mobile devices with mini screens and keyboards that plug into cellular phones, enabling the sending and receiving of emails. The user chooses one PostPet that would thereupon settle in a furnished, toy-like, virtual studio apartment in the user's PC or mobile device. Once the user enters a message it is put in a virtual envelope and delivered personally by personal PostPet to the recipient. On the recipient side, the PostPet would enter his fellow PostPet's 'apartment', deliver the envelope with the message, ask to be fed and petted, and even play with the local PostPet. After returning home, depending on the kind of reception it got, the PostPet may be happy or reluctant to deliver another message to the same recipient. PostPets can also strike up seemingly self-motivated relationships with other PostPets and decide on their own whim to pay them a visit. According to Kazuhiko Hachiya, inventor of PostPets software, 'PostPets make everything about e-mail emotionally interactive' (cited in Mann, 2001).

Comparative research on mobile texting practices shows that children and young people around the globe have become particularly adept at inventing their own language in text messaging (Plant, 2002: 80–1). What is noteworthy about the evolving Japanese teen-girl texting practices that I have described is the distinguished texting style itself, which tends to capitalize on playful cuteness as an objectification of emotional and individualistic expressiveness, as well as the attentive cooperation of media producers in enhancing this style by providing new means to apply it. In the forming of the girls' texting ecology, emotions have become a 'social practice' (see Boellstorff and Lindquist, 2004). According to Nakamura,[14] high school girls' text messages often portray an unrealistic image of the writer. The writer may seem to be *akarui* (light), *omoshiroi* (funny) and *genki* (assertive), while in reality she is quite *tsumaranai* (boring) – a rather shy and introverted person. This tendency fleshes out the play quality of this kind of text messaging, which is performed in many ways as a 'simulation game' (see Caillois, 1961 [1958]). In this game, players can express their secret wishful subjective worlds, using a specific language of emotional expression.[15]

Communication as a ludic experiential commodity

As cellular carriers introduced newer infrastructures with higher speed and data transmission capacity, new interpersonal communication applications were invented. Since 2000, messaging services that include keitai-shot photos and later keitai-shot video footage, have become extremely popular, standardizing a built-in camera as a feature of mobile phones in Japan. Bricolage platforms to personalize messages are enthusiastically received, especially among young people but increasingly among other users as well. The popularity of keitai cameras and of mobile messaging is continuously leading to the creation of new, sophisticated applications that combine the best of all worlds, emphasizing playful and emotional communication.

Following the huge success of keitai cameras, mobile videoconferencing was expected to become the third-generation killer application; nevertheless, it has not captured much consumer interest to this day, in spite of the great improvements in performance since its launch in 2002. In 2005, in an effort to make the service more attractive, DoCoMo i-mode targeted young people when it introduced a new application called *kyara den* (character telephone), in which an animated avatar can stand in for the user during videophone calls. The avatar's expressions and movements are easily controlled by the user with simple keypad operations enabling a 'playful conversation with one's intimate friends' (*DoCoMo kētai denwa katarogu*, July 2005).

The avatar concept of a preferred self-representation (*jibun no konomi no bunshin*) was taken to further playful extremes by a Duogate company[16] application called 'Team Factory'. Users can form a team of friends, which benefits from services such as checking on the present location of each member, coordinating schedules, multi-user online messaging and posting information for all members. The members' communication is mediated through their avatars, which are fully customized from their facial expressions, hairstyle and make-up to their real-life brand-name clothes, shoes and accessories, as well as the thematic backgrounds in which they appear. While some customization items are free for those subscribed to the service, others are sold separately. Users get to keep the items they have purchased for a limited time, and they can store them when not in use in a virtual closet. Team Factory is a hybrid form of Role Playing Video Game (RPG), in which players get to select the character they want to play and how this character would be dressed and accessorized, and real-life communication tools. In this RPG, users play *themselves* in real-life situations and are engaged in playing what Allison (2003: 393) has nicknamed 'a fantasy of consumer brand capitalism'. As a communication tool, Team Factory is the embodiment of the cultural construction of mobile communication technologies as play.

While the Team Factory avatars are clearly a youth-oriented product, they are not played with by youth only. Mapping the demographics of Team Factory users is of course methodologically challenging. However, the Team Factory website allows us a unique glimpse into this matter.[17] The Team Factory website regularly organizes avatar fashion competitions. The owners of the competing avatars fill out a short questionnaire in which they talk about their occupation, taste in fashion, hobbies and future dreams. Browsing through these avatars reveals that most of the users who sign up for the competition are actually *shakaijin*, working adult members of the society. Some of the highest qualifying competitors are *kaishain* (workers in large corporate firms) and *shufu* (housewives) who often attest in their questionnaire to having *atatakafamiri* (a 'warm family') as their hobby.

The rapid spread of mobile media in Japan has been leading to the commodification of communication through which the social value and the shape of interpersonal communication are engineered. 'Communications' has come to be a buzzword and, as such, it is one of the most widely used words in advertising, standing for progressiveness and well-being. Mobile communication – perhaps the most important consumer trend in Japan in the past decade – is designed to be consumed as a ludic experiential commodity and as a vehicle for experimenting with social strategies for communication. The 2005 'KDDI Designing Studio Floor Guide' articulates this clearly by addressing directly its patrons and presenting the technocentre's concept as follows: 'In this studio, *you* can share in the joy and excitement of designing new styles of communication. The leading artist is *you*. The future of communication starts here' (my italics).

Playful futuristic technologies as an expression of progressive lifestyle

The transition to third-generation cellular technology in Japan was largely completed in 2006, and upgrades to the next-stage technology are already taking place. But even before they were completed, the marketing efforts of keitai carriers to mesh mobile internet services into the fabric of Japanese society and economy have become part of the experienced urban culture of Japan. The transition to advanced mobile technologies is mostly associated with the new range and possibilities of multimedia consumption. Entertainment content for keitai, with enhanced visual and sound applications such as 3D video games,[18] music, television, and book and manga reading with special effects are becoming standardized applications of keitai. From its early days, mobile internet in Japan developed by manipulating the special characteristics of keitai and thus it has successfully avoided being stigmatized as *naichatte internet* (close but not quite like PC-accessed internet). Today, mobile carriers and mobile media content providers are looking for new ways to make multimedia consumption through the keitai unique and attractive. Media forms are domesticated to fit the keitai environment, often by converging and restructuring them as interactive and playful, and, increasingly, as multi-user experiences. The development of music consumption through the keitai would be a thought-provoking case study to explore this point.

Music downloading was pioneered in Japan by KDDI-au in 2002 with *EZchakuuta* service, which allowed users to download usually 30 seconds or less of original music that was used as ring tones. In December 2003, DoCoMo/Foma lanched its *chaku-motion* service, enabling users to combine video and high-quality music to signal incoming calls. Most commonly, these keitai-customized clips featured Japanese pop singers waving or strumming a guitar and saying something like '*Denwa da yo!*' ('You've got a phone call!'). Others featured short MTV-like videos and short clips of live performances. By late 2004 KDDI-au introduced the music download service *chakuuta full*, enabling the download of full-length original songs to mobile phones. Within six months of the introduction of *chakuuta full*, KDDI-au announced that 10 million full-length songs were downloaded. Constantly improving the data compression and data storage capacity of keitai by using memory cards, as well as the sound quality that is complemented by high-quality stereo headphones, all keitai carriers currently market cellular phones as portable music players. In January 2006, KDDI-au launched its music portal, Lismo, which allows mobile phones and PCs to share music seamlessly. The new service also enables users with mutually compatible handsets to exchange music playlists through its *uta-tomo* (song friends) service, advertised as a 'music communication service'. Moving to more experimental territories, the Hong Kong-based company Artificial Life was planning in 2005 to launch a new mobile subscription site called V-Disco that will combine chat, music streaming and music dowloading to mobile phones with interactive 3D graphics and animated virtual avatars. Users listen to the songs they choose while their avatars dance or chat with other avatars in real time (Nakada, 2005).

In the keitai cultural environment, playfulness has come to be the civilizing matrix of multimedia consumption that develops in play-forms.[19] Mobile multimedia consumption is transformed into an experience not unlike 'games of vertigo', which consists of an attempt to momentarily destroy the stability of perception in an effort to achieve a feeling of ecstasy and mental excitement (see Caillois, 1961 [1958]). The carnivalesque imageries, innovative juxtapositions, sensory overload and endless roads by which to explore the unfolding 3D multimedia keitai world fascinate consumers who have by now been educated to see futuristic mobile multimedia technologies as play. Incorporated into the ludic logic of entertainment, technology becomes friendly and inviting (see Yamaguchi, 2002). Beyond the socializing effect of play on consumers of new technologies, the convergence of play with consumption promotes further consumption. Technology consumption ceases to be merely about utilitarian materialistic commodities exchange; it becomes a fantastic, hedonic, experiential and emotive activity.[20] In sum, technology consumption becomes an expression of progressive lifestyle.

Conclusion: we shape our tools and our tools shape us

In his seminal work on how different media induce sociocultural change, McLuhan (1994 [1964]: 8) has posited that 'the "message" of any medium or technology is the change of scale or pace or pattern that it introduces into human affairs'. McLuhan argues that to fully appreciate the change introduced by new media we should look beyond the content or use of the innovation and into the change in interpersonal dynamics that the innovation brings with it (Federman, 2004). I have suggested that one aspect of the sociocultural impact of the keitai medium on the Japanese culture and society is related to the evolution of keitai as a youth-oriented platform of play in which technology develops in play-forms. Play induces sociocultural change since it has 'the power to impose its own assumptions by setting the human community into new relationships and postures' (McLuhan, 1994 [1964]: 242). I have shown in this article a variety of ways in which the keitai playscape becomes a greenhouse for new communication possibilities. I would like now to argue that the unique duality of keitai as a constant dimension of social life and as a playscape turns it into more than an arsenal of alternative cultural possibilities and strategies. Keitai is a vehicle for promoting the integration of these new possibilities in social reality.

The marketing design of keitai as playscape evolved by manipulating the 'otherness' of the keitai environment. Hanging a Hello Kitty charm on one's keitai, playing a simple cell phone digital game or having an animated character hosting one's keitai mail room are all acts of 'deviation' from reality into a play-dimension. However, as keitai is becoming seamlessly integrated into more and more settings of everyday life, the boundaries of the keitai playscape are fading as well. Keitai blurs the distinctions between the private and public, leisure and work, here and there, and virtual cyberspace and reality. As this happens, the boundaries of play as a framed act separated from real life blur as well. Rather than simply making everyday life more enjoyable, the integration of play into real life has profound implications for the production of social identities and life strategies.

The colonization of everyday life by the keitai playscape promotes a strong and irrepressible 'everyday hedonism' (see Maffesoli, 1990: 13), a cultural ambience that is deeply concerned with interpersonal communication, emotions and notions of selfhood and self-expression. This cultural ambience is expressed in the celebration of sensual pleasures, the pursuit of desires, the idealization of aesthetic experiences and affective sociability. The keitai playscape has made 'communication' one of the hottest consumer trends in Japan. Its imagery is promulgating new kinds of sociality and interpersonal communication in which emotionality rather than reserve and restraint is key. It is empowering users by giving them the tools to make their lives more pleasurable, to express and distinguish themselves by combining knowledge, information, skill and creativity. Last but not least, it also refamiliarizes a long-since alienated urban environment that is now embedded in a fun cyberspace of information and entertainment and is netted with invisible Dionysian networks. Like other favorite types of play, keitai youth-oriented playscapes arguably provide a release from the monopolistic tyranny of the 'social machine' (see McLuhan, 1994 [1964]: 238). In contemporary Japan, this social machine reflects a world order dictated by economic and political institutions identified with the 'adult society'. It is a world order that prioritizes production, high levels of conformity and a rehabilitation of Japan's conservative pre-recession middle-class values and lifestyles.

As the appeal of the keitai playscape 'imaginary'[21] is spreading, and as youth-oriented keitai accessories, services and applications are adopted by or domesticated to fit other age groups of the Japanese urban population, culturally established stylistic differentiations between mainstream and subculture, genders and generations are challenged. The cultural meanings of these styles are changing and are now hinting at a changing social environment, where 'the play of forms and the intrusion of the "futile" – the non-utilitarian – into daily life' (Clammer, 1997: 162) have become favorite pursuits. These consumption tendencies are indicators of processes that are breaking up traditional patterns of social regulation. Similar to what has been noticed in other late-consumer cultures, youth styles are migrating up the age scale, and adults are being granted greater license for childlike behavior and vice versa (Featherstone, 1991: 100–1). As we witness youth-popular-culture-driven keitai images and products migrating in various ways and degrees up the age scale, we also witness a very clear instance of how youth popular culture is changing contemporary Japanese culture and society at large. It is thus that the keitai playscape is more than a popular escapist haven; it is a mechanism of sociocultural transformation, indeed of a cultural shift.

Notes

This research was generously funded by the Japan Foundation. I am very grateful to all those who shared with me their deep knowledge of the contemporary Japanese mobile technoculture, especially to Mrs Gail Nakada, Ms Natsuko Kimura, Ms Yasuko Nakamura and Mr Neeraj Jhanji. Special thanks go to Dr Ofra Goldstein-Gidoni for her insightful comments during my research and on earlier versions of this article, and to my research assistant in Japan, Mr Alberto Fonseca-Sakai.

1   Interview conducted in Tokyo, July 2005.
2   QR codes (Quick Response codes) are an increasingly familiar sight in Japan, where they have replaced the older barcodes. The recent inclusion of QR code-reading software on camera phones has led to a variety of new consumer-oriented applications.
3   In March 2006 Vodafone-Japan was sold to Softbank.
4   As of July 2007, there were in Japan nearly 100 million users of cellular phones, and nearly 75 million subscribers to third-generation technology services (Wireless Watch Japan, 2007).
5   NTT-DoCoMo ad for the FOMA F901iS series, July 2005.
6   On the implications of a cultural idealization of play, see Sutton-Smith and Kelly-Byrne (1986 [1984]).
7   The Japanese term *mote asobe* is hard to translate since it literally means 'to play'; however, it is often used to suggest seduction and temptations in romantic relationships. This choice of vocabulary produces an image in which the user's relation with the keitai is somewhat decadent and almost sensual.
8   For this reason, after-work drinking in the Japanese corporate environment has long been considered a privileged opportunity for interpersonal communication and social bonding (Allison, 1994: 46; Ben Ari, 2002).
9   Interview conducted in Tokyo, July 2005. Wireless Watch Japan is a website covering Japan's wireless business.
10   In October 2000, Matsunaga was crowned 'Asia's Top Business Woman' by the prestigious *Fortune* magazine, and 'Woman of the Year 2000' by *Nikkei Woman* magazine.
11   Yamazaki Tsutomu is a famous actor known to Western audiences as the leading actor in many of Juzo Itami's movies, such as *The Funeral* (1984), *Tampopo* (1985) and *A Taxing Woman* (1987).
12   Interview conducted in Tokyo, July 2005.
13   Imahima website (consulted May 2006): http://www.imahima.com/ihcorpv2/container/imahima_community.php

14 Interview conducted in Tokyo, July 2005.
15 On play as an outlet for expressing wishful subjective worlds, see Sutton-Smith and Kelly-Byrne (1986 [1984]: 319).
16 Duogate was established by KDDI and Excite Japan Ltd in 2004 to create an integrated internet portal for PCs and mobile phones.
17 Team Factory website (consulted June 2006): http://pctm.ezavatar.duogate.jp/
18 The mobile gaming industry in Japan is characterized by the convergence between the traditional video game industry and the telecommunication industry. Today, with 3D graphics, excellent resolution and stereo sound, more and more familiar RPG, racing games and fighting games, formerly designed for game consoles only, are adapted to keitai with competitive performance. Accordingly, in the Tokyo Game Show of 2005 a massive third-generation mobile gaming display was particularly noticeable.
19 On playfulness as civilizing matrix, see Huizinga (1950 [1938]).
20 On the transformation of consumption into a ludic activity rather than a utilitarian activity, see Clammer (1997: 90).
21 I use the term 'imaginary' as Ito (2005: 1) does in reference to a 'shared imaginative projection of technological futures as grounded in everyday practices and the cultural present'.

References

Allison, A. (1994) *Nightwork: Sexuality, Pleasure, and Corporate Masculinity in a Tokyo Hostess Club*. Chicago: University of Chicago Press.
Allison, A. (2003) 'Portable Monsters and Commodity Cuteness: Pokemon as Japan's New Global Power', *Postcolonial Studies* 6(3): 381–95.
Auckerman, W. (2001) 'Surveys Show Cell Phone Secrets of Japanese Youth', *Asia Wireless News*, 1 January.
Beck, J. and M. Wade (2003) *DoCoMo: Japan's Wireless Tsunami*. New York: Amacom.
Ben Ari, E. (2002) 'At the Interstices: Drinking, Management, and Temporary Groups in a Local Japanese Organization', pp. 129–51 in J. Hendry and M. Raveri (eds) *Japan at Play*. London: Routledge.
Bijker, W.E. (1990) *The Social Construction of Technology*. Eijsden, The Netherlands: W.E. Bijker.
Boellstorff, T. and J. Lindquist (2004) 'Bodies of Emotions: Rethinking Culture and Emotion through Southeast Asia', *Ethnos* 69(4): 437–44.
Caillois, R. (1961 [1958]) *Man, Play and Games*. New York: The Free Press of Glencoe.
Clammer, J. (1997) *Contemporary Urban Japan: A Sociology of Consumption*. Oxford: Blackwell.
Daliot-Bul, M. (2002) 'Hahaver haselulari hatov beyoter' (The Best Cellular Friend), *Masa Aher* 129: 93–8.
DoCoMo kētai denwa katarogu (DoCoMo Cellular Phones Catalogue), July 2005.
Fasol, G. (2004) *Scenarios for Japan's Mobile Ecosystems*. Eurotechnology-Japan, URL (consulted 3 May 2006): http://www.tekes.fi/ohjelmat/vamos/Japan.pdf
Featherstone, M. (1991) *Consumer Culture and Postmodernism*. London: Sage.
Federman, M. (2004) 'What is the Meaning of *The Medium is the Message?*' URL (consulted March 2006): http://individual.utoronto.ca/markfederman/article_mediumisthemessage.htm
Fujimoto, K. (2005) 'The Third-stage Paradigm: Territory Machines from the Girls' Pager Revolution to Mobile Aesthetics', pp. 77–102 in M. Ito, D. Okabe and M. Matsuba (eds) *Personal, Portable and Pedestrian: Mobile Phones in Japanese Life*. Cambridge, MA: MIT Press.
Funk, J.L. (2003) 'Key Trajectories and the Expansion of Mobile Internet Applications', paper presented at the Stockholm Mobility Roundtable, 22–23 May. URL (consulted May 2006): http://www.iir.hit-u.ac.jp/file/FUNK%20INFO%20paper.pdf
Goffman, E. (1976) 'Performances', pp. 89–96 in R. Schechner (ed.) *Ritual, Play and Performance*. New York: The Seabury Press.
Gottlieb, N. and M. McLelland (eds) (2003) *Japanese Cyberculture*. New York: Routledge.
Green, L. (2002) *Technoculture: From Alphabet to Cyberspace*. St Leonards, NSW: Allen and Unwin.
Hakuhodo seikatsu sogo kenkyujo [Hakuhodo Research Institute of Everyday Life] (2001) *Kētai seikatsu hakusho* (White paper on keitai in everyday life). Tokyo: NTT Shuppan.
Hjorth, L. (2003) 'Cute@keitai.com', pp. 50–9 in N. Gottlieb and M. McLelland (eds) *Japanese Cybercultures*. London: Routledge.
Hjorth, L. (2005) 'Odours of Mobility: Mobile Phones and Japanese Cute Culture in the Asia Pacific', *Journal of Intercultural Studies* 26(1–2): 39–55.
Huizinga, J. (1950 [1938]) *Homo Ludens: A Study of the Play Element in Culture*. Boston, MA: Beacon Press.

Ito, M. (2005) 'Introduction: Personal, Portable, Pedestrian', pp. 1–16 in M. Ito, D. Okabe and M. Matsuba (eds) *Personal, Portable and Pedestrian: Mobile Phones in Japanese Life*. Cambridge, MA: MIT Press.

Ito, M., D. Okabe and M. Matsuba (eds) (2005) *Personal, Portable and Pedestrian: Mobile Phones in Japanese Life*. Cambridge, MA: MIT Press.

Ivy, M. (2000) 'Revenge and Recapitation in Recessionary Japan', *South Atlantic Quarterly* 99(4): 819–40.

Kinsella, S. (1995) 'Cuties in Japan', pp. 220–54 in L. Skov and B. Moeran (eds) *Women, Media and Consumption in Japan*. Honolulu: University of Hawaii Press.

Kohiyama, K. (2005a) 'The Meaning of Keitai', *Japan Media Review*, 28 July. URL (consulted May 2006): http://www.japanmediareview.com/japan/stories/050728kohiyama/

Kohiyama, K. (2005b) 'A Decade in the Development of Mobile Communication in Japan (1993–2002)', pp. 61–74 in M. Ito, D. Okabe and M. Matsuba (eds) *Personal, Portable and Pedestrian: Mobile Phones in Japanese Life*. Cambridge, MA: MIT Press.

Kontio, P. (2004) *Mobile Gaming Business*. Helsinki University of Technology, Telecommunications Software and Multimedia Laboratory. URL (consulted July 2005): http://www.tml.tkk.fi/Opinnot/T-109.551/2004/reports/mobile_gaming.pdf

Kunii, I. and S. Baker. (2000) 'Amazing DoCoMo', *Business Week*, 17 January: 24–9.

Kridel, T. (2000) 'I-opener', *Wireless Review*, 1 October: 22–8.

Machiyama, T. (2004) 'Mondo tokyo: Otaku', pp. 13–15 in P. Macias and T. Machiyama (eds) *Cruising the Anime City*. Berkeley: Stone Bridge Press.

Maffesoli, M. (1990) *Au creux des apparences: pour une éthique de l'esthétique* (At the Bottom of Appearances: An Ethic of Aesthetics). Paris: Plon.

Maffesoli, M. (1996 [1988]) *The Time of the Tribes: The Decline of Individualism in Mass Society*. London: Sage.

Mann, C.C. (2001) 'The Secret to Turning a Profit on the Web', AsiaWeek.com, 17 August. URL (consulted May 2006): http://www.pathfinder.com/asiaweek/technology/article/0,8707,170518,00.html

Matsuda, M. (2005) 'Discourses of Keitai in Japan', pp. 19–39 in M. Ito, D. Okabe and M. Matsuba (eds) *Personal, Portable and Pedestrian: Mobile Phones in Japanese Life*. Cambridge, MA: MIT Press.

Matsunaga, M. (2000) *i mōdo jiken* (The i-mode incident). Tokyo: Kadokawa shoten.

McLuhan, M. (1994 [1964]) *Understanding Media*. Cambridge, MA: MIT Press.

Nakada, G. (2005) 'Sony Music, Artificial Life Close 3G Mobile Music Deal', Wireless Watch Japan, 8 October. URL (consulted May 2006): http://www.wirelesswatch.jp/modules.php?name=News&file=article&sid=1568

Nakamura, Y. (2004) *Uchira to osoro no sedai: Tokyo joshikōsei no sugao to kōdo* (The Generation of 'Us' and 'Together': The True Face and Behavior of Tokyo High School Girls). Tokyo: Kodansha.

Norman, D.A. (2004) *Emotional Design*. New York: Basic Books.

Ohara, S. (2002) *i mōdo shakai no ware to wareware* (i-mode Society: I and We). Tokyo: Chukokoronshinsha.

Okada, T. (2005) 'Youth Culture and the Shaping of Japanese Mobile Media: Personalization and the Keitai Internet as Multimedia', pp. 41–60 in M. Ito, D. Okabe and M. Matsuba (eds) *Personal, Portable and Pedestrian: Mobile Phones in Japanese Life*. Cambridge, MA: MIT Press.

Okada, T. and M. Matsuda (2002) *Kētai gakunyʔmon* (Understanding Mobile Media). Tokyo: Yuhikaku.

Plant, S. (2002) *On the Mobile: The Effects of Mobile Telephones on Social and Individual Life*. Report for Motorola.

Rheingold, H. (2002) *Smart Mobs*. New York: Basic Books.

Shields, R. (1996 [1988]) 'Foreword: Masses or Tribes?', pp. ix–xii in M. Maffesoli, *The Time of the Tribes: The Decline of Individualism in Mass Society*. London: Sage.

Sutton-Smith, B. and D. Kelly-Byrne (1986 [1984]) 'The Idealization of Play', pp. 305–22 in P.K. Smith (ed.) *Play in Animals and Humans*. New York: Basil Blackwell.

Wireless Watch Japan (2006) Home page. URL (consulted June 2006): http://www.wirelesswatch.jp/index.php

Yamaguchi, M. (2002) 'Karakuri: The Ludic Relationship between Man and Machine in Tokugawa Japan', pp. 72–83 in J. Hendry and M. Raveri (eds) *Japan at Play*. London: Routledge.

Michal Daliot-Bul is a cultural researcher at the department of East-Asian Studies at Haifa University. Her doctoral thesis explores the deep cultural meanings of play in Japan. Her other research interests include the sociology of consumption, youth popular cultures, the production of intra- and inter-cultural imaginaries and the sociology of emotions. She has published a number of articles and is currently preparing her dissertation for publication. *Address*: Kfar-Hess, POB 545, 40692, Israel, [email: mikibul@gmail.com]

Chapter 42

SHANLY DIXON AND SANDRA WEBER

PLAYSPACES, CHILDHOOD AND VIDEOGAMES

I N T H I S E S S A Y, Shanly Dixon and Sandra Weber articulate theories of play with debates on the nature of childhood in a media-saturated culture. From the play theorists Huizinga and Caillois they draw concepts with which to address the ambiguities and fluidity of play, as well as assertions of its centrality to culture and everyday life. They reject nostalgic discourses that assume the loss of 'traditional' types of play in digital culture, finding instead strong continuities between longer-established outdoor play and the domestic, indoor and virtual activities of videogame play. The latter, they argue (and illustrate through ethnographic case studies), shares with the former creative and imaginative possibilities. And – importantly – they are not separated off from each other: the boundary between digital and analogue is thoroughly permeable. A 'game' might flow between a backyard and a videogame world, drawing on all manner of material and symbolic resources at hand and from popular media. The authors' ethnographic method is sensitive to the nuances and absurdities of children's play (notice, for example, the 'seven dwarves' rendition of 'I'm too sexy for my shirt').

Situating videogame play within the broader context of childhood

It has become a truism to state that children are growing up in an increasingly digital world. So many children play videogames that scholars, teachers, and parents are scrambling to make sense of this leisure activity. Most of the focus, however, has been on videogame play as an isolated activity cut off from the rest of childhood play forms and spaces. In contrast, like Giddings' micro-ethnography (see chapter two in this book), our research situates digital play amongst other forms that children's imaginary play can assume. Examining digital play alongside activities that occur in other playspaces such as the backyard or the neighborhood park enables us to make distinctions about digital play characteristics. It also serves to remind us that there is a fascinating continuity, flow, and ambiguity between various forms of play.

We will begin our consideration of playspaces, childhood, and videogames by framing these interrelated phenomena within a broader context, starting with a discussion of the intense nostalgia that currently surrounds children's play (see also *Boyhood spaces: play and social navigation through video games*, Dixon & Simon, 2005). After reviewing some of the literature on childhood, nostalgia, and play, we will more closely examine and reflect upon actual episodes of children at play. These ethnographic vignettes are based on extensive and unobtrusive observations of children in their natural settings, and are taken from a series of research projects we have conducted both separately and together over the course of more than fifteen years. The most recent data stems from research conducted for *The Digital Girls Project*, which we describe in the introduction to this book.

[. . .]

Nostalgia and play theory

Despite and alongside of all we have written earlier about increasing regulation of play, contemporary society seems to have much invested in maintaining the image of the purity of children's play. Dutch cultural historian, play theorist, and author of *Homo Ludens* (1961), Johan Huizinga engages in a different form of nostalgia concerning play. He establishes the importance of play in social life, asserting that "Play is older than culture," and that "all culture is a form of play" (p. 1). Huizinga's emphasis is on a higher form of play, which he characterizes through two key features—play as a *contest* for something or as a *representation* of something (p. 13). The concept of play as a contest is evident in most games and sports, including those played by adults. What is interesting to us here, however, is Huizinga's concept of play as representation. For instance, children pretending to be pirates or princesses are creating a representation of something distinct from their usual selves; something more exciting, more daring, or more magnificent. Huizinga suggests that these imaginative experiences of play can fill children with delight, enabling them to be transported beyond the self to such an extent that they almost believe they actually *are* such and such a thing, without, however, wholly losing consciousness of "ordinary reality," an imaginative experience of the truest and most fundamental kind (p. 13). Huizinga asserts that children's play embodies play in its purest form, and that as children grow into adults, their play becomes increasingly complicated and hence corrupted. His nostalgia is not only for childhood, but also for the form of unadulterated play that he believes is fostered by this stage. He associates this play with the most heroic aspects of society and views it as a civilizing force, suggesting that in past societies where play was at its pinnacle, civilization itself was at its most noble. Conversely, Huizinga notes, as a society becomes increasingly complex, technological, and overburdened with rules and systems of knowledge, it becomes more serious and, as a result, play begins to assume a less important position.

In his book, *Man, play and games* (1961), Roger Caillois builds upon the work of Huizinga using his own classifications of play and games as a means for gaining insight into particular cultures. Caillois points to a contradiction that requires reconciliation in the analysis of play. Huizinga's theory suggests that culture is derived from play and therefore he accords a cultural significance to play; however, many theorists adopt a contradictory position suggesting that games are the cast-offs of adult culture, symbolizing that which was previously integral aspects of cultural institutions, now discarded and relegated to the realm of play and childhood. According to these theorists, play and games are no longer considered serious or important cultural endeavors. Caillois reconciles this difference by suggesting that "The spirit of play is essential to culture, but games and toys are historically the relics of culture" (p. 58). Whether one argues that play produces culture or that play *reproduces* culture, Caillois suggests that much is revealed about a culture by the games that are played. Games to some extent characterize the society in which they exist and, therefore, are a valuable source of information. As Caillois relates, "They necessarily reflect its culture pattern and provide useful indications as to the preferences, weakness, and strength of a given society at a particular stage of its evolution"

(p. 83). Applying this reasoning to our present discussion of nostalgia, we suggest that the contradictions between the nostalgic yearning for the imagined innocent play of previous generations' childhoods and the current moral panic regarding media, technology, and related commercialization in contemporary children's play reveals much about our current society.

Childhood, commodification, and playspaces

From its very inception, childhood has been a social construction heavily influenced by commercial interests. In his book *The disappearance of childhood* (1994), Postman writes that childhood as a separate time and space emerged in the sixteenth century with the invention of the printing press and the subsequent rise in literacy and related need for an educated working class. Children were removed from the workforce and sent to school. But it was not until the late eighteenth century that childhood became a truly popular concept in Europe due to a developing middle class; people had newly acquired money and a desire to spend it (Postman, 1994). As families became smaller and modern capitalism resulted in children no longer being required to contribute to the family financially, having children became a conscious choice for the middle and upper classes (Dale, 2005). It was within the Victorian middle class that the idea of childhood became intertwined with the idea of consumerism. Children operated as "objects of conspicuous consumption" as adults purchased specially produced toys and clothes for their children in order to display their own economic prosperity (Du Boulay as cited in Postman, 1994, p. 44). It is perhaps this use of children as objects for conspicuous consumption that is pivotal in the Western construction of childhood. The role of children has changed; typically they no longer contribute economically to the family or to the marketplace. Young people have taken on the role of consumers rather than producers and as such they are immersed in popular culture, targeted by marketers, and inundated with media images.

Another reason that children's play has become so closely tied to media is the growing privatization and restriction of public spaces. The spaces of childhood are becoming increasingly concealed and protected whereas many public spaces have become adult-only spaces. This development has been explained in terms of two views that emerged from youth studies research around delinquency (Lucas, 1998): first, youth are thought to disrupt public space and so adults would rather they not be there; second, children are thought to be at risk in public spaces, it is too dangerous for them to be there (Jenks, 1996). This state of affairs evolved over the last century.

At the beginning of the twentieth century, it was not unusual for children to play unsupervised in the streets and empty lots. Children created their own private culture, with private spaces such as forts and clubhouses, frequently engaging in secret and forbidden activities such as gambling, fighting, drinking, and vandalism. In the second half of the twentieth century, adults began to bring children under stricter control by introducing playgrounds with commercial playground equipment; schoolyards began to be fenced in and organized clubs, such as boy scouts, and sports teams flourished (Sutton-Smith, 1997). More recently, as public spaces are viewed warily as dangerous places, children's play is becoming even further restricted, moving from streets and parks to organized, supervised activities and into domestic spaces such as bedrooms and playrooms. Adults equip children's domestic space with technologically enticing alternatives to public space in an effort to keep them safely inside (Buckingham, 2000). With this change in children's playspace, it thus becomes almost mandatory in Western society to purchase digital play equipment such as computers, videogame consoles, MP3 players, things children think are fun or "cool." Households become what Kline (1993) calls "media saturated spaces." The marketing of new technologies targets young people directly, socializing them into "the attitudes and social relations of consumerism" (Kline, Dyer-Witheford, & De Peuter, 2003, p. 244). As play becomes increasingly privatized, regulated, and supervised, it also becomes increasingly commercial and digital.

Culture, commodification, and play

For centuries, childhood, and the toys that are associated with it, has been largely a commercial construction, one that draws deeply on the well of children's popular culture to commodify children's play, opening up markets for manufacturers, advertisers, and corporations. The pervasiveness of popular culture infiltrates and, perhaps to some extent, shapes children's play as they adapt images and take inspiration from multiple influences around them. We might even go so far as to suggest that popular culture in and of itself constitutes a playspace. Adults supply children with media images (old or new) that children then use to become creators of their own playspaces, piecing together elements and mixing media to individualize their play experiences (see Weber's chapter three in this book for a detailed discussion of this phenomenon).

Cumulative cultural texts of childhood: reading children's play

A useful way to analyze children's popular culture and deepen our understanding of children's play is to regard it as part of the "*cumulative cultural text of childhood*," a text that can be "read." The concept of cumulative cultural text was described by Mitchell and Reid-Walsh (1993) and then expanded by Weber and Mitchell (1995) to refer to the culture of childhood, which carries vestiges of past images that link generations and popular images. The different, yet connected, versions of Barbie or NeoPets or Bratz Dolls or Snow White or Superman demonstrate how a strand of the cumulative cultural text of childhood evolves. Whether these "texts" begin as dolls, books, videogames, movies, or toys, if they become popular, they get spun out into a series of related toys, media, and objects, each iteration adding to the popular text. This cumulative text becomes peopled by the generations of real and fictitious characters embodied in books, films, TV programs, comics, songs, toys, software, and so on. Composite contemporary representations of Barbie and Lara Croft take their place amongst previous versions, and alongside Paddington Bears, Peter Pans, Raggedy Anns, GI Joes, Rubber Duckies, Winnie the Pooh, Spiderman, and Batman, to name just a few:

> A multitude of familiar images thus feeds the wellspring of the popular culture of childhood into which we are born and in which we are raised. These images overlap, contrast, blend, contradict, transform, amplify, address, and confirm each other as they compete for our attention in an intertextual clamour. (Weber & Mitchell, 1995, p. 167)

The extended life enjoyed by many popular images is made possible through the intertextual and generative types of variation and serialization that, for example, transformed Barnie, a popular purple dinosaur, from a TV character to a series of books, dolls, movies, knapsacks, and computer software, thus giving him presence, longevity, and power.

Both implicitly and explicitly, individual episodes and versions contextualize, influence, build on, and refer to each other, collaboratively constituting the cumulative text. A book begets a movie which begets both an audio track and a new edition of the book as well as a television series and computer games. But this serialization into multiple texts only happens if there is something commercially viable in the initial representation—something that captures children's interest, which draws them in or addresses them in a meaningful way that sells (p. 166).

In other words, popular texts such as the computer game *The Sims* or *Grand Theft Auto* wouldn't be pervasive unless they managed to tap into the particular desires of many child consumers. In that sense, they serve as a kind of mirror for childhood in our society, and reveal important truths to us about ourselves. As Caillois (1961) has suggested, the material culture of play has something to divulge about the culture within which it exists.

Returning now to our interest in videogames, while it is impossible to say with absolute certainty that the text of a child's experience of videogaming can be read or interpreted in any one particular way, we find it helpful to frame play as a meaningful text that invites a reading between the lines. Moreover, situating children's video play within the wider context of the cumulative text of childhood culture enables us see how videogame play might relate to other forms of play. How, we wonder, are social interactions and role-playing within the videogame space similar or different from children's relationships through play in other spaces such as parks, playgrounds, and playrooms? How does the experience of playing videogames shape (or how is it shaped by) the nature of contemporary childhood?

Observing and describing children's play

Our collaborative reflections on digital childhoods and children's play is based, in part, on a series of longitudinal ethnographic case studies each of us has conducted of children at play. We have followed some of the children (from three to fifteen years old) for up to six years, and our data collection includes interviews and observations. We are now sharing and combining our data, reviewing and testing our interpretations, and looking for cross-case similarities and differences. From this large corpus, we have selected a series of vignettes reconstructed from fieldnotes, each one followed by some critical reflections. Our first comes from a study done by Weber more than fifteen years ago.

Playing at Snow White: boys and girls in and out of role

I am surreptitiously watching a mixed group of mainly six-year-old children playing outside. They have been kicked out of doors by their mums who said, "get some sunshine." Let's play "Snow White," one of the girls exclaims. Most of them have recently seen the Disney movie, which seems to have impressed them. There are cries of assent, followed soon by arguing over who is going to be Snow White, who is going to be the wicked queen, and so forth. One girl has dark hair and soon convinces people she should have the role because she looks like Snow White, although another girl claims that the fact she has a Snow White lunch box gives her an edge. An older boy suddenly announces that he wants to be the wicked Queen because he has a cape he could use as a costume. No one seems to want to be the prince. The children begin enacting the story, stopping and restarting, giving each other directions (no, first she has to ask the mirror, then the woodsman takes her out to the woods), and improvising many touches that bear little resemblance to the movie. The game stops and then starts up again as one child tickles another, or someone calls attention to the mushrooms growing on the damp ground. Hilarity breaks out when one boy decides he is a deer who discovers Snow White asleep in the woods and tries to wake her by licking her. Suddenly, one of the children's mothers, who has come to fetch her child, intrudes upon the play space of the enchanted "forest." I notice that two of the children who were really "into" their roles seem startled, as if to say "what are you doing here? You're not in Snow White." One boy says "go away, we're playing." However, five minutes later, when another mother passes by and inquires, "What are you playing at," the same two children seem nonplussed and answer "Snow White." One of them says "I'm the wicked queen." "Oh, yes, I can see that you are," replies the mother gamely playing along. Snow White is called home by her mother—and another girl suggests her Barbie doll could take the part of Snow White. She proceeds to use her Barbie as a puppet, acting as ventriloquist for "Snow White Barbie." Another child goes along with this, but two others just sort of parallel play a different version of Snow White. The play keeps falling apart (to my adult observer eyes at any rate) changing directions, as a couple of boys engage in rough and tumble play, one child bursts into tears saying "I don't WANT to be Dopey," and so forth. And then the dwarfs start singing a popular song, "I'm too sexy for my shirt" and dancing around, while two girls decide the piece of cardboard they were using as the Mirror Mirror on the Wall is not very good, and announce they are going to make a "real one." When asked a few minutes after the play seemed to be grinding to a halt what they had been doing and how they had spent their afternoon, most of them said, "we played Snow White." Two of them told me "we were just playing outside." (Constructed from Weber's fieldnotes, August 1992.)

The children playing Snow White in the forest exemplify a form of childhood pretend, fantasy, or role-play that is familiar and ubiquitous, observed in children from one generation to another. Further, we see how children co-opt a variety of ideas and images to inform or guide their play, culled from various sources such as personal experiences, books, television, songs, and movies. Children adapt these images to the playspace and opportunities available to them—in this case, adapting the traditional story of Snow White to accommodate the roles the players wanted to adopt and making use of the props at hand. The play seemed to filter through *cumulative popular cultural texts*: their enacting of Snow White had an evolving script that was likely based not only on the movie but on the cumulative cultural text of Snow White that includes lunch boxes, figurines, Disney World characters, a variety of children's book versions, and so forth. It would perhaps be more accurate to say that the structure and "spontaneous" script of the children's play reflected their interpretations or responses to Disney and other forms of cultural texts. Through the children's active play, negotiations, and improvisations, the text was adapted, ignored, disrupted, and reconstructed. There was fluidity to the play despite a series of abrupt halts and changes of directions as the children moved in and out of the various roles that they had assumed.

Although the subject of the children's play (Snow White) was probably inspired by multiple sources of media and media experiences, it is nonetheless an example of the imaginary, make-believe play that many adults nostalgically reminisce about and want contemporary children to experience. This instance of play occurred unregulated and unsupervised by adults in an outdoor space. Since these fieldnotes are now fifteen years old, they may capture an experience of unsupervised outdoor pretend play that is becoming increasingly rare. And yet, as we shall see in more recent fieldnotes, children's play is not so different from contemporary examples of media-inspired play. At the time these notes were taken, movies and television (today's "old" and analog media) were still kind of "new."

Boys playing outside: pretend play and the secret spaces of childhood

Eleven years later, Dixon conducted research on children similarly at play, but using videogames as a play option; something that was not available to the children Weber observed playing Snow White. The following excerpt from her fieldnotes illustrates the children's play as it moves fluidly from an outdoor playspace to the world of a videogame.

They crouch quietly, huddled close together, scarcely daring to breathe. The clouds are low and grey overhead. They have been waiting impatiently for what seems like hours. This is a secret place they come to in order to escape, safe from prying eyes. They discovered it last fall and made it their own; in the winter they enclose themselves with fortress walls of snow, and now in the spring, it's cool and dark where the high grass surrounds them and the wild bushes make a roof above their heads. From this vantage point they can watch the comings and goings in the alleyway that runs behind the apartment building where they live. The objects of their observations are none the wiser.

It's always been like this for as long as Rowan can remember. He and Tucker are the only eleven year old boys living on the alley so they have to stick together against all those girls. They have been waiting for the girls to come out and play so they can spy on them but they have waited in vain and now big wet raindrops are starting to fall. Tucker and Rowan abandon the "secret place" and run to get their "portable forts." They use these when the rain gets heavy. The portable forts consist of pieces of plywood that they have found and nailed to long sticks. They hold them over their heads running through the rain, chasing each other up and down the alley, splashing through the mud, laughing until Rowan's mother comes out and calls them inside. She hands them towels to dry themselves off and sends them down to the basement to play. (Constructed from Shanly's fieldnotes, April 2003.)

Playing videogames inside

We now follow these same boys as they move to videogame play indoors.

Rowan and Tucker sit in the tiny playroom that Rowan's father has built in the still-unfinished basement. It is a work in progress meant to keep Rowan and his friends and their noisy television and video games safely out of earshot of the adults. The apartment is small and Rowan's dad works from home so if Rowan wants to play inside, down to the basement he goes. The room is surprisingly bright, painted white with a colourful poster on the wall, a sofa and a standing lamp from which two Spiderman action figures are perilously dangling. The focal point of the room is the television and Rowan and Tucker are sitting on the floor in front of it, a bowl of carrot sticks between them. I am sitting on the couch; here to interview the boys about videogames. They are excited at the prospect; eager to have the undivided attention of an adult who values their opinions, who regards them as experts on playing videogames. They start off by showing me their selection of games. They begin to describe their favourite game, *Pikmin*.

> Tucker: There's this guy from a planet and his name is Omar. Before he left on this journey he went to his wife who made him this soup with these carrots and when he left there was this asteroid who hit his ship and he lands down on this toxic planet and he finds a carrot and it's red and it's a carrot. He has oxygen for thirty days and so he has thirty days to recover all the parts of his ship so that he can return back home and so every day you finish you get time to picnic so you bring him to these onions and they have feet and there are these flowers and the Pikmin will destroy the flower so you actually have thirty days . . .
>
> Rowan: (Impatiently) "So we play now?"

They begin to play the game.

> Shanly: "What do you like about the game?"
> Rowan: "It's an adventure but there is action too."
> Tucker: "We like to search for the parts of the ship."

The planet in the game *Pikmin* acts as a playspace for the boys when they are unable to play outside. Their interaction on the virtual planet appears to be similar to their play in their secret hideout. In fact, at times they imagine the secret place as a spaceship, perhaps inspired from their play in the videogame. The boys say that they play videogames about three days a week, not all day long, but for a couple of hours and usually on weekends.

Comparing outdoor and indoor playspaces

Although they describe themselves as "playing a lot of videogames" when they relate the ways in which they spend their time, videogames are one of many activities in which they engage. When asked if they play at the park, they respond that they don't usually because the park is full of "old people having parties and babies." The street in front of the apartments is too busy with traffic and so they prefer to play in the alleyway behind, where they can run freely and hide in their secret place and spy. When Dixon spoke to the boys' parents, they explained that they allowed the boys to play in the alleyway because many of the kitchen windows of the apartments faced into the alley. The children who played there could be easily watched by their parents who thus felt that it was a safe, supervised place for children to play in. The alleyway was enclosed by a fence at one end and a churchyard at the other, so there was no danger from vehicle traffic, and because it was cut off, casual pedestrians rarely wandered through. The boys report that they prefer playing outside rather than inside when the weather allows, but in winter, or when it is very rainy, or in the summer when it is hot and they are bored, they play videogames.

In comparing the seemingly distinct playspace of the alleyway (an ostensibly classic childhood playspace) with the videogame (a contemporary virtual playspace) there appear to be some similarities and even some fluidity between the spaces. Our interpretation is that both spaces serve to characterize the appeal of secret childhood spaces (van Manen, 1996): they both feel concealed and secret; they are spaces where a child might slip off alone escaping from daily demands; and they are places in which to fantasize and dream. They are also places where one might engage in social interaction with peers, away from prying adult eyes.

Girls playing videogames: fluidity of play

The previous fieldnotes of boys at play reveals the permeability between the physical playspace of the alleyway and the playspace of the videogame. The following vignette from Shanly's fieldnotes of 2004 portrays the fluidity of girls' play as it moves across digital platforms and playspaces.

A group of four ten year old girls gathers around a videogame console in Anna's playroom. They are playing a videogame that they rented from the local videogame store, *Pirates; The Legend of Black Kat*, which features a female pirate described as:

> Katarina de Leon, the "Black Kat" of the high seas possessing sailing and sword-fighting skills beyond compare and unflinching bravery in the face of extraordinary dangers.

The girls spend their time in the game searching for treasure, navigating the pirate ship from island to island and fighting off pirates and giant crabs. The game is meant for a single player, but the girls take turns with the controller, advising each other on strategy and surfing the internet on Anna's laptop while waiting for their turn with the controller. They are engaged in multiple forms of play in the same space: instant messaging friends from school, listening to music, playing games online while simultaneously watching and coaching whichever girl currently has the controller. They are all invested in the success of the player, calling out encouragement or shrieking in dismay as the occasion requires. The game has captured their imaginations to such a degree that the play merges as they re-enact the adventure pretending to be pirates engaging in play sword fights and taking turns being Katarina.

Following is a short excerpt of dialogue from fieldnotes of the girls playing the videogame:

Anna: "This went so much faster than the 1st time but if I have to redo it again I'm gonna be so mad."

Anna hands the controller to Molly who explores the island looking for the treasure chest eventually encountering pirates.

Molly: "Pirates! Oh No!
I'm running through trees . . ."

Molly explores the island in the game looking for clues that will lead her to the treasure.

Molly: (handing the controller to Virginia) "Do you want to try"?

Virginia is the quietest of the girls. She is typically shy and timid on the schoolyard. She reluctantly accepts the controller.

Virginia: "You don't need to kill the monkeys cause they won't hurt you"
Anna: "Press 1, 2 right when the lock comes press 1, 2 go thru the door that opened"
Virginia: (Squealing) "Crabs, crabs, crabs, eww!" (She swipes wildly at the crabs with her sword, laughing and screeching)

In reviewing how the girls played and interacted with each other, it struck us that the videogame was being "played" simultaneously both off and online—a flowing exploration through the permeable boundaries of the digital and the analog—as the girls played at, as well as played through and around the Pirate theme. Like Seth Giddings' sons in chapter two of this book, these girls seemed at times to be both *playing at playing* a videogame and playing the game. There was a multiple layering or multitasking in the casual way they incorporated the pirate game into their play, cheering on the person playing, giving suggestions, and actually enacting or improvising around it.

Reflecting cross-cases

The play represented in the videogame episodes might serve to exemplify Huizinga's concept of play "as a contest for something" because indeed the children are playing a game and attempting to win. However, it may also be argued that they are also simultaneously engaged in Huizinga's "play as a representation of something." The videogame play provides children with an opportunity to imagine themselves as something other than that which they typically are, as they pretend to be space travelers or pirates; in Huizinga's words, they are "transported beyond themselves in a playful imaginative experience." As Virginia plays the videogame, she temporarily plays at being Katarina de Leon, pirate and legend of the high seas. Through this imaginary play she meets the criteria of Huizinga's definition: temporarily feeling magnificent, transcending the banality of the everyday, trying on identities (see Mazzarella & Pecora, 1999 for more on identity and videogames). It is interesting to note that the same analysis could apply to the example of the reenactment of Snow White, so many years earlier.

In all of the episodes, the children's play was at least partially inspired by some version of a media-generated play "text": a bedtime story, a Disney movie or book, or a videogame. There is much elitist prejudice against media-inspired play, a dismissal of such play as mere copying, not original or creative activity. Along with other scholars (e.g., Dysan, 1997; Kinder, 1991; and Seiter, 2004), we take issue with such a narrow interpretation and suggest that close examination of the kind of play we present here, reveals creativity and learning. In each of these vignettes the children adapt the text, altering the narrative in order to creatively accommodate their play intentions. The boys playing the videogame *Pikmin*, for example, can choose not to play the game as the game designer intended. Instead, they often ignore the game objective of gathering parts for the spaceship; rather, they explore the planet, hanging out and fooling around. Similarly, the girls at times seem to be playfully incorporating Katarina characters and narratives into their talk and actions around the videogame at the same time that one of them played the game itself—multitasking their play, as it were. This acting-out, inspired by the videogame, in turn feeds back into the ways they subvert or alter the game. We agree with Dyson (1997) who states that media provide the "common story material" of childhood, and urges adults and educators to acknowledge that the creative ways children reinterpret and incorporate this material in their fantasy play constitutes a form of literacy (p. 7).

In Huizinga's analysis of play, he suggests that "with the increasing systemization and regimentation of sport, something of the pure play quality is inevitably lost" (Huizinga, 1967, p. 197). He laments that the adult professional player may have greater expertise but lacks the "play spirit" of the amateur player who plays purely for fun. He even goes as far as asserting that to really play, an adult "must play like a child" (p. 199). With this assertion Huizinga relegates pure play to the realm of childhood. However, it is questionable how much of children's play fits the criteria of pure play. Moreover, Huizinga's claim that play exists most purely in childhood raises questions regarding how much of his analysis is a romanticized reflection of how children *ought* to play. At the same time, although the play we have been observing may not exactly fit Huizinga's notion of pure play, our findings do suggest that media play can be highly creative and is an important venue or space for social interaction, problem-solving, and pleasure.

The children we observed are active agents, not passive spectators in their interactions with popular images. They turn the popular culture they consume into material for their imaginative play, and use it, we would argue, to construct their own private playspaces. This interpretation of children's interaction with media is gaining currency as we revise the older and, in Seiter's (2004) opinion, classist notions that media consumption is inevitably passive mind-numbing (for in-depth discussion on this point, see Buckingham and Sefton-Green, 2004; Ito, 2007; Jenkins, 2006). This is not to say that the children's play is not shaped by media or that all play is creative. Their play is both limited and encouraged by the design possibilities (affordances) of the material at hand (see Weber & Mitchell, 2007). Like all human activity, we view the children's interaction with media as dialectical, a sense-making interaction with the environment through which they learn about the world, each other, and themselves. Through fantasy or narrative play, they are representing and interpreting their understanding of various aspects of the culture that surrounds them.

Even more important in terms of our topic of playspaces is the way that children's play flows easily on and off line, in and out of roles, weaving back and forth from the imaginative to the actual. It is in this blurring of boundaries between physical and cyberspaces, between the virtual and the actual that children create playspaces for themselves—spaces that those few scholars who still insist on separating the virtual from the "real" ignore. Most of us now argue that all play is part of real-life experience, something that is hard to deny even when we observe play media-generated spaces such as videogames. As we suggested earlier, videogame play is, perhaps in part, a consequence of adult regulation of children's outdoor playspaces. Through their anxiety and desire to monitor children at all times, adults have greatly diminished the opportunities for children to play privately with their peers. Where can a child go to carve out a secret hiding place? It is most ironic that the type of play adults long for in their romanticized past has moved to the spaces we are most concerned about; our children are finding safe harbor in the spaces created by technology and media, where in many respects they continue to play in ways not that different from generations past. When they grow up, we wonder, what childhoods will they be nostalgic for?

References

Arthur, L. (2005). Popular culture: views of parents and educators. In J. March (ed.), *Popular culture, new media and digital literacy in early childhood*, pp. 165–182. New York: RoutledgeFalmer.

Boym, S. (2001). *The future of nostalgia*. New York: Basic Books.

Buckingham, D. (2000). *After the death of childhood: Growing up in the age of electronic media*. Cambridge: Polity Press.

Buckingham, D. & Sefton-Green, J. (2004). Structure, agency, and pedagogy in children's media culture. In J. Tobin (ed.), *Pikachu's global adventure: The rise and fall of Pokémon*, pp. 12–33. Durham: Duke University Press.

Caillois, R. (1961). *Man, play, and games*. New York: The Free Press.

Coontz, S. (1992). *The way we never were: American families and the nostalgia trap*. New York: Basic Books.

Dale, S. (2005). *Candy from strangers: Kids and consumer culture*. Vancouver: New Star Books.

Dixon, S. & Simon, B. (2005). Boyhood spaces: Play and social navigation through video games. Presented at the International DiGRA Conference: *Changing Views: Worlds at Play*, June 16–20, Simon Frasier University, Vancouver, BC, Canada.

Dysan, A.H. (1997). *Writing superheroes. Contemporary culture popular culture, and classroom literacy*. New York: Teacher's College Press.

Elkind, D. (1981). *The hurried child: Growing up too fast too soon*. MA: Addison-Wesley.

Giroux, H. (1997). Are Disney movies good for your kids?. In J. Kincheloe & S. Steinberg (eds.), *Kinderculture: The corporate construction of childhood*, pp. 53–68. Boulder, CO: Westview.

Grimes, S. & Regan Shade, L. (2005). Neopian economics of play: Children's cyberpets and online communities as immersive advertising in Neopets.com. *International Journal of Media and Cultural Politics*, 1 (2), 181–198.

Huizinga, J. (1961). *Homo ludens: A study of the play-element in culture* (R.F.C. Hull, trans.). Boston: Beacon.

Ito, M. (Forthcoming). Mobilizing the imagination in everyday play: The case of Japanese media mixes. In S. Livingston & K. Drotner (eds.), *International handbook of children, media, and culture*.

Jenks, C. (1996). *Childhood*. London: Routledge.

Jenkins, H. (1999). Complete freedom of movement: Video games as gendered play spaces. In J. Cassell & H. Jenkins (eds.), *From Barbie to Mortal Kombat: Gender and computer games*, pp. 262–297. Cambridge: MIT Press.

—. (2006). *Convergence culture: Where old and new media collide*. New York and London: New York University Press.

Kinder, M. (1991). *Playing with Power in Movies, Television, and Video Games*. Berkeley: University of Berkeley Press.

Kline, S. (1993). *Out of the garden: Toys, TV and children's culture in the age of TV marketing*. London: Verso.

Kline, S., Dyer-Witheford, N., & de Peuter, G. (2003). *Digital play: The interaction of technology, culture and marketing*. Montreal: McGill-Queen's University Press.

Laumann, S. (2006). *Child's play: Rediscovering the joy of play in our families and communities*. Canada: Random House.

Lucas, T. (1998). Youth gangs and moral panics in Santa Cruz, California. In T. Skelton & G. Valentine (eds.), *Cool places: Geographies of youth cultures*, pp. 145–160. New York: Routledge.

Mazzarella, S. & Pecora, N. (eds.) (1999). *Growing up girls: Popular culture and the construction of identity*. New York: Peter Lang.

Mitchell, C. & Reid Walsh, J. (1993). "And I want to thank you Barbie": Barbie as a site of cultural interrogation. *The Review of Education/Pedagogy/Cultural Studies*, *17* (2), 143–156.

Mosco, V. (2004). *The digital sublime: Myth, power, and cyberspace*. Cambridge, MA: MIT Press.

Postman, N. (1994). *The disappearance of childhood*. New York: Vintage Books.

Quart, A. (2003). *Branded: The buying and selling of teenagers*. New York: Perseus Publishing.

Schor, J. (2004). *Born to buy*. New York: Scribner.

Seiter, E. (2004). *The internet playground: Children's access, entertainment and mis-education*. New York: Peter Lang.

Sternheimer, K. (2003). *It's not the media: The truth about pop culture's influence on children*. Boulder, CO: Westview Press.

Sutton-Smith, B. (1997). *The ambiguity of play*. Cambridge, MA: Harvard University Press.

Van Manen, M. (1996). *Childhood secrets: Intimacy, privacy and self reconsidered*. New York: Teacher's College Press.

Walkerdine, V. (2001). Safety and danger: Childhood, sexuality, and space at the end of the millennium. In K. Hultqvist & G. Dahlberg (eds.), *Governing the child in the new millennium*, pp. 15–34. New York: RoutledgeFalmer.

Weber, S. & Mitchell, C. (1995). *Reinventing ourselves as teachers: Beyond nostalgia*. London: RoutledgeFalmer.

—— (Forthcoming). Imaging, keyboarding, and posting identities: young people and new technologies. In David Buckingham (ed.), *Youth identity and digital media*. MacArthur Series on Learning and Media.

Chapter 43

MIZUKO ITO

MOBILIZING IMAGINATION IN EVERYDAY PLAY
The case of Japanese media mixes

THE WORD 'COVERGENCE' HAS been buzzing around new media debates for some time now. It can be used to refer to the possibilities digital technologies afford for connecting or hybridising previous distinct media technologies – Internet radio or cameraphones for example. At the level of the production of media texts (TV programmes, videogames, films) it refers to the tendency in commercial entertainment media to spin characters, narratives and worlds out from a single medium to a diverse, yet carefully co-ordinated, set of other media. This practice is at its most advanced in children's culture (having been pioneered by Disney in particular for decades) and Mizuko Ito here takes two of these media worlds as her focus. *Hamtaro* and *Yu-Gi-Oh!* are Japanese brands, inspired by *Pokémon*, and designed as 'multiplatform' from the start: TV cartoons, videogames, trading card games, stationery, toys and lunchboxes. Ito reviews relevant academic work on children and new media and draws out debates around active and passive consumption of popular media and products, and challenges positions that assume that these practices are 'trivial and purely consumptive', based on 'cheap and debased cultural forms'.

She is particularly concerned with the experiences of children and young people in what she calls, with echoes of Marshall **McLuhan**, a new media ecology. Her ethnographic fieldwork with children and the 'media mixes' (the popular term in Japan for these media universes) traces the 'contours' of this changing cultural landscape in everyday life. These contours include synergy with other underlying forms in new media culture, from the compulsion to personalise or remix one's media devices and texts familiar from PC and mobile phone use, to the 'hypersocial' Internet media and applications adopted by young people: chat, email, social networking, etc. (see also **Daliot-Bul**). This hypersociality links local groups of friends to wider communities and is expressed through discussion and the production of images and narratives – activities that Ito interprets as a mobilisation of collective imagination.

http://www.itofisher.com/mito/

See also Henry Jenkins' work on media convergence: http://web.mit.edu/cms/People/henry3/converge.html

The spread of digital media and communications in the lives of children and youth have raised new questions about the role of media in learning, development and cultural participation. In post-industrial societies, young people are growing up in what Henry Jenkins (2006) has dubbed "convergence culture": an increasingly interactive and participatory media ecology where internet communication ties together both old and new media forms. A growing recognition of this role of digital media in everyday life has been accompanied by debate as to the outcomes of participation in convergence culture. Many parents and educators worry about immersion in video gaming worlds or their children's social lives unfolding on the internet and through mobile communication. More optimistic voices suggest that new media enable young people to more actively participate in interpreting, personalizing, reshaping, and creating media content. Although concerns about representation are persistent, particularly of video game violence, many of the current hopes and fears of new media relate to new forms of social networking and participation. As young people's online activity changes the scope of their social agency and styles of media engagement, they also encounter new challenges in cultural worlds separated from traditional structures of adult oversight and guidance. Issues of representation will continue to be salient in media old and new, but issues of participation are undergoing a fundamental set of shifts that are still only partially understood and recognized. My focus in this chapter is on outlining the contours of these shifts. How do young people mobilize the media and the imagination in everyday life? And how do new media change this dynamic?

A growing body of literature at the intersection of media studies and technology studies examines the ways in which new media provide a reconfigured social and interactive toolkit for young people to mobilize media and a collective imagination. After reviewing this body of work and the debates about new media and the childhood imagination, I will outline a conceptual framework for understanding new genres of children's media and media engagement that are emerging from convergence culture. The body of the paper applies this framework to ethnographic material on two Japanese media mixes, *Yugioh* and *Hamtaro*. Both of these cases are examples of post-*Pokemon* media mixes, convergence culture keyed to the specificities of children's media. I suggest that these contemporary media mixes in children's content exemplify three key characteristics that distinguish them from prior media ecologies: *Convergence* of old and new media forms; authoring through *personalization and remix*, and *hypersociality* as a genre of social participation. My central argument is that these tendencies define a new media ecology keyed to a more activist mobilization of the imagination in the everyday life of young people.

The imagination in everyday life

Current issues in new media and childhood are contextualized by longstanding debates over the role of media, particularly visual media, in the imaginative lives of children. At least since television came to dominate children's popular cultures, parents, educators, and scholars have debated the role of commercial media in children's creativity, agency, and imagination. One thread of these debates has been concerned with the content of the imagination, examining issues such as representations of gender or violence. Another strand of the debate, which I will examine here, focuses on the form, structure, and practice of the imagination. What is the nature of childhood imagination when it takes as source material the narratives and characters of commercial culture? What are the modes of social and cultural participation that are enabled or attenuated with the rise of popular children's media? Does engagement with particular media types relate to differences in childhood agency or creativity? Behind these questions is the theoretical problematic of how to understand the relation between the text produced by the media producer and the local contexts of uptake by young people. Framed differently, this is the question of how the imagination as produced by commercial media articulates with the imagination, agency, and creativity of diverse children going about their everyday lives. In this chapter, I review how this question has been taken up and suggest that theories of participation and collective imagination are ways of resolving some of the conceptual problematics in a way amenable to an analysis of new interactive and networked media.

Our contemporary understandings of media and the childhood imagination are framed by a set of cultural distinctions between an active/creative or a passive/derivative mode of engaging with imagination and fantasy. Generally, practices that involve local "production"—creative writing, drawing, and performance—are considered more creative, agentive, and imaginative than practices that involve "consumption" of professionally or mass produced media—watching television, playing video games, or reading a book. In addition, we also tend to make a distinction between "active" and "passive" media forms. One familiar argument is that visual media, in contrast to oral and print media, stifle creativity, because they don't require imaginative and intellectual work. Until recently, young people almost exclusively "consumed" dynamic visual media (i.e. television and film), unlike in the case of textual or aural media where they are expected to also produce work. This may be one reason why we often do not think of reading and listening to music as "passive" or "mindless" in the same way that we view television, though all of these are mods of "media consumption." Visual media, particularly television, has been doubly marked as a consumptive and passive media form. These arguments for the superiority of "original" authorship and textual media track along familiar lines that demarcate high and low culture, learning and amusement. For example, Ellen Seiter (1999) analyzes the differences between a more working class and an upper middle class preschool, and sees the distinctions between "good" and "bad" forms of media engagement as strongly inflected by class identity. The middle class setting works to shut out television-based media and media references, and values working on a computer, reading and writing text, and play that does not mobilize content derived from popular commercial culture. By contrast, the working class setting embraces a more active and informed attitude towards children's media cultures.

Scholars in media studies have challenged the cultural distinctions between active and passive media, arguing that television and popular media do provide opportunities for creative uptake and agency in local contexts of reception. Writing in the early years of digital media for children, Marsha Kinder (1991) suggested that video games and postmodern television genres provide opportunities for kids to "play with power" by piecing together narrative elements and genres rather than absorbing narratives holistically. Arguing against the view that commercial media stimulates imitation but not originality in children's imaginings, Kinder points out the historical specificity of contemporary notions of creativity and originality. She suggests that children take up popular media in ways that were recognized as creative in other historical eras. "A child's reworking of material from mass media can be seen as a form of parody (in the eighteenth-century sense), as a postmodernist form of pastiche, or as a form of Bakhtinian reenvoicement mediating between imitation and creativity" (Kinder 1991, 60). In a similar vein, Anne Haas Dyson (1997) examines how elementary school children mobilize mass media characters within creative writing exercises. Like Seiter (1991), Dyson argues that commercial media provide the "common story material" for contemporary childhood, and that educators should acknowledge the mobilization of these materials as a form of literacy. "To fail to do so is to risk reinforcing societal divisions of gender and of socioeconomic class" (1997, 7).

These critiques of culturally dominant views of the "passivity" of children's visual culture are increasingly well established at least in the cultural studies literature (for reviews, see Buckingham 2000; Jenkins 1998; Kinder 1999). Here I build on these critiques and propose frameworks for understanding the relation between media, the imagination, and everyday activity. Engagement with new media formats such as what we now find on the internet, with post-*Pokemon* media mixes, and video games suggests alternative ways of understanding the relation between children and media that do not rely on a dichotomization of media production and consumption or between active and passive media forms. These binarisms were already being corroded by reception studies in the TV-centric era, and they are increasingly on shaky ground in the contemporary period. As digital and networked media have entered the mix, research has foregrounded active and participatory dimensions of media engagement, fundamentally undermining longstanding distinctions about children's relations to media.

In their analysis of *Pokemon*, David Buckingham and Julian Sefton-Green (2004) suggest that it has continuities with early media forms and trends in children's popular culture. But they also suggest some important new dimensions. Their analysis is worth reproducing as it prefigures my arguments in the remainder of this essay.

> We take it for granted that audiences are 'active' (although we would agree that there is room for much more rigorous discussion about what that actually means). The key point for us is that the texts of *Pokemon*—or the other *Pokemon* 'phenomenon'—positively *require* 'activity.' Activity of various kinds is not just essential for the production of meaning and pleasure; it is also the primary mechanism through which the phenomenon is sustained, *and* through which commercial profit is generated. It is in this sense that the notion of 'audience' seems quite inadequate.

In other words, new convergent media such as *Pokemon* require a reconfigured conceptual apparatus that takes productive and creative activity at the "consumer" level as a given rather than as an addendum or an exception. One way of reconfiguring this conceptual terrain is through theories of participation that I derive primarily from two sources. The first is situated learning theory as put forth by Jean Leave and Etienne Wenger (1991). They suggest that learning be considered an act of participation in culture and social life rather than as a process of reception or internalization. My second source of theoretical capital is Jenkins' idea of "participatory media cultures" which he originally used to describe fan communities in the 1970s and 1980s, and has recently revisited in relation to current trends in convergence culture (1992; 2006). Jenkins traces how fan practices established in the TV dominated era have become increasingly mainstream due to the convergence between traditional and digital media. Fans not only consume professionally produced media, but also produce their own meanings and media products, continuing to disrupt the culturally dominant distinctions between production and consumption. More recently, Natalie Jeremijenko (2002) and Joe Karaganis (2007) have proposed a concept of "structures of participation" to analyze different modes of relating to digital and interactive technologies. As a nod to cultural context and normative structures of practice, I have suggested a complementary notion of "genres of participation" to suggest different modes or conventions for engaging with technology and the imagination.
[. . .]
A notion of participation, as an alternative to "consumption," has the advantage in not assuming that the child is passive or a mere "audience" to media content. It is agnostic as to the mode of engagement, and does not invoke one end of a binary between structure and agency, text and audience. It forces attention to the more ethnographic and practice based dimensions of media engagement (genres of participation), as well as the broader social and cultural contexts in which these activities are conducted (structures of participation). Jenkins writes, "Rather than talking about media producers and consumers occupying separate roles, we might now see them as both participants who interact with each other according to a new set of rules that none of us fully understands" (2006, 4). Putting participation at the core of the conceptual apparatus asserts that *all* media engagement is fundamentally social and active,

though the specificities of activity and structure are highly variable. A critically informed notion of participation can also keep in view issues of power and stratification that are central to the classical distinctions between production and consumption. The structure of participation can be one that includes the relation between a large corporation and child, as well as the relation between different children as they mobilize media content within their peer networks. Notice that in this framing, the site of interest is not only the relation between child and text—the production/consumption and encoding/decoding relations (Hall 1993) that have guided much work in reception studies—but also the social relations between different people who are connected laterally, hierarchically, and in other ways. The research question has been recast from the more individualized, "How does a child interpret or localize a text?" to the collective question of "How do people organize around and with media texts?"

Let me return this to creativity and the imagination. A notion of participation leads to a conceptualization of the imagination as collectively rather than individually experienced and produced. Following Arjun Appadurai, I treat the imagination as a "collective social fact," built on the spread of certain media technologies at particular historical junctures (Appadurai 1996, 5). In my framing, imagination is not an individualized cognitive property, but rather is the shared store of cultural referents, common cultural source material that exceeds individual experience. This collective imagination requires not only ongoing interpretation, performance and expression, but also media technologies for representing and circulating products of the imagination. Benedict Anderson (1991) argues that the printing press and standardized vernaculars were instrumental to the "imagined community" of the nation state. With the circulation of mass electronic media, Appadurai suggests that people have an even broader range of access to different shared imageries and narratives, whether in the form of popular music, television dramas, or cinema. Media images peruade our everyday lives, and form much of the material through with we imagine our world, relate to others, and engage in collective action, often in ways that depart from the relations and identities produced locally. More specifically, in children's toys, Gary Cross (1997) has traced a shift in the past century from toys that mimicked real-world adult activities such as cooking, childcare, and construction, to the current dominance of toys that are based in fantasy environments such as outer space, magical lands, and cities visited by the supernatural. The current move towards convergent and digital media is one step along a much longer trajectory in the development of technologies and media that support a collective imaginative apparatus. At the same time, Appadurai posits that people are increasingly engaging with these imaginings in more agentive, mobilized, and selective ways as part of the creation of "communities of sentiment" (1996, 6–8). The rise of global communication and media networks is tied to an imagination that is more commercially driven, fantasy-based, widely shared, and central to our everyday lives *at the same time* as the imagination is becoming more amenable to local refashioning and mobilization in highly differentiated ways.

Taking this longer view enables us to specify much of the current debate on children and media as defined by historically specific structures of participation in media culture. Until recently these structures of participation were clearly polarized between commercial production and everyday consumption. Yochai Benkler (2006) argues that computers and the internet are enabling a change in modes of cultural production and distribution that disrupts the dynamics of commercial media production. He lays out a wide range of cases such as Wikipedia, open source software development, and citizen science to argue that cultural production is becoming more widely distributed and coordinated in internet-enabled societies. While people have always produced local folks and amateur cultures, with the advent of low-cost PCs and peer-to-peer global distribution over the internet, high-end tools for producing and sharing knowledge and culture are more widely accessible. My argument about children's culture parallels Benkler's arguments. "Reception" is not only active and negotiated but is a *productive* act of creating a shared imagination and participating in a social world. The important question is not whether the everyday practices of children in media culture are "original" or "derivative," "active" or "passive," but rather the structure of the social world, the patterns of participation, and the content of the imagination that is produced through the active involvement of kids, media producers, and other social actors. This is a conceptual and attentional shift motivated by the emergent change in modes of cultural production.

Understanding new media

Drawing from theoretical frameworks of participation and collective imagination, I would like to outline in more detail my conceptual toolkit for understanding emergent changes in children's media ecologies, and introduce the Japanese media mixes that are my topic of study. Digital or new media have entered the conversation about childhood culture holding out the enlightened promise of transforming "passive media consumption" into "active media engagement" and learning (Ito 2003). Ever since the early eighties, when educators began experimenting with multimedia software for children, digital media were seen as a vehicle for more engaged and child-centered forms of learning (e.g. Papert 1980; Ambron 1989). Although multimedia did not deliver on its promise to shake the foundations of educational practice, it is hard to ignore the steady spread of interactive media forms into children's recreational lives. Electronic gaming has taken its seat as one of the dominant entertainment forms of the twenty-first century and even television and film have become more user-driven in the era of cable, DVDs, digital download, and Tivo. In addition to interactive media formats where users control characters and narrative, now the internet supports a layer of social communication to the digital media ecology. Young people can reshape and customize commercial media, as well as exchange and discuss media in peer-to-peer networks through blogs, filesharing, social networking systems, and various messaging services. While there is generally shared recognition that new media of various kinds are resulting in a substantially altered media ecology, there is little consensus as to the broader social ramifications for the everyday lives of young people.

[. . .]

New media produced for and engaged with by young people is a site of contestation and construction of our technological futures and imaginaries. The cases described in this chapter are examples of practices that grow out of existing media cultures and practices of play, but represent a trend toward digital, portable, and networked media forms becoming more accessible and pervasive in young people's lives. I propose three conceptual constructs that define trends in new media, *form*, *production*, and *genres of participation*: *convergence* of old and new media forms; authoring through *personalization and remix*, and *hypersociality* as a genre of participation. These constructs are efforts to locate the ethnographic present of my cases within a set of unfolding historical trajectories of sociotechnical change. These characteristics have been historically present in engagement with earlier media forms, but now synergy between new media and the energies of young people has made these dimensions a more salient and pervasive dimension of the everyday lives of a rising generation. Let me sketch the outlines of these four constructs in turn before fleshing them out in my ethnographic cases.

Contrary to what is suggested by the moniker of "new media," contemporary media needs to be understood not as an entirely new set of media forms but rather as a *convergence* between more traditional media such as television, books, and film, and digital and networked media and communications. By bringing together interactive and networked media with traditional media, convergent media enable consumers to select and engage with content in more mobilized ways, as well as create lateral networks of communication and exchange at the consumer level. Today, the internet and digital media are no longer ghettoized as marginal geek phenomena: they are becoming central to the ways in which all media are distributed and engaged with. Jenkins (2006, 2) writes that convergence culture is "where old and new media intersect, where grassroots and corporate media collide, where the power of the media producer and the power of the media consumer interact in unpredictable ways." In a related vein, I have used the term in popular currency in Japan, "media mix," to describe how Japanese children's media relies on a synergistic relationship between multiple media formats, particularly animation, comics, video games, and trading card games. The Japanese media mix in children's culture highlights particular elements of convergence culture. Unlike with US-origin media, which tends to be dominated by home based media such as the home entertainment center and the PC internet, Japanese media mixes tend to have a stronger presence in portable media formats such as Game Boys, mobile phones, trading cards and character merchandise that make the imagination manifest in diverse contexts and locations outside of the home. Although the emphases are different, both Euro-American and Japanese children's media are exhibiting the trend towards synergy between different media types and formats.

Digital and networked media provide a mechanism not to wholly supplant the structures of traditional narrative media, but rather to provide alternative ways of engaging with these produced imaginaries. In children's media cultures, the Japanese media mix has been central to a shift towards stronger connections between new interactive and traditional narrative forms. Children engaging with a media format like *Pokemon* can look to the television anime for character and backstory, create their own trajectories through the content through video games and trading card play, and go to the internet to exchange information in what Sefton-Green has described as a "knowledge industry" (2004, 151). Convergent media also have a transnational dimension, as media can circulate between like-minded groups that cross national borders. The case of Japanese animation and media mixes are a particularly intriguing case in this respect, though the transnational dimension is not something that I will have space to address in this essay.

These changing media forms are tied to the growing trend toward *personalization and remix* as genres of media engagement and production. Gaming, interactive media, digital authoring, internet distribution, and networked communications enable a more customized relationship to collective imaginings as kids mobilize and remix media content to fit their local contexts of meaning. These kinds of activities certainly predate the digital age, as kids pretend to be superheroes with their friends or doodle pictures of their favorite characters on school notebooks. The difference is not the emergence of a new category of practice but rather the augmentation of these existing practices by media formats more explicitly designed to allow for user-level reshuffling and reenactment. User-level personalization and remix is a precondition, rather than a side-effect of engaging with gaming formats and media mixes like *Pokemon* and *Yugioh*. When gaming formats are tied into the imaginary of narrative media such as television and comics, they become vehicles for manifesting these characters and narratives with greater fidelity and effect in everyday life. While the role of the collective imagination in children's culture probably remains as strongly rooted in commercial culture as ever, the ability to personalize, remix, and mobilize this imaginative material is substantially augmented by the inclusion of digital media into the mix.

At the level of everyday practice and social exchange, the tendency towards remix and personalization of media is also tied to the growth of deep and esoteric knowledge communities around media content. I've described the kind of social exchange that accompanies the traffic in information about new media mixes like *Pokemon* and *Yugioh* as **hypersocial**, social exchange augmented by the social mobilization of elements of the collective imagination. Hypersociality is about peer-to-peer ecologies of cultural production and exchange (of information, objects, and money) pursued among geographically-local peer groups, among dispersed populations mediated by the internet, and through organized gatherings such as conventions and tournaments. Popular cultural referents become a shared language for young people's conversations, activity, and social capital. This is a genre of participation in media culture that has historically strong roots in cultures of fandom, or in Japan, the media geekdoms of "otaku" (Greenfeld 1993; Kinsella 1998; Okada 1996; Tobin 2004). While otaku cultures are still considered subcultural among youth and adults, children have been at the forefront of the mainstreaming of these genres of participation. It is unremarkable for children to be deeply immersed in intense otaku-like communities of interest surrounding media such as *Pokemon*, *Digimon*, or *Teenage Mutant Ninja Turtles*, though there is still a social stigma attached to adult fans of science fiction or anime.

Japan's media mix

Like otaku culture, the Japanese media mix is both culturally distinctive and increasingly global in its reach. A certain amount of convergence between different media types such as television, books, games, and film has been a relatively longstanding dimension of modern children's media cultures in Japan as elsewhere. Japan-origin manga (comics), anime (animation), and game content are heterogeneous, spanning multiple media types and genres, yet still recognized as a cluster of linked cultural forms. Manga are generally (but not always) the primary texts of these media forms. They were the first component of the contemporary mix to emerge in the postwar period in the 1960s and 1970s, eventually providing the characters and narratives that go on to populate games, anime, and merchandise. While electronic gaming was in a somewhat separate domain through the 1980s, by the 1990s it was well integrated into the overall media mix of manga and anime characters, aided by the popularity of game-origin characters such as Mario and Pikachu. These media mixes are not limited to children's media (and include a wide range of adult-oriented material), but children's media does dominate.

Pokemon pushed the media mix equation into new directions. Rather than being pursued serially, as in the case of manga being converted into anime, the media mix of *Pokemon* involved a more integrated and synergistic strategy where the same set of characters and narratives was manifest concurrently in multiple media types. *Pokemon* also set the precedent of locating the portable media formats of trading cards and handheld networked game play at the center rather than at the periphery of the media ecology. This had the effect of channeling media engagement into collective social settings both within and outside the home as they looked for opportunities to link up their game devices and play with and trade their *Pokemon* cards. Trading cards, Game Boys, and character merchandise create what Anne Allison has called "pocket fantasies," "digitized icons . . . that children carry with them wherever they go," and "that straddle the border between phantasm and everyday life" (Allison 2004, 42). This formula was groundbreaking and a global success; *Pokemon* became a cultural ambassador for Japanese popular culture and related genres of participation in media culture. Many other media mixes followed in the wake of *Pokemon*, reproducing and refining the formulas that Nintendo had established.

In the wake of the *Pokemon* phenomenon, I conducted fieldwork from 1998 to 2002 in the greater Tokyo area among children, parents, and media industrialists, at the height of *Yugioh's* popularity. My research focused on *Yugioh* as a case study, as it was the most popular series in currency at the time. My description is drawn from interviews with these various parties implicated in *Yugioh*, my own engagements with the various media forms, and participant observation at sites of player activity, including weekly tournaments at card shops, trade-shows, homes, and an afterschool center for elementary-aged children. Among girls, *Hamtaro* was the most popular children's series at the time, so it became a secondary focus for my research. I also conducted research that was not content-specific, interviewing parents, participant observing a wide range of activities at the afterschool center, and reviewing diverse children's media. I formally interviewed 30 parents, educators, and adult game-players, and spoke to many times that number of children during the course of participant observations at the afterschool center, at events, and in card duel spaces. I turn now to descriptions of *Yugioh* and *Hamtaro* at the levels of media form, authorship, and genres of participation to illustrate how these media mixes were mobilized in the everyday lives of children in Japan.

Yugioh

Like other media mixes, *Yugioh* relies on cross referencing between serialized manga, a TV anime series, a card game, video games, occasional movie releases, and a plethora of character merchandise. The manga ran for 343 installments between 1996 and 2004 in the weekly magazine *Shonen Jump* and is still continuing as an animated series. In 2001 the anime and card game was released in the USA, and soon after in the UK and other parts of the world. The series centers on a boy, Mutoh Yugi, who is a game master, and gets involved in various adventures with a small cohort of friends and rivals. The narrative focuses on long sequences of card game duels, stitched together by an adventure narrative. Yugi and his friends engage in a card game derivative of the US-origin game Magic the Gathering, and the series is devoted to fantastic duels that function to explicate the detailed esoterica of the games, such as strategies and rules of game play, properties of the cards, and the fine points of card collecting and trading. The height of *Yugioh*'s popularity in Japan was between 1999 and 2001. A 2000 survey of three hundred students in a Kyoto elementary school indicated that by the third grade, *every* student owned some *Yugioh* cards (Asahi Shinbun 2001).

Compared to *Pokemon*, where games are only loosely tied to the narrative media by character identification, with *Yugioh* the gaming comprises the central content of the narrative itself. In media mixes such as *Pokemon* and *Digimon*, the trading cards are a surrogate for "actual" monsters in the fantasy world: *Pokemon* trainers collect monsters, not cards. In *Yugioh*, Yugi and his friends collect and traffic in trading cards, just like the kids in "our world." The activities of children in our world thus closely mimic the activities and materialities of children in Yugi's world. They collect and trade the same cards and engage in play with the same strategies, rules, and material objects. Scenes in the anime depict Yugi frequenting card shops and buying card packs, enjoying the thrill of getting a rare card, dramatizing everyday moments of media consumption in addition to the highly stylized and fantastic dramas of the duels themselves. The convergent media form, as well as the narrative that focuses on esoteric game knowledge, channels engagement into otaku-like participation in genres of remix personalization. This is similar to a series like *Beyblade* that followed *Yugioh*, which involves kids collecting and battling with customized battle tops. The objects collected by the fantasy characters are the same as those collected by kids in real life. When I was conducting fieldwork, *Yugioh* cards were a pervasive fact of life, a fantasy world made manifest in the pockets and backpacks of millions of boys across the country.

Personal authorship through collection and remix is at the center of participation with *Yugioh*. While many children, and most girls, orient primarily to the manga or anime series, game play and collection is the focus of both the narrative and the more high-status forms of

Yugioh engagement. Players can buy a "starter pack" or "structure deck" of cards that is ready to play, but none of the children I met in my fieldwork dueled with a preconfigured deck. Players will purchase "booster packs" which are released in different series that roughly correspond to different points in the narrative trajectory of *Yugioh*. The booster packs cost ¥150 (a little over $1US) for five randomly packaged cards from the series, making it a relatively lightweight purchase that is integrated into the everyday routines of kids stopping at local mom-and-pop shops on their way home from school, or accompanying their parents to a convenience store or a bookstore. The purchase of booster packs supports a collection and trading economy between players, because they quickly accumulate duplicate cards or cards that they do not want to keep or use. In duel spaces, players will buy, sell, and trade cards to one another in order to build their collections and design their own playing decks of 40 or more cards. Since there are several thousand different cards on the market now, the combinations are endless.

Players I spoke to had a wide range of strategies that guided their collection and deck combinations. Some players orient toward the narrative content, creating decks and collections that mimic particular manga characters or based on themes such as dragon cards, insect cards, or occult cards. Serious duelists focus on building the most competitive deck, reading up on the deck combinations that won in the national and international tournaments, and pitting their deck against local peers. Others with more of a collector or entrepreneurial bent prioritize cards with a high degree of rarity. All cards have a rarity index that is closely tracked by internet sites and hobby shops that buy and sell post-market single cards. While most children I played with or spoke to did not have easy access to internet sites which are the clearinghouses for most esoteric collection knowledge (card lists, price lists, and rarity indexes) they were able to acquire knowledge by visiting hobby shops or through a network of peers which might include older children or young adults. Even young children would proudly show me their collections and discuss which were their favorite cards that reflected their personal taste and style. When I would walk into the afterschool center with a stack of cards I was quickly surrounded by groups of boys who riffled through my deck, asking questions about which cards were my own favorites, and engaging in ongoing commentary about the coolness and desirability of particular cards. While there is a great deal of reenactment and mimicking of existing narrative content in the practices of card collection and play, the game enables subject positions that are highly differentiated and variable. The series sports thousands of cards and dozens of duelist characters that Yugi has encountered in his many years on the air. The relation between the subjectivities of players and the commercially produced narrative apparatus of *Yugioh* is indicative of the mode of authorship of remix and personalization that I have been working to describe in this chapter. Players draw from a massive collectively shared imagination as source material for producing local identities and performances. The practices of talking about and exchanging cards are an example of hypersociality as a genre of participation: the merging of local social negotiations with the exchange of media-based knowledge and signifiers.

The practices of card collection and deck construction are closely tied to the modes of participation and sociability of *Yugioh* play. The structure of the media mix is built on the premise that play and exchange will happen in a group social setting rather than as an isolated instance of a child reading, watching, or playing with a game machine. It is nearly impossible to learn how to play the card game rules and strategy without the coaching of more experienced players. My research assistants and I spent several weeks with the *Yugioh* starter pack, poring through the rule book and the instructional videotape and trying to figure out how to play. It was only after several game sessions with a group of fourth graders, followed by some coaching by some of the more patient adults at the card shops, that we slowly began to understand the basic game play as well as some of the fine points of collection, how cards are acquired, valued and traded. Among children, this learning process is part of their everyday peer relations, as they congregate after school in homes and parks, showing off their cards, hooking up their Game Boys to play against one another, trading cards and information. We found that kids generally develop certain conventions of play among their local peer group, negotiating rules locally, often on a duel-by-duel basis. They will collectively monitor the weekly manga release in *Shonen Jump* magazine, often sharing copies between friends. In addition to the weekly manga, the magazine also featured information about upcoming card releases, tournaments, and tournament results. The issues featuring the winning decks of tournament duelists are often the most avidly studied. When kids get together with their collections of *Yugioh* cards, there is a constant buzz of information exchange and deal-cutting, as kids debate the merits of different cards and seek to augment both their play deck and their broader card collection. This buzz of hypersocial exchange is the lifeblood of the *Yugioh* status economy, and what fuels the social jockeying for knowledge, position, and standing within the local peer network of play.

[. . .]

Hamtaro

When we turn to media mix content oriented to girls, this shift toward otaku-like genres of participation has not been as pronounced, but is still visible. With girls, in contrast to boys, the status economy of skill in competitive play is less central to their social lives. They tend to engage in a wide range of media and play that differs depending on their particular playmate. The girls I spoke to preferred the more subtle competitive exchange of stickers to develop their connoisseurship and cement their friendship circles and did not participate as avidly in the hypersocial buzz of card trading. When *Yugioh* tournaments were held at the afterschool center I observed at, a handful of girls might participate, but they tended to watch in the sidelines even though they likely had their own stash of cards. None of this is news to people that have looked at the gendered dimensions of play. Although *Pokemon* crosses gender lines because of its cute characters, the same is not true for most Japanese media mixes. Overall, boys' content is culturally dominant. It sets the trends in media mixing that girls' content follows. But girls' content *is* following. The trend is slower but as of the late 1990s most popular girls' content will find its way to Game Boy, though not to platforms like Nintendo consoles or Playstation. Otaku-like forms of character development and multi-year and multiply threaded narrative arcs are also becoming more common in series oriented towards girls. There is yet to be a popular trading card game based on girls' content, but there are many collectible cards with content oriented to girls. The gender dynamics of the media mix is a complex topic that deserves more careful treatment than I can provide here. To give one example of how the dynamics of new media mixes is making its way to girls' content, I will describe the case of *Tottoko Hamutarou* (or *Hamtaro*, as it is known in English), the series that was most popular among girls during the period of my fieldwork.

Hamtaro is an intrepid hamster owned by a little girl. The story originated in picture book form in the late 1990s and became an animated series in 2000. In 2006, the anime series passed the 300 episode mark. After being released as a television anime, *Hamtaro* attracted a wide following, quickly becoming the most popular licensed character for girls. It was released in the USA, UK and other parts of the world in 2002. *Hamtaro* is an interesting case because it is clearly coded as girls' content, and the human protagonist is a girl. But the central character, Hamtaro, is a boy. It has attracted a fairly wide following among boys as well as girls, though it was dwarfed by *Yugioh* in the boys' market during the time that I was conducting my fieldwork. The story makes use of a formula that was developed by *Pokemon*, which is of a proliferating set of characters that create esoteric knowledge and domains of expertise. While not nearly as extensive as the *Pokemon* pantheon or *Yugioh* cards, Hamtaro is part of a group of about 20 hamster friends, each of which has a distinct personality and life situation. To date the series has introduced over 50 different quirky hamster characters, and complex narratives of different relationships, compatibilities, antagonisms, and rivalries. The formula is quite different from the classic one for girls' manga or anime that has tended to have shorter runs and is tightly focused on a small band of characters including the heroine, friend, love interest, and rival. Instead, *Hamtaro* is a curious blend of multi-year soap opera and media mix esoterica, blending the girly focus on friendship and romance with otaku-like attention to details and a character-based knowledge industry.

In addition to the narrative and character development that follows some of the formulas established by *Pokemon*, the series also exhibits the convergent characteristics of the contemporary media mix. Hamtaro's commercial success hinges on an incredibly wide array of licensed products that make him an intimate presence in girls' lives even when he is not on the screen. These products include board games, clothing, curry packages and corn soup, in addition to the usual battery of pencils, stationery, stickers, toys, and stuffed animals. Another important element of the *Hamtaro* media mix is Game Boy games. Five have been released so far. The first (never released overseas), *Tomodachi Daisakusen Dechu* (*The Great Friendship Plan*), was heavily promoted on television. Unlike most game commercials that focus on the content of the game, the spot featured two girls sitting on their bed with their Game Boys, discussing the game. The content of the game blends the traditionally girly content of relationships and fortune telling with certain formulas around collection and exchange developed in the boys' media mix. Girls collect data on their friends and input their birthdays. The game then generates a match with a particular hamster character, and then predicts certain personality traits from that. Players can get a prediction of whether different people will get along as friends or as couples. Girls can also exchange data between Game Boy cartridges. The game builds on a model of collection and exchange that was established in the industry since *Pokemon*, but applied to a less overtly competitive girl-oriented exchange system. In Japan, *Hamtaro* even has a trading card game associated with it, though it pales in scope and complexity compared to those of *Yugioh* and *Pokemon*.

When I spoke to girls about *Hamtaro* they delighted in telling me about the different characters, which was the cutest or sweetest, and which was their favorite. At the afterschool center, I often asked girls to draw pictures for me of media characters, one of many activities that the girls favored. *Hamtaro* characters were by far the most popular, followed by *Pokemon*. In each case, girls developed special drawing expertise and would proudly tell me how they were particularly good at drawing a particular hamster or *Pokemon*. The authorship involved in this creation does not involve the same investments of card players and collectors, yet there are still dimensions of personalization and remix. The large stable of characters and the complex relational dynamics of the series encourage girls to form personalized identifications with particular hamsters, manifest in a sense of taste and connoisseurship of which drawing is just one manifestation. Girls develop investments in certain characters and relational combinations. If they mature into a more otaku-like form of media engagement, then these same girls will bring this sensibility to bear on series that feature human characters and more adult narratives of romance, betrayal, and friendship. The *doujinshi* (amateur comic) scene in Japan was popularized by young women depicting alternative relational scenarios and backstories to popular manga. Elsewhere I have discussed in more detail the role of doujinshi in popular youth cultures

(Ito 2006). I simply note here that *Hamtaro* engagements include an echo of the more hypersocial participation genres of remix, personalization, and connoisseurship that is more clearly manifest in boys' popular cultures and practices.

Conclusions

The cases of *Yugioh* and *Hamtaro* are examples of how broader trends in children and new media are manifest in Japan-origin media and media cultures that are becoming more and more global in their reach. Part of the international spread of Japanese media mixes is tied to the growth of more participatory forms of children's media cultures around the world. At the same time, different national contexts have certain areas of specialization. For example, where Japan has led in the particular media mix formula I have described, the US media ecology continues to remain dominant in film and internet based publication and communication. The conceptual categories—convergence in media form, personalization and remix in authorship, and hypersociality as a genre of engagement—were developed based on my ethnographic work with Japanese media mixes, but I believe also apply to the media and practices of young people in other parts of the post-industrial world. For example, Sonia Livingstone (2002, 108–116) describes trends in the UK towards "individualized lifestyled" tied to a diversification of media and forms of lifestyle expression among young people. In the USA, Jenkins (2006) describes the highly activist cultures of fandoms expanding on the internet. While a comparative look at these forms of participation is beyond the scope of this chapter, there are certainly indications of growing transnational linkages and resonances.

If, as I have suggested, young people's media cultures are moving towards more mobilized and differentiated modes of participation with an increasingly global collective imagination, then we need to revisit our frameworks for understanding the role of the imagination in everyday life. Assessed by more well-established standards of creativity, the forms of authorship and performance I have described would be deemed derivative and appropriative rather than truly original. It is also crucial that we keep in view the political economic implications of having young people's personal identities and social lives so attuned and dependent on a commercial apparatus of imaginative production. At the same time, we need to take seriously the fact that cultural forms like *Yugioh* and *Hamtaro* have become the coin of the realm for the childhood imagination, and recognize them as important sources of knowledge, connoisseurship and cultural capital. Even as we look for ways of guiding these activities towards more broadly generative forms of authorship, we need to acknowledge *Yugioh* play as a source of creativity, joy, and self-actualization that often crosses traditional divides of status and class. Further, we need to reevaluate what authorship means in an era increasingly characterized by these remix and recombination as a mode of cultural production.

[. . .]

Now as ever individuals produce new cultural material with shared cultural referents. The difference is the centrality of commercially produced source material and, more recently, the ability to easily recombine and exchange these materials locally and through peer-to-peer networks. For better and for worse popular media mixes have become an integral part of our common culture, and visual media referents are a central part of the language with which young people communicate and express themselves. It may seem ironic to suggest that these practices in convergence culture have resulted in a higher overall "production value" in what young people can say and produce on their own. Our usual lenses would insist that engagements with *Yugioh* or *Hamtaro* not only rely on cheap and debased cultural forms, but that they are highly derivative and unoriginal. What I have suggested in this essay, however, is that we broaden the lens through which we view these activities to one that keeps in view the social and collective outcomes of participation. While I am not suggesting that content is irrelevant to how we assess these emergent practices, I do believe that it is just one of many rubrics through which we can evaluate the role of new media in children's lives.

Acknowledging these participatory media cultures as creative and imaginative does not mean foreclosing critical intervention in these practices or abdicating our role as adult guides and mentors. The dominance of commercial interests in this space means that it is crucial for adults with other kinds of agendas to actively engage rather than write off these practices as trivial and purely consumptive. Many efforts in media literacy and youth media are exemplary in this respect, but I believe there is much more work to be done to make these recognitions take hold more broadly. Unless parents and educators share a basic understanding of the energies and motivations that young people are bringing to their recreational and social lives, these new media forms will produce an unfortunate generational gap. Resisting the temptation to fall into moral panic, technical determinism, and easy distinctions between good and bad media is one step. Gaining an understanding of practice and participation from the point of view of young people is another step. From this foundation of respectful understanding we might be able to produce a collective imagination that ties young people's practices into intergenerational structures and genres of participation in convergence culture.

Acknowledgements

The research and writing for this paper was funded by a postdoctoral fellowship from the Japan Society for the Promotion of Science, the Abe Fellowship, the Annenberg Center for Communication at The University of Southern California, and a grant from the MacArthur Foundation. My research assistants in Japan were Tomoko Kawamura and Kyoko Sekizuka. This chapter has benefited from comments from Andre H. Caron, Michael Carter, Henry Jenkins and Dan Perkel.

References

Allison, A. 2004. "Cuteness and Japan's Millennial Product." Pp. 34–52 in *Pikachu's Global Adventure: The Rise and Fall of Pokémon*, edited by J. Tobin. Durham: Duke University Press.

Ambron, S. 1989. "Introduction." In S. Ambron and K. Hooper (eds) *Interactive Multimedia: Visions of Multimedia for Developers, Educators, & Information Providers. Learning Tomorrow*. Redmond, WA: Microsoft Press.

Anderson, B. 1991. *Imagined Communities*. New York: Verso.

Appadurai, A. 1996. *Modernity at Large: Cultural Dimensions of Globalization*. Minneapolis: University of Minnesota Press.

Benkler, Y. 2006. *The Wealth of Networks: How Social Production Transforms Markets and Freedom*. New Haven, CT: Yale University Press.

Bourdieu, P. 1972. *Outline of a Theory of Practice*, J. Goody (ed.) R. Nice (transl.); New York: Cambridge University Press.

Buckingham, D. 2000. *After the Death of Childhood: Growing up in the Age of Electronic Media*. Cambridge: Polity.

Buckingham, D. and Sefton-Green, J. 2004. "Structure, Agency, and Pedagogy in Children's Media Culture." In *Pikachu's Global Adventure: The Rise and Fall of Pokémon*, J. Tobin (ed.). Durham: Duke University Press, 12–33.

Cohen, S. 1972. *Folk Devils and Moral Panics*. London: MacGibbon and Kee.

Cross, G. 1997. *Kids' Stuff: Toys and the Changing World of American Childhood*. Cambridge: Harvard University Press.

Dyson, A. H. 1997. *Writing Superheroes: Contemporary Childhood, Popular Culture, and Classroom Literacy*. New York: Teachers College Press.

Edwards, P. 1995. "From 'Impact' to Social Process: Computers in Society and Culture." *Handbook of Science and Technology Studies*, S. Jasanoff, G. E. Markle, J. C. Petersen, and T. Pinch (eds). Thousand Oaks: Sage, 257–285.

Giddens, A. 1986. *The Constitution of Society: Outline of a Theory of Structuration*. Berkeley, CA: University of California Press.

Greenfeld, K. T. 1993. "The Incredibly Strange Mutant Creatures who Rule the Universe of Alienated Japanese Zombie Computer Nerds." *Wired* (1).

Hall, S. 1993. "Encoding, Decoding." In S. Durin (ed.) *The Cultural Studies Reader*, New York: Routledge, 90–103.

Hine, C. 2000. *Virtual Ethnography*. London: Sage.

Ito, M. 2003. "Engineering Play: Children's Software and the Productions of Everyday Life." Anthropology, Stanford University, Stanford.

Ito, M. 2006. "Japanese Media Mixes and Amateur Cultural Exchange." In D. Buckingham and R. Willett (eds) *Digital Generations*, London: Lawrence Erlbaum.

Ito, M. 2007. "Technologies of the Childhood Imagination: *Yugioh*, Media Mixes, and Everyday Cultural Production." In J. Karaganis (ed.) *Structures of Digital Participation*, New York: SSRC Press.

Jenkins, H. 1992. *Textual Poachers: Television Fans and Participatory Culture*. New York: Routledge.

Jenkins, H. 1998. "Introduction: Childhood Innocence and Other Modern Myths." In H. Jenkins (ed.) *The Children's Culture Reader*. New York: NYU Press, 1–37.

Jenkins, H. 2006. *Convergence Culture: Where Old and New Media Collide*. New York: New York University Press.

Jeremijenko, N. 2002. "What's New in New Media." In *Meta Mute: Culture and Politics After the Net*. http://www.metamute.org/en/node/5779/print [September 2007].

Johnson, S. 2005. *Everything Bad is Good for You*. New York: Riverhead Books.

Karaganis, J. 2007. "Introduction." In J. Karaganis (ed.) *Structures of Participation in Digital Culture*, Durham, NC: Duke University Press.

Kinder, M. 1991. *Playing with Power in Movies, Television, and Video Games*. Berkeley: University of California Press.

Kinder, M. 1999. "Kids' Media Culture: An Introduction." In M. Kinder (ed.) *Kids' Media Culture*. Durham: Duke University Press, 1–12.

Kinsella, S. 1998. "Japanese Subculture in the 1980s: Otaku and the Amateur Manga Movement." *Journal of Japanese Studies* 24:289–316.

Lave, J. and E. Wenger. 1991. *Situated Learning: Legitimate Peripheral Participation*. New York: Cambridge University Press.

Lessig, L. 1999. *Code and Other Laws of Cyberspace*. New York: Basic Books.

Livingstone, S. 2002. *Young People and New Media*. London: Sage Publications.

Miller, D. and D. Slater. 2000. *The Internet: An Ethnographic Approach*. New York: Berg.

Okada, T. 1996. *Otakugaku Nyuumon (Introduction to Otakuology)*. Tokyo: Ota Shuppan.

Papert, S. 1980. *Mindstorms: Children, Computers, and Powerful Ideas*. New York: Basic Books.

Sefton-Green, J. 2004. "Initiation Rites: A Small Boy in a Poké-World." In J. Tobin (ed.) *Pikachu's Global Adventures: The Rise and Fall of Pokémon*. Durham: Duke University Press, 141–164.

Seiter, E. 1999. "Power Rangers at Preschool: Negotiating Media in Child Care Settings." In M. Kinder (ed.) *Kids' Media Culture*. Durham: Duke University Press, 239–262.

Tobin, S. 2004. "Masculinity, Maturity, and the End of Pokémon." In J. Tobin (ed.) *Pikachu's Global Adventure: The Rise and Fall of Pokémon*. Durham: Duke University Press, 241–256.

Index